Dictionary of Portuguese-African Civilization
Volume 1: From Discovery to Independence

"The Portuguese discovered in the Great Ocean new
islands, new lands, new seas, new people; and what
is more important, they discovered a new sky and new stars."

Pedro Nunes, *Tratado do Sphera*, 1537

Dictionary of Portuguese African Civilization

Dictionary of Portuguese-African Civilization

Volume 1:
From Discovery to Independence

Benjamin Núñez

HANS ZELL PUBLISHERS
London • Melbourne • Munich • New Jersey • 1995

British Library Cataloguing in Publication Data
Núñez, Benjamin
  Dictionary of Portuguese-African Civilization. — Vol. 1: From Discovery to Independence
  I. Title
  967

  ISBN 1-873836-10-4

Library of Congress Cataloging-in-Publication Data

Núñez, Benjamin, 1912-
  Dictionary of Portuguese-African civilization / Benjamin Núñez.
  560pp 24cm
  Includes bibliographical references.
  Contents: V. 1. From discovery to independence.
  ISBN 1-873836-10-4
  1. Africa. Sub-Saharan — History — Dictionaries. 2. Africa — Civilization —
  Portuguese influences — Dictionaries. I. Title.
  DT352.4.N86 1994
  967'.003 — dc20   94-17124
                                                                         CIP

Published by Hans Zell Publishers, an imprint of Bowker-Saur, a division of Reed Elsevier (UK) Limited, Maypole House, Maypole Road, East Grinstead, West Sussex RH19 1HH, United Kingdom
Tel: +44 (0) 1342 330100   Fax: +44 (0) 1342 330191

Bowker-Saur is part of REED REFERENCE PUBLISHING.

Cartography by Melanie J. Knapp
Cover illustration by Marianne Watson Núñez

Cover design by Robin Caira
Printed on acid-free paper.
Printed and bound in Great Britain
by Antony Rowe Ltd., Chippenham, Wiltshire.

To the memory of my beloved parents,

SERAFIN and EVANGELISTA DURAN DE NÚÑEZ

CONTENTS

FOREWORD

Portuguese-speaking Africa has been the object of unjustifiable neglect in Africanistics of English or French expression. Qualitative works do not abound. Fragmentary information is the rule rather than the exception. Of course rare germs of scholarship are occasionally found in this apparently fallow terrain of African Studies. In this context, Dr. Núñez's book is unprecedented in its comprehensiveness. It reminds us that in African studies one cannot be local without being global, and vice versa.

This is a monumental work, somewhat reminiscent of Father Antonio Brásio's opus deservedly titled *Monumenta Missionaria Africana*, albeit different in intent and focus. Dr. Núñez's work is nurtured with the most informative and authoritative sources. Dr. Núñez makes us realize that, due to the early and long involvement in Africa, Africanist terminology and Africanists in general are more indebted to the Portuguese and Portuguese-language scholarship than customarily acknowledged. In this regard the title of this book could be deceptive as it is seemingly restrictive to the so-called "Lusophone" Africa. In actuality, this book covers the Portuguese space (*o espacio portugués*). And what part of Africa was not touched by the Portuguese at one point or the other of her history? This is evident in the various languages, African and European-Arabic, of the entries. Each entry thus makes us cross the borders of time, space, and discipline. This is why Dr. Núñez's book is likely to remain for a long time an indispensable companion to a good Africanist.

Olabiyi Babalola Yai
Chairman
African and Asian Languages and Literatures
University of Florida
Gainesville

INTRODUCTION

The historical record on Portuguese Africa is rich and varied, spanning a period in excess of six hundred years. Every viewpoint is represented, European and African, king and slave, establishment and revolutionary, scientific and poetic, religious (in many manifestations) and secular. And virtually all this rich literature is in Portuguese, a language mostly inaccessible to English speakers. My aim in researching and compiling this dictionary on Portuguese Africa has been to provide a comprehensive study of the long Portuguese involvement in the exploration, settlement, and development of the African continent, concentrating on the period from the conquest of the North African Moslem city of Ceuta in 1415 by Prince Henry of Portugal to 1975 when Portugal's colonies became independent of European rule.

The first African lands settled by Portugal were the uninhabited Atlantic islands of the Cape Verde archepelago, discovered by the Portuguese navigator Dinis Dias in 1444 and settled two years later. Next were the islands of São Tomé e Príncipe, explored by João de Santarem in 1470 and settled in 1495. The histories of these two groups are quite different. Cape Verde, off the coast of Senegal, became a center for tropical and subtropical agriculture, sugar cane in particular. Despite concerted attempts to establish a stable cash crop economy, its history has been blighted by repeated devastating droughts resulting in out-migration, mostly to the United States. São Tomé e Príncipe fared very differently. Their crucial location in the Gulf of Guinea only 155 miles (250 km) from the African mainland made them a natural center for the transshipment of slaves to the New World. The fact that they were islands meant that Europeans could conduct trade buffered from the alien diseases and other hazards of the mainland that had repeatedly wiped out untold numbers of Europeans brave enough or foolhardy enough to persist in exploring the continent proper.

On the west coast, the first to be explored, and the most enduring source of slaves, was Portuguese Guiné, now Guinea-Bissau. Further down the coast was Angola, fourteen times the size of Portugal. It became a source of repeated challenge and disappointment as Portugal persisted over the centuries in her efforts to settle, "civilize," and develop the colony's resources, both human and natural. Its varied topography dictated that settlements spread out from strategically located centers that became virtual colonies within the colony; its varied ethnicities often frustrated and resisted Portugal's intrusion.

Mozambique on the east coast was settled almost as an afterthought. Its coastal cities, Sofala in particular, were already colonized by Arab sheiks and Portugal's eyes were set on India. Mozambique's trade centers were acquired with the dual purposes of providing way stations for ships en route to India and, secondarily, for commerce with East Africa. It was not until the late nineteenth century that Portugal's hold on Mozambique extended inland from the coast and the riverbanks on which the great *prazos* (landgrants) had been established.

Barely half a century after Portugal's position had been formally secured by the 1885 Congress of Berlin, throughout Africa nationalist movements gained the necessary momentum to launch wars of independence. In the Portuguese colonies, fifteen years of rebellion and war were only relieved when Portugal herself underwent the radical change from the fascistic rule of the Salazar regime to a democracy, the result of a coup in 1974 by the Portuguese armed forces.

Throughout Portugal's history of exploration and colonization, it should be borne in mind that her explorers actually "discovered" nothing—they stumbled upon and intruded into innumerable ancient cultures of enormous variety and high civilization. In the two volumes of this dictionary of Portuguese Africa, the first covers the history, culture, geography, and resources of Portugal and her colonies. Volume II, subtitled *From Ancient Kings to Presidents*, is biographical. It is devoted to the people, European and African, who embarked on, persisted in, and resisted Portuguese settlement in Africa. From the Carthaginian Hanno in the fifth century BC to the presidents of the now-independent African nations, every type of person, military and civilian, sacred and profane, has had a hand in the conquest and ultimate independence of Portuguese Africa. Much blood was shed, yet much learning was imparted. In the inevitable clash of cultures, many amalgams were forged and much literature, inspired by Africa and voiced in Portuguese, has emerged.

The history of Portuguese Africa is far from finished. It is hoped that these volumes will provide a window on the past and an insight into the future.

The criteria for compiling and selecting the material have been pragmatic. The entries are taken from the physical and natural sciences, economics, history, literature, politics, religion, and sociology. They are organized to bring forward a fair knowledge of the environment, culture, and society built by Africans and Portuguese colonists in the tropics.

The entries, taken from specific sources as set out and duly acknowledged in the Bibliography, have been reworded and made as much as possible dictionary entries. They are nouns, noun-phrases, idioms, maxims, sayings, proverbs, and the like. Portuguese spelling prevails in African words and their linguistic associations. These linguistic associations are the ones found in dictionaries. A key to abbreviations used in citing sources is given on pp. 515-518.

With regard to the material collected from many sources, every effort has been made to take the ideas and facts, and not the narrative. If there are mistakes, they are due to human error, and not an attempt to infringe on authors' copyrights.

ACKNOWLEDGMENTS

The author wishes to thank the staff of the Library of Congress, Washington, D.C., for the assistance and facilities provided during the eleven years from 1978 to 1989 spent compiling the material for this dictionary. The author is particularly grateful for the distinction of being named a Scholar at the Library, which facilitated access to private collections. Special thanks go to Dr. Julian Witherell, at the time chief of the Africa Division, to Dr. Everett Larson of the Portuguese-Hispanic section, and to Mr. Bruce Martin, in charge of reference facilities.

At the University of Florida Libraries, the author wishes to thank Mr. William Bennett, Chair of Access Services Department, for the Special Borrower privileges and for providing a carrel for research from 1989 to 1994. The author is most grateful to Mr. Peter Malanchuck, Africana Bibliographer, who put him in contact with Mr. Hans M. Zell, of Hans Zell Publishers, an imprint of Bowker-Saur Ltd., Oxford, U.K., an African scholar in his own right. His patience and understanding in the completion of this work, the author gratefully recognizes.

The author is deeply indebted to his wife, Marianne Watson Núñez, for her support and assistance throughout this project. Thanks also go to Melanie Knapp for the preparation of the maps and to Laura Poole and Joan Bennett of Santa Fe Community College, Gainesville, for typing the original manuscript. Finally, the author wishes to express his gratitude to Margaret Joyner for the editing and final preparation of the book.

Gainesville, Florida
October 15, 1994

A Note to the Reader

The method of alphabetizing entries for Volume One is quite straightforward. The few exceptions include treaties, congresses, and the like, which are alphabetized by the city in which they took place, and such overarching topics as slaves, Jesuits, and names of colonies, where the entries may appear as "slaves, baptism of" or "Cape Verde, discovery and settlement of." Entries for modern political organizations and similar groups are alphabetized by their acronyms. For Volume Two, kings and queens are listed by name and country to avoid confusing such entries as King João I of Portugal with King João I of Congo. A king such as Alvaro Nzinga of Congo is listed under Alvaro, like Henry Tudor or Richard Plantagenet. Such prepositions as da, de, do, and the like usually are disregarded, so Vasco da Gama is listed under Gama, Vasco da. For complex Portuguese family names, the reader is cautioned that there is little agreement on how to list them. It can be as simple as Matos, Manuel Lorenço das Neves Rives de, progressing to Mousinho de Albuquerque, Joaquim Augusto, and such tertiary entries as Mascarenhas Castelo Branco, Joaquim Maria. If the biographic entry you seek is not under the conventional last name, please look under another part of the person's name.

Abbreviations

(Afr.)	African	(It.)	Italian
(Afrk)	Afrikaans	(Kimb.)	Kimbundu
(Ar.)	Arabic	(Lat.)	Latin
(Bant.)	Bantu	(Mak.)	Makonde
(Braz.)	Brazilian	(Mand.)	Mandingo
(Crio.)	Creole	(Pg.)	Portuguese
(Criou.)	Crioulo	(q.v.)	quod videt (which see)
(Engl.)	English	(Shar.)	Sharanga
(Eth.)	Ethiopian	(Songh.)	Songhai
(Fr.)	French	(Sp.)	Spanish
(Ful.)	Fula	(Swah.)	Swahili
(Gr.)	Greek	(Xir.)	Xironga
(Hind.)	Hindi	(Yor.)	Yoruba

Acronyms

AA	Associação Africana
AASA	Associação Africana do Sul de Angola
ABACO	Associação dos Bacongo
ACAIH	Associação Commercial, Agricola e Industrial de Huambo
ACOA	American Committee on Angola
ALIAZO	Alliance des Ressortissants do Zombo
ALC	African Liberation Committee
AMA	Asociação das Mulheres de Angola
AMM	Asociação das Mulheres de Mozambique
ANM	Accão Naturais de Mozambique
ANANGOLA	Asociação Regional do Naturais de Angola
ANC	African National Congress
ANM	Association of Natives of Mozambique
ANP	Afrikaner Nationalist Party
ANU	African National Union
ARA	Armed Revolutionary Action
AREC	Association des Ressortissants de L'Enclave de Cabinda
ARNA	Associação Regional dos Naturais de Angola
ASSOMIZO	Associção dos Nativos do Zombo

AUO	African Union Organization
CANM	Centro Associativo dos Negros de Moçambique
CEI	Centro dos Estudantes do Imperio
COREMO	Comité Revolucionario de Mozambique
COTONANG	Companhia-Geral dos Algodões de Angola
DIAMANG	Comapanhia de Diamantes de Angola
DGS	Direção Geral da Seguranza
FDLA	Frente Democratico para a Libertação de Angola
FLGC	Frente de Libertação da Guiné Portuguesa e Cabo Verde
FLING	Frente de Luta Pela Independencia Nacional da Guiné-Bissau
FNLA	Frente Nacional de Liberação de Angola
FPLM	Frente para a Libertação de Mozambique
FRAIN	Frente Revolucionario Africano para a Independençia Nacional das Colonias Portuguesas
FRELIMO	Frente de Libertação de Mozambique
FUA	Frente de Unidade Angola
MABLA	Movimento Afro-Brasileiro para a Libertação de Angola
MAC	Movimento Anti-Colonialista
MANU	Mozambique African National Union
MFA	Movimento das Forças Armadas
MLEC	Mouvement pour la Liberation d'Enclave de Cabinda
MLG	Movimento de Libertação da Guiné
MLSTP	Movimento de Libertação de São Tomé e Príncipe
MNR	Mozambique National Resistence
MPLA	Movimento Popular de Libertação de Angola
NESAM	Nucleus dos Estudantes Secundarios Africanos de Mozambique
NLA	Native Labour Association
NRC	Native Recruiting Corporation
OAU	Organization of Africa Unity
OCA	Organisaçao Cultural dos Angolanos
OMA	Organisaçao das Mulheres de Angola
OMM	Organisaçao das Mulheres Moçambicanas
OPVDC	Organisação Provincial de Voluntarios e Defesa Civil
OIT	Organisation Internationale du Travail
PAIGC	Partido Africano de Independencia de Guinea-Bissau e Caba Verde

PCA	Partido Comunista de Angola
PDA	Partido Democratico de Angola
PNA	Partido Nacional Africano
PIDE	Policia Internacional de Defesa e Seguranza
RENAMO	Resistencia Nacional Moçambicana
SWAPO	South-West Africa People's Organization
UNATA	União dos Naturais de Angola
UAM	União Africana de Moçambique
UDEMO	União Democrática de Mozambique
UDENAMO	União Democrática Nacional de Moçambique
UDCV	União Democrática de Cabo Verde
UDG	União Democrática da Guiné
UDMGCV	União Democrática das Mulheres da Guiné e Cabo Verde
UDNM	União Democrática Nacional de Moçambique
UGEAN	União-Geral dos Estudantes da Africa Negra
UN	United Nations
UNDM	União Nacional Democratica de Moçambique
UNEM	União Nacional dos Estundantes de Moçambique
UNGP	União das Naturais da Guiné Portuguesa
UNHCR	United Nations High Commission for Refugees
UNITA	União Nacional para a Independencia Total de Angola
UNMI	União Nacional de Moçambique Independiente
UNTA	União Nacional dos Trabalhadores de Angola
UNTG	União Nacional dos Trabalhadores de Guiné
UP	União Progressiva
UPA	União das Populações de Angola
UPICV	União das Populações das Ilhas do Cabo Verde
UPNA	União das Populações do Norte de Angola
UT	Unidade Tribal
WNLA	Witwatersrand Native Labour Association

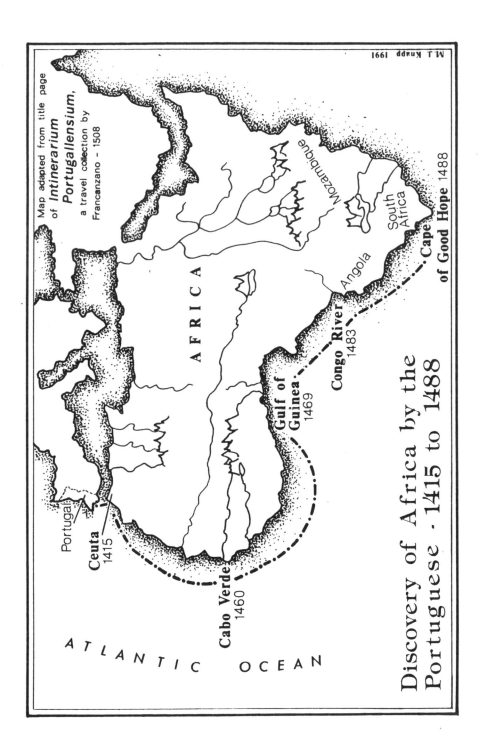

M.J. Knapp 1991

Map adapted from title page
of *Intinerarium
Portugallensium*,
a travel collection by
Francanzano - 1508

A F R I C A

Mozambique

South
Africa

Cape
of Good Hope 1488

Angola

Congo River
1483

Gulf of
Guinea
1469

Portugal

Ceuta
1415

Cabo Verde
1460

A T L A N T I C   O C E A N

Discovery of Africa by the
Portuguese · 1415 to 1488

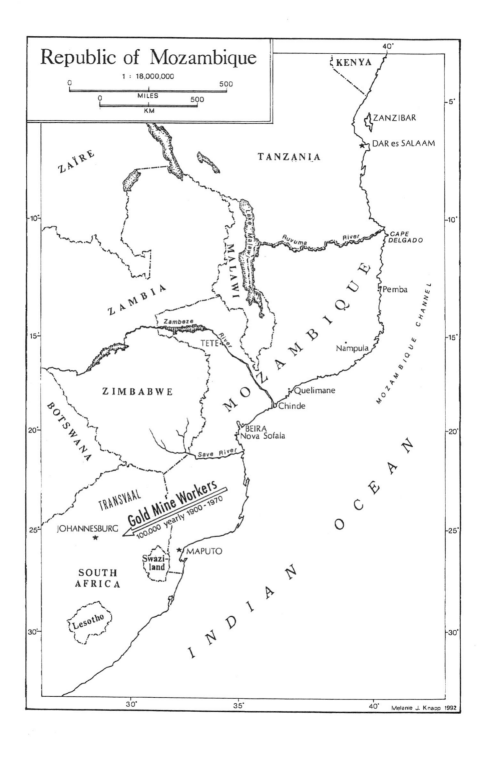

Republic of Mozambique

1 : 18,000,000

ZAÏRE

TANZANIA

KENYA

ZANZIBAR

DAR es SALAAM

ZAMBIA

MALAWI

Ruvuma River

CAPE DELGADO

Pemba

MOZAMBIQUE

Lake Malawi

Zambeze

TETE

River

Nampula

MOZAMBIQUE CHANNEL

ZIMBABWE

Quelimane

Chinde

BOTSWANA

BEIRA
Nova Sofala

Save River

TRANSVAAL

Gold Mine Workers

100,000 yearly 1900-1970

JOHANNESBURG

MAPUTO

Swazi-
land

SOUTH
AFRICA

INDIAN OCEAN

Lesotho

Melanie J. Knapp 1992

Republic of Angola

1 : 20,000,000

0   500
MILES

0   500
KM

São Tomé é Principé

CAMEROON

São Tomé
é
Principé

Equat.
Guinea

GABON

CONGO

Kasai   River

Cabinda

ZAÏRE

M'Banza
Congo

Maquela
do Zombo

Uige

Ambriz

LUANDA

Lunda

Luanda

Kawanza

MALANJE

River

Slaves
Exported to Brazil

4,000,000 from 1520 to 1850

LOBITO
BENGUELA

Bailundo

HUAMBO

ZAMBIA

Zambezi   River

Benguela

MOSSAMEDES

LUBANGO

ANGOLA

Atlantic   Ocean

NAMIBIA

BOTSWANA

BRAZIL

Melanie J. Knapp 1992

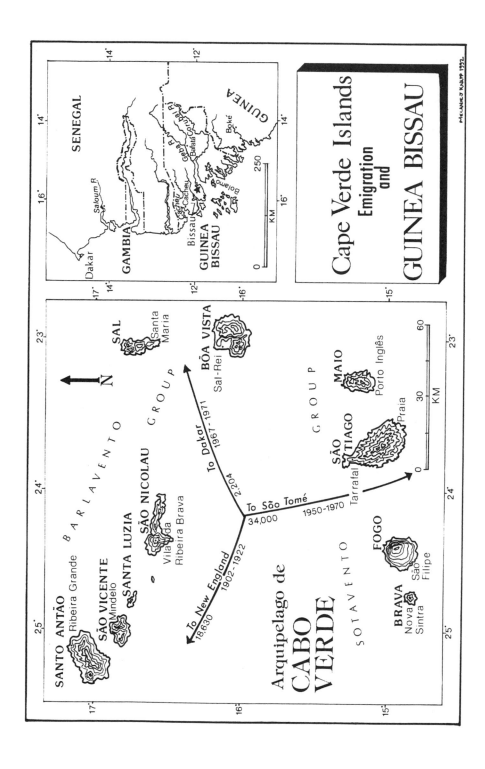

Cape Verde Islands
Emigration and
GUINEA BISSAU

MELANIE J KNAPP 1992

SENEGAL

GAMBIA

GUINEA BISSAU

GUINEA

Dakar

Saloum R.

Cacheu R.
Geba R.
Bafatá
Corubal R.
Boké

Bissau

Bolama

250

0

KM

Arquipelago de
CABO
VERDE

B A R L A V E N T O

S O T A V E N T O

SANTO ANTÃO
Ribeira Grande

SÃO VICENTE
Mindelo

SANTA LUZIA

SÃO NICOLAU
Vila da
Ribeira Brava

SAL
Santa
Maria

BÔA VISTA
Sal-Rei

MAIO
Porto Inglês

SÃO
TIAGO
Tarrafal
Praia

BRAVA
Nova
Sintra

FOGO
São
Filipe

G R O U P

G R O U P

N

To Dakar
1967-1971
2,204

To São Tomé
34,000
1950-1970

To New England
1902-1922
18,630

0   30   60
KM

DICTIONARY OF
PORTUGUESE-AFRICAN CIVILIZATION

Volume I

{ A }

AA (*Associação Africana*) (Pg.) "African Association." A society founded in Maputo in the 1950s by *assimilados* (q.v.) with moderate nationalist ideas. By 1962 many of its members became revolutionaries and joined FRELIMO (q.v.). The government charged them with sedition and closed its Maputo office. Munslow, *Mozambique,* pp. 65-6, 68.

AASA (*Associação Africana do Sul de Angola*) (Pg.) "African Association of Southern Angola." An Ovimbundu (q.v.) political group established in Nova Lisboa c.1953 by railroad workers and local African bourgeoisie with the aim of establishing local autonomy and developing their own cultural identity. It was a legal party that became more and more militant as the struggle for independence increased. It was connected with the *Liga Angolana* (q.v.). Pelissier, *La Colonie,* p. 289.

abd (Ar.) A male slave; a servant in the social and legal sense of Islamic law. It is known that Islam retained the ancient Arabian institution of slavery, the legality of which the old biblical world acknowledged. Islam allows its followers to appropriate for their own use the infidels of any country neither subject to nor allied with the Islamic Empire. For centuries the slave trade was an important business for Moslems in Portuguese Africa and elsewhere. SEI.

abobora moganga (Afr.) Tropical vines (*Cucurbita pepo* L.) with fleshy fruit, cultivated by Africans especially in times of famine; pumpkin and its relatives, introduced by the Portuguese from Asia early in the colonial period, and today is common in Angola and elsewhere in Africa. That there are many varieties is reflected in its several names, including *abobora da Guiné* and *abobora grande.* Ficalho, *Plantas Uteis,* pp. 183-4, 188.

abolition movement in Portugal The abolition movement began in Portugal at the end of the seventeenth century, influenced by an economic liberalism in Brazil where oppressed slaves and poor whites on the sugar plantations and in the mines in the northeast opposed the sugar and gold mining potentates. Manoel Ribeiro da Rocha, a Brazilian freedman and priest from Bahia who studied law at Coimbra University, published a book entitled *Ethiope Resgatado, Empenhado, Sustentatdo, Corregido, Instruido e*

Libertado (Lisbon, 1758). The author argued strongly against the slave trade and advocated the abolition of slavery. Capela, *Escravatura,* pp. 193-4; DHP.

abolition of slavery in Portugal In Portugal, the import of slaves into the country was abolished in 1761, under pressure from England. In addition, the Marquês de Pombal began a gradual abolition program on January 16, 1773, when he freed and removed all legal hindrances from children born after that date whose parents, grandparents, and great-grandparents had been slaves in the country. GEPB. *See also* abolition of slavery in Portuguese Africa.

abolition of slavery in Portuguese Africa The abolition of slavery was a slow process. In 1845, the Portuguese parliament proposed that the children of slaves be deemed free and in 1849, a project for gradual abolition was presented in Lisbon. King Pedro V of Portugal officially abolished slavery in Portuguese Africa on April 29, 1858, under pressure from liberal Portuguese politicians and the British government. The royal decree was signed in Berlin on the occasion of the king's marriage by proxy to Princess Stephanie Hohenzollern-Sigmaringen. The Marquês Sá da Bandeira promulgated the law in Angola. Abolition was neither as complete nor as drastic as the term might imply. Portuguese Africa had come to depend on this single overseas trade and was economically endangered even though there remained a market for slaves in Africa itself. Under the provisions of abolition, all Africans presently in slavery would become free within twenty years. The reasons for the delay were to make the transition from a slave-labor to a free-labor economy less painful to the slave holders. During this twenty-year period, no African could be enslaved, and children born of slaves would be free. In the meantime, former slaves would enjoy an interim status as *libertos* (q.v.), a classification neither sharply defined nor clearly understood. The trade continued in Portuguese Africa under the disguise of the contract labor policy until well into the twentieth century. Herrick, *Area Handbook,* p. 32; Newitt, *Portugal in Africa,* pp. 14, 15; DHP. *See also* abolition of slavery in Portugal.

Absinta (Afr.) A Zambezia *prazo* (q.v.) located north of Quelimane in the area of the Maganja *prazo*. It was rented c.1880 by Dona Ines, wife of João Coelho Barata, and Dona Captiva Alves. In 1884 these donas sent laborers and clients of the *prazo* to besiege the warehouse of the Opium Company at Mopea, Quelimane, partly because plundering was rife and partly to stem the advance of the commercial companies, since they were limiting the activities of the *prazo* owners. Newitt, *Portuguese Settlement,* p. 284.

abutua (Afr.) An African vine (*Tiliacora chrysobotrya*) with long and flexible stems that twine around trees in the forests. Africans use it to treat syphilis, bladder disorders, dysentery, and snake bites. It is an African plant introduced into Portugal early in the Discovery (q.v.). In 1692, *abutua* was taken from Lisbon to Paris by Miguel Amelot, ambassador of Louis XIV. Its Angolan name is *gile,* or *xile.* Ficalho, *Plantas Uteis,* pp. 82, 83.

Abutua fair (Afr.) A trading post established by a Changamire chief around 1690 in the Karanga state located between the Zambezi and the Sabe rivers in modern Mozambique. It was an important fair in the region, trading in gold and precious metals. Newitt, *Portuguese Settlement,* p. 25; Isaacman, *Mozambique: From Colonialism,* p. 70. *See also* Abutua Kingdom.

Abutua (Afr.) A Karanga chiefdom in what is present-day Zimbabwe; in 1750 it marked the southern limit of the *prazeros'* trading sphere. Large caravans led by the *prazeros* purchased gold, ivory, and small amounts of copper and medicinal roots in the Rozvi kingdom (q.v.) for sale at the Abutua fair (q.v.). At its high point in the middle of the eighteenth century, this kingdom temporarily surpassed Manica as the prime supplier of gold, and it was reputed to have supplied more than all the other trading areas combined. Isaacman, *Mozambique: From Colonialism,* pp. 81-2, 84.

Abyssinia (Pg.) Fifteenth-century Portuguese translation of the Islamic *El-Habisha,* meaning the land above the first cataract on the Nile. Also the ancient land of Cush. WTNID. *See* Ethiopia.

Academy of Sciences Originally the Royal Academy of Sciences, established by Queen Maria I of Portugal on December 24, 1779, to promote scientific research, publications, and the expansion of knowledge through the study of nature. It encompassed the natural sciences, mathematics, and arts and letters. It had a museum, a library, and a publication program. In its first session, held on July 4, 1780, a member, Pedro José Fonseca, outlined a plan for the *Dicionario da Lengua Portuguesa* (Dictionary of the Portuguese Language). The first series of publications was *Memorias Economicas* (1789-1815). DHP; GEPB. *See also* Sociedade de Geografia de Lisboa.

ACAIH (*Associação Commercial, Agricola e Industrial de Huambo*) (Pg.) "Huambo Commercial, Agricultural and Industrial Association." Established in 1961 by Portuguese citizens in Huambo, a Benguelan city in central Angola, it stressed nationality rather than cultural identity. Pelissier, *La Colonie,* p. 641.

Accão Nacional de Mozambique *See* ANM (1).

Accra, Conference of An international meeting held in Accra, the capital of Ghana, in December 1958. Its official title was First All-African People's Conference. It was chaired by Kwame Nkrumah of Ghana and attended by such prominent African leaders as Sékou Touré. The conference invited representatives of the MPLA (*Movimento Popular para Liberação de Angola*), MAC (*Movimento Anti-Colonialista*), and UPA (*União das Populacões do Norte de Angola*) with the aim of broadening its range of action in coordinating the struggle for the independence of Portuguese African colonies. At the time, Accra was a center of political activities aiming at the liberation of African territories then under the control of European nations. Marcum, *The Angolan Revolution*, I:42, 67-8.

achikunda (Afr.) In colonial Zambezia, a slave acquired by an African chief through trade, raids, or voluntary enslavement; also an African soldier on the *prazos*. Isaacman, *Mozambique: From Colonialism*, pp. 18, 53.

Achuma (Mand.) Among the Islamic Mandigoes of Guinea-Bissau, the feasts of the Islamic New Year celebrated annually on the ninth of January. Gonçalves, *O Mundo Arabo-Islámico,* p. 214.

ackee (Afr.) Fleshy aril surrounding the seed of the ackee tree (*Blighia sapida* Koenig); a diet staple for some Africans. Around 1700 the seeds were used as a weight roughly equivalent to 20 grains of gold dust in the Gold Coast. In 1790 and again in 1818, England minted a silver coin by this name for use in the West African slave trade. Seeds were brought to the Caribbean by slaves and now the tree is extensively cultivated in Jamaica. All parts, including the aril, are poisonous except for a 2- to 4-day period during ripening when the aril is safe to eat. Also spelled acky, akee. Ficalho, *Plantas Uteis*, p. 121; Polanyi, *Dahomey*, p. 152.

ACOA (American Committee on Angola) An organization based in the United States and connected with the Angolan nationalist revolution. On February 6, 1960, two emissaries of ACOA, Frank Montero and William X. Scheinman, arrived in Luanda to review the situation, and sent information on nationalist activity back to the U.S. They had previously visited São Salvador, an active center of anti-Portuguese uprisings. On their return to the U.S., they called a press conference to announce a nationalist rebellion in southern Angola. On March 10, 1960, the Lisbon government reacted by announcing that this was proof of an international plot against the Portuguese colonial government. Pelissier, *La Colonie,* pp. 305-6.

Aden (Ar.) Ancient port on the Gulf of Aden, on the southwest coast of the Arabian peninsula; a trading port since Roman times. Pero Covilha, accompanied by Afonso Paiva, visited Aden in 1487. They had instructions from King João II of Portugal to establish communication between Europe and Abyssinia (Ethiopia, q.v.), to observe the spice trade and report on commerce and navigation in the Indian Ocean. Axelson, *Portuguese in South-East,* pp. 19, 70.

afonsí (Pg.) A Portuguese coin minted by King Afonso V c.1470 and used in the expanding trade on the North and West African coasts, including Guiné and Cape Verde; also called *grosso* or *real grosso*. GEPB.

afonso de ouro (Pg.) "Golden Afonso." A coin minted c.1500 by King Manuel I and probably circulated in West and East Africa where trade by that time had expanded. DN.

"Africa" (1) "Prowess, courage, bravery." A use of the name first employed c.1600 by Portuguese historians to emphasize the heroic discoveries, explorations, and conquests of the Dark Continent that had taken place between 1444 and 1482 in the Age of Discovery. This national enterprise, achieved at the end of the Middle Ages by a small country, became a point of pride and a symbol of perseverance for the Portuguese people. GDLP. *See also* meter uma lança em Africa.

Africa (2) A bi-weekly cultural and advertising magazine published in Lourenço Marques, Mozambique, by Dr. Antonio de Sousa Neves. The first issue appeared on February 8, 1936; the last on March 2, 1936. Dias, *A Imprensa*, p. 90.

Africa at the Discovery Portugal's first contact with the Atlantic coast of Africa was made by Lanzarotto Malocello, a Genoese in the service of the Crown, who sailed along the northwest coast in 1336. After the conquest of Ceuta in 1415, Portugal expanded its explorations down the west coast of Africa and soon came to know the area between Cape Bojador and Cape Nao. Prince Henry, known in English as The Navigator, founded the Sagres nautical school on the Algarve coast in 1423 and the cartographer Jaime de Majorca and his disciples arrived in Portugal soon after to work there. These geographers were familiar with the gold and salt trade routes of the Sahara as well as with the Atlantic coast down to Arguim (q.v.). The *Atlas of Fra Mauro* (1459) revealed a good knowledge of the Kingdom of Prester John (q.v.) in Abyssinia (Ethiopia, q.v.) and shows Africa surrounded by the "Ocean." Based on this and other, anonymous, charts, Gil Eanes passed Cape Bojador in 1434. The exploration and further charting of the West African Atlantic coast began at this time. In 1435 Eanes and Gonçalves Baldaia reached Angra dos Ruivos (Garnet Bay); the following year they discovered the Rio do Ouro and the Petra da Galé. In 1444 Nuno Tristão reached the Terra dos Negros (Land of the Blacks) at the mouth of the Senegal River, and Dinis Dias reached Cape Verde in 1445. In 1446 Nuno Tristão discovered Guiné. He was killed by local Bissangos on an island off the Guiné coast. Cortesão, *History*, I:297; Russell-Wood, *A World on the Move*, p. 9; DHP. *See also* Africa, before the Discovery.

Africa before the Discovery Knowledge of the East African coast, familiar to Arab navigators, was fragmentary among Europeans. The interior was described in general terms by Arab travelers and geographers such as Masaudi, Ibn-Haukal, El-Bekri, El-Edrisi, Iacut, El-Moari, Ibn-Battuta, and Ibn-Khaldun from the tenth to fourteenth centuries, but was limited to the Sahara and the Sudan. In the fourteenth century new maps, mainly the *Catalan Atlas* (q.v.) of 1375, attributed to Abraham and Jafuda Cresque, mentioned the cities of Sijilmassa, Tabelbert, Tugurt, and Biskraat on the northern border of the Sahara, the salt mines at Tagaza, and the great Sudanese cities of Mali, Timbuctu, and Gao, spurring Portuguese travelers' interest and curiosity. A second-century Ptolemaic representation of the African continent, popularized among Europeans after 1450, had a great influence on Portuguese navigators. DHP. *See also* Africa, at the Discovery.

Africa, Our Lady of A chapel established by King João I in Ceuta, North Africa, c.1418 and the first official place of Christian worship built by the Portuguese in Africa. Prince Henry chose the name of the church and requested that a weekly mass for his soul be celebrated in perpetuity. Brasio, *Historia de Missiologia,* pp. 72-3.

Africa Ilustrada (Pg.) An illustrated monthly magazine of study, culture, and criticism published in Lourenço Marques, Mozambique, by Dr. Alexandre Sobral de Campos. Its first issue appeared in February 1945, and it folded in December of the same year. Dias, *A Imprensa,* p. 93.

Africa Medica (Pg.) A monthly journal of hygiene and tropical medicine published in Lisbon under the direction of Dr. Antonio Pacheco. Its first issue appeared on October 25, 1934, and it ceased publication in 1954. Dias, *A Imprensa,* p. 88.

Africa Oriental (Pg.) A news and literary weekly published on Mozambique Island, capital of the Mozambique province. It was founded by Joaquim José Lapa, a Portuguese journalist. Its first issue appeared on November 30, 1876; after 336 issues, it folded on December 24, 1887. Dias, *A Imprensa,* p. 51.

Africa Trading Company A commercial trading corporation formed in 1878 to develop coastal shipping and funded mainly with British and Portuguese capital. It operated in Quelimane, Inhambane, and at the mouth of the Pungué River. Herrick, *Area Handbook,* p. 38.

African dances in Portugal Between 1500 and 1550, African dances were very popular in Lisbon, Evora, and other Portuguese cities. Slaves and freedmen celebrated Christian festivals with dances and songs accompanied by the rhythm of drums and flutes. Drummers welcomed Cardinal Alexandrino's party to Vila Viçosa and Evora in 1571. The dances included the *guineo, ye-ye, zarembeque, mangana,* and *unduly,* the last apparently imported from Brazil. This popular entertainment was criticized by the clergy and by 1559 it was prohibited by law. The government also outlawed both slaves and freedmen from holding dances and meetings in Lisbon and in an area one league (48 km) around the city. Four years later, the *corregador* (judge) of Colares, a town 16 mi. (25 km) northwest of Lisbon, broke up a *festa dos negros* (negro festival) where Africans had elected a king and hanged a scarecrow from a gibbet. Saunders, *A Social History,* pp. 89, 105-7, 112; DHP.

African horse sickness A serious and often fatal viral disease of horses that is endemic in parts of central and southern Africa. It is characterized by fever, swelling, and internal hemorrhage. It is transmitted by African flies (genus *Glossina*) that includes *G. morsitans* and the tsetse, *G. vivax.* This disease is usually prevalent in heavy bush near rivers, although in Mozambique and Angola it is more often encountered in areas of open woodland. EA; GEPB.

African Lakes Company A chartered British company organized in 1889 to further trade and commerce, mainly along the Zambezi River. Up to the end of the nineteenth century, it was an instrument for British political and economic penetration into the Lake Niassa area and Central Africa. Axelson, *Portugal,* pp. 153, 162.

African Liberation Committee *See* ALC.

African literature before 1900 The first literary work penned in Africa, *Letters of King Afonso I* [*of Congo*], was written between 1510 and 1540. The Dominican friar A.D Macedo wrote *Satirical Poems* in Mozambique in 1635, but this work was not published until 1950. In 1681-3 Antonio de Oliveira Cadornega published *Historia das Guerras d'Angola.* In 1850, J. da S.M. Ferreira wrote *Espontaneidade da Minha Alma.* The first Angolan literary review, *A Aurora,* appeared in 1856, and in 1882 a group of African and *mestiço* journalists published Luanda's first newspaper, *O Futuro d'Angola.* J.C. da Matta published *Poems* in 1887. A.E.V. Pereira's novel, *Portugueses e Inglezes na Africa,* came out in 1892 and *Folktales of Angola,* edited by H. Chatelain, and Cape Verde's first literary review, *Almanach Luso-Africano,* both appeared in 1894. In Guinea-Bissau, J.M. da Sousa Monteiro published *Costumes da Guiné* in 1895. Moser, *Essays,* pp. 12-14.

African National Congress *See* ANC.

African National Union *See* ANU.

African seamen In Portugal since the Discovery (q.v.), African seamen worked alongside Europeans on some Portuguese ships. On the caravel *Santa Maria das Neves*, which sailed between Lisbon and Cantor on the Gambia River in 1505-6, seven of the fourteen ordinary seamen were Africans, as was one of the nine able seamen. There was no distinction between races in terms of pay, and one African ordinary seaman was promoted to able seaman during his service abroad, making two of the African crew able seamen. Around 1517 limitations were introduced regarding service by African seamen. They were barred from becoming captains of vessels on the route from Cape Verde to Guiné; promotions were slow, freedmen were treated in the same way as the slaves, and sea-captains needed royal permission to hire Africans. Saunders, *A Social History*, pp. 11, 145, 154; DHP; GEPB.

African sugar *See* sorghum.

African swine fever An acute viral infection (*African pestis*) involving the reticular-endothelial system and first observed among swine in South Africa by Hutchen in 1903. African swine fever occurs in Angola, Italy, Spain, and Portugal. Under natural conditions, domesticated and wild swine of all ages are subject to this infection. It is spread by direct contact or by contamination by sick swine of feed, pasture lands, and transport vehicles. GSE.

Africana A monthly illustrated magazine published in Lourenço Marques, Mozambique. It appeared in April 1933, and its editor was José Francisco Albasini. Dias, *A Imprensa*, pp. 22, 87.

Africanitude A contemporary philosophy based on the principle of integration of African and European cultures, respect for sophisticated European ideology and values, and recognition and acceptance of African human and aesthetic traditions and achievements. Africanitude involves awareness plus a degree of mystique concerning foreign and indigenous values. In the Afro-Portuguese world there has been a gradual growth of racial and cultural consciousness similar to negritude (q.v.). F.J. Tenreiro, a *mestiço* poet of São Tomé, has provided the most fully developed expression of Africanitude. His themes include revolt, anger, cosmic harmony, and important ancestral ties to the land and the culture. Chilcote, *Portuguese Africa*, p. 51; Preto-Rodas, *Negritude*, pp. 78-9.

Africanization of Islam In Guinea-Bissau and elsewhere in Africa, African cultures, religions, and traditions forced Islam to accommodate its ideology, rituals, and teaching of the Koran to a new environment; prayers, circumcision rituals, and the celebration of Ramadan were affected. Sacred trees and humble thatched huts replaced decorated mosques because Islam's rich dynamic life lost its attraction in poor isolated villages. Gonçalves, *O Mundo Arabo-Islámico*, p. 201.

Africanization of Portuguese settlers On Mozambican *prazos* (q.v.) and Angolan plantations, the newcomers often joined or married African women and adopted to various degrees their mate's life style, values, and African world view. After one or two generations, these families acquired African names, customs, and religious beliefs as well as wealth and a new identity. Various characters such as *lançados* (convicts), *pombeiros* (bush merchants), *muzungos* (Africanized Portuguese settlers), *mestiços* (mulattos), and *tangamãos* (Africanized Portuguese) began to populate the Portuguese-African human landscape. Duffy, *Portuguese Africa*, pp. 97-9; Henriksen, *Mozambique*, pp. 123-4. *See also* Afro-Portuguese dynasties.

Africanization of the slave trade *See* slave trade, Africanization of.

Africanness This literary term refers to the supposedly authentic African spirit, feeling, and traditions deeply rooted in physical, cultural, and spiritual values. The poets of Africanness stress the exploitation and suffering of Africans as they evoke the Dark Continent with its wild beasts and the mystery of African nights. Examples of contemporary writers who express Africanness include G. Bessa Victor, Luandino Vieyra, Agostino A. Neto, and Noemi de Sousa. Its overall theme is the desire to return to something that seems almost gone forever. The poets have experienced the rottenness of colonialism and wish to recapture their Africanness with a new celebration of blackness on a continental, even worldwide, scale. Burness, *Fire*, p. 7; Hamilton, *Voices*, p. 360.

Africano, O (Pg.) (1) "The African." A weekly news periodical founded and published by José Antonio Correia Pereira in Quelimane, Mozambique. Its first issue appeared on July 1, 1877, with the slogan "Education, Religion, Morality." It ended in 1881. Dias, *A Imprensa*, p. 52.

Africano, O (Pg.) (2) "The African." A weekly Portuguese-Landim periodical founded and published by José Albasini in Lourenço Marques, Mozambique. Started in 1911, this bilingual journal was very popular. It was the first to receive telegraphed news from Lisbon from the Havas and Reuter agencies and was widely read by African laborers in the South African gold fields. It ceased publishing in 1920. Dias, *A Imprensa*, p. 73.

Afrikaner Nationalist Party See ANP.

Afro-Americans In the mid-1930s the movement known as *Moïse Noire* (q.v.), or Black Moses, influenced by Garveyism and Pan-Africanism (qq.v.) spread a message in the Angolan countryside saying that Afro-Americans would come to liberate the Africans from European oppression. This notion of outside help reinforced other protest movements being organized locally. Marcum, *The Angolan Revolution*, I:47.

Afro-Brazilians in Dahomey A group of mixed Portuguese-Africans exiled or deported from Brazil to Dahomey (now Benin), in the 1800s. Many of these descendants of slaves took the names of Portuguese aristocrats or Brazilian plantation gentry. Among these names were d'Almeida, da Costa, de Souza, da Silva, and Martines. Most of the expatriates settled in Ouidah (q.v.) where they engaged in the slave trade, serving as middlemen between Africans and Europeans. One of them, Antonio de Souza, became Viceroy of Ouidah. At the time of King Glélé, Domingo Martines settled in Porto Novo and was an important palm-oil trader in the 1820s. Among the descendants of these settlers are former President Emile Derlin Zinsone and former Chief of the Army Paul Emile de Souza. Most of them were Roman Catholic, Europeanized, and well educated. During French colonial rule (1900-50) these Neo-Africans played dominant roles as professionals, politicians, and merchants. After the independence of Benin on August 1, 1960, their political power declined because, being detribalized, they were devoid of ethnic networks, the building block of Benin's post-colonial socioeconomic life. HDB. *See also* Afro-Brazilians in Lagos.

Afro-Brazilians in Lagos A community of Afro-Brazilian exiles settled in Lagos, the capital of Nigeria, c.1880. Since then they have remained a close community with both an African identity and a nostalgic feeling for their former home in Brazil. In the 1880s there were 3,000 Afro-Brazilians in Lagos, most of Yoruba origin. Their houses were built in a Brazilian style of architecture and they ate Brazilian food, including cassava (q.v.). In marked contrast to their English-speaking counterparts in West Africa, the Afro-Brazilians brought no revolutionary or reforming zeal or desire to change Africa along modern lines. Indeed, their acceptance of the slave trade and traditional African society allowed them to win positions of strong influence in the colony. They remained Roman Catholic, continued to use the Portuguese language, and strove to acquire European comforts. They considered themselves descendants of Africans and often retained a sense of being Yoruba, Fon, or Ewe in origin, but nevertheless maintained a superior attitude toward the "natives." Africans considered them to be a species of European. Flint and Geiss, *Africans in South America*, CEA, Cambridge, 1981, 5:428-30. *See also* Afro-Brazilians in Dahomey.

Afro-Lusitanism   An expression referring to the supposed ability of the Portuguese to adapt to life in tropical Africa and to adopt the ways and customs of local Africans. It stressed friendly contact and Portuguese miscegenation with Africans, a process that began in West Africa with the Portuguese expansion c.1440. It is also called *Luso-tropicalismo*. Hamilton, *Voices*, p. 11.

Afro-Portuguese dynasties   An indeterminate number of hinterland rulers who emerged early in Angola and Mozambique. Some of the earlier settlers married African women and over the generations their families became increasingly Africanized, although they often retained their Portuguese names and other trappings of their European origins which helped to maintain their identity as a group. In Luanda c.1600, the Afro-Portuguese became a dominant force by gaining access to local supplies of salt, copper, and silver, and by participating in the slave trade. It also proved more profitable for them to trade with the Dutch, English, French, and directly with the Brazilians. Indeed, until the nineteenth century, European traders used mainly Afro-Portuguese personnel to conduct trade for them. In Sofala, Mozambique, the Afro-Portuguese controlled the trade in ivory, gold, and cloth from 1584. With the connivance of the local authorities, they established their power over the local Africans, first along the lower Zambezi and later in Tete and Zumbo. By 1634, there were well-established Afro-Portuguese chiefdoms trading with the Swahili-speaking Arab and Goan merchants along the Indian Ocean coast, in Central Africa, and in the upper Zambezi area. By the eighteenth century these mixed-race families still controlled much of the Zambezi River valley and exacted tribute from their Tonga subjects in the form of foodstuffs, cotton cloth, ivory, gold dust, and slaves. They organized trading expeditions to the fairs in the Manica Highlands and to Zumbo at the confluence of the Zambezi and the Luangwa rivers. They were also granted *prazos* (q.v.) and ruled the colony through their military, economic, and judicial powers. Late in the eighteenth century they began to open up new territory north of the Zambezi. Newitt, *Portugal in Africa,* pp. 2-3, 7-8; GEPB.

Afro-Portuguese modern literature   This is a distinctive Lusophone body of literature having stylistic features, themes, and patterns of expression of real or supposed African character. This movement, still in its formative stages, includes racial characteristics and regional themes and values. The term "Afro-Portuguese Literature" offers a framework in which to assess the modern cultural and literary factors that have been at work in the five areas of Portuguese Africa: Angola, Cape Verde, Guinea-Bissau, Mozambique, and São Tomé e Príncipe. Hamilton, *Voices*, pp. 8-9. *See also* African literature before 1900.

Afro-Portuguese pride A deep sense of self-esteem and one's own dignity, publicly expressed in the press in 1929 by members of the *Partido National Africano* (q.v.). The leaders of this party were educated *assimilados* (q.v.) and Afro-Portuguese from various provinces who were influenced by Pan-Africanism, Pan-Negroism, Garveyism, and anti-slavery humanitarianism. They proposed a new multiracialism for Portuguese Africa that would allow the free development of Afro-Portuguese culture. In an article published by *A Voz d'Africa*, July 8, 1929, a writer said: "We are not simply Portuguese. Before being Portuguese, we are Africans. We are Portuguese of black ancestry." Wheeler, *Angola,* pp. 11-19.

Afro-Portuguese types After the start of the Portuguese expansion, mixed-blood individuals, often the off-spring of a Portuguese father and an African mother, identified themselves as Africans by adopting African names, language, customs, kinship, and new systems of values and religious belief. Duffy, *Portuguese Africa,* pp. 97-8. *See also* mestiço, muzungo, pombeiro.

afumu (Bant.) In Zambezia c.1650, a local chief subordinate to the *mambo* (q.v.) and in charge of resolving minor disputes. He transmitted and enforced the dictates of the *mambo*, collected taxes, and supported religious, social, and political functions. He was usually a senior member of the dominant local lineage. Also called *mfumu*. Isaacman, *Mozambique: From Colonialism,* pp. 4, 5, 128.

age-mate In Mozambique and elsewhere in Africa, a young boy who was a member of an initiation group. After a painful ritual, usually circumcision, he kept deep personal ties to his fellow group members. Age-mates were brothers for life. Herrick, *Area Handbook,* pp. 75, 137.

Age of Discovery *See* Discovery.

Agencia de Depositos e Transferencias de Fundos (Pg.) "Agency for Deposits and Transfers of Funds." An official government agency established in 1910 in Mozambique that allowed contracted mining workers in South Africa to send money back home without charge. Rita-Ferreira, *O Movimento Migratorio*, pp. 118-19.

Agencia Geral das Colonias (Pg.) "General Agency for the Colonies." A Portuguese government agency established on July 29, 1924, under the Colonial Ministry. This was the agency with authority over the juridical and commercial services, a center of information and propaganda, and in charge of specialized publications and libraries. It organized international exhibitions that showed African products and stressed Portuguese efforts to "civilize" the

Africans and modernize the colonial services. It set up awards for colonial writers and published *Boletim Geral das Colonias, Coleccão de Legislação Colonias*, and series such as *Biblioteca Colonias Portuguesa, Pelo Imperio*, and *Classicos da Expansao*. GEPB.

aggry beads   Blue glass beads, generally cylindrical, found nearly everywhere in Africa either in the tombs or tumili, reputed to be ancient or owned by the living who claim to have received them from their most distant ancestors. Africans attach great value to these beads. In the sixteenth and seventeenth centuries these beads were the objects of active commerce by English and especially Dutch navigators who bought them in countries where they were relatively abundant and sold them at a profit in the countries where they were scarce. These navigators gave them the name of *pierres d'aigris* or aggry beads, a modified form of *akori*, a word probably of Edo origin and the name for the blue coral of the Bight of Benin. Delafosse, *The Negroes of Africa*, pp. 29-30.

Agisymba (Ar.)   "Africa South of the Sahara." A term used by Claudius Ptolemy, a second-century Egyptian astronomer and geographer, to refer to the area south of Libya. Jahn, *Neo-African Literature*, p. 20.

agricultura dirigida (Pg.)   "Guided agriculture." A system introduced by the Portuguese government into Portuguese-African colonies with the purpose of teaching Africans to grow modern agricultural products and raise cash crops. Cotton cultivation on a large scale was introduced into Angola and Mozambique c.1946 and land was selected for cultivation, commercialization, and industrialization of cotton production. In Portuguese Africa cotton out put increased from 800 tons in 1926 to 28,000 tons in 1951. The *colonato* (q.v.) system was established in rural areas in 1950 with the intention of further modernizing traditional African land cultivation. Caetano, *Os Nativos*, pp. 81-3.

agua branca (Pg.)   "White water." The name given by Portuguese sailors c.1500 to milky sea waters populated by millions of protozoans, especially those belonging to phosphorescent subgroups that glow at night. DMA.

Agua-Izé   A large cocoa plantation in São Tomé that in 1898 built 30 mi. (50 km) of decauville (narrow gauge) rail to bring in supplies and to take its produce to the seaport. GEPB.

agua-vermelha (Pg.)   "Vermilion water." A poisonous beverage made from the bark of a tropical tree (*Erythrophleum guinense*) found in Angola, the Congo, and elsewhere in Portuguese Africa and used in tribal ordeals (q.v.).

A sorcerer would force an accused individual to drink *agua-vermelha* to test his innocence or guilt. This potion taken in small amounts is purgative, inducing violent peristalsis; in larger quantities it is emetic, causing vomiting. In the first case, the accused dies shortly of cardiac arrest; in the second, he survives. Portuguese law punished this practice as a serious crime. Carvalho e Vasconcellos, *As Colonias Portuguesas,* p. 160; Ficalho, *Plantas Uteis,* pp. 64. *See also* ambundu, eseré, muave.

agulha (Pg.) A white cotton cloth, usually printed with blue or red stripes, woven in Santiago and Santo Antão, Cape Verde. It was very popular during the colonial period in Guinea-Bissau and elsewhere in West Africa. Carreira, *Panaria Cabo-Verdiana,* p. 90.

agulha de marear (Pg.) *See* compasso di navigare.

agulha magnetica (Pg.) A navigational instrument used by the Portuguese at the time of the Discovery (q.v.). It consisted of a magnetized needle mounted at the center of a graduated board. The needle swings freely in the horizontal plane to find magnetic north. GEPB.

Agulhas, Banco de (Pg.) A stormy and dangerous bank near the Cape of Good Hope where the ocean current is deflected to the south by the bank and meets the northeast drift from the Antarctic. Here the conflict between warm and cold currents between June and July produces about 30 percent of the gales. It was discovered by Portuguese navigators around 1488. Axelson, *Portuguese in East-Africa,* pp. 214-5.

Agulhas, Cabo das (Pg.) Cape Agulhas, the southernmost point of Africa, 120 mi. (190 km) east-southeast of Cape Town. It serves as the dividing line between the Atlantic and the Indian Oceans. The Portuguese navigator Bartolomeu Dias discovered this cape in 1498. Originally it was called *Ponta de São Brandão*. Raper, *Portuguese Place Names*, in Valkhoof, *Miscelanea,* p. 274; DHP.

Agulhas e Alfileres (Pg.) "Needles and Pins." A humorous illustrated magazine published in Lourenço Marques, Mozambique, between 1924 and 1925. Dias, *A Imprensa,* p. 22.

Agulhas, Gulf of (Pg.) A deep, wide gulf on the east coast of South Africa where on April 23, 1488, Bartolomeu Dias anchored to repair his ships. This gulf is located three miles (4.8 km) east of Cabo das Agulhas (q.v.). Axelson, *Portuguese in South-East,* p. 16.

Aid-el-kebir (Ar.)   Among the Mandingoes in Guinea-Bissau, an annual Moslem festival of glorification of the prophet Mohammed as the origin of the Arab race and to celebrate family unity. Also called *Bana sali* and, by the Fulas, *Donquim*, it falls on the twelfth day of the twelfth month of the Moslem year, which is two lunar months after Ramadan (q.v.). Gonçalves, *O Mundo Arabo-Islámico*, p. 213.

"Ainda que somos negros, gente somos, e alma tenemos" (Pg)   "Although we are black, we are people, and we have souls." An old saying used by Africans in Portugal. Chaves, *O Preto da Guiné*, Congresso Commemorativo, Lisbon, 1946, 2:562.

aindé (Afr.)   In the coastal zone of Guinea-Bissau, a broad depression covered by water or streams with a thick stratum of fertile soil. In the Bafata-Gabu and Boe region of Futa-Djallon the term *aindé* is applied to deep river-beds with seasonal streams. Mota, *Guiné Portuguesa,* I:24, 52. *See also* felo.

aiu (Crio.)   An African table game, popular in Cape Verde, Guinea-Bissau, and elsewhere. It consists of a wooden board with twelve wells where dried, lead-colored beans are dropped. In the Portuguese-African version, players move all the beans from a well, dropping one bean in the next and the next and so on. The winner is the player whose strategy results in the greatest number of beans while simultaneously leaving his opponent without a move. Known in English as *warri*. *Boletim de Propaganda e Informaçao*, Cape Verde, 1967, 148:11; HDRGC.

aiué! (Kimb.)   An exclamation of distress used in Angolan poetry. "Our youngest son,/ they sent him to São Tomé./ He had no papers,/ *Aiué!*/ Our son cried,/ Mamma raved./ *Aiué!*" Hamilton, *Voices*, p. 108.

Ajuda   *See* Ouidah.

Ajuda, Biblioteca da (Pg.)   "Ajuda Library." An important library founded in 1721 by King João V containing valuable historical material on Portugal and its colonies, including a collection of 200 codices known as *Rerum Lusitanicarum* and the collection *Symmicta O Lusitanica*. Silva Rego, *O Ultramar*, p. 18.

Ajuda, São Baptista de   *See* São Baptista de Ajuda.

ajudas (Pg.)   In São Tomé and elsewhere around 1600, slaves brought from São Baptista de Ajuda and Dahomey (qq.v.) to work on the plantations. After

1875, it meant free contract laborers doing temporary work on the sugar and cocoa plantations on the island. Almada Negreiros, *Historia*, pp. 256-7.

akee *See* ackee.

Alagoa Bay A bay on the southeastern coast of South Africa about 420 mi. (680 km) east of Cape Town, discovered by the Portuguese in 1498. Alagoa Bay appeared in the *Perestrello Survey* of 1575. Port Elizabeth was founded by the British on its shore in 1820. Axelson, *Portuguese in South-East,* pp. 15, 3; Valkhoff, *Miscelanea,* p. 267.

Albasini Town A town at the foot of the Southparensberg Range in the Transvaal, South Africa, named for the Portuguese-African leader João Albasini who settled in the Transvaal in the mid-nineteenth century. Valkhoff, *Miscelanea,* p. 268.

ALC (African Liberation Committee) An organization established by the OAU (q.v.) in Dar es-Salaam, Tanzania, in 1967 to help Portuguese-African nationalists in their struggle for independence. Soon it became the main source of aid for FRELIMO (q.v.). Herrick, *Area Handbook,* p. 172.

Alcacer-Qibir, Battle of (Afr.) Battle which took place on August 4, 1578, between Arab Moslems and the Portuguese, the latter led by King Sebastião. The Moslem forces of Abde Almelique numbered 40,000 cavalry and 8,000 infantry; King Sebastião's army numbered 16,500. The battle, one of the largest conflicts in North Africa up to that time, ended with the complete defeat of the Portuguese and the death of Sebastião. From that time can be traced the decline of the Portuguese monarchy and the Portuguese Empire. Because young King Sebastião was unmarried and left no heir to the throne, the crown passed to his uncle, Cardinal-King Henrique. When he, too, died without issue in 1580 the crown passed to Philip II of Spain, the closest relative of the late king and known in Portugal as King Filipe I. The Spanish, more concerned with their own empire in the New World, neglected to stop the Dutch and other Europeans from infringing on Portuguese territory in Brazil, Africa, and India. DHP; GEPB.

Alcaçovas Peace Treaty A treaty signed in Castile in 1479 between Afonso V of Portugal and Ferdinand and Isabella, the Catholic rulers of Spain, that ended the Spanish War of Succession. Among its provisions were the recognition of Portuguese sovereignty over Guiné, Madeira, the Azores, and Cape Verde, the Portuguese right to colonize the Kingdom of Fez, and Spanish sovereignty over the Canary Islands. DHP.

aldeamento (Pg.) In Mozambique, Angola, and elsewhere in Portuguese Africa, a protected settlement organized by the Portuguese government at the beginning of the War for Independence (1960). By the early 1970s there were at least one million Angolans, and possibly as many Mozambicans, resettled in *aldeamentos*. These villages were guarded by their own armed militia. The *aldeamentos*, the lineal descendants of the *colonatos* (q.v.), ended the traditional free economy of the local Africans. Kaplan, *Area Handbook,* pp. 6, 60, 170, 197; Newitt, *Portugal in Africa* pp. 124, 131.

alforria (Pg.) "Manumission." In Portugal in the 1500s, the practice of freeing slaves by their master or by his heirs if he had made provision in his will. *Alforria* was often conditional on the slave's payment of a certain sum of money. As a rule, the price of freedom seemed to have been equivalent to the market price of a slave, although considerably more might have been paid in duties and incidental expenses. Saunders, *A Social History,* p. 138; GEPB. *See also* carta de alforria.

Algarve Coast The coastal strip of the Algarve province of southern Portugal. It played an important role in providing safe ports and supplying sailors for the exploration of the West African coast and the Atlantic Islands initiated by Prince Henry around 1420. The Sagres nautical school (q.v.), founded and supported by Prince Henry, was located on the Algarve coast with branches in Lagos, Faro, Olhão, and other towns. Portuguese trade with Africa was so successful that by 1500 about 10 percent of the population in this area were slaves. Livermore, *A New History,* p. 7.

Algodão de Moçambique (Pg.) A biweekly technical periodical published by Ismael Alves da Costa in Lourenço Marques, Mozambique. It began on October 5, 1925, and ended on March 15, 1926. Among its writers was J.A. Evans, an American cotton specialist. Dias, *A Imprensa,* pp. 22, 81.

algodoeiro (Pg.) *See* cotton.

ALIAZO (*Alliance des Ressortissants de Zombo*) (Fr.) "National Alliance of Zombo Nationalists." A moderate nationalist party organized in 1960 with headquarters in Leopoldville, former Belgian Congo. ALIAZO was nonviolent and conciliatory in tone, reflecting the Christian training and middle-class values of its Zombo ethnic leadership. ALIAZO's rank and file included large numbers of businessmen, teachers, civil servants, and journalists, many of whom were imbued with a tradition of communal self-help and self-determination, a tradition that Simão Toco had done much to foster. As late as 1960, the aim of the party was to win self-government within an independent Angola. Marcum, *The Angolan Revolution*, I:88-9; Pelissier, *La Colonie,* pp. 280-1. *See also* ASSOMIZO.

Aljube prison   A prison in Lisbon where African nationalists were held at various times. One prominent personality imprisoned in Aljube was Joaquim Pinto de Andrade, a Catholic priest and chancellor of the archdiocese of Luanda, Angola. After protesting the arrest of Agostinho Neto, he was arrested on June 25, 1959, and sent to Aljube. On October 17, 1961, Dr. Agostinho Neto was arrested and sent to Aljube; subsequently, he was permitted to live outside under house arrest. Marcum, *The Angolan Revolution*, I:203, 334.

Alliance des Ressortissants de Zombo   *See* ALIAZO.

alma arsinaria (Pg.)   "Arsinarian soul." An expression used in contemporary Cape Verdian literature to express a deep nationalistic feeling connected with Cabo Arsinario (q.v.). Araujo, *A Study,* p. 30.

alma negra (Pg.)   "Black soul." Expression used by F. Castro Soromenho to refer to the spirit of the African man oppressed by custom and circumstance, a picture quite different from the world of the "happy darkies" of white American folklore. Moser, *Essays,* p. 50.

Almagest (Ar.)   "The Greatest." Name applied to two books by the second-century geographer Claudius Ptolemy. Highly respected by Arab scholars and influential in Europe, around 1195 the books were translated into Latin by Gerard de Cremona, then at Toledo. The *Almagest* was well known in Europe and used in the Sagres nautical school (q.v.) around 1440. The books' heliocentric picture of the universe was accepted by scholars until the Copernican revolution of 1540. Parry, *The Discovery of the Sea,* pp. 57-8; EI.

almami (Ar.)   A high religious office in Islam. In Guinea-Bissau and elsewhere, an *almami* must exhibit strict moral conduct and be an example for the community. Gonçalves, *O Islamismo na Guiné,* p. 38.

Almanach Perduravel de Coimbra (Pg.)   "Perdurable Calendar of Coimbra." An astrologic/astronomic table describing the relative positions and motions of the heavenly bodies, compiled and composed in Portugal c.1380 and influenced by Levi ben Gerson's *Milhãmot Adonai* (Wars of the Lord) written in Hebrew c.1300. Cortesao, *History*, I:210.

Almanach Perpetuum (Lat.)   "Perpetual Almanac." An astronomic calendar composed by Abraham Zacuto for the years 1473-8 and published in Hebrew

(Leiria, 1496). It contained mathematical calculations of planetary movement, declination of the sun in degrees/minutes/seconds, and solar cycles. This almanac was a vital factor in improving Portuguese navigation at the time of King João II and King Manuel I. Because there were a number of methods to determine solar declination, in 1484 King João II of Portugal convened a commission of mathematicians to devise the best method to find latitude by solar observation. Among the most accurate and detailed were those in the *Almanach Perpetuum*. Costa, *A Marinha*, pp. 85-92; Parry, *The Discovery of the Sea,* pp. 148-49; GEPB.

Almanach Statistico da Provincia d'Angola e Suas Dependencias (Pg.) "Statistical Calendar of the Province of Angola and Its Dependencies." An almanac published in Luanda in 1852 by Inocencio Francisco da Silva. It contained information about government offices, administrative employees, population, climate, the production of rural and trade industry, commerce, legislation, military forces, religion, public education, a catalog of the governors, and information about the inhabitants of the colony. Among the merchants and industrialists mentioned was the rich entrepreneuse and widow Ana Joaquina dos Santos Silva. Lopo, *Journalismo,* pp. 41-5.

almeidina (Pg.) A cultivated tropical plant (*Carpodinus gracilis*) yielding a commercially useful but inferior rubber, known on the London market c.1870 as potato-gum rubber. The name *Almeidina* was given to this crop by João Duarte de Almeida, a Portuguese pioneer in Mossâmedes. Around 1880, *almeidina* became an important product exported to Portugal and Europe; the *almeidina*, or rubber, boom ended in 1910, partly because of international competition. Clarence-Smith, *Slaves, Peasants,* pp. 25, 49, 95.

Almirante-mor (Pg.) "Fleet Admiral." The naval officer commanding a fleet, a post created in Portugal c.1288. At the beginning of the fifteenth century there were admirals in Porto and Lisbon and probably a third admiral in Lagos where Prince Henry resided after 1423. King Afonso V added duties and honors to this position in 1450. At that time, one of the *almirantes-mor* had a few Genoese sea captains in his service. DHP.

almiscar (Pg.) A strong-scented substance from any of several varieties of plants used as the base of many perfumes. *Almiscar* was exported by the Portuguese from West Africa to Portugal after the establishment c.1480 of factories in Gambia, along the *Malagüeta* (Pepper) Coast and the Slave Coast. Godinho, *A Economia,* p. 210.

almoxarife (Ar.) "Official receiver." In Portugal, a treasurer in charge of collecting the duties, rents, and taxes on import/export commodities, including slaves, at the time of the Discovery (q.v.). Due to the development of commerce, several receivers were appointed under the control of the royal treasurer. In 1516 it was established that each *almoxarife* had to give an annual account of his activities to the *tribunal das contas* (accounting tribunal). Saunders, *A Social History,* pp. 15-6; GEPB.

almoxarife dos escravos (Pg.) "Official receiver of slaves." In Portugal early in the Discovery (q.v.), a royal controller serving at the *Casa dos Escravos* (q.v.). The first *almoxarife dos escravos* was appointed in 1486 and immediately came to play a key role in the organization of trade with the West African coast. His principal duty was to oversee the slave trade carried out by vessels belonging to or chartered by the Crown, and to receive and sell the slaves on the ships' return to Lisbon. The *almoxarife* also acted as paymaster, giving slaves or their value in cash to persons designated by the king. In addition, he was entrusted with the sale of licenses to merchants engaged in the West African slave trade, the leasing of trading monopolies of certain sections of the West African coast, and the granting of tax reduction to farmers in Cape Verde and São Tomé e Príncipe. Finally, he collected a 5 percent duty on all goods, including slaves, imported from Africa. Saunders, *A Social History,* pp. 8-9; GEPB.

Alvor (Pg.) "Dawn." A magazine published in 1948 by African students in Lourenço Marques. It was the voice of young Mozambicans like Eduardo Mondlane, who had been expelled from South Africa when a change of government revised the rules governing non-citizen African students. As the official organ of NESAM (q.v.), its aim was to enlighten ordinary Africans about the need to acquire a basic education, to preserve cultural identity, and to end colonial abuses. Besides Mondlane, the editorial staff included A. Guebuza, J. Chissano, M. Matsinda, and other, less prominent, leaders. Henriksen, *Revolution*, pp. 18, 180; Munslow, *Mozambique,* p. 66; HDM.

Alvor Accord A treaty signed on January 15, 1975, between representatives of Portugal and the leaders of FNLA, MPLA, and UNITA (qq.v.) at the Angolan town of Alvor. This agreement set down the basic principles of government for Angola during the transition period leading to independence. The major provisions set the dates for a general cease-fire and for independence, affirmed the integrity of Angola (including Cabinda), and determined the composition and powers of the transitional government. Portugal suspended the Accord in August 1975 after the outbreak of civil war between liberation movements had made its provisions unworkable. HDA.

Alvorada (Pg.) "Daybreak." A cultural periodical published by the *Tecnica Sá da Bandeira* in Lourenço Marques, Mozambique. Issues appeared between

July 1943 and September 1944. Its editor was Fernando Pearson. Dias, *A Imprensa,* pp. 22, 93.

AMA (*Associação das Mulheres de Angola*) (Pg.) "Angolan Women's Association." A women's political group organized in Luanda in 1962 and closely allied to such other nationalist parties as the MPLA (q.v.). Wheeler, *Angola,* p. 206.

Ambaca (Afr.) Town and municipality, Cuanza-Norte district, Luanda province, Angola. Established as a *presidio* (q.v.) in 1618, it later became an important trade center for slaves, ivory, wax, and wild rubber, all controlled by *mestiços* (q.v.). In 1926, cotton began to be widely cultivated and by 1933 Ambaca's population was 71,175, including 990 Europeans. An important coffee producing area, it is served by the Ambaca railway. Ambaca played a dominant role in the struggle for independence in 1960, when the MPLA (q.v.) organized guerrillas in the region. Pelissier, *La Colonie,* pp. 257, 403; GEPB.

Ambaquista (Afr.) A term for an active and "civilized" (Europeanized) Mbundu individual settled around Ambaca (q.v.) where a *presidio* was built in 1618. *Ambaquistas* soon became entrepreneurs or jacks-of-all trades who did clerical work for illiterate chiefs or Portuguese in the 1840s. They wore European dress and bribed Portuguese officials to avoid army service. They read Portuguese and developed a Mbundu-Portuguese *lingua franca* c.1850 to carry on their trade in the interior of northeastern Angola in ivory and slaves. *Ambaquistas* were in the forefront of the struggle for independence in 1961. In Luanda, the center of anti-Portuguese resistance, there were about 13,000 *ambaquistas* dedicated to obtaining economic and political freedom. Pelissier, *La Colonie,* pp. 237, 450; GEPB.

ambergris A valuable grayish, waxy digestive substance found in or ejected from the stomach of sperm whales. Ambergris is often found floating around Cape Verde and is used as a fixative in perfumes. In colonial times it was also used to remove hair from animal skins prior to tanning. On March 14, 1732, King João V of Portugal ruled that ambergris found inside whales landed on Cape Verde beaches was the property of the Royal Treasury. The authorities had the right to oversee its trade and collect taxes on it. Carreira, *The People,* pp. 42-3.

Ambriz (Afr.) An Angolan seaport north of Luanda which between 1830 and 1840 was one of the most important outlets for the exportion of slaves to the Brazilian plantations. Ambriz was the terminus of the central route from the interior of the colony. GEPB.

Ambuila, Batalha de (Pg.) A decisive battle fought in northern Angola on October 29, 1665, between the army of the African king Antonio I of Congo and that of Luis Lopes de Sequeira, governor of Angola. This confrontation brought chaos and anarchy to the Congo Kingdom. Antonio was decapitated and his head taken to Luanda and buried at the Church of the Hermit of Nazareth. Gabriel, *Angola,* pp. 65, 122; DHP.

ambundu (Bant.) A poison prepared from the bark of a tropical tree (family Lagoecieae) used in folk medicine. In tribal ordeals (q.v.) a sorcerer forced an accused person to drink the *ambundu* to prove his innocence or guilt. Africans believed that divine protection would assist the sinless to survive. The tree is found in northern Angola, Zaire, and elsewhere. Ficalho, *Plantas Uteis,* pp. 164-5. *See also* agua-vermelha.

American In Cape Verde, the term for a non-white immigrant to the United States who, after years abroad, returns rich to his homeland. When poverty increased in the islands in the 1920s, "Americans" bought land and houses from their former employers. These one-time servants, *mestiços*, and "dark skins" humiliated the country's whites by imposing themselves on the traditional ruling class. Carreira, *The People,* p. 54.

American Board of Commissioners for Foreign Missions An American congregation that in 1884 established a mission among the Ovimbundu people in southern Angola. Soon its missions and schools began to spread through Angola. Two of its members, William H. Sanders and Wesley M. Stover, both linguists, published an Umbundu vocabulary and grammar in 1884; they later translated the New Testament into Umbundu. In 1921, the congregation built a hospital, opened a secondary school, and organized a printing press in the town of Dondi. The missions published bilingual literature that introduced the Umbundu language to modern literary culture. Henderson, *Angola,* pp. 150-1.

American Committee on Angola *See* ACOA.

amoreira (Pg.) Iroke fustic tree (*Chlorophora excelsa* Welw.). Tall tropical tree of up to 430 ft. (130 m). Its thick straight white-yellow trunk supports massive dense foliage. It grows in primeval wooded areas such as Cazengo, Golungo Alto, and Dembos, Angola, in São Tomé, and elsewhere. Its abundant fruit feeds thousands of birds; its wood is used in housing and furniture. Its African name is *mucamba-camba*. Ficalho, *Plantas Uteis,* pp. 265-6.

ANC (African National Congress) A political party founded in South Africa by D.P. Seme, G.P. Montsioa, R.W. Msimang, and A. Mangena. Its first president was the Rev. J.L. Dube. Annual conferences are held. The ANC was banned in 1960 by the South African government and its leaders were either jailed or went into exile in Maputo, Mozambique. The Mozambican nationalists supported and recognized the ANC as the sole legitimate representation of the South African people, a move that intensified the guerrilla war and weapon smuggling into South Africa. In January 1981, a raid by clandestine South African forces killed several ANC leaders. In 1982 President Samora Machel of Mozambique heightened the armed struggle. Hanlon, *Mozambique Revolution*, pp. 256, 60-2; SESA.

ancestors, cult of the   In traditional African religion, a cult devoted to worship of the spirits of the ancestors, practiced by many people throughout southern Mozambique and in many other parts of Portuguese Africa. Adherents believe that their ancestors take a direct interest in human activities and provide rain, increase crops, and stimulate agricultural and human fertility. In the north, where emphasis is placed on the maternal line of descent, it is the maternal ancestors with whom persons are most concerned. In the south, where patrilineal social organizations are believed to be most influential in affairs of the family, paternal ancestors are particularly worshipped. These beliefs inspire strong ties with the supernatural world in general, and with the ancestral family spirits in particular. Herrick, *Area Handbook,* pp. 102, 111, 137.

Anglican Church in Mozambique   In 1893 the Anglican Church created the Diocese of Lebombos and a mission in Lourenço Marques, Mozambique. One reason it was established was to take care of the Mozambican workers who had returned from the Johannesburg gold fields in South Africa, because some of these workers during their stay in the mines had joined the Church of England. In spite of local Portuguese opposition, the mission survived and extended its work until 1975 when Mozambique became an independent country. Newitt, *Portugal in Africa*, pp. 125-6; Pereira da Lima, *Edifícios Históricos*, p. 124.

Anglo-German Agreement, 1898   A secret agreement between England and Germany signed on August 30, 1898. This accord authorized Germany to acquire Angola as "an economic sphere of influence," except for a British area in central Angola that included Luanda, the customs revenue of which had been offered as security if the Portuguese government defaulted on repaying loans. Wheeler, *Angola,* p. 74.

Anglo-Portuguese Peace and Friendship Treaty, 1810   An accord signed on February 19, 1810, in which the Prince Regent, later King João V, of Portugal agreed to take measures against the slave traffic between his African colonies and Brazil. This treaty was never ratified. Cunha, *O Trabalho Indigena,* p. 18.

Anglo-Portuguese Secret Declaration, 1899 An agreement signed in 1899 between England and Portugal that pledged Britain to protect Portuguese Africa "against future as well as present enemies." This helped Portugal consolidate its hold on the African territory it possessed after the partition treaties of 1885, 1886, 1891, and 1894. Wheeler, *Angola,* pp. 61, 62.

Anglo-Portuguese Treaty, 1642 An agreement signed in 1642 between King João IV of Portugal and Charles I of England giving England "most favored nation" status in trading with Portuguese colonies, granting Englishmen religious freedom in Portugal, and giving Portugal the right to buy arms and ships from England and to hire English troops. Livermore, *A New History,* pp. 173-4.

Anglo-Portuguese Treaty, 1661 An accord between England and Portugal signed June 23, 1661, according to which England would defend Portugal and its overseas territories "as if they were England itself," and have the right to trade with Portuguese colonies, including Bombay. Livermore, *A New History,* pp. 190-1.

Anglo-Portuguese Treaty, 1815 A treaty between England and Portugal signed in July 1815 declaring slave trading in Portuguese vessels to be illegal and establishing a mixed commission and court of arbitration over captured vessels in Luanda. Wheeler, *Angola,* p. 52.

Anglo-Portuguese Treaty, 1879 An agreement signed between the two countries on May 30, 1879, "For the development of commerce in South Africa and the more effectual suppression of the slave trade on the East coast and in the Interior of the African Continent." Axelson, *Portugal,* p. 28.

Anglo-Portuguese Treaty, 1884 An agreement signed on February 26, 1884, by which the British government acknowledged the authority of the king of Portugal over the Atlantic coast between 8°12' S and Porto da Lenha. The inland border was to be defined and demarcated as soon as possible. The territory was to be open to all nations; foreigners would enjoy the same privileges as the subjects of Portugal. Trade and navigation along the coastline and on the Congo River and other waterways was to be open to all nations and not subject to any monopoly or impediment, customs duties, or tolls, except those agreed upon. The parties further agreed to appoint a commission to draw up regulations for the navigation and supervision of all rivers. Axelson, *Portugal,* pp. 62-3.

Anglo-Portuguese Treaty, 1943 A treaty between England and Portugal giving British forces the right to occupy the Azores and guaranteeing the integrity of Portugal and her possessions by the United Kingdom, the Dominions, and the United States. Livermore, *A New History,* p. 337.

Angoche (Afr.) A Portuguese ammunition steamer destroyed by sabotage late in April 1971. The burned ship was found, abandoned and adrift, off the northern coast of Mozambique. Since FRELIMO (q.v.) spokesmen at the time declined responsibility for the gutted ship and the missing crew, this incident has remained unexplained. Henriksen, *Mozambique,* p. 123.

Angola, agriculture in The Portuguese arrived at northern Angola in 1483 and found a sedentary Bantu society with an economy based on hunting, fishing, collecting wild fruits, and practicing a primitive agriculture called vegeculture (q.v.) that included cultivation of grains such as fonio, sorghum, and millet (qq.v.) as well as watermelon and sweet potato. The newcomers introduced species of wheat, rice, figs, grapes, and other plants cultivated in Europe. Around 1550, the Portuguese brought manioc (cassava), maize, chilies, and potatoes from Brazil. These crops were planted around São Salvador do Congo and spread throughout the colony, providing food for millions of Angolans and their neighbors. The second period of agricultural expansion began around 1830-40 when the Luanda hinterland was developed. At this time, sugar and coffee plantations, together with small farms known as *arimos* and *roças* (qq.v.) were established. Soon these cash crops were complemented by sugar cane, a rum and brandy industry, sisal-growing, and the ubiquitous manioc for cassava flour. In 1850, agriculture began expanding outwardly from near the urban centers into the *sertões* (q.v.). Export crops increased on European-owned plantations north of the Cuanza River as well as near the Atlantic coast at Benguela and Mossâmedes. Wild rubber from eastern Angola became a boom crop between 1870 and 1900. In the twentieth century cotton acquired a dominant role in the economy. Kaplan, *Angola,* p. 8; Wheeler, *Angola,* pp. 2, 51-55, 136-7; GEPB; OED. *See also* Mozambique, agriculture in.

Angola, armed forces in According to a Portuguese law of 1684, there could be no distinction between whites, *mestiços,* or free Africans in the army. During the colonial period the Angolan army was mostly composed of *mestiços* (q.v.) and free Africans up through the mid-nineteenth century. By 1900 there was a preponderance of *assimilados* (q.v.), either *mestiços* or Africans, in the colonial army. Wheeler, *Angola,* pp. 36(n), 70, 94, 96.

Angola Bund (Germ.) "Angolan Confederation." An organization established in Germany in 1898 by colonists wishing to incorporate southern Angola into

South West Africa, then a German colony. In the period from 1898 to 1903 and again from 1912 to 1914 the Angola Bund tried to win over public opinion to their annexation plan with articles in the German press. Wheeler, *Angola*, p. 75.

Angola Capelo e Ivens A single-issue magazine published in Luanda in 1885 to commemorate the crossing of Africa from Angola to Mozambique and back by H.C.B. Capelo and R. Ivens. Lopo, *Jornalismo*, p. 59.

Angola, colonization of Colonization in Angola began with the charter granted to Paulo Dias de Novais in 1571. He accepted the obligation to bring one hundred families from Portugal, including farmers to whom within six months he was to give seeds and tools. The hostile climate and the attacks by Africans made agricultural work difficult and by 1589 the venture failed. In 1666 a second attempt also failed. Still another serious attempt was made by Governor Sousa Countinho in 1765. Bringing plants from Portugal, Brazil, and the Atlantic Islands, he tried to cultivate the Benguela *planalto* in southern Angola. In 1819, Governor Tovar de Albuquerque encouraged the planting of cotton and coffee which soon became the most exported crops in the colony. Between 1836 and 1840, the Marquis Sá de Bandeira, a reformer, declared the need for capital investment and the need to settle Portuguese farmers in the interior. Finally, between 1900 and 1950, the government devised several modern colonization programs for Africans and Europeans. By 1932, the *colonato* (q.v.) system was established along the Benguela railway in the central highlands near the Cuanza and Cunene rivers. The Provincial Settlement Board (1961-8) abolished the distinction between non-civilized and non-citizen farmers and created local administrative bodies to coordinate general and customary laws. Bender, *Angola*, pp. 95, 100, 104-5; HDA.

Angola commercio com Brazil (Pg.) "Angolan commerce with Brazil." This trade was declared duty-free and tax-free by a royal decree signed on January 11, 1758, in Lisbon. All Portuguese subjects, in Portugal or her colonies, were entitled to trade in slaves and goods from Angola and the other colonies to Brazil through the ports of Rio de Janeiro, Bahia, and Penambuco. Until then, commerce had been the king's monopoly. Silva Rego, *O Ultramar*, pp. 164-5.

Angola, coup attempt in On May 27, 1977, there was an unsuccessful attempt at a *coup d'état* on the government of President Antonio A. Neto. The civil war, the closing of schools, and the departure of most Portuguese administrators, military, colonists, and merchants generated popular discontent. The dislocation of public services and food distribution brought chaos to urban centers, especially in the *musseques* (slums) of Luanda. The people, encouraged by the nationalist slogan "Power to the People," came to the conclusion that new leaders were necessary. In a bloody encounter in Luanda, several MPLA (q.v.) leaders, including Minister of Finance Saydi Mingus, were killed. The discontent coalesced around Nito Alves, a charismatic leader who offered to provide an alternative to the *mestizo* intellectuals in government. The coup attempt failed and its leaders fled the country. HDA.

Angola, Cubans in In 1966, Fidel Castro sent military forces to Angola to train nationalist guerrillas who were fighting the Portuguese from the base they had established in Brazzaville, capital of the Republic of Congo. Initially the Cubans were concentrated in Guinea-Bissau and Cape Verde. At the time Angolans were also trained in Cuba, which provided money and weapons. Direct participation in combat began on November 5, 1975, when nationalist forces approached Luanda. In February 1976, the 14,000 Cuban soldiers turned the tide of war in favor of the MPLA (q.v.). In May 1977 their numbers had increased to 23,000, of whom 19,000 were military. The balance had important roles in health, education, housing, and other fields. During this time Castro characterized his nation as Latin-African, in sympathy with Angola, a Portuguese-African country. Kaplan, *Angola,* pp. 54, 159-60.

Angola, diocese of The diocese of Congo-Angola was established c.1580. Its name was changed in 1655 to the diocese of Angola. Its first bishop was Manuel de Natividade (1675-1685), a Portuguese Franciscan friar and superior of the Alenquer Monastery in Lisbon at the time of his nomination. Gabriel, *Angola*, pp. 156-7.

Angola, discovery and settlement of Explorer Diogo Cão reached the mouth of the Congo River in 1483. He learned of a king residing about 100 mi. (160 km) south subsequently identified as King Nzinga-a-Cuum (King João I of Congo after his baptism). Cão sent explorers to meet him but, without waiting for their return, he sailed back to Lisbon. On his second trip in 1484-6, Cão sent a mission with gifts to the African king; a message of peace included an invitation to convert to Christianity. In 1576, Paulo Dias de Novais organized the government of the colony, a status that continued with almost no modification until 1975 when Angola became an independent nation. DHP; GEPB.

Angola, education in Since the beginning of the colonial system of government around 1506, the Portuguese policy was to convert the Africans to Christianity and to educate and assimilate them. King Afonso I of Congo built churches and schools and brought missionaries, teachers, and artisans to "civilize" the Africans. Many young Congolese were taken to schools and universities in Portugal to teach them Portuguese, the Christian faith, and European culture and traditions. São Salvador and later Luanda were centers of education. In 1614 a private secondary school was opened by the Jesuits in Luanda. For over a century primary and secondary schools were the main sources of education in urban centers. Consequently, after the expulsion of the Jesuits in 1759, education was largely unavailable. By 1869 there were fewer than 600 students enrolled in the elementary schools. With the arrival in northern Angola of the Holy Ghost missionaries and Protestant mission schools in 1872, Africans again began enjoying the benefits of education. By 1909 there were 43 mission schools with a total enrollment of 2,235 students. The government delegated the task of "civilizing" through education to Catholic missions in 1919. Later that year, laws were passed making the use and teaching of Portuguese in all schools mandatory and forbidding the use of any other European language. Finally, the 1933 Constitution of the Portuguese Republic provided for the assimilation of the African population through education. Herrick, *Area Handbook,* pp. 121-135; DHP.

Angola, evangelization of The conversion of Angola to Christianity began with the opening of missions in 1560. A group of two Jesuits priests and two lay brothers met the expedition of Paulo Dias de Novais, the founder of Luanda, at the Cuanza River near Ambaca and accompanied him into the interior. This first attempt to convert Africans failed, as did the expedition. The Jesuits returned in 1575, established a parish, and built a church and residence. They limited their activities to Luanda and the surrounding area, baptizing numerous Africans, educating Portuguese children, and taking care of the spiritual needs of Africans and colonists. The Jesuits, assisted by the army, penetrated the interior. By 1593, twenty-five missionaries had arrived in Angola. Of these, half died of tropical diseases, mainly fevers. From 1660 on, the Jesuits concentrated on educating Africans, *mestiços*, and Portuguese children. In 1624, the Jesuits opened a college from which emerged both an African clergy and the *mestiço* caste who became the backbone of the civil service. Reports that the Society of Jesus participated in the Angolan-Brazilian slave trade were based on the belief that the way to convert Africans was to enslave them and force them to work on the Brazilian plantations. In 1759, the Marquês de Pombal expelled the order and closed the college, schools, and missions and the colony lost the educational institutions built during the past 200 years. For nearly 100 years more, until 1865, the Angolan people were left without missions or schools. Evangelization began its modern renaissance with the arrival of the French Holy Ghost missionaries in 1865 and the diocesan priests from the *Sernache do Bom Jardim* (q.v.) in 1875. Duffy, *Portuguese Africa*, pp. 52-3, 118-9; GEPB. *See also* Angolan missionaries, caravan of.

Angola, fairs in In the colonial period, Angolan markets were held in several towns at different intervals. These were important trade centers in Central Africa, bartering European ironwork, guns, and cloth for gold, ivory, and wax. Portuguese, Dutch, English, and French merchants organized large caravans to travel from the coast to the fair at Cassange, west of the Cuango River, which during the nineteenth century was one of the largest and most lucrative Angolan markets. Silva Rego, *O Ultramar*, pp. 149-50, 183; GEPB.

Angola, forced labor in The policy of forced labor, necessitated by the shortage of willing available labor in Portuguese Africa, was carried on until the twentieth century. Despite the Native Labor Code of 1878 which enabled Africans to decide for themselves whether they wanted to work, as "no one should be compelled to hire out his services except persons judged to be vagrants," in 1899 a government committee urged revision of this liberal labor policy and decided that force was necessary, both for economic development and for the "intellectual and moral betterment of the Africans." This latter policy was reinforced in 1928 with the provision that "all Africans should be subject to their social conditions. If they fail to fulfill it, the authorities may force them to do so." Herrick, *Area Handbook,* pp. 342-44; GEPB.

Angola, independence of *See* Angola, People's Republic of.

Angola, land tenure in Landholding in Angola was governed by both Portuguese law and the traditional African system based on customary law. The latter saw land as part of the economic structure of the community. It involved a complex system of rights and obligations which differed in detail among the various ethnic groups, although all shared the concept of collective ownership. The land was held in common by the village or the family; it was neither salable nor rentable, but remained under continuous use. The Portuguese government granted land concessions to settlers, and its effect on land traditionally held by Africans was evident by the late nineteenth and early twentieth century. The major legislation regarding landholding in Angola and elsewhere in Portuguese Africa was established in the Portuguese constitution of 1933 and in the Native Statute of 1954. Herrick, *Area Handbook*, pp. 277-8.

Angola, major language in Among the African languages and dialects spoken in contemporary Angola, Bantu is the most important. Bantu-speaking people already lived in the area of São Salvador do Congo when it was settled by the Portuguese in 1500. By the sixteenth century, the Bantu people had spread over most of the regions they occupy today and their language was adopted by people of diverse races and cultures. GEPB; HDA.

Angola, markets in   *See* Angola, fairs in.

Angola, modern settlers in   Although the Portuguese arrived at São Salvador in 1483, there were few settlers until 1800. Most of the colonists were *degredados* (q.v.), administrators, soldiers, or missionaries. The introduction of coffee in 1830-40 to Uige, the Zaire district, north and south Cuanza, and Cabinda attracted a few more colonists. Around 1850, Portuguese settlers were concentrated in Luanda, Benguela, Mossâmedes, and along the Atlantic coast. After World War II (1939-1945), tenants were lured to the hinterland by subsidies, free transportation, and offers of land ownership, housing, animals, and tools. During the War for Independence from 1960 to 1975, about 90 percent of these colonists were forced to return to Portugal. After independence, the new government encouraged repatriation of those who wished to come back to Angola. HDA.

Angola Negra (Pg.)   "Black Angola." A pre-war nationalist movement organized in 1948 by *mestiços* and students in Angola and Portugal to work for independence. This clandestine group emerged in 1952 as the *Conselho de Libertação de Angola.* Wheeler, *Angola*, pp. 162-3.

Angola, People's Republic of   This former Portuguese overseas province proclaimed its independence on November 11, 1975. Angolan president Antonio Agostinho Neto had signed a peace treaty with Portugal in January 1975, and Angola's independence was recognized by the Lisbon government on December 1, 1976. The United Nations accepted Angola as a member of the World Community on March 21, 1977. The following year Portugal established friendly relations with the former colony by sending Rosa Coutinho as its first ambassador. Adrian Sebastião presented his credentials in Lisbon as Angolan ambassador to Portugal on March 31, 1978. Soon after, a civil war broke out led by Jonas M. Savimbi the head of UNITA (q.v.). After seventeen years of war, the Angolan President Eduardo dos Santos and Savimbi signed the Lisbon Accord on May 31, 1991, which ended the conflict. *The Guardian Weekly*, June 9, 1991, p. 8; Pelissier, *La Colonie*, pp. 604-5; HDA.

Angola, plantation slavery in   Around 1850 slave labor was found mainly in cotton plantations in southern Angola and by 1870, there were between 3,000 and 4,000 slaves in the Mossâmedes area. Daily life was hard and workers labored from sunrise to sunset with a two-hour break at midday, and a rest on Sunday. Men and women performed the same tasks and labored in large gangs under the supervision of drivers and overseers who were slaves themselves. Women outnumbered men, partly because they were said to be more accustomed to agricultural tasks (women, not men, being the traditional

African farmers), and partly because, after the introduction of token salaries in the late 1870s, they were paid less than men. In 1869, a decree was passed whereby all slaves were declared *libertos* (q.v.). The changes in the former-slaves', now-contract laborers', conditions took place at the turn of the century as a result of international pressure and internal rebellions such as the Bailundo Revolt of 1902. Clarence-Smith, *Slaves, Peasants,* pp. 33, 36-8.

Angola, Provincial Settlement Board of A government agency created by decree in September 1961 to supervise and coordinate all rural settlements in the colony. In selecting settlers, the need was stressed to attract former soldiers to the *colonatos* (q.v.) and to emphasize racial integration. The idea was to establish multiracial agricultural communities. In 1967 the Board admitted 2,294 Portuguese and Cape Verdian colonists to Cela and other *colonatos*. The project eventually failed. Bender, *Angola*, pp. 109-11.

Angola, Revista Mensual de Doutrina e Propaganda Educativa de (Pg.) "Monthly Review of Education, Information and Propaganda of Angola." Published in Luanda by the *Liga Africana* (q.v.) in the 1930s, it was a mouthpiece for African interests in education and colonial policy and a medium in which to air grievances. In petitions, reports, and monthly articles, this periodical presented the views of *assimilados* (q.v.), the so-called "civilized" Africans. Wheeler, *Angola,* p. 147.

Angola, slave trade in *See* slave trade in Angola.

Angola, Soviet influence in From the beginning of the Angolan War for Independence in the 1960s, Soviet economic and military aid was rendered to Antonio A. Neto, the leader of the MPLA (q.v.). When the struggle began in earnest in 1967, Soviet military equipment was provided for guerrilla warfare. In 1971 as much as 70 to 80 percent of MPLA arms came from the Soviet Union and its satellites. In October 1976 Neto and Leonid Brezhnev signed a twenty-year friendship and cooperation treaty in Moscow. It provided for increased economic, technical, scientific, and cultural cooperation and the further strengthening and broadening of the links between the Soviet Communist Party and the MPLA. Kaplan, *Angola*, pp. 53, 134, 158-9.

Angola, United States' relations with In May 20, 1993, President William J. Clinton recognized the former Marxist government of President José Eduardo Santos as the government of the Republic of Angola. Although UNITA (q.v.), led by Jonas M. Savimbi, had been militarily, politically, and financially sustained for more than fifteen years by the United States, it was pressured to agree to a peace accord to end the eighteen-year war in which 400,000 people were killed. The United Nation secretary-general Boutros

Boutros-Ghali issued an ultimatum to Savimbi to pull his troops out of Angola before May 21, 1993, and to share power with the government of President Santos. The U.S. warned him that then was the time for an agreement to accept the May 1991 peace treaty signed in Lisbon (q.v.). The outcome is doubtful in view of Savimbi's intransigence. *The Washington Post*, Washington, D.C., May 21, 1993, p. 17.

Angola University The first university in Angola was opened in Luanda in 1963. It was integrated into the Portuguese university system and professors were often sent to Luanda from metropolitan Portugal. It awarded degrees for the first time in 1968. It was geared to the technical needs of a developing country, offering courses in engineering, medicine, veterinary science, agronomy, forestry, and secondary education. After independence, professors were selected to guarantee the implementation of the political line of the MPLA (q.v.). Beginning in the 1978-9 academic year, the faculties for the academic year included agrarian sciences, medicine, economics, engineering, and sciences and letters. Angola looked to the Soviet Union and its associates for faculty. Abshire, *Portuguese Africa,* p. 182; Kaplan, *Angola,* pp. 114-5.

Angola, War for Independence in The War for Independence started in 1961 with an armed revolt, sometimes called the Cotton Revolt, led by Bacongo and Mbundu (qq.v.) groups as well as *assimilados* (q.v.) in Baxa de Cassange, east of Malange. It was an act of defiance against the system of compulsory cotton cultivation for COTONANG (q.v.). In 1966, the MPLA (q.v.) was recognized as the movement representing the Angolan people. On February 4, 1971, an African mob stormed the São Paulo prison in Luanda. In April 1975 Portuguese armed forces deposed the government of Marcello Caetano, established a provisional *junta*, and offered selfdetermination to Angola. On November 11, 1975, Antonio A. Neto, leader of the MPLA, declared the independence of the colony. This act ended the nearly 500 years of Portuguese domination begun in 1483. Pelissier, *La Colonie*, p. 664; HDA.

Angolan Communist Party The Angolan Communist Party was founded in Luanda in October 1955. Organized by European leftists and *mestiço* civil-service intellectuals, its goal was to achieve independence and redeem the masses. Throughout the War for Independence (1961–1975) the party and its aggressive members sought Soviet assistance in the fight for the liberation of the colony. Marcum, *The Angola Revolution*, I:146. *See also* Angola, Soviet influence in.

Angolan missionaries, caravan of In 1777 Queen Maria I of Portugal sponsored a well-organized group of missionaries to work in overseas missions. Arriving in Angola in 1779, the caravan included the African priest

Fr. André do Couto Goudinho, four canons of the order of Saint Augustine, ten Franciscans, a Augustinian, a Benedictine, and a Hermit of Saint Paul. The group also included three Carmelites traveling to the Luanda monastery, two Italian Capuchins going to their Congo missions, Bishop Luis da Anunciação e Azevedo and Governor Gonçalo da Camara. The caravan arrived at Luanda on December 4, 1779, and from there the missionaries continued to their posts. The mission was of limited success because its members were unfamiliar with the customs and languages of the Africans. A few died on the road from tropical illnesses and inappropriate diet. Gabriel, *Angola,* pp. 136-9.

Angolanidade (Pg.)   "Angolanity." A concept developed by Angolan intellectuals, including future-president Antonio A. Neto and his fellow nationalists. It was based on the notion that the new Angolans are rooted to their ancestral land yet want to build a modern civilization and way of life with its own set of moral, cultural, and spiritual values. Recognizing both African and European traditions, *Angolanidade* aims at creating a free, respected, and progressive commonwealth. Ervedosa, *Itinerario,* p. 98.

angolar (Pg.)   An Angolan monetary unit established in 1928 and equal to the Portuguese *escudo.* It was used by the People's Republic of Angola until January 1977, when it was replaced by the *kwanza* (q.v.). The quoted value of the *angolar* just before the introduction of the *kwanza* was 31.57 *angolars* to US$1. Kaplan, *Angola,* p. 275; WTNID.

Angolares (Pg.)   Descendants of Angolan slaves who were shipwrecked c.1540 in the Angra de São João (q.v.) in São Tomé. They settled along the western coast and became skillful fishermen. Isolated by rugged mountains, they developed a deep sense of independence and refused to work on the plantations. Today they are settled in the town of São João dos Angolares. Tenreiro, *A Ilha,* pp. 182-90; Newitt, *Portugal in Africa,* pp. 204, 206-9. *See also* Angolares, São João de.

Angolares, Republica dos (Pg.)   "Republic of the Angolares." A small settlement on the western coast of São Tomé populated by *Angolares* (q.v.). It was organized under the authority of their local king in 1693. Almada Negreiros, *Historia,* p. 209.

Angolares, São João dos   A modern village on the northwestern coast of São Tomé, populated exclusively by *Angolares* (q.v.). It is completely surrounded by plantations owned by Portuguese. During the colonial period it was part of the Republica dos Angolares. Tenreiro, *A Ilha,* pp. 118-121. *See also* Angolares, Republica dos.

Angonia (Afr.) A highland region in northern Tete, Mozambique, with fertile soil and a moderate climate; an area of crops and cattle-raising. In 1961 it was considered free of tsetse fly. Herrick, *Area Handbook*, pp. 8, 122, 161.

Angra das Aldeias (Pg.) "Bay of Villages." A bay where Diogo Cão anchored in 1485 during his second trip to the Congo and where Porto Alexandre subsequently was built. Cão named it *Angra das Aldeias* because of the presence of two African settlements. Axelson, *Portuguese in South-East,* p. 10.

Angra de São João The site on the southern coast of São Tomé where a group of Angolan slaves were shipwrecked in 1540. Later it became the center of the community of São João dos Angolares. Almada Negrerios, *Historia,* p. 294. *See also* Angolares.

Angra do Negro (Pg.) "Black Bay." A spacious bay on the Atlantic coast near Mossâmedes in southern Angola. In 1876, the Barão de Mossâmedes organized an expedition to Angra do Negro to explore Benguela and the Cunene River. The explorers carefully surveyed the bay as a possible port of entry to the *sertão* (interior). Duffy, *Portuguese Africa,* pp. 72-3.

Angra dos Ruivos (Pg.) A bay named for a local fish and located near Cape Bojador in West Africa and discovered by Gil Eanes in 1434. In its deep waters there was an important fishing ground exploited by Portuguese fishermen at the time of the Discovery (q.v.). Mota, *Mar, Alem Mar,* p. 65.

Angra Fria (Pg.) "Chilly Bay." A bay on the southwestern Atlantic coast, today part of Namibia. On December 30, 1886, a treaty between Germany and Portugal was signed declaring Angra Fria to be German territory. GEPB.

Anguaze (Afr.) A small Mozambican *prazo* (q.v.) in the Quelimane area north of the Zambezi River where a small factory for the manufacture of groundnut (peanut) oil was started in 1870. On the same *prazo*, facilities for making bricks, tiles, and boats have been in operation for many years. The boats, constructed from local timber, were tailored to the Zambezi market. All these activities were part of the Portuguese policy of colonial development. In 1897, the Zambezia Company (q.v.) rented this *prazo*. Newitt, *Portuguese Settlement,* pp. 351, 364.

anime (Pg.) In Angola, a resin, called copal, extracted from several species of tropical trees, including *Trachylobium hornemannianum* and *T. verricosum,* or dug in semi-fossil form from the soil. This substance, widely used in paints, is known commercially as *sandarusu za miti* (copal from trees). *Anime* is also known as *elemi*. Ficalho, *Plantas Uteis,* pp. 155-8.

animism Religion based on the belief that all life springs from and is governed by a spiritual force and that natural objects have souls. Animists believe in the cult of ancestors and the existence of demons. Animism is found among groups throughout Africa, including Balantas, Brames, Banhuns, Papeis, and Felupes. Gonçalves, *O Mundo Arabo-Islámico,* pp. 148, 158, 162.

ANM (1) (*Accão Nacional de Mozambique*) (Pg.) "National Action of Mozambique." A political pressure group organized by white settlers in Lourenço Marques in 1920 to introduce reforms in the colonial administration. It was hostile to the Lisbon government. Newitt, *Portugal in Africa,* p. 173.

ANM (2) (*Associação dos Naturais de Mozambique*) (Pg.) "Association of Native-born Mozambicans." A group organized in the 1950s by European settlers in Lourenço Marques. This club for whites of Mozambican birth was later opened to people of other races. It aimed, among other goals, to strengthen the political voice of managers, planters, businessmen, and professionals in Mozambican politics. By the time it was banned in 1961, it had 10,000 members, the majority of whom were educated Africans plus a few Europeans and East Indians. It offered vocational instruction in several trades; future leader Armando Guebusa attended a typing course and Marianho Matsinha received a bursary from the association to study in Portugal. Munslow, *Mozambique,* p. 69.

ANP (Afrikaner Nationalist Party) A South African political party which in 1960, together with the Portuguese government under Antonio Salazar, proposed a United Nations investigation into political dissention and the activities of nationalist guerrillas in the Portuguese colonies. Although Portugal rejected apartheid, the economic and political ties between South Africa and the Portuguese were so strong that the Afrikaner Nationalists found an ally in the Lisbon government. Newitt, *Portugal in Africa,* pp. 48, 198.

ANU (African National Union) A regional nationalist movement formed by Mozambican exiles in Blantyre, Malawi, in the 1960s. It laid claim to the land and loyalties of peoples living between the Rovuma and Zambezi rivers in Mozambique. The idea was to establish an independent country in that territory. The exiles were encouraged by the Malawi government and white business people in Beira, but the movement disbanded when threatened by FRELIMO (q.v.). Henriksen, *Mozambique,* pp. 98, 197.

Antilla (Lat.) A legendary group of islands said to be 200 leagues (970 km) west of the Canaries and Azores. It was said that around the year 1430 a Portuguese caravel was driven by the winds to these islands, believed to be the smallest in the West Atlantic. The *Antilla* appeared in Portuguese charts up to Columbus's voyages and even afterward, when the *Antilla* began to be represented in *Portulani* (q.v.) as the Islands of the Seven Cities. Also spelled *Antilia*. Cortesão, *History,* I:130-32.

Anti-Slavery Society An abolitionist society organized in London in 1823 and dedicated to the amelioration of slaves' conditions and to their ultimate release. In 1906 it put pressure on the British Foreign Office to intervene and investigate the status of the *trabalhadores contratados* (contract laborers) on the plantations of São Tomé and Angola. It was suspected that the laborers had been bought as slaves in the African interior, then sold to planters. That same year the issue assumed the dimensions of an international scandal when Henry Nevinson published his articles describing illegal abuses in *Harper's Magazine*. In 1961 Thomas Fox Pitt, president of the society, recommended to ACOA (q.v.) that action be taken concerning the arrest of Dr. Antonio A. Neto. It also tried, together with Bishop Ralph E. Dodge of the Methodist church, to obtain a medical internship for Dr. Neto in the United States. Newitt, *Portugal in Africa,* p. 39; Marcum, *The Angola Revolution,* I:202.

Antonianos (Pg.) "The Antonians." A Christian sect founded in 1703 by an African, Pedro Constantino, in Manca, Quibango, Angola, with Saint Anthony as their patron saint. This sect quickly gained followers among the African population until 1707, when its founder, convinced of heresy, returned to the official church in São Salvador. Also known as *Santantoniozinhos*. Gabriel, *Angola,* pp. 133-6.

Antonio Silva Corporation One of the two biggest export companies in Guinea-Bissau by 1950. It had large investments in shipping, insurance, light industry, and import/export concerns. HDRGC. *See also* Casa Gouveia.

Antwerp, Portuguese commerce with From 1488 to 1795 commercial exchange between Lisbon, Africa, and Antwerp was very active. In 1499 Antwerp was established as a royal diplomatic and trading post, and in 1510 the city council gave the Portuguese the favored-nation privilege and a consulate was established. Spices, medicinal plants, sugar from São Tomé, *malagüeta* (q.v.) from Guiné, Madeiran wine, and Portuguese fruits and oil were imported, and guns, tools, metal ingots, and textiles were exported to Africa. The Portuguese settlement in Antwerp grew and by 1570 there were eighty families and seventeen unmarried merchants in Antwerp, most of whom were expelled Spanish Jews. This *feitoria* (trade center) was abolished in 1795. DHP.

Anuário de Lourenço Marques   *See* Delagoa Bay Directory.

apartheid (Afrik.) "Separateness." The policy of strict racial segregation and discrimination against Africans, mulattoes, East Indians, and other "colored" people in South Africa. It was a principle conceived and supported by the National Party and first put before the public in 1949. Although derived from an earlier principle encountered in one form or another throughout South Africa's history and previously referred to as segregation, apartheid caused worldwide controversy. Its basic idea involved the separate development, settlement, economic existence, and government of whites and non-whites in South Africa. This policy, very different from the Portuguese multiracial tradition in Africa and elsewhere, was strongly rejected by Portugal. In 1960 the United Nations called for a program of boycotts and sanctions against the apartheid regime of South Africa. Herrick, *Area Handbook,* pp. 171, 191; Marcum, *The Angolan Revolution,* I:70.

ARA (Armed Revolutionary Action)   An underground military group organized in 1973 to conduct a guerrilla war in Portugal against the Portuguese government to pressure for the independence of the Portuguese African colonies. It also tried to infiltrate cadres in the colonial army to encourage the troops not to fight. Munslow, *Mozambique,* pp. 126, 132.

Arabs in East Africa   Arab economic, political, and religious influence in Mozambique began in the eighth century when Arabs settled on the island of Pemba. By the ninth century they held strategic points as far south as Mozambique Island and Sofala. These fortified coastal communities and offshore islands became relatively independent and sometimes luxurious city-states. At the time of the first contact with the Portuguese in 1487, all settlements, and the trading posts along the Mozambican coast, were linked to coastal cities such as Pate, Mogadishu, Mombasa, Zanzibar, Kilwa, and Pemba. When Vasco da Gama encountered Inhambane and Quelimane in 1498 he was surprised at the sophisticated society he encountered. The ports were filled with ships, some as large as his own, and the settlements were impressive, many containing multi-storied buildings. Kaplan, *Area Handbook,* pp. 20-2.

Arabian coffee (Ar.) A tall shrub (*Coffea arabica*) native to tropical Africa. A number of genetic varieties are cultivated in tropical and subtropical regions for their seeds, called beans, from which most coffee is made. Arabian or arabica coffee cultivation was imported to Brazil, then introduced into São Tomé e Príncipe from Brazil in 1822. The fertile volcanic soil of the islands was excellent for coffee cultivation and coffee soon replaced the declining sugar industry, stripped of profits by the abolition of slavery. After 1870 the coffee industry was so well developed in São Tomé e Príncipe, it brought economic success to both islands. Carvalho e Vasconcellos, *As Colonias Portuguesas,* pp. 229-30; Tenreiro, *A Ilha,* pp. 78-9.

archil *See* orchil.

Ardra (Afr.) An African kingdom in coastal Dahomey (q.v.) where the Portuguese engaged in the slave trade beginning c.1550. The slaves were taken to São Tomé, then to Brazil. From 1670 to 1704, Ardra together with Ouidah (q.v.) were raised to world prominence because of the unprecedented supply of slaves. The English, Dutch, French, and Portuguese all paid heavy taxes to the Ardran king for the passage through his kingdom of slaves brought in caravans from the interior. The Portuguese exerted a formative influence in Ardra reflected in the Portuguese names for such important cultural features as the monetary unit, fetishes, and religious rituals. Polanyi, *Dahomey,* pp. 105-7, 180-1.

AREC (*Association des Ressortissants de l'Enclave de Cabinda*) (Fr.) "Association of Cabinda Enclave Nationalists." A nationalist party organized in Cabinda in 1958. It was a moderate group led by the self-proclaimed descendants of eleventh-century African aristocracy, a party that felt itself distinct from the Angolan colony in general and wanted a separate negotiated independence for Cabinda. Pelissier, *La Colonie,* pp. 286-87.

Arguim (Ar.) A peninsula and town on the northern coast of Mauritania, about 50 mi. (80 km) southeast of Cape Blanc on the Atlantic. It was explored by the navigator Nuno Tristão in 1443. The Portuguese traded at a Moorish trade center, exchanging European goods for gold, slaves, and other exotic products. It has been identified with Cerne, mentioned by the Carthaginian navigator Hanno. In the sixth century BC, he reported an island "full of cosmetics, Egyptian ceramics, elephants' paws, panthers, ivory, and wine, and very hot." Arguim, still a center of the gum arabic (q.v.) trade and turtle fishing, became part of the Islamic Republic of Mauritania in 1960. Godinho, *A Economia,* p. 190; WNGD. *See also* Awlil.

arimo (Afr.) In Angola and elsewhere in Portuguese Africa, a farm where food crops are cultivated for family consumption, the surplus sold in urban markets. After 1830, sugar cane, sisal, and manioc began to be cultivated on *arimos.* In São Tomé they are known as *roças* (q.v.). Boxer, *Portuguese Society,* p. 121; Wheeler, *Angola,* p. 54.

aringa (Afr.) An African system of fortified settlement developed during the violent times of the nineteenth century. Much-enlarged versions of the fortified village of a chief, they could be up to a mile in circumference and contain all the huts of the chief's followers, their wives, and children, housing many hundreds and even thousands of people and attaining the dimensions of a considerable town. Within the *aringa* would be a walled enclosure where the chief and his family lived. *Aringas* were built on river banks, both for a secure supply of water and as defence against the possibility of piracy from the boats passing by. Most were defended by redoubts and bastions reinforced with stonework which were used to mount the artillery that most chiefs seemed able to secure. In times of siege, an *aringa* could hold out indefinitely. Livestock was stabled and even pastured inside the walls. The stockades, made of living trees (also a source of forage and firewood), easily defied such small calibre guns as could be dragged through the bush and brought to bear against them. Newitt, *Portuguese Settlement,* pp. 227-8; GDLP.

Armageddon In the Bible, the site of the last, deciding battle between good and evil. Visualized in 1961 by fanatic African Protestant nationalists (especially by the Bembe in northwest Angola) as being a present reality, these illiterate Africans, carrying sticks and rocks and led by their sorcerers, were possessed by a mystic feeling that Armageddon was imminent. Pelissier, *La Colonie,* pp. 573-4.

Armed Revolutionary Action *See* ARA.

ARNA (*Associação Regional dos Naturais de Angola*) (Pg.) "Regional Association of Angolan Natives." A moderate nationalist movement established in Luanda in 1936 by a group of *mestiços* and *assimilados* (qq.v.) trying to improve the economic, social, and educational status of the African population. Among its members there was a strong sense of loyalty to the Portuguese nation. In 1948, the Communist Party tried to take advantage of this movement. Among other initiatives, this association established scholarships for promising young Angolans and by 1963 there were six graduates sponsored by the group. One of its contributions was the replacement of the term "indigenous" with that of "citizen." Wheeler, *Angola,* pp. 224, 36-8, 641; GEPB.

arratel (Pg.) measure of weight, equivalent to approximately 1 lb. (454 g). In São Tomé around 1530, a *lobe* (standard small portion) of molasses or a *pão-de-açucar* (a loaf of sugar) weighed between 15 and 20 *arratels.* Tenreiro, *A Ilha,* p. 69.

arroba (Ar.) An Arabic measure of weight equivalent to approximately 33 lbs. (15 kg), adopted by the Portuguese from the Iberian Moors. It was used in colonial Mozambique and elsewhere in Portuguese Africa and in the countryside of Portugal. Axelson, *Portuguese in South-East,* p. 243.

Arte da Guerra do Mar, A (Pg.) "The Art of War on the Sea." A book by Fernão de Oliveira, a Dominican monk, published in Coimbra, Portugal, in 1555. This extraordinary anti-war, anti-slavery essay is divided into two sections. First was a discussion on the nature of unjust wars that Christians carry out against Moors, Jews, and Africans. Oliveira asserts that imprisoning slaves is unjust because it ends in their exploitation and bondage. In the second part, the author describes war on the high seas, the size and armaments of the ships, the art of navigation, the sea currents, patterns of winds, astronomic observations, and naval laws. Saunders, *A Social History,* p. 43; GEPB.

Aruangua fair (Afr.) A trading post established by the Portuguese c.1720, located south of the Zambezi River in the Manica Mountains. Like other fairs in Mozambique, Aruangua was under the protection of a local African chief. Portuguese traders dealt in gold and dabbled in African politics, garnering the lucrative by-products of land concessions, slaves, and loot. It was the first post reached by traders coming from Sena. It had no permanent garrison, but there were two small pieces of artillery there by the end of the eighteenth century. The main fair for that region was in Massakisse (q.v.). Newitt, *Portuguese Settlement,* pp. 46, 74; Silva Rego, *O Ultramar,* p. 333.

arvore-da-agua-vermelha (Pg.) "Vermilion-water tree." A tropical tree (*Erythrophleum guinense*) that grows in Guinea-Bissau, Mozambique, and elsewhere in Africa, also known as the *mueve* (sorcerer) tree. A poison extracted from its bark is used in tribal ordeals (q.v.). Local people believe that this poison does not affect innocent defendants. Its victims amount to thousands per year in Africa. Carvalho e Vasconcellos, *As Colonias Portuguesas,* p. 160.

assiento dos escravos (Pg.) (1) "Registry of slaves." An official license given by the king of Portugal to a trader allowing him to buy and sell a specific number of slaves within an established period (10-20 years) along the West African coast. Carreira, *As Companhias Pombalinas,* BCG, 1968, xxiii(89/90):16. *See also* Companhia Geral do Grão-Pará e Maranhão.

assiento dos escravos (Pg.) (2) "Registry of slaves." The official record of slave traders' sales and the amount of taxes paid. The *assiento dos escravos* system was common from about 1450 to 1650 when it was replaced by commercial companies with quantities of capital, trade monopolies in manufactured goods, and the right to unlimited slave trading. The first was the *Companhia da Costa de Guiné* (q.v.), established in 1664. Carreira, *As Companhias Pombalinas,* BCG, 1968, xxiii(89/90):16. *See also* Companhia Geral do Grão-Pará e Maranhão.

assimilação cultural (Pg.) "Cultural absorption." The Portuguese policy of incorporating at least the African élite into the broad socioeconomic order of Portugal. Proponents advocated the conversion of "the heathen" to Christianity, the conquest and domination of Africans, and the exploitation of the land. The notion of Portuguese multi-racialism based on the spoken and written language and on Luso-European ideology and values was a Pan-African concept and a policy that has shaped the Afro-Portuguese world. Cunha, *O Sistema Portugués,* pp. 66-7. *See also* assimilaçao espiritual.

assimilação espiritual (Pg.) A policy of spiritual absorption of Africans by converting them to Christianity. Since the Discovery (q.v.), Portugal felt it had the "civilizing mission" of educating Africans to be citizens of the mother country and of European society. This missionary effort was mainly evident in the fifteenth and sixteenth centuries. Mota, *Guiné Portuguesa,* II:43. *See also* assimilado.

assimilado (Pg.) "Assimilated." A broad term meaning a "civilized African," one who has adopted Portuguese ideologies, values, and language. The first *assimilado* was the African king of Congo, Afonso I, educated at Coimbra University after his conversion to Christianity. He became a model for Africans of succeeding generations. This long and arduous education process reached its zenith in 1921 when Africans were first elected to the Legislative Council in Luanda. In 1926, a legal definition of *assimilado* was established, calling for strict standards for qualification that included character, sufficient income, proven ability to speak Portuguese, and fulfillment of military service. This status was abolished in 1961. Duffy, *Portuguese Africa,* p. 295; Wheeler, *Angola,* pp. 29, 49, 97-8. *See also* assimilação cultural.

Associação Africana *See* AA.

Associação Africana do Sul de Angola *See* AASA.

Associação Commercial, Agricola e Industrial de Huambo *See* ACAIH.

Associação Commercial de Loanda (Pg.) "Loanda [Luanda] Commercial Association." Organized in 1863 by a conservative group of European merchants in Luanda to promote economic interests and to oppose Lisbon's liberal and humanitarian ideals and programs, including the abolition of slavery in the colony. Apparently some members of this organization envisioned independence, including the liberation of Angola from Portugal, with Angola becoming a republic joined with Brazil, or even the offer to the United States of Angola as a colony. Wheeler, *Angola,* p. 92.

Associação das Mulheres de Angola *See* AMA.

Associação de Defesa Mutua (Pg.) "Mutual Aid Association." Founded in 1936 by Custodio Dias Bento Azevedo in Caxito, a coffee plantation area in northeastern Luanda. He led about thirty other *mestiços* (q.v.) in a mutual assistance program to end planters' abuses. Pelissier, *La Colonie,* p. 237.

Associação dos Assimilados (Pg.) "Association of the Assimilated." An ethnic association of Afro-Portuguese, mostly government employees, whose original aims were social rather than political. It was organized in Luanda in 1912, the forerunner of the *Liga Angolana* (q.v.). From 1910 onward, these *Associaçãos dos Assimilados* were established in Lisbon by *assimilados* from various Portuguese-African provinces, influenced by contemporary ideas of Pan-Africanism, Negroism, Garveyism, and anti-slavery humanitarianism. The organizations accommodated the republican politics officially adopted with the proclamation of the Republic of Portugal in Lisbon in 1910. Wheeler, *Angola,* pp. 118-9. GEPB.

Associação dos Bacongos (Pg.) A political movement started c. 1955, it was based in São Salvador do Congo, the old capital established c. 1520 by King Afonso I of Congo. Its aim was not the independence of Angola, but the ending of Portuguese rule in the northern Congo and re-establishing the Old Kingdom of Congo through negotiations. This ethno-nationalistic organization was inspired by a deep loyalty to King Pedro VII of Congo, who died on April 17, 1955. Their goal was the proclamation of a new Catholic king of Congo under Portuguese protection. As pressures escalated, culminating in the War for Independence, nationalist leaders forced the association to disband in 1960. Pelissier, *La Colonie,* p. 272, 82; DHP.

Associação dos Funcionarios Publicos (Pg.) "Association of Civil Servants." Founded in Luanda in 1917 to improve the economic, cultural, and social position of government workers, of whom the majority were *mestiços* and *assimilados* (qq.v.). Accused of political activities, it was banned in 1921 by High Commissioner J.M.R. Norton de Matos. Wheeler, *Angola,* pp. 122-1.

Associação dos Naturais de Mozambique *See* ANM (1).

Associação Mutua dos Nativos de Zombo (Pg.) "Mutual Aid Association of Native-born Zombos." A Protestant cultural and educational group organized in 1956 by Emmanuel Kunzika and André Massaki in Leopoldville, Belgian Congo. It was a legal organization whose activities were limited, only becoming a political force after the Congo gained independence. Pelissier, *La Colonie,* p. 277.

Associação Regional dos Naturais de Angola   *See* ARNA.

Association des Ressortissants de l'Enclave de Cabinda   *See* AREC.

Association Internationale Africaine (Fr.)   "International African Association." A European association organized in September 1876 by representatives of Belgium, Germany, France, England, Austria, Italy, and Russia. It had the threefold purpose of philanthropy, science, and commerce. At a meeting in July 1877, the Netherlands, Spain, and the United States joined the original group and it was decided to send an expedition from the eastern coast of Africa to establish a scientific station on or near Lake Tanganyika from which subsequent expeditions would explore west toward the Atlantic. Axelson, *Portugal*, pp. 45, 59-61.

Association Mutuelle des Ressortissants de Zombo   *See* ASSOMIZO.

ASSOMIZO (*Association Mutuelle des Ressortissants de Zombo*) "Mutual Association of Zombo Nationalists." A nationalist movement for the independence of Angola founded by Emmanuel Kuzinga and others in 1956 in Leopoldville, Belgian Congo. They preached nonviolence and published a party newspaper, *Mondo*. In 1962 Kuzinga helped to found ALIAZO (*Alliance des Ressortissants de Zombo*), serving as its vice president and representing the organization at the United Nations. The same year they also founded the PDA (*Partido Democratico de Angola*). Pelissier, *La Colonie*, p. 277; Marcum, *The Angolan Revolution*, I:83-4, 88, 170-1, 219-20. *See also* ALIAZO, PDA.

astrolabe   An astronomic instrument developed in ancient Greece for measuring the altitude of a heavenly body. The user aligned his body with a pointer that pivoted across the face of a vertical disk marked off in degrees of a circle. Portuguese navigators replaced the traditional astrolabe with the nautical astrolabe c. 1450. In the late fifteenth century, the German geographer Martin Behaim adopted the astrolabe for navigational use to determine latitude. Costa, *A Marinha dos Descobrimentos,* pp. 21-2; GEPB.

astrology   The science of the stars and formerly the equivalent of astronomy, but now restricted to mean the pseudoscience that claims to foretell the future by studying the supposed influence of the relative positions of the moon, sun, and planets on human affairs. The development of Portuguese nautical science c. 1435 was assisted by the then-current vogue for astrology; Portuguese mathematicians and Jewish scholars were its principal exponents. A royal astrologer drew up the horoscope of Prince Henry, which Gomes Eanes de Zurara gives us in his *Chronicle of Guinea*. In 1451 a fleet carrying King

Afonso V's sister Princess Leonor to meet her husband King-Emperor Frederick III of Germany was led by sea captains and astrologers "who knew the route by observing the stars and the pole." Costa, *A Marinha dos Descobrimentos,* p. 35; Prestage, *The Portuguese Pioneers,* pp. 315, 316. *See also* astronavigation.

astronavigation Navigation by observing the positions of celestial bodies at precise times to determine position. This ancient science, used in the Mediterranean by measuring the altitude of the sun and the stars, was advanced by Portuguese navigators when they reached Guiné and other points south of the equator c.1450. As ships drew nearer to the equator, the Pole Star gradually descended towards the northern horizon, then disappeared, so a new guide became necessary. Around 1480 King João II's astronomers and mathematicians suggested a method of calculating latitudes by the height of the sun at midday and prepared tables of declination for the use of navigators. They did not invent this method, but ingeniously applied the existing technology to the southern hemisphere. The Jewish astronomer José Vizinho was sent to Guiné in 1485 to test it. Costa, *A Marinha dos Descobrimentos,* p. 38; Prestage, *The Portuguese Pioneers,* pp. 316, 317.

astronomical latitude The angle between the plane of the equator and the plumb line (direction of gravitational force) at a given point on the earth's surface. The first recorded observation of latitude by the Portuguese was made by Diogo Gomes using a quadrant in 1462. His method of calculation used the height of the sun at midday and its declination in the southern hemisphere. Until then the position of the sun in the Zodiac was known, but the distance from the pole, an indispensable element for calculating latitudes, was not indicated. Prestage, *The Portuguese Pioneers,* pp. 316, 317.

Atlantic Ocean At the time of the Discovery (q.v.) this ocean was little-known beyond folktales of danger and of lost adventurers such as the Genoese brothers Ugolino and Guido Vivaldi who c.1291 crossed Gibraltar and, sailing near the Canary Islands, had their ship destroyed by a storm. Ancient writers referred to the Pillars of Hercules; Hanno, a Carthaginian navigator of the sixth century BC, apparently reached Cape Bojador (q.v.), the southernmost point known to Europeans in the Middle Ages. The patterns of ocean currents and winds were as yet uncharted. Once latitudes were established by observing the Pole Star and the height of the sun at midday, Portuguese navigators c.1450 began exploring the Atlantic region far away from the African coast. Astronavigation (q.v.), developed by scholars at the Sagres nautical school (q.v.), signaled a new scientific era that extended exploration over the western Atlantic to the New World. In the fifteenth century, Portuguese navigators returning to Lisbon from Guiné had to sail west up to the latitude of the Azores to avoid the Guinea Current and find favorable westerly winds. This extended trip was known as the *volta do largo* or *volta da Mina*, (qq.v.). Prestage, *The Portuguese Pioneers*, pp. 228-30; DHP; EI.

atumbu (Bant.) The basic unit of community into which the Bailundo (q.v.) kingdom in southern Angola was divided c.1920. At the time, there were about 200 *atumbus* under the authority of the king. Each subkingdom was ruled by a headman called an *etumbu*. Henderson, *Angola*, p. 51.

Aviz, Portuguese Royal House of The second Portuguese dynasty. The first was the House of Burgundy, the third, when Portugal was ruled by Spain, was what is known as the Catalian Usurpation, and the fourth, the House of Bragança. The House of Aviz initiated the great maritime and colonial expansion in the fifteenth century. The Age of the Discovery (q.v.) was led by members of this royal house which included Afonso V, Prince Henry, João II, Manuel I, and João III, and ended with Cardinal-King Henry in 1580. With the end of the Aviz line, Portugal became associated with Spain under King Felipe I (Philip II of Spain). Newitt, *Portuguese Settlement*, pp. 4, 11; GEPB.

Awlil (Afr.) An ancient African settlement on the Atlantic coast north of the mouth of the Senegal River. Around the year 1000, Arab geographers referred to Awlil frequently because it was situated on an important trade route to Morocco. Its salt mines were celebrated, for salt was a basic commodity of trade with Africans and played a role in history comparable to that of gold. Awlil is generally identified with the Arguim (q.v.) Peninsula which was visited by the Portuguese navigator Nuno Tristão in 1443. Trimingham, *A History of Islam*, pp. 41-2.

Axim (Afr.) A coastal town in West Africa at the mouth of the Ankebra River about 30 mi. (48 km) west of Takeradi on the Gulf of Guiné. The town was visited by Portuguese navigators in 1466. King Manuel I built a fortress there first to protect the gold trade and later the slave trade. It was taken by the Dutch in 1642, and by the English in 1872. Today it is part of the Republic of Ghana. In 1970 it had a population of 8,100. Dantzig, *A Short History*, p. 7; Prestage, *The Portuguese Pioneers*, p. 185; WNGD.

Azamor (Afr.) An Arab city in Morocco on the left bank of the Morbea River on the Atlantic coast. A town of great interest to the Portuguese in the fifteenth century, its inhabitants declared themselves vassals of the Portuguese in 1486 by paying tribute to King João II. At that time, the city was nominally ruled by the King of Fez (q.v.). In 1513 King Manuel conquered the city and fortified its defenses. King João III left the fortress, together with the town of Safim, to the Arabs in 1542. GEPB.

Azenegue (Afr.)   A Berber ethnic group settled near Rio do Ouro on the African coast, reached by Portuguese navigators c.1436. The first slave raid occurred in 1441 when the crews of two Portuguese vessels landed there, attacked the inhabitants, and carried off several citizens from Idzagen (q.v.). Captives seized included one of the Azengues' African slave women. The Portuguese would take Moorish captives who could provide military information and also be ransomed or sold as slaves. In 1443 a caravel returned to ransom a pair of Idzagen citizens for ten Africans and a little gold. In campaigns in 1444 and 1445, the merchants and nobles of the Algarve, Portugal, sent two massive expeditions against Idzagen. In the first some 235 Idzagen Arab and African prisoners were captured and sold at auction in a field outside Lagos; the second expedition was less successful. Saunders, *A Social History,* p. 5; GEPB.

Azores (Pg.)   A Portuguese group of nine islands and several islets in the North Atlantic about 800 mi. (1300 km) off the coast of Portugal. Although the date of their discovery is obscure, their existence was known in Europe in the fourteenth century. The Azores were visited by Diogo de Seville in 1427-31. They were known for a time as the Flemish Islands because of a settlement that followed the gift of the island of Faial to Isabella, Countess of Flanders, in 1466. In 1479 the Alcaçovas Peace Treaty (q.v.) assigned the islands to Portugal. Prestage, *The Portuguese Pioneers,* pp. 31, 51, 142; DHP; WNGD.

azungu (Afr.)   A young male member of the Nomi Society (q.v.) who, as an ordinary worker, occupied the lowest social rank in the group. Vail, *Capitalism,* p. 72.

Bacongo nationalism (Afr.)   This ethnic movement, based in the São Salvador do Congo region of northern Angola, was one of the first nationalist groups. It was organized by A.H. Roberto in 1960 in Leopoldville under the name of UPA (q.v.). It was a rural political movement, as opposed to the MPLA (q.v.), the Mbundu urban intellectual party organized in Luanda. Marcum, *The Angolan Revolution*, I:10, 49, 50-1; HDA.

Bacongo people (Afr.)   A large Bantu (q.v.) group whose language is Kikongo, the language spoken in São Salvador do Congo. In the fifteenth century, the Bacongo settled in the Old Kingdom of Congo and in region of northwestern Angola known as the Cabinda Enclave (q.v.). These agricultural people, in close contact with Europeans since the arrival of Diogo Cão in 1482, welcomed the white strangers, accepted their priests, and seemed eager to learn their ways of life and adopt their religion. Cão took four youngsters to Lisbon where they were baptized and taught Portuguese. The relations between Portugal and Nzinga-a Cuum, later King João I (q.v.) of Congo, were cordial. King João I of Portugal invited the *manicongo* (q.v.), as the king of Congo was also known, to convert to Christianity; he accepted and was baptized in May 1491. Since then, the Bacongo people have been the most Christianized Africans in Angola and perhaps in all of Portuguese Africa. It is no coincidence that, in modern times, many Bacongos led the way to religious and political separatism from Portugal. Pelissier, *La Colonie*, p. 12; GEPB.

Bacongo royalists   A small group of Bacongo nationalists who tried to revive the Old Kingdom of Congo at São Salvador do Congo in 1955 to create a political instrument for accomplishing economic and social reform. This group was divided into a Protestant branch led by José Eduardo Pinock and a Catholic opposition headed by Manuel M. Kidutu. After hard negotiations, Antonio José da Gama, a Catholic member of the Kivuzi clan (q.v.), was selected and enthroned as King Antonio III; he reigned from 1955 to 1957. Marcum, *The Angolan Revolution*, I:53, 63; HDA.

badzo (Afr.) An African slave in colonial Zambezia (q.v.) who was assigned to be chief of a military unit in charge of the *prazos'* (q.v.) security c. 1700.

Being versed in African customs and law, he was called on to mediate in legal disputes among slaves or Portuguese settlers. It was a prestigious position in the slave hierarchy. Isaacman, *Mozambique: From Colonialism*, p. 34; GEPB.

Bafur (Afr.) A racially mixed group who settled in northern Africa early in the Christian era (c.100 AD). These seminomadic people wandered in the southern Sahara then, around the year 1000, they settled in the Sahel (q.v.), giving origin to the so-called "Sudanese Negroes." Soon after, several Sudanese states began to emerge. They are known historically as the Songhai in the east, the Serere in the west, and the Wangara in the south. When the Portuguese reached Senegal in 1445, they met such "Sudanese Negroes" as the Mandingoes, the Wolof, and the Serere (qq.v.). King Mansa Mandu of Senegal requested Portuguese protection in 1481. Carreira, *Mandingas*, pp. 4, 19.

bafureira (Pg) A tropical shrub (*Ricinus communis* L.), the oil from the seeds of which has been used since ancient times in Asia and Europe to produce castor oil and for fuel and medicine. In Portugal, *bafureira* is called *carrapateiro* and in much of the rest of Europe *Palmachristi*. In Mozambique it is known as *ambona* and as *mbono* in Zanzibar. Africans use the oil from its seeds to treat itching, scurvy, and skin infections. The leaves are also popular folk remedies for various illnesses. Ficalho, *Plantas Uteis*, pp. 255-7.

Bagamoyo (Afr.) Bagamoyo, FRELIMO's (q.v.) first guerrilla training camp, was established in Tanzania in 1964. Such camps were ideological, political, and guerrilla training enterprises. Because national unity had to become more than a slogan, men drawn from many different groups and regions would have to fight side by side. A guerrilla fighting far from his family and region had to develop a deep feeling of group loyalty to help win freedom, so it was imperative that the Bagamoyo training instructors weld together a truly national army to succeed. Munslow, *Mozambique*, p. 88.

Bailundo (Afr.) A town in the Huando district, Benguela province, southern Angola. It produces wheat, maize, rice, horse-millet, beans, and coffee. GEPB.

Bailundo people (Afr.) An ethnic group related to the Ovimbundu (q.v) and settled in the Benguela highland of central Angola. An energetic people who have been known as long-distance merchants, warriors, and skillful *carregadores* (packers) hired by the army and by explorers. GEPB.

Baiote people (Afr.) In Guinea-Bissau, a numerically small ethnic group of the Diola cluster of the Senegambian shore region. They live mostly in the

Casamance area, the northwestern area around the town of Suzanna, and are related to the Felupes (q.v.), the other member of the Diola cluster. The Baiotes are animists (q.v.) and depend on rice cultivation. They have neither a political organization nor a leader, but in some cases have petty local chiefs. HDRGC.

Baixo Cubango (Pg.) "Cubango Valley." A rich agricultural region along the Cubango River in southwestern Angola. It has four administrative posts; Cuangar is the provincial seat. The region has had as much as 8,500,000 acres (3,500,000 hectares) dedicated to rubber production. GEPB.

Baixo Cunene A district of the Huila province, southern Angola, comprising eight administrative posts. Its capital is Vila Pereira de Éça. The first Catholic mission was organized there in 1884 and the Portuguese army established itself at Fort Humbe, carrying out a punitive campaign against the Ovimbundus (q.v.) who they claimed had massacred colonists. Surrounded by hostile African peoples, Baixo Cunene was the scene of bloody attacks and reprisals in 1904, 1906, and 1915. In 1926 Portugal signed a treaty with South Africa establishing Baixo Cunene as the official southern frontier of Angola. It was and remains an important agricultural and commercial center. GEPB.

Baixo de Cassange A productive region in northern Angola where cotton was first cultivated by the COTTONANG (q.v.) about 1950. The revolt against the company and the Portuguese government began in this area in 1960 and marked the beginning of the struggle for independence. Pelissier, *La Colonie*, pp. 19, 78, 86; GEPB.

Baixo Lucala A bountiful agricultural region that comprises Golungo Alto, Cazengo, and Cambaque in west-central Angola, near the Malange-Luanda railroad. It is part of the so-called "rich zone," the forests. GEPB.

Baixo Molocué A fertile region in the Quelimane district of Mozambique. In 1907 the Portuguese government subjugated local chiefs and established a military fort there. GEPB.

Baixo Zambezi A prosperous agricultural region near the lower mouth of the Zambezi River in the Quelimane district of Mozambique where sugar cane is cultivated in great quantities. GEPB.

Bakongo *See* Bacongo.

balafão (Afr.) An African musical instrument, a kind of xylophone or marimba comprised of nineteen thin wooden planks connected to the same number of empty gourds that function as resonance boxes. It has a diatonic scale of any standard major or minor scale of eight tones without the chromatic intervals and is played by being struck with small mallets. GEPB; WNWD.

balafon (Afr.) In Guinea-Bissau, a wooden drum with animal skin heads. Among the Felupes and the Papeis the *balafon* is also used as a means of communication. Guerra, *Terras da Guiné*, p. 18.

Balantas (Afr.) A Guinea-Bissau ethnic group settled between the Geba and the Cacheu rivers, living by fishing and rice cultivation; animism and polygamy are common. GEPB.

Balesty, Philip and Co. An English trading company that purchased a six-year contract (1745 to 1751) to buy and export *urzela* (orchil, q.v.), a dye-producing lichen that uses a perennial plant of the Orchidaceae family as host. *Urzela* was in great demand for the developing English textile trade. The company paid the Portuguese government 60,000 *cruzados* (over £6,000) for the contract that covered all the Cape Verde Islands. Duncan, *Atlantic Islands*, p. 191.

Balombo (Afr.) A town and administrative center in the province of Benguela in southern Angola which until 1937 belonged to the Bailundo municipality. By 1960 it had telegraph facilities, a Catholic mission, and mineral waters. During the War for Independence from 1961 to 1974 there was bloody fighting in this heavily cultivated region. Pelissier, *La Colonie,* pp. 555, 556(n).

baloubeiro (Afr.) In some of the ethnic communities in the Bijagos region of Guinea-Bissau, a sorcerer who is believed to have enormous magic power. Often he is also a leader of a secret society. Also called a *jambacosse*. Mota, *Guiné Portuguesa*, I:262.

balsamo de São Tomé (Pg.) A medicinal resin extracted from *Sorindeia trimera* Oliv., a tall tree with enormous leaves. Incisions in the trunk ooze a viscous, semi-solid substance collected in gourds. Found in São Tomé, the resin is used by Africans to treat ulcers and wounds. Early in the colonial period, due to exaggerations of its medicinal properties, it was eagerly sought and at one time was exported to Germany. Ficalho, *Plantas Uteis*, pp. 111-12.

Baluarte de Bolar (Pg.) A fortress built by the Portuguese over the Cacheu River in Guinea-Bissau c.1831, apparently on the site of an old village. Later the garrison was transferred to São Domingo, and then to Cacheu. GEPB.

Balunda (Afr.)   An ethnic group settled in the region of the Luena, Kasidi, and Lungue, all tributaries of the Zambezi River, Mozambique. A matriarchal society familiar with metals, the Balunda traded with the Portuguese and other Europeans around 1600. GEPB.

Balunganga (Afr.)   An important center of cattle ranches located in the Cuanhama region of southern Angola. After defeating rebel African chiefs, the Portuguese army established a fort there in 1915. It is 25 mi. (40 km) from Vila Pereira de Éça. GEPB.

bamba (Afr.)   An old Spanish coin minted c.1510 by King Ferdinand. King Sebastião authorized its circulation in Portugal in 1570 with a value of thirty-six *reis* and two *ceitils* (qq.v.). It was discontinued in 1641. GEPB.

Bamba Kingdom (Afr.)   An old kingdom located in northeastern Angola between the Ambriz River in the north, the Dande River in the south, the Pemba Kingdom in the east, and the Atlantic to the west. In 1480 it was allied with the Old Congo Kingdom with its capital in São Salvador. Pigafetta reported mines of silver and precious metals in the territory c.1590. Later its new capital of Pamza, 60 mi. (96 km) inland from the Atlantic coast, was the center of a chiefdom whose main business during the fifteenth and sixteenth centuries was salt trading, fishing, and collecting *zimbos* (q.v.). The language spoken was Mbundu, a dialect of Kimbundu. GEPB.

Bambaras (Afr.)   An animist ethnic group found in the vicinity of Gabu (Nova Lamego) in northeastern Guinea-Bissau. Originally they were members of the Mande group that is concentrated around the upper Niger River in Mali. In 1675 the Bambaras revolted against Mali rule and created the two independent states of Segou and Kaarta. Because of attacks by the Fulani, their influence declined after 1854. HDRGC.

bambi (Afr.)   A kind of antelope (*Cephalophus* spp.) that lives in the rain forests of Angola; also the name for a small deer-like animal (*C. mergens*) found in the Mossâmedes jungle of southern Angola. GEPB.

Bambos (Afr.)   An African ethnic group settled in the Lunda district of northeastern Angola who often formed small groups to attack Portuguese colonists in the region. In 1900 the Portuguese army instigated punitive campaigns against the Bambos. After some of their chiefs were defeated, they were subdued. GEPB.

bambu africano (Pg.)   "African bamboo." In Mozambique, a large, woody tropical grass (*Oxytenanthera abyssinica* Munro) with hollow stems that attain a diameter of five to six inches and are so hard and durable that they can be used to make furniture, cooking utensils, and structural framing. PDM.

bambum (Crio.) In Cape Verde, the position in which a mother carries her baby. The child is tied around the mother's body with a cloth in such a way that the mother has her hands free to work. Carvalho e Vasconcelhos, *As Colonias Portuguesas*, p. 79.

baméa (Afr.) A tropical shrub (*Tephrosia vogelii*) that produces an acid, poisonous substance used by African fishermen to stupefy fish. It is also an ornamental plant with beautiful flowers, grown in gardens and used as living fences. It is often found wild or cultivated on Príncipe Island. In Pungo Andongo, Angola, it is called *cafoto*. Ficalho, *Plantas Uteis,* pp. 128-9.

banana (Pg.) Any tree-like, tropical herbaceous plant of the genus *Musa* with long, broad leaves and large clusters of edible fruit. Early Portuguese navigators discussed at great length the relative merits of the Asiatic and Guiné varieties of sweet fruit, called banana in both English and Portuguese. The starchy types are also called *plátanos* (plantains). The Asiatic species (*Musa sapientum*) is described in the *Roteiro do Viagem da Vasco da Gama* (Lisbon, 1498). GEPB.

banana-prata (Pg.) A type of banana (*Musa sapientum satama*) native to São Tomé. Known on the West African coast and in Brazil as *banana de São Tomé*. Africans eat its fruits unripe, ripe, dried, or boiled. This starchy substitute for grain has become a basic food for some. Tenreiro, *A Ilha,* p. 92.

Banco Nacional Ultramarino (Pg.) "National Overseas Bank." The official central institution for Angola, Mozambique, and the other Portuguese African colonies. Established in 1907, it had a strict monopoly over economic affairs until independence in 1975. It was empowered to undertake all commercial banking operations as necessary, including participation in private enterprises, some of which it inherited through the transfer of assets. It had several privileges, including the sole right to issue currency and was responsible for enforcing monetary and credit policies and foreign exchange regulations. It also held the country's foreign exchange reserves and the funds of the treasury and government agencies. The officers of the bank were appointed by the government, but the bank was chartered as an autonomous agency. Kaplan, *Area Handbook,* pp. 45, 136, 183; GEPB.

bandeira (Crio.) One of the most important religious festivals on Fogo Island, Cape Verde. It is celebrated with banquets, songs, dances, and with a Te Deum on the eve of the feast. Cardoso, *Folclore Caboverdeano,* p. 43.

Baneane (Pg.) *See* Banyan.

Bangalas (Afr.) A Bantu ethnic group originally settled on both banks of the Congo River and in northern Angola. During the sixteenth and seventeenth centuries they gradually moved into the Old Congo Kingdom. Henry Morton Stanley, a British journalist working for an American newspaper, found Bangalas in Zaire in 1868. GEPB.

baniu (Afr.) Among the Islamic Manjacos (q.v.) of Guinea-Bissau, a compound where boys and girls, once through the puberty rite, are allowed to sleep together and to select a mate. This sexual experience does not incur any social stigma. Guerra, *Terras da Guiné,* p. 73. *See also* fanado.

Bank of Lisbon and South Africa A financial institution created in 1964 to further develop the commercial relations between Portugal and South Africa, at that time isolated by hostile free African countries. It was located in Johannesburg, South Africa. Herrick, *Area Handbook,* p. 170.

bantan (Mand.) The silk-cotton or kapok tree (*Ceiba pentandra*) found in Guinea-Bissau and elsewhere. Its fibers were used to make cloth, often woven in six bands, worn by the Wolof, the Mandingo, and other neighboring groups in Senegambia around 1600; and was also known as wool of poilão. Carreira, *Panaria Cabo-Verdiana,* p. 86.

banto faro (Mand.) "Beyond the swamps." In West Africa, a low area of grassland submerged in the flood season but above water in the dry period, a time when its coarse grass withers. GGT.

Bantu culture A way of life once characteristic of a large portion of Portuguese Africa, mainly in Angola and Mozambique. The ancestors of the Bantu were a Negroid people who, it appears, began their eastern and southern expansion from an area near the present-day Nigeria-Cameroon border. They arrived in Angolan territory c.1300. Although a matter of scholarly dispute, it seems certain that one of the factors that contributed to their success in the savannas was their involvement in vegeculture (q.v.). The Bantu culture was based on food production, ironworking, and a loose social and political organization. Their main crops were sorghum and millet (qq.v.); the latter was called *oilia* (food). Millet had a three-fold advantage over sorghum: it grows in more porous soil, resists long dry spells better, and can be stored for two to three years. The Bushmen, the original inhabitants of south-central Angola, were easily displaced further south by the newcomers. The Bantu established a sedentary society based on land cultivation and on an extended family group living in *libatas* (q.v.). The authority of the chief and the family headman controlled the economic, social, and religious life of the people residing in settlements called *mbanzas* (q.v.), giving a sense of unity and stability to the Bantu way of life. At the end of the fifteenth century, this culture was disrupted by the Portuguese who introduced their own culture. Henderson, *Angola*, p. 52; Kaplan, *Angola*, pp. 8-12; DHP; OED.

Bantu languages (Afr.) A large group of over 300 languages of the central branch of the Niger-Congo language family, spoken south of a line from Cameroon to Kenya. These languages are quite similar in phonology and grammar with a highly developed system of noun classes marked by prefixes, each dependent word having a prefix of the same class as the noun. Although Portuguese was the official language, the great majority of people in Angola (more than 95 percent of the total population) used other languages, some of which were closely related, others remotely so. The Bantu language family once was spoken by most Africans living south of the equator and by substantial numbers north of it. Kaplan, *Angola*, pp. 10, 11, 64-5; WTNID.

Bantu migration into Angola Around the year 1000 the Bantu people migrated southeast from a nuclear area in eastern Nigeria-Cameroon. Between 1300 and 1600 the Bantu penetrated the territory of present-day Angola from the north and the east. This diaspora established a sedentary society based on cultivation of the land, metalworking, and a loose political organization. In the fourteenth century the Bantu were located astride the lower Congo River. By that time they had added *fonio*, root tubers known as Guinea yam, and okra to their original crops of sorghum and millet. At the beginning of the fifteenth century, a Bantu state (q.v.) with a king, called a *manicongo*, was established in Mbanza Congo, later called São Salvador do Congo. Today they inhabit about one-third of the African continent, Wheeler, *Angola,* p. 20; GEPB.

Bantu migration into Mozambique Spurred presumably by population pressures and ecological changes in the Sahel, the initial migrations started from the savannas near the current Nigeria-Cameroon border at about the time of the birth of Christ. The vanguard reached the coast of Mozambique between one hundred and four hundred years later. After displacing the original settlers, the San (Bushmen), the Bantus became a sedentary society. They were vegeculturists and grew grains such as sorghum and millet, a tuber called Guinea yam, okra, and watermelon. As iron workers, they made tools in blast-furnaces. Each group of immigrants was divided into independent chieftaincies, ruled by a *mambo* (hereditary chief) with absolute authority over economic, social, and religious matters. They never established a powerful centralized state. The early Bantus living south of the Zambezi first experienced the power of an organized military state, not from the Portuguese, but from the Karanga, a Shona subgroup. Isaacman, *Mozambique: From Colonialism*, pp. 3-4; GEPB.

Bantu state   A territorial and political organization established at the beginning of the fifteenth century in northern Angola and ruled by a king, called a *manicongo* (q.v.). The Portuguese came in contact with this state in 1482 at Mbanza Congo, later called São Salvador do Congo. Its ruler Nzinga-a-Cuum, who later took the name João I when he was baptized by the Portuguese, was an absolute chief who completely controlled his subjects. The people had a subsistence economy based on rudimentary agricultural cultivation combined with collecting wild fruits, hunting, and fishing. The Portuguese in close alliance with the hereditary *manicongo* began a long process of "civilizing" these African societies. The manner and degree of this socioeconomic and cultural change is still controversial. Underlying centuries of Portuguese domination, Bantu kinship has remained a factor of unity in the minds of Angolans. King Antonio III of Congo warned his subjects in 1956 that "they should occupy and cultivate the land of their ancestors as a symbol of their unity and identity." Wheeler, *Angola,* pp. 19-22; DHP. *See also* Bantu culture.

Banyan (Hind.)   The name for both a Hindu merchant and a trading caste who immigrated from India to Mozambique c. 1600. They formed a close community, bartering in Mozambique and along the East African coast. As a money-lending class with connections to trading houses in Bombay, they acted as financiers for the trading expeditions into the interior. They lent money to *prazo* (q.v.) leaseholders and, on occasion, to the government. They did not mix with or marry Christians. Their role in colonial Zambezia much resembled that of the Asians today. In Portuguese, they are called *Baneanes*. Herrick, *Area Handbook,* p. 68; HDM.

Banyun (Afr.)   In Guinea-Bissau, a small Senegambian ethnic group related to the Cassangas and the Cobianas, living in the southern Casamance area. During the period of Mandingo expansion in the sixteenth century the Banyuns were pushed toward the Atlantic coast and were largely absorbed by the Diolas, Manjacos, and Balantas. Agricultural animists, like the Cassangas they are known as skilled weavers and dyers. In the late sixteenth and the seventeenth centuries, the Cassanga slavers expanded into Banyun territory, capturing many of these people. HDRGC.

banzo (Kimb.)   In Angola and elsewhere, a deep, often deadly, melancholy and sadness among African slaves or captives violently separated from family and relatives. In the colonial period, it frequently was manifested as depression, apathy, even suicide. GDLP. *See also* saudade.

baobab (Afr.) A tall and useful tropical tree (*Adansonia digitata* L.) having a trunk that often grows to a diameter of 30 ft. (9 m) and a height of 60 ft. (18 m), living to a very old age. In favorable conditions it is relatively luxuriant, often forming dense thickets mixed with succulents such as aloes. This type of drought-resistant vegetation covers large arid tracks of land from the Sudan to the Transvaal, and from Cape Verde to Ethiopia. In Angola, Africans drink the rainwater stored in the tissues of its enormous trunk. It is a tree of the savannas, and its bark is used to make coarse cloth, rope, and bags to collect cotton, coffee, nuts, and fruit. In Mozambique the bark is employed in the manufacture of wrapping material for articles to be exported. The gourd-like fruit, which contain edible seeds, are used as buckets and containers. Its fruits also yield a pleasant, edible pulp, used to produce a popular drink. Its light and porous wood is used in making chairs, tables, and other domestic furniture. The young leaves are edible and the dried seeds, called *lalo*, form the base of a dish much esteemed by Angolans. The baobab, in Portuguese *imbondeiro*, was discovered and described by navigators in 1447, three hundred years before the scientific description given by Michael Adanson (1727-1806). In early colonial times, the baobab pulp was exported to Europe under the name of *terra de Lemnos*, and was used to treat dysentery, hemoptysis, and fevers. Carvalho e Vasconcellos, *A Colonias Portuguesas*, p. 345; Ficalho, *Plantas Uteis*, pp. 92, 133; Leathart, *Trees of the World*, p. 189.

Baptist Missionary Society An English Baptist congregation established in 1878 in São Salvador do Congo among the Bacongos of northern Angola. Apparently they were the first Protestant group in the area. Protected by the Congress of Berlin (1885), they spread quickly, helped by booming commercial activity in the area. Churches, schools, and hospitals were established. In 1903, the Portuguese government forbade the use of English in the schools but the rubber-based economic expansion brought the Baptist missions into favor once more. In 1913 a messianic movement was started by an African Baptist, Alvaro Tulante Buta. His preaching resulted in an anti-Portuguese uprising, bloody reprisals, and the burning of São Salvador in 1938 by a mob he led himself. Other popular messianic leaders have included Simão Kimbangu in 1921 and Simão Toco in 1957. Newitt, *Portugal in Africa*, pp. 65-6, 124-5, 131-2; Pelissier, *La Colonie*, p. 265(n).

bar An ancient East Indian measure of weight, equivalent in Mozambique in 1554 to 25.4 lbs. (11.5 kg) and at Sofala to 27.3 lbs. (12.4 kg). Also spelled *baar*. Axelson, *Portuguese in South-East*, p. 244.

barafula (Mand.) In West Africa, a traditional hand-woven six-banded dyed cotton cloth, often with alternating strips of white and blue; used as a unit of currency. In Gambia and on the Benin coast c.1600, it was avidly sought by

Portuguese and European traders for resale elsewhere. Duncan, *Atlantic Islands,* p. 212.

baraka (Afr.) In Guinea-Bissau, the spiritual power of an Islamic holy man. Recognized as close to Allah, he is the intermediary between the supernatural world and the faithful. This mystic holiness is believed to be transmitted from father to son. Trimingham, *Islam in West Africa,* p. 66.

Barclay's Bank A London financial institution created on July 26, 1896. In 1967 it had branches in Lourenço Marques and Beira, Mozambique. NEB.

bare (Pg.) Measure of weight varying from sixteen to twenty *arrobas,* equivalent to between 518 and 648 pounds (235 and 294 kg). *Bares* were used in colonial Zambezia, Mozambique. Newitt, *Portuguese Settlement,* p. 379.

bare mining camps Camps in colonial Zambezia, Mozambique, to mine precious metals, especially gold. Originally the digging was sporadic. Later, when installations were built, it became a permanent operation. The two largest *bares* in Tete each had an officer with the title of *Capitão-mor* appointed as supervisor. In 1767 the post of *Capitão-mor das Terras de Bares de Tete* was created. He presumably had general supervision over all the mining operations. In 1759, Manuel da Costa, *capitão-mor* of the important Mixonga *bare,* complained to the government that the camps were full of undesirables who had come not to dig but to make trouble. Java *bare,* north of the Zambezi, was the personal preserve of Caetano Pereira, and the Cassunca mining camp was operated by the Dominicans. The most important *bare* in Mano c.1820 was the private domain of J.P.X. de Silva Botelho. Newitt, *Portuguese Settlement,* pp. 81-4; GEPB.

Bares, Capitanias das (Pg.) "Mining Captaincies." Official name given to colonial regions where precious metals, especially gold, were found. They were subject to special laws and regulations due to the number of miners and traders attracted by their wealth. Silva Rego, *O Ultramar,* p. 194.

bark cloth A type of cloth made from the bark of an African tree (*Ery-throphleum guinense*). Trade in bark cloth was stimulated by Portuguese merchants c.1500 who exported it from the Congo for sale in Benin and other parts of Portuguese Africa. The tree from which this cloth is made is also called sassy bark. Newitt, *Portugal in Africa,* p. 2; WNWD.

barley A cereal grass (*Hordeum vulgare* L. and related species) with dense, bearded spikes of flowers, each made up of three-seeded spikelets. Its seeds are used in Western Sudan for food and fodder. It was observed cultivated in the fifteenth century in the Baffor Mountains and Wada (Mauritanian Adrar) according to the explorers Valentim Fernandes and Alvise Cadamosto. Barley is still grown under the palm trees of the Atar Oasis and is sold in the market there. The people of the western Sahara may have learned the cultivation of barley in the early Middle Ages from Arab merchants from Wargla where it is still grown. Lewicki, *Western African Food,* pp. 42, 150-2, 160.

barracoon Large enclosure or barrack used on the West African coast and elsewhere for temporary confinement of slaves waiting transportation to Portugal or Brazil and the New World plantations. Large *barracoons* were built by the Portuguese at São Jorge de Mina on the Gulf of Guiné in 1482. In 1574, the Crown erected large barracks on São Tomé for slaves brought from Angola to wait to be shipped to Brazilian plantations. *Barracoons* were constructed in Bissau in 1696. When the slave trade increased between 1680 and 1710, the Dutch, French, and English built extremely large *barracoons* on the Slave Coast and the Gold Coast to house hundreds of Africans waiting to be transferred to the New World. Tenreiro, *A Ilha,* p. 72; GEPB. *See also* factory.

Barué Kingdom (Afr.) An African kingdom located south of the Zambezi River Delta in the triangle between the Sena, Sofala, and Zambezi rivers. According to Portuguese sources, it was already established in 1506, surviving under many different rulers until 1902. It was a crossroad for traders going from Sena to Manica, and a center of wars and struggles among African chiefs resulting from a racial mixture of Tongas, Shonas, and many other ethnic groups. In pre-Portuguese times, it was dominated by Monomotapa (q.v.) chiefs, and during the colonial period by Portuguese and *muzungos* (q.v.). In the 1830s the kingdom was briefly but repeatedly attacked by the Gaza Ngoni (q.v.). In 1880 it was occupied by Manuel Antonio de Sousa, a fact that gave Portugal the right to claim sovereignty and repel Cecil John Rhodes's intrusions into the region. Henriksen, *Mozambique,* pp. 9, 80, 82, 88; GEPB.

Bassas da India (Pg.) Small islands in the Mozambique Channel along which Vasco da Gama sailed on his first trip to India in 1498. Today they belong to the Malagasy Republic (Madagascar). DHP.

bastaards (Afrk.) South African mulatto renegades who arrived in southern Angola in 1884. The Portuguese always disdained Boer settlers and for this reason were eager to neutralize them by allowing the settlement of about one thousand *bastaards* near Humpata in southern Angola. Wheeler, *Angola,* p. 72.

batuque (Afr.) In Cape Verde and elsewhere, a noisy African dance accompanied by a viola and other instruments with a lead singer plus choir that repeats his lyrics. It is often performed with hand clapping, body contortions and exclamations such as *"Olé, lé, lé, lé!"* When alcoholic beverages are served, the *batuque* can turn wild. Carvalho e Vasconcellos, *As Colonias Portuguesas,* p. 81.

bazaruco (Pg.) A copper coin introduced into East Africa by the Portuguese in the sixteenth century, It was used as small change in Mombasa and other coastal towns. Also called *buzuruco.* Freedman-Granville, *East African Coins,* JAH, Cambridge, 1960, I(1):40. *See also* larin, thaler.

Bazombo (Afr.) An ethnic group settled in a small region northeast of São Salvador, near the Zaire border. In 1960 the Bazombos, some of them settled in Leopoldville, tried to mediate between the extremist nationalists and the Portuguese. Pelissier, *La Colonie,* pp. 15, 174.

Bazoruto Islands A group of islands in the Indian Ocean in the vicinity of Sofala, visited by Portuguese navigators in 1505 to chart the shoals and currents in the area. In 1580-90 these islands were often visited to trade for ivory, amber, sesame, and slaves. Commerce continued throughout the colonial period. Axelson, *Portuguese in South-East,* pp. 108, 173, 221.

Beafadas (Afr.) An ethnic group that occupied the Gabu area in Guinea-Bissau until their expulsion by the Mandingo in the fourteenth and fifteenth centuries. The Beafadas acquired many Mandingo characteristics including the system of secondary kingship, especially in the sixteenth century when they paid tribute to the empire of Mali. In the nineteenth century they resisted the incursions of the Futa-Djallon led by Coli Tenguella and forced his diversion northeast of the Beafada territory. Today the major concentration of Beafadas is in the region just north of Bambadinca and along the Fulacunda-Buba axis. The period of Portuguese colonial penetration was punctuated by numerous instances of Beafada resistance including those in 1880-2, 1886, 1900, and 1907-8. After 1908 they were considered pacified. HDRGC.

beça-ngana (Afr.) In Angola and elsewhere in Portuguese Africa, a mulatto girl who chooses to identify herself with her African heritage. Hamilton, *Voices,* pp. 96, 148.

Beira (Pg.) Seaport and capital of the Manica and Sofala districts on the southeast coast of Mozambique 120 mi. (190 km) southwest of the mouth of the Zambezi River. It is the chief port for Zimbabwe, Malawi, and central Mozambique, exporting ores, hides, cotton, and sugar. Founded in 1891, it was the headquarters of the Mozambique Company and a growing European city by 1900. In 1950 its deep water capability was greatly expanded. Its population in 1960 was 58,970. By 1991 its population was estimated at 269,200. GEPB; HDM.

Beira News, The A bi-weekly bilingual publication edited in Beira (q.v.), Mozambique. An English-Portuguese periodical that the Portuguese journalist Victor Gomes began publishing on September 1, 1917. It was distributed in Angola, Katanga (Zaire), Nyassaland, South Africa, and Zimbabwe. GEPB.

Beira-Umtali Railroad Opened in 1891, 195 mi. (314 km) long, it is the oldest and most important Mozambique railroad. Financed by the British South Africa Company and its subsidiaries, it remained in non-Portuguese hands until its purchase in 1949 by the Portuguese finance ministry. Two years later, the Beira Convention between Great Britain and Portugal guaranteed the rail traffic of the Federation of Rhodesia and Nyassaland through Beira, justifying the financing of improvements in Beira. Abshire, *Portuguese Africa*, p. 331.

beirame (Afr.) A standard length of very fine cloth used in Angola for barter. During the devastating drought and famine of October 1857, in markets in Dondo, Mbaka, Duque de Braganza, Malange, and elsewhere, people sold their own children as slaves for five or six *beirames* of cloth to exchange for cassava flour, maize, and groundnuts. Dias, *Famine and Disease*, JAH, Cambridge, 1981, 22(3):360.

Bejé (Afr.) A settlement established by the Angolan governor, Antonio de Vasconcelos, in Huila province in 1759 with the aim of centralizing the African population by organizing a market, building a mission and dwellings, and cultivating land. Bejé was one of the several centers founded in outlying regions as a means of "civilizing" their inhabitants. It was an "enlightenment project" that soon failed. Silva Rego, *O Ultramar,* pp. 166-7.

beldroegas (Pg.) A succulent herb (*Portulaca oleracea* L.) with fleshy and juicy tissues, found in sandy soils in Luanda, Pungo Andongo, Angola, and São Tomé. It is also called *bemoe* and, in English, purslane. Ficalho, *Plantas Uteis,* p. 87.

Bembe (Afr.) A municipality in the Congo district, Luanda province, Angola. A modern economic center, it is a rich cotton-producing area that includes the county seat, Vila Uige, Bembe and Songo. GEPB. *See also* Bembe copper mines.

Bembe copper mines A mining complex in Bembe (q.v.) that, with the authorization of King Afonso I of Congo, had been exploited by the Portuguese since 1515. In 1665 the Battle of Ambuila (q.v.) was fought for control of these mines. They were explored and mined by succeeding Angolan governors, then abandoned in 1769. In 1855 governor J.R.C. do Amaral authorized a Brazilian, Francisco Antonio Flores, to extract ore and export it to Brazil. Flores transferred his concession to the Western Africa Malachite Copper Mines Company in 1857. The mines became inactive again after 1887. In 1919 the *Sociedade Mineira do Bembe* (Mining Society of Bembe) installed facilities for the extraction of ore. In 1937 the Portuguese government tried to modernize the mines with the assistance of the colonial ministry. GEPB.

bembom (Pg.) A thick-lipped African; a feature considered handsome in São Tomé and elsewhere in Portuguese Africa. In Cuba, *bembom* (Spanish: *bembón*) has a derogatory meaning. Hamilton, *Voices*, p. 369. *See also* catinga.

Bengo River (Afr.) A river that starts in the Canganze Mountains in central Angola and empties into the Atlantic at Bengo Bay, north of Luanda. It irrigates a rich agricultural region where since colonial times there have been prosperous cattle ranches and farms producing grain, vegetables, and fruit. GEPB.

Benguela-a-Velha An old coastal settlement near the Atlantic port of Amboim in southern Angola. At the beginning of the seventeenth century it was a small, isolated village but after the expulsion of the Dutch in 1648, the slave trade with Brazil increased greatly and by 1759 it was considered a strategic center for the colonization of the rugged territory east of the town. Duffy, *Portuguese Africa,* p. 60; Silva Rego, *O Ultramar,* pp. 62, 167. *See also* Benguela sertão.

Benguela Current A strong cold current flowing northward along the southwest coast of Africa formed by the West Wind Drift and the Agulhas Current. The Benguela Current flows toward the equator, gradually leaves the coast, and becomes the South Equatorial Current. The Benguela Current substantially reduces precipitation along the coast, making the region south of Benguela arid or nearly so, and forms the northern extension of the Namibian Desert. This is locally called the Mossâmedes Desert, and is quite dry even in its northern reaches. The far south coast is marked by sand dunes which give way to scrubby vegetation in the middle section. Kaplan, *Angola,* p. 61; WNGD.

Benguela Dutch Village   A colonial settlement on the southern coast of Angola that Dutch invaders occupied in 1641. In 1648 they were expelled by Salvador Correa de Sá. Silva Rego, *O Ultramar*, pp. 285-6.

Benguela Sertão   "Benguela forest." An extensive wild region east of the town of Benguela that in 1759 was slated to be colonized by establishing missions, military forts, villages with enough land for agriculture, and markets for centers of trade. This idea of colonizing the interior of Angola was one of the important government projects of the time. Silva Rego, *O Ultramar*, pp. 166, 262.

Benin, Bight of   Wide-mouthed bay in the Gulf of Guiné on the former Slave Coast of West Africa. The Portuguese merchant Fernão Gomes visited this area in 1450 and 1460. Later the Portuguese established an important trade center there. DHP; WNGD. *See also* Benin, Peoples' Republic of.

Benin Gap   A natural break through the eastern and western forests of the Gulf of Guiné that connects inland Benin with the coastal lagoons. Over a stretch of less than 300 mi. (483 km) out of some 2,000 (3,218), the coast remained unforested, and over a span of some 30 mi. (48 km) the rainy season becomes considerably milder, thereby improving the climate and, particularly on a short stretch due south of Benin, the fertility of the soil. Through this gap the more moderate Sudanese climate reaches the coast, decreasing the rainfall and providing better conditions for human settlement and social development. Here the palm tree is established, yet cereal plants, especially maize, thrive. Portuguese navigators reached this area c.1450-60 to trade in spices, gold, and slaves. Today Benin Gap is part of the People's Republic of Benin (q.v.). Polanyi, *Dahomey,* pp. 5-6.

Benin, Kingdom of   An ancient African kingdom centralized under the political control of an hereditary king. In the fifteenth century it manufactured cloth and domestic artifacts and dealt in gold, spices, and slaves. Around 1486, the Portuguese navigator and explorer João Afonso de Aveiro visited and befriended King Ogané, who ruled the kingdom at the time. King João II of Portugal established formal relations and exchanged gifts with the monarch. Soon after, King Ogané's son converted to Christianity. In 1625, Benin became known as Dahomey and was a major source of slaves. Portuguese and other European traders bought thousands of slaves for the Brazilian and Caribbean plantations, and the country was called the Slave Coast. By 1767 Dahomey depended entirely on the slave trade with British, Dutch, and French slavers. When the slave trade was abolished at the beginning of the nineteenth century, Dahomey's prosperity declined. Prestage, *The Portuguese Pioneers*, pp. 212-3; DHP.

Benin, Peoples' Republic of (Afr.)   From 1625 to 1976, the country was known as Dahomey. In 1960 it achieved independence from France and in 1976 restored its ancient name, Benin. It includes the former Slave Coast and the Niger Delta region on the Gulf of Guiné. When Fernão Gomes, a Portuguese explorer and merchant, visited the area between 1450 and 1460, he found it already active in trade. Gomes, a wealthy Lisbon merchant, established a trade center, buying gold and slaves in exchange for European goods. The country was one of the most highly organized of the African states of West Africa before the coming of the Portuguese in 1485. It exerted great influence in the seventeenth century and was known to Europeans as both Dahomy and Great Benin. HDB; WNGD.

Berberia (Pg.)   A fifteenth-century name for a loosely defined zone on the Atlantic coast between Ceuta and Cape Bojador (qq.v.), and inland up to the Saharan oases and south to the empires of Mali and Ghana. The Portuguese believed it to be a region rich in gold, spices, and slaves. Mota, *Mar, Alem Mar,* pp. 86-7.

beriberi (Sinh.)   A disease caused by a deficiency of thiamine, endemic to those who live mainly on a diet of polished rice. It is characterized by multiple neuritis, general weakness, paralysis, progressive edema, mental deterioration, and finally heart failure. It was first reported in Ambriz in 1875 and in Luanda in 1877. *Revista Medica de Angola,* Luanda, 1923, 2:424.

Berlin, Congress of   An international meeting in Berlin, 1884-5, at the invitation of German Chancellor Otto von Bismarck. Representatives of all European nations, the United States, and Turkey met in Berlin to consider problems arising out of the European penetration of West Africa. The stated purpose of the meeting was to guarantee free trade and navigation on the Congo River and on the lower reaches of the Niger River. In fact, the main results were the territorial agreements made among the attending powers. The sovereignty of Great Britain over southern Nigeria was recognized and the claims to the greater part of the Congo made by the International Association, a private corporation controlled by King Leopold II of Belgium, were more or less acknowledged. These accords ignored French claims to parts of the Congo and Nigeria and the historical claims of Portugal to the mouth of the Congo River. The attempts to guarantee free trade and the neutrality of the region in wartime and to set up rules for future colonial expansion in Africa were applauded, but these understandings soon proved too vague to be workable. Portugal kept control of the right (south) bank of the Congo River and connected with the road built on the Angolan side to facilitate trade with São Salvador do Congo. It also agreed to recognize religious freedom and to protect all missionaries, irrespective of their affiliations. Before the conference, Europe had more or less ignored the interior of Africa and there was remarkably little knowledge of the size and resources of the continent, resulting in the artificial and controversial boundaries that still exist today. The partitioning of Africa brought almost the whole of the continent under European control and the imposition of European authority brought a previously unknown security to many indigenous people over wide areas, contributing greatly to their immediate material welfare and their ultimate political development. GEPB; HDRGC.

Best & Williams Company   A British shipping company with its headquarters in Lourenço Marques. In 1894 they proposed a plan to the local government to organize a steady migration of Africans to work in the Witwatersrand gold mines in the Transvaal. At the time it was calculated that two-thirds of the coastal labor force was employed in the Rand (q.v.). In 1894, 12,000 laborers boarded ships in Inhambane (q.v.) to work in South Africa. Best & Williams was in charge of recruiting young workers, receiving in exchange a percentage of their earnings from the mining companies. By the end of the century the migration had increased substantially. In 1899 there were about 80,000 African workers from southern Mozambique employed in the Transvaal and Natal goldfields. Rita-Ferreira, *O Movimento Migratorio*, pp. 15-16.

bicho cortado (Pg.)   A cotton cloth woven in the Cape Verde Islands in a variety of colors, often stamped with animal figures, and sold in West Africa during the colonial period. Carreira, *Panaria Caboverdiana*, p. 96. *See also* bantan, oxó.

Bidonville   In the 1920s, a shantytown on the outskirts of São Tomé. Since then, there has been a campaign to improve conditions in this neighborhood. Tenreiro, *A Ilha,* p. 124. *See also* caniço.

Bié Plateau (Afr.)   A highland region in central Angola, altitude c.5000 ft. (1500 m). It is the watershed of the Zambezi, Cuanza, Cuando, and Cubango, major rivers that irrigate the most important agricultural regions of Angola. GEPB; WNGD.

Bié Province   Angolan province created in 1934. A rich agricultural area, part of the of the Benguela Kingdom during the colonial period. Portuguese authorities established military control there in 1772, and the Congress of Berlin (q.v.) recognized Portuguese rights in 1885. In this province are the important Atlantic ports of Lobito (q.v.), Novo Redondo, and Port Amboim. GEPB.

Bijagos Archipelago A group of low islands belonging to Guinea-Bissau and situated southwest of Bissau (q.v.). The largest are Orango, Formosa, and Caravela. On the easternmost island is Bolama, a seaport and the capital of the archipelago. HDRGC; WNGD.

Bilad-as-Sudan (Ar.) "Land of the Blacks." A region in north-central Africa, south of the Sahara and Libyan deserts. This geographic area extends 4,000 mi. (6,400 km) across the African continent from the west coast to the mountains of Ethiopia, with the widest part nearly 1,000 mi. (1,600 km) across; its approximate area is 2,000,000 square miles (5,000,000 sq. kilometers). It includes major parts of the republics of Senegal, Gambia, Burkina Faso, and the northern parts of those countries from Guinea-Bissau to Cameroon bordering on the Atlantic; it occupies the basin of the Senegal River and the central part of the Niger and Nile basins as well as the Lake Chad region, and consists of desert, grassy savannahs, and extensive plains. Ethnologically, it is that part of Africa north of the equator inhabited by black Africans under Moslem influence. In medieval times, it was the site of the African empires of Bornu, Songhai, and Fula (q.v.). Since ancient times the Sudan has provided Mediterranean countries with small amounts of gold and slaves in exchange for cloth, copper, and metal tools. The introduction of the camel (q.v.) and the spread of Islam in the tenth century helped the Sudan to become more closely associated with North Africa and the Middle East due in great part to Sudanese Moslems undertaking pilgrimages to Mecca. The Portuguese explorer Alvise Cadamosto reached the Senegal River in 1455 and reported that the Mandingo people of Gambia regarded the Emperor of Mali, with whom Cadamosto tried to establish commercial relations, as their overlord. King João II, c.1490, sent two delegations, one by the Gambia River, which failed, and the other by way of the fortress of São Jorge da Mina (q.v.) to the king of Songo, also know as Songhai (q.v.), whose capital was one of the most populated of the great cities of the Bilad-as-Sudan region. It is also known as Bilad-al-Sudan or Bilad-es-Sudan. Trimingham, *A History of Islam*, pp. 13, 42, 74; DHP; WNGD.

bilharziasis Also called schistosomiasis. A disease, usually tropical, caused by schistosomes transmitted to man in contaminated water using snails as alternate hosts. It is characterized in man by disorders of the liver, bladder, lungs, and central nervous system. This infection affects 75 percent of the population in Mozambique. A medical team recorded the rate of incidence in the Zambezia district in 1960 as 82 percent. It was reported in Lubango, Cabinda, and Ambriz in 1902 and later appeared throughout Angola. Herrick, *Area Handbook,* pp. 117, 121; *Revista Medica de Angola,* Luanda, 1923, 3:115-16.

bilhete de identidade (Pg.) "Identity card." A formal identification card issued to Africans in colonial Portuguese Africa. This card would prove that a person had served in public office, had been employed in the colonial administrative corps, had received a secondary-school education, or was a licensed merchant, partner in a business firm, or proprietor of an industrial establishment. Duffy, *Portuguese Africa*, p. 295. *See also* caderneta.

bimba (Afr.) In Angola and elsewhere, an aquatic plant (*Herminiera elaphroxylon* Guill.) that forms thick clumps in ponds and lakes. Its soft and light wood is used to make rafts for fishing and unloading cargo in ports. Ficalho, *Plantas Uteis*, p. 130.

Bisa traders Professional African traders of the Bisa people of northern Zambia who, by the end of the eighteenth century, were the most active itinerant traders in Central Africa. At one time they organized trade caravans that traveled from the Luanda territory across Africa through Marawe, Tete, Zumbo, and along the Zambezi to the Swahili/Arab settlements on the coast of Mozambique. The transcontinental expedition headed by F.J. de Lacerda e Almeida in 1797-8 had, among other aims, the purpose of dealing with the Bisa traders who were long familiar with crisscrossing the continent. The Bisa traded small amounts of copper, ivory, and other surplus goods to Zumbo and Tete. About 1800 trade routes to the Indian Ocean coast were disrupted by war, so the Bisa, by then slave traders, started exporting their captives to the Angolan markets. Bisa caravans visited Lake Niassa and the Swahili coast until 1850. Isaacman, *Mozambique: From Colonialism*, pp. 80-1; GEPB.

Bissagos (Afr.) An ethnic group who migrated from mainland Africa and occupied the Bijagos archipelago (q.v.) long before the arrival of the Portuguese in the fifteenth century. They are animists with a social system based on petty chiefdoms. They have ethnic affinities with the Diolas, Cocolis, Padjadincas, and Papeis (q.v.). Their economy is largely based on fishing and palm products. They are famed for their large ocean-going canoes which enabled them to conduct slave raids on the coast with little fear of retaliation. The first Portuguese explorer to reach the islands was Nuno Tristão who landed in 1447 and was killed during his attacks on the Bissagos people. In the period 1840-50 the Bissagos again mounted a stiff resistance against British and French intrusion and were certainly not under Portuguese control. Attempts to suppress the Bissagos' tax revolts occurred in 1900, 1906, 1917, and 1936. GEPB; HDRGC.

Bissau (Afr.) Seaport and capital of the People's Republic of Guinea-Bissau, situated on the north shore of an island at the mouth of the Geba River (q.v.).

Discovered by Nuno Tristão in 1446, the island soon became a base for the slave trade. By 1696 Bissau had a fort, a church, a hospital, and a monastery with a few missionaries. It controlled the trade on the Geba and Corubal rivers. Frequent attacks by Africans on ports and forts were common in the colonial period. In 1879 the administration of Guinea-Bissau was separated from Cape Verde and the capital was transferred to Bolama. The first three decades of the twentieth century saw almost continuous resistance by the Papeis in the Bissau area and in 1941 the capital was moved from Bolama to Bissau. A high death rate from tropical diseases plus unrest among Africans strongly discouraged colonization. Originally occupied by the Papeis (q.v.), its population in 1979 was 105,273; the island's area is 460 sq. mi. (1200 sq. km); besides Bissau city, one finds villages such as Antula, Bandim, Bifimita, Biombo, and others. The fertile land produces rice, peanuts, coconuts, and other tropical fruits, usually grown by Africans. In modern times sugar cane, cattle, goats, and pigs have been introduced. Since independence in 1974 progress has been made on expanding port facilities and in other areas of urban planning including improvement of the electric power and piped water systems. GEPB; HDRGC.

Bissau, captaincy of   A military fort and trade center on the north bank of the mouth of the Geba River, central Guinea-Bissau, licensed by the Portuguese government on March 15, 1692. For some years this settlement had been a trade center for Portuguese and French merchants dealing in agricultural products and slaves. In 1609 the first chapel was built there by the missionary José de Bequo. Barreto, *Historia*, pp. 125-6.

black brotherhoods   Since the Middle Ages there have been religious brotherhoods in Portugal. Around 1490, the church established slave brotherhoods in Lisbon, Evora, and other cities to accommodate the increasing arrival and conversion of African slaves. By 1525 there were many black brotherhoods dedicated to honor saints such as St. Anthony and St. Francis. These congregations served the spiritual and social needs of their members, helped to gain freedom for their members, and lobbied to get government assistance for sick or imprisoned slaves. Through these congregations the Crown channeled complaints and found solutions to social and economic problems. The earliest black confraternity is believed to be the Lisbon Brotherhood of the Rosary. It was created in 1484 and coincided with the first generation of slaves born in Portugal. The brotherhoods appeared in Faro by 1518, in Lagos by 1555, and overseas in São Tomé by 1526. These fraternities were associated with the Dominican Order which had promoted devotion to the rosary during the later Middle Ages. The semi-magical, almost talismanic, nature of the rosary itself may have appealed to Africans, as it did to Portuguese. By 1550 the brotherhoods were well organized, having their own government confirmed by the Crown in 1565. This government consisted of a judge, two stewards, and a clerk who met every Sunday and holy day, morning and afternoon, to transact business. There was also a general counsel and a high government official nominated by the king to ensure adherence to the brotherhood's regulations. In this task he was aided, especially in matters concerning religious orthodoxy, by the prior of the St. Dominic monastery in Lisbon. Although the office of judge or steward was open to whites, it normally went to blacks. Elections of the governing body were held on the Sunday after Saint Isabel's Day (July 8). Although any male slave could join the fraternity, he could not hold a position; the officers had to be freedmen. The brotherhoods fought for manumission (q.v.) of slave children until well into the seventeenth century, and they continued to represent Africans' interests. In the same century, these organizations spread to the African colonies and to Brazil. Saunders, *A Social History*, pp. 151-6; DHP; GEPB.

Black Mother Name given to Angola c.1575 for being the most important source of slaves for the Brazilian plantations. Conservative estimates of the total number of Africans shipped from Angola as slaves over the centuries range from two to four million. This enormous number partly helps to explain the relatively small population of Angola today. Duffy, *Portuguese Africa*, p. 138; GEPB.

Blanquerna A book in Catalan written by Ramon Lull c.1283 in which he refers to several countries of North Africa, to Abyssinia, and even to Tartary, and recounts the first European voyage to the Sudan. *Blanquerna* has been deemed "one of the masterpieces of the Christian Middle Ages." Cortesão, *History,* I:205.

Blantyre A town in southern Malawi in the Shire Highlands named after David Livingstone's birthplace in Lanarkshire, Scotland. In 1876 the Church of Scotland established the first mission station there. Although borders were established at that time, Portugal claimed sovereignty over the territory. From 1879 to 1889 Blantyre was under constant threat of being taken by the Portuguese, who were concerned about its double role as a center of Protestant evangelization and an industrial settlement. Portugal regarded that area as part of its territorial expansion. In 1890 Lord Salisbury settled the problem by warning Portugal that Blantyre was under British protection. In 1963 the town had a population of 35,000; by 1977 the figure was 222,000. Axelson, *Portugal,* pp. 8, 157-60.

Blu-Blu (Afr.) One of the largest and richest farms on São Tomé and the site of the famous Blu-Blu Falls. GEPB.

bobra (Afr.) On Santiago Island, Cape Verde, an African stringed instrument shaped like an arrow; also known as a *bolombolo*. In Guinea-Bissau it is called *balimbó* in Mandingo. Lopes da Silva, *O Dialecto Crioulo*, p. 194.

Boers in Angola Led by Jacobus F. Botha, a group of 1,000 Boers with 200 carts and their cattle began a long and dangerous migration in 1875 from the Transvaal north through the Kalahari Desert, suffering hunger, sickness, and attacks by hostile Africans. Along the way, one-third of the travelers turned back. The rest wandered until 1880 when they arrived at the banks of the Cubango River. After crossing the Damaralandia region, they settled in the unhealthy area of Caoco. A Catholic missionary, Carlos Duparquet, advised them to seek government permission to settle in Humpata. There they were granted land and on January 4, 1881, fifty-five Boer families, totaling 295 individuals, established the colony of São Januario, named in honor of the Angolan governor, Januario Correia de Almeida, Conde de São Januario. Guerreiro, *Boers de Angola*, Garcia de Horta, Lisbon, 1958, 6(1):12-13.

Boer-Portuguese relations Boer-Portuguese relations in southern Angola passed through at least two stages. The first, a symbiotic period (1879-93), was marked by Boer successes as bush fighters in numerous "pacification" campaigns. They crushed African rebellions and cleared the way for the Portuguese authorities to control the areas. The second period (1893-1928) was a stage of misunderstandings and growing mutual suspicion and recrimination. The Boers had become restless; some disdained farming and raided nearby herds owned by African herders, some migrated north and east into the Congo, others, in a major exodus of several thousand trekkers in 1928, went back to South West Africa, to the area now known as Namibia. Wheeler, *Angola*, pp. 72-3; DHP.

Bolama Affair, The An intrusive British factory (q.v.) on Bolama Island, Guinea-Bissau, established illegally in 1792 in an attempt to start a colony under the guise of a philanthropic project; the enterprise came to be known as the Bolama Affair. The site selected was almost within sight of the Portuguese fortress of São José de Bissau. A few years later England put forth a territorial claim on the region as a colony. The British settlement at Bolama, a source of friction for a generation, was settled by arbitration in which President Ulysses S. Grant of the United States awarded the island to Portugal. Hammond, *Portugal and Africa*, p. 47.

bolanha (Pg.) In Guinea-Bissau and elsewhere, a cultivated field in a forest clearing with fertile and well drained soil. Often a *bolanha* is planted with white rice and sugar cane. Mota, *Guiné Portuguesa*, I:54-5.

Boletim dos Alunos do Liceu Gil Eanes (Pg.) "Bulletin of the Students of the Gil Eanes Lyceum." A literary journal published in Mindelo, Santiago Island, Cape Verde, in 1969. Only one issue appeared, but it demonstrated the intellectual and artistic activity among students in Cape Verde. Among its contributors were Corsino Fortes, Onesimo Silveira, and Rolando Vera-Cruz Martins. Hamilton, *Voices*, pp. 268-9.

Boletim Official (Pg.) "Official Bulletin." A government periodical started in Luanda in September 1845. It was published during the governorship of Pedro Alexandrinho da Cunha and was the first printed periodical published in Angola. Lopo, *Jornalismo* p. 19.

bolsas marítimas (Pg.) "Shipping insurance." A system established by King Fernando of Portugal in 1380 whereby a ship's owner was paid a certain sum, including the value of the cargo, by an insurer for a loss at sea. It was compulsory for all ships over 50 tons, including the king's fleet. Shipping insurance was imposed in Porto in 1397; in 1402 the premium was £10 for each ton of cargo. In 1512 King Manuel imposed a premium of one two-hundred-forthieth of a pound (less than one-half of one percent) for each pound sterling's worth of merchandise brought from Portugal to Africa. In the Netherlands and elsewhere in Europe this insurance was paid at the port of Bruges in Flanders, now Belgium. DHP.

Bombay An Indian city on the west coast of the continent which c. 1700 was an important financial center where Banyan (q.v.) traders obtained credit to operate in Zambezia (q.v.). Bombay trading houses acted as financiers for the trading expeditions into the interior of Mozambique, lending money to the *prazo*-holders and, on occasion, to the Portuguese government. Newitt, *Portuguese Settlement,* pp. 126, 151.

bore A high, abrupt wave moving inland on a narrow river estuary, caused by the incoming tides. It was first observed at the mouth of a river on the coast of Guiné by Alvise Cadamosto c.1454. GEPB.

Boror (Afr.) A large *prazo* developed as a plantation in Quelimane province, north of the Kwa-Kwa River, Mozambique, leased by the Boror Company (q.v.) in 1898. Situated far inland, it was first used as a trading post for merchants coming from the coast and Quelimane on their way west to what is now Malawi. In 1877 the current leaseholder controlled the local slave trade. When the Boror Company leased it, they developed successful agricultural enterprises. Copra, extracted from coconut meat, became the main product by 1906. Sisal, cotton, and sugar cane were soon introduced and a few years later the *prazo* had become a prosperous plantation that attracted

African laborers from neighboring *prazos*. The Portuguese government tried for years to directly administer the Boror and other *prazos* in an attempt to end the exploitation of African laborers, but its policy failed. Even after independence in 1974, FRELIMO (q.v.) was still trying to abolish forced labor, violence, and official corruption in Quelimane and elsewhere in Mozambique. Vail, *Capitalism,* pp. 35, 86, 112, 118, 177. *See also* Boror Company.

Boror Company One of the largest of the chartered companies, established in Zambezia (q.v.) in the 1880s. The Portuguese government, hopeful that concessions would attract capital that would stimulate economic growth, granted far-reaching monopoly rights and quasi-sovereign power to the Boror Company to colonize and develop the region in Quelimane province, Mozambique. It soon obtained a foothold in the oilseed trade, and the company made annual profits sufficient to ensure a reasonable return on its investment. In 1898 it was reorganized and obtained the lease to the Nameduro *prazo*, renamed the Bororo (q.v.), uniting a vast block of territory north and inland of the Macuse River in northern Quelimane. Because of the company's abuse of forced laborers, the government fined it in the 1920s. Vail, *Capitalism*, pp. 117-8, 120, 223-4; GEPB.

Bororo (Afr.) A large *prazo* (q.v.) in Quelimane, Mozambique, in which the African chiefs from 1892 to 1898 independently resorted to force to emphasize their grievances against the leaseholders. In 1898, they rallied around a principal chief and declared they would never pay taxes or recognize the authority of those leaseholders. Isaacman, *Mozambique: From Colonialism,* p. 162.

botaca (Afr.) A domestic slave kept in a *prazo* (q.v.) household of Zambezia. A *botaca* was often a personal servant of the *dona* (q.v.), the *prazo* leaseholder, and he would remain with his mistress when she married or if she changed her home. Also called a *butaka*. Newitt, *Portuguese Settlement*, pp. 196-7.

boval (Afr.) In Guinea-Bissau, a flat barren platform or piece of land considerably elevated above the rest of the region. Mota, *Guiné Portuguesa,* I:47.

bovalização (Pg.) In the Bové region of Guinea-Bissau, the deformation and erosion of bare soil by the *harmattan* (q.v.), a dry easterly wind. Mota, *Guiné Portuguesa*, I:47. *See also* boval.

Brado Africano (Pg.) "The African Cry." A weekly periodical of protest first published in Lourenço Marques, Mozambique, in 1918. It was owned and run from 1918 to 1936 by the brothers João and José Albasini. Dedicated to an African readership, each issue included a supplement in the Ronga language. An independent periodical, it survived until 1936 when the Salazar regime abolished it. Herrick, *Area Handbook*, pp. 132, 179, 180; HDM.

Brames (Afr.) An ethnic group located in the area between Canchungo and Bula on the north bank of the Mansoa River in Guinea-Bissau. Related to the Papeis, Manjaco, and Mancanha peoples, the Brames are slightly Islamized but mainly animist (q.v.). Their economy is based on slash-and-burn farming with a limited hierarchical political organization. The 1950 census showed 16,300 Brames, while the 1960 estimate indicated the population had risen to 35,000. The Brames have evolved the most successful non-irrigated system of farming in Guinea-Bissau. Mota, *Guiné Portuguesa*, I:381.

Brava Believed to have been discovered by Antonio de Noli in July 1455, Brava is the second smallest of the ten major Cape Verde islands. It attracted colonists from the Algarve, Portugal, and the Madeira Islands. In 1680 new settlers arrived from Fogo Island. Brava's first secondary school was founded in the 1850s. Historically, its limited arable land has resulted in a pattern of emigration to the United States, more so than for the other islands. HDRGC; GEPB.

Brazil Ward Since colonial times, a district of the city of Ouidah, Dahomey, where most of the Portuguese and Afro-Portuguese settled. Until 1954 local residents celebrated a religious festival in the same fashion as one held in Bahia, Brazil. Apparently the slave traffic and commercial relations with Brazil have contributed to a high level of acculturation. São Tomé e Príncipe, *Pequena Monografia*, p. 85.

Brazilian settlers in Angola Between 1849 and 1850 some 300 Portuguese nationals fleeing xenophobic persecution in Brazil were transported by the government to the haven of the southern Angolan coast. The settlers were given land, seeds, tools, and slaves by the state and steps were taken to ensure that their products were sold. After difficult early years, prosperity came during the cotton boom of the 1860s, and state-aided colonization success-fully extended to the foothills of the escarpment. Clarence-Smith, *Slaves, Peasants,* pp. 15. *See also* Afro-Brazilians in Benin, Afro-Brazilians in Lagos.

Brethren, Church of the Brethren missionaries, an English Protestant congregation founded in 1830, came to Angola in 1890 under the leadership of Frederick Stanley Arnot with the goal of spreading the Gospel to Central Africa in the footsteps of David Livingstone (1813-1873). In a few years they had set up missions throughout the Bié Plateau (q.v.) region. Later they pushed west and northwest into the territory of Luanda and maintained a number of smaller stations and schools in remote parts of the interior. By 1932 they had fourteen central stations and about one thousand outstations or posts that they visited regularly. At one time they were the largest Protestant group in Angola. Duffy, *Portuguese Africa*, pp. 125-26; GEPB; OED.

bride-price *See* lobola.

British South African Company A corporation founded in 1888, based in London and funded with British capital. It was established to conduct commerce and exploration under government supervision. The British government charter allowed it to trade within an area roughly between the Limpopo and Zambezi rivers in inland Central Africa with a private army to enforce its claims. It expanded British territories and helped to define borders with Mozambique, formalized in an 1891 treaty between Portugal and Britain. Axelson, *Portugal*, pp. 124, 146; Duffy, *Portuguese Africa,* pp. 90, 217-20.

Brussels, Conference of   The conference, held in 1889-90, dictated guidelines for the abolition of slavery in Central Africa and established a program for the organization of Africa under the protection of the Western Nations by building military posts and roads and developing shipping on rivers and lakes. The agreement has also been called the Anti-Slavery Code. Cunha, *Trabahlo Indigena,* pp. 33-36.

bulrush millet   A tropical cereal (*Pennisetum typhoides*), considered a distinct species, first widely grown before the thirteenth century in estuarine areas of West Africa. Derived from a wild variety from the savannah zone of Central Africa, there have been two separate centers of bulrush millet cultivation; one was in West Africa and the other around Lake Chad. Compared with *Sorghum vulgare* (q.v.), its nutritional value is somewhat inferior and it provides animal fodder of lower quality, but millet will grow in drier, less fertile areas than sorghum. In the thirteenth century it was imported from Bilad-as-Sudan (q.v.), into Walata and Mali. In addition to the names *anili* and *dukhun*, used for bulrush millet both by medieval Islamic authors and by the peoples of the present-day Sudan, some other local names are used. In the central Sudan, it is sometimes called *qasab* or *qsab*; the Wolof call this kind of millet (or a variety of it) *sanyo* or *suna*; the Hausa call it *gero* or *maiava*; the Tedas, *annera*; and the Kanuri, *argum moro*. Lewicki, *West African Food,* pp. 24-6.

bush drugs Narcotic, hallucinogenic substances found in the wilderness in northeastern Brazil. They became valuable commodities in the traffic between Lisbon, Bahia, Guiné, and Angola in the seventeenth century. Carreira, *As Companhias Pombalinas*, BCG, 1968, xxiii(89/90):7, 19.

bush school In Angola and elsewhere, a rural one-room school established in the twentieth century by the government for educating African children. By 1933, 46,000 pupils were attending primary schools in Angola, of whom eighty-six percent were at bush schools. Newitt, *Portugal in Africa,* p. 140.

"Bust Cabora Bassa" Around 1973, a slogan of FRELIMO (q.v.) guerrillas. They had been attempting to destroy the big Cabora Bassa Dam (q.v.), then under construction by the Portuguese government assisted by an international consortium. The campaign to organize a frontal attack began in 1969, but the results were meager and it never succeeded. Assaults on the dam's defended perimeter gradually gave way to somewhat more effective attacks on road and rail links. Starting late in 1971 and continuing until the end of the war, guerrillas damaged water pumps, raked moving railway wagons with gunfire, and derailed trains on the Trans-Zambezia railway connecting Beira and Moatize, Tete. Henriksen, *Revolution,* pp. 29, 35; DHP.

cabela (Afr.)   In Angola and elsewhere, a tall tropical tree (*Xylopia aethiopica* Dun.) and its fruit. This species is common along the West African coast from Senegambia to northern Angola and the islands of São Tomé e Príncipe. The pulp, seeds, and fruits all have a hot spicy taste; they are used by Africans to season food and in a drug to treat dysentery, fevers, and stomach illnesses. In 1551, it was cultivated in Benin under the name of *unias*. By 1735, this drug was sold in France under the names of *poivre long noir*, *poivre d'Ethiopia*, and *grains de selim*. Its timber is valuable for boat building. Ficalho, *Plantas Uteis,* pp. 77-78.

Cabinda Enclave   A district of Angola, north of the Congo River, 20,100 sq. m. (54,000 sq. km). Portugal occupied this area in 1723; before then, British slavers built a settlement and fort. The region was disputed, but England abandoned the area to concentrate her troops on the American War of Independence (1775-82). In 1815, Cabinda Enclave was officially recognized by the Vienna Conference as a Portuguese possession. Separated briefly from Angola in 1885 when Belgium acquired a corridor to the Atlantic along the lower Congo, it was returned to Portugal in 1886 by agreement with Belgium. It is now a district administered from Luanda, the capital of Angola. GEPB; WNGD.

Cabinda Gulf Oil Company   An American subsidiary of the Gulf Oil Company, chartered in the state of Delaware. It signed an exclusive contract with the Portuguese government on July 9, 1957, for oil exploration and extraction in the Cabinda district of northern Angola. Castro, *O Sistema Colonial,* p. 161.

Cabinda seaport   The capital of the Cabinda Enclave (q.v.) on the Atlantic coast. In 1723, Portugal built a fort there to control the maritime traffic of British and French slavers. Later England erected a barracks there to contest Portuguese sovereignty. During the American War of Independence (1775-82) the British garrison left and the Portuguese regained control of the port. In 1784, Portugal was given legal possession of the city in arbitration by the Spanish government. The Berlin Conference of 1885 formally recognized the Portuguese claim. Its population was 21,124 in 1970. GEPB; WNGD.

Cabindan nationalists A group of Africans from the Cabinda Enclave (q.v.) who, during the War for Independence in Angola, organized several radical nationalist groups aiming for the independence of Cabinda. In November 1960, twenty-eight nationalists were executed in a Luanda jail by Portuguese forces. In 1962, the *Movement pour la Liberation de l'Enclave de Cabinda* was organized in Brazzaville, under the aegis of the Congo government. Marcum, *The Angolan Revolution,* I:124-5, 173.

Cabo Delgado (Pg.) A cape extending into the Indian Ocean on the extreme northeastern coast of Mozambique. The area was explored by Vasco da Gama on his first voyage to India in 1498. After the fall of Mombasa in 1698, Cape Delgado became the unofficial frontier between the Portuguese and Arabs. This borderland today separates Mozambique and Tanzania and was the earliest formal frontier of modern Africa. Kaplan, *Area Handbook,* p. 138; GEPB.

Cabo Verde: Boletim de Propaganda e Informação (Pg.) "Cape Verde: Bulletin of Propaganda and Information." A monthly magazine, published in Praia, capital of Cape Verde, from 1949 until the mid-1960s. It carried a wide variety of essays, articles, and features dealing with the economic, political, cultural, and social life of the archipelago. Because of its regular monthly appearance, for nearly twenty years it served the useful purpose of being an outlet for the works of *claridosos* (q.v.) and members of other groups. Hamilton, *Voices,* p. 269.

caboceer A title of respect used by English speakers in colonial Africa, a variation of the Portuguese word *caboceiro*; an important person, the leader of a community. GEPB.

Cabora Bassa Dam A dam over the Zambezi River in the Tete district of Mozambique. It is the fifth largest dam in the world and Portugal's most enduring physical and economic structure in Africa. Its construction started in 1969 and was completed in 1974. The 2,075 megawatt dam is 137 meters high and can hold 57 million cubic meters of water. It is equipped with 408 megawatt generators and has the capacity to generate 18,000 kilowatt of electricity per hour (7,000 more than the Aswan Dam and 9,000 more than Kariba). It was built by a consortium of Portuguese, German, British, and South African companies, with help from Zambia and Zimbabwe. The South African government is estimated to have contributed about 20 percent to the construction cost, namely, some R350 million ($517.7 million). Managed by the Portuguese *Companhia Hidro-Electrica de Cabora Bassa*, the reservoir also irrigates some 140,000 sq. km of land along the Zambezi River. Through a 1,400 km power line, Cabora Bassa provides about 10 percent of South Africa's electricity needs. During the War for Independence, FRELIMO (q.v.) forces attacked the dam area in 1971 and 1974, aiming at the destruction of the project. In spite of the war, the Portuguese government was able to resettle 25,000 Africans in 1971. Following independence, however, FRELIMO realized the potential benefits from the dam and has done all it can to protect it against the MNR (q.v.), which on several occasions has blown up pylons. In 1984, South Africa and Mozambique, in the spirit of the Nkomati Accord (q.v.), agreed to establish a joint force to protect the dam and patrol the area. In April 1988, further talks were held to find more effective ways to implement the agreement. The dam is an impressive engineering feat and is seen as a manifest example of the spiritual ideal of Portuguese racial integration. Henriksen, *Mozambique*, pp. 138-9, 189, 190, 205-6; GEPB; HDM. *See also* "Bust Cabora Bassa."

cacao A tropical tree (*Theobroma cacao* L.) grown for its seeds, called cacao, or cocoa, beans. The tree grows to twenty feet (6 m) bearing seed-filled pods of a pointed oval shape. The numerous beans are imbedded in an aromatic white pith and, once fermented, they are the source of cocoa, cocoa butter, and chocolate. Cacao was introduced by the Portuguese into São Tomé from Brazil in 1822. The fertile volcanic soil of São Tomé e Príncipe is ideally suited to its growth. Cacao replaced the once-profitable sugar industry that had relied on slave labor. Cultivation of cacao has increased and has proved a dazzling economic success up to the present, although continued success depends on the world commodity markets. Carvalho e Vasconcellos, *As Colonias Portuguesas,* pp. 229-30; GEPB.

Cacheu River A wide river in Guinea-Bissau that flows southwest into the Atlantic Ocean. Among its numerous tributaries are the Farim and the São Domingos rivers and near its mouth it connects with the Casamansa River in Senegal through a navigable canal 80 mi. (130 km) upstream. From 1675 until the nineteenth century, it was an important waterway for the transport of slaves to the Brazilian plantations. Mota, *Guiné Portuguesa,* I:62-4; HDRGC.

cacimba (Kimb.) On the Angolan coast, a thick mist or fog formed whenever a stream of relatively warm moist air passes over the cold Benguela Current (q.v.) flowing from the Antarctic. This kind of advection fog, frequent in July and August, spreads landward over the costal plain as far as the Benguela plateau. GEPB; GGT.

Caconda (Afr.) A *colonato* (q.v.), or government settlement, in Huíla, southern Angola, established in 1957. It was an agricultural community where Africans cultivated the land under the guidance of government technicians. Around 1965, Caconda had 760 families divided into seven nuclei or centers. Caetano, *Os Nativos*, p. 85.

caderneta (Pg.) An identification card and passbook containing the tax and labor records of any African man as well as the names of his wife, or wives, and children (who were all responsible for paying his taxes in the event of his disappearance) and photographs and fingerprints. The bearer was legally obligated to show his *caderneta* on demand to officials and needed a visa before he could move from one part of the province to another. Duffy, *Portuguese Africa,* p. 304.

cafila (Ar.) At the time of the Discovery (q.v.), a caravan of merchants who traded from Arguim (q.v.) on the West African coast to Timbuctu, Mali (qq.v.), and a number of other trans-Saharan routes. Godinho, *A Economia,* p. 190.

cajágal (Afr.) In Guinea-Bissau, poor soil, also called *mato de capim,* covered by dense grass. The Brames (q.v.) cultivate it by alternating crops of groundnuts and beans for a period of five years, then leaving it fallow for several years before it is planted in a new cycle. Mota, *Guiné Portuguesa,* I:303-4. *See also* puul.

cajueiro (Braz.) The tropical American cashew tree (*Anacardium occidentale* L.) introduced into Angola and elsewhere in Africa by the Portuguese in 1506. Its sweet edible fruit, called cashew apple, can be fermented to prepare a kind of wine from which a rum is extracted. Its nuts, called *castanhas de caju* in Portuguese, are part of the local diet. Ficalho, *Plantas Uteis,* pp. 122-3.

Calabar A Portuguese trading post established in Calabar on the northern coast of the Gulf of Guiné c.1500. Portugal transferred it to Spain in 1577 and it was taken by Britain in 1810. GEPB.

Caldas Hospital A large hospital built and equipped in 1512 by Queen Leonor, the widow of King João II of Portugal. The queen established this hospital after being successfully treated for an illness at the hot springs resort located in Caldas. Once recovered, she asked her doctor, Mester Antonio, to select a place for a hospital outside the city. This institution was one of the first public hospitals in Portugal and for many years was the largest. It had one hundred beds, dozens of attending physicians, nurses, and nuns, a chaplain, and a pharmacy. Female slaves did the cleaning, washing, and cooking; male slaves baked bread and tended a farm that provided meat, milk, and vegetables. Expanded in the seventeenth century, this hospital, known as the Queen's Hospital, still serves the community today. In 1935, the city built a memorial to honor Queen Leonor and commemorate the hospital's 400 years of service. Saunders, *A Social History,* p. 69; GEPB. *See also* Misericordia.

calema (Pg.) Long and slow wave modulation along the coast of Guinea-Bissau and nearby islands. Strong winds occasionally generate swollen waves that break upon the shore, the rocks, and the shoals with a rushing noise, the noise and the condition both called *calema*. The *calema* often troubled early Portuguese navigators. GEPB.

calumba (Afr.) In Mozambique and elsewhere, a tropical vine (*Menispermum palmatum* L.) the root of which is used to prepare a drug highly appreciated by Africans and Europeans. The commercial demand makes it very valuable along the Mozambique coast. Ficalho, *Plantas Uteis,* p. 80; PDM.

camel (Ar.) This large domesticated beast of burden (genus *Camelus*), capable of storing water in its body tissues, was reintroduced into the Sahara in the eleventh century by Arabs. It had as revolutionary an effect upon life in the Sahara as the discovery of the compass did upon maritime navigation. The camel gave a new mobility and an immense range of activity to the Berbers (q.v.) and caravan traffic brought prosperity to many towns in the Sahel (q.v.). For the first time in history, West African peoples were in permanent contact with Mediterranean ports and inland cities and it led to the spread of Islam in West Africa. Berber, not Arab, merchants traveling on camels spread Islam among the Africans down to the Senegal River in Western Sudan. Trimingham, *A History of Islam,* pp. 12(n), 15, 20; DHP.

Cameroon (Pg.) Cameroon entered history when Portuguese navigators arrived at the Bight of Benin (q.v.) in 1472. It appeared in 1500 on Portuguese maps under the name of *Rio dos Camarões*. From the beginning of the fifteenth century to the early seventeenth century the Cameroon coast was the principal source of slaves for European and American slave traders. On October 1, 1961, it became the United Republic of Cameroon. Mota, *Toponimos,* pp. 306-7; WNGD.

Campo, O "The Country." A monthly periodical founded on June 29, 1984, in Maputo, Mozambique, by amateur journalists scattered around the country. Its press run is about 5,000 copies. Darch, *Mozambique,* p. 282.

Canarim (Pg.) In Mozambique, a Christian merchant from Goa, who peddled his goods in the *prazos*, villages, and towns on the Indian Ocean coast and in the interior. Newitt, *Portugal in Africa,* p. 380; GEPB.

Canary Current A south-flowing ocean current off the coast of Morocco that enabled Portuguese navigators to easily sail down the coast in the early days of the Discovery (q.v.), but made the return difficult because vessels were not yet able to sail into the wind with any facility. HDRGC. *See also* caravel.

Canary Islands   These islands, known since antiquity as the Fortunate Islands, are mentioned by Pliny the Elder (23-79AD) and others and chosen by Claudius Ptolemy (second century) for the prime meridian of longitude. In the first half of the fourteenth century, the Canaries were visited by Majorcan, Portuguese, and French navigators. Afonso IV of Portugal claimed possession in a letter to Pope Clement VI in 1345. From 1424 to 1453, Prince Henry of Portugal tried to occupy them. A long dispute with Spain ended with the Alcaçovas Peace Treaty (q.v.) of 1580, where Portugal recognized them as Spanish territory. Some navigators continued to reckon from this line until the eighteenth century. DHP; EB.

canave (Pg.)   "Hemp." A tall coarse annual herb (*Cannabis sativa*) of the hemp family grown for the tough fiber of its stem. Its leaves are used to make the drugs hashish and marijuana, which are smoked, chewed, or drunk for their intoxicating effect. Cultivated since antiquity in Asia, Europe, and Africa, it was grown in East Africa before the arrival of the Portuguese in 1498, having been introduced from Asia by Arabs. Africans usually chew the leaves, a habit David Livingstone (1813-1873) noted in the Zambezi region in 1856. The Africans in Mozambique called this herb *mutocuane*, and the Arabs *banga* or hashish. In Angola it is known as *liamba* or *riamba*. Ficalho, *Plantas Uteis,* pp. 259-265; GEPB.

Cangandala (Afr.)   An administrative post in the Malange district of central Angola with a population in 1950 of 21,279, of which 20,983 were classified as "indigenous." In 1961, this town was torn by terrorism and violence caused by fighting between the Portuguese forces and the nationalists. Many Catholic insurgents were saved from death by Methodist African sympathizers. Pelissier, *La Colonie,* p. 561.

canhangulo (Afr.)   A homemade rifle mounted on a rough stock and loaded with nails and bits of metal widely used by guerrilla fighters during the War for Independence in Angola and elsewhere in Africa. Wheeler, *Angola,* p. 174.

canhongo (Afr.)   In Zambezia (q.v.), a slave soldier who was third in command of a regiment of slaves serving under a chief of the unit. *Canhongo* was an important rank in the primitive African armies of the *prazos* (q.v.) in the nineteenth century. Newitt, *Portuguese Settlement,* p. 290. *See also* ensaca.

caniço (Pg.) (1)   A tall, slender reed (*Phragmites mauritanicus*) growing in marshy or wet land; a traditional building material in southern Mozambique and elsewhere. It is mostly used for walls and to screen dwellings, but is also employed to make domestic utensils, fishing rods, bows and arrows, and many other items. Oliver, *Shelter in Africa*, p. 200.

caniço (Pg.) (2) The name for shantytowns on the outskirts of towns, mainly in Mozambique, where servants, laborers, and the unemployed live in wattle shelters. They range from small villages scattered around towns to vast *musseques* (slums). These shantytowns surround large cities like Maputo, Beira, Quelimane, Porto Amelia, and elsewhere. The layout of a *caniço* is irregular and the huts and shacks of squatters are often built following a traditional method using reed or wattle while others are improvised from the scrap and rubbish thrown away by the adjoining city or bought from scrap dealers. Oliver, *Shelter in Africa,* pp. 200-1. *See also* bidonville.

cannabism Chronic addition to smoking or chewing *canave* (q.v.). Portuguese explorers c.1580 found that local Angolans were often addicted to this drug. Ficalho, *Plantas Uteis,* p. 263.

canon law and slavery At the time of the Discovery (q.v.), the church canon law considered slavery part of the Christian social order. By the end of the Middle Ages, canon law commentators agreed that appropriate authorities in any country could reduce prisoners of war and criminals to slavery, that children of slaves were slaves themselves, and that slaves could be bought and sold as chattel. In 1452, the pope as interpreter of canon law officially allowed the Portuguese to conquer and reduce to perpetual slavery all "Saracens and pagans [i.e. Moslems and heathens], other infidels and enemies of Christians" in West Africa. In the fifteenth century, canon law was declared to be supplementary to royal law by the Crown. Saunders, *A Social History,* pp. 35-7, 113. DHP.

Cão, Padrão Diogo *See* Padrão Diogo Cão.

Cape Arsinario (Pg.) Original name given by Portuguese navigators (c.1450) to Cape Verde. In the fifth song of his *Os Lusiadas,* Camões refers to Cape Arsinario. In modern Cape Verdian poetry this term symbolizes a deep emotional and nostalgic feeling of identification held by Cape Verdian intellectuals for their homeland. It is often expressed as *alma arsinaria* (q.v.). Araujo, *A Study,* p. 30.

Cape Bojador Cape on the west-central coast of Morocco extending into the Atlantic Ocean and the southernmost cape known to antiquity. In 1434 the Portuguese navigator Gil Eanes explored it and successfully navigated its dangerous waters. According to Arab geographers, Cape Bojador marked the border between the Sea of Darkness and the Torrid Zone in which, if white men penetrated, they would become black. It was also reported at the time that the sea off the Cape was so shallow that even a league (5 km) from land, it was only a fathom (1.5 m) deep, and that if a ship could pass it, the current would not allow the ship to return. To the astonishment of his contemporaries, Gil Eanes doubled the Cape in 1434 and brought back plants and valuable information about the Atlantic coast. By 1446 Portuguese navigators had explored more than 450 leagues (2,250 km) beyond Cape Bojador. Prestage, *The Portuguese Pioneers*, pp. 54-6, 90; DHP.

Cape Coast An important gold trading post founded by the Portuguese in the Gulf of Guiné c.1490 and soon visited by other European traders. In 1642, the Swedes built a castle, called Carlsborg, which still stands. In 1664, it was taken by the British, who rebuilt most of the present fort. It was the British headquarters on the Gold Coast from 1664 to 1877. Today Cape Coast is an important commercial, educational, and political center of Ghana. It is 8 mi. (13 km) east of Elmina (q.v.). The area between Elmina and Cape Coast is one of the most attractive in Africa. Mota, *Toponimos*, pp. 277-8; HDP.

Cape Lopes Headland that extends deep into the Atlantic Ocean south of Libreville in Gabon; it was discovered and explored by the Portuguese navigator Lopo Gonçalves between 1471 and 1475. Its original name was *Cabo de Polo Gonçalves*. Mota, *Toponimos*, pp. 331-2.

Cape Noun (Pg.) A promontory on the West African coast in what is now Mauritania, 160 mi. (260 km) north of Cape Bojador (q.v.), explored c.1412 by Portuguese captains in the service of Prince Henry. Feared by navigators for the strong Canary Current (q.v.) flowing south along its coast, it was a place of frequent shipwrecks. In addition, the westerly winds from April to October made traveling north difficult. There are no harbors between Cape Noun and Cape Bojador and the coastline is open to the prevailing winds. The Canary Current, compressed between the island and the coast, accelerates 1.25 knots (2.3 km/hr) and sets obliquely against the westward curve of Cape Bojador. A heavy continuous swell from the northwest sets across wind and current into the shore, raising a swirling and mountainous surf. Parry, *The Discovery of the Sea,* pp. 100-1, 121; Cortesão, *A Expansão,* pp. 74-75.

Cape Palmas A cape on the Atlantic coast in southern Liberia discovered and explored in 1471 by the navigators João Santarem and Pero Escobar. In 1469, King Afonso V had granted the trade monopoly in the region to Fernão Gomes under the condition that discovery be extended no less than 100 leagues (approximately 300 miles or 480 km) each year along the Sierra Leone coast and southward. Mota, *Toponimos*, pp. 247-8; WNDG.

Cape Verde *See* Cape Verde, peninsula of; Cape Verde Islands.

Cape Verde Islands (Pg.)   These islands, located at latitude 14°43'N, longitude 17°30' W, were discovered by the Portuguese navigator Dinis Dias in 1444. They were called *Verde* because of the evergreen vegetation, in contrast to the sandy and barren beaches on islands to the north; Cape was added because they are almost due west of the mainland Cape Verde peninsula (q.v.). These islands were ruled by a *donatario* (q.v.) from 1456 to 1495; they were made Portuguese colonies in 1495, and became an independent nation on July 5, 1975. Mota, *Toponimos,* p. 96; GEPB.

Cape Verde Islands, agriculture in   Since colonial times agricultural production for local consumption in Cape Verde has been problematic. Limited arable land of only 0.3 acres per capita, the prolonged effect of droughts and soil erosion, the cash crop economy, the backward system of land tenure, and the colonial monopoly on trade are contributing factors to local shortages. Cash crops include sugar, bananas, coffee, citrus fruit, and castor beans, all of which take up valuable land. The limitations on agriculture are even more evident when one realizes about 30 percent of the farmland of Cape Verde is left fallow and only 50 percent is in permanent regular crops. This situation is worsened by the exploitative system of land tenure under which 69.4 percent of the 36,309 farms are operated by sharecropping or tenant farming. For those farmers who do own land, the holdings are generally small. Apart from private capitalists, the Catholic Church is a major landowner. Although some narrow coastal areas of Fogo Island are particularly good for groundnut and coffee cultivation, most agriculture is concentrated on Santiago, Santo Antão, and São Nicolau, all of which have more regular sources of water. GEPB; HDRGC.

Cape Verde Islands, Diocese of This diocese was created by Pope Clement VII in 1532. Its first bishop was Dr. Bras Neto, a member of the royal council. In 1614, the seat of the diocese was transferred from Praia, Santiago Island, to Ribeira Grande, Santo Antão Island. Pinto Rema, *A Primeira Evangelização,* BCG, 1966, xxi(82):340-1.

Cape Verde Islands, discovery and settlement of Portuguese navigator Dinis Dias discovered these islands in 1444. On June 12, 1466, King Afonso V mentioned that the colonization of Santiago Island had begun four years earlier, led by António de Noli. Soon the Portuguese established plantations and organized a pastoral economy using slaves brought from the West African coast. Antonio de Noli died in Santiago Island around 1496. The first governor of the islands, Duarte Lobo da Gama, was appointed in 1597. Duncan, *The Atlantic Islands,* pp. 19-20; GEPB.

Cape Verde Islands, economy of Since colonial times two major factors, persistent devastating droughts and Portuguese monopolies, have limited the economic life of Cape Verde. In the 1970s, the major import items were food (about two-thirds of the total value of all imports). Approximately seventy-five percent of all imports were from Portugal and its former African colonies. Other significant imports include cement and textiles. The major recipients of Cape Verde's exports were Portugal and the former Portuguese-African colonies, which receive about two-thirds of the meager total. The other important recipient is the United States, which purchases 15 to 25 percent of exports, especially fish. DHP; HDRGC.

Cape Verde Islands, education in Since the discovery and settlement of Cape Verde, literacy levels have been very high, surpassing those of the African mainland and Portugal. The first seminary was established, at least on paper, on Santiago Island in 1570 by King Sebastião. Subsequently missionaries concerned themselves with education on the islands, and in 1845 local authorities organized a system of primary education. The National Lyceum was created in 1860, and in 1866 the seminary was rededicated. In 1894 primary education was declared compulsory on all the islands and in 1917 basic educational reform took place when secondary schools were established. As a result, by mid century, a prominent intellectual elite emerged. In the 1969-70 academic year there were 49 students with scholarships attending colleges and universities in Portugal. By 1986 there were 347 primary schools with 1,464 teachers and 49,703 students, and 16 secondary schools with 321 teachers and 10,304 students. In two commercial and industrial schools there were 53 teachers and 211 students. Brasio, *Historia e Missiologia,* p. 160; Cape Verde, *Pequena Monografia,* pp. 51-61.

Cape Verde Islands, ethnic diversity of In 1460 the first Portuguese found the islands uninhabited. Soon after settlement began, slave laborers were brought from the West African coast, especially from Guinea-Bissau. Internal and external migration resulted in a high rate of *mestiços.* Brava Island is the least Africanized while São Vicente is a rich mixture of racial types. According to the 1950 census, there were 3,000 whites, 36,000 Africans and 101,000 *mestiços. Crioulo* (q.v.), the dialect spoken in the islands, reflects the degree of Portuguese and African racial and linguistic contact. Duncan, *The Atlantic Islands,* pp. 165, 182, 195-8; GEPB. *See also* Crioulo de Cabo Verde.

Cape Verde Islands, evangelization in On June 7, 1454, King Afonso V assigned the task of preaching the Gospel in the island to the Order of Christ (q.v.). This was approved by Pope Nicolas V in his bull *Romanus Pontifex* signed on January 8, 1455. Two Franciscans, Friar Rogerio and Friar Jaime, both natives of Catalonia, Spain, came to the islands with Antonio de Noli, c.1462. The religious life was organized when the Diocese of Cape Verde (q.v.) was established in 1532 and a seminary was founded in 1570. Since that time clergy from Portugal and Africa from various religious orders have taken care of the spiritual needs of the settlers. In 1941 Bishop Faustino Moreira do Santos declared that the diocese, with its lack of priests and missionaries, was in ruins. Brasio, *Historia e Missiologia*, pp. 157-9.

Cape Verde Islands, forced migration from For the people of Cape Verde, forced migration to São Tomé was always an evil. The latter's equatorial humidity, bad housing, low wages, harsh treatment by plantation foremen, inadequate food, and lack of medical care destroyed their health and they could not break their two- or three-year contracts and go home. The emotional stress of being separated from their wives and children took its toll and workers often returned more wretched than when they set out. Of a contingent of laborers who went to the island in 1903, only one-third returned. The remainder had died having received only trifling medical attention. Carreira, *The People*, pp. 174, 175.

Cape Verde Islands, health care in Malaria has been endemic since colonial times but its incidence and severity fluctuate. While in 1934 there were only 6,559 cases reported and 75 deaths, by 1937 there were 12,527 registered cases of which 296 were fatal. Tuberculosis and dysentery are also frequent. Until 1979, health care was extremely inadequate. Not only were the colonial facilities poor, but the basic diet did not even yield the minimum necessary daily caloric intake, thus making disease and a short life expectancy the norm. At the time of independence in 1974, Cape Verde had only twelve doctors, or one for every 25,000 inhabitants, and only a 200-bed hospital in Praia, Santiago Island and a 120-bed facility in Mindelo, São Vicente, plus 21 health centers and 54 nurses. Several islands had no doctor and Santo Antão, the second largest, had only one. GEPB; HDRGC.

Cape Verde Islands, population of Since the colonial period there have been fluctuations in the population of Cape Verde caused by drought, famine, and migration. By 1850, the islands had 76,685 inhabitants. At the turn of the century the census showed 147,424. Fifty years later, the population had only grown to 150,000 because of out-migration. By 1976 the population was 303,000. Among the fifteen islands in the group there is an unequal distribution of people; Santiago Island has forty-four percent of the total population while some of the other islands have as little as five percent. DHP; HDRGC.

Cape Verde Islands, soil erosion in In Cape Verde soil erosion hastens the progressive destruction of arable land and vegetation. The two important erosive agents are the heavy, sometimes torrential, rains and the easterly wind that escalates to the infamous *harmattan* (q.v.) from November to March. Erosion from rain is relatively infrequent. It is wind erosion that is so destructive since the winds are constant and violent and batter most of the archipelago for several months of the year, particularly after the rainy season. If it has not rained, the ground is dry and often bare of vegetation. Persistent gales have laid bare large areas of the rocky substratum, barring cultivation. In many other areas, the soil is too shallow to cultivate. Carreira, *The People,* p. 15. *See also* Sahelian drought.

Cape Verde, peninsula of The westernmost projection of Africa, about 20 mi. (32 km) from east to west and 7 mi. (11 km) at its widest. The peninsula is composed of dunes and marshy areas called *niayes*, both surmounted by limestone cliffs. Cape Almadies is at its western tip. Dakar, the chief port and capital of Senegal, is on its southern coast. The peninsula was discovered about 1445 by the Portuguese navigator João Fernandes who gave it its name, meaning green cape. GEPB.

Cape Verde, Republic of Cape Verde was a Portuguese colony for five centuries. After a five-year war for independence from 1970 to 1975, it was declared a sovereign nation on July 5, 1975. It is comprised of fifteen islands with a total area of 1,577 square mi. (4,080 square km), and a population in 1976 of 303,000. Its capital, Praia, is located on Santiago, the largest island. GEPB; HDRGC. *See also* Mindelo.

Cape Verdian In contemporary usage, a citizen of the Cape Verde Islands. Originally this term meant one who was born in the Cape Verde Islands to a Portuguese father and an African mother. It has long been believed that Afro-Portuguese miscegenation produces a racial and social harmony unknown elsewhere in the tropics. Chilcote, *Portuguese Africa,* p. 48.

Cape Verdianness According to some Afro-Portuguese intellectuals, a deep emotional and psychological feeling of identification held by Cape Verdians. It is defined as a cultural coalescence in which African feelings are predominant at the spiritual and emotional level, and Portuguese ideas at the intellectual and religious level. Duncan, *Atlantic Islands,* p. 196.

captaincies in the Atlantic Islands A government policy that allowed the king of Portugal to grant land to explorers with the obligation to settle, administer, and defend them for the purposes of religion and civilization. A *capitão* (q.v.) had civil and criminal jurisdiction; as recompense he enjoyed extensive financial privileges. In Madeira, one of the Atlantic Islands granted, the first captains were J.G. Zarco and T.V. Teixeira, appointed by Prince

Henry in 1440, twenty years after the first settlement. Portuguese grantees were also called *donatarios* (q.v.). Newitt, *Portuguese Settlement,* p. 8-9.

capitania (Pg.) "Captaincy." At the time of the Discovery (q.v.), a royal hereditary grant of land to a nobleman that included wide judicial, fiscal, and manorial privileges in exchange for which the holder of a *capitania* was to divide the land into individual holdings and bring in settlers who would cultivate it. This system was established between 1418 and 1460, a period of great Portuguese expansion. The Cape Verde Islands were originally a *capitania*. Newitt, *Portugal in Africa,* p. 201; GEPB.

capitão (Pg.) "Captain." A military commander representing the Portuguese Crown, especially in Cape Verde. Each *capitão* governed a *capitania* (q.v.) with wide administrative, judicial, and military power. HDRGC.

capitão-mor do interior (Pg.) "Inland commander." A prestigious military post established early in the colonial period by the Portuguese government in the Zambezi area. The post-holder was in charge of upholding the government's authority among the many *prazos* (q.v.) settled along the Zambezi. In 1845, this position was offered to Chicururu, the Afro-Portuguese ruler of the Makanga *prazo*. Isaacman, *Mozambique: From Colonialism,* p. 129.

Capuchin missionaries in Angola   The Capuchins were the first non-Portuguese missionaries sent to São Salvador do Congo. They arrived in 1646 at the request of Manicongo (q.v.) Garcia Afonso II. These Italian friars were commissioned by the Holy Office of the Propagation of the Faith in Rome with the approval of King João IV of Portugal. They were dedicated to the conversion and education of Africans throughout the colonial period until 1834, when the Portuguese government expelled all the missionaries from Portuguese Africa. The Capuchins returned in 1948 to work in São Salvador do Congo, Luanda, Malange, and other towns and villages in Angola. In 1960, there were seventy missionaries in Angola, the second largest group of missionaries after the Holy Ghost Fathers. Boxer, *Portuguese Seaborne,* pp. 246-7; Gabriel, *Angola,* pp. 51, 101, 567, 572.

capulana (Pg.)   Traditional red and green cloth covering the body from the waist down, worn by African women in Mozambique and elsewhere in Portuguese Africa. GDLP.

Caputo (Afr.)   A *musseque* (slum) of Luanda, Angola, populated by a multi-ethnic community which in 1960 was only 63 percent Luandan. In such a complex population, Angolan nationalists could not organize a homogenous militant force to fight for independence. Pelissier, *La Colonie,* pp. 338-9.

caravel (Pg.) Lateen-rigged vessel of fine sea-going qualities, usually with five masts and of shallower draft and smaller tonnage than a *nau* (q.v.). Portuguese seamen were sailing light, long, high caravels by 1440. Relying entirely on its sails, it could be worked by a small crew and was not weighted down by supplies; its speed enabled it to cover great distances. It was sufficiently maneuverable to be in little danger from shoal-bound and foggy Atlantic shores yet stout enough for ocean sailing. By 1570, a caravel of 50 to 100 tons burden could carry up to 150 slaves and between ten and thirty officers and a crew as great as sixty-one. The officers included a captain, or master, and a pilot plus a scrivener who was provided by the Crown to oversee trade even when the vessel belonged to a contractor. The crew was comprised of able seamen, ordinary seamen, and occasionally cabin boys. Axelson, *Portuguese in South-East*, p. 224; Livermore, *New History of Portugal*, p. 116; DHP.

carbuncle A disease attacking cattle, characterized by a hard circumscribed deep-seated suppuration of the subcutaneous tissue. It is larger than a boil, having a flat surface discharging pus from multiple points. It was officially reported in Guinea-Bissau in 1944, apparently having been introduced from French Guinée. Its various local names, *ira do mato, tiro do irã, pídal*, and *calandim*, indicate the wide spread of the disease. Tendeiro, *Esboço Epizootologico,* Congresso Commemorativo, Lisbon, 2:227-28.

carepa (Afr.) Drizzling, mist-like rain caused by southeasterly and south-westerly oceanic winds on the southern coast of São Tomé; it occurs during the dry season from May to July. Tenreiro, *A Ilha,* pp. 37-8. *See also* cacimba.

carneirada (Pg.) In Cape Verde and elsewhere, a generic term for angina, coryza, dysentery, malaria, and similar, often tropical, illnesses. *Carneirada* in its many forms is endemic during the hot, rainy season of August and September. GDLP.

carrier service A system of compulsory tribute imposed by the Portuguese on Africans as a duty on goods transported inland through the forests and by the waterways in both western and eastern Africa during the colonial period. This tribute was abolished in Angola in 1856 and in Mozambique shortly after. The abundance of human labor had allowed the system to survive until the mid-nineteenth century. Newitt, *Portugal in Africa,* pp. 6, 13, 21.

Carta das Novas *See* Letter of the News.

carta de aforamento (Pg.) "Deed transferring land." A charter setting out the rights and obligations of a *prazero* (land holder) in Zambezia (qq.v.) and elsewhere in the colonial period. In 1755 it was stipulated that the land grant size should be three leagues in length and one in width (10.3 by 3.4 mi.; 16.5 by 5.5 km), tenure was to be limited to three generations, be transmitted through the female line, the annual quit-rent had to be paid, all services required by local officials had to be satisfied, a specific area of new land had to be cultivated, and that all the gold and silver mines found on one's estate had to be forwarded to the government. A family who met these requirements could apply to have its *aforamento* renewed upon its termination. Newitt, *Portuguese Settlement,* pp. 96, 380; GEPB.

carta de alforria (Pg.) "Charter granting freedom." In colonial Portugal and elsewhere, the legal document signed by a master freeing a slave. A charter of manumission could be executed by the master himself, usually to take effect during his lifetime, or by his heirs if stated in his will. Sometimes the *carta de alforria* could lay down conditions that the ex-slave had to fulfill; having done so he was given an unconditional *carta de alforria*, recognized throughout Christendom. Saunders, *A Social History,* p. 138; GEPB. *See also* alforria, freedmen.

carta de armas (Pg.) "Charter to grant coats of arms." A charter given c.1508 by King Manuel I of Portugal to his ambassador Simão da Silva to be delivered to King Afonso I of Congo, granting him the power to award titles of nobility and the habit of the Royal Order of Christ to his subjects. Gabriel, *Angola,* pp. 5, 59.

carta de libertade "Certificate of manumission." A document certifying a slave's freedom, introduced by an 1875 law. The law abolished slavery in Angola and elsewhere in Portuguese Africa within three years. After this law was enacted, slaves were able to refuse any mandatory work contract even if they had not yet been given the *carta de libertade.* Clarence-Smith, *Slaves, Peasants,* p. 38; GEPB.

Carta Organica do Imperio Colonial Portugues (Pg.) "Constitutional Charter of the Portuguese Colonial Empire." A law promulgated on November 15, 1933, stating specifically that the indigenous population should be integrated into "civilized society" by a progressive transformation of their customs, behavior, and social and moral values. Cunha, *O Sistema Portugués,* p. 143.

cartão de identidade "Identity card." A document issued by colonial authorities in Mozambique and elsewhere at the time of the repeal of the 1961 Indigenous Status Law of Africans. An individual had to produce the identity card upon demand. By this screening, the police could ascertain the identities and regulate the movements of people outside their normal work and living areas, but the program never functioned properly for lack of police agents. According to PIDE (q.v.) there were only 2,000 agents in Mozambique in 1974, a totally insufficient number. Owing to the infrequency of personal checks and searches, FRELIMO (q.v.) guerrillas were able to move freely between Mozambique and Zimbabwe and to infiltrate rural areas. Henriksen, *Revolution,* p. 67. *See also* carta de libertade.

cartography in Portugal   During the early Middle Ages there was little added to cartographic knowledge of Africa. People accepted the writings of the second century astronomer Ptolomy who stated the earth was the center of the universe and the heavenly bodies moved around it. At the Discovery (q.v.), maps derived from his *Orbis Terrarum,* drawn by monks, often located Jerusalem at the center of the earth. In contrast, Islamic geographers of the tenth century began determining the location of places by latitude and longitude. The Islamic cartographer al-Idrisi under King Roger II of Sicily produced a large rectangular world map in seventy sheets, among his most important works. The most detailed geographical description of Africa and the known world was done by an anonymous Spanish Franciscan who based his work *El Libro del Conoscimiento* (q.v.), written in Seville in 1350, on information from Arab, Jewish, and Portuguese merchants of the time. Prince Henry of Portugal, himself a scientist, greatly encouraged African cartography in Portugal beginning in 1420. In 1440 he founded the Sagres nautical school (q.v.) in southern Portugal to expand his African expeditions. He enlisted cartographers, geographers, astronomers, navigators, and explorers to further navigation. They compiled charts and mapped Arguim, Guiné, the Senegal River, and other places in West Africa. DHP; GEPB.

Casa da Guiné (Pg.)   At the time of the Discovery (q.v.), a royal institution originally entrusted with overseeing and collecting duties on the trade with Guiné and Mina (q.v.) and subsequently with similar tasks related to trade with India and Asia. Established by Prince Henry in Lagos c.1440, it was transferred to Lisbon in 1481. The *Casa da Guiné* originally shared a building with the *Armazem da Guiné* (q.v.), but later moved to the ground floor of the *Palace da Ribeira* when it was built in 1505. From 1509 on, two separate sections headed by treasurers oversaw the African and Asian trades, though the whole enterprise remained under the general direction of a *factor* (administrator). It was also known as *Casa da Mina e Tratos de Guiné* and *Casa da Guiné e India.* Saunders, *A Social History,* pp. 15, 83, 183, 263; DHP. *See also* Casa da Mina, Casa dos Escravos.

Casa da Mina (Pg.)   A government agency in charge of building ships, organizing the shipping trade, and hiring the pilots and crew for the voyages between Portugal and its colonies. It was established early in the sixteenth century in Lisbon. DHP; DMA. *See also* Casa da Guiné.

casa de alvenaria (Pg.)   Small brick house for rural African laborers built c.1920 by the government and planters to replace the traditional *cubata* (q.v.) in Angola and elsewhere in Portuguese Africa. Caetano, *Os Nativos*, p. 141.

Casa de Ceuta (Pg.)   A government agency and storehouse established in Lisbon in 1434 to control and enforce duties on trade with Ceuta and North Africa, including Morocco. J. Cortesão, *A Expansão Portuguesa,* p. 190. *See also* Casa da Guiné.

Casa do Congo (Pg.)   A seminary to prepare Portuguese missionaries for work in the Congo, founded by the Order of the Holy Spirit in Santarem, Portugal, in 1867. GEPB.

Casa dos Escravos (Pg.)   "Slaves' barracks." A department of the *Casa da Guiné* (q.v.) entrusted c.1440 with overseeing the collection of duties on the slave trade at the beginning of the Discovery (q.v.). This department's buildings were in the *Praça da Tanoaria,* just west of the *Armazem* and *Casa da Guiné* (qq.v.), on the waterfront in Lisbon. There appears to have been three units: a secured area of one or two large rooms where slaves were kept after landing, the offices of the *almoxarife de escravos* (official receiver of slaves) and his clerk at the front of the building, and a royal prison, also under the authority of the *almoxarife.* After the formalities of arrival, the slaves were taken ashore to designated lodgings, usually in the *Casa dos Escravos,* where they were divided into various lots for the purpose of levying duty upon them. The division was presumably made on the basis of age, sex, health, and physique, and whether the slaves belonged to contractors or to the Crown. Saunders, *A Social History,* pp. 8, 15; GEPB. *See also* Casa da Guiné.

Casa dos Estudantes do Imperio (Pg.)   "The House of the Students of the Empire." A semi-official center for African and Asian students opened in Lisbon in 1944 and closed in 1965. The CEI was a unifying institution for a new generation of students from the overseas territories. Among its members were such prominent future leaders of the independence movement as Marcelino dos Santos of Mozambique, Amilcar Lopes Cabral of Guinea-Bissau, and Mario Coelho de Andrade and Antonio A. Neto, both of Angola. Through literary contests, lectures, exhibitions, and publications, the CEI was at the front of a new intellectual liberation among Portuguese writers and politicians. In 1958, with the aid of a subsidy from the Gulbenkian Foundation, the center published *Coleccão de Autores Ultramarinos* (Collection of Overseas Authors) edited by Carlos Eduardo and Fernando da Costa Andrade.

In 1963 it published poetry anthologies from Portuguese-African writers. The CEI also published an influential journal, *Mensagem*. Because of its increasingly alarming political views, the Portuguese government closed the center in 1965. Hamilton, *Voices,* pp. 170-1, 267.

Casa Gouveia (Pg.) A major Portuguese-African export company specializing in the export of palm and peanut oils. It was established in Guinea-Bissau in 1950 as a subsidiary of the *Companhia União Fabril*, itself one of the largest Portuguese conglomerates with substantial investments in Portuguese Africa. HDRGC. *See also* Casa Holandesa.

Casa Holandesa (Pg.) A general storehouse founded by Jose Guerreiro Nuno in 1875 in Mossâmedes on the southern Angolan coast. One of its concerns was the export of dried fish to Zaire and to towns along the Atlantic coast. This family business was acquired three years later by Guerreiro Nuno's nephews, Lourenço Martins Morgado and João da Cruz Morgado. Iria, *Breve Noticia*, Congresso da Historia, Lisbon, 1938, I:20. *See also* Casa Gouveia.

Casa de Misericordia *See* Misericordia.

casas grandes mestiças (Pg.) "Big *mestiço* houses." A late nineteenth-century expression applied to the Afro-Portuguese planter families who had acquired wealth, prestige, and social standing in São Tomé, Cape Verde, Mozambique, and Angola. They were usually professionals who had been educated at Coimbra or Lisbon University. Pelissier, *La Colonie*, p. 223.

Casamance River (Afr.) A river and region in southern Senegal forming a portion of the general area known as Senegambia. The trade and administrative center of the Casamance region is Ziquinchor, part of Portuguese Guiné until late in the nineteenth century. After the Berlin Congress of 1885-66, Portugal gave up its claim to Ziquinchor and the rest of the Casamance region. HDRGC.

Caserna, A (Pg.) "The Barrack." A 12-page bimonthly published in Lourenço Marques in 1969 by the *Escola de Applicacão Militar Mozambique* (School of Military Strategy of Mozambique). Most of the articles were on miliary matters, commando tactics, and major military speeches. Herrick, *Area Handbook,* p. 182.

cassa (Afr.) A tropical tree (*Erythrophleum africana*) found in Ambriz, Angola, and elsewhere in Portuguese Africa. When used in ordeals (q.v.), a sorcerer would force an accused individual to drink a concoction prepared by combining pulverized bark or seed of *cassa* with water in the belief that this would prove his innocence or guilt. This drink taken in small amounts is purgative, inducing violent peristalsis, so the individual dies immediately of cardiac arrest; drunk in large quantity, it is emetic, causes vomiting and thus the person lives. Portuguese law considered ordeal by *cassa* a crime. Ficalho, *Plantas Uteis,* pp. 165, 244. *See also* agua-vermelha, eseré, tanguin.

Cassange fair An old colonial market in Angola in the Imbangala Kingdom west of the Cuango River. Merchants and traders from the area gathered at regular intervals to trade gold, ivory, wax, and cloth. David Livingstone visited the town in 1854 and "Found a village composed of thirty or forty traders' houses scattered without any regularity on an elevated level spot in the great Cuango River Valley. They were built of wattle and daub, and [were] surrounded by plantations of manioc and maize." Newitt, *Portugal in Africa,* pp. 3, 6, 149-50.

cassava (Taino) A tropical Caribbean and South American plant (*Manihot esculenta*), with edible starchy roots used to make tapioca and flour for bread. The Portuguese introduced cassava to Angola and elsewhere in Portuguese Africa around 1500. Its introduction was of great significance because it is a high-yield crop requiring a minimum of labor and fit in well with the traditional slash-and-burn agriculture. Newitt, *Portugal in Africa,* p. 13; GEPB.

Cassinga gold mines A supposedly-important goldfield east of Lubango, southern Angola, between the Okavango and the Cunene rivers. In the 1890s, this area was rumored to have vast gold deposits similar to the Rand in South Africa. Cecil John Rhodes (1853-1902) became interested and thought of building a railway to Cassinga from Mossâmedes that could be linked with the Southern Rhodesian railway system, but this speculative venture came to nothing and soon the project was abandoned. Clarence-Smith, *Slaves, Peasants,* pp. 3, 18.

Cassinga iron mines A promising iron ore area east of Lubango, southern Angola, between the Okavango and the Cunene territories, utilized in the colonial period by the Ovambo and the Nkhumi peoples. It was known to Europeans by the 1890s but its development was very slow because of its isolation, the rugged country, and the difficulties getting machinery and equipment to the site. Foreign investment was available only from the 1960s after the construction of the Matala Dam on the Cunene River provided cheap electrical power. Its production was shattered during the War for Independence (1961-75). Clarence-Smith, *Slaves, Peasants,* pp. 7, 61, 104; HDA. *See also* Cassinga gold mines.

cassoneira (Pg.)   In Angola and elsewhere, a tropical bush (*Euphorbia tirucalli* L.) that grows quickly, reaching a height of 10 to 20 ft. (3 to 6 m); Africans use it for fences and enclosures and as a source of rubber. It is widely distributed in southern Angola and along the Benguela region of the coast, as well as in India where it is believed to have originated. It was introduced to Angola by the Portuguese early in the sixteenth century and is well adapted to the semi-arid conditions. Ficalho, *Plantas Uteis*, pp. 246-7.

Cassongola (Afr.)   A messianic African movement that appeared in 1961 in Baixo do Cassange (q.v.), southern Angola; it was related to the Garveyism of Marcus Garvey and inspired political protest against the Mbundu elite of the region. Pelissier, *La Colonie*, p. 184.

castle trade   Trade carried out from fortified storehouses built by the Portuguese and other Europeans on the Guiné coast. They were provided with water, fresh food, firewood, and the necessary supplies to support a small number of soldiers, tax collectors, government officials, and merchants. The first castle was *São Jorge da Mina* (q.v.), built by the Portuguese in 1482. During the 300 years of the slave trade, forty castles were built along the 400 mi. (640 km) of the rocky coast of the Gulf of Guiné, some within gun-range of each other. African rulers owned the land and rented it to slavers who reserved exclusive trading rights. In the castles' dungeons, millions of slaves were processed and loaded in ships for the Atlantic crossing. Some of these castles have survived in Ghana where they are used by the government as post offices, prisons, offices, and museums. Dantzig, *Short History*, p. 79.

Catalan Atlas   Since the fourteenth century, Catalan and Italian nautical atlases were known by Portuguese navigators. A so-called Catalan Atlas drawn in Majorca in 1375 has been attributed to Abraham Cresque and his son Jafuda. In the *Livro de Marinha de Joan de Lisboa* there are atlases of the Mediterranean and North Atlantic seas. In 1379 Prince Joao of Portugal wrote to his representative in Majorca asking him to send a *mapamundi* (world map). The prince noted that a native of Majorca who had just returned from India and Tataria had spoken of the existence of atlases there. Barbosa, *Novos Subsidios*, Congresso da Historia, 1938, p. 255; DHP.

catana (Pg.)   In Angola and elsewhere, a large broadsword or machete used in clearing the bush or in war. During the War for Independence (1961-75), African nationalists used homemade *catanas* and *canhangulos* (q.v.) against the Portuguese. Pelissier, *La Colonie*, p. 666; GEPB.

Catembe (Afr.)   A region in southern Mozambique bordered on the north by the Espirito Santo and Lourenço Marques rivers, on the west by the Lebombo

Range, and on the south and east by the Maputo River. England disputed this area, but in 1875 it was declared to belong to Portugal. Axelson, *Portugal*, p. 96.

catequisador das libertades (Pg.) "Catechist of freedom." Because a free African could not legally be enslaved in colonial Angola c.1776, a catechist's duties included teaching Christian doctrine and conducting a detailed inquiry into the catechumen's status as slave or free, either before or just after the person had been bought by a slaver. Gabriel, *Angola,* p. 236.

catinga (Afr.) In Angola and elsewhere in Portuguese Africa, the sweaty smell of an African laborer. Hamilton, *Voices,* p. 39.

Catofe (Afr.) A private cooperative cattle ranch in Cuanza Sul near Quibala, Angola, established in 1949 by cattlemen from the Azores. There were 69 colonists out of a total of 256 persons on the settlement. From 1951 on, Catofe received a government subsidy. Pelissier, *La Colonie,* p. 36.

cattle, cultural significance of In the complex East African cattle cultures of the Shona, Tonga, Chopi, and Ngoni of southern Mozambique, cattle are important objects of wealth and symbols of prestige. Some groups believe their cattle are connected with the spirits of their deceased ancestors so their animals also have religious value. Vocabulary referring to kinship or status commonly uses references to cattle; for example, the chief is referred to as the Bull. Herrick, *Area Handbook,* p. 64.

Catumbela (Afr.) A town in Benguela district, southern Angola. The settlement was founded in 1836 by the governor of Benguela, Justiniano Jose de Reis. Catumbela was declared a city in 1905 and today is an important center with a 1960 population of 9,209 of which 7,509 were Africans. Served by the Lobito-Benguela railroad, its main industries are sugar, alcohol, palm oil, cattle, and other agricultural products. The first Benguela newspaper, *A Ventoso*, was published in Catumbela in 1886. GEPB.

Caxito (Afr.) An African town in Uige province, northwestern Angola, where Custodio Dias Bento Azevedo founded the *Associação de Defesa Mutua* (Mutual Aid Association) in 1936. A coffee-growing area, in 1961 it became a battleground of terrorism and violence during the struggle for independence. Pelissier, *La Colonie,* pp. 237, 635.

Cazengo (Afr.) A municipality and district in Cuanza-Norte province with its capital at Ndaltatando. Coffee was introduced to Cazengo in 1837, and today it is an important coffee-producing area and a prosperous agricultural center. In November 1916, a nativist movement was organized in the district and in the 1960s this territory was the scene of much fighting between nationalist and Portuguese forces that only concluded with the independence of Angola in 1974. Pelissier, *La Colonie,* pp. 266, 456; GEPB.

cazumbi (Kimb.) "Souls of the dead; ghosts of the ancestors." An elegiac term for lost African roots used by such poets as Mario Antonio in 1959. The poet lamented that his grandmother had forgotten the *cazumbi* and had exchanged traditional Kimbundu tenets for new Christian beliefs. Burnes, *Fire,* pp. 56-8.

ceitil (Pg.) An obsolete copper coin equal c.1430 to one-sixth of a *rei.* It was minted in Lisbon, Porto, and Ceuta on the order of King João I to commemorate his 1415 conquest of Ceuta, North Africa. It is also called a *cepti.* DN. *See also* thaler.

Cela (Pg.) A *colonato* (planned agricultural center) established by the government in 1953 in the Mossâmedes region of southern Angola. By 1953, with the assistance of African laborers, there were 267 Portuguese families scattered throughout the *colonato* and 35 families working on the medium-sized farms. Pelissier, *La Colonie,* pp. 40-2, 48. *See also* Cunene.

Central Africa, trade in Portuguese inroads into western Central Africa began around 1600. Under a royal monopoly reinforced by military power, Afro-Portuguese traders exported ivory, gold, civet, and slaves to Europe and Brazil and imported metalware, cloth, wheat, and horses. The Afro-Portuguese became expert backwoods merchants and, in association with African chiefs who were the traditional rulers of inland fairs, became active in markets in Karanga, Ambaca, Loanga, and elsewhere. By 1700, Portuguese traders introduced European goods to the Mozambican *prazos* (q.v.) along the Zambezi River. By the mid-eighteenth century they had reached the Zumbo Highlands. They associated themselves with the Islamic sheiks of the coastal Swahili area and maintained control over inland commerce up to the end of the nineteenth century. Newitt, *Portugal in Africa,* pp. 2, 3, 9; DHP.

Central African Airways An international air company operating in conjunction with South African Airways with passenger service connecting Lourenço Marques to Johannesburg and Durban, and Beira to Salisbury. Herrick, *Area Handbook,* p. 253.

Centro Associativo dos Negros de Moçambique "Associated Center of Mozambican Blacks." A cultural center organized by *assimilados* (q.v.) in Maputo in the 1950s. The members were moderates interested in reviving African traditions but not involving themselves in Mozambican nationalism.

Their members lived in towns and worked in government administration, commerce, teaching, and nursing. They were wage earners who tended to have, at most, a few years of secondary education. After the formation of FRELIMO (q.v.) in 1962 some of these people became violently anti-colonial. Munslow, *Mozambique,* pp. 65-6, 68; GEPB.

Centro dos Estudos Africanos (Pg.) "Center for African Studies." A Portuguese-African organization established in Lisbon in 1951 by young nationalist intellectuals, many of whom were the future leaders in the independence movements of the colonies. Pelissier, *La Colonie,* p. 243.

Certeza (Pg.) "Certitude." A short-lived literary journal first published in Mindelo on the island of São Vicente, Cape Verde, in 1944. It was a modest periodical that aimed at analyzing the anguish and insecurity of the younger generation, most of them educated at the Gil Eanes Lyceum, and its existential orientation was quite evident. Among the leaders were Arnaldo França, Francisco Tenreiro, Guilherme Rocheteau, Nuno Miranda, Antonio Nunes, and other Cape Verdian and Portuguese writers. It ceased publication after the third issue by order of the government. Ferreira, *No Reino do Caliban,* pp. 127-8.

Ceuta (Afr.) A seaport in northern Morocco situated 18 mi. (26 km) southeast of the Strait of Gibraltar. The closest African port to Europe, Ceuta is a strategic city taken by the Arabs in 711 AD. It was ruled by a succession of Moslem dynasties before it was conquered by King João I of Portugal in 1415. His son, Prince Henry, used it as a base for Portuguese expansion into Africa in the fifteenth century. In 1580 it became part of Spain. Today it is a Spanish military station and trading port. Its population in 1970 was 67,187. EA; GEPB. *See also* Ceuta, Diocese of.

Ceuta, Diocese of Pope Martin V established this diocese and appointed Friar Aimaro, a resident of Lisbon, as its first bishop. It is not clear if he was a French or English Franciscan. GEPB. *See also* Franciscans in Africa.

Chaimite, Battle of (Afr.) In December 1895, Portuguese led by J. Mousinho de Albuquerque fought the forces of Chief Gungunhana at Gaza, a territory west of Mozambique. The chief was defeated and taken prisoner. A further campaign had to be fought in 1897 to eliminate the remnants of his forces and pacify the Gaza territory. Newitt, *Portugal in Africa,* pp. 53, 58.

chamadas divinas (Crio.) "Divine chants." In Cape Verde, a traditional form of Gospel singing performed by groups who meet on Saturday nights in August and daily in September to implore God, the Virgin Mary, and the saints to send them rain after the dry season. Today this tradition is mainly observed on São Nicolau Island. Valkhoff, *Miscelanea Luso-Africana,* p. 46.

Changamire Kingdom (Afr.)   An African kingdom on the central plateau of Manica in Mozambique that flourished c.1660. It periodically attacked foreign intruders and exacted tribute from the Portuguese in return for peaceful trade. Herrick, *Area Handbook,* p. 28.

Channel British Squadron   A naval force established by Britain in 1890 to protect Mashonaland, an area occupied by Boers from South Africa in what is now Zimbabwe. A serious conflict developed regarding Portuguese claims to the territory. The dispute escalated with the threat of attack on Lisbon and certain Portuguese-African ports by the British fleet. On August 20, 1890, England issued the Ultimatum (q.v.) that effectively ended the crisis. Axelson, *Portugal,* pp. 220, 224, 232.

chaplains on shipboard   At the time of the Discovery (q.v), the Portuguese Crown required the presence of a chaplain on board all slavers. He should preferably be a friar, often a Franciscan. If not, he should at least be drawn from the most devout of the secular clergy. The chaplain taught catechism and baptized slaves, said mass, attended the sick, and gave last rites to the dying. Duncan, *Atlantic Islands*, p. 230.

chefe de posto (Pg.)   "Chief of Post." An administrator in charge of a municipality in Portuguese Africa. The system of *chefe de posto* was introduced in the colonies by the Colonial Act of 1930 signed by President Antonio Salazar. This official was a white Portuguese who supervised the collection of taxes, presided over disputes, dispensed punishment, and oversaw village agriculture and small government projects. Often he abused his authority for reasons of personal profit, spite, or lust, thus creating bitter feelings among Africans. Henriksen, *Mozambique,* pp. 100-1; GEPB.

Cheringoma (Afr.)   A *prazo* (q.v.), leased in 1750 by Dona Ignez Pessoa de Almeida Castelo Branco, a wealthy and powerful Afro-Portuguese aristocrat. It was located about 50 mi. (80 km) southeast of the mouth of the Zambezi. Isaacman, *Mozambique: From Colonialism,* pp. 20, 30, 36.

Chewa Kingdom (Afr.)   An African kingdom, located north of Tete on the north bank of the Zambezi River, that came into being c.1640. During its formative period the ruler, called the *Undi*, was at the apex of this indigenous political system. The *Undi* appointed his matrilineal kinsmen as rulers and headmen of towns and villages. As owner of the land, he controlled the system of shifting agriculture as well as commerce and slave trading with the

Portuguese and Arabs. The Chewa Kingdom reached its summit of power and wealth at the end of the eighteenth century. It began its decline about 1880 when the Portuguese government promulgated a series of laws designed to establish political control and to abolish the old *prazo* system which was closely linked to the Chewa system with their Zambezian chiefdoms. Isaacman, *Mozambique: From Colonialism*, pp. 14-15, 46-7, 159-60; GEPB.

chibalo (Afr.) A system of forced labor established by the Portuguese government in Mozambique in 1899 as a regular source of cheap labor. All African inhabitants of the province were subject to the "moral" and legal obligation of seeking to acquire through work those things they lacked for subsistence and thereby to improve their own social condition. They had "full liberty" to choose the means by which to comply with this obligation. If they did not comply, however, the public authorities were empowered to force them. Local administrators had complete discretion over determining who was "idle," and after 1930 virtually all *chefes de posto* (q.v.) supplemented their modest salaries with gifts and favors from European planters, merchants, factory owners, and farmers in return for African labor. As a result, the rural areas were transformed into large labor reserves. *Chibalo* laborers worked under grueling conditions. They were not entitled to food or lodging, were subjected to repeated physical abuses, and received little or no remuneration. Skilled *chibalo* workers, such as carpenters, earned barely ten percent of the salaries of their free counterparts. In rural areas planters and merchants regularly withheld remittances from their workers' wages and often bound them through a system of incurred debts. The system exacerbated the existing shortage of labor in Mozambique by driving thousands of illegal workers to the gold mines of South Africa. Also spelled *shibalo* and *xibalo*. Rita-Ferreira, *O Movimento Migratorio*, p. 155; DHP.

chiche (Braz.) In Angola and elsewhere, a small tropical tree (*Sterculia tomentosa* Guill. and Perr.) from which Africans extract a gum (*Icacia chiche*) eaten in time of famine. In some parts of Africa this tree is called *cola* and its seeds are chewed. Ficalho, *Plantas Uteis,* p. 101.

chick-pea A leguminous plant (*Cicer arietinum* L.), highly resistant to drought, probably brought by caravans from North Africa to Ghana c.1300; it was the staple food of the Mandingos settled at that time in Ghana, an area also known as the "land of gold dust." Lewicki, *West African Food,* pp. 56-7, 166, 320.

Chicumbane (Afr.) A Swiss Protestant mission established c.1900 in João Belo, in the Gaza district of Mozambique. This mission has a hospital which served the Africans of the surrounding region. It and other Swiss missions are particularly known for their studies of ethnography, geography, linguistics, and tropical medicine. Herrick, *Area Handbook,* p. 109.

chigger In Angola and elsewhere, the tiny red larva of certain mites (family Trombiculidae) which penetrate and lay eggs under the skin. It is thought to have been introduced c.1872 by ships arriving at Ambriz from Brazil where it was a serious problem among slaves there and in the Caribbean. Soon it was transported inland by caravans. Though harmless if promptly extracted, the eggs can cause ulcers, often followed by gangrene, resulting in the death of many people through poor sanitation and ignorance. Even when they did not indirectly kill their host, chiggers impede movement since they mainly affected the feet. As a result of chigger infestations, trading caravans were brought to a standstill. The magnitude of the problem was such that in 1875 a special hospital was established to treat the condition in Luanda. Ulcers caused by chiggers were the most frequent ailment treated and second only to smallpox as a cause of death in the hospital at Luanda between July and October 1877. Also called *jiga* and *chiggoe.* Dias, *Famine and Disease,* JAH, Cambridge, 1981, 22:368-9.

Chimoara (Afr.) A trading and customs town at the junction of the Shire and Mozambique rivers in the Tete district of Mozambique. In 1884, Africans rebelled and destroyed the village in reaction to the heavy compulsory pool taxes (group taxes) levied on men and women, and even boys and girls. The people pillaged and burned the lumber and trading station, and looted a French factory and several Dutch stores. Most Portuguese residents fled. The governor-general of Quelimane subsequently intervened to restore order and authority over the town. Axelson, *Portugal,* pp. 142, 166-67.

China, relations with Angola The People's Republic of China sided in the 1960s with UNITA and FNLA (qq.v.) against the MPLA (q.v.) which finally won the War for Independence in 1975. In 1968, Jonas Savimbi, the UNITA leader, was invited to Peking to negotiate for assistance. When Antonio Neto of the MPLA followed him in 1972, he received nothing, since he was already getting help from the Soviets who were at odds with China at the time. In 1973, China began sending military equipment and training FNLA guerrillas at the Kinkuzu base in southern Zaire. In November 1976, when the question of Angola's admission to the United Nations came up before the Security Council, China's delegate was absent. Neto, then president of Angola, contemptuously denounced China as a country that allied itself with the forces of imperialism. Kaplan, *Angola,* p. 161.

China, relations with Mozambique The People's Republic of China's relations, both ideological and military, with FRELIMO (q.v.) began in the

1960s. By 1968, Mozambican guerrillas were using Chinese weapons with great success. By 1973, there were military camps under Chinese control in Tanzania. As the War for Independence was reaching its end in 1974, FRELIMO's association with Beijing was well established and the Chinese Revolution was taken as a model. Henriksen, *Mozambique,* pp. 173-4, 200, 203-4.

Chinde (Afr.) A seaport on the only navigable mouth of the Zambezi River in Mozambique, explored by the Portuguese in 1861 and rediscovered by the British explorer Daniel Rankin in 1889. By 1890 England claimed the concession to Chinde which was finally settled in an agreement with Portugal in 1912. It was formerly the chief port for Malawi and Zambia. The city's population in 1960 was 25,671; the chief export is sugar. Vail, *Capitalism,* pp. 10, 104-5.

Chinese immigrants in Mozambique Chinese immigrants from Macao and the mainland have been coming to Mozambique since the seventeenth century. Chinese marriages were reported in lower Zambezia in 1777, and in 1832 a governor authorized the import of about 4,000 more Chinese women from Macao as prospective brides for Chinese men in the colony. In 1900, Chinese laborers, called coolies, from Mozambique were contracted for work in the South African mines. At that time there were well-organized Chinese communities in the province. By 1960 there were 2,098 Chinese with their own associations and schools. Traditionally, they kept to themselves, avoiding any involvement in politics. Henriksen, *Mozambique,* pp. 143, 251-2; Newitt, *Portuguese Settlement,* pp. 102, 142, 144, 368.

Chinfuma, Treaty of (Afr.) A treaty between Portuguese and the Bacongo (q.v.) of Cabinda signed on September 29, 1883, establishing a Portuguese protectorate in the region, making the Cabinda Enclave (q.v.) completely independent of Angola. Pelissier, *La Colonie,* p. 286.

Chire River *See* Shire River.

Chironde (Afr.) A *prazo* (q.v.) lying between the Buzi and the Pungue rivers, north of Sofala in central Mozambique. It measured six by eight leagues (48 by 64 mi.; 30 by 40 km) and was low-lying, at least half of it being swamp. Herds of elephants grazed there and there was a large African population split between two local chiefs. Besides the usual African subsistence crops, it produced indigo and tobacco for export and provided pasture for a large number of cattle. A request for a grant of the area in 1755 by Sebastião Rodrigues, a native of Goa, was denied on the grounds that Rodrigues was trying to establish a monopoly over Crown lands. Eventually

Chironde passed into the hands of Rafael Fernandes, succeeded by his daughter Antonia Fernandes in 1787. Newitt, *Portuguese Settlement,* pp. 206, 207.

chitala (Mak.) In Mozambique, a meeting hut or house for men only, built in the middle of a village and encircled by the rest of the huts. Here the Makonde chief together with the council of elders administers justice, assigns land for cultivation, and performs religious rituals. One of the most important functions is the annual consultation of the people on whether the village should move to fresh lands, a frequent event among the Makonde of northern Mozambique. Dias, *Portuguese Contribution,* pp. 33-5.

Chitato (Afr.) A region in the DIAMANG Company (q.v.) concession in Luanda. It was the seat of an African nativist cult that appeared in 1951 and preached resurrection of the dead, abandonment of the farms, and the slaughter of livestock. They called themselves "enlighteners" and were outlawed by the company and the Portuguese government. Pelissier, *La Colonie,* p. 181.

Chokwe (Afr.) A Bantu group settled in Zaire, parts of Angola, northwestern Zambia, and Catanga. This large matrilineal group began migrating into Angola c.1850; today the Chokwe have mixed with many different groups and are scattered throughout Luanda, Moxico, and Bié. In 1960 they numbered 600,000, half of whom were living in western Angola. They participated actively in Angola's War for Independence. HDA.

Cholera morbus (Lat.) A highly contagious often fatal gastrointestinal disease transmitted by contaminated food and water. Portuguese historians claim that V.C. Garcia de Horta in his *Coloquios* (Dialogue) of 1563 was the first European to scientifically describe this disease which he found in Goa. He wrote that this illness could kill a patient in twenty-four hours and was much more serious than a similar disease in Portugal. Cholera was endemic in Goa, and there are records of epidemics that occurred in 1538, 1543, 1553, 1563, and many more times. It was brought to Lisbon in 1832 and after killing 3,621 persons in the city, it spread throughout Portugal. GEPB; WTNID.

Chopi (Afr.) An ethnic group established on the coast of Inhambane and the Gaza district in Mozambique. They are divided into clans ruled by hereditary chiefs of patrilineal descent who have wide political, military, and religious powers. Together with their neighbors the Tonga (q.v.) they had a total population of 450,000 by 1970. They are accomplished musicians of the *mbila*, a type of xylophone, and users of the bow. Neither instrument is used by the Tonga. Henriksen, *Mozambique,* pp. 246, 250, 251.

choriro (Afr.) "Weeping." A mourning ritual practiced by both slaves and warriors in Zambezia (q.v.) that involved burning and pillaging to make people weep for the death of their master. On the death of Chief Choutama in 1840, six hundred warriors descended on the Tete *prazo* (q.v.) with fire and sword to make the settlers weep for the departed chief. Newitt, *Portuguese Settlement,* pp. 237-8.

chuanga (Afr.) In colonial Mozambique c.1750, an African administrator who was an intermediary between the foreign overlord and the African chief. He was in charge of collecting taxes, ivory, and game belonging to the *prazero* (q.v.). He also acted as an internal purchasing agent and in plentiful years bought the *colonos's* (q.v.) surplus sorghum, maize, rice, and other products. Isaacman, *Mozambique: The Africanization,* pp. 32-3.

chunga (Afr.) A slave in colonial Mozambique who was in charge of collecting taxes, transmitting orders and messages between his owner and local chiefs, and acting as the master's eyes and ears on the village level. His labor was rewarded by a share of the revenue, an inducement to exact the utmost. One of his unpopular tasks was that of using poor quality cloth to purchase agricultural products at below-market prices from the villagers. Henriksen, *Mozambique,* p. 63.

Chupanga (Afr.) A *prazo* (q.v.) on the southern bank of the lower Zambezi administered by the Mozambique Company (q.v.) in the 1880s. Chupanga had been an agricultural and trading post since early in the eighteenth century. Rice and other grains were cultivated by Africans while outsiders, mainly Indian merchants, controlled the slave and ivory trades. Mary Livingstone, the wife of the famous explorer David Livingstone (1813-1873), died and was buried in Chupanga on April 27, 1862. Since then, Africans have come in pilgrimage to visit her grave, now considered a shrine. Portugal established a military post there in 1883 and the following year a network of *aringas* (q.v.) were built to defend this important commercial region. In the 1890s, it became an area of increasing unrest caused by African chiefs eager to oust the Portuguese administration and in 1893, Africans attacked the settlement. As recently as 1970, in some popular songs of protest, Chupanga is portrayed as a village of hungry people. Vail, *Capitalism,* pp. 7, 29, 32-3; Isaacman, *Mozambique: The Tradition,* pp. 134, 165.

cinchona (Lat.) A Latinate term coined in 1753 by the Swedish taxonomist Carolus Linnaeus to honor the Countess del Chinchon, wife of a seventeenth-century Peruvian viceroy. She was successfully treated for malaria using a quinine decoction extracted from the bark of the evergreen *Cinchona officinalis* tree of tropical South America. The tree was introduced into São Tomé in

1864. Annual production of quinine (*quinina* in Portuguese) was 15 tons in 1887 and grew to 49 tons in by 1891. It was also introduced into Mozambique and Portugal in 1864. From 1864 to 1888 several varieties of cinchona were cultivated in the Coimbra Botanical Gardens in Portugal. From there, trees were taken to Madeira and to the Azores. Carvalho e Vasconcellos, *As Colonias Portuguesas,* pp. 230-1; GEPB; WNWD.

cinnamon The yellowish-brown spice made from the dried inner bark of several trees or shrubs of the genus *Cinnamomum* of the laurel family, native to the East Indies and southeast Asia. Known from antiquity, cinnamon was reported in Alexandria, Egypt, by Vasco da Gama on his first trip to India in 1498. At the Age of Discovery (q.v.), it became a valuable spice in the Indo-Portuguese trade. In Portugal it is called *canella.* GEPB; WNWD.

cipaio (Afr.) An African policeman usually assigned to a lower-level administrator or to an African chief in colonial Mozambique. When attached to a chief, the *cipaio*'s function was to help recruit workers, arrest and beat individuals suspected of crimes or disobedience, and carry messages. Often, the ire of the Africans was directed toward the *cipaio,* although in most cases he simply followed to the letter the orders of his superiors. It is also spelled *cipai* and *sipaio.* HDM.

cipaka (Afr.) A type of rough fortress built c.1900 by bandits in the rugged terrain and thick acacia forests of the southern highlands of Angola. This primitive palisade of sharpened stakes or great thorn bushes was often located on a rocky outcrop, the gaps being filled in with boulders. In some cases a *cipaka* could withstand sustained rifle fire and could only be taken with field artillery. Clarence-Smith, *Slaves, Peasants,* pp. 86-7.

circumcision A painful African initiation rite performed at puberty in which the foreskin is removed from boys and the clitoris is surgically reduced on girls. It is common in many ethnic groups in Portuguese Africa and elsewhere in sub-Saharan Africa. After the ritual surgery the initiates go through a period of seclusion then receive instructions regarding their roles and duties as husbands and wives. Often a new name is given afterwards. Female circumcision in particular has become increasingly controversial, considered by many to be mutilation. Herrick, *Area Handbook,* p. 65.

civet A yellowish substance with a musk-like scent, secreted by a gland of the civet cat (*Civettictis civetta*) and used in perfumery. The civet cat was found in Angola and elsewhere in Africa by the Portuguese and the musk has been exported to Europe together with ivory, pepper, and gold since the early sixteenth century. Newitt, *Portugal in Africa,* p. 2.

civil service in Africa The Portuguese overseas civil service was divided into general and special services. The general service, under the jurisdiction of the overseas ministry, included such posts as governor-general, provincial secretary, and district governor. The special service pertained to government employees working in colonial territories. Personnel such as medical or railroad workers, on special assignment to one or another service, were under civil service regulations for the duration of the appointment. Military personnel and the police were under separate regulations. Herrick, *Area Handbook,* p. 168.

Civilização da Africa Portuguesa, A (Pg.) "Portuguese African Civilization." A weekly periodical, the first of its kind in Luanda, Angola, began publishing on December 6, 1866, under the direction of Urbano de Castro and Alfredo Mantua. It was dedicated to the "Administrative, economic, commercial, agricultural, and industrial interests of Portuguese Africa and especially [those] of Angola and São Tomé." It defended European interests in matters of reform, advocating political autonomy for the Portuguese settlers. This periodical immediately came under fire from the governor-general who fined and chastised the first editor; press criticism of the government and the question of press freedom were a constant topic in the paper. Ervedosa, *Itinerario,* p. 251.

Claridade (Pg.) "Clarity." A literary journal published irregularly between 1936 and 1960 in Mindelo, Cape Verde, by a group of local writers, later known as *claridosos.* Nine issues were published: two in 1936, one in 1937, two in 1947, and one in each of the following years: 1948, 1949, 1958 and 1960. Its founders were concerned with analyzing the reality and roots of their impoverished society and writing about the land and the people's problems and frustrations. The *claridosos* thought that a Cape Verdian, with a unique Afro-Portuguese racial and cultural tradition, should be considered distinct from the Portuguese in Europe or in any other overseas province. These writers used the local language, *Crioulo* (q.v.), as a literary instrument to report to the outside world their isolation, their feelings of *saudade* (q.v.), and their poverty as well as their problems of migration, drought, ignorance, and political backwardness. It was a movement parallel to that of *negritude* (q.v.). Among its founders were Baltasar Lopes, Manuel Lopes, and Jorge Barbosa. Ferreira, *No Reino de Caliban,* pp. 77-80.

claridosos *See* Claridade.

cloth money A square of cloth stamped in Lisbon c. 1490 with the royal coat of arms. It was used along the Guiné coast as fiat money. The official value of marked cloth money was four times the value of unmarked cloth. This money was introduced by Portuguese merchants into the Ardra and Benin kingdoms (qq.v.) at the end of the fifteenth century and it was employed over the entire area that formerly used cowrie shell (q.v.) money, including the Slave and Gold coasts. Polanyi, *Dahomey,* pp. 181-3.

coconut palm A tall pan-tropical tree (*Cocos nucifera* L.) that bears coconuts. It grows on or near coastal plains. Copra (q.v.), the source of coconut oil used in cooking and soap-making, is the dried meat of the coconut. Herrick, *Area Handbook,* pp. 14, 202, 219.

coffee (Ar.) Tropical shrubs or small trees (*Coffea arabica* and *C. canephora*) that reach 5-10 ft. (2-3.5 m). The seeds, called beans, found in its red berries are, dried, roasted and ground to make coffee. Native to north-eastern and central Africa, coffee trees were imported to Brazil by the Portuguese. Coffee was introduced to São Nicolau, Cape Verde, from Brazil by Antonio Leite in 1790. By 1830 it was being cultivated in coastal Angola and quickly became an important cash crop. In 1850, in an experiment to see if it could grow in new areas, coffee was taken inland to Cazengo, a region east of Luanda. The experiment was a success and African farmers spread coffee cultivation widely throughout the area. Ficalho, *Plantas Uteis,* p. 198; HDA; WNWD.

coffee of the Negroes In West Africa in the sixteenth century, the term applied to cultivated varieties of cola (q.v.) trees (*Cola* spp.) grown for their nuts which contain caffeine. In modern times, this stimulant has replaced coffee and tea among many African groups. Lewicki, *West African Food,* p. 123. *See also* cola.

coffle A chain gang sometimes numbering over a hundred slaves, brought from the inland states of West Africa for sale along the Gold and Slave coasts c.1700. At the height of the slave trade there were hundreds of organized coffles. The vast numbers of slaves required for the trade were acquired during bloody raids on villages. Ardra, Dahomey, Ouidah, the Royal African Company, and the Dutch, Portuguese and French were all engaged in coffling, bringing slaves hundreds of miles from the interior to the coast. Polanyi, *Dahomey,* pp. 18-22.

Coimbra (Pg.) An isolated African settlement in Niassa province near the Malawi border in northwestern Mozambique, transformed by the Portuguese army in the 1970s into a fortified outpost surrounded by hostile FRELIMO guerrilla forces. By 1972, barbed wire, mines, and trenches encircled it with gun towers at the outer perimeter. This island-like Portuguese garrison was resupplied by air. Henriksen, *Revolution,* p. 48.

cola (Afr.) Tropical trees (*Cola acuminata, C. nitida*, other *Cola* spp.) found in West Africa and widely if informally cultivated by Africans since before the coming of the Arabs in 1059. From these and several other *Cola* species, cola nuts are obtained. The nuts, containing caffeine, are chewed by Africans who also use the nuts to prepare a pleasant tasting non-alcoholic beverage and a digestive aid. It also was a favorite gift between lovers. In the sixteenth century the Portuguese traded cola nuts, which they called *coleira*, in Senegambia and Sierra Leone. Mandingo traders took them to the Niger region and Timbuctu. Famed for its gold and slave market c.1550, Timbuctu was an important commercial center for the Sudan. The Moslem traveler Leo Africanus (1493-1552) gives a detailed description of this plant and its nuts. By the eighteenth century the Arabs considered cola a royal food. During the colonial period it was exported to Portugal and Brazil where slaves consumed it in great quantities. In Nigeria it is called *guro*. In modern times, cola is exported to many countries as the basic ingredient of cola drinks. In Angola a popular rhyme says: "The one who eats cola, stays in Angola." Ficalho, *Plantas Uteis*, pp. 102-4; Lewicky, *West African Food*, pp. 122-3. *See also* coffee of the Negroes.

coleira (Pg.) "Cola." The nut of the cola (q.v.) tree. Ficalho, *Plantas Uteis*, pp. 102-4.

coleus Tropical herbs (*Coleus tuberosus* and *C. esculentus*) of the mint family with edible tubers. They are part of the starchy diet in Angola and elsewhere in Africa. In Angola they are called *ucola, tamba*, and African potato. There are over 100 species of coleus, although not all are cultivated. GEPB.

colonato (Pg.) In Portuguese Africa, large agricultural settlements with each village having its own farm buildings and tools, organized by the government as recently as 1950. They were under the supervision of Portuguese immigrants using African laborers, the latter living on the margins of the *colonato*. Production goals were assigned to each family and workers who did not achieve their goals because of what was perceived as indolence were removed from the *colonato*. Duffy, *Portuguese Africa*, p. 309.

colonia de exploração (Pg.) "Colony for exploration." Term used c.1800 for what amounted to a base of operations from which small numbers of Portuguese colonists extracted only such local wealth as slaves, precious metals, ivory, and animal skins for export from coastal trade areas populated mostly by Africans. Caetano, *Os Nativos*, p. 117.

Colonial Act A Portuguese law concerning indigenous labor passed on April 11, 1933. Article 18 stated that indigenous labor for the state must be remunerated; Article 19 forbade forced labor for any corporation; Article 20 ruled that the State can only force indigenous labor for public works of common benefit by criminal court order; Article 21 stated that an indigenous labor contract is based on individual liberty and the right to a just salary under state control. Cunha, *O Trabalho Indigena,* pp. 204-5.

colonial agreement In Africa, a tacit understanding among the European powers, including Portugal, during the eighteenth and the beginning of the nineteenth centuries, based on the conviction that the major colonies should contribute to the welfare of the European power by providing labor and raw materials. Cunha, *O Sistema Portugués,* p. 11.

colonial mystique A widespread feeling among the Portuguese of the twentieth century, rooted in a military tradition and in the general beliefs of an intellectual group of *assimilados* (q.v.), stressing what they believed was a peculiar Portuguese talent for "civilizing" Africans, that is, absorbing African customs while bringing Christianity and "enlightenment" to them, and of administrating the colonies to the colorful tune of the Luso-African drummer. Wheeler, *Angola,* pp. 102-3.

colonial policy in Africa (Pg.) An empirical socioeconomic system of government administration that evolved between the fifteenth and seventeenth centuries, based mainly on the ideal of evangelization and the exploitation of natural resources; specifically, the exportation of slaves to Brazil and other parts of the New World and to Portugal. Between 1820 and 1910, colonial policy was to achieve "uniform assimilation" of the African population into the Portuguese socioeconomic structure. After 1910, with the establishment of the Republic in Portugal, colonial policy was aimed at organizing financial autonomy and qualified cultural integration according to the degree of Europeanization acquired by an African population. Cunha, *O Sistema Portugués,* pp. 112-3, 131.

colono (Pg.) "Colonist." A European agricultural settler in Portuguese Africa. In Angola, the settlers were usually poor, lacking in capital, and with little previous knowledge of farming. Many quickly gave up and turned to commerce. HDA.

coloquintida (Pg.) A tropical vine (*Citrullus colocynthis* L.) native to West Africa and Cape Verde. The pulp of the extremely bitter fruit is used to prepare purgatives. Introduced from Africa to Portugal early in the colonial period, it spread to southern Europe and other parts of the world. Roasted seeds of the *coloquintida* form part of the diet of people in the southern Sahara. Ficalho, *Plantas Uteis,* pp. 186-87.

color prejudice In Cape Verde, as in many other racially mixed communities, skin color is of great interest. A census of 1856 lists no fewer than seventeen distinctions of skin color ranging from "very dark" to "almost white." Today this colonial racism has been tempered. Cape Verdians feel that their society is neither European nor totally African and are proud of being islanders, irrespective of their skin color. Davidson, *The Fortunate Isles,* pp. 31-32. *See also* Cape Verdianness.

Comissão da Revolução Nacional (Pg.) "Commission of the National Revolution." A political group organized in the Leopoldville area of the Belgian Congo in 1960 by a young Cunhaman soldier, João Baptista Traves Pereira, a deserter from the Portuguese army. This group soon associated itself with the UPA (q.v.), the overall nationalist party fighting for independence in Angola. Pelissier, *La Colonie,* pp. 284, 543.

Comissão de Mão-de-Obra (Pg.) "Migrant Workers' Commission." A government commission established in 1900 in Mozambique to inspect and control African workers recruited to work in the South African goldfields. Rita-Ferreira, *O Movimento Migratorio,* p. 77. *See also* Witwatersrand Native Labour Association.

Comissãos Administrativas dos Bairros Indigenas (Pg.) "Administrative Commissions of Indigenous Boroughs." A municipal organization established in 1956 with the purpose of eradicating the *musseques,* the poor and unhealthy slum neighborhoods in Luanda, the Angolan capital. These multi-ethnic and potentially anti-colonial communities were considered dangerous by the government. Pelissier, *La Colonie,* p. 359(n).

Comité de Libertação dos Territorios Africanos sob Dominio Portugues (Pg.) "Committee for the Liberation of African Territories under Portuguese Domination." A nationalist organization formed by Lucio Lara in June 1959 in Frankfurt, West Germany. This was one of the first modern movements directly geared to fight for the independence of Portuguese colonies. Pelissier, *La Colonie,* p. 251.

Comité de Trabalho Indigena (Pg.) "Indigenous Labor Committee." A Portuguese colonial government organization established in 1892 by the *Câmara das Minas de Transval* (Chamber of Mines of Transvaal) to supervise the contracts, salaries, transportation, and complaints of African migrant laborers working in the South African mines. Rita-Ferreira, *O Movimento Migratorio,* p. 62.

Comité Revolucionario de Moçambique *See* COREMO.

Commission for the Promotion of Angola's Commerce   A commission founded in Luanda shortly before 1851 by a group of merchants dedicated to promoting the conservative views of the Europeans involved in the old Angolan economy, which was based on revenues from the slave trade and slave labor. This began a tradition of European organizations in Angola concerned with economic interests rather than with ideology or doctrines. Governmental reform or colonial independence was not their concern. Duffy, *Portuguese Africa,* pp. 91-2.

Communist Party of Angola   *See* Angolan Communist Party.

Companhia Africa (Pg.)   "Africa Company." A chartered trading company organized in 1884 by Donald Currie, William Mackinnon, and J.C. Paiva de Andrada, with a board in London controlling three-quarters of the capital and a board in Lisbon controlling one-quarter. The company was granted privileges to work mines in the Manica district of Mozambique. The adventure failed because of unrest among local chiefs and disputes between Portuguese and British settlers. Axelson, *Portugal,* pp. 123-4.

Companhia Carbonifera de Moçambique (Pg.)   "Coal Company of Mozambique." A concern formed in 1949 that was owned sixty percent by Belgian interests, thirty percent by the Mozambique Company, and ten percent by the Portuguese government. Coal reserves in its main 9,154 acre (3,700 ha) concession were estimated in 1951 to be about 400,000,000 metric tons. Herrick, *Area Handbook,* p. 228.

Companhia Comercial da Baia de Lourenço Marques (Pg.)   "Lourenço Marques Bay Commercial Company." A corporation established in 1825 by Vicente Tómas dos Santos and Carlos João Baptista. The owners were obliged to maintain a trading post exclusively for ivory trading and to maintain a garrison of about 100 soldiers for a period of fourteen years. Silva Rego, *O Ultramar,* p. 332.

Companhia da Costa de Guiné (Pg.)   "Guiné Coast Company." One of the first commercial corporations organized by the Martins brothers, Lourenço Pestana and Manuel da Costa. On September 1, 1664, it was granted exclusive commercial monopoly of Arguim (q.v.) for a period of eight years. GEPB.

Companhia de Cacheu e Cabo Verde (Pg.)   "Cacheu and Cape Verde Company." A chartered Portuguese trading company organized in 1690 to exploit the upper Guiné coast. The company had only limited success in the face of efficient competition from the English and French. In 1757 the powerful

Companhia Geral do Grão-Para e Maranhão (q.v.) rebuilt the Bissau port and became the leading concern in the trade of goods and slaves between Portugal, West Africa, and Brazil. Duffy, *Portuguese Africa,* p. 137; GEPB.

Companhia de Cacheu, Rios e Comercio de Guiné (Pg.) "Company of Cacheu, Rivers, and Commerce of Guiné." A corporation organized on May 19, 1676, by Antonio de Barros Bezerra, Manuel Preto Baldez, and others. It was licensed for six years to engage in commerce and the slave trade in the port of Bissau. GEPB.

Companhia de Diamantes de Angola   See DIAMANG.

Companhia de Diamantes de Moçambique (Pg.) "Mozambique Diamond Company." A corporation organized in 1967 with a concession of 13,000 square mi. (33,500 square km) of land near Pafúri at the Rhodesian border. The company had its headquarters in Mozambique and half its directors were Portuguese nationals. Herrick, *Area Handbook,* pp. 229-230.

Companhia do Estanco de Maranhão e Pará (Pg.) "Maranhão and Pará Maritime Company." A Brazilian chartered trade company organized on February 12, 1682, by Antonio de Barros Bezerra, Manuel Preto Baldez, Pedro Alvarez Caldas, Antonio da Gama Padua, and many others for exclusive trading rights with northeastern Brazil and the importation from West Africa of a total of ten thousand slaves in lots of five hundred individuals per year for twenty years. In 1676 it was replaced by the *Companhia de Cacheu e Cabo Verde* (q.v.). Carreira, *As Companhias Pombalinas*, BCG, 1968, xxiii(89/90):18; GEPB.

Companhia Geral do Grão-Pará e Maranhão (Pg.)   "Grão-Pará and Maranhão General Company." A Portuguese import-export company chartered in 1757 and based in Santiago, Cape Verde, to which the king granted the exclusive rights for twenty years for trade along the upper Guiné coast (Guinea-Bissau) and in the Cape Verde Islands. In 1765 the grant was extended. Its transactions, such as ivory, cotton cloth, brooms, slaves, and European goods, were duty free. Because local authorities could not control or inspect cargoes, the king later appointed regional officials. The Marquês de Pombal and other government members had shares in the company. In 1778, the company's request for another ten-year extension of the license was denied. This company was officially liquidated in 1914, 130 years later. GEPB. *See also* Companhia de Cacheu e Cape Verde.

Companhia Geral dos Algodões de Angola   *See* COTONANG.

Companhia Lusitana do Aluminio da Guiné e Angola (Pg.) "Lusitanan Aluminum Company of Guiné and Angola." A Dutch firm founded August 6, 1957, to prospect for and process bauxite ore in Guinea-Bissau and Angola. The Portuguese government and the a Dutch corporation were partners. As of 1993 regular production has not yet been achieved. HDRGC.

Companhia União Fabril *See* CUF.

Compasso di Navigare (It.) "Navigation Compass." A thirteenth-century handbook covering the Mediterranean and Black Seas, developed c.1290 from the accumulated experience of local pilots. The directions in the *Compasso* go port-to-port clockwise around the Mediterranean from Cape St. Vincent, Portugal, to Safi, Morocco. They include bearings, distance in miles (short, or geometric, miles of 4100 feet or 13.45 km), descriptions of landmarks and dangers, instructions for entering harbors, and information about depths and anchorages. Besides coastal passages, the *Compasso* includes directions, with courses and distances, for a number of long-distance crossings between easily-recognized points, usually capes or islands. Some of these open-sea crossings were 700 or 800 mi. (1125 or 1300 km) in length. By the fifteenth century the *Compasso di Navigare* together with *Portolani* and the *Toleta de Martelogio* (qq.v.) were familiar to Portuguese navigators and other Mediterranean pilots. Parry, *The Discovery of the Sea*, pp. 32-3.

Conferencia das Organizações Nacionalistas das Colonias Portuguesas (Pg.) "The Conference of Nationalist Organizations of the Portuguese Colonies." This organization's first meeting was held in Casablanca in April 1961 in an attempt to formalize and increase the links between the four socialist parties of the Portuguese African colonies, FRELIMO, MPLA, MLSTP, and PAIGC (qq.v.). The main activities were joint lobbying and propaganda work, especially at the OAU (q.v.), and the exchange of military information. The chief external support came from the Soviet Union and other socialist countries. HDA.

Conference des Estats Africaines à Monrovia (Fr.) "Conference of African States at Monrovia." Its first meeting was held on May 8, 1961, where Holden Roberto, one of the Angolan leaders, proposed organizing civil uprisings on the northern Angola plantations as a prelude to military action in the struggle for independence. Pelissier, *La Colonie*, p. 475.

Conference of Nationalist Organizations in the Portuguese Colonies An organization established in Dar es-Salaam, Tanzania, in 1961 to coordinate the activities of several African and Portuguese groups engaged in the War for Independence. Backed by Julius Nyerere of Tanzania and Kwame

Nkruma of Ghana, it was a significant step toward unity of all liberation forces. Members of participating organizations assumed most of the key posts, but Eduardo Mondlane of Mozambique was elected president and Marcelino dos Santos became secretary-general. In 1966 it allied itself with the Portuguese Communist Party. Together they passed out such anti-war slogans as "Pass the Word" to Portuguese soldiers in the colonies and welcomed deserters to further the growing awareness and sympathy toward their cause within the Portuguese military establishment. This alliance helped to prepare the way for the April 1974 Lisbon coup against the Caetano government. Henriksen, *Revolution,* pp. 20, 193; Munslow, *Mozambique,* pp. 108-9. *See also* Voice of Liberty.

Congo, Diocese of the The Holy See created the Diocese of the Congo in 1665; its first bishop was Manuel da Natividade, the superior of the Franciscan monastery in Alenquer, Portugal. He governed from 1675 to 1685. Gabriel, *Angola,* pp. 156-7.

Congo, evangelization in the The first missionary group to come to sub-Saharan Africa arrived in São Salvador in 1490. The six priests, members of the order of Saint John the Evangelist, were part of a group sent by King João II. The missionaries met Nzinga-a-Cuum, then instructed and baptized him on May 3, 1491, in his *kraal* (q.v.) Mbanza. He was named João I and acknowledged King of Congo by the Portuguese. The Jesuits organized missions in São Salvador in 1548, the Dominicans and Franciscans had several missions in the territory around 1570, but the most active were the Italian Capuchins who arrived in 1640. The Capuchin record is arguably the best of any missionary work in Africa up to the present. *Pratica Missionaria* was written c.1760 by a Capuchin and describes how their mission work was done at the time. Brasio, *Historia,* pp. 176-7; Duffy, *Portuguese Africa*, pp. 11-12; Gabriel, *Angola,* p. 56.

Congo Kingdom The Congo Kingdom originated sometime in the four-teenth century when King Nimi, a Lukemi of the Bungu chiefdom near the present Boma, conquered the Congo Plateau, a tableland that includes the site of São Salvador. The invaders allied themselves by marriage to the main lineages of the region and King Nimi was accepted as political overlord. He subdued several minor chiefdoms in the region and took the title of Manicongo (q.v.). One of his successors, King Nzinga-a-Cuum, met and befriended the Portuguese when they arrived in 1483. He was converted to Christianity, baptized, and took the name João I. The Portuguese established diplomatic relations with the king and promised to educate his people. His son, later King Afonso I, requested and obtained missionaries, teachers, and colonist to help develop the country. There were about twenty-four kings from 1504 to 1678 when the kingdom was destroyed by civil war. It never fully recovered. In the twentieth century, Congo nationalists re-established the monarchy, but after independence in 1975, the Angolan government did not recognized its existence. Vansina, *Kingdoms of the Savanna,* pp. 38, 41, 257; GEPB.

Congo Kingdom, restoration of the   After its destruction by civil war in 1678, the idea of restoring the Old Congo Kingdom kept recurring during the colonial period. The first recorded movement to restore the splendor of the past occurred in 1704-6 in northern Angola, headed by Chimpa Vita (Dona Beatriz), the woman who founded the Antonian sect (q.v.). This group preached radical doctrines that featured black saviors and saints and urged the restoration of the kingdom to its former strength. In 1891 in eastern Angola, another movement, led by N'Engana Zambi, preached anti-Portuguese messages and favored reviving the old empire. In the 1960s Tocoism (q.v.) espoused similar ideas. Wheeler, *Angola,* pp. 153-5; GEPB.

Congo River   The second-longest river in Africa, it is 2,716 mi. (4,371 km) long from its source in Central Africa to the Atlantic and is only exceeded by the Nile (4,157 mi.; 6,690 km). It was discovered by Diogo Cão who landed on the left bank in 1483. Its lower course was explored by a British expedition in 1816, its headstream by David Livingstone in 1867-73, and its entire length by Henry M. Stanley around 1874. Duffy, *Portuguese Africa,* pp. 5-6; GEPB; WNGD.

Congo village   In the sixteenth century, the village was the basic unit of political and social structure of the Congo Kingdom. Every village was matrilineally organized. The village compound was the place to live, cultivate the land, and die; there were no scattered huts in the countryside. In the hamlet the headman's family and the families of his dependents, related or unrelated, gathered to celebrate community events and religious festivals. The village patriarch was a direct descendant in the matrilineal lineage of the founder of the settlement. There were freemen, slaves, criminals, and captives, all residing in the village. Vansina, *Kingdoms of the Savanna,* p. 41.

conhecenças das terras (Pg.)   "Knowledge of land features." In the late fifteenth century, navigators in the Atlantic and Indian oceans described the characteristics of the seacoasts in terms of the color and current of the sea, the kinds of fish and sea birds observed in different latitudes and localities, and the dissimilar varieties of seaweed. At this time, Portuguese pilots relied heavily on their accumulated knowledge of land and sea features for the long and dangerous trips into uncharted waters. Costa, *A Marinha,* p. 344; Boxer, *The Portuguese,* p. 28. *See also* sinais da terras pela aves, sinais da terras pela plantas maritima.

conhecenças e sinais (Pg.) "Knowledge of natural history and peoples." Term used by navigators in the late fifteenth century to describe the mountains, forests, plains, plants, birds, animals, and people they encountered along the West African coast. Costa, *A Marinharia dos Descombrimentos,* p. 344. *See also* sinais da terras pelas aves, sinais da terras pela plantas maritima.

conquistador (Pg.) In colonial Portuguese Africa, an adventurer who took land and towns by force for the king of Portugal, defended his most remote holdings, acted as his ambassador, and held important bureaucratic positions in the government. GEPB. *See* degredado.

conscription In Portuguese Africa, Portugal depended entirely on draftees for its armed forces. A conscript was incorporated into regular battalions led by professional and non-commissioned officers, most of them assigned from Portugal. Around 1960, about 15 percent of the Mozambique army were Africans. In other African colonies the percentages were similar. Herrick, *Area Handbook*, p. 299.

contract labor, system of After the abolition of slavery in Angola and elsewhere in Portuguese Africa, a contract labor system was established to which all former slaves, then called *libertos*, were subjected. By a statute of 1875, a freedman was obliged to contract his services, preferably to his former master, for two years although wages, working conditions, housing, and health care were not specified. This has been called the first Portuguese native labor code. Under the vagrancy clause added to this statute any "nonproductive" African could be judged a vagrant and be forced to contract his services. Duffy, *Portuguese Africa,* pp. 152-3; GEPB.

copal (Pg.) A tropical tree (*Trachylobium hornemannianum*) from which a resin used to make varnish and lacquer is extracted. Copal, known in Africa since antiquity, is also found in fossil and semifossil form in Cabo Delgado, northern Mozambique, and the Atlantic coast of Angola. Direct reports on copal were recorded beginning in 1622. In the colonial period, copal resin was exported to Portugal and Brazil. From 1878 to 1872, the average annual export was about 300,000 kilos. In 1958 the export reached 900,000 kilos. There are many local names including *almeidina, anime, eleni tacamaca*, and others. Ficalho, *Plantas Uteis*, pp. 155-6. GEPB.

Copper Belt Name applied to the Katanda area of Zambia, near the Angolan border, where since 1923 one of the largest industrial complexes in Africa has been developed using British South African capital. This extensive copper deposit was known by Africans before the arrival of the Portuguese c.1600.

The Benguela railroad in southern Angola connects the copper belt with Lobito on the Atlantic coast. Wheeler, *Angola*, pp. 68, 136.

copra Dried pulp, or meat, of the fruit of the coconut palm (*Cocos nucifera* L.) from which coconut oil is extracted. It is used in Mozambique and elsewhere by Africans for cooking and to manufacture soap. Coconut palm plantation are established along the coastal belt of the Zambezia and Nampula provinces of Mozambique and elsewhere. Copra production is dependent on the vagaries of weather; too little rain hinders the growth of the palms and too much prevents the harvest from drying. In 1965, 65 tons of copra were produced and exported to Europe. Kaplan, *Area Handbook*, pp. 148, 151.

COREMO (Pg.) Acronym for *Comité Revolucionario de Moçambique* (Revolutionary Committee of Mozambique), a nationalist party organized in 1965 in Lusaka, Zambia, by people opposed to FRELIMO (q.v.); it was a small group engaged in limited guerrilla warfare in Mozambique. Based in Lusaka, COREMO engaged in military activities in the Tete area, where they attacked the Mukangadzi settlement near the Cabora Bassa Dam (q.v.) in 1971. COREMO subsequently faded away from lack of material and financial assistance. Henriksen, *Mozambique,* pp. 176-7, 189.

Corisco An island in the Gulf of Guiné discovered by Portuguese navigators in 1486. It soon became a slave station. Mota, *Toponimos,* pp. 131-2.

Corpo Santo, Brotherhood of A religious and mutual-aid brotherhood formed c.1440 by fishermen in several Algarve coastal towns such as Lagos, Silves, Faro, and Olhão. Apparently some of the members settled in West African ports during the period of the Discovery (q.v.). In 1679, a sailors' church was built in Luanda. Iria, *O Algarve no Descobrimento,* Congresso da Guiné, 1946, I:196. *See also* Corpo Santo Island.

Corpo Santo, Igreja do (Pg.) A church built in Luanda, Angola, c.1679 to honor St. Pedro Gonçalves, Portuguese patron saint of sailors. This seaman's parish, located near the port on the west side of the city, had a sailors' confraternity empowered to collect fees from each ship arriving at the port. Gabriel, *Angola*, pp. 121-2.

Corubal River (Afr.) One of the major rivers of Guinea-Bissau, its headwaters are in the vicinity of Labé on the Futa-Djallon (q.v.) Plateau; the river changes names several times between Labé and its confluence with the Geba (q.v.) in the upper portion of its estuary. The Corubal is about 280 mi. (450 km.) long, and provides a convenient route for the export goods and, in the colonial period, for shipping slaves to the coast. HDRGC.

Costa de Malagüeta   The West African coast roughly from the Gambia River south to the Cabo das Palmas, an area split between Sierra Leone and Liberia. It stretches about forty leagues (280 mi.; 450 km). Discovered c. 1470 by Fernão Gomes who bought the *malagüeta* (q.v.) monopoly, this area was the center of the *malagüeta* trade from 1470 to 1550. Godinho, *A Economia,* pp. 199-200.

COTONANG   Acronym for *Companhia Geral dos Algodões de Angola* ("Angola General Cotton Company.") The largest of several cotton-growing companies, COTONANG had the concession for the Cassanje region east of Malange. The local people were forced to grow cotton and sell their crops at low prices fixed by the government. In January 1961, the workers went on strike, refusing to pay taxes as a protest against the abuses of the system. Reprisals by the Portuguese resulted in villages being destroyed and people killed. This Cotton Revolt (q.v.), as it came to be known, was a precursor of the nationalist uprisings of February and March 1961. After independence, the company, along with several other foreign firms abandoned by their owners, was nationalized in 1978. HDA.

Cotonocracia (Pg.)   "Cottonocracy." A term used in 1961 government reports to refer to compulsory policy regarding Angolan cotton whereby Africans were forced to work as cotton producers in several regions of the colony and to sell the product at prices set by the government. Pelissier, *La Colonie,* pp. 422-3.

cotrim (Pg.)   An old Portuguese copper coin with a weight of 1.8 grams and a value equal to five *ceitils* (q.v.). It circulated in Lisbon and elsewhere in Portugal between 1490 and 1491. GEPB.

cotton   The soft white filaments filling the seed pods of various shrubby plants (genus *Gossypium*) of the mallow family, native to the tropics. The species *G. herbaceum* is considered to be native to West Africa but is rarely found south of the equator. The species *G. arboreum*, apparently introduced by the Portuguese from India at the time of the Discovery (q.v.), is cultivated in Angola, Cape Verde, Mozambique, and elsewhere in Africa. Since the mid-nineteenth century, Portugal had encouraged commercial production of cotton for domestic use and export. In 1953 Portugal imposed a quota, increasing production to supply Europe. By 1962 cotton production constituted between 20 and 33 percent of the total value of exports from Mozambique. Ficalho, *Plantas Uteis,* pp. 98-99; Herrick *Area Handbook,* pp. 194, 201, 237.

cotton, forced cultivation of   *See* agricultura dirigida; COTONANG; Mozambique, forced cotton cultivation in.

cotton in southern Angola Cotton was the main crop in southern Angola c.1830, and cotton production was officially encouraged by the government from 1850 on. The first spectacular increase in cotton production came about as result of the American Civil War (1861-1865) when the price of cotton rose in southern Angola, reaching a peak of about 15 percent more per kilo than previously. As a result, every scrap of available land was planted to cotton. After 1864 the price fell steadily. From the mid-1870s to the late 1900s, prices were a fraction of the old price. In 1920 average prices rose on the world market and remained high throughout 1920s in spite of violent fluctuations. Angolan cotton producers could not take advantage of these price rises due to changes in agricultural production, deterioration of cotton germ plasm, reduction of soil fertility, and a series of droughts. By 1929 cotton planting was greatly reduced. Clarence-Smith, *Slaves, Peasants,* pp. 23-4, 29-30.

Cotton Revolt A bloody uprising that occurred on January 1, 1961, in Baixo de Cassange, Malange district, against the government policy of mandatory cotton cultivation and obligatory sale at a low set price to COTONANG (q.v.). Wheeler, *Angola,* p. 174.

covado (Pg.) (1) An ancient unit of length equivalent to between 0.66 and 0.68 cms which was used c.1440 in naval construction and navigation. DMA.

covado (Pg.) (2) In Portuguese Africa in the sixteenth century, a cloth measure equivalent to 25.9 English inches, or 65.7 cms. Duncan, *Atlantic Islands,* p. 261.

cowrie (Afr.) Any of the numerous marine gastropod mollusks of the family *Cypraeidae* widely distributed in warm seas. Cowries have domed oval shells that have a beautiful sheen, like porcelain, and are often highly colored; formerly used as currency in parts of African. HDA. *See also* cowrie as currency.

cowrie as currency A unit of currency used c.1670 in Dahomey and along the Slave Coast (qq.v.). In 1679 its value was equal to one-eighth of a farthing or one-tenth of a pfennig. It was a standard currency in Ouidah, Calabar, Porto Novo, Ardra, and other slaving ports in the Gulf of Guiné. In Dahomey (q.v.) cowries were associated with different traders: the Berbers in Tuareg and later the Arabs, Portuguese, and Venetian merchants. In the Mali Empire, the cowrie was a standard currency. In 1455 Alvise Cadamosto, a Venetian explorer and merchant who had never seen a cowrie, described it surprisingly well from hearsay. Polanyi, *Dahomey,* pp. 93, 175, 179-80; Fernandes, *Description,* p. 158. *See also* Cypraea annulus, Cypraea moneta, Olivetta nana, zimbo

cría de pé (Pg.) In Guinea-Bissau c.1650, a walking infant or toddler of slave parents, usually sold as a member of a family unit in Brazilian markets. Carreira, *As Companhias Pombalinas*, BCG, 1968, xxxiii(91/92):307. *See also* cría de peito.

cría de peito (Pg.) In Guinea-Bissau c.1650, a suckling infant of slave parents, usually sold as a member of a family unit in Brazilian markets. Carreira, *As Companhias Pombalinas*, BCG, 1968, xxiii(91/92):307. *See also* cría de pé.

crioulo (Pg.) (1) "Native, creole." Anything native to or anyone or anything born in a colony. GEPB.

Crioulo (Pg.) (2) Creole dialect spoken and written in Guinea-Bissau and Cape Verde since early in the colonial period. The *Crioulo* dialect is characterized by pronunciation, grammar, and syntax differing from standard Portuguese. Wilson, *The Crioulo of Guiné*, p. vii.

Crioulo de Guiné (Pg.) A *lingua franca* of the 768,000 people of Guinea-Bissau; the first language spoken by Africans born and bred in large towns. *Crioulo* as spoken in Guinea-Bissau and São Tomé has a greater proportion of African loan-words than that spoken in Cape Verde. It is also spoken in Ziguinchor, Senegal, just north of the border of Guinea-Bissau. Wilson, *The Crioulo of Guiné*, p. vii. *See also* Crioulo de Cabo Verde.

Crioulo de Cabo Verde (Pg.) A Cape Verdian dialect of Portuguese using Portuguese morphology and African phonetic systems with words from both stocks, sometimes used to imply a mixed Cape Verdian cultural heritage. *Crioulo* has deep importance in the emotional and psychological makeup of the average Cape Verdian, having grown out of the historical exigencies of the West African slave heritage. Wilson, *The Crioulo of Guiné,* p. viii; Duncan, *Atlantic Islands,* pp. 195-6. *See also* Crioulo de Guiné.

Cristão (Pg.) "Christian." In Guinea-Bissau and elsewhere in Portuguese Africa, a detribalized and semi-Christian descendant of Africans who were converted by missionaries in the early colonial period. Mota, *Guiné Portuguesa*, I:264.

cross staff An ancient nautical instrument used to measure the altitude of stars and planets; it was a wooden rod marked with graduations 3-4 in. (7-10 cm) apart crossed vertically by smaller one-*soalha* marks. The observer looked at the star over the upper angle and at the horizon through the lower.

The angle formed between the point of observation, the star, and the horizon gave the altitude. This medieval instrument was also called a *balestrilha*, or *baculo* (staff), *do São Tiago* by Portuguese navigators, but it was not used by them before 1500. Costa, *A Marinha dos Descobrimentos,* pp. 26-27.

cruzado (Pg.)   A gold coin originally equal to 324 *reis.* In 1472 it was revalued at 300 *reis,* 390 *reis* in 1496, and 400 in 1514. At 23.75 carats, it weighed 3.54 g. In 1538 it was reduced to 22.625 carats but its value remained 400 *reis.* Axelson, *Portuguese in South-East,* p. 244; DN.

Cruzeiro do Sul, O   A progressive periodical published in Luanda in 1873 by a group of radical European and African intellectuals. It advocated republican solutions to Angolan problems and called for sweeping changes in the colony. It was a marked departure from doctrinaire Angolan journalism, signaling the earliest beginnings of Angolan nationalism. Wheeler, *Angola,* p. 93.

Cuale (Afr.)   A western Angolan village in the Malange district, the scene of terrorism and violence between nationalists and the Portuguese army c. 1965 during the struggle for independence. Pelissier, *La Colonie,* p. 561.

Cuama River (Afr.)   Also known as the Lubo-Cuama Velho, it is one of two branches of the lower Zambezi River, the other is the Quelimane. Portuguese merchants were very active along the Cuama and its many streams around 1509, trading European cloth and other goods for gold and ivory. It was described c. 1558 by Diogo Homem in his unpublished atlas now in the British Museum. Axelson, *Portuguese in South-East,* pp. 71, 78; GEPB.

Cuando River (Afr.)   A river about 500 mi. (800 km) long that rises in central Angola and flows southeast, forming part of the boundary between Angola and Zambia. It continues east along the boundary of Botswana and empties into the Zambezi River just above Victoria Falls. Although *pombeiros* (q.v.) had crisscrossed the Cuando and the Zambezi rivers for many years before, this isolated region was not formally explored until 1798 when a Portuguese force came to the area from Tete, Mozambique. Vansina, *Kingdoms of the Savannah,* pp. 172, 179; GEPB.

Cuando-Cubango province (Afr.)   Situated in the southeastern corner of Angola on the border of Zambia and Namibia. It is one of the most remote and least populated areas of Angola. The major river, the Cubango, enters the Okavango Swamp in Botswana. The Cubango's tributaries are seasonal but in the eastern part of the Cubango watershed, the area is better watered and has permanent streams, tall grass, and scattered forests with cattle and timber potential. The broad and evenly flowing Cuando River, a tributary of the

Zambezi, is a useful waterway for the people of the area. The capital of the province, Menongue, is linked to the Atlantic coast by the Mossâmedes railway. GEPB; HDA.

Cuanza-Norte (Afr.)   A district of Luanda province, its seat was Vila Salazar, now Ndalatando, situated north of the Cuanza River. The district includes the municipalities of Cazengo, Cambambe, and Ambaca with a total population in 1960 of 122,012 of which 117,410 were Africans. One of the most acculturated areas in Angola, it is an important coffee-producing region. GEPB. *See also* Cuanza-Sul.

Cuanza River (Afr.)   A river 600 mi. (965 km) long, that rises in south-central Angola and flows northwest to the Atlantic near Luanda; one of the most important waterways of Angola. The Portuguese explored the lower Cuanza around 1775 but for a long time were unable to advance because of violent opposition by the Jagas. Trimingham, *Conflict and Trade,* pp. 17, 19.

Cuanza-Sul (Afr.)   A district created in 1914, its seat is Novo Redondo. It includes the municipalities of Porto Amboim, Amboim, Libolo, Quibala, and Seles. In 1960 its population was 289,257 of whom 282,165 were Africans. It is a rich agricultural region raising cotton, coffee, grain, and cattle. GEPB. *See also* Cuanza-Norte.

Cuanza Valley (Afr.)   A land drained by the Cuanza River, the largest Angolan river after the Congo. It was a corridor of westward migration for African peoples from the east and the north. Since the founding of Luanda in 1575, the valley has acted as a highway for the eastward penetration of commerce and colonization for Portuguese newcomers and settlers. This has led to a concentration of agricultural development along the valley to the detriment of the other parts of Angola. Wheeler, *Angola,* pp. 3, 5.

Cubal (Afr.)   African village seat of the Ganda municipality in the Benguela province of southern Angola. This settlement, populated mainly by Ovimbundu people, was a center of anti-Portuguese guerrillas and of Tocoism (q.v.) in the 1960s. Pelissier, *La Colonie,* pp. 176, 555.

Cubango River (Afr.)   Also known as the Okavango; a river of southwest Central Africa about 1,000 mi (1,600 km) long rising in central Angola. It flows south and then east, forming a section of the boundary between Angola and Namibia, then crosses the Caprivi Strip and empties into the Okavango Basin, a large marsh north of Lake Ngami in northern Botswana. The Cubango territory was explored in 1886-9 by Arturo de Paiva who built two forts, Maria Pia and Princesa Amelia, to control rebellious chiefs. GEPB; WNGD.

Cubans in Angola   *See* Angola, Cubans in.

cubata (Afr.)   In Angola, a hut made of branches with a round thatched roof, occupied by a single family. GEPB. *See also* libata.

cuchá (Mand.)   In Guinea-Bissau, a tropical wild and cultivated edible herb (*Hibiscus sabdariffa* L.). Its tender leaves are boiled in oil and vinegar to prepare a popular dish, and also used in folk medicine to treat fevers. In Angola, it is called *husa*. Ficalho, *Plantas Uteis*, p. 97; Carreira, *As Companhias Pombalinas*, BCG, 1968, xxiii(91/92):324,

cuchá, arroz de (Pg.)   *"Cuchá* rice." A dish prepared by boiling rice with a mixture of salt, vinegar, and oil, popular among the Mandingos of Guinea-Bissau. This food was taken by slaves to Brazil and today *arroz de cuchá* is popular in Maranhão and Pará. Carreira, *As Companhias Pombalinas*, BCG, 1968, xxiii(91/92):324.

Cucumbi (Afr.)   An African village and Catholic mission in Lunda province in northeastern Angola, located on the route from Malange to Henrique Carvalho. In 1923 there were religious riots between followers of African cults and Protestant fundamentalists. Pelissier, *La Colonie,* p. 182.

CUF (Companhia União Fabril) (Pg.)   "United Manufacturing Company." One of Portugal's largest conglomerates representing approximately ten percent of Portugal's total corporate capital, it is a multinational concern with extensive investments in Portuguese Africa. It is involved in textiles, agriculture, petrochemicals, steel, and shipbuilding. It has its own merchant ships and has tens of thousands of employees. CUF is primarily owned by the powerful Mello family. It dominated the former colonial economies and has connections to American and French capital as well. In Guinea-Bissau, the two major CUF affiliates were *Casa Gouveia* and the Antonio Silva Corporation. In Angola it had a plantation established in 1952 on the bank of the M'bridge River which became the scene of violence and terrorism by nationalist guerrillas in March 1961. Pelissier, *La Colonie,* pp. 484, 499; HDRGC.

Cuilo (Afr.)   An administrative post, Camaxilo municipality, Lunda province, in northeastern Angola. In 1960 its population was 1,030 of whom 968 were Africans. GEPB.

Cuilo Futa (Afr.)   A village in Uige district in northeastern Angola where in 1961 nationalists attacked the settlement and killed many villagers. The

Portuguese government was forced to evacuate the town and move its inhabitants elsewhere. Pelissier, *La Colonie*, p. 571. *See also* Cuilo Pombo.

Cuilo Pombo (Afr.) A village in Uige district in northeastern Angola that was a region of terrorism and struggle between nationalist and Portuguese forces during the War for Independence. In April 1961 it was evacuated by the government. Pelissier, *La Colonie*, p. 571. *See also* Cuilo Futa.

Cuimba (Afr.) An African village located near the site of the old city of São Salvador do Congo, 19 mi. (30 km) from Leopoldville, Zaire. In March 1961 this settlement, a center of prosperous coffee plantations, was attacked and burned by nationalist forces. Pelissier, *La Colonie*, pp. 484, 499.

Cuio (Afr.) A colonial fishing village on the Atlantic coast at the mouth of the Coporo River in southern Angola. Also known as Luacho, it first appeared in a 1790 chart. GEPB.

çuku-ó (Mand.) Among the Mandingos of Guinea-Bissau, a beverage prepared from the leaves of a tropical plant (*Annona senegalensis*) and used to stimulate an increase of milk in nursing mothers. Carreira, *Mandingas*, p. 241.

culemba (Afr.) In the colonial period, an Angolan wedding ritual that included pre-marital sexual experience, dances, prayers, and a bride's payment. GEPB.

cult of the ancestors *See* ancestors, cult of the.

Cultura (Pg.) "Culture." A monthly journal of scientific, literary, and artistic news published by the *Sociedade Cultural de Angola* from 1945 to 1951, appearing a total of nineteen times. After six years of silence, *Cultura* resumed publication in 1957 under new directorship and with a metropolitan and international scope. Each issue intensified the profound nationalistic consciousness on the part of Angolan intellectuals. Hamilton, *Voices*, pp. 65-68, 129.

cultura de canna (Pg.) "Sugar cane cultivation." Sugar cane (*Saccharum officinale* L.) was introduced by the Portuguese to Madeira c.1450. In 1452, Prince Henry signed a contract with Diogo de Teive to build a water mill to press the canes. Prestage, *The Portuguese Pioneers*, p. 42; Tenreiro, *A Ilha*, p. 68. *See also* sugar, sugar cane.

cultura obrigatoria (Pg.) "Mandatory tillage." A coercive agricultural policy imposed on all able-bodied Africans by the Portuguese government in

1898 to work the land or suffer stiff penalties. The aim was to produce sufficient food for their families and their community. Cunha, *O Trabalho Indigena,* pp. 170-71. *See also* trabalho obrigatorio.

Culucumba (Ron.) In Mozambique, a high Ronga god, creator of all things. *Culucumba* is unknowable and unconcerned with the lives of the people. This is in contrast with the spirits of the ancestors who constantly protect, care for, and guide the people. Herrick, *Area Handbook,* p. 112.

Cum Sicut Nobis (Lat.) A letter sent by Pope Alexander VI on August 29, 1499, to King Manuel of Portugal granting him the right to patronage to build cathedrals, churches, monasteries, convents, and chapels in all the African lands discovered or to be discovered by Portugal. Pinto Rema, *A Primeira Evangelização,* BCG, 1966, xxi(82):316.

Cunene (Afr.) A government-planned agricultural colony established halfway up the Cunene River in southern Angola in 1953, in an area with little Portuguese control. By 1960 there were 281 families in the *colonato* (q.v.). It became a rich ranching region that resisted government control and enforced cooperative labor. HDA. *See also* Cela.

Cunene River (Afr.) A river 700 mi. (1126 km) long in southwestern Angola. Its lower course forms a section of the boundary between Angola and Namibia and in its westward descent to the coast there are several cataracts, most notably the Ruacana Falls. WNGD.

Cunga (Afr.) An African settlement in Uige province, northern Angola, 2.5 mi. (4 km) from Carmona City. This is an important coffee-producing area where as late as 1962 African laborers were forced to work under Portuguese colonial law for a meager salary and many laborers fled to the nearby forests. The year before, in 1961, Cunga had been the scene of terrorism and violence between nationalists and Portuguese forces. Pelissier, *La Colonie,* pp. 465(n), 536(n).

curador (Pg.) "Guardian." In Angola and elsewhere in Portuguese Africa around 1899, a government official in charge of protecting and defending the rights of laborers. Among his duties were checking labor contracts to see that they were written according to labor code regulations. Because the *curador* was often ignorant of the local language, the contract was usually just a formality. Duffy, *Portuguese Africa,* p. 159.

Curadoria (Pg.) "Guardianship." In Portuguese Africa, a government agency in charge of advising, defending, and protecting African laborers. In

Mozambique the *Curadoria* was also in charge of recruiting laborers for local plantations and, mainly, for the South Africa goldfields. Duffy, *Portuguese Africa*, p. 159.

Curadoria do Transvaal (Pg.) "Guardianship of Transvaal." A Portuguese government agency in charge of protecting and controlling African laborers' working conditions, housing, health, and education in the South African goldfields. Duffy, *Portuguese Africa*, pp. 159-60.

currency in Portuguese Africa   In Portuguese Africa, according to Portuguese law, each territory had its own currency, its own annual budget, and its own system of taxation. In reality, however, financial autonomy was greatly restricted throughout the colonial period. As stated in the Portuguese Constitution of 1933, "The economic organization of the Portuguese Overseas Provinces shall form part of the general economic organization of the Portuguese Nation and shall thereby take its place in the world economy." Herrick, *Area Handbook,* p. 273. *See also* kwanza.

curva (Pg.) (1)   A tax imposed in 1630 by the government requiring Portuguese residents of Mozambique Island to pay a 1,000 *curva* tax equivalent to 200 *cruzados* (q.v.) per annum to trade in the Monomotapa Kingdom.

curva (Pg.) (2)   In the colonial period, a gift of cloth given to an African chief in return for which he granted permission to trade in the chiefdom. Axelson, *Portuguese in South-East*, p. 244.

cuscuz (Afr.)   In Cape Verde and elsewhere in Portuguese Africa, cornmeal bread cooked in butter. In Mozambique it is called *alcuscuz*. GDLP.

customshouse   At the time of the Discovery (q.v.), a government office where duties were paid and ships were cleared for entering or leaving Lisbon and other ports. Customshouses were located in seaports and at the border of towns throughout Portugal. Once commerce expanded with the import of African goods and slaves, King Afonso V reorganized the system c.1460 and ordered that all merchandise, such as spices and slaves, brought from Guiné should be taken to the *Grande Alfandega* (Main Customshouse) of Lisbon to pay duties. Around 1510, King Manuel I established seven *casas* (customhouses) in Lisbon, each in charge of collecting duties imposed on clothing, spices, gold, slaves, and other goods. At one time, there were fifteen customhouses in Lisbon alone. After the discovery of Brazil in 1500, the Crown established a royal monopoly on *pau-Brasil* (Brazilwood), spices, and slaves, imposing a 10 percent duty on all precious metals and a variable percentage on other goods, such as sugar, ivory, orchil (q.v.), and other products. The register of the *Grande Alfadenga* of Lisbon began in October 1587 and lasted until 1889, a period exceeding 300 years. DHP; GEPB.

Cypraea annulus (Lat.) The scientific name for a kind of cowrie (q.v.) shell used as money. This currency reached Dahomey (q.v.) and the west coast of Africa by sea c. 1500. It was heavier and larger than the *Cypraea moneta* (q.v.) and was considered second-rate, being bluish-grayish with a yellow-ringed body. It originates on the east coast of Africa, opposite Zanzibar. As currency it had to compete with gold and the much handier and more attractive *Cypraea moneta*. Polanyi, *Dahomey,* p. 176. *See also* cowrie as currency.

Cypraea moneta (Lat.) The scientific name for a kind of cowrie (q.v.) shell used as money and considered more valuable than the *Cypraea annulus* (q.v.) shells. According to the Venetian explorer Alvise Cadamosto writing in 1455, it was used in trade in Guiné. Although the Venetian explorer had never seen a *Cypraea moneta,* nevertheless he correctly described it from hearsay, adding specific information about its use in commerce and its movement from Persian traders to Venice and from Venice by the desert route of the Western Sahara and the area of the Niger River. Fifty years later Valentim Fernandes mentions that *Cypraea moneta* was still being used in Western Sudan. Fernandes, *Description*, p. 158; Polanyi, *Dahomey,* p. 180. *See also* cowrie as currency.

{ D }

Dahomey (Afr.)   An ancient kingdom on the Gulf of Guiné established by Dakodoou, chief of the Allada, an indigenous people; also known as Benin. The navigators Pedro de Cintra and João Santarem encountered the region in 1470 and soon the Portuguese began trading in ivory, gold, and slaves brought from inland by local rulers. By the beginning of the seventeenth century, Dahomey was an important center of the slave trade. In 1680, the Portuguese built the fortress São Baptista de Ajuda, known as Ouidah (q.v.). From there, they shipped thousands of slaves to São Tomé and Brazil. Portugal was able to keep up good relations with the kings of Dahomey, particularly King Gezo (1818-58). Portugal kept Ouidah until 1960 when it was taken by the Republic of Dahomey. Duffy, *Portuguese Africa*, p. 137; HDB.

Dakar, emigration of Cape Verdians to   The capital of Senegal has been a port of entry, and often of settlement, for Cape Verde's emigrants since 1900. Children born to Cape Verdian parents have appeared in baptismal registers there beginning in 1903. In 1973, Cape Verdians and their descendants in Dakar numbered 987 households with a total of 4,585 individuals, of whom 2,166 were male and 2,419 female. Carreira, *The People,* pp. 69, 75.

damba (Afr.) (1)   The uniform and attractive bean of a tropical leguminous plant (*Abrus precatorius*) of Africa and Asia. The *damba* bean, also known as the rosary pea, is bright scarlet with a black spot. It served as unit of medicinal weight and a weight for jewelry and precious metals. This unit was used in colonial West African trade around 1732. Polanyi, *Dahomey,* p. 153.

Damba (Pg.) (2)   In northwestern Angola, a *colonato* (q.v.) settled in 1951 by 245 Portuguese and African families accompanied by fifteen white employees, all working to improve food production. This government-subsidized settlement was abandoned in 1961 due to unhealthy living conditions. Caetano, *Os Nativos*, p. 85. *See also* Caconda.

Dambu de Africa   "The African Sun." A Portuguese-Xironga bilingual newspaper published in Lourenço Marques in 1921, edited by João Tomás Chambene and Benjamin Moniz. It ceased publication in 1922. Dias, *A Imprensa,* p. 78.

dance groups In São Tomé all villages and towns have informal teams that dance competitively. Each village's group wears flamboyant clothes, distinctive for each settlement. Flags and banners of various kinds form part of the regalia. Music is provided by a band playing African instruments. Apparently this popular tradition has been the origin of several well-known folk dances, including the *danço congo* and *socopé* (qq.v.). Garfield, *History,* pp. 244-5.

danço congo (Afr.) A mute show in which the performers express themselves with gestures. It is purely African in theme and spirit, derived from Congolese festivals which were carried to São Tomé Island by slaves c.1500. It is a pantomime in which a jester plays a planter who rents his farm to his laborers; at his death they take possession of the estate and the plantation is ruined by disorder, theft, injustice, and abuses. Also called Dance of the Captain of Congo. Garfield, *History,* p. 244. *See also* socopé.

dandanda (Afr.) A protected Angolan village in an isolated region headed by a traditional African *soba*, or chief, chosen by the Portuguese when the nationalist uprising began to organize c.1960. As the war progressed, colonists' brutality and injustice made some *sobas* sympathetic to the nationalist cause, and by 1968 *dandandas* often were centers of opposition to the Portuguese government. Marcum, *The Angolan Revolution*, II:213, 219-20.

Dande (Afr.) A river in northern Angola. An old settlement in the region had a church by 1759 and in 1807 served as an army stud farm for horse breeding. The rich alluvial banks of the Dande River were developed as sugar plantations c.1840 for alternative exports to help sustain Angola's economy after the slave trade was officially abolished. Silva Rego, *O Ultramar*, pp. 62, 274, 280.

dar (Ar.) "Home, country." In Portuguese Africa and elsewhere, a house, habitation, land, or country. This Arab word is used in various combinations such as Dar es-Salaam (q.v.), the Country of Peace. Vail, *Capitalism,* p. 393.

Dar es-Salaam (Ar.) The capital city of Tanzania, formerly Tanganyika and Zanzibar. In the early 1960s two major political parties were organized in the city. The first, MANU (q.v.), with Matthew Mmole as president and Lawrence M. Millinga, both former leaders of a Kenyan trade union, was organized in 1961 to oppose Portuguese rule and establish an independent state. MANU limited itself to organizing workers in Zanzibar, Tanganyika, and Kenya. The other, FRELIMO (q.v.), was founded in Dar es-Salaam in June of 1962 by Eduardo Mondlane and others. Vail, *Capitalism*, p. 393; DHP.

days of the Congo week In the Kikongo language spoken around 1880 in São Salvador do Congo, the week had only four days, *nsona, nkandu, konzo,* and *nkenge* (qq.v.). BeAD.

decolonization *See* exodus of settlers.

deferred payment In Mozambique, a system of withholding part of the salary earned by Mozambican laborers in South African gold mines, to be paid out back in Mozambique at the end of the labor contract period (usually 18 months). The system was begun in 1906 by the South African mining industry. Rita-Ferreira, *O Movimento Migratorio,* pp. 116-7.

degredado (Pg.) In Africa and elsewhere, a convict legally exiled. These deportees, including an occasional physician and numerous politicians, had various skills and crafts but often preferred trading or tavern-keeping to other pursuits. In Mozambique and Angola, some organized trading groups that often backed rebellions, others were successful slave traders. Wheeler, *Angola,* pp. 43-5, 94; Silva Rego, *O Ultramar*, p. 209. *See also* lançado.

De Instrumento Secretorum (Lat.) A book, also known as *Tractatus Instrumenti Astronomi,* written in Hebrew by Levi ben Gerson in 1432 and translated into Latin, contains the first description of the cross-staff, called *baculus Jacobi* in some manuscripts, whence the designation "Jacob's staff." Based on the same principle as the *kamal* (q.v.), the instrument, at first only used for astronomical observations, was later adopted by the Portuguese for navigation. First, the height of the sun or another star was measured; then the latitude of a place could be calculated by taking twice the angle between horizon and star. One extreme of the cross-piece is aimed at the star, the other at the horizon. This angle is given by the ratio of the length of the staff at the point at which the cross-piece is adjusted for a given observation, or its tangent; ben Gerson was not acquainted with the tangent and used the sine of the angle instead. Cortesão, *History*, I:210.

Delagoa Bay (Eng.) A bay on the extreme southeastern coast of Mozambique, 55 mi. (90 km) long. The city of Maputo (q.v.) lies at its head. Discovered by the Portuguese in 1502, the neighboring territory was explored by Lourenço Marques in 1544. A trading settlement existed there between 1721 and 1730. The islands in the bay were occupied by the British in 1861, but were also claimed by the Portuguese. When Transvaal attempted to occupy them in 1868, this brought the dispute to a head. The islands were awarded to the Portuguese by arbitration in 1875. After the building of the Delagoa Bay Railroad, which connected Maputo with Pretoria as an economic outlet for the Transvaal in 1895, it became the subject of a British agreement with Germany in 1898 and with Portugal in 1899. GEPB; WNGD.

Delagoa Bay Directory First published by A.W. Bayly & Co. in Lourenço Marques in 1898, this annual directory of commercial businesses appeared only in English until 1914 when the Portuguese version *Anuário de Lourenço*

Marques was published. Dias, *A Imprensa,* p. 104. *See also* Delagoa Gazette of Shipping and Commercial Intelligence.

Delagoa Gazette of Shipping and Commercial Intelligence The first newspaper published in Lourenço Marques, Mozambique. Owned by Leslie Martyns and James Munro, it appeared under the editorship of James Munro and Jacinto Machado de Farias e Maia on December 22, 1903, and ceased publication after fifty-nine issues in April 1904. It reappeared in new and enlarged form as the *Mozambique Gazette* under the same editorship. In 1913 a supplement entitled *Gazeta de Mozambique,* in Portuguese and English was added. Dias, *A Imprensa,* pp. 68, 71. *See also* Delagoa Bay Directory.

Demba (Afr.) A village 40 mi. (65 km) south of the Cuanza River in Quissama, Angola. In 1583 Jeronimo de Almeida built a fort there to protect the local salt deposits. Salt trading was still active in 1784, partly because rock salt was used locally as currency. GEPB.

Dembos (Afr.) A subdivision of the district and province of Luanda, Angola, with its seat at Quilaye and comprised of the administrative posts of Pango Aluquém, Bula Atumbu, Castendo, and Danje. It is located between the Bengo River in the south and the Danje River north and east of Luanda. GEPB.

Democracia (Pg.) "Democracy." A weekly published in Lourenço Marques, Mozambique, whose first issue appeared on November 9, 1933 and its ninety-first (and last) on November 22, 1935. It was owned by Fernando Tito Martin, edited by Tito Martins, and later by Jose Leitão. Dias, *A Imprensa,* p. 87.

dengue (Afr.) In Portuguese Africa and elsewhere, a contagious, rarely fatal, fever that attacks the bones and the joints. It is transmitted by mites (genera *Repicephalus, Amblioma,* and *Boophilus*). There have been several *dengue* epidemics in Luanda and elsewhere in Angola, mainly among the African population. The most devastating outbreaks occurred in 1864 and 1877. *Revista Medica de Angola,* Luanda, 1928, 2:459-64; 4:330; PDM.

Desertas A group of four small rocky volcanic islands, part of the Madeira archipelago, discovered by Portuguese navigators c.1430. The Desertas are comprised of Deserta Grande, Bugio, Ilheu Chão, and Farilhão or Prego do Mar. An early colonization effort during the time of Prince Henry failed, but the cultivation and export of *urzela* or orchil (q.v.), the orchid lichen used for dying, was established soon after. GEPB; WNGD; *See also* Selvagens.

detribalization The process of an individual African rejecting tribal leadership, ethnic customs, traditions, and rituals and then acquiring simple economic and technological knowledge without completely assimilating Western ideology, values, or behavior. The status of a detribalized African is perceived to be between a "primitive," or non-civilized, individual and a "civilized" European. Great numbers of such Africans are concentrated in urban centers. In Luanda c.1950, there were 96,657 detribalized individuals and 40,482 classified as civilized; in Lourenço Marques c.1950, 45,070 who retained the traditional ways and 18,098 civilized. Cunha, *O Sistema Portugués*, pp. 106-7, 196-7; Caetano, *Os Nativos*, p. 17. *See also* assimilado.

"Deu creou o branco e o preto, o portuguese creou o mulato" (Pg.) "God created the white and the black, the Portuguese have created the mulatto." An old Portuguese saying, appearing during the time of the Discovery (q.v.), when unrestricted miscegenation first began. The term was originally used in Cape Verde (1470), then in Angola (1550). Goemaere, *Le Portugal*, p. 9.

Devon merchants Merchants from Devon, England, who were very active around 1663, exporting wheat to Madeira and other Atlantic Islands. They were favored by a decree of Charles II of England allowing trade between Portuguese islands and England and the English colonies. Duncan, *Atlantic Islands*, pp. 72-72.

Dialonkes A small ethnic group of Guinea-Bissau, presently located east of Duas Fontes (Bangacia). Apparently of Senegambian stock, they have very pronounced Mandingo acculturation, so they are sometimes considered Mandingos. They are partly Islamized as a result of the eighteenth-century Fulani migrations from Futa-Djallon. HDRGC.

DIAMANG Acronmy for Diamond Company of Angola, a private mineral prospecting corporation organized in 1917 in Dundo, Lunda province, eastern Angola. Although the company had no official charter, it quickly associated with the state, becoming the de facto government throughout Lunda province. DIAMANG retained its dominant position until Angola became independent in 1975. Newitt, *Portugal in Africa*, pp. 77, 92-3; GEPB.

Diario de Moçambique (Pg.) "Journal of Mozambique." A periodical published in Beira by the *Centro Social* under the sponsorship of the Catholic Diocese of Beira. Its first issue appeared on December 24, 1949. Dias, *A Imprensa*, p. 101.

Diario de Mozambique (Pg.) "Journal of Mozambique." A daily newspaper published in Beira, Mozambique. Founded on September 25, 1981, this publication was the second largest daily in the country at the time. Darch, *Mozambique*, p. 282.

Diario de Noticias (Pg.) "The Journal News." A daily paper published in Lourenço Marques by Manuel dos Nascimento Ornelas. Its first issue appeared on April 1, 1905; it ceased publication with number 626 in April, 1907. It replaced *O Districto*, a periodical edited by M.N. Ornelas and suppressed by the government of Mozambique. Dias, *A Imprensa*, p. 70.

Dieu Donne (Fr.) "God's Gift." A religious cult organized in 1955 in Leopoldville, Zaire, by Bacongo (q.v.) exiles. By gathering large crowds and awakening public feelings, this movement helped the Angolan nationalist movement initiate the Angolans-for-Independence movement in 1961. Pelissier, *La Colonie*, p. 172.

DGS Acronym for *Direção Geral de Seguranza* (General Security Administration), the Portuguese international secret police, established in 1970 to survey political dissidents. DGS replaced the *Policia Internacional e de Defesa do Estado* created in the 1960s. With 3,000 agents and a wide net of informers, it was able to drive the nationalist leadership of the rebelling colonies into exile, forcing them to direct their nationalist efforts *in absentia*. Newitt, *Portugal in Africa*, p. 226.

"Dilectus Filius. Salutem and Apostolicam Blessum" (Lat.) "Beloved Son. Greetings and Apostolic Blessing." Title of a bull signed in Rome in 1518 by Pope Leo X to Prince Henrique, son of King Afonso I of Congo. The bull gave authorization to consecrate Henrique, then twenty-four years old, titular bishop of Utica and auxiliary of the Madeira diocese. It also gave him dispensation regarding illegitimacy, if necessary. Brasio, *Monumenta*, I:419.

dilõlo (Afr.) (1) A small West African tree (*Annona senegalensis*) whose yellow-orange fruits, similar to custard apple, are eaten locally. It grows in many places in Portuguese Africa, including Angola, Mozambique, and Cape Verde. Other names are *maiolo* and *diolo*. Ficalho, *Plantas Uteis*, pp. 76-77.

Dilõlo (Afr.) (2) A municipality in Moxico district, Bié province, northeastern Angola, a commercial center for the upper Zambezi and Zaire, with railroad, roads, and telegraph service. Dilõlo is also the name for a forest zone crossed by many rivers and a lake in eastern Angola. GEPB.

dinar (Ar.) A gold coin minted in several places in the Moslem world during the Middle Ages. The coin weighed 6.15 oz. (174.35 g), and was used in Mozambique and along the East African coast c.1600. Axelson, *Portuguese in East-Africa*, p. 244.

dinhángoa (Afr.) An annual cultivated vine (*Cucurbita maxima*) from South America, introduced to Africa by the Portuguese. It produces squash used as gourds and eaten during periods of famine in Angola and elsewhere. *Dinhángoa* is cultivated in Luanda and other parts of Angola by both Portuguese and Africans. Ficalho, *Plantas Uteis,* p. 188.

dinheiro do mar "Sea money." An expression used c.1938 by Cape Verdian immigrants to São Tomé, Senegal, and New England to refer to money earned abroad. In the popular folk poem *Morna,* in which the writer expressed the high personal and emotional price paid for leaving home, one verse says, "Money from the sea, how costly you are!" The off-island Cape Verdians found escape from homesickness in the lyrics of the melancholy blues or *morna.* Duncan, *Atlantic Islands,* p. 237.

Diogo Cão An illustrated historical journal published in 1931 by Rev. Manuel Ruela Pombo, a Portuguese diocesan missionary and historian. Ten issues were published in Luanda; the fourth series appeared in Lisbon. GEPB.

Direção Geral de Seguranza *See* DGS.

Direito, O (Pg.) "The Law." A weekly published in Lourenço Marques by Manuel dos Nascimento Ornelas. Its first issue appeared on November 22, 1922. It continued publication for over forty years until it was suppressed by the Mozambican government on March 15, 1965. Dias, *A Imprensa,* p. 79.

Direito Colonial Internacional do Trabalho (Pg.) "International Colonial Labor Law." This 1949 code set out the juridical principles established by treaties, conventions, and legislation for dealing with migratory African laborers. It covered salary protection, family welfare and health, and prevention of exploitation and abuse. Cunha, *O Trabalho Indigena,* pp. xxxi, 3. *See also* Direito da Ociosidade do Indigena.

Direito Colonial Interno (Pg.) "Internal Colonial Law." A set of juridical norms and regulations governing the overseas colonies and colonization activities, promulgated in 1949. It enforced principles, rights, and duties of settlers and the indigenous population. Cunha, *O Trabalho Indigena,* pp. xxvii, 142-5. *See also* Direito Colonial International do Trabalho.

Direito da Ociosidade do Indigena (Pg.) "The Natives' Right to Indolence." An 1878 statute giving former slaves the choice of whether or not to continue in their work. This law was repealed in 1899. Cunha, *O Trabalho Indigena,* pp. 142-45.

Direitos de Trabalhadores Indigenas (Pg.) "Rights of Indigenous Laborers." These rights were recognized by law in 1926, and included the right to a just salary, to a limited number of work hours, to compensation for work-related accidents and sickness, and the right to rescind a labor contract. Cunha, *O Trabalho Indigena,* pp. 91-2. *See also* recrutamento do mão-da-obra.

Discovery   A broad term applied to the great period of Portuguese maritime expansion initiated in the late fourteenth century. Prior to this time it was generally believed that the greater part of the Earth's surface was land, a concept that would be disproven in just over one hundred years. Following King João I's marriage to Philippa of Lancaster in 1386, Portugal embarked on overseas exploration. The king set his sights on North Africa, and in 1415 conquered Ceuta. At the time, this city was a center of trade in gold and goods brought by merchants who crossed the Sahara to the legendary *Bilad es-Sudan* (Land of the Blacks). King João I's six children, called the *Santarém,* or *Inclita* (Famous) *Geração* (Generation) were impressive figures, and to one of them, Prince Henry (1394-1460), belongs the glory of initiating the Discovery. The organizer and the guiding spirit of the Discovery, Prince Henry established the Sagres nautical school (q.v.) in 1423 to encourage further exploration. Navigators in his service overcame the terror of the "Sea of Darkness," a myth spread by Arab geographers, and fear of the Torrid Zone where legend said white men would turn black. João Gonçalves Zarco visited the Madeira Islands in 1418 then the Azores in 1427. Gil Eanes passed Cape Bojador (q.v.) in 1434 and proved that the sea beyond the Cape was navigable. The first European trading post in West Africa was established in 1438 in the Arab port of Arguim (q.v.) and it was from there the Portuguese took the first African slaves, sold in Portugal in Lagos (q.v.) in 1444. The Gulf of Guiné was reached c. 1470, and Diogo Cão discovered the Congo River in 1482. He sent a mission to King Nzinga a-Cuum of Congo, later baptized with the name João I in 1490. The arrival of missionaries and advisors south of the Sahara launched an attempt to "civilize" the heart of Africa. In 1487, Bartolomeu Dias rounded the Cape of Good Hope and entered the Indian Ocean. Vasco da Gama reached India and founded Goa on its west coast in 1498; Pedro Alvares Cabral discovered Brazil in 1500. Portuguese historians called this period *O Siglo Maravilhoso* (the Miracle Century). Prestage, *The Portuguese Pioneers,* pp. 54, 56-59, 63; Livermore, *A New History,* pp. 67-82; DHP.

Distrito, O (Pg.)   "The District." A bi-weekly periodical owned by Ramos da Silva and published on Mozambique Island. The first issue appeared on March 1, 1932, with Lieutenant Colonel Viriato Lopes Ramos da Silva as editor. It ceased publication in October, 1938. Dias, *A Imprensa,* p. 102.

diwal (Afr.)   In Guinea-Bissau and elsewhere, a rural district under an African ruler. By 1710, the Islamic Fula chiefdom of Futa-Djallon had nine *diwals.* Gonçalves, *Islamismo na Guiné,* p. 181.

dizima (Pg.)   At the time of the Discovery (q.v.), a 10 percent tax was collected on all goods and slaves entering or leaving Portuguese seaports and border towns. Around 1480, this import duty was applied to all slaves to be sold in the country and was collected at all ports through which the slaves passed. By 1534, the increased number of slaves passing through Lisbon required an increase in the number of customs agents and offices. This tax apparently was not collected on slaves exported from Portugal to Cape Verde until c.1560. Saunders, *A Social History,* pp. 9-10; GEPB.

djilba (Mand.)   A long white garment worn by Moslem Mandingo men in Guinea-Bissau. It is a status symbol and required gift from a bridegroom to the bride's father. Silva, *Usos e Costumes,* BCGP, 1968, xxiii(91/92):277.

djiló (Afr.)   Itinerant Mandingo merchant in Guinea-Bissau who sells cattle, fowl, salt, spices, and homemade utensils. Fearless traders, the *djiló* crossed forests, rivers, and frontiers in search of meager earnings, spending months away from home. Until the twentieth century, the *djiló* did business by barter; today they use currency. Carreira, *Mandingas,* p. 147-8.

djoká (Afr.)   A song, accompanied by drums, performed as a harvest ritual. The lyrics retell good deeds of the landlord. It is sung at harvest time among the Mandingos in Guinea-Bissau. Carreira, *Mandingas,* p. 225.

Djolas (Afr.)   An ethnic group of Senegambian stock related to the Senegalese Serer (q.v.). These animistic rice cultivators are found today between the Casamanse and lower Cacheu rivers in the northwestern and coastal portions of Guinea-Bissau. The term *Djolas* must be distinguished from the Mandingo-derived *Dyulas* (q.v.). The Djolas were frequent targets of the Mandingo slave raiders who sold their captives to the Portuguese and other European traders. HDRGC.

djukó (Afr.)   Among Islamic Mandingos in Guinea-Bissau, a tiny amulet made of silver, bronze, or lead that hangs from the neck of a young woman as protection against evil spirits and female diseases. Carreira, *Mandingas,* p. 224.

djutó (Afr.)   Name given by the Mandingos in Guinea-Bissau to a beverage prepared from the root and leaves of a tropical plant (*Securidaca longipedunculata*), used in folk medicine to treat the poisonous bites of snakes and insects. Carreira, *Mandingas,* p. 242. *See also* fará.

dobra (Pg.)   A gold coin weighing approximately 3.6 oz. (10 grams) which circulated in Mozambique and East Africa c.1600. Axelson, *Portuguese in South-East,* p. 244. *See also* dobrão.

dobrão (Pg.) A gold coin or doubloon, minted under King João V in 1745 and circulated in Europe, Africa, South America, and the Caribbean. Duncan, *Atlantic Islands*, p. 264. *See also* dobra.

Dolisie (Afr.) An African village in Zaire, northern Angola, where in 1953 Simon Zephyrin Lassy founded an ethnic Congo cult that preceded the nationalist movements of 1961 in its opposition to Portuguese colonialism. Pelissier, *La Colonie*, p. 168. *See also* Lassyism.

dolo (Afr.) Beer made from millet flour and boiling water, filtered then fermented. Made by the Wolof of Senegambia, a people living c.1050 and later in the basin of middle Senegal and in historic Ghana, this kind of millet beer is known today throughout the western, central, and eastern Sudan by such names as *dolo*, *kimbil*, and *merissa*. Lewicki, *West African Food,* p. 130.

Dom (Pg.) "Sir." A title of nobility given in the Congo Kingdom since the time of King of Congo Afonso I. King Manuel granted this privilege to Afonso I in a royal document entitled *Carta de Armas* (q.v.). Gabriel, *Angola,* pp. 58-9. *See also* Dona.

Dombondola (Afr.) An old military fort in the Cuamato captaincy, southern Angola, on the southern border of the Dombolas, between Unda and Balando and near Ruacana Falls on the Cunene River. Originally known as *Forte Henrique Couçeiro*, it was built in 1909 by Captain João de Almeida. GEPB.

Dominicos (Pg.) Dominican missionaries, members of the Domincan Order founded by St. Dominic (1170-1221). They arrived on Mozambique Island in 1577 to minister mainly to Portuguese soldiers and traders and other Europeans in East Africa. They organized expeditions to the interior for the purpose of making conversions. These began in earnest in the seventeenth century, but never had far-reaching results. Silva Rego, *O Ultramar,* pp. 193-5.

Dominion Colonial and Overseas Bank British financial institution that by 1965 had established branches in Beira and Lourenço Marques. It supplied credit for essential enterprises producing goods for the local market. Herrick, *Area Handbook,* p. 277.

Dona (Pg.) "Lady." Female title of nobility granted by the king of Portugal c.1755 to the African wife of an Afro-Portuguese holder of a *prazo* (q.v.) in Zambezia, Mozambique, and included the right to inherit the land leased by her husband. In Mozambique, land tenure was limited to three generations and was transmitted through the female line. Upon its termination, a formal request for extension had to be submitted by her heirs. In Angola, *Dona* was a title of nobility without land tenure, according to a privilege given by King Manuel I in 1506 to Afonso I, King of Congo. Gabriel, *Angola* p. 59; Isaacman, *Mozambique: From Colonialism*, pp. 96-7. *See also* Dom.

Dona Ana   An African village on the left bank of the Zambesi River, Mutarara municipality, Tete district, Mozambique. This town began to be better known when a bridge over the Zambezi was built. It is connected by railroad with the Trans-Zambezia Railroad that links Beira (q.v.) with Nyassaland, once a British possession. GEPB.

Donataria (Pg.)   "Royal Grantee (female)." At the time of the Discovery (q.v.), a medieval system of conquest and colonization by which the Crown granted a *donataria* the responsibility of settling and defending the extent of the lands at her own expenses. In return, the proprietor received administrative and fiscal authority over the area. Usually the king reserved to himself the trade in certain commodities, such as spices and slaves. The grant was not always hereditary and, on the death of the grantee, the land might revert to the status of crown captaincy, administered by an appointed captain-general. This medieval system was introduced by Prince Henry into Madeira in the fifteenth century for the purpose of colonization. Duffy, *Portuguese Africa,* pp. 53-4; GEPB. *See also* Donatario.

Donatario (Pg.)   "Royal Grantee (male)." In Portuguese Africa the proprietor of large expanses of land granted by the Crown in exchange for the responsibility of defending and settling that territory. The grantee, usually a member of the nobility, was subject to inspection and appeal by Lisbon. The regulation of a *donatario* was sometimes in the hands of an army officer. The recipients of these royal grants farmed their holdings with slaves. Chilcote, *Portuguese Africa,* p. 7. *See also* Donataria.

Dondo (Afr.)   An African village on the right bank of the Cuanza River, 135 mi. (218 km) from Luanda, Angola. Since 1625 there has been an important market in Dondo. With the coming of the railroad in the twentieth century connecting the village to the main Malange-Luanda railroad line, trade activities have increased greatly. It is an important commercial center dealing in oil and other products produced locally. GEPB. *See also* Dondo fair.

Dondo fair (Pg.)   Important market established in 1625 in the town of Dondo, located on the bank of the Cuanza River, Angola. It was a permanent commercial center for African merchants from the neighboring regions of Libolo, Quissama, Songo, Duque de Bragança, Ambaca, Cazengo, Bailundo, and Bié. During the nineteenth century goods from this market became the most important merchandise exported through Luandan customs to Portugal. DHP.

Dondos (Afr.) African ethnic group settled in a rich agricultural zone by the Cuanza River, southeast of Luanda, Angola. The Dondos, who were in constant contact with the Portuguese, became highly acculturated in the colonial period. In the War for Independence (1961-1975), they played an important role in the struggle against the Portuguese. Wheeler, *Angola*, p. 186; GEPB.

Dongo (Afr.) An Angolan chiefdom in Luanda province north of the Cuanza River. It was ruled c.1615 by King Ngola Mbandi of Ndongo, poisoned by his sister Queen Nzinga in 1624. The Portuguese opposed her and supported Ngola Aire as the new king. In return, the latter promised to pay taxes annually and was baptized Felipe, in honor of King Felipe II (Philip III of Spain). In 1669 a new ruler, João Aire, rebelled against the Portuguese. He was defeated and executed. After that, Dongo remained a Portuguese province. GEPB.

Dongo town (Afr.) A town in the Ganguelas district, Huila province, southeastern Angola, connected by road with Vila da Ponte and Huila. It was a rich cattle and commercial center with a relatively large number of Portuguese colonists. It produces millet, *gergelim* (q.v.), maize, and other agricultural products, including wax. GEPB.

Dongüena (Afr.) A town in Gamboa district, Huila province, southeastern Angola, a region of abundant big game that during the dry season cross the area for water in the Cunene River. It was first visited by Humbo merchants in 1854. In 1891 the Portuguese army pacified the area and in 1906 a military fort was erected. African uprisings continued until 1915 when the Portuguese were able to establish complete control of the frontier zone. GEPB.

Donquin (Afr.) In Guinea-Bissau, among the Islamized Fula (q.v.), an annual festival established to celebrate both the glorification of the prophet Mohammed as the founder of Islam and the unity of the Arab family. It falls on the twelfth day of the twelfth month of the Moslem year, two lunar months after Ramadan (q.v.). Gonçalves, *O Mundo Arabo-Islámico,* p. 214.

dormideira (Pg.) In Mozambique and elsewhere, a poppy (*Papaver somniferum*) from which the narcotic opium is extracted. In 1874, a company was founded in Lisbon to cultivate the plant and produce opium for export. A plantation of *dormideira* was established in 1877 on the Kwa-Kwa River, Quelimane, by the company. Ficalho, *Plantas Uteis,* p. 84.

Doutrina Christiãa, A (Pg.) "Christian Doctrine." A catechism in Portuguese written by Marcos Jorge then translated into the Kikongo language by order of Mateus Cardoso and published in Lisbon in 1624. It was edited by Father Vetralla, a Capuchin missionary in the Congo associated with the

Congregation of the Propagation of the Faith, who translated it into Italian and Latin in 1650 for use by missionaries. This version was published as parallel texts in four columns: Kikongo, Portuguese, Latin, and Italian. In 1978 it was republished in Brussels. Gabriel, *Angola,* p. 100.

dualismo colonial (Pg.) "Colonial dualism." A policy based on the premise that colonies should be organized in pairs: Angola with Brazil, Mozambique with India, and Guiné with Cape Verde. This early Portuguese organization was changed in 1778 when the Marquis of Pombal, following the British colonial system, directed that all overseas territories should be oriented and controlled by the Lisbon government. Silva Rego, *O Ultramar,* p. 19.

Dum Diversa (Lat.) A papal bull issued by Pope Nicholas V on June 24, 1452, granting King Afonso V of Portugal and his successors the right of conquest and subjection of heathen kingdoms and lands ruled by infidels. Pinto Rema, *A Primeira Evangelização*, BCG, 1966, xxi(80):313.

Dum Fidei (Lat.) A papal bull issued by Pope Leo X on June 7, 1514, granting Portuguese kings the right of patronage, that is, to administer the church, to appoint bishops, and to distribute ecclesiastic benefits in the area from Cabo Bojador on the West African coast to Goa in India. GEPB.

Duma Fort A trading post built by the Portuguese on the Gulf of Guiné in 1628, about 23 mi. (37 km) up the Ankobra River from the coast. It was established to trade the gold thought to be in the area. The building was destroyed by an earthquake in 1636, and there is no trace of it today. HDG.

Dundo (Afr.) A village in Chitato municipality, Lunda province, northeastern Angola. It was founded in 1912 to be the seat of the *Companhia de Pesquisas Mineiras de Angola*, which ceased operations four years later. Its original population increased significantly in the 1920 census after it had become the seat of DIAMANG (q.v.) in 1917. Before the War for Independence, this important mining center had a population of 8,291 Africans and 117 Europeans working in a total of 29 mines. GEPB.

Duquela (Ar.) In North Africa, a confederation of Moroccan ethnic groups of Arab origin which in 1500 covered a large territory, including the Portuguese forts of Azamor, Mozagao, and Safim (q.v.). The area ran along the rich Atlantic coastal plain and the mountainous interior where they farmed cattle. To the north is the Azamor River and to the south, Marrakesh. DHP.

Dutch Africa Even before winning its independence from Spain in 1609, in 1596 Holland explored Guiné. They also explored the Cape of Good Hope between 1615 and 1658, discovered by the Portuguese in 1488. To further their increasing slave traffic with the New World, the Dutch attacked and took São Jorge da Mina (q.v.) in 1637, giving them control of the traffic along the Slave Coast and the Gulf of Guiné. In 1652 a Dutch colony was established there on land taken from local chiefs. Silva Rego, *Portuguese,* pp. 61-2.

Dutch dialect In South Africa c.1827, a patois used by Boers, slaves, Bantus, Hottentots, and, by the 1870s, by Boer colonists in Huila, Angola. At that time this dialect was avoided by people born and brought up in Holland who used High Dutch, that is, the correct language of the mother country. Valkhoff, *New Light,* p. 4.

Dutch East India Company A chartered trade company organized in 1602 to trade in spices with India and Java. Cornelius Houtman, a Dutch resident of Lisbon, visited Java in 1595 and was one of the people instrumental in trying to secure this profitable traffic by establishing this company, which soon rewarded its shareholders with ample dividends. The company enjoyed its highest profits in 1644. Livermore, *A New History,* pp. 167, 174, 180.

Dutch invasion In 1641 a Dutch fleet of twenty-one ships took possession of Luanda and a few months after of Benguela in the south. In 1647 Salvador Correia de Sá e Benavides, the Brazilian governor, was appointed governor of Angola with orders to retake the colony. In May 1648 Correia de Sá conquered Luanda and, shortly after, Benguela and São Tomé. Duffy, *Portuguese Africa,* pp. 66-7.

dyula (Afr.) The name for itinerant Mandingo traders in Guinea-Bissau and Cape Verde, originally from Mali (q.v.). They traded along the Volta River and spread Islam wherever they went. The *dyulas* made up a trading group that controlled commerce along the Volta River and the surrounding towns in the colonial period. They were also known as *dioula, juula,* or *wangan.* Davidson, *The Fortunate Islands,* p. 78.

Dyulas (Afr.) An pre-colonial Islamic Mandingo ethnic group with some Fula (q.v.) components. As itinerant traders during the colonial period, they integrated the Portuguese economy in the sixteenth century along the Gambia and Cacheu rivers. The Dyulas stimulated local production of gold, cola nuts, and the exchange of slaves for imported products such as salt, textiles, and firearms. Portuguese penetration of the interior broke into the territory of the Dyulas' commerce, one of the causes of the Dyula revolts in the Upper Niger and in Guinea-Conakri when they tried to re-establish their commercial authority from 1835 to the 1880s. HDRGC. *See also* Gabu.

{ **E** }

ebala (Afr.) In São Salvador do Congo region c.1880, a small clearing made at the crossing of paths where an *ensande* tree (Ficus family) had been planted. In its shade merchants sold food, wares, and beverages to passing travelers. BeAD.

ebindé (Afr.) A primitive plow made from a hardwood (*Pterocarpus erinaceus*) covered by an iron plate with a long handle; a kind of iron shovel. It was used by Balanta (q.v.) farmers in low coastal fields in central and southern Guinea-Bissau. It was also called a Balanta plow. Mota, *Guiné Portuguesa*, I:293.

Ebo (Afr.) An administrative post in the Amboim municipality, Benguela province, southern Angola. In 1961, during a nationalist uprising, 151 Europeans were massacred in this village. Pelissier, *La Colonie*, p. 593.

ebunge (Afr.) In São Salvador do Congo in the 1880s, a charm cast by a sorcerer without the knowledge of onlookers. It was believed to render actions invisible and to make an individual invulnerable in war. BeAD.

ebwela (Kik.) A dance, characterized by the rotary movement of each shoulder and hip alternately, performed in São Salvador do Congo around 1880. BeAD.

Ecavongo (Afr.) The fortified camp and residence of chief Dunduma in Bié, north-central Angola, taken by Artur de Paiva's forces in November of 1890. With the surrender of this settlement, a large region became subject to Portuguese control. GEPB.

Echo da Zambézia (Pg.) "Echo of Zambezia." A periodical first published in Quelimane, Mozambique, in 1887. Its owner and editor, Jose Peixoto do Amaral, suspended publication in 1896. Dias, *A Imprensa*, p. 59.

Echo de Angola, O (Pg.) "The Echo of Angola." The first periodical edited by Africans. It appeared in Luanda, Angola, in 1881; there is no information about the length of publication. Lopo, *Jornalismo*, p. 57.

Eco de Nyassa (Pg.) "Echo of Nyassa." A periodical published in Ibo in Lourenço Marques, Mozambique, that first appeared on February 25, 1919, with Francisco Leite Pereira as editor. In its pages it carried commentary on government opposition to its publication. Later its name was changed to *O Diario de Nyassa*. It ceased publication on August 15, 1920. Dias, *A Imprensa*, p. 103.

Eco dos Sports (Pg.) "Sports' Echo." A periodical published in Lourenço Marques, Mozambique, on May 10, 1938. Its owner and editor was Leopoldo Cerqueira Afonso. It ceased publication in 1954 with issue no. 216. Dias, *A Imprensa*, p. 90.

Ecole des Cadres Angolais (Fr.) "School of Angolan Public Administration." A school established by nationalists in Leopoldville, Belgian Congo, in November 1963, to train political commissioners and prepare for the day of liberation in Angola and elsewhere in Portuguese Africa. It was put under the direction of Walter Artho, a Swiss sympathizer, who with others had formed the Swiss Friends of Angola to assist students attending Swiss universities. Plans called for a two-year curriculum in social sciences and public administration to be taught by expatriate faculty staff excluding Americans. Marcum, *The Angolan Revolution*, II:101-102, 149.

Ecumenical Council, Vatican II (1962-65) In November 1962 Angolan nationalists led by the party's vice president Rosario Neto presented to the Council a memorandum seeking a new source of leverage against Portugal. Rosario Neto, a former Angolan seminarian, discussed the Angolan independence with Vatican officials. Earlier, on February 13, 1962, he had presented a summary to the Papal observer at the United Nations in New York. Marcum, *The Angolan Revolution*, I:303.

Effective Occupation A new fundamental principle established by the Berlin Conference (q.v.) for African territories. This principle put forward by the German government invalidated the historic Portuguese policy of taking territory by force. Hammond, *Portugal and Africa*, p. 99.

ejinga (Kik.) In São Salvador do Congo c.1880, a deep, still spot formed in a river bed at the base of a waterfall. BeAD.

ekindu (Afr.) In São Salvador do Congo c.1880, a dance conducted all night long on the occasion of the birth of a child who was supposed to be the incarnation of a *lombo* (a fairy). BeAD.

ekoko (Cong.) In São Salvador do Congo c.1880, a staff or cane cut from the stem of a tropical climbing palm (*Calamus secundifloris*); also the palm. BeAD.

Elaeis guineensis *See* palm oil.

elemi (Afr.) In Angola and elsewhere, a gum-resin substance extracted from tropical rubber trees (*Clitranda henriquesiana* and *Carpodinus lanceolatus*). Africans used this gum in making chairs and tables. Ficalho, *Plantas Uteis,* p. 155; GDLP. *See also* tacamaca.

Elephantiasis nostras (Lat.) A tropical disease characterized by a chronic enlargement, sometimes to grotesque proportions, of the subcutaneous and cutaneous tissues as a result of lymphatic obstruction. In the form commonest in the tropics, the recurrent lymphangitis is caused by the filarid nematode (*Wucheria bancrofti*) most usually affecting the legs and scrotum. It was reported prevalent in some regions of Angola in 1900. *Revista Medica de Angola,* Luanda, 1928, 3:497-503.

Elmina *See* São Jorge da Mina.

Elo (Pg.) "Link in a Chain." A periodical published in Lourenço Marques, Mozambique, by the group that also called itself Elo. Its director was Max Fernandes and its first issue appeared April 8, 1950. Dias, *A Imprensa*, p. 95.

"Em quanto o mundo dura" (Pg.) "As long as the world lasts." An expression used in the Zambezia region, Mozambique, c.1700 to characterize *prazos* (q.v.) granted to religious orders in perpetuity. Newitt, *Portuguese Settlement*, p. 99.

Emancipador (Pg.) "Liberator." A weekly published in Lourenço Marques, Mozambique. Edited by Pedro Dias Selimnae, the first issue appeared on December 6, 1919. It was an aggressive and controversial publication. Its last issue (no. 873) was published on July 19, 1937, when due to conflict with the Portuguese governor it ceased publication. Dias, *A Imprensa*, p. 76.

embala (Afr.) In colonial Angola, a compound surrounded by high palisades, occupied by the chief's household including his wives and children, his assistants, servants, and slaves with their respective families. It was built with narrow paths, big trees for shade, and special sections for cattle, other domestic animals, and possessions; the hut of the chief usually was on high ground. GEPB. *See also* quilombo.

emboto (Afr.) In Angola, a tropical shrub (*Euclea lanceolata*) with edible red fruit, that grows to 25 ft. (7.6 m). Ficalho, *Plantas Uteis*, pp. 210-11.

empacasseiro (Pg.) "Porter." In Angola, an African hired and paid by the government for duty as mailman, policeman, porter, or soldier. Wheeler, *Angola*, p. 57.

emphyteusis (Lat.) In Portugal, a contractual form of land tenure, clearly defined in the late Roman Empire. Under *emphyteusis*, land could be leased in perpetuity or for some long but limited period, usually three generations (about ninety years). In order to develop overseas lands during the period of the Discovery (q.v.), Portugal extended the system of *emphyteusis* in the Atlantic Islands and the West African coast by organizing *capitanias* (captaincies). In 1440, Prince Henry granted in *emphyteusis* the earliest *capitinias* (q.v.) on Madeira Island, twenty years after the first settlements had been founded. The individual to whom land was granted was called a *donatario* (q.v.). In Zambezia, Mozambique, c.1660, a *donatario* came to be known as a *prazero* (q.v.). Newitt, *Portuguese Settlement*, pp. 1-2, 104-5; GEPB.

emphyteuta (Pg.) In medieval Portugal, the holder of a contract of *emphyteusis* (q.v.). The *emphyteuta* had extensive rights over the property. He could leave the land to his heirs or could sub-lease or sell it. In Zambezia c.1660, the *emphyteuta* was called a *prazero* (q.v.). Isaacman, *Mozambique: From Colonialism*, pp. 173, 175.

enchada (Afr.) A short hoe with a thin, flat blade set across the end of a long handle, used on the *prazos* (q.v.) in Zambezia around 1750-1850 to weed and loosen the soil. It was introduced by Portuguese colonists to cultivate beans, cassava, maize, millet, sorghum, and vegetables. PDM.

Encoje (Afr.) Military fort built in 1759 on the Atlantic coast in Angola, north of the mouth of the Dande River. It was supposed to prevent smuggling and to control the Dembos and other groupss settled inland from the coast. Located on a well-traveled trade route from the interior to the Congo coast, it became the northernmost station to stop Dutch, French, and English slavers. In 1911, it was organized as a municipality. GEPB.

encosse (Pg.) In early Mozambique, a petty African chief in the Zambezia area who received tribute and services from his people but enjoyed no judicial authority over them; also called a *fumo*. Hammond, *Portugal and Africa*, p. 40.

encosta (Pg.) In Cape Verde and elsewhere, a mountain slope that drains into the ocean or a river. USBGN, pp. iii, 1961.

eneli (Afr.) "Sudan millet." In Western Sudan, a cultivated variety of millet (*Pennisetum typhoideum*), imported in the fifteenth century from Bilad-e-Sudan (Land of the Blacks) into Walata, at the southern edge of the Sahara, and Mali. This foodstuff could be obtained in every African village on the route from Walata to Mali. It is also called guinea corn (q.v.). Lewicki, *West African Food*, pp. 24-5.

ensaca (Afr.) (1)   A gang of female slaves composed of six to ten women governed by a *inhacoda* (q.v.) or chief in charge of agricultural and mining work in the *prazos* of Zambezia c.1750. The *ensaca* was part of a large slave force that specialized in digging goldfields, in washing alluvial ores in rivers and streams, and in pounding rocks which, once reduced to fragments, were washed through square trays to find mineral particles. Isaacman, *Mozambique: From Colonialism*, pp. 70-1.

ensaca (Afr.) (2)   A regiment of slaves trained as soldiers to guard the *aringa* (fortified camp) of a *prazero*. In the nineteenth century these corps had about 250 men. In 1861, J.B.A. da Silva, the powerful holder of the Maganga da Costa *prazo*, had twelve *ensacas* with 1000 to 1200 slaves each. This primitive form of army was used to fight neighbors and government intrusions into the affairs of the *prazo*. Newitt, *Portuguese Settlement*, pp. 195, 288; GEPB. *See also* canhongo.

ensino primario rudimentar (Pg.)   "Elementary school curriculum." A basic program of instruction for African children lasting three to five years. Since 1956 this system has been called *ensino de adaptacão* (instruction of adaptation). An African graduate of the elementary program was qualified after passing the entrance examination to enter secondary school. In Angola and Mozambique there were also private technical schools at the secondary level. Duffy, *Portuguese Africa*, p. 313.

epata (Umb.) "Family." The nuclear and extended family unit. Among the Ovimbundu in Angola the nuclear family, c.1928, included two lineages: the paternal *oluse* and the maternal *oluina* (q.v.). As a biological and social association, the *epata* assigned rights and obligations in Ovimbundu society. Henderson, *Angola*, p. 50.

epia (Umb.)   An upland field cultivated by the Ovimbundu (q.v.) c.1920. Cultivation began just before the first rains in September and, depending on the onset and duration of the rains, planting of maize and other crops took place from early October to well into December. The Ovimbundu spent the next three months hoeing and weeding, harvesting the crops after the rains ended in April or early May. Henderson, *Angola*, p. 48. *See also* onaka, ulima.

equator Portugal and Spain signed two treaties c.1448 regarding the West African coast. Under the first, the equator was considered the dividing line between Portuguese and Spanish interests, the south belonging to the former, the north to the latter. At the same time, in a second agreement, it was established as a demarcation line between the same parties regulating Portuguese fishing rights from Cape Bojador to the Rio do Ouro and giving Spain the same rights to the north as far as Ceuta. Prestage, *The Portuguese Pioneers*, p. 243.

Equator Treaty An international agreement signed in 1815 between Portugal and England outlawing the slave trade north of the equator. The Congo and Angola still remained as sources of slaves for the American South but England intensified its war against Cuban and Brazilian slavers. GEPB.

equatorial current In the tropical seas of the northern hemisphere, the clockwise southeast to northwest movement of the surface waters; in the southern hemisphere, the counterclockwise movement northeast to southwest. Where these two streams come into opposition (near the equator), the resultant movements are either east to west (equatorial current) or west to east (counter equatorial). The general result is that there are north and south equatorial currents with a counter equatorial current between, more pronounced in the Pacific than in the Atlantic. GGT.

erva-da-Guiné (Pg.) "Guinea grass." A creeping tropical grass (*Panicum altissimum*) used as forage. Also known as *capim da Guiné*. GEPB.

erva de Santa Maria (Pg.) "Herb of Saint Mary." In Angola and elsewhere, a tropical herb (*Chenopodium ambrosioides*) used in folk medicine to treat many maladies including diarrhea and dysentery. African workers moving to work in the copper belt in eastern Angola often suffer a near-fatal disease, the *maculo*, which is cured with an infusion of *erva de Santa Maria* tea. Although it has powerful principals, it is widely used by quacks. Also know as wormwood. Ficalho, *Plantas Uteis,* pp. 240-41.

erva-doce (Pg.) "Sweet grass." In Cape Verde, a tropical plant (*Foeniculum vulgare*) cultivated for forage. Also known as fennel. GEPB.

erva-do-grão-prior (Pg.) "Great prior's herb." The first name given to tobacco when it was introduced to Portugal c.1500. It was also called *erva santa* (holy herb). GDLP.

erva-dos-picos (Pg.) "Summit herb." In Mozambique, a poisonous tropical herb (*Acanthospermum hispidum*). Also called *erva-da-quinhenta*. PDM.

escola caseira (Pg.) "Private school." In Cape Verde, a family school run by parents for the benefit of their children and for those of their neighbors when they were unable to afford matriculation in public schools. This useful practice has been abandoned in recent years. Araujo, *A Study*, p. 15.

Escola Colonial de Lisboa (Pg.) "Colonial School of Lisbon." An institute of higher learning established in 1927 by the Portuguese government to educate and train colonial administrators. Later it became the *Escola Superior Colonial* (q.v.). Pelissier, *La Colonie*, p. 121.

Escola de Medicina Tropical (Pg.) "School of Tropical Medicine." An institution created in Lisbon in 1902 by the Portuguese government to foster medical research, training, and healing in the overseas territories, especially in Africa. DHP.

Escola de Quadros (Pg.) "School for staff officers." A school established by Lucio Lara under the sponsorship of MPLA (q.v.) at Leopoldville, Zaire, on February 28, 1963. Its aim was to educate leaders and teachers to improve the economic and social life of Africans in Portuguese Africa. Marcum, *The Angolan Revolution*, II:30.

Escola Superior Colonial (Pg.) A Portuguese institution of higher learning, formerly *Escola Colonial de Lisboa* (q.v.), organized by the Ministry of the Colonies in 1927. Later it became the *Instituto Superior de Estudos Ultramarinos*. The school studied the problems of the colonies and provided training to civil servants working in the colonies. Pelissier, *La Colonie*, pp. 121, 126, 138(n).

escrava (Pg.) "Female slave." In Portugal at the time of the Discovery (q.v.), an enslaved African woman owned as property by another person and absolutely subject to his will. This legal term replaced the traditional *serva* (serf) when a massive arrival of African captives from Guiné crowded Lisbon, Evora, and other cities. The *Ordenacões Manuelinas* (1514) and the *Leis Extravagantes* (1559) (qq.v) recognized the meaning of *escrava* as chattel. Saunders, *A Social History,* pp. xxiii, 14; GEPB. *See also* abd.

escrava de cria (Pg.) "Nursing slave mother." A term used in West Africa c. 1650. A young slave mother with a nursing child usually sold at a high price as a family unit in the Brazilian market. Carreira, *As Companhias Pomblinas*, BCG, 1968, xxiii(91/92):307.

escrava do peito caido (Pg.) "Old female slave." A term used in West Africa c. 1650 for an old slave mother with pendulous breasts who sold at a low price in the Brazilian market. Carreira, *As Companhias Pomblinas*, BCG, 1968, xxiii(91/92):307.

escrava lotada (Pg.) "Young female slave, highly priced." A term used in West Africa c.1650 for a young adult female slave, healthy, well-developed, and attractive, who sold at a high price in the Brazilian market. Carreira, *As Companhias Pomblinas,* BCG, 1968, xxiii(91/92):307.

escrava mascavada (Pg.) "Deformed female slave." A term used in West Africa c.1650 for a female slave deformed either by birth or accident or with ulcers or skin disease who sold at a low price in the Brazilian market. Carreira, *As Companhias Pomblinas,* BCG, 1968, xxiii(91/92):307.

escrava moçetona (Pg.) "Young female slave." A term used in West Africa c.1650 for a female slave 14 to 16 years old, healthy and attractive, who sold at a high price in the Brazilian market. Carreira, *As Companhias Pomblinas*, BCG, 1968, xxiii(91-92):307.

escrava rapariga (Pg.) "Young girl slave." A term used in West Africa c.1650 for an 8- to 10-year-old female slave, highly priced in the Brazilian market. Carreira, *As Companhias Pomblinas*, BCG, 1968, xxiii(91-92):307.

escravinho, menino, mulatinho (Pg.) "Little slave boy, little baby, little mulatto." Terms of endearment used by priests of the Lisbon archdiocese c.1500 to refer to infant male slaves given as presents to aristocratic ladies. Leite de Vasconcellos, *Antroponimia*, pp. 363-64.

escravo (Pg.) "Male slave." In Portugal at the time of the Discovery (q.v.), an enslaved African male owned as property by another person and absolutely subject to his will. This legal term replaced the traditional *servo* (serf) when a massive arrival of African captives from Guiné crowded Lisbon, Evora, and other cities. The *Ordenacões Manuelinas* (1514) and the *Leis Extravagantes* (1559) (qq.v) recognized the meaning of *escravo* as chattel. Saunders, *A Social History,* pp. xxiii, 14; GEPB. *See also* abd.

escravo canario (Pg.) "Canarian male slave." A term used in Madeira c.1341 to refer to an enslaved male from the Canary Islands working on the sugar plantations. Often these slaves were skilled in sugar manufacturing. DHP.

"Escravo chegado vivo" (Pg.) "Slave arrived alive." The phrase used when African slaves arrived alive at the port of destination after a long voyage. In 1772 at Luanda, Angola, a cargo of 5,318 *peças* (slaves) was loaded; 4,125 arrived alive at Pará, Brazil, 1,193 (22 percent) having died during the trip. The same year at Cacheu, Guinea-Bissau, a cargo of 4,698 slaves was loaded, of whom 4,415 arrived alive at Maranhao, Brazil, with the loss of 283 (6 percent). Carreira, *As Companhias Pomblinas*, BCG, 1968, xxiii(91/92):302-3.

escravo da camara (Pg.) "Slave owned by the king." At the time of the Discovery (q.v.), the Crown officially owned most of the slaves taken from West Africa to Portugal and Brazil; slavers paid a tax per head. DHP.

escravo da Casa da Misericordia (Pg.) "Slave owned by the Casa de Misericordia (Mercy House)" (q.v.). In Portugal, this charitable institution owned many slaves who worked in hospitals and hostels managed by the institution. DHP.

escravo da Igreja (Pg.) "Slave owned by the Church." In Angola and elsewhere, a Christian slave owned by the Church, who, with his family, was in charge of keeping an *hospicio* (q.v.) in rural areas to provide lodging for transient missionaries. This slave and his family were protected by law and they could not be sold. Gabriel, *Angola,* pp. 103, 138.

escravo da porta (Pg.) "Domestic slave." In colonial Mozambique, a domestic slave working at the *prazero*'s house. Also called a *mbandazi.* Isaacman, *Mozambique: The Africanization,* p. 54.

escravo do estado (Pg.) "State-owned slave." In Portuguese Africa in the colonial period there were many slaves owned not by the Crown but by the Portuguese government. These *escravo do estado* slaves worked on plantations and roads, and in hospitals and public institutions. In a law promulgated on October 25, 1853, these slaves were declared freedmen on condition that they serve the state for an additional seven years. If the slave were pagan, compulsory baptism was ordered by the same statute. Cunha, *O Trabalho Indigena,* p. 134-35.

escravo do quisico (Pg.) "Illegitimate slave child." In Matamba and Dongo in Guinea-Bissau c.1650, such a child was a ward of the master and branded with his initials. Carreira, *As Companhias Pomblinas*, BCG, 1968, xxiii(89-90):74.

escravo importado (Pg.) "Imported slave." Any slave imported into Brazil was declared a freedman by a law proclaimed in Lisbon on October 25, 1853, on condition that he serve his master an additional ten years. Cunha, *O Trabalho Indigena,* p. 134.

escravo lotado (Pg.) "Young male slave, highly priced." A term used in West Africa for a young, healthy, robust, and physically fit slave 16 to 18 years old, considered at the peak of his working life, who was sold at the highest price in the Brazilian market c.1856. This category was used by slavers calling at Cape Verde on their trip to the New World. Carreira, *As Companhias Pomblinas,* BCG, 1968, xxiii(91/92):303-4.

escravo mascavado (Pg.) "Deformed male slave." A term used in West Africa c.1600 for a male slave physically deformed either by birth or accident or with ulcers or skin disease who sold at a low price in the Brazilian market. Carreira, *As Companhias Pomblinas,* BCG, 1968, xxiii(91-92):307.

escravo mulato (Pg.) "Mulatto slave." A term used in West Africa c.1650 for a slave of mixed racial parentage. An adult male *mulato* slave sold for a high price on Brazilian market. Carreira, *As Companhias Pomblinas,* BCG, 1968, xxiii(91/92):306.

escravo negro (Pg.) "Black slave." A male African slave. The first African slaves from Guiné arrived at Lisbon around 1441. DHP.

Escravos, Ilha dos (Pg.) "Island of slaves." A settlement established by runaway slaves on an island at the mouth of the Bolala-Tombal River in Guinea-Bissau. In the sixteenth and seventeenth centuries many fugitive slaves from the Portuguese factories of Porto-da-Cruz and Bigubá settled here. In foreign charts it appears as *Bossessane* or *Montere.* GEPB.

escupila (Afr.) In São Tomé, a tall tropical tree (*Pentaclethra marcrophylla* Benth.) that grows up to 130 ft. (40 m) and provides good timber for ship building. Its seeds are used for food and in medicine. Almada Negreiros, *Historia,* p. 238.

eseré (Afr.) The seed of a tropical vine (*Physostigma venenosum*) found in Angola, Congo, and Calabar in the Gulf of Guiné. A beverage prepared by combining pulverized fruits and seeds with water was used in tribal ordeals (q.v.). A sorcerer forced an accused person to drink this concoction to prove his innocence or guilt. Drunk in small amounts this potion is purgative and induces peristalsis; in larger quantities it is emetic and causes violent vomiting. In the first case the person dies immediately of cardiac arrest, in the second he survives. Portuguese law punished this practice as a serious crime. *Eseré* is also known as *fava de Calabar* (Calabar bean) and *fava de prova* (bean of proof). Ficalho, *Plantas Uteis,* pp. 164-5. *See also* agua-vermelha, tanguin.

Esmeraldo de Situ Orbis (Lat.)   An early book on navigation by Duarte Pacheco Pereira, published in Lisbon in 1505. Among other advice, it recommended that ships should sail from the Tagus in January, preferably February, and no later than March. From Lisbon they should sail southwest for 200 leagues to 28°N, to the vicinity of the Canary Islands, then 45 leagues southeast to 25°N, from where they could coast to Cape Verde. From Gorée Bay they should sail due south for 600 leagues to 19°S; 850 leagues east-southeast would have taken them to 37°S, to a point 40 leagues west-southwest of the Cape of Good Hope. The *Esmeraldo de Situ Orbis* gives exact points to reach India and return safely to Lisbon. It was one of the most important contributions to the navigational art of the time. Axelson, *Portuguese in South-East*, pp. 106, 110; GEPB.

Espaço Portugues (Pg.)   "Portuguese Space." The geographic extent and spiritual unity of the Lusitanian family spread in Portuguese-Africa and elsewhere since the Discovery (q.v.). Each colony was supposed to have its own characteristics, being equal *inter pares*. Neither white nor black, supposedly, had any racial or political privilege over the other. Hamilton, *Voices*, pp. 14-15.

espanadeiro (Pg.)   In Cape Verde and elsewhere, the portion of a stream where the current accelerates as it descends with sufficient rapidity, without a break in the slope of the stream bed, that a waterfall forms. Carvalho e Vasconcellos, *As Colonias Portuguesas*, p. 48.

Espantalho de Angola, O (Pg.)   "The Scarecrow of Angola." A periodical published in Luanda, Angola, in 1925. Lopo, *Jornalismo*, p. 86.

Espectaculo (Pg.)   "Spectacle." A weekly periodical dedicated to theater, films, and music, published in Lourenço Marques with F.C. Martins Machado as director. Its first issue appeared August 15, 1953, and its last in May, 1954. Dias, *A Imprensa*, p. 97.

espinheiro (Pg.)   A handsome tree (*Acacia albida*) with a whitish bark and short curved thorns that grows in Luanda, Mossâmedes, Zambezia, and other parts of southern Angola and arid areas of Mozambique. This kind of acacia is characteristic of the region. Ficalho, *Plantas Uteis*, p. 170.

Espirito Santo (Pg.)   A river that flows east into Delagoa Bay, Lourenço Marques, southern Mozambique. It was explored by the Portuguese in 1544. In 1546, King João II ordered the establishment of a factory to trade with the interior. In 1780, the Dutch and the local chiefs challenged Portuguese control. After the Dutch left the area, Portugal allied itself with Chief Mfumo to regain possession of the bay and the trade. Axelson, *Portuguese in South-East*, pp. 141, 217.

esponjeira (Pg.)   A small variety of wild or cultivated tropical thorn tree (*Acacia farnesiana*). In Angola, Africans cultivate this plant to extract a black resin used to paint baskets, pots, and other domestic articles. Ficalho, *Plantas Uteis*, p. 173.

esquilo (Pg.)   In Mozambique, small rodents represented by five species, *Paraxerus cepagi*, *P. palliatus*, *P. flavivitis*, *P. vincenti*, and *Heliosciurus refobrachium*. They have small heads, big eyes, and bushy tails. The color of their hair ranges from ash gray to golden yellow. PDM.

ESSO Exploration of Guinea   ESSO (acronym for Standard Oil, now EXXON), the large American oil corporation, established itself in Guinea-Bissau in March 1958 and was given exclusive oil prospecting rights at an annual cost of US$250,000. An additional $14 to $60 was paid for each square kilometer where prospecting actually took place. Beyond this there was a 12.5 percent tax on production and a 50 percent tax on profits. In 1966 and 1973 the contract between the Portuguese government and ESSO Exploration was renewed and extended to include other minerals. The on-shore and off-shore results of prospecting were not conclusive, but conditions are propitious for finding oil-yielding strata. Since independence (1974) the new government suspended the contract with ESSO and a new contract was written with AGIP, an Italian petroleum company. HDRGC.

Estado Novo, O (Pg.)   "The New State." A right-wing corporate-state established by Dr. Antonio de Oliveira Salazar in Portugal in 1930 and lasting until 1968. Modeled in part on Mussolini's Italy, it promised continuity, stability, and centralization of power. Salazar's principal objective in Africa was to impose a uniform administration, centrally controlled from Lisbon. After the disorder and extravagance of the previous decades, this was a wise policy, but it involved challenging the privileges of foreign concession-holders, the most important of whom were British and South African. It was the first great achievement of the Salazar government in such an endeavor that, while it systematically eliminated the rights of concession-holders and reduced the opportunities for forcing interference, it was able at the same time to increase its international standing and security. At the heart of the *Estado Novo* policy were the Colonial Act of 1930 and the Overseas Administration Reform of 1933. In 1955 the key colonial policy had three fundamental aims: spiritual assimilation, administrative differentiation, and economic solidarity. Newitt, *Portugal*, pp. 43-4; DHP.

Estrela da Alva (Pg.) "Morning Star." This star, clearly seen by Portuguese navigators on the Atlantic coast at the Discovery (q.v.), was the planet Venus. It is the most brilliant planet in the solar system, second in distance from the sun, anciently or poetically called Lucifer as the Morning Star and Heperus as the Evening Star. DMA; WNWD.

Estrela do Norte (Pg.) "Northern Star." This star, well known by Portuguese navigators at the Discovery (q.v.), is in the constellation Ursa Minor which contains twenty-three visible stars that form the Little Dipper. The most important of these stars, the North Star, is at the end of the dipper's handle; it is a stationary star used for navigation. DMA; WNWD.

Ethiopia Ancient biblical Cush, the name given by the Greeks to the people of the southernmost part of the then known world. They were converted to Christianity in the mid-fourth century, but their links with the West were cut by the Moslem conquest in 639-42AD resulting in Ethiopia being isolated for over 500 years from the rest of Christianity. Beginning in the twelfth century, during the pontificate of Calixtus II (1119-24), the medieval legend of a powerful patriarch in Africa named Patriarch John or Presbyter John, who came to be known as Prester John, began to spread throughout Europe. The concept of the presence of a Christian priest-king on the other side of the land occupied by the Moslems against whom Christendom had declared war raised great hopes and enthusiasm in the West and proved an enormous influence on the literature and the voyages of discovery of the time, particularly in Portugal. A fifteenth-century ambassador from King Ogawé of Benin informed King João II of Portugal of the presence of Prester John. Bartolomeu Dias received orders from King Manuel to look for Prester John during his trip around the Cape of Good Hope in 1488. Friar Antonio of Lisbon seems to be the first Portuguese emissary sent c.1500 in search of Prester John, traveling by way of Egypt. A Portuguese envoy arrived at the Ethiopian court in 1520 during the reign of David II, or *Negus* (Emperor) Lebna Dengel. Friar Francisco Alvares, the chaplain of the Portuguese group, published a complete description of conditions in Ethiopia entitled *Ho Preste Joam das Indias. Verdadera informação das terras do Preste Joam, segundo vio e escriveo ho padre Francisco Alvares capellã del Rey nosso Senhor. Agora novamente impresso por mandato do dito senhor em casa de Luis Rodrigues livreiro de su Alteza*, Lisboa, 1540. Portuguese interest in Ethiopia came to be primarily religious. From 1557 to 1603, Portuguese Jesuits were in charge of converting them from Coptic to Roman Catholic Christianity, educating them, and attending to their spiritual life. The Jesuits were expelled from the country and Portuguese influence decreased substantially. Cortesão, *History*, I:255-7; Coutinho, *Os Portugueses na Ethiopia*, Congresso da Historia, Lisboa, 1938, II:257-60; DHP; GEPB.

Ethiopia Oriental (Pg.) "Eastern Ethiopia." A book written by the Dominican friar João dos Santos; a coherent account on life and customs of Mozambique published in Lisbon in 1609. Duffy, *Portuguese Africa*, p. 38.

etunda (Afr.) Communal pastureland on the high sandy plain in the interior of Ambo country, southern Angola c.1920. Henderson, *Angola*, p. 54.

Evangelho, O (Pg.) "The Gospel." A journal that appeared in Lourenço Marques, Mozambique, on February 5, 1927. Its last issue was published on October 29, 1949. Dias, *A Imprensa*, p. 85.

evangelization, decline of A period of decline for Portuguese missionaries in their efforts to convert Africans to Christianity began around 1650 when internal political instability in Portugal and external attacks by European adversaries undermined Portugal's political strength. Clear evidence of this decline was the conquest of Luanda and Benguela by the Dutch in 1641. It was not until the middle of the nineteenth century that a new and strong missionary spirit emerged in Portugal spearheaded by graduates of the famous missionary college *Sernache do Bonjardim* (q.v.) established in the 1840s. Cunha, *O Sistema Portugués*, pp. 105-7; Gabriel, *Angola*, p. 272.

Evora An ancient city in south-central Portugal, the capital of Alentejo and second largest city in Portugal in the mid-sixteenth century. African slaves were among the population as early as 1466. Nicolaus Clenardus, the Dutch humanist, reported on his arrival at Evora in 1535, "I thought that I had come to some city of evils: everywhere there were so many blacks, whom I so loathe, that they may just be able to drive me away from here." The 3,000 African slaves at that time amounted to 16 percent of the total population. Between 1547 and 1555, they declined to 9.4 percent. Evora was the residence of the Portuguese court during the fifteenth and sixteenth centuries. Saunders, *A Social History*, pp. 1, 57-61; GEPB; WNGD.

ewongo (Afr.) In São Salvador do Congo and elsewhere, c.1880, cassava (*Manihot esculenta* Crantz.) peeled and shredded, then soaked for a day or two in water. The cassava is then squeezed to remove poisonous alkaloids and reboiled in fresh water or dried and ground into a flour for bread or for making tapioca. It is an important source of starch. BeAD.

ewunze (Afr.) In São Salvador do Congo c.1880, a tree growing in swampy places and in standing water, the fruit of which yields a red dye or, when mixed with a crushed climbing plant and steeped in black mud, a black dye. BeAD.

ewuwa (Afr.) In São Salvador do Congo c.1880, a tree yielding a large edible sweet fruit that has sections like a pineapple, and is also similar in color and size. The large leaves of the tree do not decay as readily as other leaves so the ground beneath the tree is therefore always strewn with them; the wood is useless. BeAD.

exilu (Cong.) In São Salvador do Congo c.1880, a rock on which locals break nuts. BeAD.

Eximiae Devotionis (Lat.) A bull issued in Rome by Pope Leo X on August 7, 1513, granting the Lisbon vicar of the Church of Our Lady of the Conception the right to baptize any slave brought from Guiné, and anyone else who desired it. In need or in danger of death, such a person could be baptized by the captain of a ship. This license, requested by King Manuel I, apparently was unsuccessful; in 1553 the royal secretary Pedro Carneiro complained of the large numbers of slaves landed in Lisbon and sold without ever having been baptized. Pinto Rema, *A Primeira Evangelização*, BCG, 1966, xxi(82):321; Saunders, *A Social History*, p. 41; GEPB.

exodus of settlers Many Portuguese, East Indian, and *mestiço* settlers began to leave Angola and Mozambique for Portugal and elsewhere at the start of the War for Independence in 1961. By 1975 there were about one million settlers and their families in Portugal, crowding the outskirts of Lisbon, Porto, and other cities. The *retornados* (q.v.) created serious problems in housing, education, and health, an upheaval never before experienced in Portugal. Bender, *Angola*, pp. 227, 236-7; Harvey, *Portugal*, pp. 126-8.

Expansão Portuguesa (Pg.) "Portuguese Expansion." The early Portuguese expansion along the West African coast began in 1434, sponsored by Prince Henry. Gomes Eanes de Zurara gives five reasons for the *Expansão Portuguesa*: scientific curiosity, economic interests, to measure the forces of Islam, to form new alliances to fight against Islam, and to conquer souls for Christ. Cunha, *O Sistema Portugués*, p. 66.

Expe (Mand.) Among the Mandingos in the fourteenth century, a secret society that set values and regulated social and economic activities for itself. Rodney, Walter, *The Guinea Coast*, CHA, Cambridge, 4:280.

Exponi Nobis (Lat.) A papal brief signed by Pope Leo X in 1513 in response to a request by King Manuel I to allow Ethiopians, Hindus, and Africans from Morocco, then living in Portugal, to be allowed to become priests. The request was granted, and henceforth these non-Europeans could be invested in full holy orders, regardless of the circumstances of their birth. The pope also agreed with the king's wishes to limit the new priests' freedom of action. Consequently, they could preach, celebrate mass, and administer the sacraments only when there were no parish priests available and on no condition were they to hold a benefice or be responsible for any ecclesiastical property such as a chapel. Saunders, *A Social History*, p. 157; DHP.

exportação de-mão-de-obra (Pg.) "Exportation of laborers." Since 1880, a large number of workers immigrated to the gold fields in South Africa, farms in Southern Rhodesia (now Zimbabwe), and to work in other neighboring countries. In 1954 in Mozambique, Portugal collected £30 tax from an employer for each laborer. Caetano, *Os Nativos*, p. 38.

{ F }

factor "Business agent." Early in the Discovery (q.v.), the factor was a royal appointee representing the highest authority in a seaport or fortress, in charge of collecting duties and taxes on merchandise and slaves passing through the post. The earliest factors were stationed in Arguim (1445), Elmina (1483), and later on São Tomé Island. In Portugal there was a factor at the *Casa da Guiné* in Lagos, a post established in 1440, which in 1481 was transferred to Lisbon. In 1499, the Crown appointed a factor in Antwerp, the center of trade with Portugal and the rest of Europe. Saunders, *A Social History*, p. 13; GEPB.

factoria (Pg.) "Factory." A group of buildings occupied by factors who conducted trade in Portugal and in foreign cities and ports. Through factories the Crown was able to control and collect duties and taxes for the West African coast beginning around 1445. DHP.

fadenia (Mand.) Male lineage among the Mandingos in Guinea-Bissau; children belong to the paternal line for all juridical, social, and religious affiliations. Silva, *Usos e Costumes*, BCG, 1968, xxiii(91-92):269.

fado (Pg.) Apparently of Brazilian origin, it is a combination of song and dance. After having been taken to Lisbon in 1833, it became popular in bars, cabarets, and public dancing places. Around 1954 the Lisbon form was reported known in Lourenço Marques. Soon local composers wrote narrative, romantic, and love *fados*, usually accompanying the singing with two guitars, one Portuguese and the other Spanish. From Lourenço Marques this music was taken to Beira, Nampula, and Johannesburg, South Africa, where there was a large Portuguese-Mozambican colony. Nunes Nabarro, *The Background*, in Valkhoff, *Miscelanea*, pp. 259-62.

Faial (Pg.) Westernmost island of the central group of the Azores, discovered c.1427 by Portuguese navigators in the service of Prince Henry. Faial is actually a volcano, called the *Pico Gordo* (Fat Peak), that rises to only 3,421 ft. (1043 m), but which has an immense volcanic crater over a mile (1.6 km) wide and 400 ft. (122 m) deep. Volcanic eruptions and earthquakes occurred in April, 1672, and throughout 1957-8. Early colonization efforts between 1427 and 1452 were not successful, but in 1466 the Flemish pioneer Jos van Huerter and a group of colonists obtained *sesmarias* (land grants) that initiated development. Around 1700 wine from Faial was exported to New England and the West Indies. Also spelled *Faral* and *Fayal*. Duncan, *The Atlantic Islands*, p. 8; GEPB.

Fala de Guiné (Pg.) "Guinea-speech." A simplified Creole dialect spoken in Lisbon and other urban centers c. 1455 by newly arrived slaves from Guiné and the West African coast. Some scholars suggest that what was brought to Portugal was an early fifteenth-century trade jargon spoken by Africans on the Atlantic coast and islands. This speech has strong morphologic, syntactic, and phonetic resemblances to standard Portuguese, as demonstrated in plays by Gil Vicente, a classic playwright. It is reported that a "black king" from Sierra Leone entertained the public in 1455 by performing a song in rudimentary *Fala de Guine* to accompany a dance at the wedding of the Infanta Dona Joana. Also called *Fala de Negros*. Saunders, *A Social History*, pp. 99-101, 111-2, 168-9; DHP; GEPB.

Faná Jamá (Afr.) Among the Islamic Fulas in Guinea-Bissau, a special weekly prayer meeting that lasts over thirteen hours, held every Friday in mosques. Gonçalves, *O Mundo Arabo-Islámico*, p. 214.

fanado (Afr.) In Guinea-Bissau, a religious festival among the Islamic Balantas organized to celebrate the circumcision rite. Guerra, *Terras da Guiné*, p. 75. *See also* blufo.

fará (Afr.) Name given by the Mandingos of Guinea-Bissau to a beverage prepared with the ground bark of a tropical tree (*Bauhinia reticulata*) to treat syphilis and hemorrhoids. The bark also provides a strong fiber used to make cordage. The roots supply a mahogany-colored dye; the pods and seeds a black and blue dye, respectively. Carreira, *Mandingas*, p. 241.

faraçola (Pg.) An ancient Indian measure of weight equivalent in Mozambique in 1554 to 25 *arreteis* (25.4 lbs.; 11.5 kg), and in Sofala to 27 *arreteis* (27.3 lbs.; 12.4 kg). Axelson, *Portuguese in South-East*, p. 244.

Faral *See* Faial.

farim (Afr.) (1) In Guinea-Bissau in the Mansoa River area, a group of villages ruled by a Mandingo chief and his council of elders. At the time of the Portuguese arrival in 1460, these *farims* were under an African king settled in the upper Niger River. Mota, *Guiné Portuguesa*, I:280.

Farim (Afr.) (2)   A town founded by Gonçalo de Gambia in 1642. It is the seat of a municipality on the bank of the Farim River (q.v.) at the confluence with the Sao Domingos River in Guinea-Bissau. In 1960, before the War for Independence (1961-1975), its population of 40,000 included 563 whites. Fulas and Mandingos are the main ethnic groups established in the Farim municipality. GEPB.

Farim River (Afr.)   In Guinea-Bissau, a river with headwaters to the north of Contubel on the Geba River. The Farim River flows almost directly west until it reaches the town of Farim. At this point it begins to widen and becomes known as the Cacheu River, since it is in the vicinity of the town of that name. The Farim and Cacheu rivers, with a combined length of about 160 miles (258 km), formed an important corridor for commerce and the export of slaves to Brazil. HDRGC.

Faro (Pg.)   A seaport on the Algarve, southern Portugal, on the Atlantic coast 137 mi. (220 km) south-southeast of Lisbon. Taken from Moorish control in 1249, it was sacked by the Englishman Sir Francis Drake in 1596. At the time of the Discovery (q.v.), it was an important center of navigation and commerce with sailors and merchants crowded aboard caravels for exploration and trading, sailing to Arguim, Guiné, and São Jorge da Mina. There were earthquakes there in 1722 and 1733. In 1981 it was a municipality with a population of 42,450; today it trades in fish, wine, oil, cork, and dried and fresh fruit. Iria, *O Algarve no Descobrimento*, Congresso da Guine, Lisboa, 1946, I:196; WNGD.

fazenda-de-negro (Pg.)   In Mozambique before the twentieth century, coarse cotton fabric of various colors, made in Damascus, Syria, and imported to manufacture garments worn by African slaves on the *prazos* (q.v.). PDM.

"Fazer vida marital com a sua mulher" (Pg.)   "To live a married life with your wife." An expression used c.1625 in Angola and elsewhere to force married men who were not government officials and who had been away for a longer time than considered reasonable to return to their wives in Portugal. Boxer, *Women,* pp. 27-28.

FDLA (*Frente Democratico para a Libertação de Angola*) (Pg.)   "Democratic Front for the Liberation of Angola," a nationalist party organized by Agostino A. Neto in 1963 with the purpose of establishing a new alliance of all active separatist movements in Angola. The FDLA party faded away when it moved its headquarters from Kinshasa (formerly Leopoldville) to Brazaville, Congo. Wheeler, *Angola,* pp. 214-15, 223.

febre da carraça (Pg.) "Tick fever." A tropical disease caused by the bite of a crab-louse (*Ornithodoros moubata*, subfamily *Argasinae*). In 1909 it was reported as being endemic in Mozambique. *Revista Medica de Angola*, Luanda, 1923, 4:329-336.

fedegoso (Pg.) In Angola and elsewhere, a small tropical biennial or triennial shrub (*Cassia occidentalis* L.). Its roots are used to prepare a drug with properties similar to quinine used to treat fevers; its roasted seeds are boiled to prepare a kind of coffee. It is found on Santiago and the Santo Antão Islands, Cape Verde, and Luanda, Ambriz, and Golungo Alto in Angola and in Mozambique. Africans call it *munhanoca* or *maioba*. Ficalho, *Plantas Uteis,* pp. 149-50.

feijão cutelinho (Pg.) A tropical legume (*Dolichos lablab* L.), also called hyacinth bean, bearing edible pods and beans and widely cultivated in Portuguese Africa. It is usually found on high mountains which seems to indicate that it is indigenous to Cape Verde and cooler parts of Angola such as Luanda, and Zambezia and Mossâmedes, Mozambique. Ficalho, *Plantas Uteis,* p. 140.

feijão do Congo (Pg.) In Cape Verde, Africa, and elsewhere, a tropical legume (*Cajanus cajan* L.), the Congo or pigeon pea, widely cultivated for its edible pods and beans; a basic food among Africans. Carvalho e Vasconcellos, *As Colonias Portuguesas,* p. 48.

feitoria da Coroa (Pg.) Fortified commercial centers along the African coasts, administered by a royal factor (q.v.), protected by soldiers, and often having a church with missionaries to convert and baptize non-Christians. Early in the Discovery (q.v.), most of these ports were under the control of the king. Caetano, *Os Nativos*, p. 94.

feitoria do interior (Pg.) Scattered commercial posts c.1700, administered by a merchant in charge of buying local goods such as gold, ivory, and slaves, and selling European cloth, beverages, guns, and general merchandise. These posts were branches of a large coastal center. Caetano, *Os Nativos*, p. 95.

fel da terra (Pg.) In Guinea-Bissau, an annual wild herb (*Schultesia stenophylla* var. *larifodia* Mart.) with yellow flowers that grows in moist soil. A preparation made of its leaves is used in folk medicine to treat the discharge of blood. It has a bitter taste according to Frederic M.J. Welwitsch, the Austrian botanist (1807-1872). Espirito Santo, *Plantas Venenosas e Medicinais*, BCG, 1948, 10:403-4; Ficalho, *Plantas Uteis,* p. 222.

felo (Afr.) A grassy hill with scattered groves found at a maximum altitude of about 985 ft. (300 m) that marks the transition between the plains and the *planalto* (tableland) of Boé and Bafatá-Gabu in Futa-Djallon, Guinea-Bissau. Mota, *Guiné Portuguesa*, I:24. *See also* aindé.

Felupes (Afr.) In Guinea-Bissau, a small Senegambian ethnic group closely related to the Balantas and Baiotes (qq. v.). The Felupes are well known as rice cultivators who use the flood irrigation technique. They are mainly located in the northwest corner of the country, especially south of the Casamance and north of the Cacheu rivers, reaching to the Atlantic coast in that region. During the period of aggressive Portuguese colonization, military reports show acts of resistance by the Felupes in 1878-90, 1901, 1903, and finally in 1915. HDRGC.

Fernão Veloso Bay A deep sea inlet of the Mozambique Channel on the northeast coast of Mozambique, south of Cape Loguno. In 1829 Portugal established a colony there that was often attacked by neighboring Arab sheiks. It was one of the three captaincies into which Joaquim A. de Moushino de Albuquerque (1855-1902) divided the district of Mozambique in 1896. GEDL; GEPB.

Ferro (Pg.) One of the smallest and westernmost of the Canary Islands off the northwest coast of Africa; now known as Hierro. It is a rocky volcanic island with an area of 107 sq. mi. (277 sq. km). Its population in 1970 was 5,500. It is part of the Spanish province of Santa Cruz de Tenerife. In ancient times it was Spain's westernmost point, hence the Spanish reckoned zero longitude from it. It was used by Portuguese navigators and cartographers as the zero meridian from the sixteenth century until adoption of the Greenwich meridian in 1884. DHP; GEPB.

Ferroviario, O (Pg.) "The Railroad Worker." A periodical published in Lourenço Marques, Mozambique; its first issue appeared in July, 1951, with Anibal A. Valente as editor. After publication was interrupted in 1952, it reappeared on April 23, 1953. In November of the same year it ceased. Until 1948 it was owned by the *Clube Ferroviario* and after that by *Clube Ferroviario de Mozambique*. Dias, *A Imprensa*, pp. 93-4.

Feudalismo Luso-Africano em Angola (Pg.) "Luso-African Feudalism in Angola." A colonial system established by the Portuguese in Angola and elsewhere by which the government bound all African chiefs as vassals in exchange for military and commercial gains and, most of all, for slaves for Brazilian plantations. The governor had enough power to enforce this allegiance and keep control over Angola and its population during the reign of King João V from 1706 to 1750. This semi-feudal policy was ended in 1885 at the Berlin Conference (q.v.). Silva Rego, *O Ultramar,* pp. 63-4, 66-7; GEPB.

Feudalismo Luso-Africano em Moçambique (Pg.) "Luso-African Feudalism in Mozambique." A colonial policy that was developed in Zambezia in 1696 by the Lisbon government. The emphasis was on strict control of the African chiefs and promotion of commerce and trade out of centers like Sofala, Mozambique Island, and Manica along the Zambezi and the Sabe rivers. This policy, finally destroyed by the *prazeros* (q.v.), lasted until late in the eighteenth century. Silva Rego, *O Ultramar,* pp. 99, 263, 324. GEPB.

Fez (Ar.) A commercial city in north-central Morocco, approximately 150 mi. (242 km) northeast of Casablanca. One of the sacred cities of Islam, founded in 790, it has many mosques, including Qarawiyin (founded c.850). For many years it was the traditional capital of Morocco. After the conquest of Ceuta in 1415, the Portuguese often intervened in the Arab government of Fez. By leading his second expedition to North Africa in 1578, King Sebastião had plans to conquer the city and be crowned its king. Its population in 1982 was 488.823. It produces leather and metal goods. GEPB; WNGD.

Fico (Pg.) "We stay." The name of a political party founded in Beira, Mozambique, in 1973 by white settlers determined to take a stand and perpetuate white supremacy. Violently opposed to the FRELIMO (q.v.) Marxist policy, Fico petered out even as its constituents demonstrated great energy and courage in defending Portugal. This right-wing settler group organized an abortive coup in Lourenço Marques on September 8, 1974, the day after the signing of the Lusaka Accord (q.v.). The organizers wanted to secure a policy of continuity with the West. Munslow, *Mozambique,* p. 128.

fidalgo (Pg.) "Nobleman." A member of the Portuguese nobility. This system was also established in the Kingdom of Congo by King Afonso I after he was granted the privilege of *carta de armas* (charter to grant coats of arms) and to organize a royal aristocracy by King Manuel I in 1508. Missionaries performed a ritual in the ceremony that bestowed the title that entitled the grantee to use the honorary title of *Dom* (q.v.). Gabriel, *Angola,* pp. 58-9, 142. *See also* carta de armas.

fidalgo da selvageria (Pg.) "Gentleman of the wilderness." In Mozambique and elsewhere, the ironic term for *mestiço* Africans who rejected manual labor and lived by stealing, exploiting, and defaulting on other Africans. Around 1902 they began to migrate to East Transvaal. Rita-Ferreira, *O Movimento Migratorio,* pp. 55-6.

Fides Religio Moresque Aethiopum (Lat.) "Faith, Religion, and Mores of the Ethiopes." An historical account by Damião de Gois based on information provided by an Ethiopian priest, the ambassador of Emperor David I, who was living in Lisbon 1530-5. The book, published in Louvain in 1540, drew conclusions regarding Ethiopian religion that were used by Portuguese theologians to declare in 1555 that Ethiopians were not true Roman Christians. Coutinho, *Os Portugueses na Ethiopia,* Congresso da Historia, Lisboa, 1938, II:258.

figueira (Pg.) "Fig tree." The tropical fig tree (*Ficus carica*) that grows wild in Senegambia, near Nioro on the Niger River between Timbuctu and Gao, in Bornu, and elsewhere in Africa; its fruit is part of the local diet. It is widely cultivated in North Africa, and in the Middle Ages was taken by Arabs to Western Sudan where it is still grown extensively in such places as Katsina in Hausaland. A Mediterranean variety of fig was introduced by the Portuguese in early colonial period to Angola, Mozambique, and Cape Verde. Ficalho, *Plantas Uteis,* p. 269; Lewicki, *West African Food,* pp. 70-1.

filariasis   A tropical disease caused by filarial nematodes (*Wuchereria bancrofti)* transmitted by mosquitoes. The nematodes invade the lymphatic vessels and lymphoid tissue, causing chronic swelling of the lower extremities and other parts of the body. It is endemic in coastal regions of Mozambique. The actual incidence is poorly documented, but from 85 to 100 cases were usually reported annually. It is also known in West Africa. Simmons, *Global Epidemology,* II:220; GEPB.

filho da terra (Pg.) "Son of the land." Term used to refer to the *mestiço* child of a Portuguese father and an African mother, sometimes an outlawed individual. These mixed-race people formed an acculturated group, part Christian and part animist, that played important roles in such colonies as Guinea-Bissau. Mota, *Guiné Portuguesa,* I:25.

Filhos da Terra   "Sons of the Land." Term used to refer to a generation of Angolan writers who flourished in the 1890s and began a literary movement centered in Luanda where a group of African intellectuals found cultural and political expression through an incipient African press. The movement coincided with the publication of *O Echo de Angola* (q.v.), a periodical founded in Luanda on November 12, 1881. This signaled the beginning of African participation in the formerly white-controlled press. One member of the *Filhos da Terra* generation was Joaquim Dias Cordeiro da Matta. Hamilton, *Voices,* p. 28.

Filhos do Ibo (Pg.) "Sons of Ibo." An African Moslem ethnic congregation formed of Africans and *mestiços* whose forebears originated in India. Their mosques are very modest and their religious practices and rituals do not conform with strict Islamic rules. Gonçalves, *O Mundo Arabo-Islámico,* p. 270.

fina (Afr.) In São Salvador do Congo c.1880, a practitioner of black magic who supposedly transforms himself into a strange sprite and, sitting on a beam in his victim's house, sings and looks at his sleeping victim. What he did and how he did it, no one would admit to knowing because to know would make a man a warlock. BeAD.

finaçon (Crio.) A type of folksong sung at *batuque* (q.v.) dance meetings on Santiago Island, Cape Verde, and in Guinea-Bissau. This music, performed by a soloist and a choir, according to historians has as its main characteristic the "expression of moral rules [and] norms of individual and social behavior." A *finaçon* can be satirical or obscene or even be a praise song based on African traditional music. Hamilton, *Voices,* pp. 251-3.

Fisico-mor de Angola (Pg.) "Surgeon General of Angola." A position established in Luanda by the Portuguese government in 1703. *Revista Medica de Angola,* Luanda, 1923, 2:195-96.

flagellation A term applied c.1966 by Portuguese soldiers to a guerrilla tactic consisting of a burst of gunfire against a stalled convoy or ambushed patrol followed by a quick getaway. Such tactics inflicted physical and psychological damage on the incumbent forces while minimizing the attackers' losses and swelling the confidence of the guerrillas and their civilian adherents. It was a strategy that accelerated the defeat of the Portuguese government. Henriksen, *Revolution,* p. 41.

Flanders A major European commercial center in what was then the Low Countries (now Belgium). Also, the name of a group of Dutch colonists who in 1456 made the first shipment of Madeiran sugar ever sent to England. Later, the colonists shipped considerable quantities to Flanders. The exported sugar had been boiled only once and was very raw so most of the refining had to be done in European sugar factories. The Madeiran cultivation was so successful, and production so plentiful, that the price of sugar on European markets fell by about 50 percent between 1470 and 1500. Duncan, *Atlantic Islands,* p. 10.

Flanders, voyages to In the fifteenth century, Flanders was a region of the Low Countries on the North Sea comprising the Scheldt (Escaut) River and the hills of Artois. It was involved in trade in Guiné, Cape Verde, the Madeira Islands, and the West African coast during the early part of the Portuguese expansion. One of the first traders in Flanders was Alvise Cadamosto, a wealthy Venetian merchant who had a trade patent from Prince Henry to import into Flanders wine, sugar, goat's leather, Madeiran wood, *urzela* (orchil, q.v.) for dyeing, and other products of the land. Because Flanders was at the crossroads of Europe, Portuguese trade with that region increased greatly until the eighteenth century. It is now part of Belgium. Duncan, *Atlantic Islands,* pp. 10, 151, 225; Prestage, *The Portuguese Pioneers*, pp. 95, 97.

Flechas (Pg.) "Arrows." Name given to agents of a paramilitary branch of PIDE (q.v.) that began operating in the Portuguese colonies in mid-1973. The *Flechas* comprised squads of Africans commanded by Portuguese. Trained in military skills and parachuting as well as intelligence, the *Flechas* took on not only military intelligence missions but acted occasionally as a commando force against insurgents. First utilized in Mozambique, the *Flechas* began operations in Vila Perry, Manica district, in 1973. Their ruthlessness and success struck a responsive chord among those settlers who favored a get-tough policy toward FRELIMO (q.v.) and its rural sympathizers. Professional soldiers resented the *Flechas'* intrusion into their own operating zones. The army moreover believed that the *Flechas'* brutal methods undermined their efforts to win over local Africans to the Portuguese banner. Made up of secret police agents, former guerrillas, and people of disreputable reputation, the *Flechas* gained an unsavory reputation for torture and summary executions. Henriksen, *Revolution,* pp. 54, 62, 107; DHP.

Flemish Islands Name given to the Azores on Dutch maps c.1460 when Prince Fernando of Portugal inherited them from his uncle Prince Henry, known as The Navigator. After the death of Prince Henry, who had been lord-proprietor of the islands, Flemish merchants and adventurers were called in to develop the territory. Flemings established the first settlements in Terçeira, and were wholly responsible for the initial colonization during the late 1460s and early 1470s. Duncan, *Atlantic Islands,* p. 16; Prestage, *The Portuguese Pioneers*, p. 48.

FLGC (*Frente de Libertação da Guiné Portuguesa e Cabo Verde*) (Pg.) "Front for the Liberation of Portuguese Guiné and Cape Verde," a political movement that emerged in 1960 led by Henri Labery, also the founder of the *União das Populações da Guiné* (UPG, q.v.) in 1957. Essentially FLGC replaced three smaller parties based in Dakar, Senegal and provided an effective base to oppose the leadership of Amilcar L. Cabral. HDRGC.

FLING (*Frente de Luta pela Independencia Nacional da Guiné-Bissau*) (Pg.) "Front for the National Independence of Guinea-Bissau," an extremely militant party, founded in July 1962 in Dakar, Senegal. In 1963 it began military operations against the Portuguese. Jaime Pinto Bull became president in 1966, and the main operation continued from the Dakar office. After quarrelling with PAIGC (q.v.), FLING lost influence in the nationalist struggle. In 1970 Domingos Joseph da Silva took over as the new secretary-general and in 1973 the leadership passed to Mario Jones Fernandes. FLING was accused by other nationalists of creating disturbances in Bissau, Bolama, and Bafata in May 1974. After independence, members of FLING were arrested in April 1976 by the new government of Guinea-Bissau. HDRGC.

Flores Island (Pg.) The westernmost, most isolated, and stormiest island of the Azore archipelago. Its existence, if not its exact location, was known to Portuguese navigators before 1439. In 1452 it was rediscovered by Diogo de Teive. By 1680 it produced about 69,300 English bushels (2.2 million lbs.; 2,442 kl) of wheat. It has an area of 58 square miles, with a population in 1980 of 22,431. Duncan, *Atlantic Islands,* pp. 12, 16, 261; WNGD.

floresta do fanado (Pg.) "Circumcision grove." In Guinea-Bissau and elsewhere a sacred grove where circumcision rites take place. Gonçalves, *O Mundo Arabo-Islámico,* p. 103.

fodeo (Afr.) In Guinea-Bissau and elsewhere among the Fulani and Mandingos, an Islamic cleric holding spiritual and temporal powers in his community, in charge of youth education. Gonçalves, *O Mundo Arabo-Islámico,* p. 196.

Fogo (Pg.) The third largest island of the Cape Verde Archipelago, discovered around 1450 by Portuguese navigators and the second island in the group to be settled. It attracted colonists from Madeira who farmed and dealt in slaves. By 1582 the slave population had reached 2,000. After independence in 1975, the Cape Verde government began a reforestation program, built roads, constructed schools and dikes for water conservation, and increased coffee production on the island. In 1980 it had a population of 31,115. HDRGC.

foleo (Afr.) A woody tropical vine (*Landolfia heudelotii* A.DC.) found in Guinea-Bissau and elsewhere in West Africa. It yields a valuable latex, used in the rubber industry, and edible fruits. Carreira, *Mandingas,* p. 132.

fonio (Afr.) A wild and cultivated grass (*Digitata exilis*); a type of grain with many varieties, found in the basins of the upper Senegal and Niger rivers, pointing to early domestication in the area. It is very resistant to drought and needs little cultivation. It prospers in areas too infertile for other crops. The earliest reference to it (1352-3) comes from the old Mali Empire. Europeans first called it "hungry rice" in the seventeenth century. It is currently consumed in Western Sudan. In Portuguese, *fonio* is known as *fundo*. Lewicki, *West African Food,* pp. 22, 35, 37-38; HDRGC.

Fontismo (Pg.) An economic theory developed mainly by Antonio Maria de Fontes Pereira de Mello in the 1870s based on the assumption that Portuguese economic weakness could be remedied without fundamental institutional change by borrowing heavily on the international money market to build up a communications infrastructure. Once this was achieved, industrialization would automatically follow. This policy was embraced by the Portuguese government, anxious for improved industrialization. But approach could only work if there were adequate control over expenditure and a willingness to liquidate the international debt as rapidly as possible. Neither of these conditions was met and *Fontismo* caused dislocation in the economic development of Mozambique and Angola, especially with the agricultural change brought about by the introduction of sugar, coconut, groundnut, and other new crops in Zambezia and parts of Angola. The *Fontismo* policy was abandoned around the time of the British Ultimatum (q.v.) in 1890. Vail, *Capitalism,* pp. 125-7.

Football Clube de Luanda (Pg.) "Soccer Club of Luanda." A periodical published in Luanda, Angola, in December 1937. Lopo, *Jornalismo,* p. 59.

forced labor policy In Portuguese Africa, forced labor policy was established around 1850. It was based on the view that, since farming traditionally was a woman's task, men could and should work in other areas as a "civilizing" experience. In addition, it had the advantage of providing cheap labor for government and commercial enterprises. While the Native Labor Code of 1878 enabled Africans to decide for themselves whether they wanted to work or not and only vagrants could be compelled to work; however, the vagrancy clause included all Africans engaged in their traditional work instead of laboring for Europeans. On November 9, 1899, the government ruled that forced labor was necessary for economic development and the moral and intellectual improvement of Africans. Subsequent legislation intended both to eliminate major abuses and to end international controversy over Portuguese labor policy. The Native Labor Code of 1928 forbade the use of forced labor by private individuals or enterprises, but the government retained the right to enlist the labor of any African who did not fulfill certain criteria for self-sufficiency and economic contribution to society. The Rural Labor Code of 1962 replaced the 1928 code, abolishing forced cultivation of commercial crops and repealing all legislation that enforced the moral obligation of Africans to work. A new labor agency had the responsibility of safeguarding Africans against violations and abuses of the law. Herrick, *Area*

Handbook, pp. 3, 153, 172; Kaplan, *Area Handbook,* pp. 40-1. *See also* chibalo.

foreiro (Pg.) In Mozambique around 1700, a *prazo*-holder with a contract of *emphyteusis* (q.v.). The *foreiro* had the right to prospect for gold and to farm the land. Beside paying rent, his obligations included carrying out almost all the functions of government, such as collecting taxes, controlling custom duties, maintaining the church, and initiating the celebration of religious festivals. Newitt, *Portuguese Settlement,* p. 123.

fornecido (Pg.) In Mozambique and elsewhere, a laborer who by law was forced to work for the government or for private employers. In 1927 there were 14,939 *fornecidos* in Lourenço Marques alone. Rita-Ferreira, *O Movimento Migratorio,* p. 159. *See also* requisitado.

forro (Pg.) (1) "Free man." An African slave, c.1500, freed by his master on certain conditions, including the payment of a certain sum of money. A tax of about 10 percent of the purchase price was also part of the manumission requirements. Sometimes the term *meio forro* (half-quit) was used. If a slave were owned by two people, often husband and wife, their joint consent was required for him to be freed. Saunders, *A Social History,* pp. xiii, 140, 144; GEPB.

forro (Pg.) (2) "Free man." In São Tomé, a free man who was the African descendant of freed colonial slaves, either African or *mestiço.* The *forros,* for the most part, formed a economically- and socially-deprived illiterate lower-middle class. It was believed that *forros* felt antipathy toward regular productive labor and that many were inclined to enjoy drinking, dancing, gambling, and were often guilty of criminal acts, despite the fact that the rural police and clothing merchants include a large number of *forros.* Tenreiro, *A Ilha,* p. 189; Almada Negreiros, *Historia,* pp. 108-12.

Fort Jesus A fortress built (1593-8) by the Portuguese at the entrance of the port of Mombasa. It is so solid that much of the original structure has remained undamaged through the centuries. Although it was abandoned by the Portuguese in 1726, it remains a remarkable product of sixteenth-century Portuguese architecture and construction. Axelson, *Portuguese in East-Africa.* p. 193.

Fortaleza de São Pedro da Barra A sinister fortress used by the Portuguese police in Luanda to imprison Angolan nationalists after February, 1961, when the War for Independence began in force. Pelissier, *La Colonie,* pp. 367-68.

FPLM (*Frente para a Libertação de Mozambique*) (Pg.) "Front for the Liberation of Mozambique," created by FRELIMO (q.v.) in 1970, a military and political front founded to increase pressure against Portuguese forces throughout central Mozambique and Sofala, Manica, and Tete provinces. The FPLM was a well-structured organization having at the top was secretary of the province and under him a secretary of defense with a chief of operations, a chief of security, and a political commissioner. Below these positions there were the sectors, departments of sabotage, education, culture, and production and commerce. There were periodic meetings of all the leaders and a constant re-examination of problems of strategies and of the propaganda war. Training was essential and the unity created was used to mobilize the people and raise the political consciousness of why they were fighting. Munslow, *Mozambique,* pp. 116-18.

FRAIN (*Frente Revolucionaria Africano para a Independencia Nacional das Colonias Portuguesas*) (Pg.) "Revolutionary African Front for the National Independence of the Portuguese Colonies," a political party established by Lucio Lara and others in January 1960 in Tunis with its headquarters in Conakry, French Guinée. The role of FRAIN in the war was weakened by internal power struggles. Wheeler, *Angola,* pp. 164-65, 170; HDRGC.

Franciscanism A late-medieval religious movement inspired by St. Francis of Assisi (1181-1226). It identified with nature and stressed a pragmatic Christian doctrine of love, communication, contemplation, and mystical aspiration that dissipated the shadow of malediction and terror which hung over life on the earth and opened a new road for Christians to march on the planet. Based on the imitation of the evangelical life of Christ and on love of the poor and of all things, animate and inanimate, it appealed strongly to intellectuals and influenced scientific development, especially in travel and geographic expansion. This new spirit and love for mankind was very influential during the Discovery (q.v.), directly and indirectly impacting on scientific investigation and inquiry into the secrets of nature. Cortesão, *History*, I:189-90; DHP; GEPB. *See also* Franciscans in Africa, Franciscans in Portugal.

Franciscans in Africa Early in the Discovery (q.v.), c.1385, the Franciscans as apostles of the outcast, promoters of peace, and preachers of a new mystic love for nature, became an inspiration for Portuguese navigators. In 1417 or 1418 Aimaro de Haurillack, a French or English Franciscan, resident in Portugal, was appointed first bishop of Ceuta by Pope Martin V. In 1421, the first Franciscan monastery on the African continent was opened. In the sixteenth century others were established in Cape Verde, São Tomé, and Angola. Cortesão, *History*, I:189; DHP; GEPB. *See also* Franciscans in Portugal, Franciscanism.

Franciscans in Portugal   In 1218 St. Francis of Assisi (1181-1226), the founder of the Franciscan order, sent a group of five friars to Morocco by way of Lisbon. The first Franciscan monastery in Portugal was founded in 1216 in Lisbon. Like many people in Europe, he wanted to convert Moslems to the Christian faith and missionaries from the order traveled to Fez (q.v.), where they were martyred in 1220. Prince Fernando brought back their remains for burial in Coimbra. The Franciscans, as champions of the poor and preachers of a new mystic affection for mankind and nature, got the attention of kings and nobles. They built monasteries in Lisbon (1216), then in Porto (1224), and Coimbra (1250). A few years later, they established the Lisbon Theological College. Because Franciscans were attracted by the sea, they had been an inspiration to Portuguese explorers and navigators since the beginning of the Discovery (q.v.). DHP; GEPB. *See also* Franciscanism, Franciscans in Africa.

francolin   A species of Old World partridge (*Perdrix francolinus*) found in Africa and southern Asia. This partridge with richly colored plumage is now extinct in Europe but has survived in Mozambique and elsewhere in Africa. Isaacman, *Mozambique: From Colonialism*, p. 65.

freedman   In Portugal c. 1437, any slave, male or female, who was freed from bondage by a *carta de alforria* (q.v.). The practice was based on the principle that freedom is the natural state of man. Freedmen were citizens of the town where they lived. They could own, sell, and bequeath property, could trade, and were entitled to a proper trial in court. King Manuel I required freedmen to show respect to their former masters and their former master's parents and children, under penalty of having their freedom revoked. Saunders, *A Social History*, pp. 141-147; GEPB.

FRELIMO (*Frente de Libertação de Mozambique*) (Pg.)   "Front for the Liberation of Mozambique," the nationalist party organized in Dar es-Salaam, Tanzania, at a conference held June 20-5, 1962, by several Mozambican leaders including Marcelino dos Santos, Eduardo Chivambo Mondlane, Matthew Mmole, and Uria Simango. Julius Nyerere of Tanzania and Kwame Nkrumah of Ghana pressed for a unified front against Portuguese rule. In 1969 after the assassination of Mondlane, Samora Machel became head of FRELIMO which was the official government party after independence in 1974. Henriksen, *Mozambique*, pp. 169-70, 172.

FRELIMO and education   After Mozambican independence in 1974, FRELIMO (q.v.) was the government's official party. Their first move was to take education under state control and inaugurate a rapid expansion of primary and secondary education and adult literacy training. After five years of independence, the results were remarkable. The school population totalled 1.5 million, with 90,051 in secondary schools, 12,707 in technical schools, 1,744 taking pre-university courses, and the remainder, 1.38 million, being in primary schools. Between 1974 and 1978, 8.75 million Mozambicans had attended literacy courses, and in 1980 225,000 were registered, up over 10 percent on the previous year. A new department of adult education was created, and a plan was drawn for an adult education structure within every economic and social unit, whether state or private. Given a total population of 12,130,000 in the 1980 census, these statistics are confirmation of the government's success in this field. Munslow, *Mozambique,* p. 168.

FRELIMO, goals of The goals of FRELIMO (q.v.) leaders in 1962-9 were to reconstruct Mozambique society away from traditional rule by ethnic groups, Portuguese colonial domination, and individual gain and toward a nation of party government and collective endeavor. They looked to China and Tanzania for models and inspiration. In the economic sphere, the nationalists organized agricultural cooperatives to expand food production for local populations and a self-sufficient guerrilla force to open a small export trade to Tanzania and to help shape a collective society. To stimulate production and individual initiative the traditional *shambas* (individual lots) for private tillage stayed in the new program. Henriksen, *Mozambique,* p. 203.

FRELIMO, Women's Detachment of Women's auxiliary corps of FRELIMO (q.v.), the nationalist party, organized during the War for Independence. Founded in 1967 in Mozambique, it quickly grew to become a central component of the party. The tasks of the women guerrillas were to make contact with the population in new areas and approach their own relatives in regions where enemy troops were stationed. They collected intelligence and began the work of politicization. By the end of 1970, the women's detachment was fully involved in the revolutionary process, acting with courage, determination, and cool heads. According to their leader, Elisa Geteo, they won the support of the local people. Munslow, *Mozambique,* pp. 106, 123-4, 134.

Frente de Libertação da Guiné Portuguesa e Cabo Verde *See* FLGC.

Frente de Libertação de Mozambique See FRELIMO.

Frente de Luta Pela Independencia Nacional da Guiné-Bissau *See* FLING.

Frente de Unidade Angola *See* FUA. (Pg.)

Frente Democratico para a Libertação de Angola *See* FDLA.

Frente para a Libertação de Mozambique *See* FPLM.

Frente Revolucionaria Africano para a Independencia Nacional das Colonias Portuguesas *See* FRAIN.

"From the Cape to Cairo" Imperialist slogan coined by the British scientist Sir Edwin Arnold (c.1880) and used by Cecil John Rhodes and other British South African politicians who wanted to expand the Cape Colony north to Egypt, including Mozambique and other East African coastal areas. EA.

fruit fly Any of several small flies (family *Tephritidae*) whose larvae feed on fruits and vegetables. Apparently they originated in West Africa, and around 1800 infested European farms; in the twentieth century, farms in California and Florida were struck. GEPB; WNWD.

fruta do conde (Pg.) Small New World tropical tree (*Annona reticulata* L.) imported into Africa by the Portuguese in the early colonial period. It is cultivated for its aromatic heart-shaped and heart-sized fruit, known in English as custard-apple and bullock's heart and in French as *coeur-de-boeuf*. Ficalho, *Plantas Uteis,* p. 75. *See also* dilolo.

FUA (*Frente de Unidade Angola*) (Pg.) "Front for Angolan Unity," a nationalist movement formed in January 1961 by white settlers in Benguela, Lobito, and Nova Lisboa along with Ovimbundu leaders from central Angola and a few *mestiços*. It was a multi-racial separatist group active until May 1961 when its leaders were arrested by PIDE (q.v.). Wheeler, *Angola,* pp. 271; HDA.

fuba (Afr.) A finely ground cassava (q.v.) flour that, when boiled with water and milk, makes a popular Angolan dish called *infundi*. *Fuba* is much used in the preparation of bread and fermented beverages. Cassava was introduced by the Portuguese from Brazil c.1550. In October 1857, during a devastating drought and famine around Dondo, Mbaca, and other villages, people sold their children as slaves for three or four dishes of *infundi*. Ficalho, *Plantas Uteis,* pp. 26, 249-53; GEPB.

Fuesse (Afr.) A military headquarters near São Salvador do Congo that served as a hideaway for Jose Manuel Peterson, a chief of UPA (q.v.) in 1961. From there he directed the armed struggle for independence. This complex of huts of mud and grass coordinated a rudimentary system of self-defense and attack on many African villages. At one time the *Fuesse* camp was under the charge of Federico Deves, a veteran UPA organizer in the São Salvador region. Marcum, *The Angolan Revolution,* I:213, 230.

Fula (Afr.)   In Guinea-Bissau, one of the groups of Islamized Sudanese people of African stock with a Mediterranean Caucasoid admixture. They have a highly variable skin color that is often reddish-brown, hair which varies from wavy to crisp, and a slender build. Within the Fulas there are two main further distinctions: the sedentary, more fully Islamized, Fula and the migratory, pastoral, Fula who observe a syncretic form of Islam and animism. The former are rather strongly hierarchical in sociopolitical organization and have been influential in the spread of Islam through the sub-Saharan region. In their southward migration to and through Guinea-Bissau, some of the latter group adopted Mandingo cultural patterns and came to be known as Fulacundas or Fula-Pretos (q.v.). They were able to establish their own rule, and often served as herdsmen to Western Sudanese kingdoms. Modern Fulas can easily be traced to Futa-Toro and Tekrur (qq.v.) on the Senegal River. They are related to the Berber, Wolof, and Serer people. In 1950, the Guinea-Bissau Fulas were estimated at 108,400, or 21.5 percent of the total population. Fula is also spelled *Fulbe*. HDRG; WTNID.

Fula-Burure (Afr./Pg.)   A nomadic Fula (q.v.) subgroup of cattle raisers, always on the move looking for pasture throughout Guiné in the colonial period. This group is now nearly extinct. Mota, *Guiné Portuguesa*, I:275-6.

Fula-Forro (Afr./Pg.) In Guinea-Bissau, a subgroup of the Fula (q.v.) who, under the leadership of Moló, fought against the Mandingos in the 1860s. They settled as free and independent people in eastern Guinea-Bissau. Their economy is a mixture of pastoralism and subsistence agriculture. They are also known as the Fulacundas. Carvalho e Vasconcellos, *As Colonias Portuguesas,* pp. 148-9. *See also* Fula-Preto.

Fula-Futa (Afr./Pg.)   A subgroup of Moslem Fulas (q.v.) heavily influenced by Arab culture who, after a struggle against the Mandingos in 1860, settled in the easternmost part of modern Guinea-Bissau; they grow groundnuts and gather rubber and wild tropical fruits. They are related to the Fula-Forro and the Fula-Preto (qq.v), although they consider themselves superior to both. Carvalho e Vasconcellos, *As Colonias Portuguesas,* p. 150.

Fula-Preto (Afr./Pg.)   In Guinea-Bissau, the most numerous subgroup of the Fulas (q.v.), concentrated in a wide area between Gabu (q.v.) and Bafata and in scattered communities in the southeast. The Fula-Pretos also include the Fula-Forros, or Fulacundas, found in the northeast and in sizable groups in the vicinity of Aldea Formosa and the south-central area. The large numbers and widespread distribution of this major Fula group attest to the centuries of intermingling with local Mandingo people. Carvalho e Vasconcellos, *As Colonias Portuguesas,* pp. 148-9; HDRGC. *See also* Futa Toro.

Fulacunda (1) *See* Fula-Forro.

Fulacunda (Afr.) (2) A town seat and district, south-central Guiné, bordered by the Geba and Buba rivers. This area offered suitable conditions for cattle-raising and the nomadic Fulas (q.v.) settled here in the colonial period. Rodney, *The Guinea Coast,* CEA, Cambridge, 1975, 4:287; GEPB.

Fulanization (Afr.) Among the Fulas in Guinea-Bissau, the practice of mixing animistic beliefs with Islamic rituals, such as the five daily prayers and kneeling in mosques. Fula devotions include, when building a hut, consulting Islamic holy men and sacrificing a chicken accompanied by prayers to Allah, after which the roasted meat is distributed among the participants as sign of unity and brotherhood. Gonçalves, *O Islamismo na Guiné,* p. 181.

Funchal (Pg.) Situated at the head of a large bay on the southeast coast of Madeira, this seaport, winter resort, and capital of Madeira was discovered and settled by explorer Gonçalves Zarco in 1419, now buried in the cathedral (built 1485-1514). King Afonso V granted special privileges to Funchal village in 1452, declared a city by King Manual I in 1508. In 1981 it had a population of 119,022. GEPB; WNGD.

Funchal, Diocese of (Pg.) An ecclesiastic jurisdiction created in 1514 by Pope Leo X in response to a petition by King Manuel I of Portugal. At the time, the diocese comprised the African coast from south of Morocco to the Cape of Good Hope, including the African Kingdom of Congo and the Gulf of Guiné, plus the Orient and Brazil. Prince Henrique, son of King Afonso I, titular Bishop of Utica, was an auxiliary of this diocese and vicar of the Congo Kingdom, the seat of which was in São Salvador. Gabriel, *Angola,* pp. 81, 96; Felgas, *Historia,* pp. 35-36, 122.

Funchal, English community in A group of English merchants resided in Funchal, Madeira, and dominated commerce from 1680 until the twentieth century. In 1687, of a dozen foreign traders, more than half were English. Among them were Obadiah Allen (the English vice consul), Henry Criton, George Fryer, Lawrence Gay, Samuel Hutchinson, Matthew Martson, and Richard Miles. These merchants dealt in textiles from Europe that were shipped to West Africa and the West Indies. In 1690 local authorities ordered the English merchant William Ray, on pain of a fine, to secure special permission from the city before unloading any more Brazilian sugar. By the end of the seventeenth century, these merchants bought Madeira wine with the proceeds from the sale of English textiles and other imported commodities and shipped the wine to Jamaica and Barbados. In the West Indies, the ships would load sugar, molasses, and rum then return to Europe by way of New England and Newfoundland, taking on salted codfish, fish oil, lumber, and barrel staves. A single voyage around the grand circle of North Atlantic maritime commerce yielded enormous profits for the English merchants. Up to the present, the Funchal English community has occupied a pivotal position in the economy of Madeira. Duncan, *Atlantic Islands,* p. 5, 42, 46, 54-60; GEPB.

Funcionario, O (Pg.) "The Civil Servant." A periodical published in Lourenço Marques, Mozambique, by the Association of Civil Servants of the province of Mozambique, and edited by Anibal Duarte and Raul Neves. Its first issue appeared on September 15, 1926. It was suppressed by the government on August 13, 1927. In 1928 it reappeared with the same format but as a two-page handbill. After the liquidation of the Association, its balance account of 26,135 *reis* was given to charity. Dias, *A Imprensa,* p. 84.

funco (Crio.) A rural hut or shack on Cape Verde that for modern Cape Verdian poets has become a symbol of poverty in the islands. Hamilton, *Voices,* p. 252.

fundo *See* fonio.

Futa-Djallon (Afr.) A highland in what is now the Republic of Guinea-Bissau with elevations up to 4500 ft. (1372 m). It is the source of the Gambia, Senegal, and Niger rivers as well as a number of other smaller rivers that flow directly south and west into the Atlantic. In the early eighteenth century, Fulani reformers created a theocracy there with the state controlled by elected *almanis* (aldermen). This Futa-Djallon experience served as a model for Islamic reformers in other areas of West Africa. The state of Futa-Djallon underwent several expansions. The first was between 1654 and about 1700, during which they lived peacefully with the Mandingo state to which they paid tribute. Due to pressure from the slave trade, by the mid-eighteenth century Futa-Djallon was in conflict with its neighbors at such places as Cacheu, Bissau, on the Casamanse and Gambia rivers. By 1788 the Fula (q.v.) were the dominant power in the Guinea-Conakry and Guinea-Bissau regions. Around 1888 the French defeated the Fulas and Futa-Djallon became a colonial dependency. HDRGC. *See also* Futa Toro.

Futa-Fulas (Afr.) In Guinea-Bissau, an ethnic group settled in the north-central Gabu-Peche area. Also called Futa-Jalonkas, they include groups of Boencas. The are found just north of Gabu and in the extreme southeast, near Madina, and Boe, adjacent to the former province of Labé, from which they originated. HDRGC. *See also* Futa-Toro.

Futa-Jalonkas *See* Futa-Fulas.

Futa Toro (Afr.) In Guinea-Bissau, an old Fula (q.v.) kingdom in the plateau region adjacent to the Senegal River. It was established around the tenth century by Berber, Tokolor, and Soninke ethnic groups and Islamized in the eleventh century. From Futa Toro, the Fula peoples spread widely in the twelfth and thirteenth centuries, becoming the most important pastoralists in West Africa. In the fourteenth century the Mali Kingdom (q.v.) dominated Futa Toro, and in 1490 the Fula rebelled. In 1534 King João III of Portugal sent a mission to Mali. At this time, Portuguese trade in slaves, gold, ivory, guns, and textiles was conducted along the Senegal River. Throughout the fifteenth century, Fulas from Futa Toro drifted eastward and southward to Guinea-Bissau where they settled peacefully with the existing Mandingo-speakers and other Senegambians. After 1770, there were several Fula migrations toward the east accompanied by holy wars. During these migrations the Fula crossed over eastern Guinea-Bissau and settled among the Fula population centers already there. HDRGC. *See also* Futa-Djallon.

Futuro, O (Pg.) "The Future." A weekly, bilingual Portuguese-English periodical published in Lourenço Marques, Mozambique, whose first issue appeared on April 28, 1898. In 1899 it was owned by the *Sociedade Anonima de Responsabilidade Limitada* with L. Cohen as editor and A.F. Berg as administrator. In 1898 it printed 1,000 copies and in 1899, 1,200. It was published until 1908. Dias, *A Imprensa,* p. 23, 60.

Futuro de Lourenço Marques, O (Pg.) "The Future of Lourenço Marques." A weekly publication in Lourenço Marques, Mozambique. The first issue appeared on July 12, 1894. It ceased publication May 18, 1895, by order of Antonio Enes, governor of Mozambique. Its successor was *O Futuro* (q.v.). Dias, *A Imprensa,* pp. 23, 58.

fuxi (Kimb.) In Angola c.1880, the third child born in the same delivery; the last-born of a set of triplets. EDK.

{ G }

"G" At the time of the Discovery (q.v.), the letter "G" was branded on the right arm of slaves. This referred to Guiné, the origin before 1500 of most of the slaves brought for sale in Lisbon and other cities. This identification also indicated that the taxes ordered by King Manuel in 1519 had been paid. Runaway slaves when caught occasionally were branded on both cheeks, as was the case in 1519 of a slave in Evora. Before the use of the letter "G," the official brand had been a cross. Saunders, *A Social History,* pp. 13, 108; GEPB.

Gabon (Afr.) River, estuary, and adjacent coast in West Africa. Portuguese navigators reached it around 1475. At the time, part of the coast was inhabited by the Mpongwe (also spelled Spongoué), part of the Omyéné ethnic group, who may have come into the area as late as the thirteenth century. The Tang, who became the dominant group in the region, arrived in Gabon from the north at the beginning of the nineteenth century. Following the Portuguese, traders and explorers from the Netherlands, Great Britain, France, and America cruised the Gabonese coast in search of slaves, wood, rubber, adventure, and opportunities to make converts to Christianity. GEPB; WNGD.

gabu (Afr.) (1) "Hippopotamus." A large plant-eating mammal (family *Hippopotamidae*) that the Portuguese found on their arrival on the West African coast in the fifteenth century. In the Middle Ages, the hippopotamus was hunted and eaten in Songhai, Mali, and Bornu. A Songhai legend tells of a king of Gao named Farang who was a great hippopotamus hunter. It is reported that there were numerous herds of hippopotamus on the lower Senegal River in the middle of the eighteenth century. In Arabic the *gabu* is called *qafu*. Lewicki, *West African Food,* p. 201.

Gabu (Afr.) (2) A town in eastern Guinea-Bissau (now part of Angola) and seat of an old Islamic state that played a dominant role in the area in the seventeenth and eighteenth centuries. Portugal changed the name from Gabu to Nova Lisboa in the nineteenth century. After independence in 1975 it was renamed Huambo. HDRGC.

Gabu Empire (Afr.) A thirteenth-century Islamic Mandingo Kingdom in northeastern Guinea-Bissau and the Casamande River area. Control of this location on the coastal river estuaries secured Portuguese dominance of the trade in salt and gold plus slaves for the Brazilian market. In the seventeenth and eighteenth centuries various military operations explored Gabu territory and many towns were raided in search of slaves for the Brazilian plantations. In 1867 the Fulas (q.v.) conquered the Gabu Empire and by 1912 Portugal occupied the territory. The eastern city of Guinea-Bissau was renamed Nova Lamego to commemorate this military conquest. HDRGC.

Galangue (Afr.) A military *presidio* built in 1780 at the head of the Cunene River in the Benguela *sertão* (interior), southern Angola. In the twentieth century, some of the Ovimbundu settled in this region have converted to Christianity and at the same time the area has become a center of African cults organized by detribalized Africans. It 1955 Galangue was the scene of violence organized by Ovimbundus fighting for independence. Silva Rego, *O Ultramar*, p. 264; GEPB.

Galangue Grande (Afr.) A commercial settlement established in 1760 by Governor Miguel Antonio de Melo on the banks of the Cunene River in southern Angola. Soon it became an important trade center for the Benguela *sertão* (interior), a densely populated region. This market is mentioned in a 1769 report. Today Galangue Grande has become a commercial and trade town. Silva Rego, *O Ultramar,* pp. 167, 175.

galé (Pg.) In the early fifteenth century, a small, swift galley propelled both by sails and oars, having one mast and sixteen or twenty seats for rowers, originally used on the Mediterranean. At the beginning of the Portuguese expansion c.1415, there were two kinds of *galés*: one light, fast, and armed for war; the other heavy, for cargo. Both were used along the African coasts and in India and Asia. GEPB; HDP.

galeão (Pg.) "Galleon." A large, armed, four-deck ship of between 500 and 1000 tons with four masts, built in Lisbon after 1415. In the years following the Discovery (q.v.), *galeãos* were used for cargo in West Africa and India. GEPB.

galhina (Pg.) A unit of currency c.1600 equal to 1000 cowrie shells. The shells were collected along the Luandan coast of Angola and used in the area of the Gulf of Benin in the cloth and slave trades. Polanyi, *Dahomey*, p. 181. *See also* cowrie, olivetta nana.

Galhinas (Pg.) Island in the Bijagos archipelago, southern Guinea-Bissau, mentioned for the first time by Valentim Fernandes in 1507. In 1828 a local African chief granted it to Joaquim Antonio de Matos, a merchant and an interim governor of Guiné. It became a possession of the Portuguese Crown in 1832. Mota, *Toponimos,* p. 168.

Gambia, Christian missionaries in The Portuguese navigator and explorer Diogo Gomes visited the Gambia River in 1456. On his return to Portugal, he conveyed a request from the Gambian ruler, Nomi-Mansa, to Prince Henry for instruction in the Christian faith. Shortly after, a group of missionaries was sent to the Gambia Kingdom (q.v.). Prestage, *The Portuguese Pioneers,* p. 153.

Gambia Kingdom A fifteenth-century Islamic chiefdom located at the mouth of the Gambia River, discovered by Alvise Cadamosto in his trip of 1455-6. He explored the region and found that the river, even at its narrowest part, was not less than three miles wide, enabling ships to sail a considerable distance upstream. They found settlements and observed Africans rowing with great speed on the river. In the villages they saw handsome men, each clad in a white cotton shirt and wearing a white hat with a plume. To the Portuguese, the headgear was reminiscent of that worn by Germans, except that the hats had a white wing on each side and a feather in the middle, as though they were warriors. Through interpreters, the Portuguese gathered information about the Gambia Kingdom and its ruler, Nomi-Mansa, who requested Prince Henry to send missionaries. Prestage, *The Portuguese Pioneers,* pp. 107, 117, 153; GEPB.

Gambia River A river in West Africa, about 700 mi. (1130 km) long that rises in Futa-Djallon, Guinea-Bissau, flows northwest through Senegal then west to the Atlantic Ocean at Bathurst, now Banjul. The lower 200 mi. (320 km), navigable at all seasons, are in the Republic of the Gambia. The river was discovered by Diogo Gomes, a Portuguese navigator, between 1454 and 1458. Around the same time, Alvise Cadamosto explored the region because, according to reports by slaves in Portugal, it was a densely populated area. Prestage, *The Portuguese Pioneers,* pp. 124, 131(n), 132; DHP.

Gambia settlement The Gambia River and the Gambia Kingdom were discovered and explored by Diogo Gomes between 1454-6. Soon after, explorer Alvise Cadamosto established a factory to trade with the Africans. Between 1618 and 1619, agents of a British trading company moved up the river. Fort James, built on a small island about 20 mi. (32 km) from the mouth of the Gambia River, was established in 1664, and captured by the French in 1779. British claims to the region were recognized by the Treaty of Versailles in 1783. The Gambia settlement was placed under the control of the government of Sierra Leone in 1807. It became a British colony in 1843 and a protectorate in 1894. It achieved independence in 1965 and became a republic in 1970. Prestage, *The Portuguese Pioneers,* pp. 117, 153; WNGD.

Gambos (Afr.) A municipality, Huila province, southern Angola, with its capital at Chibemba. It is an important millet-producing area and cattle center. The first Europeans in the region came in 1840-1. In 1857 a military fort was built. Continuous unrest among the local African chiefs forced the few European merchants to abandon Gambos and settle in Mossamedes. In 1888 a new fort was built to control the region. When the Portuguese forces occupied the upper Cunene River area, peace and security allowed agricultural and commercial development. Modern progress was assured after 1914 when a military captaincy-general was established in Angola. GEPB.

gamela (Afr.) In São Tomé, a tall tropical tree (*Bombax buonopozence*) which reaches as high as 100 ft (30 m). Its timber is used to make planks, studs, and other construction material; its fruit bears a type of cotton- or vegetable-wool used to make mattresses and other domestic articles. Also called the silk-cotton tree. Ficalho, *Plantas Uteis,* p. 95.

Gango (Afr.) African village, capital of the Chiengue municipality, southern Angola. In 1643 the Dutch attacked and captured governor Cesar de Menesses there. The governor escaped and fled to Massangano then Luanda where he continued Portuguese opposition to the Dutch invaders. GEPB.

Ganguela (Afr.) Angolan municipality with its capital at Vila-da-Ponte. It is a vast region at the headwaters of the Cubango and Cuanza rivers, south of Bié and east of Caconda in the Huila tableland (q.v.). It reaches an altitude of 4,750 ft (1,450 m), and has an area of 11,690 square miles (30,285 square km). It is a rich agricultural area producing millet, groundnuts, maize, castor oil, and cattle. Historically the Africans at Ganguela have been known as shrewd merchants who deal in rubber, wax, and honey. In 1853 Silva Porto visited this area for the first time. A fortress called Fort Amelia was built in 1886 and in 1889 the region was occupied by military forces. The Ganguela municipality, including the towns of Cassinga, Dongo, and Galangue, became part of the Bié district. Also spelled *Nguela*. Wheeler, *Angola,* pp. 6, 9; GEPB.

Ganguelas (Afr.) Ethnic group of Central Africa that in the colonial period was settled in the Huila province, southeastern Angola along the Cussave River, a tributary of the Cunene, up to the Cubango River and the headwaters of the Cuchi River. The area is also known as North Ganguela. GEPB.

"Gardá feiticera" (Criou.) "Protect him from the sorceress." A Cape Verdian expression referring to the need to defend a newborn from the dangers of being bewitched. Carvalho e Vasconcellos, *As Colonias Portuguesas,* p. 83.

garé (Criou.) A twisted cotton thread, a term used c. 1930 on Fogo Island, Cape Verde. Cardoso, *Folclore,* p. 81.

Garveyism A social and political philosophy based on African-American self-pride and separatism, preached in New York in the early twentieth century by Marcus Mosiah Garvey. Its influence reached African students in Lisbon around 1920 and soon spread to Portuguese Africa. In 1922, in Luanda and Mossamedes, Angola, a group of elite *assimilados* (q.v.) accused some white merchants of trying to establish Garvey as "President of Africa." In Sá de Bandeira in 1922 there was a movement to organize what was called a Republic of Blacks. Wheeler, *Angola,* p. 118.

Gaza (Afr.) A district producing rice and cattle, located between Lourenço Marques and the Sabe River in Mozambique. Although arid, it has many small lakes and slow-moving marshy rivers. Its capital is João Belo. The district has an area of 31,000 sq. mi. (80,310 sq. km). For centuries the Portuguese were unable to control the territory. In 1889 Gungunhana, a Vatúa African chief, organized a strong campaign against the Portuguese. Joaquim A. Mousinho de Albuquerque (1855-1902) defeated and imprisoned Gungunghana in 1895. Its population in 1980 was 999,900, most of whom were Africans. Herrick, *Area Handbook*, pp. 7, 12, 19, 51; GEPB.

Gaza Ngoni (Afr.) An important migrant ethnic group who fled the dominant Shaka chief in South Africa and entered the Zambezi region in 1832. In 1834 the invaders approached the outskirts of Missonge, the capital of the Barué Kingdom. But instead of conquering the Barué to incorporate them into a larger Ngoni state, the Gaza Ngoni chose to plunder the fertile fields, rustle cattle, and kidnap women and children who were then absorbed into the Gaza society. Despite the brief period of their activity, the cumulative effect of the Gaza Ngoni raids severely weakened the Barué Kingdom. In the 1870s part of the outlying chiefdom of Gorongosa was incorporated into the Ngoni Empire. Isaacman, *Mozambique: The Tradition,* pp. xi, 8-9.

Geba (Afr.) A river that has its headwaters in northernmost Guinea-Conakry and curves through the Casamance area of Senegal before turning back toward the southwest, emptying into the Atlantic in the northeast of Guinea-Bissau. The Geba is about 340 mi. (548 km) long and was an important route for commerce, including slaves, bound for Brazil. Gabu, capital of the Gabu Kingdom, is on the Geba. HDRGC. *See also* Corubal River.

genero pobre (Pg.) "Inexpensive goods." An expression used in the colonial period by farmers in the Portuguese African territories to refer to produce consumed locally, such as millet, *cassava*, groundnuts, chilies, sweet potatoes, and greens. Caetano, *Os Nativos*, p. 113. *See also* genero rico.

genero rico (Pg.) "Expensive goods." An expression used in the colonial period by farmers in Portuguese Africa to refer to commodities exported to

Portugal and other European countries, such as gold, silver, ivory, sugar, and animal skins. Caetano, *Os Nativos*, p. 113. *See also* genero pobre.

gengibre (Pg.) "Ginger." An Asiatic plant (*Zingiber officinale*) grown for its aromatic rhizome, used as a spice or in perfume or medicine. It was introduced by the Portuguese into Africa, possibly around 1550. Today it is widely cultivated in São Tomé e Príncipe and Cuanza Norte and Dembos in Angola. DHP.

Genoa, relations with Portugal Relations between Genoa and Portugal were established around 1200. In 1260 the Genoese merchant Vivaldo Vivaldi lived in Lisbon; his wife, Dona Inez, founded the Santa Clara Convent for Franciscan nuns in 1282. In 1317 King Dinis appointed Manuel Lesanha, a Genoese, admiral of the Portuguese navy. In 1336 another Geonoese in the service of Portugal, Lanzarotto Malocello, sailed down the Atlantic coast of Africa. It was also the Genoese who introduced the sugar industry to Madeira c.1425. In the service of Prince Henry, the Genoese navigator Antonio Noli discovered the Cape Verde Islands in 1460, Antonio Usodomare explored the Guiné Coast, and Alvise Cadamosto discovered the Canary Islands. Christopher Columbus, also a Genoese, traded in sugar between Lisbon and Madeira around 1470 and sailed with Portuguese navigators to the Gulf of Guiné several times in the period around 1480. Cortesão, *History*, I:297-8.

Genoese, seafaring of the In the thirteenth century, the Genoese were among the most active seafarers in Europe. The position of Genoa as the northernmost Mediterranean port and its growing commercial importance favored its expansion. The development of the *portolano* (q.v.) chart, and the movement of the Crusaders, whom the Genoese often supplied with sea transport, increased their maritime experience and the wish for new adventures. The first Atlantic voyage along the northwestern coast of Africa was made in Portuguese ships under the command of Lanzarotto Malocello, a Genoese, in 1336. Cortesão, *History*, I:297. *See also* Genoa, relations with Portugal.

"gente da terra" (Pg.) "People of the land." An expression used at the time of the Discovery (q.v.) to refer to Africans. In the nineteenth century the Portuguese replaced the term with *indigena* then in 1950 with *Africano*. Duffy, *Portuguese Africa,* p. 290.

"gente do mesmo navio" (Pg.) "Passenger on the same ship." An expression used in São Tomé and elsewhere to refer to slaves who made the crossing from Africa to São Tomé or the New World in the same ship; the experience often forged a deep feeling of lasting kinship among the survivors. Also called *malungo* in Brazil. Tenreiro, *A Ilha,* p. 191.

Gentilis Angolae (Lat.) "Heathen Angolans." Title of a catechism written in Kimbundu by Father J. Pacconio, a seventeenth-century Italian Jesuit. After his death it was published by Antonio do Couto in a simplified form (Lisbon, 1642) for use by Congo missionaries. In 1661 it was re-edited by the missionary Antonio Maria do Monteprandone, who added a Latin version for missionaries who did not know Portuguese. The text is arranged in three columns: Latin, Kimbundu, and Portuguese. Banned by the Marquis of Pombal, who expelled the Jesuits in 1759, the book was re-edited again after his death. Gabriel, *Angola,* p. 100.

Geographical Society of Lisbon A scientific corporation founded on November 10, 1875, with Luciano Cordeiro as its first president. It extolled Portugal's role in Africa and helped to organize quasi-scientific expeditions into the interior. Between 1877 and 1885 it sponsored the expedition of A.A.R. Serpa Pinto and that of Capelo and Ivens. It also supported Portuguese claims in Africa, especially in east-central Africa where the Portuguese faced the intrusions of Cecil John Rhodes. It had a library and archives and published a bulletin. In 1896 it had 1,600 members, including eight explorers. Newitt, *Portugal in Africa,* pp. 29-30; DHP.

gergelim (Afr.) "Sesame." A tropical East Indian herbaceous oil plant (*Sesamum indicum*; syn. *S. orientale*), widely cultivated in Africa. It is grown for its flat seeds which yield a valuable oil used in cooking and medicine; the seeds are often added whole to breads and pastries. This plant was introduced to Mesopotamia at a very early date, then apparently the Arabs took it to East Africa where it was found by the Portuguese in Mozambique in 1554. It is widely cultivated in Zambezia up to the Rovuma River. It is also found in western Angola and Cape Verde. Today it is also found in northern Nigeria and the Sudan. Since it is a basic food in many African diets, it has many other names including *sem-sem* or *sim-sim* (Arabic); *ocoto, ricota,* and *nguila* (Angola); and variations on the name *gergelim,* including *gingeli, jingili,* and *gergeri.* Ficalho, *Plantas Uteis,* pp. 234-7; Lewicki, *West African Food,* pp. 110, 211.

Germans in Africa German interest in acquiring African colonies began around 1867 when Chancellor Otto von Bismarck encouraged private German groups to settle in Africa south of the Sahara. In 1883 the Bremen merchant Adolph Luderick bought from local African chiefs the area of Angra Pequena and its surrounding territory on the southern Atlantic coast of Angola, an area of 835,000 sq. mi. (2.16 million sq. km) including a considerable coastline. When England sent a protest to the German government, Bismarck answered by saying that this settlement was under the protection of the German Empire. Togo was organized as a colony in 1884.

In East Africa, the *Gesellschaft für Deutsche Kolonisation* sent an expedition from Berlin to the region of Dar es-Salaam where, after being established as the *Ostafrikanische Gesellschaft* in 1884, this group bought 54,000 sq.mi. (140,000 sq. km) of territory. An Anglo-German treaty in 1886 established its borders, just to the north of Mozambique, limiting it to 384 sq. mi. (995 sq.km) and 620 mi. (1,000 km) inland from the Indian Ocean coast. Silva Rego, *O Ultramar,* pp. 51-2.

gero (Afr.) In the lower Zambezi, in accordance with Sena custom, a big hut in which the adolescent girls of a village live together immediately after initiation rites are performed at the end of the dry season. Once these rites are performed, they receive young men in the *gero* for intercourse; once a girl becomes pregnant, marriage occurs. A young man living in a *gero* was not charged his annual tax. Vail, *Capitalism,* p. 72. *See also* azungu.

Ghana Kingdom (Afr.) A medieval Sudanese state between the Senegal and Niger rivers, visited by the Portuguese around 1480. Two years later Portugal built the fort and trade center of São Jorge da Mina (q.v.) on the Gulf of Guiné in the Ghana Kingdom to trade in gold, spices, and slaves. The region became known as the Gold Coast because of the enormous profits from trade. Trans-Saharan caravans brought gum arabic (q.v.), ostrich feathers, slaves, and gold for trade with the Europeans. Beginning in the sixteenth century there were bloody confrontations between Portugal and Britain, Holland, France, and Denmark over trade. In 1859 the British took control of the area and it was a British Trust Territory until 1957 when the Gold Coast, as it was known in England, achieved independence as the Republic of Ghana. HDG; WNGD.

giboía (Pg.) A snake of enormous size and power often conceived of as a mythical serpent. African poets such as Agostino A. Neto often use it in their poetry as a symbol of the mystery and greatness of the African world. Burness, *Fire,* p. 32.

gila (Afr.) In Guinea-Bissau, an itinerant merchant among the Mandingos (q.v.). At least since the sixteenth century, as noted by Valentim Fernandes c.1520, the Mandingan *gilas* have been peddling their merchandise among the many ethnic communities controlled by the Gabu Empire (q.v.) in northwestern Guinea-Bissau. Mota, *Guiné Portuguesa,* II:282-3.

gleba (Pg.) In São Tomé, a small landholding owned by a *forro* or a *filho da terra* (qq.v.) family. Traditionally its size is less than three acres (1.3 ha), producing barely enough for family subsistence. Its owner never worked his *gleba* full-time; he also pursued a trade or worked in the city. In 1979, *glebas* amounted to 10 percent of cultivated land in the island. This land system, introduced in the sixteenth century, has survived colonialism and lasted until the present. Hodges, *São Tomé e Príncipe,* p. 57, 59, 130.

glossina (Lat.) Tsetse (q.v.) flies (*Glossina morsitans*), two-winged with long slender sharp proboscis and plumose aristae. They are found in open woodlands and in dense bush near rivers in Mozambique, Angola, and elsewhere in tropical Africa. Tsetse flies are the vector that transmits the sleeping sickness trypanosomes to humans and animals. EA; WTNID. *See also* nagana and suoma.

gnu (Afr.) Any of several large but compact African antelopes (genera *Connochaetes* and *Gorgon*) having large heads like that of an ox, short manes, long, flowing tails, and, in both sexes, heavy horns that curve downward and outward, then upward, forming a frontal shield in mature individuals. Their habitat is south of the equator, including Mozambique and Angola. They have several indigenous names, including *hyrax, hessa,* and *huxlu.* GEPB; PDM.

Goan A Portuguese native of Portugal's Indian colony of Goa. At first the Goans were traders on the lower Zambezi in Mozambique. By the 1700s some had became holders of *prazos* (q.v.). The Goans believed themselves Portuguese and came to Mozambique to take up military and administrative posts. They were also very active in trade. Maintaining their close links to Goa on the west coast of India, the Goans were a more resourceful and vigorous group than the European Portuguese. Gradually they came to take over senior posts and gained control over more and more *prazos* until, in the nineteenth century, they were almost the only support for the Portuguese Crown that remained in the colony. Hammond, *Portugal and Africa,* p. 40; Newitt, *Portuguese Settlement,* p. 144; GEPB.

Goan prazero Originally a merchant from Goa, India, who settled in the Zambezi area. By 1833 many had become grant-holders, called *prazeros* (q.v.), often holding grants of land too small to repel attacks from local African chiefs. Isaacman, *Mozambique: From Colonialism,* pp. 116-17. *See also* Goan priests, Goan traders.

Goan priests Priests from the Diocese of Goa in India, occasionally were sent to Mozambique and Angola to do missionary work. In 1885, it was reported that there were eight Goan priests in Angola. Gabriel, *Angola,* pp. 276, 394.

Goan traders In the Zambezi region of Mozambique and elsewhere, beginning in the seventeenth century, traders from the Portuguese colony of Goa on the west coast of India peddled their wares in African towns and villages. They were on the road for months before returning to their base of operation. After the abolition of trade restrictions in 1789, many settled permanently in Mozambique. Many soon prospered, becoming wealthy *prazeros*, marrying local women, and attaining a dominant social and economic position in the Afro-Portuguese society. Later, when Inhambane became an important trader center, it was dominated by Goan merchants. They traded with African laborers coming from Natal, the gold fields of Witwatersrand, and the cities of South Africa. Isaacman, *Mozambique: From Colonization*, p. 59; Rita-Ferreira, *O Movimento Migratorio,* pp. 45-6.

"God gave the Portuguese a small country to live in, but the whole world to die in." A saying first popular at the time of the Discovery (q.v.) c.1500. Cardini, *Europe in 1492*, p. 204.

goeiro (Afr.) Outside villages in southern Zambezia c.1890, a sacred hut where adolescents lived temporarily during the time leading up to the onset of puberty. In some instances, Africans refusing to pay exorbitant taxes for their children used to lodge them in a *goeiro*, since residents were, by law, tax-exempt. Isaacman, *Mozambique: The Tradition,* p. 105; GEPB. *See also* gero.

gold This precious metal was highly valued in Europe at the time of the Discovery (q.v.). Around 1444, Portuguese found gold in Guiné and the Gulf of Guiné (present-day Benin and Ghana, respectively). To protect and control the gold trade, Portugal built the fort and trade center of São Jorge da Mina in 1482. By the end of the fifteenth century, Portugal was the principal gold trader in Europe, exporting 100,000 pounds (45,360 kg) per year of the precious metal from West Africa. By 1600, however, the slave trade had superseded that of gold and dominated all other Portuguese commerce. Henderson, *Angola,* p. 76; Prestage, *The Portuguese Pioneers,* pp. 202; 207.

gold bar Twisted pieces of gold wire, worth an *ackee* (q.v.), or one-sixteenth of an ounce of gold. The gold bar was used as a conventional unit of trade on the Slave Coast c.1720. In 1737, in Sierra Leone, the price of a female slave about twenty years old was 50 gold bars. Polanyi, *Dahomey,* p. 152.

Gold Coast European name for the coastal area between present-day Côte d'Ivoir (Ivory Coast) and Togo. In 1874, the English adopted the name of the Gold Coast for the area under their protection. As their rule extended over the Ashanti and the Northern Territories, the name came to be applied to those areas also. In 1957 the Gold Coast became the Republic of Ghana. HDG.

Gold Coast trade The gold trade in this area originally was carried on by Europeans bartering their wares for gold, either as castle trade, that is from warehouses (called factories, q.v.), or from their ships. This trade was conducted on or near a narrow strip of land between the beach and the thickly-wooded mountains. The area was mostly a sandy waste, stretching to the Volta River where river-gold from the coast and hinterland ended abruptly. The Portuguese established their first offical gold trade center in 1482 at the fortress of São Jorge da Mina (q.v.). Polanyi, *Dahomey,* pp. 11, 101, 102; WNGD.

gold in Mozambique In the fifteenth century the gold in the rivers south of the Zambezi River and the gold-bearing granite nearby began to be exploited commercially. Gold nuggets and dust were panned in the rivers and dug out of the termite hills, but deeper-level mining was also known and modern operations have uncovered old pits and galleries, some as far as 150 ft. beneath the surface. At the time of the Portuguese arrival in 1550, the gold collected in the country traditionally was brought to Sofala, Kilwa, and the Swahili villages on the Indian Ocean. The Portuguese altered this pattern of trade, causing the decline by the sixteenth century of Sofala and Kilwa. In 1693 the Portuguese had dominated the Monomotapa Kingdom and had taken over the gold trade. Newitt, *Portuguese Settlement,* pp. 22-5; GEPB.

gold mines in South Africa The Witwatersrand gold fields of South Africa were discovered in 1886. Within four years, Mozambican laborers began to migrate to the area to work on the mines. Rita-Ferreira, *O Movimento Migratorio,* pp. 76-77. *See also* Witwatersrand gold fields.

gold rush in Zambezia The first eighteenth-century gold rush in Zambezia occurred around 1744 when gold-bearing rocks were found by some *sertanejos* (backwoodsman, q.v.) near the Mano settlement, an area that had been ravaged by disorders. Newitt, *Portuguese Settlement,* p. 81.

Golungo (Afr.) A municipality in the Cazengo district, Cuanza-Norte province, Angola. It is located at an elevation of about 2200 ft. (675 m) and is linked by rail to Luanda, Vila Salazar, Lucala, Camana, and other towns built in this rich agricultural area that produces coffee, coconuts, palm oil, and timber. In 1658 Bartolome de Vasconcelos secured Portuguese control of the region. By 1760 Golungo was reported to be the richest town in that area. The Carmelites established several missions there and in 1765 Governor F.I. de Sousa Continho built an iron factory in nearby Oeiras. The botanist Frederick Martin J. Welwitsch (1807-1872) studied its rich flora from 1854 to 1856. In 1857 it was organized as the Golungo Alto district and an army garrison was established there in 1876. GEPB.

gombo (Afr.) The magic box of a sorcerer, said to contain infants' bones, shiny stones, birds' heads, lions' paws, hyena teeth, the small horns of animals, and similar objects. In Ganguela and the Luanda area, Angola, a *gombo* filled with amulets is believed to be the source of the power that a sorcerer uses to treat mental and physical illnesses. GEPB.

gongon (Afr.) A mythical animal, a kind of werewolf; a fantastic creature that haunts a Cape Verdian child's world. Writers often refer to the *gongons* as remnant vestiges of the African heritage. Hamilton, *Voices,* pp. 320-1.

Gorée (Afr.) Island in the Atlantic, 1.9 mi. (3 km) off the Cape Verde peninsula, Senegal, West Africa. It is a rocky wasteland discovered in 1444 by Dinis Dias, a Portuguese navigator in the service of Prince Henry. A warehouse was quickly established to trade in gold and slaves. Originally called *Ilha da Palma*, the name was changed by the Dutch when they occupied it in 1667. It was taken by the French in 1677 on behalf of the Senegal Company and converted into a busy slave-trading center that later served as a justification for French claims to Senegal. It was held by the British during the Napoleonic Wars but restored to France in 1817. Today it provides historical evidence of the development of the slave trade. Mota, *Mar Alem Mar,* p. 253; WNGD.

Gorongoza (Afr.) In Mozambique, a large *prazo* situated between the Pungue and Zambezi rivers about 100 mi. (161 km) inland from the Indian Ocean. It was rented c.1750 by Bernardo Caetano de Sá Botelho. Isaacman, *Mozambique: From Colonialism*, pp. 38, 57, 59.

Governador Perpetuo do Algarve (Pg.) "Perpetual Governor of the Algarve." Title given to Prince Henry in 1419 by his father, King Jaão I, in the Church of Santa Maria do Castelo after the prince had returned from his triumphal victory at Ceuta (q.v.), North Africa. Iria, *O Algarve no Descobrimento*, Congresso da Guiné, Lisboa, 1946, I:193.

Graciosa (Sp.) Island northwest of Terçeira in the Azores with an area of 24 sq. mi. (62 sq. km). Discovered c.1450 by Terçeira fishermen, its first settler was Vasco Gil Sodre and the first *capitão* and *donatario* (qq.v.) was Duarte Barreto. It was owned by descendants of the first settlers until 1730 when it was incorporated by the Portuguese Crown. Throughout its history the island has often been attacked by pirates. Its capital is Santa Cruz da Graciosa; in 1980 the island had a population of 5,462, down from 8,700 in 1960. GEPB.

Grain Coast Section of the West African coast of Upper Guinea, now Liberia, from Cape Palmas to the Sierra Leone border; so-called from the colonial trade in *malagüta* (q.v.), called in English Grains of Paradise (*Amomum clusii*; syn. *A. malagüeta*); it is a substitute for cardamom and used as a kind of pepper in Europe. Navigator Pedro de Sintra discovered and explored this area around 1460. Soon *malagüeta* became an important export to Portugal and Europe. The area's original Portuguese name was *Costa da Malagüeta*. Mota, *Toponimos,* pp. 217-8; WNGD. *See also* Slave Coast.

Grammatica Aethiopica (Lat.)   A Latin grammar written by Nicolaus Clenardus, who founded Latin schools in Evora and Braga (c.1530-40). He taught Latin to his three slaves so that they could assist him in the classroom. In his grammar, Clenardus includes simple dialogues based on questions and answers between him and his slave assistants. Saunders, *A Social History,* pp. 101-2.

grant land In Portugal, a medieval system of land bestowal exercised by the king who granted royal estates to noblemen and prominent citizens in recognition of military or civil service to the Crown. Around 1500 this practice in the form of *capitanias* and *sesmarias* (qq.v.) was extended by King João I to the new Portuguese-African territories. DHP.

grão de maluco (Pg.) A tropical tree (*Jatropha curcas* L.) found in Angola, Mozambique, and elsewhere in Africa. The fruit, called physic nut, contains a powerfully purgative oil. Africans prepare a beverage using two or three nuts, said to be sufficient to cure a patient's illness. In Cape Verde, breast-feeding mothers take a liquid preparation of *grão de maluco* to increase the flow and amount of milk. Ficalho, *Plantas Uteis,* p. 248.

gravana (Pg.) A cool and dry south-southeasterly wind along the São Tomé coast lasting about three weeks between the dry season from May to July and the rainy season from October to January. The wind is influenced by the oceanic current from the South. Africans call this time *tempo da gravana* and consider it the best time of the year. In the sixteenth century sailors used to call it the "season of winds." GEPB. *See also* gravanito.

gravanito (Pg.)   In São Tomé, a dry south-southwesterly and west-southwesterly continental wind that blows from January to March, raising dense clouds of dust and sand. Tenreiro, *A Ilha,* p. 37. *See also* gravana.

Green Sea of Darkness Name given c.1200 by the Arabs to the Atlantic Ocean around the Canary Islands off the west coast of Africa. Abshire, *Portuguese Africa,* p. 35.

Gregorianos (Pg.) On São Tomé after 1875, the name given to former slaves freed by the local governor, Gregorio José Ribeiro. He applied the royal decree of King Pedro V of Portugal who declared the emancipation of all slaves in the Portuguese Empire on February 25, 1859. Tenreiro, *A Ilha,* p. 78.

Gremio Africano (Pg.) (1) "African Union." A labor organization formed in 1913 by a moderate group of Luanda-based *assimilados* (q.v.). It was a breakaway section of the Liga Angolana (q.v.). Its moderate aims chiefly concerned the improvement of the educational and social conditions of *mestiços* and Africans. In 1920 the government allowed *Gremio Africano* to send representatives to serve on the legislative Council; by 1928 it had been virtually silenced due to its increasing nationalist tendencies. HDA.

Gremio Africano (Pg.) (2) In Mozambique, a nationalist group organized in 1960 in Lourenço Marques by *mestiços*. Later its name was changed to *Associação Africana* (q.v.). Herrick, *Area Handbook*, p. 165.

griot (Afr.) A greatly respected poet, oral historian, itinerant musician, arbitrator, and keeper of lineages. *Griots* were well-known in Guinea-Bissau, Senegal, and elsewhere in West Africa since colonial times. HDRGC.

grumete (Pg.) Historically, an African deckhand aboard Portuguese ships. Later *grumete* meant an African or *mestiço* who handled cargo and worked on boats. Duncan, *Atlantic Islands,* p. 212. *See also* lançado, tangomau.

Grupo Unido de Moçambique "United Group of Mozambique." A political party established in 1973 just before the military coup of April, 1974. It came into existence with the tacit support of the prime minister, Marcello Caetano. The party's leader, Maximo Dias, held a meeting with the Portuguese premier in September, 1973. Among its goals was the progressive autonomy of Mozambique including the election of Africans and *mestiços*, "the intellectual class," to rule the country. This party soon fell apart and its members joined other nationalist groups. Munslow, *Mozambique,* p. 128.

Grupos Dinamizadores (Pg.) "Dynamizing Groups." A state institution organized by FRELIMO (q.v.) in Mozambique after independence in 1975. These groups were established in every place of work or study, as well as in residential areas. They served a number of social functions, but in particular they were intended to incorporate the people into the political process by holding meetings and acting as a local catalyst for change. By 1976 the groups were engaged in organization, information, education, culture, women's activities, social affairs, production, and commerce. Propaganda was dispensed in the form of songs, dances, and films, devices used to change the society according to the principles of socialism and Marxism established by the Mozambique revolutionary government. Munslow, *Mozambique,* pp. 151-2.

Guadalupe Entrevista (Pg.) A meeting in 1576 between King Sebastião of Portugal and his uncle, Philip II of Spain, later Filipe I of Portugal. On this occasion King Sebastião requested assistance for his Moroccan expedition, being prepared at the time. He also asked his uncle for the hand of his uncle's daughter, then ten years old. Philip opposed the expedition, which ended in 1578 with the defeat and death of Sebastian in Alcacer-Quibir (q.v.), and dismissed his nephew's marital ambitions. GEPB.

Guerra do Mato (Pg.) "War in the Bush." Early, bloody slave revolts repressed in São Tomé. In 1595 and 1693 there were violent uprisings by *Angolares* (q.v.), who attacked the *roças* (small farms) and burned sugar plantations on the island. Tenreiro, *A Ilha,* p. 73.

guerras pretas (Pg.) "Black wars." In the colonial period, skirmishes between hostile African and Portuguese forces stationed in forts and towns in central Angola. Friendly local Jaga chiefs assisted the Portuguese, serving as auxiliaries. Childs, *The People of Angola,* JAH, Cambridge, 1960, I:2:274.

guila (Afr.) In São Tomé and West Africa, two species of the same genus, *Parinari.* One is a tall tree (*P. excelsi*) with edible fruits, in Sierra Leone called gray-plum, and the other a tree (*P. macrophylla*) bearing a fruit called gingerbread in English. In Angola, a third member of the genus is a tree (*P. capensis*) that is uncultivated. Ficalho, *Plantas Uteis,* p. 176.

Guiné, Armazem de (Pg.) "Guinea Department." A government agency in Lisbon, founded by King Manuel I in 1494, in charge of building ships, organizing overseas trade, and hiring crews for voyages between Portugal and Guiné and other West African posts. In 1497 it became *Casa da Guiné.* DHP. *See also* Casa da Mina.

Guiné (Guinea) (Afr.) A geographic term applied by the Portuguese to an extensive and poorly defined territory on the West African coast south of Cape Bojador and extending inland up to the Upper Volta. At the time it was an active commercial region visited by Saharan caravans that traded European bracelets, carpets, horses, English and Irish textiles, copper, and lead for African gold dust, *malagüeta* (q.v.), parrots, monkeys, cotton, and raffia. The name Guiné began to appear on maps after the voyage of the Vivaldi brothers in 1291 and the area called Guiné was expanded after the expedition to the Mandingo Kingdom by Jaime Ferrer in 1346 to include that area. Around 1480, Portugal's kings began to claim territorial rights in the region, and in 1486 King João II assumed the title of Lord of Guiné. Until 1880, Guiné was one of the most active slave-trading areas. In 1975 Portugal recognized its independence and it became People's Republic of Guinea-Bissau. From the beginning of maritime expansion, Guiné and the West African coast were considered virtually synonymous. Chilcote, *Portuguese in Africa,* p. 86;

Cortesão, *Expansão dos Portugueses,* pp. 57-8; Duncan, *Atlantic Islands,* p. 213; Godinho, *A Economia,* pp. 28-1, 112-3; Mota, *Guiné Portuguesa,* p. 15.

Guiné, Lord of A title that King João II of Portugal assumed in 1486 at the time he bestowed the privileges of a municipality on São Jorge da Mina (q.v.) in the Gulf of Guiné. Prestage, *The Portuguese Pioneers,* p. 204.

Guinea *See* Guiné.

Guinea-Bissau, agriculture in The agriculture in Guinea-Bissau may be divided into subsistence and cash-crop farming. During the colonial period, the majority of farms were small African holdings often farmed under an extensive slash-and-burn system of crop rotation. There were only a few large plantations and, as late as 1945, non-whites, who made up 0.4 percent of the population, controlled only 4 per cent of the total area. The leading cash crops were and are rice, maize, millet, manioc, coconuts, groundnuts, and palm oil. Since independence in 1975, agriculture has been substantially expanded in terms of arable land and production. The Portuguese trade monopoly has ended, and today the main crops are exported to African and European countries, including the former Soviet Union. In 1976 over 12 percent of the land was under cultivation. HDRG; Mota, *Guiné Portuguesa,* II:239-40.

Guinea-Bissau, discovery and settlement of Navigators reached the mouth of the Senegal River in 1445, and in 1446 sea captains Gil Eanes and Nuno Tristão explored the estuaries and islands of Guinea-Bissau. Portugal's earliest slaving activities began in this territory. According to the chronicler Gil Eanes de Zurara, one object of the discovery was to expand trade with inland Africa in gold dust, spices, and other products by diverting traditional Saharan trade from the Mediterranean to Senegal. Guiné and Bissau became captaincies with big warehouses or factories (q.v.) to receive slaves brought from the interior on foot and in light river craft. Soon the labor requirements of Brazilian plantations prompted an energetic traffic in slaves during the sixteenth, seventeenth, and eighteenth centuries. Several companies were established, such as the *Companhia da Costa de Guiné* (1664) and the *Companhia Geral do Grão-Pará* (1757), which had an exclusive monopoly on the slave trade. As the slave system drew to a close in 1850, production of palm oil, coconuts, and salt increased the cash-market economy and replaced slave-trading. Few Portuguese and Europeans settled in the colony. According to 1950 census figures, in a population of 502,457 there were only 2,263 Europeans. Prestage, *The Portuguese Pioneers,* pp. 30-1; HDRG.

Guinea-Bissau, economy of Under colonialism, approximately 90 percent of the exports of Guinea-Bissau went to other Portuguese-African colonies an

Portugal. West Germany was the next largest importer of products from Guinea-Bissau, but this represented only a very small portion of the total. The largest segment of imports were from Portugal, representing between 50 and 55 percent in the early 1970s, with the rest shared between other European powers, Japan, and the United States. The current trend in trade policy has been to diversify trading partners, with some export now going to socialist nations in eastern Europe, the former Soviet Union, and Cuba. During the heyday of Portuguese rule, Guinea-Bissau's major exports were rice and groundnuts but the War for Independence (1963-74) seriously eroded this source of hard currency. The present government expects that food will again be an important export. HDRG.

Guinea-Bissau, education in   In Guinea-Bissau, as in Metropolitan Portugal, the educational provision since colonial times has been particularly low. Just before independence there were 11,827 students and 162 teachers in primary education, and 987 students and 45 teachers in secondary schools in the 1962-3 school year. In the whole colony there were a total of fourteen university graduates. During the War for Independence and after, the educational level has increased greatly. In 1975 the country claimed a substantial decline in illiteracy from about 98 percent of the population to 75 percent once peacetime conditions prevailed. There were also 60,000 primary students with 800 teachers in 400 primary schools, 2,000 students at the secondary level, and 5,000 in other educational training, including some 495 in a variety of foreign countries receiving secondary, university, or specialized education such as medical, vocational, construction, and organizational training. HDRG.

Guinea-Bissau, ethnic diversity in   Portuguese Guiné recognized about twenty local ethnic groups. In 1950, the most numerous were the Balanta (146,300) and the Manjaco (71,700) in the coastal zone, the Mandingo (63,800) in most of the central portion, and the Fula (108,400) throughout the northeast and east. Some twenty dialects and a *lingua franca*, *Crioulo*, a Cape Verdian variety of Portuguese, are spoken. Islam is the principal religion in the north and animism in the south; imported Christianity has had little impact. Abshire, *Portuguese Africa,* pp. 20, 110, 112. *See also* Guinea-Bissau, languages of.

Guinea-Bissau, evangelization of   From the beginning of the Discovery (q.v.), Portugal spread the Gospel among Africans. On June 7, 1454, King Afonso V charged the Order of Christ to convert Africans. In 1460, Prince Henry authorized the same order to establish missions. Merchants and soldiers who had settled along the coast were visited by traveling priests. On December 12, 1470, a Spanish Franciscan, Afonso de Bolaños, opened missions in the area, where he died in 1473. The territory was incorporated into the Cape Verde Diocese by the Holy See on January 31, 1533. Pinto Rema, *As Primeiras Missões*, BCG, 1967, xxii(87/88):230, 238, 240. *See also* Jesuit missions in Guinea-Bissau.

Guinea-Bissau, health in In Guinea-Bissau there are numerous debilitating tropical diseases such as malaria, bilharzia, filariasis (qq.v.), and various intestinal disorders. Tuberculosis and nutritional deficiencies are also common problems. In 1959 there was one doctor for every 20,000 inhabitants, the same ratio as for the former French colony of Senegal and far better than that for Mali, which had only one doctor for 39,000 people in 1962. By 1964, the doctor-to-patient ratio had improved to one for every 15,400 people. During the War for Independence (1963-74), PAIGC (q.v.) improved its own health and military facilities to treat war casualties and to serve the increasing numbers of people in liberated zones. Throughout the war, PAIGC sent people overseas for nursing and medical training, while significant numbers of foreign doctors, especially from eastern European nations and Cuba, came to serve as doctors in the liberated regions. Since independence health services have been greatly increased. HDRGC.

Guinea-Bissau, languages in Beside Portuguese, the official language, the languages spoken in Guinea-Bissau include the Senegalese-Guinean and Nigerian-Senegalese groups of languages as defined by Delafosse. According to Westerman's more recent classification they come under two great linguistic divisions termed western Atlantic languages and Mandé languages. There is a great variety of languages, but the Cape Verde *Crioulo* (q.v.) dialect is the *lingua franca* in Guinea-Bissau. Mota, *Guiné Portuguesa*, II:377. *See also* Guinea-Bissau, ethnic diversity in.

Guinea-Bissau, literacy in In 1990, of a total population of 510,800, the literacy ratio among adults was 19 percent, the lowest in Portuguese Africa. *ASOS*, 1991, p. 560.

Guinea-Bissau, mourning in Funeral rites among the Islamized Fulani are performed at a mosque by the family and friends of the dead person. They include prayers, songs, and the sacrifice of a calf which, once roasted, is distributed among the participants. Gonçalves, *O Mundo Arabo-Islámico*, p. 211.

Guinea-Bissau, population of The census in Guinea-Bissau must be considered approximate. In 1950 the total population was 510,777, of which 502,457 (98.3 percent) were "uncivilized," essentially the illiterate or rural population or both; 4,568 (0.8 percent) were *mestiços* (mulattoes) involved mainly in small-scale commerce and local government administration; 2,263 (0.4 percent) Europeans; 1,478 (0.2 percent) *assimilados* and, finally, 11

Hindus. In 1979 the population was estimated at 767,700. *ASOS,* 1991, p. 560; HDRGC.

Guinea-Bissau, Republic of In 1975 the army rebellion that began in 1962 against Portugal ended. On September 10, 1975, Portugal granted independence to its former colony and Luis Cabral was elected president of the new republic. HDRG. *See also* Guinea-Bissau, War for Independence in.

Guinea-Bissau, slave trade in *See* slave trade in Guinea-Bissau.

Guinea-Bissau, War for Independence in In 1956 Amilcar Cabral organized PAIGC (*Partido Africano da Independencia da Guiné e Cabo Verde,* q.v.) in Bissau. The anti-colonial struggle that lasted from 1963 to 1974 took many lives, including that of Cabral who was assassinated in Conakry, French Guinée, on January 20, 1973. Portugal officially recognized the new republic on September 10, 1975. HDRGC.

Guinea coin An English gold coin minted from 1663 to 1813. The coin was intended to have the same value as the pound sterling, 20 shillings, but the purity of the reddish-colored "guinea gold" was so great and the coins were in such high demand that in 1694 they were worth thirty shillings of silver. Eventually the value of a guinea was fixed at 21 shillings (one pound, one shilling) in 1717. In present-day Britain luxury goods and private medical fees are still priced in guineas. Davidson, *Black Mother,* p. 28; WTNID.

guinea corn (Afr.) A wild and cultivated tropical seed-producing grass (*Sorghum vulgare*) native to West Africa and used as food and for animal forage. It is believed that there are three locations where guinea corn was domesticated: West Africa, the Nile-Abyssinia area, and East Africa. Today it is a basic food in many African diets. In Senegal this grain was cultivated before 1300. Its many names such as *anili, argum moro, gero,* and *sanyo,* in various Sudanic languages, testify to its antiquity in the region. Lewicki, *West African Food,* pp. 28-9. *See also* African sugar.

guinea-fowl A domesticated African fowl having a full body, small head which is partly naked of plumage, and a short or depressed tail; especially the common domesticated *Numida meleagris.* It has several African names such as *canga* (Angola) and *omborolo* (Guinea-Bissau). In Portugal it is known as *galhina da India* and *galhina de Angola.* GDLP.

Guinea Portugalexe A collection of charts drawn in Venice c.1489. One of these charts shows the line of the West African coast beyond *Cabo do Lobo* going southeast, then east, then northeast, and ending in what was then an unknown ocean. Apparently *Guinea Portugalexe* reflected information given by Diogo Cão to King João II of Portugal who, in 1484, informed Pope Innocent VIII that "his men nearly reached the Prassum Promontorium the year before." Cão actually had only reached Fish Bay on the northern Mossamedes coast of West Africa. King João, who was looking for a route to the Indian Ocean, either misunderstood or overestimated Cão's discovery. Parry, *The Discovery of the Sea,* pp. 125-26.

Guinea spade gold An English monetary unit first coined by King Charles II in 1663 from gold obtained from the area of West Africa known as Guiné or Guinea. The term was used until 1813. FWNSD. *See also* Guinea coin.

Guinea-worm A thread-like nematode (*Filaria medinensis*) common in Portuguese Africa and elsewhere, sometimes 6 feet long when adult. The larva bores into a cyclops (a type of water flea), completes one stage of its life cycle, then exits into the water. When humans drink this water, the nematode enters the stomach whence it makes its way to the subcutaneous connective tissues, especially of the legs and feet, where it causes abscesses. FWNSD; WNWD.

gum arabic A gum obtained from several African acacias, mainly *Acacia albida*, used for stabilizing emulsions in medicine, other pharmaceutical products, and candy. It was one of the goods brought by Arab traders c.1450 to the Arguim factory on the Mauritanian coast to exchange for red and blue cloth, shawls, coarse kerchiefs, and other articles of slight value made in Alentejo, Portugal. Prestage, *The Portuguese*, p. 167.

Gunga Cabolo (Afr.) An African settlement in the Benguela *sertão*, southern Angola, established by F.I. de Sousa Coutinho in 1759. Colonists were brought to clear and cultivate the land and promote commerce, and missionaries opened a mission to convert Africans in the region. Silva Rego, *O Ultramar*, pp. 166-7.

"Gwa, Eee!" (Afr.) A song sung by migrants and named after Gwa, a Sena village on the lower Zambezi close to Maganja aquem-Chire. In the 1930s rural Mozambican people migrated from there to Nsange, now Malawi. Its content refers to the hunger and famine the migrant workers experienced in places like Missongue, Mutarara, or Mulolo, all places where they suffered. The song stresses the feeling that there can be no going back to their villages. One line of the song said, "The Children of Gwa are crouched, waiting for food like baboons." Vail, *Capitalism*, pp. 349-50. *See also* Jemwe songs, massamanga songs, paiva songs, varajim songs.

{ **H** }

Habito de Cristo (Pg.)   A robe worn by members of the Military Order of Christ at the time of the Discovery (q.v.). After the Order was introduced into Angola by King Manuel I in 1506, many Congolese noblemen, as members of the order, publicly wore this robe in royal ceremonies. Tradition decreed that the donning of this robe should be blessed by missionaries, and that only after this ritual was performed could the robe be worn. Gabriel, *Angola*, p. 146.

hadith (Ar.) (1)   "Communication, narrative."   A narrative record of the sayings or customs of Mohammed, the founder of Islam, and his companions.

hadith (Ar.) (2)   "Communication, narrative."   The collective body of traditions related to Mohammed and his companions. In the Hausaland of West Africa and in Portuguese Guiné around 1450, the *hadith* played an important part in the expansion and political influence of Islam. Gonçalves, *O Mundo Arabo-Islámico*, p. 27; Trimingham, *A History of Islam*, p. 132.

hafiz (Ar.)   In Mozambique and elsewhere, a Moslem who has memorized the Koran. PDM.

haisikoti (Afr.)   In the grassy savanna regions of southeast Angola, a path flattened by cows. Ervedosa, *Itinerario*, p. 19.

Haji (Ar.)   In Guinea-Bissau and elsewhere, an honorific title acquired by a devout Moslem after a pilgrimage to Mecca. GEPB.

Haji qasim (Ar.)   A Moslem pilgrim who frequently performs a pilgrimage to Mecca. Such a person is held in great esteem in the Moslem World. DI. *See also* hajj.

hajj (Ar.)   "Getting out." Among the Moslems in Guinea-Bissau and elsewhere, "the start" or "commencement" of a pilgrimage to Mecca performed in the twelfth month of the Moslem year. It is the fifth pillar of Mohammed, an incumbent religious duty founded upon express injunctions in the Koran. According to Mohammed, it is a divine institution and has the authority of the Koran for its due observance. DI.

hajlij (Afr.)   In Guinea-Bissau and the Western Sudan, a small thorny tree (*Balanites aegyptiaca*) that produces large oval fruit with sweet, slightly sharp-tasting pulp, used as food for both people and cattle. The leaves of this tree are cooked and eaten in many Sudanese regions, often as a common ingredient in sauces. The trees and their fruit were described by Valentim Fernandes on his exploration of 1506-10. He noted that the fruits were usually eaten after being dried, which caused them to become sweet. The fruit of the *hajlij* is also used by other peoples of the Sudan, from the Senegalese Wolof to the people of Lake Chad. Fernandes adds that these trees grew in Mauritania. The *hajlij* is known in English as the desert date. Lewicki, *West African Food*, p. 69.

halíb (Ar.)   In Guinea-Bissau and elsewhere, fresh cow's milk drunk by Sudanese people in West Africa c.1150. Leo Africanus reported in 1540 that milk was used by the people of the Sudanese town of Ghinea (Jenne), people of incontestable African origin. It was probably the Berber people and also some of the African groups living in the Sahel borderlands who were being referred to in a remark made c.1068 by al-Bakri about "all the desert people," that is, all the inhabitants of the Sahara. He said that milk was drunk instead of water, of which they sometimes did not drink a single drop for months on end. Lewicki, *West African Food*, pp. 124-5.

Hamallism (Ar.)   An Islamic-animist sect founded around 1920 by the Marabu Hamallah in Niovo, a town located about 16 mi. (25 km) northwest of Bamaco, Guinea-Bissau. The Hamall are violently opposed to the traditional Asiatic sects of Qadiriya Tariqa and Tidjania Tariqa (qq.v.). For the Marabu Hamallah, Niovo replaced Mecca as center of pilgrimage. Hamallism is considered heretical by other Islamic sects. Gonçalves, *O Mundo Arabo-Islámico*, pp. 166-7.

Hanha (Afr.)   An African town, Ganda municipality, Benguela district, south-central Angola. Hanha is located between the Hanha and Coporlo rivers, a rich cattle area that produces timber, sugar cane, millet, manioc, and sweet potatoes. The first military fort in the area was built in 1685. In 1846 the army pacified the area. In 1925 the population was moved to the town of Cubal, linked by rail to Benguela. GEPB.

Hanno, Periplum of   *See* Periplum of Hanno.

hansansheré (Afr.)   In Guinea-Bissau, a kind of shifting sandy soil formed by material transported by water and wind. It forms extensive low-lying plains where open forest grows. Mota, *Guiné Portuguesa*, I:52. *See also* aindé, boval.

harmattan (Afr.) A cool dry dust-laden parching wind that blows from the interior of Africa toward the Atlantic, especially from November to March; it clouds the air with red dust. In Cape Verde it withers the vegetation and parches human skin, but relieves the endemic climatic fever and dysentery. In Guinea-Bissau and Cape Verde it is called *vento del este* (easterly wind). Mota, *Guiné Portuguesa*, I:30; GGT.

hashish (Ar.) "Dried hemp." A drug formed from the resin obtained from the flowering tops of Indian hemp (*Cannabis sativa*), that grows wild or cultivated. Hashish is chewed or smoked for its intoxicating and euphoric effects. It is probable that the Portuguese reintroduced it into Portugal and Europe at the time of the Discovery (q.v.). In the Sudan this drug was used by members of a medieval religious sect in the eleventh and twelfth centuries to induce mystical dreams and revelations. From *hashshash*, the Arabic plural for hashish addict, comes the English word assassin. Also spelled *haxixe*. GEPB.

haspa (Pg.) In Mozambique and elsewhere, a generic name given to copper coins circulated around 1800 and minted locally in the shape of the letters H, I, and X. At the time they were equal to US 0.9 cents. They were widely used in commerce in central Africa, Transvaal, and Angola. PDM.

heller (Germ.) In Mozambique, a German copper coin that circulated between 1914 and 1918. PDM.

Herero (Afr.) A migratory group of Bantu herdsman from southwestern Angola living in arid coastal regions. Cattle are highly prized and central not only to the Herero economy but also to their culture, for they despise sedentary pursuits. Unlike many of their Angolan neighbors, the Herero have no chiefs. They belong to the cultures of Namibia as much as to those of southwest Angola. In 1970 they numbered around 20,000. Wheeler, *Angola*, pp. 6, 7, 9; GEPB.

herva de Santa Maria (Pg.) In São Tomé and elsewhere, a tropical plant (*Chenopodium ambrosioides* L.) bearing leaves that when boiled and mixed with rum are administered in folk medicine as an enema to treat diarrhea and worms. Also known as wormwood. Almada Negreiros, *Historia*, p. 242.

herva tostão (Pg.) In São Tomé, a wild tropical plant (*Boerhaavia plumbaginea*) that bears leaves used in folk medicine to treat liver and stomach complaints. Almada Negreiros, *Historia*, p. 242.

Hesperides (Lat.) A legendary cluster of islands in the Atlantic claimed sight unseen by Portugal early in the twelfth century. Around 1350, Pope Clement

VI granted Prince Louis de La Cerda the right to conquer and settle the Hesperides. After the Portuguese made their first recorded landfall on them in 1456, they were called the Cape Verde Islands (q.v.). NDLP.

High Commission for Indigenous Affairs A Portuguese agency created by law on November 20, 1946, under the overseas ministry. Its duties included protection of African laborers in the colonies and elsewhere, enforcement of taxation and civil and criminal statuses, and supervision of housing, food, education, and information about customs and mores. Cunha, *O Sistema Portugués*, pp. 225-6.

Hilara In Mozambique, a large estate in the Luangwa River territory controlled by Xavier Araujo Lobo, an Afro-Portuguese who settled in the area around 1890. Xavier Araujo Lobo was the brother of J. Araujo Lobo who pioneered Portuguese penetration north of the Zambezi River in the region of Zumbo Mozambique. In 1891, as the result of a partition accord with England, the Hilara *prazo* area was transferred to the latter and became part of modern Zimbabwe. Newitt, *Portuguese Settlement*, pp. 300, 308.

hippopotamus *See* gabu.

Hodie Ecclesia (Lat.) A bull issued in Rome by Pope Clement X on June 15, 1672, appointing Dom Fabio as bishop of the Cape Verde Islands, with Santiago Island as the seat. Dom Fabio replaced the former bishop, Dom Vicente. The Pope requested Prince Dom Pedro to protect and help the new dignitary. GEPB.

Holy House of Mercy *See* Misericordia.

Holy Orders in Portugal At the beginning of the Discovery (q.v.), devout Africans were not allowed by canon law to receive minor orders in the church. After 1518, the hierarchy changed its attitude, granting orders to Prince Henrique, son of King Afonso I of Congo. Soon after, between 1533 and 1535, several Congolese studying in Portugal were ordained as priests. In 1553, Isabel Borges of Beja freed her mulatto slave João Fernandes, left money for him to be trained as a priest, and endowed a chapel to which she appointed João and his European father the administrators. Saunders, *A Social History*, pp. 157-8; GEPB. *See also* slave children, baptism of.

homem de negocio (Pg.) "Businessman." A term applied in the nineteenth century in Portugal and Africa to a financier and money-lender. The *homem de negocio* enjoyed a superior social status and was considered a member of the nobility. He was a merchant-prince, as opposed to an ordinary merchant-trader or shopkeeper who weighed, measured, and sold or packed goods with his own hands. Boxer, *The Portuguese Seaborne*, p. 33.

homem grande (Pg.) Among the Balantas in Guinea-Bissau in the colonial period, the ancestor of a family or its larger ethnic group. The *homem grande*, a unifying religious link, is worshipped as a protective spirit by these animist people. Mota, *Guiné Portuguesa*, I:249.

homosexuality At the time of the Discovery (q.v.), homosexuality was considered a crime punishable by death or time in the galleys. In 1544 the Inquisition drafted a special statute called the *Livro do Mau Pecado* (Book of the Evil Sin) containing a list of all those denounced as being homosexual. Saunders, *A Social History*, pp. 160, 219.

hoof-and-mouth disease An acute, highly contagious disease of cattle, deer, and other hooved animals caused by a virus and characterized by fever and blisters in the mouth and around the hooves. In Guinea-Bissau and elsewhere, it is an epidemic sickness first officially reported in 1883. Apparently it was introduced from India by Goan (q.v.) merchants. Tenderio, J., *Esboço Epizootologico*, Congresso Commemorativo, Lisboa, 1946, 2:221.

Horizonte (Pg.) "Horizon." A news magazine published in Lourenço Marques, Mozambique. Its first issue appeared on February 24, 1945; its last, no. 43, on June 15, 1946. Dias, *A Imprensa*, pp. 23, 93.

Horta (Pg.) A seaport and capital of the four islands of Faial, Pico, Flores, and Corvo, the westernmost Portuguese settlement in the Azores. In the colonial period, it was the greatest entrepôt between Europe and North America, supplying food and fuel. In 1981 its population was 15,749. It has a radio station, telegraph center, and air base. Its exports include wine, oranges, and grain. Duncan, *Atlantic Islands*, pp. 11, 111, 137; WNGD.

hospicio (Pg.) In colonial Angola, a rustic thatched hut used by transient missionaries in rural settlements. These primitive shelters were tended by Africans known as *escravos da igreja* (slaves of the church) who gardened and provided facilities for the occasional guests. In the first half of the seventeenth century there were *hospicios* in Pinda, near Santo Antonio do Zaire, São Salvador, Incusso, in the Damba area, and elsewhere. Gabriel, *Angola*, pp. 103-04, 138.

Hospital de Todos-os-Santos (Pg.) "All Saints Hospital." The first centralized hospital for the general public established in Lisbon in 1492. It was authorized by Pope Sixto V, opened by King João II, and finished by

King Manuel I, c.1515. It had 150 beds with resident physicians, a pharmacy, and secular administration. The hospitals of Florence and Siena served as models. It took care of Lisbon patients and had facilities to attend sick navigators, sailors, merchants, and government officials returning from overseas. In its first year it treated nearly 3,000 patients. In 1504 the first school of tropical medicine opened there. Around 1550 similar hospitals were established in Angola and Mozambique. DHP; GEPB. *See* slaves working in hospitals.

Hospital dos Indigenas de Luanda (Pg.) "Hospital for Indigenes at Luanda." An institution for infectious diseases established in 1883 when the Military Hospital was built. *Revista Medica de Angola*, Luanda, 1923, 2:479. *See also* Hospital Militar.

Hospital Geral da Caridade em Luanda (Pg.) "General Hospital of Charity at Luanda." A colonial institution that was replaced in 1883 by the Military Hospital and the *Hospital dos Indigenas de Luanda* (qq.v.). *Revista Medica de Angola*, Luanda, 1923, 2:478-79.

Hospital Militar (Pg.) "Military Hospital." A hospital built in Luanda, Angola, in 1883. For some time it was considered the best in West Africa; around 1920 a new clinic and several specialized facilities were added. *Revista Medica de Angola*, Luanda, 1923, 2:479.

Houser Mission A religious institution connected with the Methodist Church in the United States. They led several delegations to assist Angolan refugees in Leopoldville, Zaire, and the São Salvador region in northern Angola in 1954 and 1962. Marcum, *The Angolan Revolution,* I:228-33.

Hualondo (Afr.) A Protestant mission established c.1900 in Bié, south-central Angola, with an agricultural school, hospital, and other social services supported and serviced by African-Americans in the United States. GEPB.

Huambo (Afr.) Town in the highlands of west-central Angola at an altitude of 5,580 ft. (1,700 m), founded in 1912. Until 1975 it was known as Nova Lisboa. In 1969, the population was 49,823. This densely populated area was settled by the agricultural Ovimbundu people who, between 1957 and 1962, were under pressure to register as contract laborers to work in the Cuanza-Norte plantations deserted by the Kimbundu nationalists. Eventually the Huambo people came under the influence of UNITA and MPLA (qq.v.) in 1961. Some of the workers in the Huambo district protested Portuguese rule by heeding their nationalist leaders and ceasing to pay taxes. In 1961 in the Huambo region, the armed revolt began that finally ended with the independence of Angola in 1975. Wheeler, *Angola*, pp. 178-9, 188; WNGD.

Huila, A (Afr.) "Huila." A periodical published in Lubango (formerly Sá da Bandeira), Huila district, southern Angola. Actually this paper was the continuation of *Mossamedes*, a periodical founded in 1932 in Mossamedes and transferred to Lubango in 1937. On January 1, 1940, with issue 169, this publication appeared under its new name *A Huila* (The Huila). Lopo, *Jornalismo*, p. 90.

Huila planalto "Huila plateau." In central Angola, a tableland at an altitude of 8,200 ft. (2,500 m) with a moderate climate and little rain that has attracted Portuguese and other European settlers since early in the nineteenth century. The predominant vegetation is savanna with isolated baobab and acacia trees. The small section of the Huila *planalto* near the town of Lubango (q.v.) has long been among the most densely settled areas of Angola. Kaplan, *Angola*, p. 61.

Huila province (Afr.) A province of southern Angola with Lubango (formerly Sá da Bandeira) as its capital. It is bordered to the north by Benguela, to the south by Namibia, to the east by Bié, and to the west by the Atlantic Ocean. It comprises the *planalto* (highland, plateau), the healthiest region of Angola. It was explored in 1770 under F.I. de Sousa Coutinho, although Portuguese forces had superficially penetrated the area as early as 1627. It was officially occupied in 1845. After several attempts at colonization by the Portuguese army in 1857 and by the Germans in 1858, a group of 222 colonists from Madeira established the first Portuguese colony in Humpata on the banks of the Lubango River in 1884 near a colony of Boers who had settled in the area in 1881. The economic development of Huila province was improved by farming and cattle. In 1934 it was declared a province, one of the five then established in Angola. Today Lubango is a modern booming city. GEPB.

Humbe (Afr.) An African village, Gamboa county, Huila district, southern Angola, on the banks of the Cunene River. In the sixteenth century it was a territory inhabited by the aggressive Jagas. Portuguese merchants penetrated into the area in 1852 and in 1857 the government established the county of Humbe. Portuguese settlers were forced by powerful local chiefs to abandon this region in 1867. At the same time, a group of Boer settlers came to colonize Caoco, a village on the left bank of the Cunene. After several campaigns the Portuguese were able to control the local chiefs, and pacified the territory around 1914. GEPB.

Humpata (Afr.) A town and administrative post in the Lubango municipality, Huila district, southern Angola. A large region centered around Humpata was settled by convicts and colonists between 1868 and 1872. In 1877 a group of Boers led by Jacobus Botha arrived from Transvaal, South Africa. They settled near the Cunene River and obtained official permission to establish a colony in 1890. Soon after Portuguese and settlers from Madeira arrived and joined the new agricultural settlement. Due to internal unrest, a result of English attempts to have the Boers repatriated plus threats from local African chiefs, Portugal sent a force led by Auturo de Paiva to establish order. Disagreeing with government policies, most of the Boers left the area in 1908. In 1927 the South African government finally decided to bring back the remaining colonists unable or unwilling to adjust to new economic and political conditions. The Humpata region was reorganized, and in 1918 and 1923 several agricultural and cattle services were created to help modernize production. In 1928 the *Norton de Matos* colony was established in the area. Today Humpata is a modern and progressive town, well known for its excellent climate. DHP; GEPB.

hunguva (Chop.)   In the Chopi region of southern Mozambique, fog, mist, or haze. DPC.

husa (Afr.)   A tropical plant (*Hibiscus acetosella* Welw.) cultivated by Africans for its edible leaves which are also used to treat fevers. It grows wild at the edge of humid forests in Golungo Alto, Angola. Ficalho, *Plantas Uteis*, p. 97.

hut tax   *See* palhota tax.

hyrax (Gr.)   In Mozambique and elsewhere, a small mammal (order *Hyracoidea*) characterized by a broad body with a rudimentary tail and short legs and ears. Its teeth have molars resembling those of the rhinoceros and incisors like those of rodents. PDM.

{ I }

Ialala Falls (Afr.)   Well-known waterfalls on the Congo River, 93 mi. (150 km) from its mouth. The Ialala Inscriptions (q.v.) are found nearby. GEPB.

Ialala Inscriptions   Anonymous inscriptions on three rocks, referring to the first Portuguese trip to the Congo by Diogo Cão in 1482. They are in Angola about 93 mi. (150 km) from the mouth of the Congo River. One inscription reads, "Here arrived the ships of the noble King João II of Portugal," then follow the names of Diogo Cão, Alvaro Pires, and Pero Escobar. Their authenticity is questionable. DHP.

Icolo-e-Bengo (Afr.)   Municipality and capital of Vila Catete, Luanda district, Angola, established in 1932. Originally settled by the Bantu Gingas, it is an important commercial and agricultural center linked by road and railroad with Luanda. It produces cotton, sugar, beans, and sorghum, the last grown for grain, fodder, and pasture. This is a Kimbundu-speaking region. GEPB.

Ideal (Pg.)   "Ideal." A publication that appeared in Lourenço Marques, Mozambique, on August 1, 1902, to commemorate the fourth anniversary of the foundation of the Association of Employees of Commerce and Industry. There was only one issue and its distribution was free. Dias, *A Imprensa,* p. 8.

Idzagen (Ar.)   An inland Moslem settlement near Cabo Blanco on the Atlantic coast of what is now Mauritania. They were cattle herders and, most of all, caravan traders in the Sahara. Around 1450, they traded with the Portuguese in gold dust, gum arabic, hides, and rock salt at the commercial center of Arguim. Since medieval times the Idzagen had been engaged in commerce with Timbuctu and the Mali Empire in the interior of Africa. Prestage, *The Portuguese Pioneers*, pp. 74-7, 105, 110; GEPB. *See also* Azenegue.

Idzagen slaves (Ar.)   Around 1445 Portuguese merchants bought Idzagen slaves at the market on the island of Arguim, at the time an important slave trade center controlled by West African Moslems. Apparently these were the first slaves brought to Lagos, southern Portugal, and sold in the public market. According to the chronicles, some of the slaves were white Arabs, considered hard workers. Saunders, *A Social History,* p. 167; DHP.

Idzagen trade (Ar.) The Idzagen were nomads engaged in the caravan trade in Mauritania and the western Sahara. Gomes Pires concluded the first transaction with the Idzagen of the Rio de Oro in 1445, exchanging European goods for African and Arab slaves. Afterward trade with the Idzagen was pursued at the permanent trading post at Arguim (q.v.), an island off the Mauritanian coast. Trimingham, *A History of Islam,* pp. 20-21; GEPB.

Ile (Afr.) A municipality created in 1919, now capital of Errego, Quelimane district, Mozambique. A fertile mountainous region 159 mi. (256 km) from Quelimane city, it has several rivers including the Moliquela, Mutuaze, Metebuade, Mugade, Mulemade, and Nipiode. It is an active commercial center with an attractive climate and it had a few European merchants and farmers raising cattle and sheep. By 1927 it had been linked with other centers by 125 mi. (200 km) of paved roads. The Africans in the district make excellent sisal cloth and mats, bamboo baskets, and other crafts, some of which have won prizes at exhibitions in Seville and Paris. GEPB.

Ilha-Nova (Pg.) A legendary island thought to be in the Azores region and often mentioned in official documents and by adventurous navigators in the sixteenth and seventeenth centuries. The last expedition undertaken to find it was in 1770. GEPB.

Ilhas Perdidas (Pg.) "Lost Islands." At the time of the Discovery, a term applied to a number of legendary islands believed to be near the Cape Verde Islands. Apparently the name originated after the disappearance of a criminal sentenced to be banished by a Portuguese judge. Sometimes these islands were called the Garças Islands, the Maiadas Islands, or São Mateus Island, all still seen on maps up until the beginning of the nineteenth century. GEPB.

Illius Qui (Lat.) A bull signed by Pope Eugene IV on December 19, 1443, granting plenary indulgence to those soldiers and lay brothers of the Order of Christ (q.v.) who died with contrite hearts in battle against the Moslems in North Africa. Pinto Rema, *A Primeira Evangelização*, BCG, 1966, Porto, xxi(82):313.

Ilundo (Afr.) In Angola, a cult mixing Bantu spiritism, animism, and Christianity that appeared around 1900 among uprooted Africans settled in Angolan cities, mining camps, and plantations. It was an occult movement that held ceremonies where the faithful invoked spirits who manifested themselves through the body of an entranced medium. Therapeutic magic was practiced, as was sorcery. *Ilundo* was gradually transformed into an ingredient of nationalism once an African working class began to coalesce later in the twentieth century. Chilcote, *Protest,* pp. 238, 240.

Ilustrado, O (Pg.) "The Illustrated." The illustrated magazine of the Louren-ço Marques newspaper *Noticias*. Its first issue appeared on April 1, 1933, and its last on April 1, 1934. Its director was Dr. Alexandre Sobral de Campos; it was owned by Empresa de Tipografia. Dias, *A Imprensa,* pp. 18, 87.

iman (Ar.)   Among Moslems, the spiritual leader in charge of the services and school in a mosque. In Western Sudan there are reports of *imans* in Mali (1050) and Ghana (1067). In Futa-Djallon)q.v.) in 1840 *imans* were elected. Trimingham, *A History of Islam,* pp. 52, 81, 179.

Imbo (Umb.)   An Ovimbundu village in Angola which around 1920 was composed of about fifty households, and included as many as 1,000 people. Among the Ovimbundu, villagers commonly bore the name of the founder of whom the current elder would probably be a descendant. Only the village elder, the *sekulu,* could speak of "my village"; for everyone else it was "our village." Henderson, *Angola,* p. 49.

imbondeiro (Pg.)   A variety of baobab tree (*Adansonia digitata* L.), used metaphorically by some modern Angolan poets to describe personal feelings. For them it is a symbol of nostalgic identity with the African past. In Mozam-bique it is called *malamabeira.* Hamilton, *Voices,* p. 80. *See also* baobab.

impala (Afr.)   In Mozambique and elsewhere in Africa, a large antelope (*Aepyceros melampus*) of brownish-bay color, white below, with a black crescent-shaped stripe on the haunch, the male being distinguished by slender annulated lyrate horns. Around 1500 navigators served impala meat to slaves on their voyages from West Africa to Portugal. Saunders, *A Social History,* pp. 13, 14; GEPB; WTNID. *See also* slaves, food for, on shipboard.

Impirire (Afr.)   A *prazo* (q.v.) in the Zambezia granted to João Fernandes do Rosario. According to an inventory carried out in 1788, it had twenty families and forty-five slaves and their children. In addition, a *mestiço* goldsmith, presumably a dependent, also lived on the *prazo.* Isaacman, *Mozambique: From Colonialism,* pp. 177, 195.

Imprensa de Moçambique, A (Pg.)   "Printing Press of Mozambique." A single-issue 70-page magazine published on May 13, 1954, in Lourenço Marques to commemorate the centennial of the first printing press in Mo-zambique. Published by Gabriel de Medina Camacho of Imprensa-Nacional de Moçambique, 3,500 copies were printed. Dias, *A Imprensa,* pp. 97-8.

Incomati (Afr.)   A river that rises in the Transvaal, South Africa, flows across the Marracuence, Manhica Magude, and empties into the Indian Ocean. At its mouth are the islands of Xefina-Pequena, Xefina-Grande, and Bengalane. In this area in 1894, the Portuguese army fought and defeated African chiefs opposed to the government. Hammond, *Portugal and Africa,* p. 181.

Incondicional, O (Pg.) "The Unconditional." A weekly published in Lourenço Marques, Mozambique, from 1916 until 1921. Dias, *A Imprensa,* pp. 19, 23.

Indian merchant In Mozambique from about 1685 until modern times, a tradesman from Goa, India, who peddled his wares among Africans along the coast and inland. Because these traders controlled the trade center of Inhambane and dealt with laborers coming from the gold fields of Transvaal, South Africa, Maputo, and other cities, they were economically and socially influential. Rita-Ferreira, *O Movimento Migratorio,* pp. 45-46.

Indian Ocean The ocean east of Africa and south and west of India which King João II of Portugal wanted to reach to search for both Prester John, the legendary Christian king of Abyssinia (q.v.), and the route to the Oriental spice trade. In 1487 the king sent an expedition led by Bartolomeu Dias who reached the Indian Ocean after sailing around the Cape of Good Hope. In 1498 Vasco da Gama crossed the ocean from Sofala and Kilwa, East Africa, to Goa in India, Axelson, *Portuguese in South-East,* pp. 19, 21, 33; GEPB.

Indian-Portuguese dynasties From around 1634 onward, adventurers from Portuguese India established large estates or *prazos* (q.v.) south of the Zambezi River. They created a succession of landholders by marrying African women whose children freely intermarried. The land was granted by the Portuguese government to these settlers for three lifetimes in return for rent and the obligation to recruit soldiers for the defense of the colony. The more powerful of these *prazo*-holders built large followings of slaves and clients who were supported by goods produced on the *prazos*, including from their mines, and raiding neighbors. The Africans whom they supplanted became dispossessed. Many of these landholders established dynasties which came to control enormous estates and thousands of landless people. The Araujo, Moraes, Pereira, Vas do Anjos, and other Indian-Portuguese dynasties arose in this fashion. Newitt, *Portuguese Settlement,* pp. 61-3, 68, 76; GEPB.

Indians in Mozambique Generations of Indians migrated to Mozambique from the northwest area that is present-day Pakistan and the former Portuguese-Indian enclaves of Goa, Diu, and Damao. In 1960 there were 17,243 people of Indian heritage employed in government and small business, particularly in the up-country. These people adhered to Hinduism or Islam and, when clustered together in communities, strengthened their ethnicity by conducting school lessons in Urdu and Gujarati and by forming welfare societies. Their economic competitiveness and their practice of sending profits back to India have been resented by Portuguese, other Europeans, and Africans. Henriksen, *Mozambique,* p. 251.

indigenato (Pg.)   In Portuguese Africa, a generic term applied by the Portuguese after 1891 to any indigenous population or community ruled by a chief and subject to African customary law with access to communal land. An *indigenato* paid the native tax and was subject to being contracted to perform such services as being a carrier, working for the police, laboring on public works, and acknowledging a general obligation to contract themselves as workers. *Indigenato* as a way of life was supposed to change them into "civilized" individuals. This legal status was abolished in 1961. Newitt, *Portugal in Africa,* pp. 100-1; Bender, *Angola,* p. 25.

indigenous   In the nineteenth century, an African was identified as indigenous if he were a member of an ethnic group or community and racially different from the white Portuguese settlers. Under the policy of the New State (q.v.), those classed as indigenous were placed in a separate legal category with none of the rights of Portuguese citizens although they were subject to taxation and forced labor. The only way an African could escape from this status was through education, becoming an *assimilado*. This status was ended in 1961 as a result of opposition and open rebellion. Its abolition ended a racial discrimination historically inherent in Portuguese African policy toward the African population. Cunha, *O Sistema Portugués,* p. 180; Duffy, *Portuguese Africa,* p. 291; HDA. *See also* assimilado.

indigenous public health officer   A member of a corps of African medics created by the Portuguese government in Luanda, Angola, on September 14, 1844. The same year a medical school was established to train them. *Revista Medica de Angola,* 1923, 2:196. *See also* fisico-mor de Angola.

Indirect Rule   A Portuguese colonial policy advocating the preservation of traditional ways of life for the indigenous population. Their chiefs were limited and controlled by the colonial power, represented by white colonists segregated from the Africans. The policy was known as Lugardism in English Africa. Cunha, *O Sistema Portugués,* p. 18.

informer   In Angola and elsewhere, an African informer recruited by the Portuguese secret police during the War for Independence (1961-75) to supply information about individuals cooperating with nationalist guerrillas. He was exempt from taxes and paid a small monthly retainer. If the information were important, he might receive a substantial sum. Bender, *Angola,* p. 162.

"Inglaterra, la nação mais negreira de Europa" (Pg.)   "England, the greatest slaver nation in Europe." An expression applied by Portugal to

England after they both signed the Utrecht Peace Treaty of 1713-15 which gave the British the monopoly of the slave trade. Silva Rego, *O Ultramar,* p. 4. *See also* Utrecht, Peace Treaty of.

Inhabanzo Chiefdom in what is now Zimbabwe. In 1609 it was granted to the Portuguese pioneer D.S. Madeira. Newitt, *Portuguese Settlement,* pp. 50-1.

Inhaca (Afr.) A small island in a channel linked to Lourenço Marques Bay, Mozambique. Inhaca is the southernmost limit of tropical East African flora and fauna. In 1588 a group of shipwrecked Portuguese going to Cochim, India, landed here. At the end of the nineteenth century it was occupied by England, but after a long dispute it was returned to Portugal. Darch, *Mozambique,* p. 223.

inhacoda (Afr.) The female chief of a group of six to ten women in charge of digging in gold fields in the *prazos* of Zambezia c.1750. These gangs used several methods to extract gold. During the rainy season, when it was impossible to dig, they went out daily and brought back several pounds of rock which they reduced to a coarse powder by pounding them together, banging one against the other. The fragments were then washed down a trough and the gold particles were removed. After the rainy season ended, the *inhacoda* took her squad to rivers and streams to wash alluvial ores in search of the precious metal. Isaacman, *Mozambique: From Colonialism,* pp. 70-1.

Inhacororo (Afr.) A *prazo* on the lower Zambezi River held in 1798 by João Fernandes de Rosario. According to an inventory done that year, the *prazo* had a slave village of twenty men and sixty women, plus their children. Newitt, *Portuguese Settlement,* pp. 177, 195. *See also* Impirire, prazo.

Inhambane (Afr.) An Indian Ocean seaport and capital of the Inhambane district, Mozambique. Vasco da Gama arrived at this Arab port on January 10, 1498. He called the area *Terra de Boa Gente,* the name under which it appeared on Portuguese maps for many years. By a royal order of May 9, 1761, it was elevated to the rank of city. In 1895 it was the headquarters of Joaquim Mousinho de Albuquerque who commanded the bloody campaign against Gungunhana, the Vatúa chief. Today it is the center of municipal government with schools, a hospital, an observatory, courts, and a chamber of commerce. GEPB.

Inhambane district A Mozambican district with an area of 26,436 sq. mi. (68,500 sq. km). In 1940 the Inhambane district was assigned to the Lourenço Marques archdiocese. Part of the Sul-do-Save province, it includes the townships of Vilacu, Morrumbene, Homoine, Inharrime, and Zavala. It is a densely forested area with valuable timber. In cleared areas sugar and sisal production are important. As the region is free of the tse-tse fly, it has developed a prosperous cattle industry. It has a moderate climate, so it was more amenable to European colonists. In 1980 its population was 977,000. GEPB.

inhame branco (Pg.) The edible starchy root of the tropical vine *Dioscorea cayenensis* L., this yam is grown in São Tomé and elsewhere in Africa. It was introduced by the Portuguese from the New World c.1550. GEPB.

inhame gudú (Afr.) The edible root of the greater yam (*Dioscorea alata* L.), a tropical vine grown in São Tomé and elsewhere in Africa. GEPB.

Inhampende (Afr.) A *prazo* (q.v.) in the Sena area, lower Zambezi, that around 1750 was bequeathed to the Jesuits by the widow of a settler. She left it to them in return for their saying masses for her soul. Newitt, *Portuguese Settlement*, p. 123.

inhamucangamiza (Afr.) The policy of forced sale of millet, sorghum, and cassava (qq.v.), in effect in the *prazos* of Zambezia from 1750 to 1850. The *prazeros* imposed this obligation on African farmers even during periods of famine and shortage of food. It invariably produced tensions and instability within the estates and was responsible for the downfall of a number of *prazos*. Isaacman, *Mozambique: From Colonialism*, pp. 36-7, 73, 114.

Inhangona (Afr.) A *prazo* in the central Barué Kingdom, south of the Zambezi River in Mozambique, that was attacked c.1885 by the adventurer M.J. de Sousa. Newitt, *Portuguese Settlement*, p. 330.

Inhassunge (Afr.) A *prazo* in the lower Zambezi held by Caetano de Piedade Sousa in 1877 at a time when industrialized agriculture was being promoted by the Portuguese government. Sousa established a sugar plantation and sugar mill on the estate. Newitt, *Portuguese Settlement*, pp. 347, 351.

Inn of the Black Lady Alley The name of a street in the San Justa parish of Lisbon where around 1550 a freed African woman owned and managed a hostelry. Innkeeping was an occupation open to free Africans, especially women. Saunders, *A Social History*, p. 145.

inoculation Originally, the process of physically transmitting smallpox from an infected person to uninfected persons. The recipient contracted a mild case and became immune to the disease. It was introduced into Luanda, Angola, in 1803. Dias, *Famine and Disease*, JAH, Cambridge, 1981, 22(3):363(n). *See also* vaccination.

Inquisition, African slaves and the   At the end of the fifteenth century, African slaves, whether born in Africa or in Portugal, came under the scrutiny of the Inquisition. Around 1495 the tribunal, established in Lisbon, Evora, and Coimbra, began accepting the testimony of slaves regarding heresy, sorcery, and religious misconduct on the part of their masters and fellow slaves. Due to the number of slaves unable to speak Portuguese, by 1533 the Inquisition provided interpreters. In 1541, Vicente, a mulatto, told the tribunal that his master's family observed the Jewish Sabbath. A slave girl in Setubal was reported to the Inquisition for encouraging a young boy in her care to lean out of the window and to make the sign of the horn while the Holy Sacrament was passing by. Africans were denounced for such alleged sins as bigamy and homosexuality. Tribunal records show that most of the African defendants were people who, through ignorance, deviated from Christian dogma and practices. Saunders, *A Social History,* pp. 99, 101, 137, 164; DHP; GEPB.

Insaca-saca (Afr.)   In southern Mozambique, a tropical tree (*Olea verrucosa* L.) that grows up to 33 ft. (10 m). It has black wood, the density of which exceeds that of iron. It is used for furniture, wagons, and mill wheels. In the Cape province of South Africa it is called "perpetual wood." GEPB.

In Sacra Petri Sede (Lat.)   A bull delivered by Pope Leo X in Rome on August 14, 1514, that, at the request of King Manuel I, granted plenary indulgence and other privileges to all soldiers in the African and Indian wars. GEPB.

Institute for Aid to National Refugees   A Portuguese governmental agency established in 1976 in Lisbon to assist the *retornados*, both European and African settlers, who had come back to Portugal since 1961, particularly after the independence of the former Portuguese African colonies in 1975. The agency had a budget of US $308 million, over one-third of which went on housing; the balance was spent on medicine, clothes, and schools. Harvey, *Portugal,* pp. 127-8, 131.

Instituto de Medicina Tropical   The Institute of Tropical Medicine was created in Lisbon in 1937. It grew out of the *Escola de Medicina Tropical* (School of Tropical Medicine), founded in 1903. Of the two kinds of students, one group comprised physicians who would work in overseas hospitals and the other was physicians who would be assigned to the armed forces in Portugal and its colonies. The course lasted three years and the main subjects taught were pathology, clinical hygiene, climatology, bacteriology, and parasitology. DHP; GEPB.

Instituto Negrofilo   A militant group that broke away from the Associação Africana (q.v.) in the 1960s. Established in Lourenco Marques, its leaders demanded an end to forced labor and wanted guaranteed land ownership for Africans. The group placed emphasis on Africanness, access to education, and the breakdown of racial barriers. Henriksen, *Revolution,* p. 17.

Instituto Superior Catolico (Pg.) "Catholic Higher Institute." An institute established in Nova Lisboa, southern Angola, in the 1960s. With Vatican approval, three Holy Ghost priests, F. Jorge Sanches, A.F. Santos Neves, and Waldo Garcia, the last a Spaniard, freely expressed their opposition to the Portuguese government. Bishop Daniel Junqueira of Nova Lisboa allowed them to teach and preach in the diocese. Rev. Sanches became rector of Christ the King, the largest seminary in Nova Lisboa, with his two companions assigned to his staff. They organized seminars to study theological, political, and social problems for laymen, priests, and seminarians. The ISC gave strong support to those opposing Portuguese rule. Under pressure from the government, the Catholic hierarchy exiled the three missionaries to Luanda. In 1968 they were expelled from the colony. Rev. Sanches worked in the offices of the general council of the Holy Ghost Order in Rome, Rev. Santos Neves went to Paris and later left the priesthood, and Rev. Waldo Garcia settled in Spain. The loyalty of the Catholic hierarchy to Portuguese colonialism hid the fact that more Catholic than Protestant missionaries were expelled from Angola during the War for Independence. Rev. Santos Neves became the chief publicist for the religious opposition, publishing five books between 1968 and 1975. Henderson, *Angola,* pp. 218-9.

Instituto Superior de Estudos Ultramarinos *See* Escola Superior Colonial.

Instituto Teresiano (Pg.) "Theresian Institute." A Spanish lay organization dedicated to working among young people in Angola. In 1971 it sent two women to the offices of *Mocidade Portuguese Feminina* (Portuguese Young Women) in Nova Lisboa to assist its members in their work. Later the superior assigned two female teachers as staff at the Minor Seminary in the Caala Diocese. Gabriel, *Angola,* p. 593.

Insulae Fortunatae (Lat.) "Fortunate Islands." According to Ptolemy (c.150 AD), a legendary group of islands located west of Portugal and considered the westernmost habitable point on earth; they were variously identified by Portuguese cartographers c.1300 with either the Canary Islands or Madeira. Cortesão, *History,* I:195, 248.

insurrection, center of In Angola in the 1960s, the term for an isolated farm or abandoned barracks, located in a remote area and used as a base of operations by bands of trained revolutionaries. These militants, often far from their command posts and fighting with a minimum of political or administrative structure, had their own immediate logistical priorities. They attacked government posts, farms, and military installations and reviled local officials as exploiters of the poor, thus helping to create and perpetuate revolution. Their incursions into rural areas in the form of depredation or as agents of modernization or both often resulted in the recruitment of rural people to the revolutionary cause. Basing his systematic approach on Eduardo (Che) Guevara's formulation, Regis Debray developed his Theory of Centers of Insurrection in his book, *Revolution in the Revolution* (F. Maspero, Paris, 1967). Henriksen, *Revolution,* p. 215.

Inter Coetera (Lat.) A bull promulgated by Pope Calixto III in 1456 granting the Grand Master of the Order of Christ a spiritual jurisdiction over Portuguese territories overseas with the power to establish ecclesiastic benefits and nominate their holders. Gabriel, *Angola,* p. 48.

International Labor Organization An international agency that deals with labor affairs. Although Portugal had ratified the ILO conventions of 1956 and 1959, in 1961 Ghana made an official complaint against forced labor in Portuguese Africa. An ILO commission was appointed to investigate the complaint and presented its findings in early 1962. After spending only one week in Mozambique, the ILO rejected many of the complaints, but there were reports that forced labor continued until the early 1970s. A secret Angolan government report in 1969 by the director of labor, clearly showed that widespread abuses were still common. Munslow, *Mozambique,* p. 43.

Intransigente, O (Pg.) "The Intransigent." Illustrated humorous magazine published in Lourenço Marques, Mozambique, in 1912. Its editor was Albino Revés. Dias, *A Imprensa,* p. 73.

ira (Afr.) In Guinea-Bissau and elsewhere, any charm or object, animate or inanimate, such as a fork, knife, tree, or forest, regarded with a feeling of awe and belief that it had mysterious powers residing in it or that it was the representative or habitation of a deity. Gonçalves, *O Islamismo,* pp. 102, 166.

Irmaosinhos de Jesus (Pg.) "Little Brothers of Jesus." A religious order of men and women that settled in 1958 in Xamavere on the Namibian border of southeastern Angola to work among the pygmies living in that region. They organized small communities of nomadic pygmy families in southwestern Namibia and, after a few years, built schools and chapels to educate and serve the spiritual needs of their wards. Around 1963 the War for Independence forced the *Irmaosinhos de Jesus* to close their schools and missions and move elsewhere in Angola. In 1965 the missionaries returned to Portugal, victims of the political turmoil in the colony. Gabriel, *Angola,* pp. 579-80.

iron bar currency An iron token used as currency by Portuguese and other Europeans around 1700 to trade goods and slaves and to pay taxes in Dahomey and along the Slave Coast. It was the only standard that expressed the rates of all locally grown staples and those of most European goods as well, although its actual value varied a great deal. The Royal African Company valued iron bars in Dahomey at 4 shillings, in Gambia it was 5 shillings, and in English trade it was generally 6 shillings. Polanyi, *Dahomey,* pp. 144-5.

Islam (Ar.) A religion founded by Mohammed (c.570-632), the prophet of Islam. Islam emphasizes obedience and submission to the will of Allah (God). It is the third major monotheistic religion, the others being Judaism and Christianity. An adherent of Islam is called a Moslem or Muslim. In Africa, Islam has been a highly successful missionary faith. The Portuguese came into contact with Islam around 1444 in the Senegal region. Soon they captured and brought Wolof slaves, followers of Islam, to Lisbon and other cities. DHP; WTNID. *See also* Islamic civilization.

Islam among the animists The animistic belief that all life is produced by a spiritual force and that all natural phenomena and objects have souls has been a tenet of many isolated groups in Western Sudan. Around 1450 the Portuguese found that these Africans had incorporated magic, sorcery, and rituals into Islam. The Africanization of Islam varies widely among ethnic groups. In urban communities, animism and Islam peacefully coexist even today. Trimingham, *A History of Islam,* pp. 4, 82, 94.

Islam among the Fulas Islam reached the upper Senegal River around 1390 with Fulas among the first sub-Saharan Africans to become Islamized. These pastoral nomadic people moved west to Guiné c.1200-1500. Around 1490, they organized the Futa Toro Kingdom south of the upper Senegal River. Trimingham, *A History of Islam,* pp. 47, 150-1; HDRGC.

Islam among the Mandingos The Mandingos were a Sudanese people settled along the upper Niger and upper Senegal rivers who embraced Islam around 1393. Their first Islamized king, Baramandana, made a pilgrimage to Mecca at that time. A settled agricultural ethnic group, they soon after moved west into Portuguese Guiné, establishing the Gabu state in 1546. Until 1847 this was an important center of Islamic education and proselytizing. This proud Islamic state did not accept Portuguese domination until 1900. Trimingham, *A History of Islam,* pp. 62-3; HDRC. *See also* Mandingo.

Islam among the Serer The Serer were a small ethnic group, originally living north of the Senegal River, who rejected Islam around 980 AD. Later, under pressure from the Soninke Kingdom, the Serer group crossed the

Senegal and just before the arrival of the Portuguese in 1445 settled in the southwest on the Atlantic coast north of the Gambia River. According to the testimony of Valentim Fernandes in 1505, under their Fula rulers the Serer became semi-Islamized. It was a small independent chiefdom until 1864, when the French captured their land because it had become a center of anti-European struggle. Trimingham, *A History of Islam*, pp. 45, 174-5; DHP.

Islam among the Wolofs The Wolof Kingdom, a Moslem society, settled around 1390 on the Senegal and Gambia rivers. At the time of the Portuguese arrival at the mouth of the Senegal River in 1446, the Wolofs were part of the Mali Empire. During the early period of the Discovery (q.v.), Moslem Wolof slaves were well known in Lisbon, Evora, and other cities. Trimingham, *A History of Islam*, pp. 40-1, 174-5.

Islam, conversion of Africans to African chiefdoms such as the Fula and Mandingo in the Western Sudan were converted to Islam around 1300. Valentim Fernandes describes in detail the Islamic Mandingo state whose capital Gabu was about 230 mi. (375 km) from the mouth of the Senegal River on the Atlantic coast. Often only the elite professed an orthodox Islam, while the rest kept their animistic rituals, sorcery, and magic. In marginal forest regions, animism coexisted with Islamic law and faith. Fernandes, *Description*, pp. 37-49; Trimingham, *A History of Islam*, pp. 82-3, 86.

Islam in Futa-Djallon (Futa-Jalon) This Fula state south of the middle Senegal River converted to Islam at the end of the eighteenth century then attached itself to the Qadiriya Tariqa brotherhood (q.v.) gaining considerable popularity. Since 1850 the religious and political success of the Tekrur (q.v.) people, the Futa-Djallon joined the Tidjania Tariqa (q.v.), a much older and more powerful brotherhood. Trimingham, *A History of Islam*, pp. 159, 161-2.

Islam in Futa-Toro The Futa Kingdom on the south bank of the Senegal River, sometimes identified with the Tekrur, was Islamized c.980 AD. It reached a high point of development in 1067 when its influence through clerics or representatives reached throughout Western Sudan. At the beginning of the nineteenth century, an Islamic revivalism introduced a theocratic state in Futa-Toro. In 1805 an *almami* (q.v.) claiming the power of Allah promulgated Islam by *jihad* (holy war), expanding his power and authority in Senegal, Gambia, and parts of Guinea-Bissau until French intervention in 1882. Gonçalves, *Os Islamismo*, p. 96; Trimingham, *A History of Islam*, pp. 41-7, 161-2, 176; GEPB.

Islam in Mozambique *See* Mozambique, Islam in.

Islam in Senegal Islam penetrated into the forest region at the mouth of the Senegal River and along the Atlantic coast c.836 AD, assisted by Moslem missionaries and merchants. Around 1040 there were several Islamic states, one of which was Tekrur (q.v.), forerunner of Tokolor (q.v.), a powerful kingdom that soon controlled the trade routes connecting Arguim (q.v.), an old Islamic trade center on the north bank of the Senegal River, to the Sahara Desert and Sahel to the east. From 1076 the tropical forest from the mouth of the Senegal to the Niger River, crisscrossed by caravans, was slowly absorbed by Islam and influenced religious traditions among animistic and pagan groups of the area. Trimingham, *A History of Islam,* pp. 21, 30, 40-5; HDRGC.

Islam in Tokolor (Afr.) Tokolor, an Islamic African kingdom located south of the Senegal River, was closely allied with the Futa-Toro (q.v.) state. Valentim Fernandes reported in 1506-10 that Tokolor was under the rule of a Moslem chief. Around 1700, Tokolor began to expand, so much so that by 1776 it was a well organized, independent state and the home of widely-celebrated Islamic schools where many foreign students came for legal training. Tokolor clerics scattered throughout the Sudan belt in both Moslem and pagan villages. Local chiefs believed them to be practitioners of magic and granted them land to cultivate. In the nineteenth century a revival led to a kind of theocracy or divine commonwealth whose clerics represented the rule of Allah. One of the great leaders was Ahma Bamba, a Senegalese who died in 1927. He founded the Muridiya brotherhood, a truly African Islamic order that today has over one-half million adherents. Trimingham, *A History of Islam,* pp. 28-9, 41-7, 174-5.

Islam in Western Sudan This region covered a large and heavily populated territory that extended from south of the Sahara and east of the Atlantic to the upper Niger River. In this area were the empires of Ghana and Mali, both Islamized in the tenth century. When the Portuguese arrived in 1450, they found several chiefdoms, including the Mandingo, Songhai, and Senegal, well organized under Islam rulers having thousands of followers of the Sunni (q.v.) sect representing over 90 percent of the population. Gonçalves, *O Mundo Arabo-Islámico,* pp. 29-30; Trimingham, *A History of Islam* p. 34.

Islamic civilization At the time of the Discovery (q.v.), Portuguese explorers in the Senegal River area found well established Islamic kingdoms. During the colonial period Islam was a religion concentrated on mosque activities such as rituals, festivities, and education. In West Africa as elsewhere, Islamic missionaries were very active. In the nineteenth century Islam was transformed into a political force, inaugurating a new age. Theocratic states based on loyalty to a common goal were established in West

Africa. This change affected Tokolor, Futa-Djallon (qq.v.), and other states in Guinea-Bissau. Trimingham, *A History of Islam,* pp. 232-3; GEPB.

Islamic civilization and the African way of life A high level of religious, social, juridical, political, and educational development was achieved under the influence of Islam that around 800 AD penetrated into what would be Portuguese Africa along the Indian Ocean coast of Mozambique. On the West African coast, Portuguese navigators c.1440 found Islamic groups in Arguim (q.v.), Senegal, and Gambia. In 1445 Alvise Cadamosto reported that some Senegalese chiefs professed Islam. Islamic civilization shaped local cultures to various degrees; significantly in some places, such as Futa-Djallon (q.v.), and only very slightly, as in Gabu and Tokolor (qq.v.). Early in the colonial period, Islam was incorporated into and modified by African institutions, forming another element within African cultures and becoming the religion of the urban classes. In Western Sudan from the sixteenth to eighteenth centuries, Islam was neutralized by being emptied of those elements that challenged African ways of life, and Moslems were accommodated into African society. The many Sudanese chiefdoms around the middle of the Niger River and west toward Senegal retained their own organizations, customs, and domestic animistic religion upon which their communal identity was based. In the nineteenth century Islam was transformed into a political force, ushering in a new age. These theocratic states were entirely different from anything the Western Sudan had seen before. They represented an attempt to introduce into the African milieu a concept of the state based upon the universal adherence of all subjects to a common religion. The change affected Tokolor, Futa-Djallon, Futa-Toro (qq.v.), and other chiefdoms in Guinea-Bissau and elsewhere. Trimingham, *A History of Islam*, pp. 4, 46-7, 97-8, 141-5; HDRGC.

Islamic Law A body of rules, practices, modes of conduct, and rituals prescribed or formally recognized as binding by the prophet Mohammed and made obligatory by sanctions established in the Koran and its institutions. Traditional Islamic Law is divided into 1) Sunnatu 'l-Fi'l, or what Mohammed did; 2) Sunnatu 'l-Qaul, or what Mohammed enjoined; 3) Sunnatu 't-Tagrir, or that which was done or said in the presence of Mohammed and which was not forbidden by him. It was enforced in all the Western Sudanese chiefdoms and states, and introduced into Sanghana in 1030 when its king, War-Jabi, converted. While visiting Cairo around 1300, Mansa Musa, king of Mali, learned to his surprise that Islamic law limits to four the number of wives a man may take. He said, "By God, I did not know that. I renounce it from this moment." Islamic law is still the code observed by all Guinea-Bissau Moslem communities. Trimingham, *A History of Islam,* pp. 43, 71; DI.

Islamic schools In Guinea-Bissau and elsewhere in West Africa, Islam has stressed learning the Koran by heart and, often, reciting it in schools and public rituals. In several chiefdoms, such as the Tokolor on the upper Senegal River, Koranic schools were organized c.1776. These widely celebrated Islamic schools attracted many foreigners who came for legal training; some settled in the country, but others returned to their homeland to extend the knowledge of Islam. Long before, in the Mali Empire c.1258, the Koran schools were greatly valued as a link between East and North Africa. Trimingham, *A History of Islam,* pp. 47, 81; DHP.

Ismailis (Ar.) In Mozambique and elsewhere, followers of the Shiite (q.v.) sect of Islam who recognize the Aga Khan as the *Imam* (spiritual leader) of the community. There are well organized sects of Ismailis, mainly along the Indian Ocean coastal towns. The name originated as the result of a controversy in 765 AD about the legitimate successor to Jaafar al-Sadiq, who was the sixth of the Shiite *imams* (q.v.). A majority accepted the claims of Jaafar's son Musa al Qazim, but the rest preferred Jaafar's older son, Ismail, and upon Jaafar's death, the Ismailis accepted Ismail as their *imam.* EA; GEPB.

Istorica Descrizione de Tre' Regni Congo, Matamba et Angola (Ital.) "Historical Description of the Three Kingdoms of Congo, Matamba and Angola." A book by João Antonio Cavazzi, an Italian Capuchin who came to Africa in 1658 and worked in the region for twenty years. He returned to the Capuchin monastery in Rome in 1678. Originally written in Portuguese, this book appeared in Italian, published in Bologna, in 1687. A French Capuchin translated it into French and published it in Paris in 1732. GEPB.

Itinerario, O (Pg.) "The Itinerary." Monthly periodical dedicated to literature, criticism, arts, and science, published in Lourenço Marques, Mozambique. It was first published on February 7, 1941, by Dr. Alexandre Sobral de Campos (nos. 1 to 21). Later Dr. Manuel Francisco dos Remedios (nos. 22 to 53) and H.V. Soares de Melo (nos. 54 on) were editors. Its owners were Fausto Leitão Britos and the *Editorial Itinerario.* Dias, *A Imprensa,* pp. 23, 92.

ivory A hard, off-white form of dentin that makes up the tusks of African elephants (*Loxodomia africana*) and other large tusked animals. Trade in ivory was begun by the Portuguese in Guiné, West Africa, around 1460. Soon it became one of the most valuable items of trade, together with slaves, gold, wax, and *malagüeta* pepper. After the discovery of the Gulf of Guiné around 1469, the ivory bought along the coast was traded in Cape Verde, Lisbon, Europe, and the New World. Duncan, *Atlantic Islands,* pp. 17, 214-5, 218; GEPB. *See also* Ivory Coast.

Ivory Coast A loosely defined region along the western coast of the Gulf of Guiné, explored by João Santarem and Pedro Escobar in 1469. This coast, covered by a primeval forest, was populated at the time by fragmented communities of peoples from the east who had migrated during the course of the centuries across Yoruba land to the Mono River, the western border of the coast. Today the main coastal peoples are the Kru and the Agni. Since August 4, 1960, the Ivory Coast has been the *République de Côte d'Ivoire* (Republic of Ivory Coast). Polanyi, *Dahomey,* p. 11; GEPB.

ivory trade in Angola Ivory was one of the most valuable commodities traded in southern Angola from about 1840 to 1890. This vast semi-arid region was well provided with abundant game and its ivory was in growing demand in the West. The abolition of the royal monopoly over ivory in 1834 was also a powerful stimulus to hunting in the dry savanna country. Indeed, the town of Mossamedes was originally founded in 1840 as a coastal trading center to intensify the traffic in ivory from the southern marshes of the colony. The ivory boom only lasted about fifty year but at the price of the near-extermination of elephants in the region. Clarence-Smith, *Slaves, Peasants,* pp. 52-3, 61-2. *See also* ivory trade in Mozambique.

ivory trade in Guiné According to Valentim Fernandes, ivory was highly prized and traded in Guiné around 1506. All along the coasts of Guiné and Sierra Leone people had ivory made into jewelry or incorporated by skillful craftsmen into silverware. Fernandes, *Description,* pp. 77, 79, 97, 105. *See also* ivory trade in Angola.

ivory trade in Mozambique As a valued European and Asian trade commodity, ivory has been a highly prized item since 1550 when the Portuguese arrived in East Africa. Both early settlers and, around 1700, the holders of *prazos* organized systematic hunting parties to obtain this precious trade item. At the time of the abolition of the slave trade (c. 1840) ivory increased greatly in value. In 1860 the Portuguese trader José Anselmo Santana returned from an expedition to the interior of the Zambezi River with 25,000 lb. (11,340 kg) of ivory from the 210 elephants he and his hunters had killed. Santana was introduced to David Livingstone in 1853 in the Mozimkwa village in Zambezia, Mozambique. Newitt, *Portuguese Settlement,* p. 296. *See also* ivory trade in Angola.

jabacoso (Crio.) In Cape Verde, an African dance accompanied by singing. It is a rude and ingenuous lyrical-satirical expression of a humble and strong people who have struggled to maintain their African traditions. Hamilton, *Voices*, p. 250.

jaca (Afr.) In São Tomé, a tropical cultivated tree (*Artocarpus integrifolia* L.) introduced from India by the Portuguese in early colonial times. Its large edible starchy fruit, 20 in. (50 cm) long, is also used in folk medicine to induce abortion. According to some authors it was introduced from Brazil in 1808. Also known as *arvore pão* and *fruta pão*. Tenreiro, *A Ihla*, p. 92.

Jagas (Afr.) Savage groups from southeast of the Congo and Cuango rivers who c.1580 repeatedly attacked and ransacked São Salvador and other settlements. At the time, the Jagas also invaded Benguela in central Angola. They are related to the Iacas and Gingas. Felgas, *Historia*, p. 66.

jahliyya (Ar.) "Ignorance." A term often applied to the pre-Islamic period when what is called the true religion of Islam was unknown in Futa-Djallon and the Islamic regions of Guinea-Bissau. Dias Farinha, *Lingua Arabe e Islamismo, Ultramar*, 1973, 3:8.

jamaia (Pg.) In São Tomé, a tropical plant (*Eryngium foetidum*) of the carrot family having a cluster of flowers on stalks of nearly equal length which spring from a low whorl. The roots have an offensive odor but, when combined in soups or meat stews, impart an agreeable flavor. It was introduced from the New World by the Portuguese in the colonial period. GEPB.

jami (Cong.) Cemetery, burial ground in the Luanda area, c.1880. BeAD. *See also* poço dos negros.

Janierinhas (Pg.) New Year festival held in January coinciding with the election of local officials on São Tomé Island c.1600. Garfield, *History*, p. 258.

jasmineiro de Africa (Pg.) "African jasmine." A tropical wild shrub (*Diplorhynchus angolensis*) with white flowers that are intensely aromatic and very much appreciated by Africans and Portuguese settlers. It is found in Golungo Alto, Cazengo, and elsewhere in Angola. Also called *jasmineiro de Cazengo*. Ficalho, *Plantas Uteis*, p. 219.

Jazirat al-Milh (Ar.) "Salt Peninsula." A region south of the Awlil settlement on the Atlantic coast on the bank of the Senegal River. Since medieval times, sea salt extracted from this area has been exported into Western Sudan and beyond, along the Senegal River up to Silla, Tekrur, Barissa, and Ghana in the east, and the Upper Niger. Salt is of great importance in the food preparation of the people of Sudan. Portuguese navigators explored this area at the time of the Discovery (q.v.). Even today, the Mandingo and Fula population of Guinea-Bissau are "sea salt" eaters. Lewicki, *West African Food*, pp. 116-18.

Jemwe Song of admiration and praise named after the Portuguese representative at Maruro Joaquim de Paiva Andrada, the holder of the Luabo *prazo* in the 1890s before the arrival of modern capitalism. These melodies belong to the so-called canoe-songs sung by canoemen on the Kwakwa River in Mozambique. They reflect the paternalistic feeling of many of the *prazeros* toward their workers, a relationship undermined with the arrival of the plantation companies in the late nineteenth century. Although the government regulations of 1892 still gave *prazo*-holders responsibility for the welfare of their dependents, the plantation companies were interested only in large supplies of cheap labor. Vail, *Capitalism,* p. 167. *See also* Shamwale Ngawona song, work songs.

Jenne (Afr.) A mainly agricultural African state east of the middle Niger River on the southern border of the savanna and the Sahara Desert. Around 1270 it had a very active commerce through Kabara on the Niger and with a Berber settlement a few miles inland as well as at Timbuctu (q.v.). It traded with merchants and travelers crossing the Sahara. During the colonial period Jenne expanded its commerce to Tokolor in Portuguese Guiné. In 1893 it was taken by the French. Trimingham, *A History of Islam*, pp. 31, 67, 244.

Jesuits Members of the Society of Jesus, a religious order founded in 1534 by Ignatius of Loyola (1491-1556) and confirmed by Pope Paul III in 1540. One of its goals was the spread of the Church by preaching, converting non-Christians, and teaching. Saint Ignatius himself sent the first missionaries to areas south of the Sahara, the first group arriving at São Salvador do Congo in 1548. They opened mission schools and gave instruction in Christianity in ways that could be chanted. They made notable contributions to scholarship in both theology and the secular disciplines. In 1760 they were expelled from the country by the Marquis de Pombal. FWNE; DHP.

Jesuits in Angola In March 1548 the first Jesuit mission consisting of three priests and a lay brother led by Diogo de Soveral arrived on the banks of the Congo River at the request of King Diogo I of Congo. With the assistance of King Pedro Afonso II, in 1625 that remained open until 1669. With their characteristic energy, they started work, performing 2,100 baptisms in the first four months. Three churches were erected, one of which, dedicated to the Savior, gave the capital city of Mbanza its new name of São Salvador. At one time six hundred children were being educated under the leadership of Soveral. The Jesuits were less successful in bringing moral order to the Portuguese community in general and, at times, the Jesuit community in particular. In his first year of residence, Father Jorge Vaz collected sixty slaves for embarkation and sale in Brazil. As time went on, further evangeization was difficult because of internal conflicts in the kingdom. In this atmosphere of antagonism their work was of little profit and by 1552 the Jesuit mission in the Congo Kingdom was closed and the missionaries departed in what they perceived as failure. They returned in 1560 with the expedition of Paulo Dias de Novais who granted them land in Luanda. The superior, Francisco de Gouveia, built a residence, church, and school in the city. By 1593 they again were well established. The Jesuit Mateus Cardoso brought the first catechism in Kikongo, *Doutrina Cristiana* (Lisbon, 1624), to the Congo missions. In the same year they began operating a college sponsored by a Luandan philanthropist, but young African men were slow to enroll and by 1650 only seminarians were left. Soon after, the Jesuits decided to concentrate their efforts in the hinterland, organizing several missions to convert Africans and establishing schools to educate youth. By the middle of the eighteenth century, their rural missions and schools were flourishing and in Luanda the college enrollment of African and Portuguese youth had greatly increased. Despite these successes, in 1759 the Marquês de Pombal expelled the Jesuits and closed their institutions. The Angolan people, Portuguese as well as African, suffered a great loss. Duffy, *Portuguese Africa*, pp. 20, 52-3, 69, 114; Gabriel, *Angola*, pp. 98-106; DHP. *See also* Congo, evangelization in the; Jesuits in Ethiopia; Jesuits in Guiné and Cape Verde; Jesuits in Mozambique.

Jesuits in the Cape Verde Islands and Guiné Portuguese Jesuits organized missions in Guiné from 1604 to 1642. The first group of missionaries led by Baltazar Barreira arrived at Ribeira Grande, Santiago Island, on June 20, 1604. From there they went to Guiné where they worked from Senegal to Sierra Leone until 1617, when, due to sickness and lack of help from the bishop and authorities, they left and did pastoral work in the Cape Verde Islands. In 1642 they were replaced by Franciscan missionaries. The last Jesuit superior, Antonio Dias, and his companions left Ribeira Grande, Santiago Island, on July 23, 1642. Pinto Rema, *As Primeiras Missões*, BCG, 1967, xxii(87-8):256, 261-2, 268.

Jesuits in Ethiopia The first two Portuguese Jesuits arrived in Abyssinia, now called Ethiopia (q.v.), in 1555. They were followed two years later by six more Jesuits. Many more continued to come until 1635 when the Abyssinians expelled them. Begore their explusion the Jesuits built the first Ethiopian churches and other buildings in the European style, as remaining ruins demonstrate. Cortesão, *History*, I:272-3. *See also* Jesuits in Angola, Jesuits in Mozambique.

Jesuits in Mozambique St. Francis Xavier, on his way to Goa in 1541, spent six months in the Portuguese settlement on Mozambique Island preaching and assisting in the hospital. In 1560, two Jesuit missionaries and a lay brother arrived at Mozambique, establishing missions in Sena, Tete, and Sofala. One of these missionaries was Gonçalo de Silveira, who died a martyr in Monomotapa. This incident was one of the reasons why the Jesuits left Mozambique in 1570 and returned to Goa. In 1610 the Jesuits came back and settled again on Mozambique Island, building their headquarters and establishing a college that survived for one hundred and fifty years as a training center for local clergy. In 1628 the Monomotapa king was baptized by a Jesuit, taking the name Sebastião. The Jesuit missions declined around 1680, as did all the others in the region. In 1759 they left Mozambique by order of the Marquês de Pombal who banished nine Jesuits priests from the colony. In 1881 the order made a reappearance in Mozambique and four members of the society, led by J.C. Paiva de Andrade, settled in Zambezia. They opened mission stations and schools on several *prazos*. They themselves were granted and managed the *prazo* Boroma where they built a magnificent baroque palace for their headquarters. From then until 1910 they built schools, missions, and hospitals in the region. The Portuguese Republic, established in 1910, the same year expelled about one hundred members of the Society from the colony. The Jesuits turned their missions over to the Divine Word Society, a German order. Duffy, *Portuguese Africa*, pp. 107-8, 111, 113; Herrick, *Area Handbook*, pp. 28, 30, 105; GEPB. *See also* Jesuits in Angola, Jesuits in Ethiopia.

Jewish children In 1493, at the time of the Spanish Inquisition, about 2,000 Jewish children were separated from their parents in Portugal and brought to São Tomé to convert them to Christianity. According to Valentim Fernandes, only six hundred of them had survived by 1499, and in 1532 there probably were not more than fifty or sixty adults. Thus, this group disappeared, mostly due to the high mortality rate; those who lived to maturity mixed with the African population. Abshire, *Portuguese Africa*, p. 109.

Jewish immigration to Angola In June 1912 the Portuguese Chamber of Deputies passed a bill authorizing Jewish communities the right to establish individual settlements in the colony. In 1913, on the eve of World War I, there were negotiations between the Portuguese government and the Jewish Territorial Organization of London for the establishment of an autonomous Jewish community in Angola, but the potential new immigrants wanted collective colonization, communal autonomy, and an initial grant of 5000 sq. mi. (12,950 sq. km) of land. No agreement was reached, partly due to a lack of consensus and partly due to the renewed interest in Palestine as a Jewish state. Marcum, *The Angolan Revolution*, I:4.

jideus (Pg.)   In Guinea-Bissau, an itinerant African Islamic teacher, genealogist, and storyteller who goes around the countryside narrating stories of Islamic heroes and spreading the prophet Mohammed's teachings. Gonçalves, *O Islamismo*, p. 159.

jiefo (Afr.)   In Angola, São Tomé, and elsewhere, a tropical vine (*Piper guineense*) bearing pungent fruit similar to true black pepper. It was discovered by João Afonso de Aveiro who c.1486 took it to Portugal where it soon became very popular. It was also introduced to Flanders and other European markets, but in a few years it was replaced in the markets by the true pepper (*Piper nigrum*), known as *pimenta da India*, which was of better quality. Ficalho, *Plantas Uteis*, pp. 242-3.

jihad (Ar.) "Holy contest, holy war." A war against unbelievers or enemies of Islam, and even against ideas opposed to the teaching of Mohammed, the founder of Islam. In the Koran it is a divine institution, enjoining followers to wage *jihad* to advance Islam and repel evil. In Guinea-Bissau c.1850, *jihads* were frequently organized to fight Islam's enemies. Hiskett, *Nineteenth Century Jihads*, CEA, 1976, 5:163; DI. *See also* jihad al-qalb, jihad al-sayf.

jihad al-qalb (Ar.) "War of the heart." In Islam this term implies a personal battle against carnal lust, required to purify the soul. It is a theological interpretation of the Koran propounded c.1850 by the West African Moslem mystic al-Hajj Umar, an ardent follower of the Tijaniyya Tarika (q.v.), a brotherhood in Western Sudan. Hiskett, *Nineteenth Century Jiahds*, CEA, Cambridge, 1976, 5:163.

jihad al-sayf (Ar.) "War of the sword." A violent military action against infidels resisting Islam, a theological interpretation of the Koran propounded by al-Hajj Umar, a Moslem mystic and reformer in Hausaland in the period 1850 to 1860, who incorporated it as a doctrinal pillar of the Tijaniyya Tarika (q.v.) movement in Western Sudan together with *jihad al-qalb* (q.v.). Hiskett, *Nineteenth Century Jihads*, CEA, Cambridge, 1976, 5:163. *See also* jihad.

ji-nongongo (Kimb.) A puzzle in the form of a question or statement with a tricky answer that is hard to guess; a form of amusement and foretelling popular in Luanda, Angola, c.1880. Ervedosa, *Literatura Angolana*, p. 12.

jinsonge (Afr.) A tropical leguminous plant (*Cajanus cajan* L.) native to Africa, bearing edible pods and seeds. A staple food among Africans, it is widely cultivated in Angola and elsewhere in the tropics. Also known as Congo peas, pigeon peas, and *quisonge*. Ficalho, *Plantas Uteis*, p. 160.

ji-sabu (Kimb.) A short popular saying expressing a moral truth or an accepted form of behavior, taught by an elder or chief to the members of his ethnic group in Luanda, Angola, around 1880. Ervedosa, *Itinerario*, pp. 11-12.

jizya (Ar.) In Western Sudan and elsewhere, a tax imposed by Islamic leaders around 1270 on Africans who refused to accept the new religion. Many African farmers moved to the southwestern regions of West Africa to avoid this economic burden and to keep their own way of life. Trimingham, *A History of Islam*, pp. 16, 58, 200, 212. *See also* kharaj.

João Belo (Pg.) A small seaport and village near the mouth of the Limpopo River, the seat of the Gaza district, southern Mozambique. It became Vila Nova de Gaza on December 12, 1922, then João Belo on March 10, 1928. After independence in 1975 its original African name, Xai-Xai, was restored. In 1972 its population was 3,000. By 1980 the Gaza district had a population of 999,900. Herrick, *Area Handbook,* p. 151; WNGD.

Jornada de Africa (Pg.) "African Journey." An account by Jeronimo de Mendonça of the famous battle of Alcacer-Quibir in 1578 in which the Portuguese forces were destroyed and their leader King Sebastião killed. After the first edition in 1578, this book was reissued in 1785, 1904, and 1941. GEPB.

Jornal a Libertade (Pg.) "Journal of Freedom." A periodical published in Lourenço Marques, Mozambique, by the Rev. Manuel da Cruz Boavida. Its first and only issued appeared on January 29, 1926. The same editor also published *O Jornal da Libertade, A Libertade, O Jornal Libertade, O Jornal,* and *O Jornal da Provincia de Moçambique.* Dias, *A Imprensa*, p. 82.

Jornal de Loanda (Pg.) "The Journal of Loanda." A Luandan periodical founded in 1878 by Dr. Alfredo Troni. It published local and provincial news and commercial and industrial activities as well as bitter personal and political accusations and denunciations of the government. Lopo, *Jornalismo*, p. 35.

Jornal de Medicina (Pg.) "Medical Journal." A journal first published in 1749 in Lisbon and originally entitled: *O Zodiaco Lusitanio Delphico, Anato-*

mico, Botanico, Chirurgico, Dermatologico e Pharmaceutico (Lusitanian Delphic Anatomic, Botanic, Surgical, Dermatologic, and Pharmaceutical Zodiac), read in Portugal and her colonies. GEPB.

Junta Central do Trabalho e Emigração (Pg.) "Central Board of Labor and Migration." A Portuguese governmental agency created in 1928 in charge of enforcing labor laws protecting Africans in the gold fields of South Africa, Zimbabwe, and other countries. They set norms to protect health, housing, and wages, spreading the Portuguese language and keeping close contact with ethnic chiefs back in Mozambique. Cunha, *O Sistema Portugués*, pp. 228-9.

Junta das Missões (Pg.) "Board of Missions." Agency established by the Portuguese government in 1682 to promote missionary activities in Angola. In 1755 the *Junta* reported that "many missions are abandoned and that it is crucial to remedy the situation." Gabriel, *Angola*, pp. 161, 172.

Junta de Defesa dos Direitos de Africa (Pg.) "Committee for the Defense of the Rights of Africans." An organization founded in Lisbon by a group of *assimilados* in 1912 concerned with the average African's lack of education, health facilities, and decent housing in Maputo and other Mozambican urban centers. There also was great concern about the exploitation suffered by the migrant laborers taken to work at the Witwatersrand gold fields in South Africa. The group published a short-lived newspaper, *A Voz d'Africa* (The Voice of Africa). Later the *junta* was reorganized as the *Partido National Africano*, presided over by João de Castro, a deputy representing São Tomé. Newitt, *Portugal in Africa*, p. 145; Pelissier, *La Colonie*, pp. 224-7.

Junta de Desenvolvimento Industrial (Pg.) "Board of Industrial Development." A government agency established in Angola in 1962 to preside over the diversification of Angola's local industries, which experienced an annual growth rate of 13 percent during the 1960s. The growth was concentrated in textiles, chemicals, food and beverages, petroleum products, tobacco, paper, cloth, footwear, cement, and construction. Newitt, *Portugal in Africa*, p. 238.

Junta de Saude de Angola (Pg.) "Board of Public Health of Angola." An agency established by the Portuguese government in Luanda on September 14, 1844. Its purpose was to improve health care and to upgrade hospital facilities. The members of the board were the surgeon general, two physicians, and a pharmacist. The agency also supervised the Luanda Medical School. *Revista Medica de Angola*, Luanda, 1923; 2:196. *See also* fisico-mor.

Junta-Geral (Pg.) "Overall Board." A factotum governmental agency established in Angola in 1869 to increase commercial and agricultural development in the colony. Its members included teachers, government officials, merchants, and farmers representing the municipalities of Luanda, Benguela, and Mossâmedes. A qualified African spoke for each district. Originally the *Junta-Geral* had been intended as a first step toward self-government, but until 1953 it served only as a consultative body. Newitt, *Portugal in Africa*, p. 172.

Juntas Protectoras dos Escravos e Libertos (Pg.) "Protective Boards of Slaves and Freedmen." An agency established by law in 1845 anticipating the abolition of slavery in the Portuguese colonies. Their tribunals, created in Luanda, Angola, and other capitals of the overseas provinces, were in charge of enforcing statutes regulating the gradual liberation of slaves and the protection of freedmen. Cunha, *O Trabalho Indigena*, p. 134.

juramento da agua vermelha (Pg.) "Vermilion water oath." In Angola, Guinea-Bissau, and elsewhere in Portuguese Africa, a tribal ordeal in which a defendant was exposed to danger of death by being forced to drink *agua vermelha* (vermilion water), a poison prepared from the bark of a tropical tree (*Erythrophloeum guinense*) from which the innocent was supposed to be divinely protected. The earliest report of this practice, which has taken thousands of lives over the years, is from 1594. Ficalho, *Plantas Uteis*, p. 164.

Justificação da Colonizacão Portuguesa (Pg.) "Justification of Portuguese Colonization." Since 1490 Portugal has tried to justify its colonial expansion and domination by characterizing it as a providential undertaking meant to convert Africans to Christianity and to secure and improve their economic, social, and educational status. Through the Gospel, Portugal has labored for the spiritual transformation and the material betterment of Africans, a position they have in common with most colonial and many modern thinkers. Cunha, *O Sistema Portugués*, pp. 169-70.

Juventude Cristiana de Angola (Pg.) "Christian Youth of Angola." A secret nationalist society organized by young African intellectuals in Nova Lisboa in 1959. Its first president was João da Cruz Chisseva, an Ovimbundu and a former seminarian. He tried to establish revolutionary cells in Luanda and other urban centers, but in January 1960 he was arrested by PIDE (q.v.). The movement greatly influenced the MPLA (q.v.), especially in 1961 when violence broke out in Angola. In Nova Lisboa, the JCA evolved an Ovimbundu expression of nationalism comparable to that of the Congo. Duffy, *Portuguese Africa*, p. 168; Pelissier, *La Colonie*, pp. 289-90, 374.

{ K }

Kabasa (Afr.)   The royal settlement of the Ndongo Kingdom in central Angola. King Ngola moved there in 1564 after his capital, Ngoleme, was burned. Later the Ndongo Kingdom expanded westward to the Atlantic coast. Its growth and power was directly influenced by the arrival of the Portuguese explorers around 1600. Birmingham, *Trade and Conflict,* pp. 40, 44, 50-1.

kadiva (Afr.)   In southwest Angola, a track of low, soft, wet land covered by grass and weeds; a marsh. Ervedosa, *Itinerario,* p. 18.

Kalahari Desert Border (Afr.)   Semi-desert region southeast of the Kalahari Desert and one of the provinces of Angola. This *sertão* (hinterland) was a marginal territory, sparsely populated and with little economic activity even before Portuguese contact in the sixteenth century. Wheeler, *Angola,* pp. 2, 4, 20.

Kalonga (Afr.)   A Central African Kingdom, south of Lake Malawi on the Shire River, settled around 1614. Having established Mankhoma as a capital, the ruler of Kalonga controlled the ivory trade in the territory north of the Zambezi River. The area went from expansion and consolidation in the seventeenth century to decline in the early eighteenth century. Isaacman, *Mozambique: From Colonialism,* pp. 12-13, 154.

kalundu (Afr.)   A powerful and omnipresent spirit conceived of as a supernatural being having power over nature and men. The *kalundu* is manifest in everything, the earth, the mountains, the sea, the sky, and the forest. The well-known Luandan poet G.B. Victor in his poem *Kalundu* describes the nature and power of this spirit. Andrade, *La Poesie Africaine,* p. 87.

kalunga (Kimb.)   In Kimbundu this term means both sea and death, each possessing the quality of being endless. It has frequently negative connotations, but in *Mussunda Amigo* (Mussunda Friend), a poem by Antonio A. Neto, it is an affirmative destiny, ineluctable as death or the sea, a destiny of freedom and peace. Burness, *Fire,* p. 26.

kamal (Ar.)   An Arabic navigational instrument used in the fifteenth century to measure the angle formed between a star and the horizon. In 1498 a *kamal* was given to Vasco da Gama by Ibn Madjid, the Arab pilot who guided the Portuguese expedition to Goa, India. Vasco da Gama brought the *kamal* to Portugal. Under the names *tavoleta da India* or *tabua da India*, it was used by navigators of the period. Costa, *A Marinha,* p. 29; DHP.

kangaza (Chop.) A light, fine, wild straw found in flat plains areas and used by the Chopis in southern Mozambique to thatch roofs. DPC.

kaper (Dutch) A warship built by the Dutch government to capture or destroy Portuguese ships trading between Africa and the New World. In 1649 a fleet of *kapers* intercepted a convoy of eleven caravels bound from Madeira to Luanda with military stores and reinforcements, and captured or destroyed most of them. Boxer, *Salvador de Sá,* p. 284.

kapok (Afr.) In Angola and elsewhere in Africa, the silky fibers around the seeds of the tropical silk-cotton or kapok tree (*Ceiba pentandra*) used for stuffing pillows and mattresses. In Portuguese they are called *capoca*. GEPB.

karamokõdjo (Afr.) A Moslem man among the Islamized Fula in Guinea-Bissau who is learned in theology. He enjoys an important role in the Islamic community as teacher, advisor, and missionary in charge of expanding the faith and winning converts. Gonçalves, *O Mundo Arabo-Islámico,* pp. 214-5. *See also* almudo, tahibadjo.

Karanga Kingdom (Afr.) An early African kingdom established by migrant Shonu groups who invaded and conquered the territory occupied by the Bushman people living along the Zambezi River in Mozambique. By the fourteenth century the Karanga, with their well organized empire, migrated into what is now Zimbabwe and are credited with having built the complex know as the Acropolis. At the time of Portuguese contact c.1550, the Karanga were a large confederation of chieftaincies north and south of the Zambezi. Isaacman, *Mozambique: From Colonialism,* pp. 3, 5-11.

Kariba (Afr.) A town on the upper Zambezi River in the Tete district, Mozambique, settled by several African ethnic groups. In 1888 they were supposed to be under Portuguese dominion. Axelson, *Portugal,* p. 155.

kariti (Afr.) In Portuguese West Africa, a semi-wild tree (*Butyrospermum parkii*) found by explorers early in the Discovery (q.v.). It bears oval fruit with a pit containing considerable quantities of oil, up to 60 percent of the whole. The pit is a major source of vegetable oil, used in cooking, soap-making, lamp oil, and to whitewash houses. It is also known as the shea-butter tree. Lewicki, *West African Food,* p. 104.

Karonga (Afr.) An African settlement at the northern end of Lake Malawi (then Lake Niassa) that in 1878 was proposed by Portugal as the terminal point of a railroad originating in Tanganyika in Central Africa. In 1887 the town was found in ruins and deserted. Today there is a town with the same name in Malawi, at the north end of Lake Malawi. In 1966 the population of this town, which is a lake trading post and had been an important headquarters during World War I, was about 1,000. Axelson, *Portugal,* pp. 161, 171-3; WNGD.

Kasai province A northwestern region of Angola that in 1887 was annexed by Belgium to the Congo Free State, now Zaire. Newitt, *Portugal in Africa,* p. 30.

Kasai River (Afr.) The Kasai is 1338 mi. (2155 km) long, rising in central Angola, flowing east, then north, forming part of the border between Angola and Zaire. It continues north and northwest, through south-central and western Zaire, flowing into the Congo River on the Congo border, forming the chief south tributary of the Congo. It is navigable to Stanley Pool on the eastern fringe of the Loango region. Communication and commerce probably existed along this route in pre-European times in the same way they did during the height of the Portuguese Atlantic slave trade (1600-1800). Birmingham, *Trade and Conflict,* p. 8; WNGD.

Kasanje (Afr.) A warrior among the Inbamgalas in Angola c.1520. A *kasanje* was in charge of ambush and guerrilla war against the Portuguese and other intruders. At the time of Queen Nzinga, the Inbangalas retired to the Lui-Cuango Valley, south of the Cuanza, where the *kasanjes* organized an irregular struggle against the invaders. Miller, *Nzinga of Matamba,* JAH, Cambridge, 1975, 16(2):201-216.

Kasoko (Afr.) An island with a *prazo* and settlement, located twelve days' journey above Zumbo on the upper Zambezi River, Mozambique. The Portuguese established a trading center there in 1888. At that time, a number of African chiefs came to Kasoko to pay homage to the Portuguese. Axelson, *Portugal,* p. 154.

Katalunga (Kimb.) In Angola, a tropical shrub used in folk medicine to treat a variety of sicknesses including scurvy, hemorrhage, headaches, skin inflammation, wounds, and other maladies. EDK.

Katanga copper mines A rich copper field in southwest Zaire that around 1880 was a center of economic contention among the governments of Germany, Britain, and Portugual. In 1902 a British engineer, Robert Williams, obtained a Portuguese concession to build a railroad to move the copper across Angola to Luanda. He built the line as far as Benguela on the Atlantic coast; in 1930 it had been extended north along the coast to Luanda. Newitt, *Portugal in Africa,* pp. 37, 89.

kati (Chopi)   Among the Chopis of Mozambique c.1900, the village where a man paid the *lobola* (q.v.) to acquire a wife. DPC.

Katima Rapids   Falls on the Katima River near the Andra village on the upper Zambezi River. In 1886 the rapids were established as the eastern boundary of Angolan territory in the Mashonaland region. Axelson, *Portugal,* p. 186.

Katunga (Afr.)   An African settlement on the Shire River, upper Zambezia, in the area of the Massingire *prazo* which was under Portuguese control. In 1787 Katunga was occupied by force and illegally by H.H. Johnstons, the British consul in Mozambique. Axelson, *Portugal,* pp. 205, 207-8.

Kazembe (Afr.)   A sixteenth-century African chiefdom located north of the Zambezi River. In the middle of the eighteenth century it prospered by its contact with the Portuguese. Around 1793 it developed an active slave trade both with the Atlantic coast through Angola and with the Tete and Sena fairs along the Zambezi. In 1829 Kazembe carried on slave trade with the Pereira family, holders of the Makanga *prazo*. Isaacman, *Mozambique: From Colonialism,* pp. 75, 80-1.

Kazonzola (Afr.)   An Afro-Christian revivalist movement organized among the Ovimbundu of central Angola in the 1930s. It was a syncretic religion, anti-white and hostile to Christian missions. Newitt, *Portugal in Africa,* p. 132.

Khaki Uniform Movement   An anti-white nativist religious group organized in 1940 by Simon M'Padi, a Bakongo born in the Belgian Congo. Emphasizing Bible-reading and the destruction of idols, he preached anti-Portuguese sermons and encouraged his followers to look toward a future of great happiness for Africans. Wheeler, *Angola,* pp. 153-4.

kharaj (Ar.)   A hut tax that African kings allied with Arab sheiks imposed c.1394 on African farmers settled in the southwestern region of Western Sudan on the border of the Sahara and the savanna. The farmers were also obliged to supply manpower for their kings' armies. Trimingham, *A History of Islam,* pp. 30, 58, 212.

Khoisan (Afr.)   A non-Bantu people living in southern Angola for centuries prior to the Bantu invasion in the fourteenth century. This hunter-gatherer population was soon dominated by the newcomers; by 1900 the Khoisan were represented by only a few thousand souls. *Khoisan* is a compound of *Khoi*, the Hottentots' name for themselves, and *San*, their name for Bushmen. If there ever were Hottentots in Angola, they have long been eliminated or displaced. By the first two decades of the twentieth century, a few thousand Bushmen in small family bands wandered across southern Angola and into the Kalahari Desert living a nomadic life with no permanent settlements. They built simple semicircular windbreaks of saplings stuck in the ground, tied together at the top, and covered with grass. They practiced no formal agriculture and owned no domestic animals except occasional dogs. Henderson, *Angola,* pp. 63-4.

khumur, al- (Ar.) An alcoholic beverage made from millet, used in rituals for the dead in Guinea-Bissau, southern Mauritania, and what is now Mali. *Al-khumur* is a generic word for drink but it is probably with this ritual meaning that the Arabic chronicler al-Bakri used the term c.1050. Lewicki, *West African Food,* p. 130.

ki-beta (Kimb.) "Great Punishment." An expression used in Congo, Kwanza, and elsewhere in Angola around 1864 for the suffering and death caused by devastating smallpox epidemics. Dias, *Famine and Disease*, JAH, Cambridge, 1981, 22(3):367. *See also* ki-ngongo.

Kibentele (Afr.) The name of a refugee camp in northern Angola. In 1963 it was visited by the Rev. David Grenfell, a minister associated with the American Baptist Missionary Society and involved in relief work. Marcum, *The Angola Revolution*, I:19.

Kidism (Afr.) A religious sect whose members called themselves Followers of Christ. It was a syncretic Afro-Christian movement that appeared in the Maquela do Zombo region of northern Angola in 1941. At that time hundreds of detribalized Africans had abandoned their traditional culture and were in need of an institution for spiritual guidance. Kidism also was one of several Protestant sects that served as outlets for African protests against European domination. In the Kikongo language the correct appellation would be *nzambi-a-tosi* (drop of water), indicating acceptance of Christ by baptism. Marcum, *The Angola Revolution*, I:79. *See also* Kimbanguism, Tocoism.

kidney bean Kidney-shaped legume (*Vigna sinensis*), also known as cowpea and black-eyed pea. Cultivated in Western Sudan since early medieval times, it is a part of the basic local diet in Ghana, Mali, and Mauritania. It originated in Central Africa, where it was presumably domesticated; from there it had already spread eastward in remote times, reaching India and other tropical countries of the Old World. In Egypt it is called *lubiya* and in West Africa *niébe*. It was introduced to the West African coast by Arabs in the thirteenth century, and its cultivation was spread by Africans who had been converted to the Moslem faith as they went deeper and deeper into the forest zone of West Africa. Today it is important in the diet of the Mandingos of Guinea-Bissau, among other groups. Kidney beans should be distinguished from the New World common bean (*Phaseolus vulgaris*), now so popular in the Old World. Lewicki, *West African Food,* pp. 53-4, 57, 164.

Kikongo (Afr.)   One of the major Angolan languages, it is spoken by the Bacongo people, the northernmost group in the Cabinda Enclave and the northwestern areas of Angola. Since contact with the Portuguese in 1482, Kicongo has been used to communicate with outsiders for commercial as well as social and religious purposes. In 1960 Kikongo speakers numbered around 400,000. Wheeler, *Angola,* pp. 7-8; GEPB. *See also* Kimbundu, Umbundu.

Kilifi (Afr.)   An Arab sultanate on the Indian Ocean in the Mombasa region, visited by Portuguese navigators early in 1500. Later the Portuguese established control over trade with the sultanate. Continued struggle among neighbors brought war and in 1586 Portuguese and Arab allied forces attacked the capital, Marani, and killed the sultan's brother. Another raid took place in 1592 when the Portuguese, allied with the Sultan of Malindi, razed the town to the ground. Axelson, *Portuguese in South-East,* pp. 182, 190-2.

Kilindini (Afr.)   A deep safe natural harbor at Mombasa that offered anchorage to the Portuguese fleet led by Vasco da Gama on the route to India in 1498. Portuguese pilot Manuel Monteiro surveyed the bay for the first time in 1599. Axelson, *Portuguese in South-East,* p. 197.

Kilwa (Ar.)   Island town with an excellent harbor, 25 mi. (40 km) off the southeast coast of Tanzania. It is an ancient settlement founded in 975 AD by a Persian prince. Many remains of its historic capital Zanguebar (forerunner of the name Zanzibar) still stand. In 1505, it was occupied by the Portuguese and became a slave trade center. Today it is a modern town. GEPB; WNGD.

kimbanda (Kimb.)   A diviner and folk healer, either male or female, who uses personal spiritual power and idols to assist people in trouble. They may also have substantial knowledge of herbal medicine and at least part of a *kimbanda*'s work is devoted to curing the sick. *Kimbandas* are believed to have inherited or acquired the ability to communicate with spirits. They charge for their services and may journey from village to village within a district in search of people in need of assistance. The greater the reputation of the *kimbanda*, the more he or she charges for services. Kaplan, *Angola,* p. 104-5.

kimbangila (Kik.) In São Salvador do Congo c.1880, the last layer of grass and mud put on a hut roof. BeAD.

Kimbanguism (Afr.) A nativist and messianic religious movement founded by Simão Kimbango in 1922 in the São Salvador do Congo area. It was a syncretic ideological group that mixed animistic and Christian beliefs and practices. From the beginning, *Kimbanguism* was anti-fetish and anti-Portuguese, preaching a militant Bacongo ethnic nationalism. It was a close-knit politicized congregation that remained underground until 1961 when the War for Independence began in Angola. *Kimbanguism*, besides being against magic practices and what they considered obscene African dances, preached abstaining from polygamy, reading of the Bible, and cultivating a deep feeling of God's presence. Once the movement was recognized by the authorities as being nationalistic and anti-European, the Belgian government intervened and imprisoned Simão Kimbango. As a messianic movement, *Kimbanguism* still has many followers in Angola and elsewhere. Estermann, *O Tocoismo*, Garcia de Horta, 1965, 13(3):329-30; Pelissier, *La Colonie,* pp. 165, 168, 172; GEPB.

kimbares (Afr.) African soldiers trained by the Portuguese and used around 1620 to control rebellious local chiefs. In 1625 Queen Nzinga gave asylum to many of these fugitive soldiers, receiving them into her own Matamba army, promising them land and other rewards. Vansina, *Kingdoms of the Savanna,* pp. 134-5.

Kimbari (Afr.) An African settlement located along the Atlantic coast of Mossâmedes, southern Angola. Its inhabitants are descendants of slaves brought to the region in the nineteenth century. These fishermen speak a modified form of Kimbundu, the language of Luanda and the surrounding area. Their culture is a syncretic mixture of Portuguese and Mbundu elements. They are essentially integrated into European forms of social and political organization. From their base in the coastal zone, the Kimbaris have spread inland to towns and other centers of economic activity. During the Salazar regime (1926-1969), many Kimbaris were acculturated, becoming full Portuguese citizens. Clarence-Smith, *Slaves, Peasants,* p. 8.

Kimberly diamond mines The discovery of the Kimberly mines in South Africa around 1875 had a devastating impact on the economy and society of Mozambique. The acute shortage of labor in South Africa forced the Kimberly company to import cheap labor from Mozambique, one of the main suppliers of workers, and elsewhere. The flow of laborers was strictly regulated in several agreements between Portugal and the South African government in 1897, 1909, and 1928. Cash crops and food production were neglected, and the absence of fathers weakened the family and contributed to child vagrancy. Munslow, *Mozambique*, pp. 18-9, 26. GEPB.

Kimbo (Afr.) In Angola, small villages where Africans cultivate manioc, millet, maize, and other vegetables in family plots. In 1970 nationalists obtained much of the food for their forces from these *kimbos*, which became targets of airborne herbicide attacks by the Portuguese. Marcum, *The Angolan Revolution*, II:213.

Kimbundu (Bant.) In Angola, a Bantu language spoken by four major, closely related, groups, the Mbundu, Mbaka, Ndongo, and Mbondo. Totaling about 1,100,000 people, they live mostly in Luanda province and the Kwanza Valley. The Mbundu are the second most populous ethnolinguistic group in Angola and have comprised the majority of the Western-oriented intelligentsia since the mid-nineteenth century. These groups have staunchly resisted European intrusion and authority in the colony. Pelissier, *La Colonie*, p. 12; Wheeler, *Angola*, pp. 8, 32(n), 34, 36.

Kimpasi (Afr.) A secret society organized by the Bacongos (q.v.) in northern Angola in 1960. It began as a militant syncretic group aiming at independence and at the same time preaching a messianic revivalism that they believe will bring peace, happiness, and justice for the oppressed African masses. It was a rebirth of the old religious movements of the seventeenth century that tried to create a non-European church for Africans. Pelissier, *La Colonie*, p. 163.

kinaxixi (Kimb.) In Luanda, Angola, a large public market. In his poetic imagery Antonio A. Neto often uses Kimbundu words such as *kinaxixi*, *umbuneiro* (tree), and *giboia* (snake) to link his poems with the Angolan people. Burness, *Fire,* p. 32.

ki-ngongo (Kimb.) "Great suffering." An expression used in the Congo, and Kwanza and elsewhere in Angola around 1875 to refer to devastating smallpox epidemics. In the second half of the nineteenth century smallpox epidemics were of the virulent, eruptive strain (*Variola major*) rather than the milder form (*Variola minor*). The spread of the disease was increased by the African rejection of European medical aid, preferring remedies prescribed by their *kimbandas* (q.v.). Dias, *Famine and Disease*, JAH, Cambridge, 1981, 22(3):367. *See also* ki-beta.

Kinkuzu (Afr.) A nationalist training camp in Congo-Kinshasa (later Zaire) organized by anti-Portuguese dissidents in the 1960s that on August 21, 1962 was put at the disposal of the UPA (q.v.) by the rebel Congolese government. It is claimed that the nationalists trained about 3,000 guerrillas in a short time, but there are reports that these officers and soldiers felt more at home in the independence parade in Kinshasa than among the guerrilla units. Wheeler, *Angola,* pp. 206-7.

Kinsembo (Afr.) A trading post established in 1855 by the English on the Angolan coast near Ambriz to trade baobab fiber (for paper making), coffee, sesame, rubber, ivory, and palm kernels. Axelson, *Portugal,* pp. 39, 60.

Kintwadi (Kik.) "Association." A social-aid organization established in 1959 in northern Angola by Simão Kimbangu to assist African workers. At one time membership numbered about 100,000. Gabriel, *Angola,* p. 611. *See also* Kimbanguism.

Kintwadi Kin Luvuzlu (Afr.) "Health Union." A religious-nationalist group organized by C. Teixeira in Kinshasa, Zaire, in 1951. In 1960 the group was accused by the Portuguese government of organizing a revolt in north-western Angola. Pelissier, *La Colonie,* p. 166.

Kipini (Afr.) A settlement in the Rovuma River area, East Africa, established in 1886 along the border between German and English possessions. Axelson, *Portugal,* p. 87.

Kisama (Afr.) A region of the Angolan hinterland between the Cuanza and the Cunene rivers that from the time of Paulo Dias de Novais, the founder in 1576 of Luanda, to 1920 was independent of Portuguese control. Overland travel between Luanda and Benguela and between Benguela and Mossâmedes was dangerous, even suicidal, and the Kisamas acted as guides, assisting travelers crossing the area. Wheeler, *Angola,* p. 58.

Kishicongo (Afr.) A Bantu group, part of the Bacongo (q.v.) in northern Angola. It was a member of the Congo Kingdom c.1482. Wheeler, *Angola,* p. 8.

Kishili laws (Afr.) A set of rules governing infanticide and human sacrifice introduced around 1650 by Temba Ndumba, queen of the territory in the upper Cuango River, Angola. Birmingham, *Trade and Conflict,* p. 71.

kissari (Afr.) The edible carrot-like root of a tropical creeping shrub that grows between coffee trees in the Cazengo highland and elsewhere in Angola. Since early colonial times Africans collect and eat this wild root during drought and famine. Dias, *Famine and Disease,* JAH, Cambridge, 1981, 22(3):355.

Kissembo (Afr.) A small colonial town and port north of Ambriz that c.1850 was settled by a few *sertanejos* (backwoodsmen) and used as a base to penetrate the Angolan hinterland to trade in slaves for Brazilian markets. In this port, Prince Nicolas of Congo was murdered in 1860 by a mob of Africans who considered him a pro-European stooge, a Westernized traitor who rejected the independence of the Congo Kingdom. Wheeler, *Angola,* pp. 54-5, 88-9.

Kiswahili (Ar.) A variation of the Bantu language spoken today as mother tongue by an Afro-Moslem people settled along a narrow coastal strip of arid land in southern Mozambique on and near the border with Tanzania and including its capital, Dar es-Salaam. Before the arrival of the Portuguese in 1498, Kiswahili was used as a language of trade. A variation of Swahili (q.v.), it is grammatically Bantu and shows close lexical similarity to other Bantu languages. It differs, however, in that it is not tonal and its noun-class system is somewhat less complex than those of most Bantu languages, differences which are, perhaps, the result of the process of simplification characteristic of many languages that, like Kiswahili, have been used as *lingua franca* over a period of time. In the mid-twentieth century Kiswahili became a symbol of unity and later the official language of Tanzania. EA; SESA.

kitata (Bant.) Patrilineal kinship transmitted from father to son in the old Xicongo culture. *Kitata* was recognized but not counted in the family clan organization because land inheritance, marriage and family structure, loyalty, and social stability were transmitted through the female line from maternal uncle to nephew. Male descents of a common matrilineal line crossed the blood boundaries beyond which security, solidarity, and affection were no longer guaranteed in all circumstances. Henderson, *Angola,* p. 42.

Kitawala (Afr.) A Protestant sect; a branch of the Watch Tower Association of Brooklyn, New York, introduced in the Katanga region in 1925 by a self-proclaimed prophet, Tomo Nyirenda, from Nyassaland, called by his followers *Mwana Lesa* or Son of God. Accused of ritual killings, Nyirenda was arrested by Belgian police, and the followers of *Kitawala* were expelled. The group moved to the Cambande region, southern Angola, where in 1942 they were accused of killing a Portuguese settler. In 1951 *Kitawala* reappeared among the Quioco in Teixeira de Sousa, southern Angola. Among the population along the Benguela railroad, the leader of the sect was thought to perform miracles. This dissident sect secretly organized resistance against the Portuguese government. In 1953 its leader in Angola was arrested by the authorities. Comhaire, *Societés Secrets,* 1955, 25:54-59; Pelissier, *La Colonie,* pp. 101-2, 187.

kitomi (Afr.) Among the Congo people c.1600, an animist priest believed to be the intermediary between spirits from the supernatural world and mortals. The *kitomi* or *kitongo* was a man able to communicate with mysterious, intangible, and unknowable powers. Vansina, *Kingdoms of the Savanna,* pp. 32, 324.

kitongo *See* kitomi.

Kitwe (Afr.) A mining village in Zambia. In 1958 refugees working in the mines at Kitwe organized *Chijilochalimbo,* a mutual-aid association presided over by Dickson Mukuma, an itinerant merchant. The society was made up of Luena workers from Ganguela, Angola, who settled in Zambia, then called Northern Rhodesia. Pelissier, *La Colonie,* p. 295.

Kivusi (Afr.) An African clan or family group who consider themselves descendants of the same ancestor. It is one of about twelve royal clans in São Salvador, Angola, that for generations have provided the kings of the Congo monarchy. The Kivusi are a conservative, Catholic branch from which originated the dynasty that ruled the Old Congo Kingdom. Its seat is in São Salvador and has been represented by such monarchs as Pedro V in 1959 to Pedro VIII in 1962. Marcum, *The Angolan Revolution,* I:51; Pelissier, *La Colonie,* pp. 264, 266-8.

Kiyoka (Afr.) An ethnic-religious movement organized around 1870 in the São Salvador region of Angola that preached destruction and the burning of fetishes. It was a colonial nativist group with radical anti- European overtones considered to be a precursor of such modern sects as *Kimbunguism* and *Tocoism* (qq.v.). Pelissier, *La Colonie,* pp. 163-4.

Kizamba (Afr.) An African village on the Congo-Angola border where Antonio Mariano, a self-proclaimed religious prophet, established his base of operation in 1966. At one time his political-mystic movement had several thousand followers who called themselves Marianos. Marcum, *The Angolan Revolution,* I:420.

kõdi kõió (Afr.) "White coin." Name given by Mandingo merchants in Guinea-Bissau to Portuguese coins. Carreira, *Mandingas,* p. 148.

Kololo (Afr.) An African ethnic group in the upper Zambezi region of Central Africa that around 1650 began an expansion that eventually assimilated such other groups as the Lozi and the Nsenga. Isaacman, *Mozambique: From Colonialism,* pp. 155-6.

Komati (Afr.) A river in southern Africa about 500 mi. (800 km) long. It rises in the North Drakensberg Mountains of southeastern Transvaal, flows east through northern Swaziland, and then turns north. About a mile below its junction with the Crocodile River it flows through a cleft 600 ft. (80 m) deep at Komati. It crosses the boundary between Mozambique and the Republic of South Africa and flows north then south in a wide curve, emptying into Delagoa Bay. Along the river around 1861 African chiefs settled disputes with the Portuguese and English authorities regarding spheres of influence. Axelson, *Portugal*, pp. 9, 98; WNGD.

Konde (Afr.) Central African chiefdom, under Portuguese control, located northeast of Lake Niassa, now Lake Malawi. Around 1880, it was a fertile and populous area for raising cattle and sheep. Its chief, Kasote, was attacked and killed at that time by Arab slavers from Zanzibar. Axelson, *Portugal*, p. 171.

Kongwa (Afr.) A FRELIMO (q.v.) training camp created in 1965 in Tanzania. Its instructors were recruited from different regions and ethnic groups in Mozambique. The fundamental aim of the movement was to develop a national ideology; the camp's purpose was to train a guerrilla force capable of fighting a successful war for independence. In terms of the people involved, Kongwa was one of the most important FRELIMO training camps. Two men of exceptional political and military ability, Samora Machel, future president of Mozambique, and Joaquim Chissano, the first prime minister of the country after independence in 1975, acted as instructors to the young revolutionaries. Munslow, *Mozambique,* pp. 88, 149. *See also* Bagamoyo.

konzo (Kik.) The third day of the four days of the traditional African week in São Salvador do Congo c.1880. The others, in order, are *nsona, nkandu,* and *nkenge.* Henderson, *Angola,* p. 43; BeAD.

korah (Ar.) Among the Islamic Mandingos of Guinea-Bissau, a stringed instrument made from a large gourd wrapped in an animal skin and attached to a long flat wooden stick with twenty strings, now nylon, and a bass string made of gazelle sinew; a kind of jazz instrument. Guerra, *Terras da Guiné,* p. 18.

Koran (Ar.) "Recitation." The sacred book of Islam, written in Arabic. It is regarded by Moslems as the infallible word of Allah, the perfect transcription of an eternal conversation preserved in Heaven and revealed to the prophet Mohammed over a period of twenty years through the medium of the angel Gabriel. It is also spelled *Quran.* WNWD.

Kosi Bay (Afr.) A bay south of Delagoa Bay that in 1889 was considered a boundary between the Republic of South Africa, Swaziland, and Mozambique. Axelson, *Portugal,* pp. 109, 245.

Kota-Kota (Afr.)   An African settlement along the Shire River, central Mozambique. It was an area occupied by *prazeros* (estate-holders) under Portuguese protection. In 1889 in Kota-Kota H.H. Johnston, an English negotiator, made an illegal treaty with local African chiefs favorable to British claims to the area. Axelson, *Portugal,* pp. 208-9.

kraal (Afrk.)   A word used in South Africa and elsewhere to designate an African settlement, usually surrounded by a stockade. The word may be derived from the Portuguese *curral*, meaning a cattle pen or fold. In southern Mozambique, a *kraal* has hundreds of huts with conical grass-thatched roofs arranged in an arc surrounded by a circular fence of thorny branches. In 1805 Portuguese explorers lived for an extended period in the *kraal* of the king of Kazambe in Central Africa. Chief Gungunhana conducted official business in his *kraal* in 1893. Duffy, *Portuguese Africa,* p. 192; Hammond, *Portugal and Africa,* p. 178; GEPB.

Kropatcheck rifle   A weapon provided by British forces in 1889 to African chiefs in the Makololo territory, Central Africa. This rifle was used against the Portuguese soldiers led by A.A.R. Serpa Pinto. Axelson, *Portugal,* p. 212.

ku-lemba (Kimb.)   "Bride price." In Angola, a Kimbundu expression used by modern writers wishing to stress African traditions. In Mozambique its equivalent is *lobola* (q.v.); in Portuguese, *alabamento*. Burness, *Fire,* p. 59.

Kuruman (Afr.)   In Mozambique, a village and Protestant station north of the Limpopo River, Matabele district, Zambezia, established in 1888 by Robert Moffat, a British missionary. Axelson, *Portugal,* p. 146.

kutado (Afr.)   Name given by the Mandingos in Guinea-Bissau to a tropical annual plant (*Gossypym herbaceum*), the American short staple cotton, apparently introduced by the Portuguese in the sixteenth century. It is described by Andres Alvares de Almada in his *Tratado Breve dos Rios de Guiné*, Lisbon, 1594. Widely used by Africans to make fabrics traded all over the region. In the nineteenth century the introduction of European cloth eclipsed the traditional domestic industry. Carreira, *Mandingas,* p. 134.

Kwaaihoek (Afr.)   A point of land on the Indian Ocean coast north of modern Port Elizabeth, South Africa, where the Portuguese explorer Bartolomeu Dias erected a *pardão* (q.v.) on March 12, 1488, dedicated to Saint Gregory. Axelson, *Portuguese in South-East,* p. 16.

Kwa-Kwa (Afr.)   A river that flows west from the Zambezi River to the port of Quelimane, central Mozambique. In the colonial period it was used by barges and canoes to transport gold, ivory, other goods, and slaves from the Shire and Zambezi rivers to the Quelimane coast. Vail, *Capitalism*, pp. 10, 13, 103.

Kwanjulu (Afr.) An African village and Protestant mission near Belmonte, Bié district, southern Angola. In 1890 the Plymouth Brethren from England opened a station to care for Africans. Axelson, *Portugal*, pp. 250-1.

Kwanyama (Afr.) An African chiefdom, related to the Ambo people. Early in the nineteenth century it was under Chief Aimbiri. In 1915 Portuguese forces invaded the territory and deposed the last king, Mandume. This ethnic group is considered the most developed in Angola. Wheeler, *Angola,* pp. 26-7.

kwanza (Kimb.) Angolan unit of currency that replaced the Angolan *escudo* on January 8, 1977. The *kwanza*, named after the Kwanza River, consists of 100 *lweis*, named after one of the river's tributaries. The *kwanza* was a nonconvertible currency until late 1978 when exchange rates for authorized transactions were established at US $1 to kw 29.622. Kaplan, *Angola,* pp. 275-6. *See also* angolar.

kwashiorkor (Afr.) In Ghana, Guinea-Bissau, and elsewhere in developing countries, a severe disease of young children caused by a chronic deficiency of protein and calories in the diet and characterized by stunted growth, edema, unnaturally light reddish-colored hair, and a protuberant belly. GEPB; WNWD.

{ L }

laban (Ar.) Camel's milk drunk by the West African Idzaul Azuregue and Berber people in Mali, Songhai, and the Tuareg from the eleventh century to modern times. It was drunk fresh and still warm every morning and evening; alternatively, dried meat was cooked with butter in this milk. Today camel's milk is a luxury for the people of the Sahara. Lewicki, *West African Food,* pp. 125-6.

Labor Code for Natives On December 6, 1928, the Portuguese government promulgated a labor code for laborers in the Portuguese African colonies. It contained 428 articles enumerating such items as labor contracts, salaries, nutrition, housing, central and local offices, and the like. There is no information about its degree of enforcement. Cunha, *O Trabalho Indigena,* pp. 137, 140.

labor contract A written legal agreement between a laborer and the Portuguese government, introduced around 1890. By the terms of the contract, a African was entitled to work in the Zambezi *prazos*, on Rhodesian plantations, or in South African gold fields. Wages were shared between the laborer and the government. The recruitment of laborers for São Tomé sugar and coffee plantations and Belgian Congo rubber plantations was considered a new form of slavery. From its inception, abuses of this system attracted world attention. Newitt, *Portuguese Settlement,* pp. 368-9.

labor for South Africa The discovery in 1886 of gold fields in South Africa some 200 miles (320 km) from the Mozambique border escalated the traditional migration of Tonga, Chopi, and Shangana men. Soon the exodus reached 250,000 workers per year of whom 100,000 were believed to be illegal. To regulate and profit from the influx of laborers, starting in 1890 the Portuguese government entered into a series of international agreements with the Republic of Transvaal. The Portuguese-South Africa Convention of 1928 set provisions that lasted until independence in 1975. In return for labor south of the 22nd parallel, the Portuguese were guaranteed 47.5 percent of the seabound rail traffic from Johannesburg, Pretoria, and Kurgesdorp; they also received payment for each worker recruited, custom duties on the goods of returning workers, and deferred wages from the mines given to the government in gold then paid to the laborers in provincial *escudos* once they returned to Mozambique. A steady revenue flowed to the government and a lucrative transit trade enriched the port of Lourenço Marques, but emigration caused depopulation and the denationalization of Africans. Henriksen, *Mozambique,* pp. 120, 121; GEPB.

labor, principle of the maximization of ultra-cheap   An economic principle put forward by English scholars; specifically, the use of labor to exploit the diamond and gold deposits in South Africa shortly after their discovery in 1871 and 1878, respectively. The cycle of operations of the mines expanded or contracted more or less in direct ratio to the number of Africans employed, most of them recruited in Mozambique. From 1896 the Witwatersrand Native Labour Association (q.v.) monopolized labor recruiting. In Mozambique, which had the cheapest labor force in Africa, this recruiting was done with the official collaboration of the Portuguese government. Munslow, *Mozambique,* pp. 18-9.

ladino (Pg.) "Cunning." In colonial Portuguese Africa, an African domestic who was skillful in his chores and able to speak Portuguese. Often he served as an interpreter and middleman in towns with large African populations. HDRGC.

lagoa (Pg) "Lagoon." On the Atlantic coast of Guinea-Bissau and elsewhere, a shallow body of salt water separated from the sea by sand dunes. During the rainy season *lagoas* often are covered with dense tropical vegetation. Mota, *Guiné Portuguesa,* I:73, 368. *See also* lala.

Lagos, Nigeria   The capital of Nigeria; a seaport on the Atlantic coast founded c.1700. It comprises two islands (Lagos and Iddo) settled by the Yoruba. These islands were discovered in 1472 by Portuguese navigators who named the area Lagos either because of its many lagoons or because the sailors were from Lagos, Portugal. In the colonial period it was a notorious slave market. The city and the territory became a British protectorate in 1851 and the British colony of Nigeria in 1861. Lagos was made the capital of Nigeria in 1914. It is the terminus of a railroad to the interior and it exports petroleum, palm oil, and groundnuts. In 1971 it had a population of 1,112,463. Costa, *Descobrimentos Maritimos,* Congresso da Historia, 1938, Lisboa, II:26; CE; FWNE; WNGD.

Lagos, Portugal   An Atlantic seaport in southern Portugal; the largest city in Portugal in 1400. During the Discovery (q.v.), it became a flourishing commercial and maritime center for exploration of the Atlantic islands and the

West African coast. Gil Eanes, the discoverer of Cape Bojador, departed from this town in 1434. Many of his crewmembers were local fishermen, sailors, and merchants. Here the *Companhia de Lagos* established the first slave market and the *Casa de Guiné* (q.v.) was organized. In 1587 Sir Francis Drake sacked Lagos. Marques, *History of Portugal*, p. 143; DHP.

Lagos Companhia (Pg.) One of the oldest colonial Portuguese commercial corporations, organized in 1444 to develop fishing and commerce in West Africa. Among the charter members were Gil Eanes and Estevão Afonso. The company, which was given its charter by Prince Henry, had the obligation of continuing beyond Cape Bojador (q.v.) and was granted a monopoly on gold, spices, and the slave trade. GEPB.

Lagos, Rio dos (Pg.) A river that empties into the Gulf of Guiné; discovered and explored by Portuguese navigators between 1471 and 1475. It was called Rio dos Lagos because of the many lagoons at its mouth. Today is part of the Republic of Nigeria. Mota, *Toponimos,* pp. 287-8.

lala (Afr.) In Guinea-Bissau, a piece of level fertile land covered with crops sowed and cultivated by African farmers, mostly women. Mota, *Guiné Portuguesa,* I:90-91.

lançado (Pg.) "Outcast." A Portuguese outlaw living in the African bush who, although illegally supplying foreign competitors with goods, helped Portugal to maintain its hold in colonial territories. A *lançado* usually married an African woman and adopted her customs, language, and values. At the sufferance of local chieftains, *lançados* managed the water-borne commerce of rivers and coast. Around 1750 they fused indistinguishably into a single Afro-Portuguese *mestiço* trading class. Chilcote, *Portuguese Africa,* pp. 87, 88; HDRGC. *See also* tangamãos.

Lanzarote Island Easternmost island of the Canaries, about 85 mi. (137 km) off the northwest African coast. In 1326 the Genoese navigator and explorer Malocello Lanzarotto, for whom the island is named, visited it. The island was colonized c.1350. Duncan, Atlantic Islands, p. 7.

langua (Afr.) In Mozambique, a coastal lowland of treeless brackish swamps formed on alluvial sedimentation laid down by periodic floods. GDLP.

larim (Afr.) A rare silver coin shaped like a fishhook that circulated in Mombasa, Mozambique, Arabia, and Persia c.1666. Freeman-Granville, *East African Coins,* JAH, Cambridge, 1960, I:39.

Lassyism A religious movement founded in 1953 in the mid-Congo area by Simão Zepherine Lassy. The movement was composed of Congolese Africans who believed in the second coming of Christ and the cure of illness by prayer and the drinking of holy water. Its ritual was strongly influenced by Catholic liturgy although it emphasized the destruction of fetishes, medals, and images of saints. It preached obedience to civil authorities and rejected nationalistic activities, considering them illegal. It soon penetrated into the Cabinda Enclave of Angola and in 1954 they established a religious center in Bavil, a village in the Cacongo municipality. In 1956 Lassy officially requested the Luanda authorities to recognize the movement as a legal church, claiming to have about 8,900 members. Its rapid expansion and the numerous desertions of Africans from Catholic missions in Cabinda forced the Archbishop of Luanda to organize a campaign against the sect. Many of the Lassy chapels were destroyed and in July 1957 the missionaries built a Catholic church and a mission in Bavil itself at a time when there were about 10,400 followers of Lassyism. After 1959, the sect began to decline. It is also known as *N'Zambi Kunguna.* Pelessier, *La Colonie,* pp. 169-71. *See also* Kimbanguism.

league A measure of distance usually equal to about 3.5 mi. (3.63 km). The relation between the league and the Portuguese *grade* varied at the time of the Discovery (q.v.). According to João de Lisboa (1500) there were 16.75 leagues to a *grade.* His contemporary, Duarte Pacheco, reported 18 leagues per *grade.* At the end of the fifteenth century it was accepted that there were 17.5 leagues per *grade.* DMA.

Lebombo, Diocese of (Afr.) An Anglican diocese south of the Sabe River, created in 1893 to minister to the Mozambican Africans who had joined the Church of England during their stay in the Rand gold fields in South Africa. It was incorporated as a small Anglican enclave into northern Mozambique by the partition of 1891. In spite of its remoteness and the hostility of the local Portuguese, it survived and modestly expanded after the independence of Mozambique in 1975. Newitt, *Portugal in Africa,* pp. 125-6.

Leis Extravagantes (Pg.) "Vagrants' Law." A legal code c.1570 that regulated the status and behavior of vagrant slaves who in a changing society were becoming a social problem. These laws recognized shifts in the racial composition of the slave population by distinguishing among African, Christian, and Moorish (Moslem) slaves settled in Portugal around and after 1500. Each category was clearly defined by a code drawn up by Duarte Nunes Leão that included laws promulgated in Portugal up to 1569. Saunders, *A Social History,* p. 114; GEPB.

lemba-lemba (Afr.)   The name for a tropical woody vine, most likely the strangler fig (*Ficus pynaerti*), the seed of which germinates near the top of a tree then sends out aerial roots that descend to the ground. The foliage and roots of the *lemba-lemba* eventually completely envelop the host tree, killing it and leaving the *lemba-lemba* free-standing. It is common in Sao Tome where is also called the *corda*. Carvalho e Vasconcellos, *As Colonias Portuguesas*, p. 227.

lemon   The name for both a small thorny semi-tropical evergreen tree (*Citrus limon*) and its oval fruit with a sour juicy pulp. A native of southern Asia, the lemon and other citrus were introduced to Europe and sub-Sahel Africa by the Arabs and the Portuguese. In 1506, Valentim Fernandes reported seeing a lemon tree on the Senegal River. Fernandes, *Description*, p. 127; Ficalho, *Plantas Uteis,* pp. 1089.

lenga (Afr.)   An individual or a group of young men serving as personal bodyguard to a chief in the Mossamedes region, southern Angola, and else-where in the colony around 1880. Armed with efficient weapons such as repeating rifles, these guards were skilled in protecting their chiefs and forcing their rules upon the people. In the process of these change, the chiefs mercilessly seized people's wealth. At this time ivory and the revenue it produced was scarce, so the *lengas* were used to rustle cattle, hijack other products, raid unfriendly settlements, and impose heavy taxes on other Africans. By 1910, after thirty years of pillage, the *lengas* had enriched themselves by impoverishing their people, who at that time were starving and dying in one of the worst famines ever known in southern Angola. Clarence-Smith, *Slaves, Peasants,* pp. 76-7.

Lestadas (Pg.)   "Easterlies. " In the Cape Verde Islands, a dry, parching, dust-laden wind that blows across the archipelago from Africa during January and February; it obscures visibility with a pall of red dust and is considered a scourge to agriculture. Carvalho e Vasconcelos, *As Colonias Portuguesas,* p. 46. *See also* harmattan.

letrados, clase de (Pg)   "Educated class." In Mozambique and elsewhere c.1950, a newly-emerging social class in indigenous societies. The *letrados* were a small group of young Africans raised and educated in Catholic mission schools, deeply indifferent to ethnic traditions, values, and allegiances, and lacking in respect for their headman and ancestors. Rita-Ferrira, *O Movimento Migratorio*, p. 142.

"Let's discover Angola!"   *See* "Vamos descobrir Angola!"

Letter of the News   A letter comprised of a portfolio of fourteen leaves (pages) written by Diogo de Sequeira, governor of Goa, in 1520 and sent to King Manuel I of Portugal. It reports the visit of ambassador Rodrigo de Lima to Prester John, Christian king of Ethiopia. The letter reached Lisbon in April 1521; officials considered it so important that it was immediately edited and printed in Lisbon with the title *Carta das Novas y Vieram a El Rey Nosso Senhor do Descobrimento do Preste Joha* (The Letter That Came to the King, Our Lord, with News of the Discovery of Prester John). It describes the land of Prester John, a legendary Christian king of great power who for many years had been sought after by the kings, captains, and fleets of Portugal. At the end of the letter is appended the well-known letter of Queen Helena, the regent for Negus (Emperor) Lebna Dengel of Abyssinia, also known to Europeans as David II. Cortesão, *History,* I:268-70; GEPB. *See also* Ethiopia.

levirate   Among polygamous households in Guinea-Bissau, the mandatory marriage of a widow to her deceased husband's brother. It also extends this obligation to a cousin or any other male relative of her deceased husband if there is no suitable brother. Mota, *Guiné Portuguesa*, I:190.

liambra (Afr.)   The term for the narcotic drug hashish, extracted from the hemp plant (*Cannabis sativa* L.). It was brought to Portugal by *retornados* (refugees) returning from Africa in 1976. Beside *liambra*, they also introduced marijuana (cannabis leaves) and hard drugs into a virtually drug-free Lisbon. Harvey, *Portugal*, p. 128.

libata (Afr.)   In Angola and elsewhere, a African compound or group of huts of an extended family, consisting of a maximum of fifty huts. Vansina, *Kingdoms of the Savanna*, p. 334. *See also* quilombo.

Liberia   Portuguese navigator Pedro de Sintra explored what is now the Liberian coast in 1460. He called it *Costa de Malagüeta* because of the abundance of *malagüeta*, a pepper substitute, harvested by Africans. Soon an active commerce in *malagüeta* was established with Lisbon. The earliest inhabitants of the area probably arrived during the early fifteenth century as refugees from the military destruction of the Moslem Kingdom of Songahi on the Niger River. Free and manumitted African Americans began arriving at this coast in 1817, sponsored by the American Colonization Society. Settlers severed their ties with the Society in 1847 and established the only independent black republic in Africa until the independence of Ghana in 1957. Mota, *Toponimos*, pp. 217-18.

liberto (Pg.)   The term for an African slave who had secured his provisional freedom by the government decree signed on December 14, 1854. Under the law, he was to be paid for his labor by his former master who also became his protector. Minors under thirteen years of age became free on reaching the age of twenty. A *liberto*'s legal status was never clearly defined; although freed, he was obliged to work as a servant for additional twenty years. This system was abolished in 1878. Cunha, *O Trabalho Indigena,* pp. 132-3; GEPB.

libongo (Afr.) A local form of currency used for trade in colonial Portuguese Africa; it was made of square pieces of palm bark-cloth and was also known as "straw money." In 1649, ten *libongos* were valued at 500 *reis.* Boxer, *Portuguese Society*, p. 125. *See also* macuta.

Libro del Conoscimiento de Todos los Reinos Y Senorios que Son por el Mundo, El A fictional geographic account written in Seville c.1350 by an anonymous Spanish Franciscan born in 1305. It describes what was known of sub-Saharan Africa up to 1348 and was well known by such explorers as Jean de Bethencourt, who in 1402 tried to colonize the Canary Islands, and certain Portuguese geographers of the Sagres nautical school (q.v.). *El Libro del Conoscimiento*, based on oral accounts of Jews, Moors (Arabs), and other travelers and merchants, gives a fair description of the West African Atlantic coast. Reflecting two versions of the same account, it describes the coast from Ceuta to Cape Bojador, down to Senegal and what appears to be the Gulf of Guiné, Western Sudan, and the Kingdom of Prester John, thought to be in Central Africa but actually in what is now Ethiopia (q.v.). Regarding distances, the author states that the distance between Cape Bojador and the Canary Islands is 110 mi. (177 km); the 1505 *Esmeraldo de Situ Orbis* by Duarte Pacheco Pereira (q.v.) says 120 mi. (193 km), remarkably close to the earlier account. Between the Rio de Oro and Senegal, the friar says 620 mi. (1000 km); the *Esmeraldo* says 820 mi. (1320 km). Modern scholars such as Charles de la Ronciere have identified some place names given in *El Libro del Conoscimiento* as those found in Ethiopia and central Sudan. It was first published in 1877 (T. Fortanet, Madrid), edited and with a critical analysis by Marcos Jimenez de la Espada who also compiled a geographic glossary (pp. 172-267). It was translated into English by Clements Markham and published in London in 1912. Cortesão, J., *A Expansão*, pp. 512, 517, 626-8, 634.

lichamba (Afr.) Cultivated field in the Maconde region, northern Mozambique. RLM.

lichue (Afr.) In Mozambique, a variety of grass (*Imperata cylindrica*) used by Africans to roof huts. PDM.

licongue (Afr.) In Angola and elsewhere, a woody vine (*Landolphia owariensis*) that produces a type of latex, the basis of various commercial products, notably rubber. It is found on the West African coast from Sierra Leone to Angola. *Licongue* is abundant in Golungo Alto, where Africans have extracted this latex for the Luanda market since 1880. It is also cultivated for export in Zambezia, Cabo Delgado, northern Mozambique, and Zanzibar. This latex has various names, including *mbungu* in Mozambique, *matire* or *mtiri* in Zanzibar, and *mtolia* or *matatu-bonsu* elsewhere in East Africa. Ficalho, *Plantas Uteis,* pp. 212-18.

liconte (Afr.)   In Angola, the fiber from bark taken from the *imbondeiro* or *baobab* (q.v.) (*Adansonia digitata* L.) used to make sacks to collect cotton, coffee beans, and charcoal, and for other domestic uses. Ficalho, *Plantas Uteis*, p. 22.

lidembe (Afr.)   Among the Macombe in northern Mozambique, an abandoned village or settlement. RLM.

life span   A legal term in Mozambique c. 1600 meaning a generation or about 30 years of life; used to set the length of the lease of a *prazo* in Zambezia. Often such a land grant lasted for the legal equivalent of three lives or generations before returning to the grantee or to the king of Portugal. Newitt, *Portuguese Settlement*, p. 385.

Liga Africana (Pg.)   "African League." An organization founded in Lisbon c. 1920 through a coalition of *assimilados* (q.v.) from Portuguese African colonies. For its time, its goals, including the repeal of all discriminatory legislation, were radical. Like other nationalist organizations it ran into trouble with the Portuguese government which closed its offices and shut its presses. In 1931, the *Liga Africana* was allowed to merge with other nationalist groups in the *Movimiento Nacionalista Africano*, a government sponsored movement. Herrick, *Area Handbook*, p. 46; HDA.

Liga Angolana (Pg.)   "Angolan League." A recreational and cultural social club founded in Luanda, Angola, in 1912. It was not a political group, although it achieved some influence among Luanda's *mestiços* since some of the league's members were politically active. In the growing hostility of Europeans toward it, and in the attempts made to link it with rural rebellion in the Congo region in 1914 and 1917, its importance and authority became evident. In 1921, it was suppressed. In 1938, the *Liga Angolana* was replaced by the *Liga Nacional Africana* (q.v.). Newitt, *Portugal in Africa,* pp. 144-S.

Liga Filoafricana (Pg.)   "Friends of Africa League." A Protestant association established in Luanda in 1896 by the Swiss linguist and missionary-entrepreneur Heli Chatelain. It was an independent organization aimed at spreading the Gospel, the promotion of the catechism, education, and protection of the faithful. HDA.

Liga Nacional Africana (Pg.) "National African League." A movement founded in Luanda around 1929 as the heir to the previously purged *Liga Angolana* (q.v.). It was led by Luanda-born, middle class, Catholic *assimilados*. If its activities and goals were limited by government interference, from 1930 to the 1950s it kept alive the tradition of nationalist protest. By the middle of the 1950s, young militant nationalists had broken away to found their own clandestine groups, one of which was the MPLA. Wheeler, *Angola*, p. 117.

Limpopo (Afr.) A river in southeast Africa about 1,100 mi. (1,770 km) long. It rises near Johannesburg in the Transvaal, flows north and northeast to form the border of Transvaal, turns southeast and south across Mozambique, then empties into the Indian Ocean near the port of Xai-Xai. Its entire course and its headwaters are sometimes called the Crocodile River. In Portuguese territory, it was known as the Bembe, and at its mouth on the Indian Ocean it was known as the Inhampura. It was explored by the British in 1885 and by Xavier Caldas in 1889. GEPB; WNGD.

lineage A line of kinship descent, the members of which can, in principle, trace their descent unilineally through either male or female forebears from a common ancestor. Lineages in the communities of Angola and southern Mozambique are generally matrilineal. In any system of lineage, those of greater genealogical depth may include lineages of lesser depth, the lineages at each level having different social, political, and economic implications and ramifications. Kaplan, *Angola*, p. 276.

Lisboa (Pg.) Lisbon, a city and port; capital of Portugal. It is an ancient Moorish settlement conquered by the Portuguese in 1147, becoming the capital of Portugal when King Afonso III established the center of the kingdom's administration in Lisbon c.1275 and began buying property and building palaces, houses, storehouses, and monasteries. With the opening of the Atlantic or western sea route by the Crusaders, who previously only sailed the Mediterranean, Lisbon's trade within Western Europe greatly expanded. In 1353, Lisbon's merchants opened a trade center in Bruges to export wine, oil, figs, cork, *esparto* (broom) grass, and other products. During the Age of Discovery (q.v.) and expansion (1400-1550), Lisbon was the center of Portuguese trade, explorations, and politics. Prince Henry established a royal monopoly in Lisbon c.1415, controlled by the *Casa de Ceuta* that levied special duties on all goods brought from Africa. After 1444 Lisbon was the port of entry for most of the goods and slaves from Africa, and in 1512 officially became the sole port of landing. At one point, Lisbon had the largest slave market in the world. In 1486 the *Casa de Mina e Guiné* was organized in the city. After the voyage of Vasco da Gama to India in 1498, the *Casa de India* was specially created to supervise Asiatic trade. The economic control was under an *almoxarife* (q.v.), an official entrusted with the collection of rent and taxes for the Crown. Around 1500, German and Genoese merchants and financiers opened branches in Lisbon to buy and sell spices, slaves, and African products. Its prosperity began to decline at the end of the sixteenth century. On August 4, 1755, an earthquake destroyed most of the city and took more than 50,000 lives. Saunders, *A Social History,* pp. 8-10; DHP; GEPB.

Lisbon Military Coup of 1974   A political uprising that took place on April 24, 1974, led by General Antonio de Spinola, head of a *junta* formed by military officers. President Admiral Americo Tomaz and Prime Minister Marcello Caetano were arrested and confined to a fortress in Funchal, Madeira. In a proclamation, Spinola announced the immediate release of all political prisoners, the end of all press censorship, and the total disbanding of the Portuguese international secret police known as PIDE (q.v.). In addition, the new government established that the political status of African territories and other overseas provinces should now be decided by a consensus of their inhabitants. There was little resistance from loyalist forces. Only five people are known to have been killed and some fifty to seventy injured, most in an incident outside PIDE headquarters. It was a remarkably bloodless coup that toppled in less than thirty hours the monolithic regime hitherto considered impregnable. Bruce, *Portugal,* pp. 9, 23, 113-4.

literacy in Angola   The post-independence literacy rate in Angola was estimated in 1977 at 15 percent, later rising to 20 percent. In 1977 there were 1 million children in primary schools and about 100,000 in secondary schools, but quality education suffered from a shortage of resources. The government has promoted an education policy based on free and universal learning and nationalization of all schools, including mission schools. The policy is linked to results and ideologically to the power of the people. Kaplan, *Angola,* p. xii; HDA.

literacy in Cape Verde   In 1973, just before independence, the literacy rate was estimated at between 25 and 28 percent; about 90 percent of these were literate only at the primary level. HDRGC.

literacy of Africans in Portugal   In Portugal c.1500, African slaves were allowed to learn to read and write, although in fact only a few Africans, free or slave, were able to write their own names. Inquisition records show that there were many slaves who signed with a mark on their depositions. At the same time it was reported that João Pinto, a Wolof, signed his name with a colorful signature. He also claimed to be able to read a Book of Hours in his possession, most likely as a result of the Portuguese belief that African slaves were human beings who should be converted to Christianity and educated. Around 1515, the first group of Congolese youth were brought to Lisbon and registered at Coimbra University and other schools. Saunders, *A Social History,* pp. 39, 91, 101; DHP.

literature, depiction of Africans in early Portuguese   Early in the Discovery (q.v.), Europeans reported that the skin color and facial features of African slaves were unattractive. When the playwright Gil Vicente (1470-1536) wished to describe ugly peasant women he endowed them with dark skin, broad noses, and kinky hair. Recording the first landing of African captives in Lagos in 1444, Gomes Eanes de Zurara (1444) notes that "They were so deformed in their faces and bodies, that they almost seemed images from the lowest hemisphere." European physiognomy remained the standard of beauty in the sixteenth century, but some whites began to make distinctions, favoring some African racial groups over others. Saunders, *A Social History,* pp. 99-100, 106-7; GEPB.

Livro das Rotas (Pg.) "Book of the Sea Routes." A log written around 1514 by João de Lisboa, a seaman at the time of King Manuel I. It also includes a compilation of several books that describe the West African coast up to Cape Guardafui and mention Príncipe Island in the Gulf of Guiné. Costa, *A Marinha,* pp. 2967.

Livros de Marinharia (Pg.)   "Books of Navigation. " This navigational material was compiled between 1530 and 1580 by Portuguese historians and scientists. At the time of the Discovery (q.v.) c.1400, the art of navigation entered an era of innovation, change, and adaptation. Until then, sea captains had used guides, astrolabes, *tavoletas, portolanis* (qq.v.), navigation compasses, and other aids and guide books. The *Livros de Marinharia* have two sections: one on astronomy and the rules to determine latitude, the position of the Pole Star, Southern Cross, and so on; the other comprises *roteiros* (q.v.) and logs, especially those describing the route from Lisbon to India. Among the compilers were João de Lisboa, Andre Pires, Bernardo Soares, and Manuel Alvares. DHP.

lo (Kik.)   In São Salvador do Congo around 1890, the time that an African sleeping on his hard mat would spend before turning over onto his other side; it was supposed to indicate sleeping for an unbroken period of time. BeAD.

Loango (Afr.)   Atlantic coast port and city in Equatorial Africa (now Congo) about 100 mi. (160 km) north of the mouth of the Congo River. In the 1770s this was an important center for the slave trade. A Portuguese expedition reported that on the Loango coast it found seventeen ships comprised of nine French, four English, and four Dutch, and heard that six others had recently sailed. The report estimated the volume of trade to be about 20,000 slaves a year. Birmingham, *Trade and Conflict*, p. 157; WNGD.

Loango Kingdom   A Bantu kingdom encountered by early Portuguese explorers north of the Congo River, probably founded earlier than the Congo Kingdom. In a 1610 account by Andrew Battell, the king of Loango was described as an absolute ruler like the king of Congo. He had a large compound in which he gathered his noblemen around him. In an inner court he kept his wives and ate alone in a small hut. One of the king's major functions was that of rain-maker. The kingdom had four provinces ruled by the sons of the king's sister. The Queen Mother had a special political status, an ethnic trait found in other Bantu kingdoms further east. Wheeler, *Angola,* pp. 8-11.

Lobito (Pg.)   Seaport on Lobito Bay, west-central Angola founded a league north of Catumbela (q.v.), in 1843 by the Angolan governor, Manuel Bernardo Vidal. The early Portuguese navigators Cristofero Soligo and Henrique Martelo made reports in 1486 and 1496, respectively, about the bay where Lobito was later built. It is a center of road and rail transport, and also has an airport. Industries include shipbuilding, metalworking, and food processing; agricultural products include grain, fruit, sisal, coconuts, and groundnuts. The city had a population in 1970 of about 60,000. GEPB; WNGD.

lobola (Zulu)   The term for the wealth passed from the family of a man to that of a woman to validate a marriage. It is the Zulu term for what is properly termed "bride-wealth" or, mistakenly in the earlier literature, "bride-price." This latter phrase is a misnomer because the goods that change hands, cattle in the case of the Rongas of Southern Mozambique, Zulus, and other East African people, do not represent a purchase price; rather, they indicate the ability of the bridegroom to head a family, of his position in his family's own relationship group, and is a pledge that he will not mistreat his future wife. The passage of *lobola* wealth is a sign of the highest social sanction to a given marriage. Among the Zulus and other East African peoples, the position of a man in society is largely determined by the source of the cattle given for his wife. In modern times in more cosmopolitan areas this practice of the groom compensating his father-in-law for marrying the latter's daughter has seen hard cash become the usual tender. As a result certain additional hardships have been forced on the male who often must go to the gold mines of South Africa to earn the necessary money. Also spelled *lobolo*. In Angola the comparable Kimbundu word is *ku-lemba* (q.v.). Hamilton, *Voices,* pp. 122-3, 225; FWNSD.

locais (Pg.) "Locals." In South Africa, a name given in 1906 by the Witwatersrand Native Labour Association to Mozambican mine workers illegally employed beyond the period of their contract. They were also called "volunteers." Rita-Ferreira, *O Movimento Migratoria,* pp. 122-3.

locust invasions Swarms of migratory locusts typically precede and accompany droughts in various parts of Angola and elsewhere in Africa. They eat virtually all vegetation in their path, often resulting in famine further exacerbated by the ensuing drought. In Angola, this has happened at least once every decade. Such plagues were reported nine times in Congo between 1642 and 1664. Luanda was threatened around 1835 and again in 1841 by clouds of locusts coming from the northeast, darkening the sky over the town for several hours as they headed southward in search of more abundant vegetation. The inhabitants used to fear such visitors as precursors of drought. Dias, *Famine and Disease,* JAH, Cambridge, 1981, 22(3):368-9.

Loios Conegos (Pg.) "Blue Canons." Arriving in 1490, they were the first Portuguese religious order at São Salvador do Congo and the first missionaries to preach the Gospel in a sub-Saharan chiefdom. A *Loio* missionary is said to have baptized King Nzinga-a-Cuum of Congo, giving him the name João I. Apparently Prince Henry, son of King Afonso I of Congo and future bishop of Ostia, was taken to be educated at their Santo Eloi monastery in the Alfana neighborhood in Lisbon around 1520. *Loios Conegos* were also known as *Conegos de São João Evangelista* or *Conegos Azueis,* the latter derived from the color of their habits. In the same monastery, Angolan youngsters were housed to study Portuguese and attend primary and secondary school. From the beginning of African colonization, the Portuguese were concerned with bringing Africans to Portugal to be educated and "civilized." Brasio, *Historia,* p. 176; Gabriel, *Angola,* pp. 95-6.

London Convention England and Portugal signed a treaty in London on January 22, 1817, authorizing warships of both nations to inspect merchant vessels suspected of transporting slaves, and creating a court of justice to punish illicit traffic. Cunha, *O Trabalho Indigena,* p. 23.

Loulé (Pg.) An important commercial and fishing seaport in the Algarve, southern Portugal, 10 mi. (16 km) northwest of Faro (q.v.). Merchandise from Loulé included leather, porcelain, *esparto* (broom) grass, and palm products. It was a medieval town, originally Moslem, that at the beginning of the Discovery (q.v.) served as a port of embarkation for the exploration of the West African coast and the Atlantic Islands. In 1415, Loué was rich and populous, providing a substantial number of sailors and merchants who filled the caravels of such navigators as Gil Eanes, João de Santarem, and Diogo de

Azambuya. Iria, *O Algarve no Descobrimento,* Congresso Commemorativo, Lisboa, 1938, I:194.

Lourenço Marques Originally a Mozambican fort and warehouse established by order of King João III in 1554; it was named for Lourenço Marques, the explorer and trader who settled in Maputo Bay in 1546. Soon the town became a port of call for merchants trading with Sofala and Goa. Around 1668, the slave trade and ivory exports attracted the attention of the British and Dutch. Guilherme Bolts, a Dutch merchant, founded a trading post in the area in 1777. In 1781 Joaquim de Araujo, manager of the warehouse, built a fort called Espirito Santo on the left bank of the bay in the same place where Maputo, the capital of Mozambique, is located today. French pirates attacked the fort in 1796, and in 1833 the Vatuas pillaged and burned the settlement. After a protracted struggle with England over the sovereignty of the Maputo region, on July 23, 1875, President Marie Edme Patrice MacMahon of France ruled that the territory under dispute was a Portuguese possession. Since then Lourenço Marques has prospered and expanded. After independence in 1975, Lourenço Marques was renamed Maputo. DHP: GEPB.

Lourenço Marques, medical services in This colonial capital of Mozambique was founded as a trade center by King João III in 1554. As in Angola, it had a medical facility for government officials, merchants, and colonists. Its first modern hospital (today the Miguel Bombarda Central Hospital) was established in 1877. Early in the 1900s, the Portuguese government expanded the hospital's facilities at the time when infirmaries were opened in Tete, Inhambane, and other towns. In 1917, a modern military and civilian hospital was built in the city. A significant advance in health care occurred in the 1940s when departments for mental illness and leprosy were established and a center for research in tropical medicine was inaugurated. In 1964 the University of Lourenço Marques was founded, including a medical school to train doctors, nurses, and medics. After independence in 1975, the Republic of Mozambique began a complete reorganization of the public health services in the city. At the same time the city was renamed Maputo and the university renamed Mondlane. DHP; GEPB; HDM. *See also* Luanda, medical services in.

Lourenço Marques railway A railway linking Lourenço Marques with the Transvaal, built between 1880 and 1894. At that time the Boers still controlled the Transvaal region, and they preferred the line pass through Portuguese territory rather than through the British-controlled port of Cape Town. The railway served to transport labor quickly to the Transvaal mines and to export coal through the port of Lourenço Marques. In 1929 the South African government forced the Portuguese to nationalize the port and the railway to improve efficiency. Attempts to take over the port by South Africa were met with a sustained resistance by the Portuguese government. Munslow, *Mozambique*, p. 27.

Lourenço Marques, relations with Transvaal Since the discovery of gold in the Transvaal in 1886, Africans in Portuguese districts in Mozambique have sought work in the mines. Lourenço Marques has been the main border crossing to and from South Africa. Mozambican workers have worked legally (and illegally) for months and even years in the Witwatersrand region. Transvaals' shippers showed a persistent preference for Lourenço Marques over the British ports for their exports. At the turn of the twentieth century, the WNLA (q.v.) had control of the laborers working in the South African mines. Hammond, *Portugal and Africa*, p. 326; Rita-Ferreira, *O Movimento Migratorio*, p. 74.

Lourenço Marques University *See* Mondlane University.

Losna de Humpata (Afr.) A tropical herb (*Artemisa afra*) related to absinthe and wormwood with an aromatic scent and a bitter taste, used in folk medicine in Angola. It is found in Luanda, Mossâmedes, and elsewhere. Ficalho, *Plantas Uteis*, p. 207.

Lower Zambezi People For thousands of years the Zambezi Valley attracted a rich cultural diversity of African and non-African immigrants, traders, and conquerors. Although they have intermarried for many generations, the lower Zambezi peoples speak distinct dialects and maintain their separate identities. Today the region of Mozambique below the Zambezi is inhabited by a variety of highly acculturated people. In 1970, its population was 900,000. Henriksen, *Mozambique,* pp. 247, 249.

loxodromic sailing The art or practice of sailing on rhomb, or oblique, lines against the wind. In the sixteenth century Portuguese sailors called this navigation practice a *linha do rumo*. It was well described in 1534 by Pedro Nunes, a Portuguese mathematician. Costa, *A Marinha*, pp. 224-7; GEPB.

Luabo Company (Afr.) One of the first commercial corporations in Zambezia, established in 1895 on the Luabo *prazo* (q.v.). The company received a thirty-year monopoly to extract rubber, to experiment with planting cotton and sugar cane, and to supply laborers to nearby plantations. In 1910, J.P. Hornung took control of the company. Vail, *Capitalism,* pp. 116-17, 120

Luabo prazo (Afr.) In Mozambique, a *prazo* straddling the Luabo River, a branch of the Zambezi where it passes through the delta. Luabo was settled around 1630 and soon flourished as an agricultural center and port, becoming more important than the nearby Quelimane. This fertile valley produced all sorts of provisions, including millet, rice, and maize, not easily produced elsewhere in the region. The first tenant was Belchior Dias de Sá Camello who leased it in 1676. His wife, Maria da Guerra, succeeded him in 1680. Manuel Gonçalves Guião inherited the *prazo* in 1714, and his widow, Dona Urdula Ferreira inherited it from him in 1716. Luabo passed through several more holders and in 1824 was granted to Caetano Camillo Vas dos Anjos. *Capitalism,* pp. 10-1, 30, 306; GEPB.

Luabo River (Afr.) A river at the southernmost branch of the Zambezi after the main stream splits to find its way to the sea through the delta. The Luabo mouth of the Zambezi had been recognized early as the best point to enter the river, since it was deep enough at all seasons of the year. Swahili merchants were very active in the area even before the Portuguese arrived in 1498. Newitt, *Portuguese Settlement*, pp. 20, 30, 154-6.

Luanda Carnival (Afr.) An annual festival of dancing and parading in colorful costumes that originated in the seventeenth century to celebrate religious and saints' days. Today it is a national institution typified by a special creole mixture of cultural traditions dominated by African singing, dancing, and masquerading with the joyful participation of the whole population. As early as the 1870s, dancers and musicians from the African quarters of the city would prepare new songs and dances satirizing life in Luanda. This African mimicry of European dress and manners was always an important part of the celebrations. During the years between 1880 and 1910 the Luanda carnival became the counterpart of the more famous carnival in Rio de Janeiro, Brazil. In 1967 and 1968 creole carnivals still retaining something of the old cosmopolitan feeling of coastal West Africa were celebrated. Birmingham, *Carnival at Luanda,* JAH, Cambridge, 1988, 29:93-103.

Luanda City (Afr.) City founded by Paulo Dias de Novais in 1575, and capital of Angola since 1627. A Dutch fleet captured Luanda and briefly controlled the city until 1648 when a Portuguese fleet led by Salvador de Sá e Correia, a Brazilian hero, arrived from Brazil and retook the city and reorganized the colony. Luanda then became the most important colonial slave port until 1836 when Portugal abolished its slave trade. By 1950 Luanda, the main seaport of Angola, had became a city dominated by the Portuguese, and many services and trades once controlled by Africans were now filled by Portuguese administrators and politicians. In 1952, 35 percent of the Europeans were native-born Angolans while 65 percent had been born outside Angola. While Luanda had the largest *mestiço* population (over 6 percent) of any city in Africa, nevertheless it looked more like Rio de Janeiro than any other Portuguese-African metropolis. A new European immigration, directed to the interior, modernized agriculture and developed commerce while greatly expanding the missions and schools. This new population stayed in close contact with the urban centers, especially Luanda, and made the capital more than ever like a European city. By 1961 Portuguese Angolans were claiming, with some justification, that Luanda was now in size and loyalty the "third city" of Portugal, surpassing all others except Lisbon and Oporto. In 1970 Luanda had a population of 475,328. After independence, Luanda, as capital of a new nation, continued to grow in population, commerce, and industry. The city's early name was *Loanda*. Kaplan, *Angola,* pp. 66-7; Wheeler, *Angola,* pp. 143-4; GEPB; HDA.

Luanda Commercial Association A powerful lobby established in Luanda in 1863-4 by a group of European merchants with interests in the traditional Angolan economy based on revenues from the slave trade and slave labor. Duffy, *Portuguese Africa*, p. 92. *See also* Commission for the Promotion of Angola's Commerce.

Luanda Medical School Since the Discovery (q.v.), the king of Portugal traditionally concerned himself with the study of medicine. Around 1550 the government established the *Aula de Medicina e Cirugia* (School of Medicine and Surgery) in Goa to educate physicians and care for local patients in an adjacent hospital. The famous physician and scientist, Castelo de Vite Garcia de Horta (c.1490-1558), was associated with the school. He also was one of the first botanists to collect plants to study the effect of plant-derived drugs. The Marquis of Pombal reformed the medical studies in Portugal in 1750. Around 1830 the study and practice of medicine further expanded in Coimbra, Lisbon, Oporto, and the colonies. As a result, on September 14, 1844, the government opened the Luanda Medical School to train Portuguese and Africans physicians and medical auxiliaries to serve in rural clinics throughout the colony. In 1963 the medical school became a department of the new University of Angola. *Revista Medica de Angola,* 1923, Luanda, 2:196; DHP; GEPB.

Luanda, medical services in In 1605 a hospital directed by Alexio Abreu was established in Luanda. Abreu was a Portuguese physician who came to Luanda in 1595 to supervise the construction of the hospital and organize the medical services for the city. He treated many Portuguese and African patients and soon discovered the devastating effects of tropical fevers and scurvy (q.v.). While there, he wrote *Tratado de Las Siete Enfermedades* (Treatise of the Seven Illnesses), and a treatise on the *Mal de Luanda*, the name given at the time to scurvy. He returned to Portugal in 1510 and published both studies in Lisbon in 1526. In 1750 the Marquis of Pombal reformed several hospitals in Portugal and her colonies, including the hospital at Luanda. In 1864 the Military and the Misericordia hospitals merged and were named the Central Hospital. This hospital was expanded in 1883 and renamed Maria Pia Hospital. When the University of Angola was reorganized in 1963, the hospital was named University Hospital. *Revista Medica de Angola,* 1923, 2:196; DHP; GEPB.

Luanda Museum   This museum was founded by ministerial decree in 1938 in the historic fortress of St. Michael, the construction of which was started by Paulo Dias de Novais in 1575. The museum contains a comprehensive collection of more than 10,000 items, many of considerable value and historical interest. Among its principal sections are history, archeology, ethnography, natural history, fine arts, and sacred art. There are displays of geologic, numismatic, ichnographic, and other collections. The museum includes the library and archives of Angola. In the history and archeology section are found ancient arms, engraved sepulchral monuments, stones with heraldic emblems and inscriptions, early Portuguese relics, and diverse archeological objects. The natural history section contains sixty-one dioramas and displays many zoological specimens such as the rare giant sable antelope (*Hippotragus grandiformis*) and the gemsbok (*Oryx gazelle*). The museum has an impressive list of publications, most in the series *Arquivos de Angola.* In 1963 the museum was incorporated into the Angola Institute for Scientific Research, directed by Virgilio Cannas Martin. GEPB; SESA.

Luangwa (Afr.)   A river that rises east of Lake Malawi, flows south, and empties into the Zambezi at Zumbotown. In 1891, at the time of the partition of Zambezia between England and Portugal, many *prazos* on both the east and west banks of the Luangwa River came under British rule. Vail, *Capitalism,* pp. 219, 308.

Luanze fair (Afr.)   The site of the fair was an African settlement and fort in the Barué Kingdom south of Tete in western Mozambique. The fair was established by Estevão de Ataide in 1689 to control the commercial traffic in the area. He built a storehouse, an arsenal, and huts inside an earthen enclosure fortified with ditches and bastions. The settlement, an important market for trade in gold, ivory, and slaves, was situated in a rich gold mining region. The Luanze fair was held until the 1850s. Newitt, *Portuguese Settlement,* pp. 43-4, 321.

Lubango (Afr.)   A municipality in the Huila district, southwestern Angola, a rich agricultural and cattle region. Lubango comprises two administrative posts, Umpata (q.v.) and Hoque. It had a large Ovimbundu population under the care of several missions including São José da Mucha, established in 1881, the Mission of the Sacred Heart of Mary in Munhino, founded in 1896, and the São Bento mission, organized in 1892. The capital of the municipality is Lubango City (q.v.). GEPB.

Lubango City (Afr.) Formerly Sá da Bandeira, it is in southwest Angola about 95 mi. (153 km) east-northeast of Mossamedes at 5,820 ft. (1,774 m) above sea level. In 1960 the population of the metropolitan area was 15,129. Lubango is a modern city with government buildings, schools, hospitals, churches, and army barracks. GEPB; WNGD. *See also* Lubango.

Lubango, European migration to This major European agricultural area began to develop in 1885 when immigrants from Madeira attempted to settle. They faced violent opposition from the Africans, but they persisted and their farming formed the basis of the area's modern agricultural development. Other settlers came from Portugal in 1950 and 1960. In the 1960s a period of modernization began with road building and cheap electricity from the new Matala Dam on the Cunene River. This growth was stimulated by government aid and foreign investment. By 1969, 42 percent of Angola's maize exports came from the Lubango region and elsewhere in southern Angola. The railway, built in 1923 and later modernized, has aided economic growth. Clarence-Smith, *Slaves, Peasants,* pp. 86, 89, 98-100.

lucasse (Afr.) In Mozambique, a tribal ordeal in which a sorcerer forced a defendant to drink a potentially poisonous drink in order to prove his innocence. It is believed that under divine protection, the innocent survive, the guilty die. Ficalho, *Plantas Uteis,* p. 166. *See also* esere, muave.

Luderitz Bay (Germ.) A small German settlement on the Atlantic coast south of Angola, established by Chancellor Otto von Bismarck in 1883. The following year the chancellor declared the whole area south of 26 degrees latitude up to the Angolan border to be German territory. This declaration specifically excluded Walvis Bay (q.v.). Axelson, *Portugal,* pp. 70, 73.

Luderitz Town An Atlantic seaport with a well-sheltered harbor 520 mi. (837 km) northwest of Cape Town. Portuguese navigator Bartolomeu Dias explored the area in 1488 and named it *Angra dos Iheus*, a name that was subsequently changed to *Angra Pequena*. Today it is the western terminus of the railway. The modern town was founded in 1883 by Germans who changed its name to Luderitz. In 1970 it had a population of 6,642 and was the site of a well known health resort. Valhoff, *Miscelanea,* pp. 271, 272; CE.

Luena (Afr.)   Town in east-central Angola, formerly called Luso. In 1960 it had a population of 40,000. DHP; WNGD.

lukusu (Kik.)   A skin condition that causes white spots on the hands, face, and other part of the human body; prevalent in São Salvador do Congo around 1880. BeAD.

lumbu (Afr.)   In São Salvador do Congo c.1880, the compound and residence of a chief surrounded by a stockade. BeAD.

lunda (Afr.)   A small African farm in Benguela, southern Angola. GEPB.

Lunda   A jurisdiction created in 1895 as part of the Malange province in east-central Angola with Capenda-Camulemba as county seat, later transferred to Vila Henrique Carvalho, today Saurimo. It comprises the counties of Camaxilo, Cassai-Sul, Chitato, and Minungo. In 1945, it had a population of 261,804 of which 452 were whites. It is an agricultural center and rich in diamonds and rubber. GEPB. *See also* Lunda Kingdom.

Lunda Kingdom (Afr.)   A kingdom settled around 1600 in east-central Angola bordering the Ovimbundu people to the west. At the capital town, Musumba, the king and his nobility comprised the centralized government. The relations between the ruler and the people were based on kinship. The king nominated court officials, created new titles, could strip officials of their ranks, presided over the state council, and was believed to have sacred attributes. The Portuguese noted in 1624 that the Cassange fairs in Lunda were a center of active bartering and commerce; it was beyond Portuguese control until 1895. By 1650 a trade route to Luanda and the Atlantic coast was opened. It is along this route that the first cloth, guns, and, more importantly, the cultivation of manioc and possibly maize spread to Lunda. It is also along this route that slaves were moved to the Atlantic coast for transport to the New World plantations. In 1895 the government established administrative towns and villages under the control of the army and further commerce was developed. Vansina, *Kingdoms of the Savanna,* pp. 70, 78-85; GEPB.

lundum (Afr.)   An African dance which originated either in São Jorge da Mina or Angola. It was brought by slaves to Bahia around 1600, and soon became very popular among Afro-Brazilians. It was introduced into Lisbon and the rest of Portugal between 1712 and 1721. The Brazilian mulatto poet Caldas Barbosa, while visiting Lisbon in 1750, praised the beauty of the *lundum,* thereby opening the way for this dance to enter the aristocratic salons of the time. The *lundum* is still danced in São Tomé and in Cape Verde, where it is called the *landum.* Tenreiro, *A Ihla,* p. 187; GEPB.

lunga-lassoge (Afr.) A wild tropical tree (*Combretum glutinosum*) the bark and roots of which yield a resin used by Africans as a yellow textile dye. Ficalho, *Plantas Uteis*, p. 180.

Lurio (Afr.) A municipality in the coastal Cabo Delgado district, northern Mozambique; its large territory is occupied by Macuas and other ethnic groups. Historically its population has been predominantly African. Its more important towns are Ocua and Xiure, the latter having a few European settlers prior to independence. The Lurio municipality is a forested area with valuable timber and abundant game. The major African population is concentrated in the Megaruma River Valley about 25 mi. (40 km) inland from the Indian Ocean. GEPB.

Lusaka Accord (Afr.) An official agreement signed between FRELIMO (q.v.) and the Portuguese government in Lusaka, Zambia, on September 7, 1974, to end the War for Independence and to transfer power to the revolutionary forces. As a result, there was a three-day revolt organized by Europeans in Lourenço Marques followed by the surrender of marines at Chire in Zambezia province, Namil in Cabo Delgado, and other garrisons. The Lusaka Accord was a direct result of the military coup that took place in Lisbon on April 25, 1974. Munslow, *Mozambique,* pp. 112, 126-7.

Lusitanian civilization A state of material and social well being, deeply rooted in Portuguese and Christian principles and values that was believed to infuse Europeans and Africans with national fervor and pride, a sense of cultural unity, and a commonality of interests and aspirations. Moral and spiritual unity were strengthened by trust in hierarchic authority and confidence in the leadership of the Portuguese nation. Chilcote, *Portuguese Africa*, pp. 46, 47.

Lusitanian Integralism A monarchist movement founded in 1914 and supported by the Coimbra periodical *Naçáo Portuguesa* (Portuguese Nation). It demanded the return of the monarchy and the king as head of state and repudiated the republican government, founded in 1910. This movement ended in 1935 with the death of its leader, Antonio Sardinha. DHP.

Lusotropicology A theory and discipline postulated in the 1920s by Gilberto Freyre, a Brazilian sociologist. He argued that with the Portuguese expansion in the fifteenth century, a new type of civilization evolved in Africa and elsewhere and since that time, the Portuguese have been transforming the tropics, not by introducing European values but by themselves changing into *Lusotropicals* in body and soul through miscegenation and by socially Christianizing the Africans. Lusotropicology has come to be the academic expression of these values, attitudes, and myths. Chilcote, *Portuguese Africa,* pp. 47, 48; Hamilton, *Voices,* pp. 10-11.

lussango (Afr.) A wooden child's toy made of two small gourds containing seeds. It is found in Angola and elsewhere in Portuguese Africa. GEPB.

lwei (Kim.) Angolan subunit of currency; there are 100 *lweis* to one *kwanza,* the major unit. The *lwei* is named after one of the tributaries of the Kwanza (Cuanza) River. It was first used in 1977. Kaplan, *Angola,* pp. 275-5.

lyceum The term for secondary school for which, after graduating from the primary level and passing an entrance examination, a African registers at the age of thirteen. In 1959 there were five lyceums in Angola, two in Luanda, and one each at Sá da Bandeira, Benguela, and Nova Lisboa. There were two in Mozambique, one each at Lourenço Marques and Beira, and one in Mindelo, Cape Verde. Duffy, *Portuguese Africa,* pp. 313-4; DHP.

{ M }

"M" The letter "M" for Mozambique was used in the colony in the period around 1760 for branding slaves by order of the captain-general of the colony, Pedro de Saldanha de Albuquerque. The king of Portugal exacted a tax for each slave bought in the territory. Once bought, slave traders took these slaves to the markets in the New World, particularly Bahia, Rio de Janeiro, and elsewhere in Brazil. This heavy slave traffic brought the slavers enormous profit. GEPB; PDM.

mabala (Afr.) A tropical leguminous plant (*Psophocarpus palustris* Desv.; syn. *P. longepedunculatus* Hassk) cultivated for its edible pods, seeds, and roots in Ambriz, Libongo, and Luanda, Angola. In Mozambique it is grown in the Zambezia region. Ficalho, *Plantas Uteis,* p. 140.

mabandazi (Afr.) A group of domestic slaves in charge of working around the *prazero's* house in Zambezia, Mozambique, c.1850. These slaves constituted only a small percentage of the total slave population owned by a *prazero*; their absolute number rarely exceeded fifty and most often was between fifteen and thirty. On Cheringoma *prazo*, twenty of the 946 slaves were *mabandazi;* on one Dominican *prazo* in Quelimane, of 154 slaves, again twenty were *mabandazi.* Isaacman, *Mozambique: From Colonialism*, pp. xvii, 54.

MABLA (*Movimento Afro-Brasileiro para a Libertação de Angola*) (Pg.) "Afro-Brazilian Movement for the Liberation of Angola," a political party organized by students at São Paulo University, Brazil, to work for the independence of Angola. Marcum, *The Angola Revolution*, I:202.

maboca (Afr.) Tropical shrub (*Strychnos* spp.) cultivated in Angola for its edible seeds. The shrub also yields a toxic substance, used in medicine. Ficalho, *Plantas Uteis*, p. 222.

MAC (*Movimento Anti-Colonialista*) (Pg.) "Movement of Anti-Colonials," nationalist movement formed in Lisbon in 1957 by revolutionary intellectuals from Portuguese African colonies. It was the precursor of *Frente Revolucionario Africano para a Independencia Nacional.* Its strong unity played an important role in the liberation of the African colonies in 1975. HDRGC.

macaco fidalgo An endangered forest monkey (*Colobus polykomus*) protected by law; in English, a macaque. Mota, *Guiné Portuguesa,* II:189.

macamblala (Afr.) In São Tomé and elsewhere a tropical tree (*Crasterispermum aetiopium* Mart.) bearing roots said to yield an aphrodisiac; from its bark, Africans extract a substance used in folk medicine. Almada Negreiros, *Historia,* p. 245.

macareu (Pg.) A bore or tidal wave of extraordinary height, caused either by the meeting of two tides or by the tide rushing up a narrowing estuary or river. On certain rivers of peculiar configuration or location, such as the Geba River and estuary in Guinea-Bissau, a *macareu* is a regular occurrence. Carvalho e Vasconcellos, *As Colonias Portuguesas,* pp. 111-12.

maceira brava (Afr.) A medium-size tropical tree (*Zizyphus jujuba* Mill.) bearing edible fruit similar to small apples from which Africans make a kind of rum. It was introduced by the Portuguese to Angola from India early in the colonial period; it is also found in Mozambique. Ficalho, *Plantas Uteis,* pp. 118-9.

machamba (Afr.) A small plot of land on which one person cultivates crops, usually cotton; the plot varies from 0.2 hectares to 1.2 hectares. On average the amount of work required to cultivate a *machamba* planted to cotton is about 150 days a year. To prevent shortages of food, the grower often has to mark out a *machamba* for food production as well. The *machamba* system was introduced by the Portuguese government in the 1940s, arousing African resentment. At its height, cotton growing employed a substantial portion of the population of Mozambique; in 1944, it was estimated that 790,000 people were involved. Newitt, *Portugal,* pp. 122-3.

machilla (Pg.) A litter or palanquin used in the eighteenth century in Zambezia to transport passengers; it was manned by professional carriers, often slaves. Newitt, *Portuguese Settlement,* p. 383.

machim (Pg.) In São Tomé and elsewhere, a large heavy-bladed knife used to cut sugar cane and dense underbrush; a machete or cutlass. GEPB.

machongo (Afr.) In Mozambique, a soil rich in organic matter, found in swampy areas. PDM.

macoda (Afr.) A special slave in charge of a group of domestic female slaves owned by a *dona* (q.v.) in Zambezia, Mozambique, c.1740. Newitt, *Portuguese Settlement,* pp. 197, 383. *See also* butaka.

Macombe (Afr.) A dynasty of Shona-speaking people in Barué, central Mozambique, c.1500. During the colonial period, the Macombe state was closely allied to the Barué kingdom. These dynasties, often rising together against Portuguese *muzungos* (q.v.) and other outsiders, managed to survive until the late nineteenth century. The Macombe effectively controlled large areas of southern Zambezia. Isaacman, *Mozambique: From Colonialism,* pp. 19, 21, 154.

macua (Afr.) In Angola, a tall tropical tree the timber from which was used to make vessels in the colonial period. Ficalho, *Plantas Uteis*, p. 93.

macuata (Afr.) In Angola and elsewhere, a tall tropical tree (*Trachylobium hornemannianum* Hayne) that is the source of a red resin used for domestic and industrial purposes. This resin is also known as Mozambique copal. Africans call it *ocote, cocoto,* and *mucocoto.* Ficalho, *Plantas Uteis,* pp. 155-58.

macundi (Afr.) A tropical leguminous vine (*Vigna catjang* Walp.) bearing edible pods and seeds; widely cultivated by Africans in Angola and elsewhere. The Portuguese call it *feijão macundi.* Ficalho, *Plantas Uteis,* p. 139.

macuta (Kimb.) A copper coin equal to 200 *reis,* minted in Angola in 1694. Apparently the first of its kind in Portuguese Africa. DN. *See also* kwanza.

Madal Society An agricultural and commercial company organized by Gongoza, Bouvay & Company, a French corporation with headquarters in Marseille. In 1904, they leased several Mozambican *prazos,* including Madal, Chiringona, Mahindo, and others in the Quelimane area. After obtaining the backing of the prince of Monaco, the company cleared virgin forests, planted heavy-yielding varieties of trees, introduced machinery for the production of oil, sugar, cotton, and foodstuffs, and used compulsory means to recruit laborers. By 1916, it had 406,832 coconut trees producing 788 tons (715,500 kg) of copra (q.v.). After independence in 1977, FRELIMO (q.v.) allowed the company to continue business, subject to an annual review of its profits. Vail, *Capitalism,* pp. 61, 120, 155-8, 401; GEPB.

Madagascar An island in the Indian Ocean, separated from the continent by the Mozambique Channel. Portuguese navigator Rui Pereira and his crew visited the island in 1506. Friendly locals welcomed them with yams, fowl, and ginger. Geologically and culturally the island is related to southeast Asia, not Africa, as are the flora and fauna. Axelson, *Portuguese in East-Africa,* pp. 61-2.

Madeira Islands, discovery and settlement of These islands were discovered by Portuguese navigators c.1419 then developed in 1425 by João

G. Zarco who established settlements in Funchal and Michico. It is believed that the Genoese introduced sugar cane from Sicily into the islands, which were well suited to its cultivation. Diogo de Teive built a sugar mill and in 1456 sent the first sugar shipment to England, later expanding to Flanders. Duncan, *Atlantic Islands,* pp. 7-10.

Madeiran settlers in Angola   Between 1884 and 1892, the Portuguese government brought about 1,500 Madeirans to the Huila Highlands in southern Angola. These Maderians were desperately poor small farmers, often illiterate, who were accustomed to intensive irrigated agriculture on tiny plots of land in their native islands. They were therefore given two-hectare plots of irrigable lands along the small streams of the northern highlands. Wheat and sugar cane were tried but they proved unsuccessful as cash crops because neither the farmers nor the government were able to organize an efficient system to transport their products to distant markets. Many of the farmers therefore limited their efforts to producing just enough for family subsistence while others opted for repatriation to Madeira after the expiration of their contracts. Still others took to trade or entered the inflated local bureaucracy or the church. Clarence-Smith, *Slaves, Peasants,* pp. 44-5, 46.

Madi (Ful.) According to the beliefs of the Islamized Fulas in Guinea-Bissau around 1900, Madi is the last prophet, still to come to guide the Islamic people. Gonçalves, *O Islamismo*, p. 138(n).

madonto (Afr.)   Tribute paid to chiefs for permission to pass through their land. Around 1760, during the height of the Manica fairs in Zambezia, Mozambique, the payment of these duties was a source of bitter quarrels between the Portuguese and African chiefs. These disputes ultimately led to the closing of trade routes in the interior of Central Africa. Newitt, *Portuguese Settlement,* pp. 151, 383. *See also* milando.

Madrid, Convention of   A treaty signed by Portugal and other European powers on January 30, 1876, that obliged Portugal to recognize the slave-trading interests of all European nations in the area from 5°12'S latitude to the Congo River. Axelson, *Portugal*, p. 40.

madjan-candjan (Afr.)   In São Tomé, the godmother who holds a candle during an infant's baptism. Tenreiro, *A Ilha*, p. 198.

madjan-glande (Afr.)   In São Tomé, the godmother who pays for the swaddling clothes for an infant and the church fees, including the tip to the sexton, for a baptism. Tenreiro, *A Ilha*, p. 198.

madjan lu-lu-lu (Afr.) In São Tomé, the godmother who buries the placenta of a newborn child. Tenreiro. *A llha*, p. 198.

madzi-a-manga (Afr.) A secret water-based medicine used for the investiture of a Barue king c.1750. Early in the eighteenth century, the Portuguese wrongly thought that this holy water, traditionally required for the coronation of the king, converted him to Christianity. As a result, colonial officials periodically attempted to withhold the water in an effort to influence the outcome of succession crises or to wrench concessions from the king. In response, Barue soldiers invariably attacked Portuguese Crown estates and disrupted commerce between Sena and the Manica fair until the Portuguese yielded the water. Isaacman, *Mozambique: The Tradition*, pp. x, 3.

Mafalala (Afr.) A slum on the outskirts of Maputo, capital of Mozambique. Andrade, *Antologia Tematica*, I:260.

mafe (Afr.) In Guinea-Bissau, a fish that is part of the regular diet among Africans; meat is usually reserved for rituals. Mota, *Guinéa Portuguesa,* II:93.

mafumeira (Pg.) In Angola and elsewhere, a handsome tropical tree (*Ceiba pentandra*) with a thick straight trunk, abundant foliage, and fruit that produces a kind of silk-cotton or kapok used as a textile. The wood is used for timber. It grows to a height of 200 ft. (60 m) and is also known by Africans as *mufumu*, in Guinea-Bissau as *poilão* and *tagarra,* and in São Tomé as *ocá.* Carvalho e Vasconcellos, *As Colonias Portuguesa*, p. 226; Ficalho, *Plantas Uteis*, p. 93. *See also* mafumeira encarnada.

mafumeira encarnada (Pg.) In Angola and elsewhere, a tropical tree (*Bombax buonopozence*) with characteristics similar to the *mafumeira* (q.v.). The soft wood is used in construction; the woolly pods produce a silk-cotton used to make mattresses and a fiber employed in domestic utensils. It is found in the Golungo Alto forests, Angola. In Guinea-Bissau, it is known as *poilão.* Ficalho, *Plantas Uteis*, p. 95.

mafura (Afr.) An oil extracted from the *mafumeira* (q.v.) tree (*Ceiba pentandra*) that Africans in Mozambique used as a condiment in many dishes. In Inhambane, southern Mozambique, this oil is called *metiana.* Ficalho, *Plantas Uteis,* pp. 114-15.

magaissa (Afr.) In Mozambique, a contract laborer returned from the South African Transvaal gold mines. He enjoyed great social prestige among his fellow villagers c.1920. Caetano, *Os Nativos*, p. 39.

Maganja Aquem Chire An important *prazo* east of the Shire River and north of the Zambezi in Mozambique. It was leased by I.J. Paiva Raposo in 1877. Soon after, it became part of the famous Mopeia (q.v.) *prazo* and village, operated and controlled by the Paiva Raposo-Hornung family until the 1950s. Vail, *Capitalism,* pp. 9, 60.

Maganja da Costa One of the largest and wealthiest nineteenth century Zambezian *prazos.* It was located on the Indian Ocean coast between Quelimane and Angoche. Leased by A. Alves da Silva in 1853, Maganja da Costa soon became a center for the trade in slaves, ivory, and gold. By 1870, it challenged the Portuguese authorities who had neither the resources nor the personnel to control the area. By 1892 the Alves da Silva family was finally deposed and the Portuguese took possession of the *prazo.* Newitt, *Portuguese Settlement,* pp. 286-7, 338, 361.

Maganja d'Alem A *prazo* to the northwest of the Zambezi River near the Sena *prazo.* In 1879 it was controlled by the *Campanhia da Zambezia* whose forced labor and maltreatment of Africans caused the latter to flee to the Indian Ocean coast in 1898. The brutal methods employed to collect the *mussoco* (official tax) resulted in the loss of thousands of *colonos* (q.v.) who left the estate to work on neighboring plantations, also in 1898. At the turn of the century, cotton, sugar, rice, and tea were introduced into the *prazo.* In the 1920s, a system of large all-wage-labor plantations increased production of cotton by African growers under European supervision and yielded some profit. Vail, *Capitalism,* pp. 9, 115, 169-70, 273.

Maghreb (Ar.) "Sunset." An area comprising western Mediterranean Africa, including Morocco, Algiers, and Tunisia, conquered by Moslems around 700 AD. They imposed Islam on the local Berber people, who resisted Arab violence and racial arrogance. After several generations, the Berbers adopted Islam and spread their new faith in the western Sahara. The Portuguese came into contact with them in Ceuta in 1415 and in Arguim in 1442, on the eve of the great expansion. Also spelled *Maghrib.* Trimingham, *A History of Islam,* pp. 14, 18.

magic Black magic was widely used in rural areas in Mozambique during the civil war between the government and RENAMO (q.v.). Leaders of RENAMO had sorcerers and witches who used charms, rituals, and spells to create feelings of courage and fearlessness among their fighters preparatory to going into action. The use of magic prolonged the war, and groups like the N'dau (q.v.) made a profession of practicing magic to better fight their enemies and to gain control over other groups. Andersson, *Mozambique,* p. 61, 169.

Mahindo (Afr.) A *prazo* in the Quelimane region of Mozambique, leased by João Antonio Correa Pereira in 1873. At that time it was not producing any export commodities and the local labor was in revolt. The new lessee reorganized the estate, promoted agriculture, and within ten years transformed it into a highly profitable business by producing sugar and cotton for export. Later it was taken over by the *Companhia de Mozambique.* Isaacman, *Mozambique: The Tradition,* pp. 77, 106.

maindo (Afr.) In colonial Zambezia, a Goan merchant who peddled his wares in the *prazos* and towns along the Indian Ocean. PDM.

Maio One of the islands of the Cape Verde archipelago, discovered by the Portuguese around 1460 and settled 1520. Its early economy, based on livestock, was repeatedly decimated by drought. By 1643, slave ships from New England were trading in Maio and the slave trade helped sustain the colonists who also engaged in salt trading, important until the 1950s. Since independence in 1975, an airport and tourist facilities have been developed. HDRGC.

maize or **Indian corn** Cultivated New World cereal plant (*Zea mays*), introduced into West Africa by early Portuguese slave traders. Between 1510 and 1540 cultivation of this grain had spread to Western Sudan, particularly the Saharan borderlands. Leo Africanus (1493-1552) claimed to have seen maize in the Timbuctu and Kano markets in 1512. This implied that this grain, which greatly enriched the African diet beginning in the sixteenth century, had already been known and cultivated for some time. This tropical American plant, with its high yield requiring a minimum of labor, is of great economic and social significance in Portuguese Africa. Combined with beans in the diet, the two supply all necessary amino acids, important in diets low in animal protein. Lewicki, *West African Food,* pp. 20, 134, 141; Newitt, *Portugal in Africa,* p. 13.

maka (Kimb.) In Angola, an oral story, real or fictitious, with a moral. *Makas* are used as a means of teaching ethical values to children. Ervedosa, *Itinerario,* p. 11.

Makanga (Afr.) An African kingdom in an old Chewa chieftaincy on the Upper Zambezi River, north of Tete, organized in the middle of the nineteenth century by the Afro-Portuguese Pereira family to recapture land taken by the government. After acquiring European weapons, they established an army of about 4,000 soldiers. The family underwent the customary Chewa rites of royal investiture, received African praise names, and maintained a royal shrine at which they periodically propitiated the *mudzimu,* or ancestor spirits.

Although Portugal would not tolerate the existence of new states, they initially tried to accommodate the leaders of Makanga whose power was largely dependent on European technology and markets. Gradually Portugal established a strong military presence throughout the Zambezia and by the end of the nineteenth century Makanga disappeared. Isaacman, *Mozambique: The Tradition*, pp. 23, 29, 30, 35-9.

Makanga prazo   A large estate in Mozambique, originally part of the old Chewa chieftaincy, leased by the Pereira family (flourished 1800-1902), located north of the Zambezi River and extending as far as the Ruareze and Muchingue mountains. The first family member to enter the territory c.1775 was Gonçalvo Caetano Pereira, but the actual founder of the *prazo* in 1800 was Pedro Caetano Pereira, better known as Chamatowa. Isaacman, *Mozambique: The Tradition*, pp. 119-20.

Makanja (Afr.)   An African state established around 1850 in the eastern region of Malawi and centered in the lower Shire Valley. Makanja greatly disrupted Lisbon's imperial policies in Mozambique. After acquiring European weapons, the leaders of Makanja organized a sizable army that until 1902 opposed Portuguese penetration into the northern reaches of the Zambezi River. For years it dominated strategic waterways and threatened Portuguese army bases, but the combination of internal political instability and intense military rivalries caused its sudden and rapid decline at the end of the nineteenth century. Even after its disappearance as a state, in 1902 its inhabitants joined forces with other ethnic groups to continue anti-Portuguese activities. Isaacman, *Mozambique: The Tradition*, pp. 10, 23, 39.

Makololo (Afr.)   An Angolan ethnic group that first arrived in Mozambique in 1856 as carriers for David Livingstone. Awaiting Livingstone's return they settled on the middle reaches of the Shire River where they attracted the sympathy and protection the Scottish missionaries (q.v.) in Blantyre, Malawi. The Makololo amassed a military force and began raiding Massingire lands, soon organizing a chiefdom headed by strong leaders. They played important roles in helping the British or the Portuguese, according to the circumstances. In 1889, A.A. da Rocha Serpa Pinto organized a force to attack the Makololo, but the 1890 British Ultimatum (q.v.) forced the Portuguese to withdraw their forces and leave the area. Henriksen, *Mozambique*, pp. 82-83, 93; Isaacman, *Mozambique: The Tradition*, pp. 23, 33-34, 38.

Makonde (Afr.)   An ethnic group, possibly part of a Bantu migration centuries ago from lands south of Lake Malawi, settled on a northeast plateau in the Cabo Delgado district, Mozambique. In 1970, they numbered 175,000.

They are known for their wood carvings and for the elaborate patterns of scarification of the body and face. Traditionally they have cultivated the soil because the presence of the tsetse-fly precluded cattle raising. They live in small family groups, recognizing only the authority of the village headman. The Makonde have not only ably defended themselves in their high-ground sanctuary but in the past have proved aggressive toward their neighbors, the Makua, whom they enslaved. A constant defense against becoming themselves enslaved has been offered as the chief explanation for their bellicosity and resistance to Islam and the Portuguese. Until the War for Independence in 1964-74, Christian missionaries tried to convert them. Henriksen, *Mozambique,* pp. 247-8.

Makua-Lomwe (Afr.) These two culturally similar ethnic groups live in an area from south of Lake Nyassa across Mozambique to the Indian Ocean coast; they were the largest and possibly the least known of the indigenous groups prior to independence. The Makua, one of the few groups now spread in large numbers into bordering states, are believed to have been the first Bantu immigrants to reach the Indian Ocean, arriving around the eleventh century. In 1970, the Makua population was calculated at 3 million; they outnumber the Lomwe by more than three to one. They are Swahili-speaking and have been highly influenced by Arab customs and Islam. The Lomwe have been categorized as a distinct group because of their language, life style, and beliefs. After 1900, many Lomwe moved to Malawi, where they now constitute the second largest ethnic group. They are related to the Nyanja in the Tete district and to the Chuabo on the coast. Henriksen, *Mozambique*, pp. 247-9.

makulu (Pg.) "Dysentery." Any of the various inflammatory intestinal diseases characterized by abdominal pain and intense diarrhea with bloody mucus. This disease was common among slaves crowded in barracoons (q.v.) in African ports from the seventeenth to the middle of the nineteenth century. The slaves were often kept for months waiting to be shipped to the New World. Their exposure to disease during this time caused numerous deaths at the port or during the subsequent and lengthy middle passage (q.v.). *Makulu* is derived from the Portuguese word *maculo* (stain, impurity). EDK; GEPB.

Makvolk (Afrk.) This ethnic group was originally an African community who worked as servants to the Boers in South Africa. Around 1880, these speakers of Afrikaans immigrated with a group of Boers to southern Angola and were granted land in the Huila Highlands by the Portuguese government. They remained in the highlands after the departure of the Boers in 1928 and prospered modestly as small farmers. Clarence-Smith, *Slaves, Peasants*, p. 45.

mal de Luanda *See* scurvy.

malagüeta (Pg.)   Pungent seeds from an African shrub (*Aframomum melegüeta* or *A. melehueta,* Rosc.; syn. *A. granum paradisi*) used as a condiment and in liquors and medicine. It has been known in Europe since the thirteenth century and was used there as a pepper and cardamom substitute. It was originally collected along the coast of Guiné and caravans transported it from the West African coast across the Sahara to the Mediterranean where Italian merchants distributed it in Europe. It was little known in Portugal until the Portuguese navigator Antoniotto Usodimare brought *malagüeta* from Gambia in 1455. Cabo das Palmas on the coast was the center of *malagüeta* exchange in Africa, and Lisbon, Antwerp, and Flanders the centers of distribution in Europe. Until 1513, Portugal had absolute monopoly on its trade. After 1550, the Portuguese *malagüeta* trade declined due to British and French competition. It is also known as grains-of-paradise. Alternate spellings include *malegüeta* and *melegüeta.* Godinho, *A Economia,* pp. 199-200.

malaria (Ital.)   A generally intermittent and recurrent infectious disease, caused by any of various sporozoans (genus *Plasmodium*) that are parasitic to the red blood corpuscles and are transmitted to man by the bite of an infected mosquito, especially of the genus *Anopheles*; it is characterized by severe chills and fever. Of an expedition of 700 European troops dispatched from Lisbon in 1860, over half died of malaria and dysentery in the Cassange region. Malaria is endemic in upper Zambezia in Central Africa east of the Kasai River and in many parts of the humid tropics and subtropics. It is a major cause of death among Africans in affected areas, especially children under the age of five. Wheeler, *Angola,* pp. 40,54-6; GEPB.

Malawi (Afr.) An ethnic group that inhabits the Tete district, Mozambique. Like most other Mozambican ethnic groups, the Malawi are found across the frontiers in the countries of Zambia and Malawi, crossing the borders in search of jobs and educational opportunities in neighboring states. The Malawi, extensively studied by British and Portuguese scholars, have been classified into three principal subgroups: the Nyanja, the Chewas, and the Nsenga. In Mozambique, the branches of the Chewa are called the Chipeta and the Zimba (q.v.). In 1970, the Malawi numbered about 26,000. Henriksen, *Mozambique,* pp. 247, 249.

Mali Kingdom (Afr.)   An Islamic empire in Western Sudan organized c.1090 AD. Based on trade in slaves, gold, and ivory, it flourished in the fourteenth century and by 1375, even though the African coast was still to be explored, Mali was noted on European maps of Africa. Around 1460, Mali supplied as much as one-sixteenth of the western world's gold. Weakened by internal wars, King Mansa Mamoud I sent emissaries to King João II of Portugal in 1530 requesting military assistance without success. In 1534 a request was made to King João III and Mali ambassadors actually traveled to Lisbon. Portugal again declined to provide aid. In 1546 Songhai invaders sacked Niani, the capital, bringing to an end a major West African empire. GEPB; HDRGC.

ma-lunda (Kimb.) In Angola, an esoteric, sacred folktale known only to the ruling class and kept from the common people. This type of story, part of the educational process, also is called *mi-sendu.* Ervedosa, *Itinerario*, p. 11. *See also* maka, mi-soso.

mambari (Afr.) In colonial times, Ovimbundu traders from Bié and Benguela on the Atlantic coast traveled the long distance to the Barotse Kingdom on the Upper Zambezi River. Their main commerce was in ivory, wax, dye plants, slaves, and wild rubber. Ovimbundu merchants organized transcontinental caravans between Angola and Mozambique and, during the rubber boom (1874-1916), they had the monopoly of the trade. Since 1912, epidemics, famine, the railroad, and new roads have weakened the Mambari's commerce, but even today they continue to trade overland as far as Namibia and South Africa. Wheeler, *Angola*, p. 26.

mambo (Afr.) In Mozambique, a local African chief with hereditary secular and spiritual powers. These powers are used to assure the well-being of his people. Isaacman, *Mozambique: From Colonialism*, p. 8.

Mambone (Afr.) A large *prazo* situated between Sofala and the Sabe River, Mozambique, established around 1780. It extended over a hundred miles of coastline along the Indian Ocean from Sofala to the Barazuto Islands. In 1806, it was divided into four and granted to four *donas* (q.v.). In 1832, the Mambone *prazo* included six villages and a small garrison at the mouth of the Sabe, with a chief to collect tribute and taxes for the government. Newitt, *Portuguese Settlement,* pp. 209-10.

mamoeiro (Afr.) In Portuguese Africa and elsewhere, the papaya (*Carica papaya*), a single-stemmed tree resembling a palm in that it has a cluster of large leaves at the top, and bearing a large, oblong, yellowish-orange fruit similar to a melon. It is native to tropical America, and was introduced to Africa by the Portuguese early in the colonial period. Its fruit is also called *mamão.* Ficalho, *Plantas Uteis*, p. 182.

mamote (Afr.) A tropical fruit tree (*Solanum thonnigianum*) found around Luanda province, Angola, that bears a sweet edible fruit tasting somewhat of tangerine. Ficalho, *Plantas Uteis*, p. 229

mamparra (Pg.)   In Mozambique, the name given to an African laborer registering for the first time as a contract mine worker for work in the Rand in South Africa. Traditionally, a *mamparra* is considered ignorant, lazy, and disinclined to work until seasoned by the hard labor in the mines. Rita-Ferreira, *O Movimento Migratorio*, p. 58. *See also* magaissa.

manchilla (Pg.)   Length of African-made cotton cloth historically used as a standard measure in trade. It was used by Africans to pay taxes to their local chief. Isaacman, *Mozambique: From Colonialism*, pp. 17, 31; Newitt, *Portuguese Settlement,* pp. 189, 383.

mancone (Afr.)   In Guinea-Bissau, a tropical tree (*Erythophleum guinense*) used locally and exported as timber for industrial construction and ship building. Its boiled leaves and branches were used to prepare a poison employed throughout Portuguese Africa in tribal ordeals (q.v.). Ficalho, *Plantas Uteis*, p. 167; Mota, *Guiné Portuguesa*, I: 167.

Mandingo (Afr.)   A large Islamized African ethnic group centered in the Upper Niger Valley and widely spread over West Africa. The Mandingos include the Bambara, Dyula, Malinke, and others. Traditionally grouped in states, they had to shift their grounds in the last century as the result of the Fula Wars. They are divided into castes and are strongly patriarchal. They are farmers but poor cattle herders. Shifting cultivation is their traditional method of cultivation and groundnuts their chief commercial crop. They are considered good traders. Also known as Sahelian Sudanese. Mota, *Guiné Portuguesa*, I:379.

Mandingo-Mouro (Afr.)   In Guinea-Bissau, a large Islamized community that came from southern Gambia around 1819, traveling along the Cacheu and Casamansa rivers and settling in the Farim region. For many years the Mandingo-Mouros extended their territory beyond the Cacheu River and were able to Islamize the Balantas. Carreira, *Evolução do Islamismo,* BCG, xxi(84):442-43. *See also* Mandingo.

Mandinguization   Among the Mandingos of Guinea-Bissau, a process of combining traditional animism with Islamic devotions incorporating such abridgments as observing four daily prayers (not five), using churches and chapels (not mosques), performing nontraditional rituals, and having a rigid hierarchical order of religious chiefs. They wear amulets inscribed with verses from the Koran as protection against evil. Gonçalves, *O Mundo Arabo-lslamico*, pp. 1767, 202.

manganaz (Crio.)   In Guinea-Bissau, a white-flowered tropical shrub (*Icacina senegalensis*) up to 3 ft. (1 m) high. The red velvety fruit was used in folk medicine as a tonic or in a bath to treat smallpox and similar sicknesses. Espirito Santo, *Algumas Plantas Venenosas e Medicinais,* BCG, 1948, 10:398-9.

mangrove In Africa, tropical shrubs, rarely trees, of the genera *Rhizophera,* especially *R. mucronata, Bruguiera,* and *Ceriops,* growing in swampy land along riverbanks or in brackish or salt water, that spread by sending down aerial roots, forming thick groves over a large area. Mangroves play an important role in land and island building. They grow along rivers in Guinea-Bissau, Mozambique, and Angola. In Angola, there are large mangrove areas along the mouths of rivers north of Luanda and Lobito. GEPB.

mangue (Pg.) Marshy ground along the seacoast and on the banks and at the mouth of rivers where mangroves (*Rhizophera mucronata*) grow; earth mixed with the decaying leaves of these trees serves to dye cotton. In Guinea-Bissau, *mangue* is characteristic of low areas flooded by rivers and the sea. *Mangue* grounds are associated with many different forms of herbaceous vegetation. Mota, *Guiné Portuguesa,* I:88. *See also* mangrove.

Manica (Afr.) A municipality, capital Macequece, in the Beira district, Mozambique. Even before the arrival of the Portuguese in 1506, its gold fields in the Monomotapa state were well known and it was an important gold trading center controlled by Swahili-speaking Arabs. Francisco Barreto visited the region in 1559. From 1600, important fairs were held in the Manica area. In 1889, the British South Africa Company, under Cecil John Rhodes, took their chief, Mutassa, prisoner and seized the gold mining concession. Portugal made an agreement with England and recovered Manica in 1891. Soon after Manica and its capital, Macequece, became one of the richest regions in Mozambique. Newitt, *Portuguese Settlement,* pp. 39-41; GEPB.

Manica-e-Sofala A province of west and south central Mozambique that includes the Tete and Beira districts, with its capital at Beira. In colonial times important kingdoms such as Barue, Monomotapa, and Gaza were part of this province. It is a rich agricultural area with plentiful trade along the Zambezi River and through the coastal towns. The Beira Railway Company links the port of Beira with Zimbabwe and Malawi. The province covers an area of 50,137 sq. mi. (129,888 sq. km) and in 1970 had a population of 1,085,290. GEPB; WNGD. *See also* Manica.

Manica fair This fair, located in a gold mining area in the Manica Kingdom, was established by the Portuguese around 1590. For years they struggled for control of the area in spite of continuous rebellions of local chiefs interested both in digging and trading gold. In 1719, the fairs in the area were re-established by a leading trader from the Sena settlement. He befriended local chiefs and maintained several trading posts, one of which was Massikisse (q.v.). Newitt, *Portuguese Settlement,* pp. 48, 73-4.

Manica gold mines These well-known gold mines, located in the mountains between Sofala and the Matzoe River, were originally subject to the authority of Quiteve Kingdom (q.v.). The Portuguese settled there in 1550 and established three fairs at the important settlements of Manica, Chipangura, and Sofala at each of which a Portuguese *capitão* resided. The Portuguese tried to keep control of these mines throughout the colonial period and Manica continued to be a center of gold trade in the region south of the Zambezi. Today the Manica gold mines are in the Beira district of Mozambique. Newitt, *Portuguese Settlement,* p. 46.

Manica Kingdom Originally part of the Monomotapa Kingdom; established as a separate state in 1589. Located between Sofala on the Indian Ocean coast and the Matzoe River inland in central Mozambique, it served as a crossroad for traders and government forces trying to control this vast territory. By 1630, the Portuguese were the dominant power in the area, although the chiefdom kept its independence until 1890 when a daughter of the chief married the famous English adventurer George Taylor. Newitt, *Portuguese Settlement,* pp. 48, 70, 335.

Manica Mining Journal A weekly published in Manica and Sofala Territory in 1911. The *Manica Mining Journal* appeared in English and French, with references in Portuguese. Dias, *A Imprensa,* p. 25.

Manicongo (Afr.) Title of the hereditary Congo king whose seat was in São Salvador do Congo. The first *Manicongo,* met by explorer Diogo Cão in 1482, was Nzinga-a-Cuum, named João I after being baptized in 1491. Before and after their encounter with the Portuguese, the *Manicongos* ruled a unified chiefdom in northern Angola that endured throughout the colonial period. This strong ethnonationalism was still felt in 1938 when King Pedro VII of Congo met the President of Portugal, General Antonio Oscar Fragoso Carmona (1869-1957). On this occasion the king expressed his and his ancestors loyalty to Portugal. Pelissier, *La Colonie,* p. 265; GEPB.

manioc (Braz.) An economically important genus (*Manihot* spp.) of herbs and shrubs, introduced from tropical areas of the New World by the Portuguese early in the sixteenth century. These valuable commercial plants are widespread throughout Portuguese Africa and are a standard food for many Africans. The most common manioc species, *Manihot esculenta,* is cultivated for food and fermented beverages. It was most probably introduced to Africa on the Angolan coast where today its cultivation, harvesting, and preparation still show Brazilian influence. After it is processed, often into a flour, it is known as cassava (q.v.). Ficalho, *Plantas Uteis,* pp. 249-254.

Manjaco An ethnic group of Senegambian cultural stock who live mainly along the Niger and Congo rivers. The Manjacos who settled in the northwestern region of the Cacheu and the Mansoa rivers are slightly Islamized through contact with the Mandingos. The Manjaco economy is based on shifting agriculture, mainly rice cultivation. They provided stiff resistance to Portuguese settlement between 1878 and 1890 when they were among the first to try to halt Portuguese penetration into the interior. They also fought the Portuguese between 1913 and 1915. In 1960, the Manjaco population was estimated at 80,000. HDRGC.

Mansa (Afr.) A Mandingo chief, also called a *Farin,* in charge of a group of villages in Guiné c.1600. At that time, Mansa-controlled villages were located along the Upper Niger River, Western Sudan, under the rule of an emperor called Mandimansa. Mota, *Guiné Portuguesa,* I:280.

Mansoa (Afr.) The fourth-largest river of Guinea-Bissau; the Mansoa travels about 120 mi. (193 km) to the coast, and is navigable for at least two-thirds of the way. Its course is roughly parallel to that of the Farim-Cacheu, which flows to the north. The headwaters of the Mansoa are found to the east of Mansaba in the Farim municipality. The Mansoa was the corridor, through the coastal swamps, up which the Portuguese sailed for trade with the interior. HDRGC.

MANU (Mozambique African National Union) A nationalist party established in February 1961 in Mombasa, Kenya, by Mozambican plantation and dock workers settled in Kenya. Matthew Mole was its first president and Lawrence M. Millinga, secretary-general; several leaders were English-speaking. In June 1962, they met with MANU (q.v.) representatives and other nationalists in Dar es-Salaam, Tanzania, and formed FRELIMO (q.v.) as the sole official group of all Mozambican liberation movements. Henriksen, *Mozambique,* pp. 169, 170.

Manzanes Company A commercial navigation company organized in India c.1687 by Banyans (q.v.), a Hindu trading caste, to trade with Mozambique. A powerful corporation protected by the Portuguese in India, it soon monopolized commerce, establishing agents in all the major trading posts in Mozambique. Its activities created hostility in Mozambique because it was owned by foreigners and non-Christians. The Manzanes Company disbanded in 1777. Silva Rego, *O Ultramar,* pp. 96, 97.

mão-de-obra (Pg.) "Labor." Around 1900, under Portuguese government supervision, thousands of African migrant workers from Mozambique signed labor contract with South African companies to work in the gold fields of the Rand. Both the companies and the government took a substantial portion of the laborers' salary. This was considered forced labor and was bitterly denounced by nationalist Mozambicans and international agencies. Rita-Ferreira, *O Movimento Migratorio*, p. 61.

mapiko (Mak.) A secret meetinghouse or large hut set away from the village and used for the puberty initiation rituals of Makonde boys. By tradition, a narrow, tortuous path through dense thickets leads to it and females and non-initiated boys must avoid it. Under the direction of elders, boys perform nocturnal dances imitating wild animals or walk on tall stilts. Dias, *Portuguese Contribution*, pp. 36-37. *See also* nalombo.

maprere (Afr.) In Mozambique c.1700, an annual tribute for land use paid by a *colono* (q.v.) to a *prazo*-holder or an African to a chief. Newitt, *Portuguese Settlement*, pp. 175, 181. *See also* madonto.

Maputo (Afr.) Formerly Lorenço Marques, the colonial capital of Mozambique; in 1975 it was renamed Maputo and became the capital of the People's Republic of Mozambique. Maputo has been modernized with expanded port facilities for loading and unloading ships and additional warehouses. The city produces cement, pottery, cosmetics, footwear, rubber products, and furniture. It is the largest port in Mozambique for export of agricultural products and timber. The university founded in 1962 was renamed Mondlane University (q.v.) in 1987. The city had a population of 383,775 in 1970 that grew to 1,250,000 by 1980. HDM; WNGD.

Maputo River (Afr.) A navigable river in southern Mozambique, 50 mi. (81 km) long. It is formed by the convergence of the Usutu and Pongono rivers, and flows east to Delagoa Bay. The mouth of the Maputo River and the surrounding bay were explored in 1552 by Captain Manuel Sousa de Sepulveda. Axelson, *Portuguese in South-East*, p. 206; WNGD.

Maquela do Zombo A town and municipality in the Congo district, northern Angola, close to the Zaire border. Located on a plateau 2,966 ft. (904 m) high, it is an agricultural area with roads to Damba, São Salvador, Quimbata, and Cuango. It is an important economic and cultural center. During the War for Independence (1960-75), it played a decisive role in the anti-Portuguese insurrection. Simão Toco, founder of a messianic movement, and Antonio Mario, one of the most distinguished writers of modern Angola, were born in this municipality. Wheeler, *Angola*, pp. 152, 178, 186; GEPB.

Mar Tenebroso (Pg.) "Dark Sea." Name given in the Middle Ages to the Atlantic Ocean off the west African coast, south of Cape Bojador (26°08'N, 14°39'W). The area was considered to be populated by monsters and extremely dangerous. It was believed that those who entered it would never return. In 1291 these waters, dominated by the Canary Islands current going south coupled with strong winds from April to October, were reported to have swallowed the brothers Ugolino and Guido Vivaldi. The two Genoese navigators, looking for a route to India, disappeared mysteriously after crossing the latitude of Cape Bojador. Rosario, *Genoveses*, p. 84.

marabout (Ar.) In Moslem North Africa, an ascetic, a holy man, or a saint. In Guinea-Bissau and elsewhere, an itinerant Moslem missionary. In sub-Saharan Africa, a *marabout* is associated with the cult of saints among Islamic Africans. Birmingham, *Islam in West Africa*, p. 68; Gonçalves, *O Mundo Arabo-Islamico*, p. 192. *See also* Marabout cult.

Marabout cult (Ar.) In Guinea-Bissau and elsewhere, an unorthodox Islamic system of outward forms and religious ceremonies used in worship, centered around an ascetic Moslem leader admired and respected by his fellow believers. Birmingham, *Islam in West Africa*, p. 68; Gonçalves, *O Islamismo*, pp. 148, 152. *See also* marabout.

Marangue (Afr.) A *prazo* managed by the Jesuits c.1746 and located facing the Massangano *prazo* just across the Luenha River near its confluence with the Zambezi River. This Crown *prazo* was one of the eight *prazos* rented and developed by the Jesuits in the Tete region of Mozambique. Newitt, *Portuguese Settlement*, p. 89.

Marca de Guiné (Pg.) "Mark of Guiné." Originally the initial "G" branded on the right arm of a slave. It was replaced by the mark of a cross in 1519. After 1532, the *marca de Guiné* identified all slaves who landed at São Tomé from Benin, the Slave River (Guiné), and the Congo. Saunders, *A Social History*, p. 13; GEPB. *See also* "M"; "G"; slaves, branding of.

Maria Sect (Pg.) A nativist African messianic movement that began in 1960 with the reported appearance of the Virgin Mary to people in a Cassulo-Cuenda village in central Angola. This miracle included a message of redemption for the exploited laborers of the cotton plantations. According to the reports, the Virgin Mary requested her devotees to refuse to work for white masters, boycott Africans doing otherwise, build a chapel on each farm, avoid certain foods, take a daily bath, and clear roads leading to cemeteries to facilitate the final gathering of the dead at the Last Judgment. This nativist movement contributed to the general uprising of the agrarian class against

Portuguese domination in Baixa Cassange in 1960. Pelissier, *La Colonie,* pp. 185, 410-12. *See also* Maria War.

Maria War   An agrarian revolt staged and sustained by followers of the Maria Sect (q.v.) that began in Malanje in central Angola in 1960. It was a bloody uprising of African laborers protesting the Portuguese policy of forced cotton cultivation in Baixa de Casanje. The rebellion, rooted in a messianic movement, was crushed by Portuguese forces in February of 1961 after heavy air bombardment. One report revealed that the massacre included the destruction of seventeen villages that left 5,000 dead. Many rebels died singing hymns to the Virgin Mary and to Patrice Lumumba, the Angolan nationalist. Marcum, *The Angolan Revolution,* p. 2; Pelissier, *La Colonie,* pp. 415-8.

marimba   An African xylophone made of wooden slabs fixed to a frame. Beneath each slab is an acoustically matched resonator, usually of calabash. The *marimba* is found among the Mandingos in Liberia, the Chopi in Mozambique, the Yaswa in Congo-Brazzaville, and the Venda in South Africa. HDM.

mariner's compass   An ancient navigational instrument consisting of two magnetized iron bars. On long voyages, Portuguese sailors would re-magnetize these bars with lodestones mined near Alvito, Portugal. Around 1345, Portuguese navigators decided that the mariner's compasses used in the Mediterranean Sea were inadequate for navigating the Atlantic coast. They demanded a new chart based on latitude and longitude, unlike the current charts based on bearing and distance. Costa, *A Marinha dos Descobrimentos,* p. 164; GEPB. *See also* astrolabe.

market days   In São Salvador do Congo around 1880, there were four market days, *konzo, nkenge, nsona,* and *nkandu,* that coincided with the four Congo weekdays. Markets held on the day on which *konzo* fell were called *konzo* throughout the Lower Congo, the markets held the next day were named *nkenge,* and son on. At the beginning of this century, men collected goats, pigs, sheep, various kinds of farm produce, palm wine, manufactured goods, and even, in some areas, slaves, and took them along on any of the four market days. In addition, every village had at least one weekly market within reasonable walking distance. Henderson, *Angola,* p. 43.

marlota (Afr.)   In Guinea-Bissau, a small hooded cotton cape worn by children. Carreira, *Panaria,* p. 12.

maroon settlements (Sp.)   Isolated settlements established by fugitive slaves (*marrons* or *marróns*) and free Africans in protest against oppression and poverty. These settlements, each led by a chief, were beyond the control of the colonial authorities. Like their New World counterparts, these groups were situated in inaccessible, often inhospitable, regions such as the swampy coastal areas of Quelimane and the rugged mountains along the Mozambique-Zimbabwe frontier. Not being completely self-sufficient, its members engaged in raiding inland estates and *prazos* to acquire food and weapons. Maroon communities had antecedents dating back to the seventeenth century in Mozambique. They rejected promises by the colonial administration to redress grievances in return for their submission. Around 1884 in the Tete district, chiefs like Boroma fled and established fugitive settlements in the area. Isaacman, *Mozambique: The Tradition,* pp. 98-99, 107-10.

maroonage   The act of abandoning a village or *prazo* by a group of slaves under the leadership of a indigenous ruling family to flee into the wilderness to organize a fugitive society beyond the control of established authorities. Maroonage, also spelled *marrónage*, was practiced in the eighteenth and nineteenth centuries in Zambezia, Mozambique, and elsewhere. Isaacman, *Mozambique: The Tradition,* p. 98. *See also* maroon settlements.

Marral (Afr.)   An inland estate north of the Kwa-Kwa River, Quelimane province, Mozambique, held in 1855 by João de Jesus Maria. At the time, he was engaged in raiding villages for captives to be sold at a slave-trading post on the coast in exchange for ivory and gold. In 1873 his son Romão de Jesus Maria started to cultivate groundnuts and planted coconuts for the production of copra. These products were sold to Banyans (q.v.) along the rivers and the Indian Ocean coast. Romão was so popular among his laborers in the 1890s that Africans hailed his canoemen with a song entitled *Muzungo Romão Has Arrived.* Although the formal *prazo* system was abolished in 1930, Marral laborers were still employed in the region as late as 1945. Vail, *Capitalism,* pp. 33, 61-4, 166-7; GEPB. *See also* Muzungo Romão.

marrónage   *See* maroonage.

Marvelous Century, The   The most glorious and resplendent age enjoyed by Portugal, lasting from 1415 to c.1515; also known as the Discovery (q.v.). Beginning with Prince Henry and ending with Afonso de Albuquerque, this was an age that included captains and explorers like Bartolomeu Dias, Diogo Cão, Gil Eanes, Nuno Tristão, Tristão da Cunha, Vasco da Gama, and Francisco de Almeida. They have furnished a seemingly endless source of inspiration to chroniclers, poets, and scientists in Portugal and abroad, who so defined and elaborated these glories that this century has become an age of superhumans whose inspiration is still a living presence in Portugal and Portuguese colonial ideology. DHP; GEPB.

mascavado (Pg.) In Portuguese Africa, a slave physically handicapped either by birth or by accident, a defect registered in the slave trade c.1856. Carreira, *As Companhias Pombalinas*, BCG, 1968, xxiii(91/92):307.

Mashonaland (Afr.) An open fertile plateau in northeast Zimbabwe rich in gold and inhabited by the Mashonas, a Bantu people. In the 1880s it was under the control of Chief Gungunhana. The area was explored in 1887 by J.C. Paiva de Andrada and was acquired by the British South Africa Company in 1890, becoming part of Southern Rhodesia in 1923. It is now a province of Zimbabwe. Axelson, *Portugal,* pp. 128, 131-2; WNGD.

massamanga (Afr.) A protest song that satirized and ridiculed co-workers who were not doing their fair share of joint tasks on the sugar or coconut plantations in the lower Zambezia region in the late 1890s. Vail, *Capitalism,* pp. 340-1. *See also* Jemwe, Paiva.

Massangano (Afr.) In Angola, a town situated about 110 mi. (177 km) from the coast. It is east of Luanda at the confluence of the Lukaba and Kwanza rivers. A fort was established by Paulo Dias de Novais at this point in 1583 during his advance along the Kwanza against the Mbundu (q.v.). Massangano was the temporary Portuguese capital of Angola from 1641 to 1648 when the Dutch occupied Luanda. HDA.

Massangano Army Around 1860 the Massangano *prazo* organized an African military force of about 14,000 slave-soldiers along Portuguese and European models. It had a *ukazambo* (leader), and was divided into *butakas* (regiments), and subdivided into *ensa-cas* (squads). This force was intended to protect the estate's borders, quash internal revolts, and engage in slave raids and offensive forays against neighbors. Isaacman, *Mozambique: The Tradition,* pp. 27-9. *See* Massangano prazo.

Massangano prazo A large *prazo* granted by the king of Portugal to Joaquim José da Cruz c.1820. It was located along the south bank of the Zambezi River between the towns of Tete and Sena. The *prazo* was taken by the government around 1900 after the death of its last chief, Motontora. Isaacman, *Mozambique: From Colonialism,* pp. 138-47. *See* Massangano Army.

Massapa fair (Afr.) One of the most important markets, it was established around 1580 in the Mount Darwin area a short distance from the Monomatapa *kraal* (q.v.) in what is now Zimbabwe. A great number of Arab, Goan, Portuguese, and African traders converged on Massapa to deal in gold, ivory, slaves, and European and Asiatic goods. The chief of the fair, called the *capitão das portas* (captain of the gates), collected the dues that the merchants had to pay to the Monomatapa, settled disputes among Portuguese, and heard cases between Europeans and Africans and purely African cases. The office itself was unpaid but his income was assured by participants' fees. This fair declined and the Monomatapa state faded away in the late colonial period. Newitt, *Portuguese Settlement,* pp. 42-3.

massape (Braz.)   Fertile, highly alkaline soil in which many plants grow well; found in particular in the Cape Verde Islands. GDLP.

Massikisse fair (Afr.)   An important market in the Manica gold mining area, it was established around 1695 and prospered until 1890. Located on a crossroad between the southern Zambezian *prazos* and the interior of Mozambique, it attracted a great number of Arab, Portuguese, and African traders. Here gold, ivory, wax, pearls, rock crystal, and animal skins were traded for liquor, cloth, beads, firearms, and powder. Newitt, *Portuguese Settlement,* pp. 46, 74. *See also* Aruangua fair.

Massingire (Afr.)   A large *prazo* located in central Quelimane, Mozambique, established c.1859 by the Vas do Anjos family. Its vast territory north of the Zambezi River was bounded by the Lupata gorge, the Murchison cataracts, and the confluence of the Shire and Zambezi rivers. Isaacman, *Mozambique: From Colonialism,* p. 137; Newitt, *Portuguese Settlement,* pp. 275-87.

Masters of Biscayne   A group of four skilled Basque iron technicians brought to a Benguela iron factory in 1768 by the Angolan governor, F.I. Sousa Coutinho. These technicians were José E. Echeverria, the chief, José de Retolaza, Francisco Zulo, and Francisco de Chinique. The high expectations faded shortly after their arrival as all became ill with tropical fevers and died within a year of beginning their work. Silva Rego, *O Ultramar*, pp. 186-7.

Matabele (Afr.)   A South African ethnic group that came into contact with the Portuguese attempting to settle in the Gaza district, inland from Inhambane, Mozambique, c.1840. They often raided the Zumbo and the Manica mountain areas for goods and slaves. Until the 1880s, their relations with the Portuguese were friendly because the Portuguese were eager to sell them slaves, particularly women captured north of the Zambezi. It was David Livingstone who first drew the attention of British people to the extent of this purely internal slave traffic that evaded the British cruisers and the diplomatic sanctions so elaborately deployed in 1858-64 to stop the seaborne slave trade. Henriksen, *Mozambique,* pp. 225, 300.

Matamba (Afr.)   An eastern Mbundu Kingdom situated between the Cuango and Wamba rivers. In the mid-seventeenth century during the reign of Queen

Nzinga, Matamba became one of the most powerful states in the area. Together with its southern neighbor Kasanje (q.v.), it held a key position on the slave-trade routes from areas east of the Cuango River to the coastal markets to the west. In the eighteenth and nineteenth centuries, the traders and rulers of Matamba (usually called *Jinga* in contemporary sources) directed much of the trade to ports such as Cabinda, north of the Zaire River. Relations with the Portuguese at Luanda fluctuated from periods of uneasy peace to sporadic attempts at direct intervention by the Portuguese in the affairs of Matamba. It was only in the early twentieth century that the kingdom was finally brought under colonial rule. Birmingham, *Trade and Conflict,* pp. 18, 75, 101, 130; HDA.

Matamba mission   A Catholic mission established in 1654 in the Matamba Kingdom by the Congregation for the Propagation of the Faith. It was staffed by Italian Capuchins and its first superior was Friar Serafim de Cortona. Queen Nzinga officially received the first group, headed by Friar Antonio Romano, with kindness. Friar Antonio built a church in honor of Saint Mary of Matamba and opened a school for African children in 1659. A few years after the death of Queen Nzinga in 1663, the mission was abandoned due to internal wars among her heirs. Gabriel, *Angola,* pp. 75-6.

Mata-Frades (Pg.)   "Killer of Friars." The name given to an anticlerical decree abolishing all the religious orders in Portugal and its colonies, signed by the cabinet minister Joaquim Antonio de Aguiar in 1834 during the reign of Queen Maria II. Gabriel, *Angola*, p. 128.

Matemo (Afr.)   One of the twenty islands of the Querimba group, located between Pemba and Cabo Delgado, northern Mozambique. At the time of Vasco da Gama's visit in 1498, was ruled by Swahili merchants who carried on a prosperous trade in gold, ivory, and slaves. The Portuguese later occupied the island, ruining the trade, and poverty replaced wealth. In 1744, several *prazos* in the area were granted. The holders brought slaves and developed agriculture and a prosperous commerce in the area. Newitt, *Portuguese Settlement*, p. 213.

mato santo (Pg.)   "Holy grove." In Guinea-Bissau, an isolated wooded area outside a town where young Islamic men are segregated for several days while they undergo the circumcision rites. A *mato santo* is found outside every Moslem village. Carvalho e Vasconcellos, *As Colonias Portuguesas*, p. 167.

Mauritanian coast   After the explorer Gil Eanes rounded Cape Bojador (q.v.) in 1434, Portuguese navigators began exploring the Mauritanian coast. Further south, Afonso Gonçalves Balaia explored the Rio Ouro and Nuno

Tristão visited Arguim in 1443. Arguim was a medieval center of commerce where gold, gum arabic, slaves, and many kinds of African produce were traded. In 1445, the Portuguese occupied the town and began the export-import of goods to and from Lagos and Lisbon. Around 1460, the Portuguese began to seize slaves in warlike raids on the coast and started an active slave trade with African chiefs and Arab merchants. Today Arguim is still an important commercial city, part of the Islamic Republic of Mauritania. Godinho, *A Economia*, p. 190; DHP.

Mazagão (Ar.)   A Portuguese fortress built around 1520 on the Moroccan coast on the southern bank of the Azamor River. It was well fortified and in 1550 became the center of the Portuguese defense, replacing Azamor and Safim, abandoned in 1542, and Arzila and Alcacer-Ceguer, dismantled by King João III. After the battle of Alcacer-Quibir (q.v.) in 1578, Mazagão began to lose importance. During the seventeenth century it was continuously attacked by Arab sheiks. In 1769 the Marquis of Pombal abandoned the fortress and the Moors established a defense complex on the site. GEPB.

mbandazi   *See* escravo da porta.

Mbanza (Bant.)   In the Congo Kingdom c.1500, a village consisting of a minimum of two hundred huts. Vansina, *Kingdoms of the Savanna*, p. 334; GEPB.

Mbanza Congo (Kik.)   Name given by the nationalist government to São Salvador do Congo (q.v.) after the independence of Angola in 1975. *Mbanza* was the Kikongo name for a settlement, specifically the king of Congo's settlement, and the name for the area prior to contact with the Portuguese. Kaplan, *Angola*, p. viii.

mbuemba (Bant.)   One of two ritual sticks, the other being the *nidcua,* used by *mambos* (local chiefs) in the Sena region, Lower Zambezi, during the rain ceremony c.1650. With the *mbuemba* and *nidcua*, a *mambo* summoned the spirits of the ancestors. After the invocation, he cast the two sticks into a hole previously dug for the purpose and, according to tradition, it began to rain. Isaacman, *Mozambique: From Colonialism*, p. xvii, 27.

Mbundu (Kimb.)   A large Kimbundu-speaking ethnic group, located mainly in the Luanda area and on the lower Cuanza River. Traditionally they were hunters and farmers, and many were traders. They came to the area from central and east-central Africa before the fifteenth century. They had contact with Portuguese traders and missionaries by 1500 and many Mbundu were converted to Christianity, adopting European culture. They settled in towns and learned Portuguese agriculture and cattle farming. In 1970, the core

Mbundu population was over 700,000, plus another 400,000 people whose cultures reflected Mbundu influence. Wheeler, *Angola*, p. 8; GEPB.

Mbundu slave trade   The Portuguese first established contact with the Mbundu people of Angola around 1500 and noted that one large group of Mbundus were settled on Luanda Island on the southern Atlantic coast. For the next half century Mbundu-Portuguese relations were fairly peaceful and the Portuguese were free to explore the hinterland. In 1576, Paulo Dias de Novais occupied the region and founded the Portuguese settlement of Luanda, subsequently the capital of Angola. Afterward a Mbundu-Portuguese slave trade was established at the Luanda port from which millions of slaves were eventually exported to the Brazilian and Caribbean plantations until the slave trade was abolished in 1836. Wheeler, *Angola*, p. 34; DHP. *See also* Mbundu.

Mbungu (Bant.)   In Mozambique and elsewhere, the generic name for tropical vines (*Landolfia kirkii* and other species) that yield a type of rubber. They are found in several regions of Mozambique, especially on the Cabo Delgado coast and Ibo Island. On Zanzibar, *mbungu* rubber was an important product for export. Ficalho, *Plantas Uteis*, p. 216.

Mburuma (Bant.)   An important chiefdom established around 1690 at the confluence of the Lungwana and Zambezi rivers in western Mozambique, an area rich in gold and ivory. This state grew in importance up to the end of the nineteenth century despite continuous Portuguese intrusions. The Mburuma justified their territorial claim by citing their descent from Monomatapa (q.v.) royalty. For many years the Mburuma chiefs controlled the famous Zumbo fair. In 1860, a chief was murdered by the powerful Portuguese ivory trader José Anselmo Santanna and replaced by a rival of the slain chief. This situation did not last and the people rallied around the legitimate chief's heir, mounting an impressive resistance to the Portuguese between 1887 and 1890. Tired of war, in 1891 the Mburuma made peace with the Portuguese government and the majority of the chiefdom was incorporated into the territory of the British South African Company. Newitt, *Portuguese Settlement,* pp. 78, 296-7, 305; GEPB.

mead (Engl.)   A honey-based alcoholic drink common in West Africa. Traditionally, the Wolof in Guinea-Bissau prepared mead by mixing honey and water and exposing the combination to the heat of the sun to aid fermentation. Mead is common in Mali and there is evidence that in the eleventh century this drink was made in southern Morocco, in the country then called Sus al-Aqsa. Lewicki, *West African Food,* pp. 175-6.

medical services in Angola In 1576 in Luanda, Angola, the Misericordia built a hospital to care for navigators, explorers and slaves. Under the supervision of Aleixo Abreu, a physician, another hospital was begun in 1594 and finished in 1605. In 1756 the Marquês de Pombal founded a school of medicine that provided health care to Europeans and Africans. In the twentieth century a large leprosarium was built in Angola, near the Zimbabwean border, in 1950, which prior to independence was under the technical direction of the Institute of Tropical Medicine in Lisbon which was founded to conduct research in tropical diseases, notably sleeping sickness. In 1954, Angola had 53 state-operated hospitals, 60 infirmaries, and 55 private hospitals, the last often quite small and antiquated. The *Anuario Estadistico* listed 156 government doctors plus about 100 private and missionary doctors, figures inadequate for a population in the millions. Duffy, *Portuguese Africa,* pp. 316-7; Saunders, *A Social History,* pp. 16-89; DHP; GEPB. *See also* Luanda Medical School; Luanda, medical services in.

medical services in Mozambique At the beginning of the Discovery (q.v.), medical services in Mozambique were deficient and limited to treatment of the Portuguese. In 1704, a small hospital was opened on Mozambique Island by Francisco de São Tomé, a Franciscan in charge of the Brothers of São João, a medieval brotherhood. In the colonial period small infirmaries were created in Tete, Quelimane, Inhambane, and other urban centers along the Indian Ocean trade routes. Early in the twentieth century, medical facilities were increased in the colony. In the 1920s, the government forced companies with more than one hundred African workers to maintain infirmaries. At the time, Lisbon took the Portuguese civil service patients from Africa to special hospitals in Portugal. In the 1950s, the number of hospitals doubled in the colony. Mozambique had fifty government hospitals, thirty-five private ones, and eighty-two infirmaries. The figures for medical staff in Mozambique were about the same as those provided in Angola (q.v.). By 1980, there were ten first-class hospitals in the Republic. HDM.

medico auxiliar indigena (Pg.) "Native auxiliary medic." African medic trained at the Luanda Medical School. First aid, nursing, and general disinfection were parts of this popular medical education. Once qualified, a medic would be placed in charge of a rural Angolan clinic, providing first aid and nursing services to families and teaching general hygiene and primary medical care. *Revista Medica de Angola,* Luanda, 1923, 2:190; GEPB.

meia peça (Pg.) The name for an African slave, male or female, between the ages of eight and fifteen and in good health; a category of slave that sold for a good price in the Brazilian markets around 1600. DHP. *See also* peça enteira.

meio-forro (Pg.) "Half-free." In Portugal c.1500 the law clearly distinguished between a free and a half-free slave. The half-free slave often was owned jointly by a husband and wife. If only one of them gave his or her consent to free the slave, the slave was legally half-free, not wholly free. DHP.

Melinde (Afr.) An ancient African coastal city across from Zanzibar. It was one of the most active ports on the Indian Ocean, trading with Oman and Calcutta. In 1498, Vasco da Gama visited Melinde and its sultan. Here the Portuguese navigator met the pilot Ibn Madjid, who guided him on the trip to Goa on the west coast of India. Around 1520 Melinde is referred to as a booming Arab trading post by Luis Camões in his book, *Os Lusiadas*. GEPB.

melon (Lat.) "Cantaloupe." This tropical vine (*Cucumis melo* L.) and its large succulent fruit. In 1506 Valentim Fernandes observed it growing in the westernmost part of the Sudan to the north of the lower Senegal. Africans and Moors grew *melon* to quench their thirst. It was observed growing in the shade of palms in Walata, an extremely hot place on the southern borders of the western Sahara, on the Niger River, and in Goa. Lewicki, *West African Food*, p. 64.

Memba (Afr.) Seaport and municipality, Nampula district, northern Mozambique, covering an area of 2027 sq. mi. (5,250 sq. km). Memba is an important agricultural and commercial center located on Memba Bay, Mozambique Channel. In 1902, the Portuguese government stationed a military garrison there. GEPB.

Memba Bay (Afr.) An inlet of the Mozambique Channel on the Indian Ocean coast, explored by the Portuguese c.1500. The bay is 7 mi. (11.3 km) across at the point where the Mecuburi, Moendaje, and Cumbo rivers empty into the ocean. GEPB. *See also* Memba.

menino (Pg.) In Guinea-Bissau around 1650, the name for the infant son of slave parents; a *menino* usually was sold in the Brazilian market as a member of a slave family unit. Carreira, *As Companhias Pombalinas,* BCG, 1968, xxiii(91/92):307.

Mensagem (Pg.) "Message." A journal of arts and literature published in Luanda, Angola. There were only two volumes, the second including numbers 2, 3, and 4, (1951 and 1952). This periodical, closed by the government, represented the renaissance of an authentic Angolan literature. Among its founders were Viriato da Cruz, Angostinho A. Neto, and Mario de Andrade, members of the group Young Intellectuals of Angola. Wheeler, *Angola*, p. 150.

mentalização (Pg.) "Mentalization." A controversial program of Portuguese political indoctrination established by General K. Arriaga to counter the independence movement in Mozambique at the beginning of the War for Independence in 1962. Its aim was to instill and maintain the patriotism and loyalty of the population to Portugal. Elite soldiers, African and European, had one hour of political drill each day. *Mentalização* began in boot camp where pamphlets and slogans were memorized and discussed. Soldiers often chanted marching songs about Mozambique being Portuguese or Africans being citizens of Portugal. In crack garrisons and units, *mentalização* was always part of the daily routine. Henriksen, *Revolution*, p. 99.

mercadoria defesa (Pg.) "Protected merchandise." Special kinds of goods imported to Portugal c.1450 and distributed under a strict royal monopoly enforced by heavy fines and corporal punishment. The large list of these goods included guns, tools, cowrie and black shells, wrought iron, clothing, upholstery, bracelets, cloth from India, brocades from Flanders, silk and cotton shirts, and many other items. This merchandise was used in exchange for slaves. Carreira, *As Companhias Pombalinas*, BCG, 1968, xxiii(89/90):12-13. *See also* resgate de escravos.

Mercantil (Pg.) "Mercantile." The third periodical published in Luanda, Angola; it was a weekly commercial magazine that first appeared on July 1, 1870. Beginning with number 1311, on October 3, 1896, it added news, features, and literary material. Lopo, *Jornalismo*, p. 57.

merceiro (Pg.) "One who prays." In Portugal at the time of the Discovery (q.v.), the term for a pious person who lived without charge in a house with the obligation of attending mass and praying for the dead relatives of his or her benefactor. Around 1450 there were many *merceiros* living in private houses in Lisbon and other cities. In 1491, Queen Leonor, the wife of King João II, established five houses for *merceiros* in Obidos, a resort town near Lisbon. At the time, she was mourning the loss of her son, Prince Afonso, who had died in an accident in 1491. GEPB.

Mesa da Consciencia e Ordens (Pg.) "Board of Conscience and Regulations." A tribunal established in Lisbon by King João III in December 1532 to seek advice on cases of conscience and morality that could not be decided by an ordinary court of justice. The tribunal, headed by prominent bishops and superiors of military orders and under the supervision of Coimbra University, held daily meetings to discuss litigation pertaining to the country. On Wednesdays they dealt with cases related to Guiné and Brazil. On August 16, 1833, it was abolished by King Pedro IV. DHP: GEPB.

mestiço (Pg.) "Mixed blood." In Portuguese Africa at the time of the Discovery (q.v.) an African mulatto, the offspring of a Portuguese father and an African mother. In São Tomé, a *mestiço* is a mixed-blood person descended from slaves brought to the island from the Gulf of Guiné, the Congo, or Angola c.1500. These mulattoes are also known as *filhos da terra* (children of the land). A Portuguese law of 1684 decreed that there was to be no distinction between Europeans, *mestiços,* and Africans. Eventually *mestiços* were incorporated into middle administrative and economic strata in the Portuguese colonial government. Hamilton, *Voices*, p. 62; Wheeler, *Angola*, p. 36(n); HDRGC. *See also* mulatto honrado e casado.

"Meter uma lança em Africa" (Pg.) "To thrust a spear in Africa." An old Portuguese saying from the time of the Discovery (q.v.) referring to the courage and bravery displayed by the Portuguese while exploring and settling Africa and converting Africans to Christianity. GDLP.

Methodist Missions The first Methodist missionaries arrived at Luanda in 1885 from Switzerland. Among the early missionaries was the remarkable linguist and ethnologist Heli Chatelain. The Methodist, Baptist, and Congregational missionaries stressed the importance of speaking Kimbundu and transcribing European and American texts into Kimbundu for the purpose of religious instruction. Chatelain and his co-workers learned Kimbundu, wrote its grammar, and published a dictionary. In 1888, the Gospel of St. John was published in Kimbundu. Reading and writing Kimbundu was part of the Christian school curriculum. In 1897, the Methodists established the Filafricana (Friends of Africa) Mission Society to spread interest in Kimbundu language, traditions, and customs. The Methodist missionaries had to deal with divisions between the Kimbundu, Ambanquistas, Bacongo, and other groups. Ironically, of the major Angolan languages, Kimbundu is the least used today. Henderson, *Angola,* pp. 149-50.

metical (Ar.) In Mozambique and East Africa, an ancient gold coin used as currency in Ormuz. In 1498, Vasco da Gama found the *metical* in use in the Arab world and determined its value to be about 880 *reis*. It was also used as a measure of weight for gold and silver c.1550; one *metical* was equal to 4.85 grams. GEPB; PDM.

mfecane (Bant.) "Time of trouble." A Zulu expression referring to periods of unrest, disruption, and crisis in their midst. One of these crises took place around 1823 when, due to population pressures and struggles for grazing land, the Zulus were forced to leave Natal and migrate to southern Mozambique. They settled for nearly half a century along the Indian Ocean coast before returning to South Africa c.1870. Henriksen, *Mozambique,* pp. 75-6.

mfumu (Bant.) A local chief in the Zambezian *prazos* around 1750. He was a kinsman and member of the dominant local lineage and in charge of resolving minor disputes, enforcing decisions of the chief, and collecting taxes. Often the *mfumu* was also the headman of an African village. Isaacman, *Mozambique: From Colonialism*, pp. xvii, 25.

Mfumu Kingdom (Bant.) An African chiefdom located at the mouth of the Espirito Santo River, Delagoa Bay, southern Mozambique. In 1554, the Mfumu king allowed the Portuguese to build a fort and a trading center in his territory. This settlement evolved into Lourenço Marques (q.v.). Internal unrest and bloody rebellions forced the Portuguese to abandon their Mfumu allies around 1700. When forces from the Province of Natal occupied the kingdom in 1888, Portugal reasserted its authority and forced the invaders to leave the region. In 1975, the People's Republic of Mozambique changed the name of Lourenço Marques to Maputo, and declared it the capital of the new nation. Henriksen, *Mozambique*, pp. 49-50.

mhondoro (Afr.) Among the Shona in Mozambique, the ancestor-spirit who is their protector and source of unity, magic strength, and invisibility in battle. The *mhondoro* often has been associated with great chiefs such as Kabudo Kagaro, who in 1900 fought the Portuguese. The Shona believed that the magic inspired by the *mhondoro* neutralized their enemies' weapons, and the death of their warriors was blamed on witchcraft. Henriksen, *Mozambique*, pp. 5, 10; Isaacman, *Mozambique: The Tradition*, pp. 67, 129, 138.

Micaune (Afr.) A Zambezian *prazo* near Chinde municipality, Quelimane district granted to the Portuguese corporation of *Correia e Carvalho* in 1870. Micaune started as a copra (q.v.) plantation in 1877, and in 1904 it was sold to the Madal Society (q.v.) who used it as its headquarters. Vail, *Capitalism*, p. 120.

middle passage The name for the voyage of slave ships from the West African coast to Pernambuco, Brazil, and the Caribbean, first begun c.1525. The middle passage was also the second leg of a trade triangle originating in Europe or North America. This long trip was first conducted by Spain as early as 1517. Early in the sixteenth century, the Portuguese had a monopoly on the Guinean (African) slave trade, forcing England, France, and Holland to buy slaves from them. Apparently the first organized cargoes of Benin slaves shipped from São Tomé to Santo Domingo and Puerto Rico took place in the 1530s. The Portuguese control of the middle passage phase was constantly challenged by the other European powers and in the early eighteenth century, after they had lost the slave monopoly to England, they still enforced their monopoly on slave transportation. Garfield, *History*, p. 36.

Mignon, O (Fr.) "The Darling." A humorous illustrated weekly published in Lourenço Marques, Mozambique. It first appeared on February 23, 1902, and suspended publication late the same year. It reappeared on April 21, 1905, as a news and political weekly. The magazine was closed by the government on May 19, 1905. Dias, *A Imprensa*, p. 67.

migração definitiva (Pg.) "Definitive migration. " In Angola, the internal movement of families and individuals from rural areas to urban centers where they settled permanently. After the move their ethnic and family ties were weakened and eventually the migrants merged into the colonial society. In the 1920s, this population movement was intense, particularly to Lobito, Huambo, and Nova Lisboa in southern Angola. According to the 1950 census in the Luanda district, there were 117,195 newcomers representing a 152 percent increase over the 46,500 migrants of 1940. Caetano, *Os Nativos*, p. 31.

migração internacional (Pg.) "International migration. " In Mozambique, the seasonal international migration of Mozambican laborers to work under contract in the Witwatersrand gold fields in South Africa, on Rhodesian farms, and in other neighboring countries. This massive movement was supervised by the Portuguese government. Caetano, *Os Nativos*, p. 26.

migração legalizada (Pg.) "Legal migration." In the 1920s, a legalized seasonal migration of African laborers to neighboring countries supervised by government officials. It required documentation, health examinations, absence of no more than six months, payment of the state tax, and the deposit by the employers of a part of the salary in a "special system" payable to the laborer once he was back in his village. Caetano, *Os Nativos*, pp. 37-8. *See also* migração temporaria.

migração temporaria (Pg.) "Seasonal migration." In Portuguese Africa, a transient migration of African laborers within the same region, province, or to neighboring countries to work in the mines or on farm harvests. It was supervised by the government, but not as stringently as the *migração definitiva* (q.v.). Caetano, *Os Nativos*, pp. 31-2.

mi-imbu (Kimb.) "Folk song." In Angola, a traditional Kimbundu song with repetition of the beginning two or more words; a kind of poetry which according to H. Chatelain constituted a typical folk poetry in the colony c. 1880. Ervedosa, *Itinerario*, p. 12.

milando (Afr.) "Violation of the law." In Zambezia, Mozambique, and in Central Africa, the disregard of local regulations by merchants. They often avoided inspections of merchandise and payment of taxes along trade routes.

The local chief and his council examined any allegations of violations and, if the merchant were found guilty, pronounced sentence. Around 1870 these violations led to bitter quarrels. Newitt, *Portuguese Settlement,* pp. 151, 383. *See also* madonto.

Military Coup of 1974 in Lisbon *See* Lisbon, Military Coup of 1974 in.

millet Tropical cereal grasses (*Panicetum* spp.) used for food and fodder that are related to New World maize, or corn, (*Zea mays*) but much more drought tolerant. Millet, a annual that produces abundant foliage and fibrous root systems, was widely cultivated in northern Sudan and West Africa from the tenth to the sixteenth centuries, after which it was somewhat eclipsed by maize (q.v.). In medieval Arabic literature, in early Portuguese sources, and in reports of explorers and travelers of the nineteenth century, millet appears under various names, often hard to identify. In West Africa there are two common types of cultivated millet, *Panicetum typhoideum,* commonly known as bulrush millet, and *P. miliaceum,* plus another maize relative, guinea-corn (q.v.), also known as sorghum (*Sorghum vulgare*). Lewicki, *West African Food,* pp. 23-4.

millet dos negros (Pg.) "Millet of the Negroes" or guinea-corn. A tropical grain (*Sorghum vulgare*) found in West Africa, where it is grown for food. Since the fourteenth century, it has been cultivated by the Berbers in North Africa. It is grown either using available rainfall or under irrigation. Valentim Fernandes reported finding it grown by Africans on the Senegal River in 1506. This cereal is related to New World maize, or corn, (*Zea mays*), as is true millet (*Panicetum* spp.). In the fifteenth century, Arab writers called it *banj as-Sudan* (wheat of the blacks) and gave details for cultivation similar to that for maize. Lewicki, *West African Food,* p. 26; HDRGC. *See also* millet.

Mina, Costa da (Pg.) Name given early in the Discovery (q.v.) to the West African coast from Sierra Leone to the Gulf of Guiné. This territory was granted by King Afonso V to the wealthy Lisbon merchant Fernão Gomes in 1469. The grantee had an exclusive trade monopoly for five years to all this region except the Cape Verde Islands and Arguim (qq.v.). Prestige, *The Portuguese Pioneers,* pp. 184-5, 207.

mindele (Kimb.) In the Kimbundu language in Angola, the term for a white or swarthy person. As a sign of respect, Africans applied this term to a *mestiço* or African dressed as a European. GEPB.

Mindello (Afr.) Seaport and resort in northwest São Vicente Island, Cape Verde, founded c.1550. The Portuguese essentially ignored it for centuries until 1838 when the Marquis Bernardo Sa da Bandeira (1795-1876) declared Mindelo a city and the capital of the Cape Verde archipelago. In 1850, the British consul John Randall obtained a government license to establish a coaling station there to serve ships sailing between England and Brazil. By 1870, it had a population of 17,000. In 1970, its population was 28,000. It is also called by its Portuguese name of Porto Grande. HDRGC; WNGD.

Misambadzi (Afr.) A *prazo* in Mozambique that was a center of the slave trade. Its holder traveled to the interior of the continent to barter cloth, beads, alcoholic beverages, and firearms for slaves and ivory. Isaacman, *Mozambique: The Africanization*, p. 53.

Misericordia (Lat.) "Mercy." The Misericordia was a lay brotherhood dedicated to serving the poor, the sick, and pilgrims during the Middle Ages. These *homens bons* (good men) also maintained shelters and infirmaries and provided aid to the needy in cities and towns. In 1380, the government authorized the Misericordia to open a public hospital in Lisbon, administered by the Trinitarian Order. During the maritime expansion in the fifteenth century, the Misericordia expanded its social services in Portugal, Africa, and elsewhere. Despite this expansion, this brotherhood kept its tradition of being a lay association, supporting its services by private funds and donations and, after the sixteenth century, by government subsidies. The Misericordia and the *Senado de Camara* (q.v.) were the pillars of the Portuguese colonial society, remaining unchanged until 1822. Boxer, *The Seaborne*, p. 273-4, 278; DHP; GEPB. *See also* Misericordia in Luanda. Misericordia in Zambezia.

Misericordia in Luanda A Misericordia (q.v.) hospital and its social services was established in Luanda as early as 1580 by Paulo Dias de Novais. It was supported by private and, later, government funds. The Misericordia in Luanda also had a share in the slave trade. Gabriel, *Angola,* pp. 88-9; *See also* Misericordia, Misericordia in Zambezia.

Misericordia in Zambezia The Misericordia (q.v.) was introduced into Zambezia, Mozambique, in 1555. As was the case in Portugal, this lay institution supported its social services with contributions from its members and friends. In Mozambique it also held *prazos* to support and extend its social services. In 1830, the society leased the Tirre *prazo* on the condition that the brotherhood sublease it to the Velasco family. This was necessary because as early as 1600 church charitable institutions had been forbidden to rent land. Gabriel, *Angola,* pp. 88-9; GEPB. *See also* Misericordia, Misericordia in Luanda.

Missão Africana (Pg.) "African Mission." A weekly that promoted religion, published in Beira, Mozambique. Its first issue appeared on October 3, 1931, and its last on July 27, 1940. Its directors were Martinho da Rocha Barbosa, Antonio Ribeiro, and Joaquim Marques. Dias, *A Imprensa*, p. 100.

Misside (Afr.)   Among the Islamic Fulas in Guinea-Bissau, a group of hamlets built around a mosque, headed by an *almami* (q.v.). Mota, *Guiné Portuguesa*, I:279.

Missombo (Bant.)   An Angolan prison camp for political prisoners located near Serpa Pinto. Its inmates included Methodist ministers, Catholic catechists, merchants, professionals, and politicians. In September 1966, there were 468 prisoners in Missombo with 132 of them working under supervision in the Serpa Pinto community. Wheeler, *Angola*, p. 270. *See also* Tarrafal.

Missongue (Afr.)   An African settlement, capital of the Barué Kingdom. Between 1880 and 1900, it was a center of political activities. Protected by a network of *aringas* (q.v.), it had a small factory that provided guns for the kingdom and its allies. In 1902, the Portuguese captured Missonge and took its king prisoner. Isaacman, *Mozambique: The Tradition,* pp. 53, 55, 68.

mi-soso (Kimb.)   In Angola, a traditional oral story of marvelous and supernatural content using the adventures of anthropomorphic animals to teach children moral values. Ervedosa, *Itinerario,* p. 11. *See also* ma-lunda.

mitete (Afr.)   In Mozambique, a voluntary ritual to make oneself slave to a master, usually a chief, headman, or other influential African. The ceremony, a symbolic act of servitude carried out in silence, included breaking domestic utensils, tearing clothes, and destroying other belongings. It was common in the eighteenth century. Newitt, *Portuguese Settlement,* pp. 190-1, 383.

mizimu (Afr.)   In Zambezia, Mozambique, the spirit of the ancestor believed to be the protector and guide of the chief. A number of religious ceremonies were performed on the chief's behalf to obtain the blessing of the deities. Around the 1880, it was believed that pleasing the *mizimu* was crucial for the well-being of the chiefdom and its people. Isaacman, *Mozambique: From Colonialism*, pp. 26-7.

MLEC (*Mouvement pour la Liberation d'Enclave de Cabinda*) (Fr.) "Movement for the Liberation of the Cabinda Enclave," a nationalist party organized in 1962 in Brazzaville, Congo, by Luis Ranque Franque. Its goal was the independence of Cabinda, an idea rejected by the MPLA (q.v.), the most powerful Mozambican nationalist group. The MLEC, inspired by F. Yalou, president of Congo-Brazzaville, was accused of being a tribal faction. Marcum, *The Angolan Revolution*, I:24-5, 173.

MLG (*Movimento de Libertação da Guiné*) (Pg.) "Movement for the Liberation of Guiné," a nationalist group headed by François Mendy Kankola, based in the Manjaco ethnic community in northwest Guinea-Bissau. The MLG, one of the most militant parties, began attacking Portuguese positions in Guinea-Bissau in 1961 and were responsible for breaking relations between Portugal and Senegal. In 1962, the movement joined forces with FLING (q.v.). It was dissolved in 1964. HDRGC.

MNR (Mozambique National Resistance) A terrorist organization established in 1974 by foreign security forces in Arare, Zimbabwe. Among its founders was Ken Flowers, former head of Rhodesian Central Intelligence. Their members included agents of PIDE, anti-FRELIMO (qq.v.) fighters, and South African "special forces." It began a bloody guerilla war against Mozambique in 1977. The MNR indiscriminately attacked schools, hospitals, villages, and economic development facilities in the countryside. From 1981 onward, the problem of this armed banditry, sponsored by the South African government, has increasingly come to dominate public thinking about Mozambique. The war, waged mainly against defenseless rural people, has brought famine and misery in its wake to all parts of the country. A disturbing first-hand account of the suffering of the people of Southern Mozambique by Inia Magoia is found in *Dumba Nengues* (Riches Abandoned), published in Maputo in 1987 by Cuadernos Tempo. Darch, *Mozambique,* pp. xx, 140, 142, 196; Hanlon, *Mozambique: Revolution,* pp. 219, 228-30.

Moçambique (Afr.) "Mozambique." The organ of the League of Defense and Propaganda of Mozambique, published in Lourenço Marques, Mozambique. Its first issue appeared on January 1, 1931; its last in May, 1946. Its owners were Ramos da Silva and Acacio Silva. Dias, *A Imprensa,* p. 86.

Moçambicanismo (Pg.) "Mozambicanism." The name for a literary movement that embraced the collective voice of Mozambican poets and writers expressing social concern for African traditions and values; they tried to express in new stylistic forms the essence of an African spiritual and intellectual world. Hamilton, *Voices,* p. 195.

Moçamedes *See* Mossamedes.

Mocasambo (Afr.) Around 1750, a slave acting as the leader of a slave gang and closely associated with his master, the holder of a *prazo* in Zambezia, Mozambique. In raids and in war, the *mocasambo* took part in looting and burning and the capture of slaves to be sold at fairs and to outside merchants. In peaceful times the *mocasambo* collected taxes and supervised the work done by other slaves on the estate. In 1760, in an inventory of two large

prazos, Cheringoma and Gorongosathe, each had twenty-eight *mocasambos.*
Newitt, *The Portuguese Settlement,* pp. 146, 196-7, 383.

Mogadishu (Ar.)   Seaport about 720 mi. (1,160 km) south of the Horn of
Africa on the Indian Ocean, first visited by the Portuguese in 1509. It was a
stone-built city, already prosperous, trading cloth, spices, ivory, gold, and
wax with Aden (q.v.) and the Indian settlement of Cambay. In 1975, it had
a population of 349,245. Today Mogadishu is the capital of Somalia.
Axelson, *Portuguese in South-East,* p. 70; WNGD.

Moïse Noir (Fr.)   "Black Moses." In Angola, an Afro-Christian cult
organized c.1920 that opposed missions and the colonial government. It was
a syncretic religion that tried to spread Garveyism (q.v.) in Africa. Newitt,
Portugal in Africa, p. 132.

Mombasa (Afr.) Island and seaport off the southern coast of Kenya, 150 mi.
(235 km) north of Zanzibar at the mouth of a deep bay. Believed to have been
settled by Arabs in the eleventh century, it was visited by Vasco da Gama in
1498. In 1593 the Portuguese built the famous Fort Jesus which even today
is used for offices by the Kenyan government. In 1698, the Portuguese left
Mombasa and in the eighteenth century it was subject to Oman rule. Between
1887 and 1907 it was a British protectorate. GEPB; WNGD.

Mondlane University   Formerly the University of Lourenço Marques,
founded in 1962 by the Portuguese government. It was organized according
the official Portuguese program and had the same rights to award degrees and
privileges as Portuguese universities. Many professors were transferred to
there from Portugal. In 1962, there were 540 students; that number rose to
1,852 by 1983. In 1987, it was renamed Mondlane University by The
Peoples' Republic of Mozambique. Darch, *Mozambique,* p. 224; HDM.

Monomatapa Dynasty (Afr.)   The dynastic title of the rulers of a Shona-
speaking kingdom in modern Zimbabwe (q.v.), formerly Southern Rhodesia.
During the sixteenth and seventeenth centuries, Portuguese traders along the
East African coast obtained gold and ivory from the kingdom. In Europe, the
Monomatapa earned the reputation of being the head of a powerful and
wealthy African state, believed to have been established by Karanga Bantu
people. The name *Monomatapa* is widely used in Central Africa but with
various spellings, including *Muenemutapa, Mwene Mutapa,* and *Munhumtapa.*
Isaacman, *Mozambique: From Colonialism,* pp. 3, 4-7, 8-10; DAHB.

monsoon A seasonal wind with heavy rains found in various latitudes in the
Indian Ocean and southern Asia. It generally blows from the southwest in the

period from the latter part of April to the middle of October. There is a counter, dry wind from the northeast from the middle of October to April. On April 24, 1498, Vasco da Gama and his squadron sailed from Mombasa to India borne on the southwest monsoon and guided by Ibn Madjid, an Arab pilot. They anchored in Calcutta on May 18, 1498. This was the first time Portuguese navigators had sailed with the monsoon. Da Gama set out on his return voyage before the onset of the northeast monsoon and the result was a three-month crossing of the Arabian Sea, all the time sailing into the prevailing southwest winds. Scurvy so incapacitated and decimated the crew that only seven or eight men were fit to handle each ship. Axelson, *Portuguese in South-East,* pp. 27-8; WTNID.

monsoon in Cape Verde In the Cape Verde Islands, a prevailing summer wind that blows from the southwestern Atlantic toward the African continent in August-September. Its direction can depend on changes in temperature of the surrounding land surface. Carvalho e Vasconcellos, *As Colonias Portuguesas,* p. 45.

Moor The term for a dark-skinned North African Moslem, often a prisoner of war legally enslaved in Portugal early in the Discovery (q.v.) and considered chattel; sometimes manumitted by his master. In a broader sense, the term for the Arabs who occupied the Iberian peninsula, including much of Portugal, in the eighth century. They were expelled from Lisbon by King Afonso I in 1147 Saunders, *A Social History*, p. xiii.

mopané (Afr.) In Angola, a common broad-leaved tree (*Copalifera mopané* Kirk) having two bent leaflets on a single petiole. This tree provides dense shade for people and animals. In the northern veld of South Africa, it forms extensive and monotonous forests. It also grows in Cunene in northern Namibia, Mossâmedes in southern Angola, and elsewhere. Its trunk produces a reddish blood-colored resin called Congo copal. Ficalho, *Plantas Uteis,* pp. 160-1. *See also* copal.

Mopeia (Afr.) A *prazo* located in the Zambezia, Mozambique. At one time an opium plantation, it was leased by Ignacio J. Paiva Raposo in 1877. The lessee introduced coconut palm, groundnut, sorghum, millet, rice, and other agricultural crops. In 1890, Mopeia was modernized by bringing machines from Europe and soon became the most important plantation in Mozambique. After 1940, persistent labor shortages and African unrest culminating in the War for Independence (1961-75) destroyed its economy. Mopeia lost its role as a successful example of an African capitalist venture and prosperous corporation. Vail, *Capitalism,* pp. 60-2, 99-100, 353-4, 403; GEPB.

morabeza (Crio.) "Kindness." A *Crioulo* (q.v.) expression considered to be characteristic of the Afro-Portuguese culture of Cape Verde. Local poets such as Manuel Ferreira in his book *Morabeza* (Lisbon, 1958) analyzed the expression and concluded that it represents an ethnic theme rooted in the community ethos. Hamilton, *Voices,* pp. 238, 350, 426.

morgado (Pg.) In Portugal, an entailed estate. *Morgados* were often formed by businessmen returning from Africa and elsewhere. One of those business-men was Antonio Coelho Guerreiro who was established in Angola between 1678 and 1705 and, on his return, invested part of his fortune in a *morgado*. Boxer, *The Portuguese Seaborne,* pp. 326, 389.

morna (Pg.) A nostalgic dance song peculiar to Cape Verde, originating at the end of the nineteenth century. Although the *morna* is Cape Verdian Creole folk music mixed with European forms, many critics, including Jean-Paul Sartre, have preferred to see the *morna* as an expression wholly Lusitanian in origin; others have argued that the *morna* is similar to the Martinican *beguine* and the Brazilian *João Conde*. Such local poets as Eugenio Tavares, in his book *Morna* (Lisbon, 1932), and Manuel Ferreira have found in *mornas* deep inspiration based on a traditional ethos rooted in an Afro-Portuguese context. Hamilton, *Voices,* pp. 244, 249, 350.

Morocco At the time of the conquest of Ceuta by King João I in 1415, Morocco comprised several Islamic states that often fought among them-selves. King João's son, Prince Henry (1394-1460), opened the western coast of Africa to commerce and trade, especially slave trade. In 1445, Gomes Pires concluded the first transaction with the Idzagen (q.v.) on the Rio do Ouro by exchanging African slaves for European goods. The first West African trading center taken from the Arabs by the Portuguese was Arguim (q.v.) on the Atlantic coast. Saunders, *A Social History*; GEPB.

morocunda (Mand.) In Guinea-Bissau towns, a quarter or ward populated exclusively by Mandingos. Since the earliest Portuguese contact in the fif-teenth century, Mandingo merchants have traded in Fula and Hausa settlements and in each town they form a close community. Mota, *Guiné Portuguesa,* I:283.

Mossâmedes (Pg.) An area explored by the Barão of Moçâmedes, governor of Angola in 1785-6. It comprised a stretch of desert coast 200 miles (320 km) south of Benguela. From the Atlantic coast where the sand ends, a plateau rises sharply to the east. The southern part is bordered by the Cunene River. In 1840, the town of Mossâmedes, also spelled Moçamedes, was founded to honor the baron. Wheeler, *Angola,* pp. 2-4, 20.

Mossãmedes, Companhia de (Pg.) A company chartered by the Portuguese government in 1894 to cultivate a large and mainly barren stretch of land along the southern frontier of Angola. The company could not survive because much of the area was occupied by warlike peoples. The terms of the concession were changed in 1923, and the company established a cattle ranch. Clarence-Smith, *Slaves, Peasants*, pp. 17-8.

Mossel Bay A seaport and bay on the Indian Ocean south of Cape Town, South Africa. The area was explored by the Portuguese navigator Bartolomeu Dias in 1488 and by Vasco da Gama, who named it *Aguada do São Bras*, in 1498. Explorer João da Nova built a chapel there, the first Christian place of worship in South Africa, in 1501. In 1970, it had a population of 15,574. Its main activity is the harvest of oysters and mussels, whence its name. Valkhoff, *Miscelanea*, p. 268; WNGD.

Mossuril (Afr.) Town and municipality, Nampula district, Niassa province, northern Mozambique. In 1750, the Portuguese built a fortress to defend the settlement against attacks by the Macuas, but it was burned by Africans in 1775. In the 1890s Joaquim A. Mouzinho de Albuquerque organized several campaigns in Mossuril against rebel African chiefs and finally pacified the area in 1896. Today it is an agricultural and commercial center. GEPB.

Mother Angola Name coined in Brazil after troops led by Salvador Correia de Sá reconquered Angola in 1648, driving out the Dutch invaders. After that time the colony became the main source of slave labor for the sugar plantations in Brazil. Portuguese and *mestiço* traders organized military campaigns into the interior of the colony to capture and buy slaves for the New World market. By a royal decree signed of 1758, the monopolies were rescinded and all Portuguese subjects were entitled to trade in slaves and goods between Angola and the other African colonies and Brazil through the ports of Rio de Janeiro, Bahia, and Pernambuco. Silva Rego, *O Ultramar*, pp. 62-3, 164-5.

Mourimi (Afr.) A Messianic movement that appeared in southern Mozambique during the devastating famine of 1913-14. It was an Islamic cult mixed with witchcraft, fetish worship, and Christian practices. Africans thought the famine was due partly to the defeat of their chief, Gungunhana, by the Portuguese and partly to sorcerers. In the 1950s, the Mourimi cult reappeared in the Maghrib (q.v.) and West Africa. Gonçalves, *O Mundo Arabo-Islamico*, pp. 33-4; Newitt, *Portugal in Africa*, p. 130.

Mouvement pour la Liberation d'Enclave de Cabinda *See* MLEC.

Movimento Afro-Brasileiro para a Libertação de Angola *See* MABLA.

Movimento Anti-Colonialista *See* MAC.

Movimento de Libertação da Guiné *See* MLG.

Movimento Popular de Libertação de Angola *See* MPLA.

Moxico (Afr.)   A district, Bié province, southern Angola; Vila Luso is its capital. It was explored in 1794 by José de Assunção e Melo, an Afro-Portuguese merchant from Benguela. This easternmost district of Angola, situated between the Cuanza, the Lungue-Bungo, and the Luengue-Lumana rivers, was visited by David Livingstone in 1843. In 1895, many exiles settled in the area. Moxico was pacified and brought under government control around 1905. GEPB.

Mozambique, abolition of slavery in   *See* slavery, abolition of, in Mozambique.

Mozambique African National Union   *See* MANU.

Mozambique, agriculture in   Until 1790, traditional African farming, based on staple food crops, fruits, and vegetables, was the dominant form of agriculture. Before that time, Mozambican contact with the outside world was limited to Lourenço Marques and the clandestine slave ports. After 1790, more modern agricultural practices were implemented with the establishment of an official agency in charge of introducing new crops and European techniques. Since 1850, the major cash crops have been cotton, sisal, cashew nuts, copra, *afurra* (a kind of tomato), sugar, rice, manioc (q.v.), maize, groundnuts, tobacco, and sorghum, most intensively cultivated for export. Inland agricultural areas are located mainly in the highland region north of the Zambezi River, and south to the Sabe River. The richest inland centers are in the river valleys where a plentiful supply of water is assured. Duffy, *Portuguese Africa,* pp. 2-3, 102; Herrick, *Area Handbook,* pp. 202-4. *See also* Angola, agriculture in.

Mozambique, Captaincy General of   A military division established in 1577 to govern the colony; before that time it was a dependency of the viceroy of Goa in Portuguese India. From 1837 to 1975, the colony was renamed the Overseas Province of Mozambique. The captaincy had jurisdiction over Inhambane, Sofala, Sena, Zambezia, and Cabo Delgado. Boleão, *Moçambique,* pp. 149-57; Silva Rego, *O Ultramar,* p. 192.

Mozambique Channel   The strait between the Malagasy Republic (formerly Madagascar) and the Mozambique coast. It is about 625 mi. (1000 km) at its widest. Portuguese navigators explored this area in 1506, and in 1525 it was forbidden to sail along the channel, possibly due to the danger of the many shoals along the coast. In 1530, there were reports that the channel was marked in the wrong latitude. Axelson, *Portuguese in South-East,* pp. 109, 198; WNGD.

Mozambique Company A corporation organized by Portuguese traders in 1891 to promote agriculture, commerce, and industry, to exploit mines, and to build a railroad in the Manica and Sofala districts in Mozambique. With initial capital of £40,000, it was supposed to pay the government 5 percent of the net proceeds of the mines and 5 percent of the profits of the subcontractors. Its charter expired in 1942. Axelson, *Portugal,* pp. 133-45; WNGD.

Mozambique Current A warm ocean current flowing from the Indian Ocean south through the Mozambique Channel (q.v.), past Natal (hence also called the Natal Current), and along the coast of the Cape Province of South Africa, where it is known as the Agulhas Current; off Cape Agulhas, it is deflected to the left and flows southeast toward Australia. It is believed to have a decided effect on the climate of the Cape Province. WNGD.

Mozambique, diocese of From the Discovery (q.v.) until the beginning of the seventeenth century, Mozambique was part of the archdiocese of Goa. In 1612, Pope Paul V declared it a *Prelatura Nullius* with a prelate as administrator. The first appointed prelate of Mozambique, Dr. Domingos Torrado, governor of the archdiocese of Goa, died before he could take possession. In 1782, Queen Maria I nominated the Dominican friar Amaro José de Santo Tomas to be bishop of Mozambique. He was confirmed by Pope Pius VI the following year. Since that time, all prelates were consecrated bishops. The first seat was in Sena but in 1780 it was transferred to Mozambique Island. In 1940, a concordance signed between the Portuguese government and the Holy See created three dioceses: Lourenço Marques, Beira, and Nampula. Brasio, *Historia e Misionologia,* pp. 555, 562; GEPB.

Mozambique, discovery and settlement of In 1487 Pero Covilha was the first Portuguese to arrive, by way of Cairo, at Sofala on the Mozambique coast in search of Prester John, the legendary Christian king of Ethiopia (q.v.), and to obtain information about the lucrative Indian spice trade. In 1498, Vasco da Gama touched Inhambane and stopped at Mozambique Island, Kilwa, Mombasa, and Malindi. He found a sophisticated Arab-Swahili trading society, ports filled with ships, and well-built towns. As a result of da Gama's trip, in 1515 Portugal decided to take Sofala. Once conquered, they established their trade center on the Mozambique coast. Soon the Portuguese exercised authority over Mombasa, Kilwa, and Malindi and controlled navigation on the Indian Ocean. Originally the entire area of East Africa from the Cape of Good Hope to Mombasa was administered as part of Portuguese India, governed by the viceroy in Goa. In 1752, Portuguese East Africa became an independent captaincy. The Dutch and English established fortified trading centers on Delagoa Bay in 1750, and the Portuguese built the fort of Lourenço Marques in 1782. The city of the same name became the capital of the colony and, after independence in 1975, the capital of the country under its new name, Maputo. Kaplan, *Area Handbook,* pp. 22-3, 28-9, 32.

Mozambique, diseases in Early Portuguese sailors fell victim to scurvy, the result of vitamin C deficiency, during the long trip to the Indian Ocean. Vasco da Gama's crew, in Malindi c.1498, discovered that oranges appeared to cure some tropical fevers endemic in the area. In 1530, in the trade center of Sofala, it was reported that about 370 Portuguese had died of tropical diseases. When it was discovered that Mozambique Island was healthier than mainland Africa, many colonists settled there. By 1570, in addition to scurvy and malaria, the Portuguese had identified such serious maladies as trypanosomiasis, various intestinal disorders, tuberculosis, leprosy, and the almost always fatal bilharziasis (schistosomiasis). Axelson, *Portuguese In East-Africa,* pp. 8, 30, 65, 150; Herrick, *Area Handbook,* pp. 120-1.

Mozambique, education in Since 1500, in Mozambique and elsewhere in Portuguese Africa, Portuguese missionaries were responsible for the education of colonists and Africans. In the Indian Ocean coastal towns, Jesuits and Dominicans maintained schools and hospitals where Europeans and Africans were cared for. Whatever cultural advantages the Africans achieved from 1500 to 1900 were gained almost exclusively through the guidance of Catholic mission schools. Until 1534, all missionaries in Mozambique were under the jurisdiction of the Diocese of Funchal (q.v.) in Madeira. With the establishment of a bishop in Goa that year, supervision of educational activities in East Africa came from India until 1783 when Mozambique became a prelacy. Goan Dominicans settled in the Monomatapa Kingdom in 1590, establishing missions and schools. A number of the king's royal youngsters, including a son baptized Filipe Domingos, as well as other aristocratic youths prepared themselves for the priesthood at the Dominican seminary in Goa. The majority of them, captivated by the cosmopolitan glitter of Goa, remained there; those who returned to Mozambique did not notably contribute to the spiritual progress of their people. The Jesuits had a college on Mozambique Island from 1610 to 1760, when they were expelled by the government, acting on orders from the Marquis de Pombal. After the Jesuits left, there was a near-absence of educational opportunities in the colony for over a century. In modern times, the University of Lourenço Marques was founded in 1963 by the government, but to complete their studies and earn a degree, students had go to Portugal. The Organic Law of 1972 (q.v.) established that the purpose of education in Mozambique and elsewhere was to foster a sense of national identity with Portugal and to produce the skilled technicians and professionals needed for economic development. Duffy, *Portuguese Africa,* pp. 47, 85, 108-112; Herrick, *Area Handbook,* p. 91.

Mozambique, evangelization of Vasco da Gama's fleet of 1498 had several priests, but they did not do mission work. In 1500, Alvares Cabral's fleet carried a number of Franciscans who served as chaplains in several forts and trade centers on the Indian Ocean coast. The Jesuit St. Francis Xavier, on his journey to India and China, visited Mozambique Island in August 1541. Goncalo de Silveira, a Portuguese Jesuit, was the first to work in Zambezia and the Monomotapa Kingdom (1560-61). Despite great initial energy, over the years missions declined. In 1760 the Jesuits were expelled on orders from the Marquis de Pombal. By 1806 there were reports of other orders having become corrupted by the wealth acquired from holding large *prazos* (q.v.). Duffy, *Portuguese Africa,* pp. 46-7, 85; Brasio, *Historia,* pp. 547-8.

Mozambique, fairs in Seasonal gatherings of people for barter and trade gold, ivory, cloth, and slaves was an old practice among Arabs and Africans along the Indian Ocean costal towns. Long before the arrival of Vasco da Gama in 1498, Swahili-speaking merchants traded over vast areas of East Africa and Malawi. In 1630 the first *prazos* were established and from 1750 to 1850 fairs appeared along the Zambezi River. Traders and colonists also organized seasonal fairs. During the winter from May through July, important fairs operated in Sena, Tete, Zumbo, and Manica. These were large gatherings that included Africans, Arabs, Goans, and Portuguese. New goods such as cloth, iron tools, firearms, spices, grain, and forest products were added to the pre-Portuguese merchandise. Under the *Junta do Comercio* (Commerce Ministry), represented locally by the *Fazenda Real* (Royal Treasury), the fairs were organized to coordinate with the monsoon season and the local harvest schedule. Profits of 200 and 300 percent were frequently realized. The Zumbo fair was the most famous of all. In 1860, David Livingstone reported that Bisa traders from Angola would come to Zumbo to trade ivory, rubber, and other items. Isaacman, *Mozambique: From Colonialism,* pp. 12-3, 75-9; GEPB.

Mozambique, forced cotton cultivation in In the 1930s, the Portuguese *Estado Novo* (New State) under President Antonio Salazar reinforced the policy of forced cotton cultivation in the colony by passing the Native Labor Law. In 1938, the Cotton Export Board began rigidly enforcing the labor code with a strictly imposed work schedule. At the beginning of this crackdown, a chief organized his crew to work a small field. From 1942 onward, each married couple was forced to cultivate an 8x8 m cotton field. The wives of men in the armed forces were exempt, as were those of the cotton oveseers, but the wives of migrant laborers in South African gold fields were not. Cotton cultivation occupied eight months of the year, from January to August. In Mozambique, local workers were obliged to work three days a week on their cotton fields under the overseers' supervision. If production was too low, the person could be beaten or imprisoned and punishments were severe. The number of people brought into cotton production in Mozambique was enormous; by 1944, it reached 791,000, later stabilizing at around one-half million. This modern feudal system so weakened farm workers' ability to produce their own subsistence crops that, in parts of Inhamane, many suffered acute hunger according to the Rt. Rev. Sebastião Soares de Resende, Bishop of Beira. Munslow, *Mozambique,* pp. 36-7.

Mozambique, forced labor in In Mozambique and elsewhere, forced labor was dictated by the economic needs of the colonists. The choice to work or not to work, given to the Africans by the Native Labor Code of 1878, was radically revised by 1898, when a legislative committee headed by Antonio Enes made recommendations establishing forced labor as necessary for "the moral and intellectual advance of the Africans" and the economic development of the colony. Europeans viewed the discipline of regular labor by Africans as a compulsory step toward the goal of their attainment of European values and "civilized" ways of life. In 1891, the Mozambique Company (q.v.) required male Africans to work on its sugar plantations and on public works carried out in its settlements. Women were forced to grow cotton and other cash crops but were allowed to sell their products to the company. Forced labor was legal throughout the company's territory and the company did not hesitate to use it. As an extra measure it set the hut taxes so high that Africans had to work for extremely long periods just to pay them. Conditions were even more cruel on the lands managed by the Nyassa Company (q.v.), which received its charter in 1891 but was not fully functional until 1893. Africans resisted when they could and many fled to Nyassaland and Tanganyika. When abuses became intolerable, Africans in Mozambique revolted. Between 1890 and 1905 there were at least sixteen uprisings in the Zambezia valley alone. In 1961 and 1963, legislation was passed establishing forced cultivation of commercial crops and repealing laws that mandated the moral obligation of Africans to work. The Rural Code of 1962 replaced the Native Code of 1928 which forced Africans to work on government construction projects under certain conditions and imposed penal labor for failure to observe the provisions of a labor contract. Herrick, *Area Handbook,* pp. 258-60; Kaplan, *Area Handbook,* pp. 41, 44-46, 49.

Mozambique, German invasion of At the outbreak of World War I, Portugal tried to remain neutral, but in 1916 the decision was made to enter the war on the side of the Allies. Germany briefly invaded northern Mozambique in November 1917, withdrawing its forces in September 1918. Newitt, *Portugal in Africa,* pp. 40-1.

Mozambique, governors of   Portuguese occupation of present-day Mozambique began in 1505, when they built a fort in Sofala (q.v.) to trade with the interior for gold. Until 1752, the governors were appointed in Goa. After that time and until the 1970s, they were appointed by Lisbon. After the Portuguese revolution in 1974, Mozambique has advanced rapidly to self-government, with full independence achieved in 1975. DAHB.

Mozambique Institute   A secondary school established by Eduardo Mondlane and his American wife Janet in 1963 in Dar es-Salaam, Tanzania. Its aim was to prepare Mozambican students for higher education abroad and to teach nursing and other skills to secondary school students. The institute was conceived as the apex for the FRELIMO (q.v.) educational system. It enjoyed success in obtaining aid, securing foreign instructors, and placing students abroad. Dissatisfaction with the curriculum and with the slow progress of the War for Independence, and uneasiness about Mrs. Mondlane's control over the school and her alleged ties to the CIA caused disagreements between students and teachers and the eventual failure of the institute. Henriksen, *Mozambique,* pp. 177-78.

Mozambique, Islam in   Islam came to the East African coast around the year 800 AD by Arab traders along the coast and took strong root in the north. When Vasco da Gama arrived at Mozambique in 1498, he found a sophisticated Islamic society along the Indian Ocean coast in commercial towns such as Sofala, Mombasa, Kilwa, and Malindi. Arabs controlled the trade in gold, silver, cloth, cloves, pepper, ginger, ivory, pearls, and slaves. Swahili (q.v.) was spoken along the coast and the trade routes into the interior of Mozambique. In Malindi, da Gama met and hired the famous Arab pilot Ibn Madjid, whose services he secured to travel to India. Angoche, Sancul, and Quitangonha in the northeast became important bastions of Islamic resistance to Portuguese penetration. Today it is estimated that there are more than two million Moslems scattered throughout the northern part of the country, the northeastern coast, and the hinterland, especially among the Yao (q.v.); the center and the southern parts of the country have practically no Moslems. Axelson, *Portuguese in South-East,* pp. 25, 27, 213; HDM.

Mozambique Island   An island in the Indian Ocean coast, 200 mi. (322 km) north of the Zambezi Delta, where the Portuguese built a factory and a fort in 1507. In 1508, Portugal strengthened the fort with a battery of guns. Soon it became the center of the colony's government replacing Sofala. In 1763, after

Mozambique was separated from Goa, it became a city and municipality. Newitt, *Portuguese Settlement,* pp. 33; GEPB.

Mozambique, land tenure in   Before the arrival of the Portuguese in Mozambique in 1500, Africans occupied and cultivated the land according to ethnic custom. Africans did not own land because in their cultures land had no economic, only communal, value. The clan or lineage collectively controlled and assigned plots and hunting and fishing grounds to families. The Portuguese introduced a land system based on European legal principles. According to Portuguese law, the land was owned by the Crown, but it was leased to individuals or families for a fixed number of lifetimes. This practice was the basis of the *prazo* or estate system. Along the Zambezi River, the most typical lease of a *prazo* was for three lifetimes with the possibility of renewal. During this time the successive leaseholders were free to develop their holdings to the maximum. These estates, where the holder exercised judicial authority over the holding's inhabitants, were known as *prazos da coroa* (q.v.) and the leaseholders as *prazeros.* After independence in 1975, the constitution of the People's Republic of Mozambique stated that the country's land and subsoil were the property of the state, which determines its development and use. Although personal property is also recognized and foreign capital enjoys some protection, the government clearly indicated that, at least in the short term, private property was to be replaced by collective, socialist ownership. Kaplan, *Area Handbook,* pp. 27, 90, 143; GEPB.

Mozambique, languages in   Contemporary scholars divide the linguistic map of Mozambique into nine major African languages: Makua-Lomue, Marawi, Maconde, Yao, Nguni, Tsonga, Shona-Karanga, Chopi, and the Sena cluster in the Lower Zambezi. In addition, there are three non-African languages: Portuguese, English, and Afrikaans (q.v.). In 1969, the African languages spoken in radio broadcasts were Shangana and Ronga (Tsonga group), Makua, Makua-Medo, Chuabo, and Seneca (Lower Zambezi cluster). Herrick, *Area Handbook,* pp. 182-5; Kaplan, *Area Handbook,* pp. 84.

Mozambique, migrant labor in   Since the discovery of the Witwatersrand gold fields in South Africa in 1884 and the commencement of mining operations in 1886, Mozambique has provided the highest proportion of laborers to work in the mines. Between one-quarter and one-third of the total Mozambican work force was annually exported to South Africa and other adjacent countries. South of the Zambezi River, a class of workers was formed and a transport infrastructure was built to facilitate the easy flow of men to and from the mines. Broadly, one can distinguish two periods of migration: the first from 1886 to 1925, the time of mining hegemony; the second from 1925 to the 1975, marked by the dominance of manufacturing and the emergence of South Africa as an industrial power. Apart from a brief period during the Great Depression (1930-39), every year between 80,000 and 115,000 Mozambicans worked in the Transvaal mines. The mine labor organization had an extensive recruiting network throughout Mozambique so that Africans could reach a Witswatersrand Native Labour Association (WNLA, q.v.) station within twenty-four hours of leaving their *kraal* (q.v.), no matter where the latter was situated. Herrick, *Area Handbook,* 258-9; Munslow, *Mozambique,* pp. 16, 26.

Mozambique National Resistance *See* MNR.

Mozambique, People's Republic of The former Portuguese East Africa became the People's Republic of Mozambique in June 1975 when it proclaimed its independence. Its first elected president was Samora Machel, the leader of the *Frente de Libertação de Mozambique* (FRELIMO, q.v.). Lourenço Marques, the former colonial capital of Mozambique, was renamed Maputo, the capital of the new republic. WNGD.

Mozambique, refugees from In 1987 it was estimated that 80,000 to 130,000 Mozambican refugees were in Johannesburg and Soweto, South Africa. In fact, this was a latter-day organized slave trade. People who were sold described themselves as *izigcila* (slave in the si-Tonga language). For about $100, these Mozambican victims of the war between the government and RENAMO (q.v.) could be bought as concubines, slave laborers, or for *muti* (body parts needed for ritual sacrifice). Andersson, *Mozambique,* p. 126-7.

Mozambique Revolution A magazine in English published by FRELIMO (q.v.) which first appeared on December 1, 1963, the day after the most successful stevedore strike in the history of the port of Lourenço Marques, staged to protest Portuguese colonial policy. Throughout the War for Independence, *Mozambique Revolution,* a polished publication, pleaded for international help and was instrumental in exerting heavy pressure by both Communist and non-Communist countries on Lisbon. Its editorials and war documentation were an outstanding testimony to the dedication of those who waged the long struggle for independence. Henriksen, *Revolution,* pp. 41, 125, 184; Munslow, *Mozambique,* pp. 75, 112.

Mozambique, slave trade in *See* slave trade in Mozambique.

Mozambique, slavery in *See* slavery in Mozambique.

Mozambique, trade with India Since 1600, the Mozambique-Indian maritime trade was controlled by the Banyans (q.v.), a Hindu caste of merchants centered in Dio, India. First settled on Mozambique Island and, in 1750 in Maputo, these energetic traders monopolized the commerce in gold, ivory, cloth, iron, wheat, cotton, and foodstuffs by organizing the Manzanes Company (q.v.). All through the colonial period there were protests against the Banyans, and Portuguese merchants tried unsuccessfully to compete with them. Silva Rego, *O Ultramar*, pp. 96-7, 326-9.

Mozambique-Transvaal Convention An international agreement between the Portuguese government and Transvaal Province, signed in 1909. It regulated Mozambican laborers migrating to work in the South African gold mines. The colony received a bonus for each worker crossing the frontier plus a percentage of his wages at his return. These payments were in gold in South Africa, but in Mozambique, were in *escudos*. In the currency conversion, the workers lost half of their original salary. Vail, *Capitalism*, p. 202. *See also* Tete Agreement.

Mozambique, War for Independence in   African nationalists, whose protests were fueled by forced labor laws, inadequate education and health care, internal censorship, and police control, organized a formal opposition to Portuguese rule in the colony. In June of 1962, several groups met in Dar es-Salaam, Tanzania, under the sponsorship of President Julius Nyerere of Tanzania and other leaders, and organized the FRELIMO (q.v.) movement with Eduardo C. Mondlane as its first president. The armed struggle began in September 1967 with forces led by Samora Machel attacking Tete and the Maconde Plateau. The Portuguese army was forced to retreat south and east of the region. The nationalists, well trained in Marxism and guerrilla warfare, crossed the Zambezi, bringing the war close to Beira. On April 24, 1974, the Lisbon government was overthrown by a military coup and the war came to an end on September 7, 1974, with a peace agreement signed in Lusaka, Zambia. A few days later, FRELIMO Defense Chief Alberto J. Chipande entered Lourenço Marques (now Maputo). Kaplan, *Area Handbook*, pp. 4952, 193-4.

Mpinda (Bant.) A town and seaport on the south side of the Congo River in the territory of the Old Congo Kingdom. This was the scene of the first important slave trading in the region c. 1510. By 1550, Portuguese ships were taking African slaves at the rate of some 10,000 a year to São Tomé, the Brazilian markets, and elsewhere in the New World. Wheeler, *Angola*, pp. 30-1; GEPB.

MPLA (*Movimento Popular de Libertação de Angola*) (Pg.)   "Popular Movement for the Liberation of Angola," the main urban-based Angolan political party organized in December 1956 in Luanda, Malanje, and Benguela by a group of Portuguese-African Marxists. Its leadership was drawn from elite Angolan intellectual exiles and Angolan students attending foreign universities. Headquarters were opened in Conakry, French Guinée (1960), Leopoldville (now Kinshasa), Zaire (1961), and Brazzaville, Congo (1963). The MPLA's main sources of aid were the Soviet Union and Eastern European countries. In 1962, at the First National Conference in Leopoldville, Antonio A. Neto, a physician and poet, was elected president, a position he held until his death in 1980. In 1962-74, guerrilla offices were opened up in the Cabinda, Moxico, Malanje, Bie, and Cunene districts. Factionalism caused by ideological and personal divisions were a constant problem. In November 1974, a Luanda office was opened and started organizing the movement in the urban Mbundu area. In 1975, Angola became independent and Antonio A. Neto was chosen president. In December 1977, the first Party Congress was held in Luanda. It declared that Angola was a Marxist-Leninist nation. Marcum, *The Angolan Revolution,* 1:29-31, 43-46, 94100; HDA.

mtolia (Bant.)   In Mozambique and elsewhere, a tropical shrub (*Landolfia kirkii*) that yields an edible fruit and latex used to manufacture rubber. Since 1873, it has been cultivated on the Luabo and Mopeia *prazos* by such pioneers as I.J. de Paiva Raposo and his son-in-law J.P. Hornung. A commercially profitable plant that later was taken to Zambezia, it is also called *matatubonsu.* Ficalho, *Plantas Uteis*, p. 217.

muave (Afr.)   A toxic beverage extracted from the bark of a tropical tree (*Tanghinia venerifera* Dup.). Found in Zambezia, Mozambique, Angola, Congo, and elsewhere in Portuguese Africa, it is used in ordeals. A sorcerer forces an accused individual to drink *muave* to prove his innocence or guilt. This beverage is prepared by combining ground bark with water. If taken in small amounts, it is purgative and induces violent peristalsis and the defendant dies immediately of cardiac arrest. If taken in large quantities, it is emetic, causing vomiting, and the accused survives. Portuguese law punished this practice as a serious crime. Ficalho, *Plantas Uteis,* pp. 164-5; Isaacman, *Mozambique: From Colonialism*, p. 15. See also esere, tanguin.

mucanda (Kimb.)   In Angolan tradition, a message or order sent by word of mouth by a new chief to his people. *Mucanda* became popularized in Angolan poetry at the time of the War for Independence (1960-1975) when they became a series of poetic messages from nationalist leaders to the soldiers, asserting a collective optimism of winning the war when defeat seemed imminent. The Angolan poet Geraldo Bessa Victor published *Mucanda* (Braga, 1964) in which he conveys a message of hope and victory in a time of hardship and despair. Victor felt that the new Angola would be a nation enriched by mingling African and Portuguese values. Burness, *Fire,* pp.35-9; Hamilton, *Voices,* pp. 51-2.

mueia (Afr.) In Angola, a mid-size tropical tree (*Terminalia sericea*) yielding a compact yellowish hardwood timber considered very valuable for furniture and construction. It grows in forests at high altitudes in Huila and in dry areas such as Ambaca and Pungo Andongo. Ficalho, *Plantas Uteis*, p. 179; GEPB.

muenga ia muchito (Afr.) "Tree of the forest." In Angola, a wild tropical tree (*Bosquea angolensis*) with spreading branches. After cutting, its wood turns from yellow to pink; used for construction, cabinet work, and torches. It also bears edible fleshy fruit and seeds. Ficalho, *Plantas Uteis,* p. 269.

mukomowasha (Afr.) A Barué royal adviser and, often, the interim ruler when there were problems over the succession to the throne. In the nineteenth century, King Samaconde and King Hanga sought the advice of their *mukomowasha* before making important government decisions. Isaacman, *Mozambique: The Tradition,* pp. 52, 54.

mulato honrado e casado (Pg.) "Honest and married mulatto." In São Tomé, an expression referring to honest *mestiço* citizens who could be elected members of the city council. In 1535, the council requested King João III to allow these residents to serve on the municipal board beginning in 1540. Tenreiro, *A Ilha*, p. 67.

mulattitude (Pg.) In the Cape Verde Islands and elsewhere, the consciousness among mulattoes of their cultural heritage, together with an affirmation of the distinctive qualities and values of this heritage in an ambivalent Portuguese society. It is also an expression of norms of behavior shaped through experience and education; neither white nor black, just mulatto, a new personality born from both cultures. Around 1530, when a mulatto appeared on stage in Lisbon, he was always educated, spoke fluent Portuguese, and behaved according to accepted norms. Hamilton, *Voices,* pp. 14, 15, 251; Saunders, *A Social History*, p. 101. *See also* negritude.

mulemba (Afr.) A handsome evergreen tree (*Ficus verruculosa* Warb.) with strong branches and abundant leaves. Its small cherry-like fruit are eaten by Africans and its brightly colored roots are used in medicine. Modern Angolan writers consider the *mulemba* a symbol of a lyric African identity associated with feelings of sadness, nostalgia, and disillusionment. Ficalho, *Plantas Uteis*, p. 267; Hamilton, *Voices,* pp. 8, 114.

multiracial theory The notion of building in Africa and elsewhere a multiracial Christian society; held, if not always adhered to, by the Portuguese nation from the time of the Discovery (q.v.) to 1960. Under the regime of President Antonio O. Salazar, from 1930 to 1960, this traditional policy was proclaimed and pursued by the *Estado Novo* (New State). In the 1960s several English-speaking scholars violently rejected this tenet. They argued that multiracialism extended to only a few thousand people in coastal settlements yet "was something that commended universal approval among the Portuguese governing class" of the time. These scholars also felt that the myth of racial harmony in the African territories had its basis in the fact that Portuguese men freely coupled with African women. To this, the Portuguese answered that from 1436 to 1974 the Lusitanian nation had enforced a civilizing mission and had carried out the historic function of colonizing Africa and spreading among Africans the benefits of its Christian civilization. And if its aims did not always become reality, it did not render invalid such "civilization." The fact is, five newly independent Portuguese African nations kept the Portuguese language and culture, and they enjoy a racial harmony unknown in South Africa and other English-speaking African countries. Munslow, *Mozambique,* pp. 7-8; GEPB.

mungaba (Afr.)   In the nineteenth-century *prazo* society in Mozambique when *prazo* slaves were organized into an occupational hierarchy, a female slave, chief of a gang of female slaves either living in a village compound or in seasonal mining camps. Isaacman, *Mozambique: From Colonialism,* p. xvii. 54.

muntu (Kik.)   Person, man or woman, living or dead, in São Salvador do Congo around 1880. Jahn, *Muntu,* pp. 100-1; BeAD.

musitu (Afr.)   A fortified bush hamlet first developed by anti-Portuguese Africans in the Zambezia area around 1600. It was comprised of a group of huts surrounded by thorny shrubs and wooden stockades, protected mainly by its isolation and difficult terrain. It was a precursor of the *aringas* (q.v.) built in the eighteenth century to protect the *prazos* and African villages in the Zambezia region of Mozambique. Isaacman, *Mozambique: The Tradition,* p. 26.

mussambaze (Afr.)   A professional African trader, an old institution in Zambesia, possibly predating the arrival of the Portuguese in the region in 1550. Around 1760 *mussambazes* were active in the Zumbo territory. They entered the Portuguese colonial service and, at the same time, traded on their own behalf in the regional fairs. The Portuguese often referred to the *mussambazes* as their slaves, but this specialized class of traders was anything but servile and never hesitated to make their own livings at the expense of their employers. Newitt, *Portuguese Settlement,* p. 78; GEPB.

musseque (Afr.)   Slum districts surrounding Luanda and other African cities. In 1922, when High Commissioner Norton de Matos cleared out one section of African huts from a European residential area, a contemporary observer in Luanda called this proper social hygiene, claiming that in this residential pattern local and foreign Africans became Europeanized. In the 1960s, there were dozens of *musseques* in Luanda inhabited by several hundreds of thousands of Angolans and refugees from other African colonies. It is also spelled *muçeque.* Wheeler, *Angola,* p. 70; Hamilton, *Voices,* p.227; GEPB.

Mussungo   One of three large *prazos* established on the coastline north of Quelimane, Mozambique, after 1750. This was a low-lying area dotted with Islamic coastal towns. Mussungo *prazo* was established by Dona Maria da Guerra c.1750, but she had neither property deed nor developed the land by 1777 when she died. After her death, the *prazo* was taken by a new grantee. Newitt, *Portuguese Settlement,* p. 87.

mutopa (Afr.)   A pipe used by Angolans to smoke hashish extracted from the tropical plant *Cannabis sativa.* Often the *mutopa* is smoked in groups, with each individual inhaling three or four times. The hashish produces intoxication and, in large doses, hallucinations; it is habit-forming and induces sickness. Ficalho, *Plantas Uteis,* p. 264.

muxiri (Afr.)   A handsome tropical shrub with clusters of woolly flowers that grows wild along the banks of the Cuanza River and elsewhere in Portuguese Africa. In Pungo Alto, Angola, it is cultivated by local farmers for its sweet roots which are mixed with millet and sorghum to make a popular beer. Ficalho, *Plantas Uteis,* pp. 140-1.

muzinda (Afr.)   A *kraal* (q.v.) or settlement where an African chief resided protected by a *prazero* in Zambezia, Mozambique, c.1700. Here the local chief was the center of government and exercised military, political, religious, and judiciary power. The term *muzinda* appears throughout the Zambezia region. Isaacman, *Mozambique: From Colonialism,* p. 25.

muzungo (Afr.)   A Portuguese, prominent and well respected, living in a rural village in the Zambezia region of Mozambique. In the nineteenth century, it specifically meant a member of a class of old Zambezian *prazo-*holders. These men married African women, adopted African names and customs, practiced a folk religion, and dressed as Europeans. At the time, they held power, wealth, and political influence in the *prazo* society. Newitt, *Portuguese Settlement,* pp. 141, 384; GEPB.

Muzungo Romão (Afr.)   A praise song popular around 1890 among the canoemen of Romão de Jesus Maria, beloved holder of the Marral *prazo,* Quelimane, Mozambique. His men would greet him on his return home with a song that went: "Muzungo Romão has arrived, and he is going to Marral, *e-e*. Muzungo Romão *ofia, e-e*. No Marral *odoa, e-e*." Vail, *Capitalism*, p. 167. *See also* Paiva song.

mwene (Afr.) An African headman in charge of governing a village in the Zambezia around 1890. It was one of several positions in a bush society with the authority to distribute land and exact taxes and with power over village and family life. The *mwene* was someone who could use, or abuse, his people, usually with impunity. The term appeared in Mozambican songs of protest and rebellion until independence in 1975. Vail, *Capitalism,* pp. 25, 74, 350.

Mwene Mutapa Dynasty *See* Monomotapa Dynasty.

"My son is *mestiço* by the grace of God!" A remark made by a white male Portuguese, an official of the Luanda government, who around 1950 married an African woman from Mutano, Angola. He was referring to his mulatto first-born son. Goermaere, *Le Portugal*, p. 53.

Naboangongo (Afr.)   A large territory of Angola province west of Encoje and southeast of Ambriz, crossed by the Lifune and Hongo rivers and inhabited by the Dembo people. In 1759, the Dembo attacked the São José de Encoge fort, built to protect the area. GEPB.

Nacala (Afr.)   Town and municipality in Nampula district, Niassa province, Mozambique; it includes the towns of Itoculo and Netia. The region is rich in timber and produces beans, manioc, groundnuts, sesame, and cotton. The county seat is Nacala, located on Fernão Veloso Bay, an area explored by Portuguese navigators around 1560. GEPB.

nagana (Afr.)   An infectious encephalitic disease of horses and cattle, common in tropical Africa. It is caused by a trypanosome (*Trypanosoma brucei*) transmitted by the bite of infected tsetse flies. It is prevalent in dense bush near rivers and in open woodland areas of Mozambique, Angola, and other sub-Saharan countries. GEPB.

Nagusa Nagast (Ethiop.)   "King of Kings." Title given to Prester John by the people of Ethiopia (q.v.). This information was reported to King Manuel I of Portugal in 1520 by his ambassador, Rodrigo de Lima, who had traveled there in 1518. *Nagusa* is also spelled *Negus*. Cortesão, *History*, I:272.

nahni (Crio.)   "Misery, starvation." A term used in Cape Verde to refer to the famines caused by prolonged droughts in the islands. The resulting shortages of food forced people to migrate. *Nahni*, not the endemic tuberculosis or syphilis, causes the greatest suffering and death among the islanders. Carreira, *The People*, p. 219.

naka (Afr.)   In Angola, a traditional agricultural method used to cultivate a low field seasonally flooded by a nearby river. Mendes, *Cabela*, Garcia de Horta, 1974, 2(1):53.

nakaka (Afr.)   Among the Islamic Manjaco community in Cacheu, Guinea-Bissau, the first of multiple wives. She is in charge of household chores and the education of the household's children. Guerra, *Terras da Guiné*, p. 72.

Nakuru Agreement   The result of a summit meeting held by Angolan revolutionaries Holden Roberto, Agostino Neto, and Jonas Savimbi in Nakuru, Kenya, June 16 to 21, 1975. The leaders discussed and signed an accord to have "A peaceful transference of powers in Angola at the time of independence." This much-publicized meeting, presided over by Kenyan president Jomo Kenyatta, in fact did not bring peace. On the contrary, it signaled the beginning of seventeen years of bloody civil war. Henderson, *Angola,* p. 250. *See also* Lisbon Accord.

nalombo (Mak.)   Among the Makonde in the Tete district, Mozambique, a priestess who performed the female puberty initiation ritual. This took place at the end of a long seclusion in a secret place in the bush where the young girls danced, prayed, and roared, imitating lions to terrorize the other participants. Led by the naked *nalombo,* the older women sing, dance, and utter obscenities. At the climax of the ritual, drums are played and the priestess deflowers the girls with a pottery phallus. *Nalombos* still performed these rituals in the second half of the twentieth century. Dias, *Portuguese Contribution,* p. 53.

Nalus (Afr.)   In Guinea-Bissau, an ethnic Senegambian group Islamized by the Mandingos. In the fifteenth century they settled in the Bissago region on the Atlantic coast. Now they are concentrated near the modern town of Catio in eastern Guinea-Bissau where they cultivate rice. HDRGC.

Namacunde (Afr.)   A town and administrative post in Baixo Cunene municipality, Huila district, southern Angola. This was an area of unrest and violence until Portuguese forces took control of the territory in 1915 and established the town of Namacunde, later connected by rail with Vila Pereira de Eça. GEPB. *See also* Ngiva.

nambwa (Kik.)   A fetish consisting of a stick shaped like a cone used in the hope of securing good luck in rat hunting in São Salvador do Congo, Angola, c.1880. BeAD.

não indigena (Pg.)   "Not indigenous." Expression used in Mozambique in accordance with a 1954 statute to refer to a "civilized" African who was baptized, spoke Portuguese, had attended school, and served in the government or the army or was self-employed. Henriksen, *Mozambique,* pp. 126, 127; GEPB.

Napraprama (Afr.)   The name of a group of pro-government African fighters in Mozambique during the civil war between the government and

RENAMO (q.v.). It is said that these young Africans fought with sticks and slings and, by using magic and incantations, turned their enemies to stone. In reality, the Napraoranas chased RENAMO's soldiers from areas the government, using automatic weapons, had been unsuccessfully trying to recapture for years. Because witchcraft appeared to be so effective, its practice gained the support of the people. Andersson, *Mozambique*, p. 61.

Nampula (Afr.) A district in northern Mozambique. Its town seat, created in 1946, has the same name. The Holy See organized a diocese with a resident bishop there in 1948. Nampula district had a population of 103,985 in 1960 and such modern facilities as paved streets and a railroad. In 1980 the population had risen to 2,402,700. Today it is a prosperous commercial and industrial center with well-developed agriculture, gold mines, forestry, and game. GEPB; WNGD.

Natal A coastal city on the South African-Mozambican border in an area discovered by Vasco da Gama on December 25, 1497, which he named *Terra Natalis* (Nativity Land). The tropical climate along the level coast favored the production of crops, especially sugar and tobacco, and the Portuguese founded a settlement on a nearby bay on the Indian Ocean coast. Around 1550 they built a fort and established a trade center that they named Lourenço Marques, now Maputo. In 1684 the Dutch established a commercial post in Natal. The British annexed the area in 1843 and in 1856 made Natal a Crown Colony. In 1910 the colony became a province of South Africa. By 1967 it had a total population of 3,419,000. CE; GEPB.

Native Labor Code A Portuguese law to protect contract laborers in the South African mines, promulgated in Lisbon on December 6, 1928. It contained 428 articles regulating labor contracts, salaries, nutrition, housing, central and local labor offices, penalties, and other matters. It was a radical revision of the law of 1898 which was the outgrowth of a legislative committee headed by Antonio Enes that made recommendations establishing forced labor as necessary for "The moral and intellectual advance of the Africans" and the economic development of the colony. Cunha, *O Trabalho Indigena*, pp. 201-02. *See also* Mozambique, forced labor in.

Native Recruiting Corporation *See* NRC.

Native Statute A law promulgated by the Portuguese government in 1954 that defined the political and legal status of local Africans and the requirements necessary for aliens to obtain citizenship in the colonies. Herrick, *Area Handbook*, p. 141; GEPB.

native tax A tax instituted in 1908 in Angola by the Portuguese government. It mandated that the head of each African family pay a tax to raise revenues. Its purpose was to force Africans into the money economy by paying in currency. Before this time, Africans used shells, salt, cloth, and goods, the traditional means of exchange, to meet their obligations. By 1928, each African male head of family paid an annual tax of 80 *angolares*, equal to 100 days of labor. In 1945 this tax was raised to 100 *angolares*. Many Africans preferred to flee to the Belgian Congo and Southern Rhodesia rather than pay these taxes. Those who stayed had to work even harder under oppressive labor contracts. Henderson, *Angola*, pp. 119-20. *See also* palhota tax.

nativism and revivalism In Portuguese Africa around 1930 there were organized efforts on the part of Africans to create a more satisfying spiritual life and cultural environment. Both nativists and revivalists wanted to return to an idealized former era of happiness, a supposedly golden age. These leaders aimed at purging the society of unwanted foreigners and reviving the nearly forgotten Bantu gods. In contemporary Portuguese Africa, both nativists and revivalists are still active. GEPB; IESS. *See also* Kimbanguism, Mourinism.

nativos extra-união (Pg.) "Non-unionized natives." A category of illegal laborer coming from various regions of Mozambique to work in the Transvaal gold mines. Attracted by the high wages paid in the Rand mining area, the numbers of illegal migrants working in South Africa steadily increased, reaching 80,000 by 1928, 100,000 by 1940, and 185,479 by 1956. These workers were not protected by labor laws regarding payment, health care, housing, or transportation facilities. Rita-Ferreira, *O Movimento Migratorio*, pp. 91-2.

natu (Kik.) In Angola c.1880, a small gift given to a shaman or medicine man by his patient. BeAD.

nau (Pg.) A broad, heavily built but lightly gunned merchant ship of about 400 tons with a large, well developed forecastle and aft. This class of ship was used from the time of the Discovery (q.v.) to the eighteenth century. By the middle of the sixteenth century, the size of a *nau* increased to between 600 and 1,000 tons. They were also called carracks or galleons. Boxer, *The Portuguese Seaborne*, p. 207.

nautical astrolabe A simplified instrument to measure the altitude of the stars. It was developed by Portuguese navigators at the time of the Discovery (c.1450). Made of wood or brass, it was useful for both astronomic and geographic measurements. The oldest description of a Portuguese nautical astrolabe appeared in 1528 in *Repertorio dos Tempos* by Valentim Fernandes. In the eighteenth century, the nautical astrolabe was replaced by the sextant. Costa, *A Marinha dos Descobrimentos*, pp. 21, 22.

navigational manual *See* regimento do astrolabio.

N'Dau A Mozambican ethnic group that allied with RENAMO (q.v.) in the civil war against the government. They believed in the power of magic and enlisted sorcerers and witches to impart courage and fearlessness to the fighters. They used charms, spells, and rituals, claiming that these would make the men immune to bullets. The N'Dau played an important role in fighting the war. Andersson, *Mozambique*, pp. 62, 169.

ndembu (Bant.) (1) The term for an African chief who was in charge of protecting trade routes in the Matamba Kingdom (q.v.) c.1630. At the time, Queen Nzinga of Matamba opened a road from just west of her kingdom to the Atlantic on which to transport groups of hundreds of slaves to the coast for transport to the Brazilian plantations. Miller, *Nzinga of Matamba*, JAH, Cambridge, 1975, 16(2):212.

Ndembu (Bant.) (2) A secret society organized around 1960 among the Bacongo (q.v.) people of northern Angola. It was a syncretic organization that combined political struggle for independence with messianic goals. This movement was a revival of a seventeenth-century anti-Catholic, anti-missionary attempt to create a church for Africans. Pelissier, *La Colonie*, p. 163. *See also* kimpasi.

ndendo (Bant.) In the Golungo Alto forest, Angola, a tropical tree (*Diospyros dendo* Welw.) that yields a hard heavy white wood with a beautiful black center. The wood is used for construction and furniture. Ficalho, *Plantas Uteis*, p. 212.

ndjele, ti- (Ron.) A musical instrument consisting of a gourd filled with seeds or stones that when shaken produces a rapid succession of sharp, clattering sounds. It is popular among the Rongas of southern Mozambique. DRP.

ndoma (Bant.) In Mozambique, a lip-plug worn for personal decoration by Makonde men and women. This fashion is said to assure submission and enchantment among lovers. In a hole in the upper lip they place a stick resembling a hen feather and in the lower lip they insert a large lead cork, so heavy that it turns the lip inside out almost to the chin. A fashion still common as late as 1961, mainly among women. Dias, *Portuguese Contribution*, pp. 38-39.

ndomba (Bant.)   The term for a Bantu labor society composed of married men who hired themselves out as temporary workers to earn money c.1890 at a time of great change in the Sena plantation system. The introduction of the sugar economy put economic pressure on traditional institutions like the *ndomba*. Vail, *Capitalism*, p. 72. *See also* nomi societies.

Ndongo (Bant.)   A sixteenth-century chiefdom ruled by an Ngola (q.v.) that covered a vaguely defined territory between the Dande and Cuanza rivers. The Portuguese considered its chief to be the second most powerful ruler in the western region of Central Africa. Birmingham, *Trade and Conflict*, pp. 29, 30-1; GEPB.

ndungu (Bant.)   In Angola and elsewhere, the leaves of the *molungo*, a New World tropical shrub (*Capsicum* spp.). Its fruit, the chili pepper, is widely used as a condiment by Africans. Also called *malagüeta*, chili, Cayenne pepper, and *poivre de Guinée*. Ficalho, *Plantas Uteis*, pp. 230-1.

Negritude (Fr.)   An African ethnic revival stressing a conscious awareness of cultural heritage, together with an affirmation of the distinctive values of their ancestors. This revival inspired a literary movement that first appeared in the French colonies c.1950. It expresses a sense of racial and cultural identity, stressing an awareness of shared humiliation and suffering based on skin color, years of slavery, and exploitation by dominant social groups. Poets like the celebrated African Martinican, Aimé Césaire, and others plunged to the depths of collective misery and despair, exacerbated by the suspicions of demoralized Africans themselves that they were accused of being inferior. This movement soon extended to the Afro-Portuguese colonies, including Brazil. The writers and poets of *Negritude* agreed that only by contemplating the Africans' past and their present abasement could they foment the anger necessary to overcome their passive dejection. The early aggressive tone of *Negritude* was later softened and the later writers discovered the positive aspects of rhythm, sensuality, mystery, and the communal feelings of the African world that embraces all things including the person himself. The movement, stressing a surrealist approach to literature, has been one of the most important African literary movements of our time. Preto-Rodas, *Negritude*, pp. 3-5; GEPB.

negro (Pg.)   "Black." A term used since at least the time of the Discovery (q.v.) to signify an African, specifically a person with dark skin, thick lips, and kinky hair, all considered unattractive features by Europeans at that time. It also meant misfortune and sadness. During the Middle Ages many Europeans believed that black was the color of the devil's skin. The first African slaves brought to Lagos, Portugal, in 1444 were described as "so deformed in their faces and bodies, that they almost seemed to emerge from the lowest hemisphere [of Hell]." In modern times, the term *negro*, and especially its pejorative derivatives, can be considered offensive. Saunders, *A Social History*, pp. xii, 167; GEPB.

Negro, O (Pg.) "The Negro." A short-lived periodical published in Lisbon by a group of Luso-Angolan *mestiços* to promote Angolan interests, including improved public education, health care, and workers' condition. These young Angolans apparently were under the influence of Marcus Garvey and his Back to Africa Movement. This periodical, believed to be the organ of the *Partido Africano* (q.v.), first appeared on March 9, 1911, and published three issues. Pelissier, *La Colonie*, p. 223.

negro barbado (Pg.) "Bearded black." A term used in West Africa c.1760 for a young bearded slave between 15 and 20 years old. This type of slave would sell for a high price in Brazil. Carreira, *As Companhias Pombalinas*, BCG, 1968, xxxiii(91/92):306.

negro boçal (Pg.) "Rude, or ignorant, black." An idiom c.1650 referring to an "uncivilized" slave, baptized but uneducated and unable to speak Portuguese. NDLP.

negro ladino (Pg.) "Cunning black." Early in the Discovery (q.v.) in Portugal, a slave who spoke Portuguese and was a skillful artisan. GEPB.

Negus *See* Nagusa Nagast.

ne-ko-o (Afr.) Among the Mandingos of Guinea-Bissau, a tropical tree (*Spondias purpurea* L.) brought to Africa from South America by the Portuguese. It bears edible fruit and a powder from its ground leaves is used to treat conjuntivitis. Also called red mombin. Carreira, *Mandingas*, p. 243.

NESAM (*Nucleo dos Estudantes Secondarios Africano de Moçambique*) (Pg.) "Mozambican Secondary School Students' Group." An association founded in 1948 in Lourenço Marques. Among the founders of NESAM was Eduardo Mondlane (1920-1969) who was studying at the time at Witwatersrand University in South Africa. The group's main objectives were to improve educational opportunities for Africans, to preserve cultural identity, and to end colonial abuses. Its official organ was the magazine *Alvor* (Dawn). When some of the students also joined FRELIMO (q.v.), the secret police became suspicious of NESAM and arrested several members. In 1964 the government banned the association. Henriksen, *Revolution*, pp. 18, 180; Munslow, *Mozambique*, p. 66; HDM.

neto (Mand.)   Name given by the Manidingos of Guinea-Bissau to the African locust tree (*Parkia biglobosa*) that bears edible seeds and whose leaves and seed pods are used for forage. Carreira, *Mandingas*, p. 133.

new man   A term used early in the Discovery (q.v.) to refer to a person of mixed racial parentage, a *mestiço* (mulatto), usually with a Portuguese father and an African mother. Large-scale misgenation began c.1480 in many of the Atlantic Islands and c.1495 in São Tomé and Angola. Tenreiro, *A Ilha*, p. 239.

New State   *See* Novo Estado.

nfingo (Bant.)   In Cabinda, northern Angola, and elsewhere in the tropics, a leguminous vine (*Abrus precatorius* L.) that bears beans that are bright scarlet with a black spot at the end. They were used in Dahomey and elsewhere on the West African coast c.1650 as a unit of weight for medicinal herbs, jewelry, and precious metals. Commonly know as the rosary pea, in Mozambique it is called *muasassa-musambere*. Boxer, *Portuguese Society*, p. 153; Ficallho, *Plantas Uteis*, p. 137.

nganga-a-moko (Kik.)   In São Salvador, Angola, a witch called to the bedside of a sick person to identify the cause of, or the individual responsible for, the illness. BeAD.

nganga-a-nazji (Bant.)   A fetish found c.1880 among Africans in the Congo, northern Angola. It was believed to have magical powers that could be used by a sorcerer to cure various illnesses. Henderson, *Angola*, p. 44.

nganga-a-ngombe (Bant.)   "Witch-finder." A sorcerer who specialized in identifying the individual responsible for having a spell cast on another. In the colonial period the *nganga-a-ngombe* was a well respected medicine man among the Xicongos in the Congo Kingdom, northern Angola. Henderson, *Angola*, p. 44.

Ngangela (Bant.)   An ethnic group settled along the course of the upper Okavango River in the central highlands of southeastern Angola. Interspersed among them are small groups of Cokwe immigrants from east-central Angola who entered the region during the nineteenth century. In the colonial period, the population density was low in this cattle grazing region although individual villages were large. The village headman, rather than the chiefs, made most of the decisions regarding local government. Matrilineal lineage appears to have been the rule except for candidates for local political office. In that instance, the Ngangela could have patrilineal succession. In the nineteenth century, scattered Ngangela villages were subject to intense

Ovambo raiding. This led to the formation of small missions under the care of the Holy Ghost fathers in the twentieth century. Clarence-Smith, *Slaves, Peasants*, pp. 11, 88.

Ngangela, missionaries in   Missionary members of the French Order of the Holy Ghost worked among the Ngangelas (q.v.) in southeast Angola in the 1880s. They settled in the region, organizing mission stations under Portuguese protection. They respected the Africans' social and cultural customs, used the indigenous languages, and maintained traditional communal land tenure and redistribution of wealth. At the same time, the missionaries introduced monogamy and insisted on a strict sexual morality. Their paternalistic rule and their belief in the natural inferiority of non-European peoples (a concept common in Europe at the time) brought opposition and later rebellion by African factions. Between 1890 and 1900, the missionaries faced open violence from bandits, forcing them to organize a militia of Christian youths. From 1910 to 1926, the Republican government of Portugal waged an official anti-missionary campaign. The *Novo Estado* (q.v.) under Salazar's direction, on the contrary, helped and encouraged the Holy Ghost fathers to intensify their educational and social work to the benefit of the Ngangela people. Clarence-Smith, *Slaves, Peasants,* pp. 17, 89-93.

Ngangela, slave raids in   During the colonial period the scattered Ngangela villages in southeast Angola were subject to frequent slave raids by such predatory peoples as the Wiko, Ovambo, Cokwe, and Luvale. Slavery was linked to the ivory and rubber trades and slaves were often used to carry merchandise to the Atlantic coast. As a result of the suppression of the Atlantic slave trade, these raids drastically declined in the 1840s. Clarence-Smith, *Slaves, Peasants*, p. 64.

ngangula (Kik.)   A skilled blacksmith in São Salvador do Congo c.1880. BeAD.

ngila-sonde (Bant.)   Name given to a tropical tree (*Pterocarpus angdensis*) with hard wood that was used to make domestic utensils, drums, canoes, paddles, furniture, and spears for war and fishing in Angola. Ficalho, *Plantas Uteis,* p. 144.

ngiló (Bant.)   In Angola, the name for the tropical cultivated eggplant or aubergine (*Solanum melongena* L.) used by Africans as a meat substitute and in salads. Ficalho, *Plantas Uteis*, p. 229.

ngimo (Bant.)   In Angola, a tropical creeping shrub (*Chrysobalanus icaco* L.) that grows wild in moist soil and flooded areas near the sea. Its red and yellow apple-sized fruit is edible. Africans obtain a resin from it that is used to repair fish nets. Ficalho, *Plantas Uteis*, p. 175.

Ngiva (Bant.)   Town seat of the Baixo Cunene municipality, southern Angola. In 1960 its name was changed to Vila Pereira de Eça. This old African village, originally settled by the Cuanhama, was occupied by the Portuguese government in 1915. It is linked by road to Benguela and Huila. GEPB.

Ngola (Bant.)   Name for the ruler of the Ndongo kingdom (q.v.), the capital of which was at Kabasa. This culture, which worshipped its chief, was located c.1550 between the Dande and Cuanza rivers. Its people possessed skills in ironwork and weaving and traded within the chiefdom and with foreigners. Around 1660, the Portuguese forced them to move beyond the Cuanza into the interior of the colony. GEPB.

Ngola ritmos (Bant.)   "Angolan Rhythms." A musical movement made popular by Liceu, a band and vocal group founded in the 1950s by Carlos Vieira Dias. This was the first and perhaps the most telling artistic contribution to the cultural revival of Luanda. The musical compositions were inspired by folk music motifs and played on guitar and African percussion instruments with lyrics in Kimbundu. One song, *Mbiri Mbiri, Ngongo* (Ay, Ay, My Suffering) composed by Vieira Dias, in its rhythmic and melodic structure defies the stereotypic noisy, chaotic *batuque* (q.v.) label generally applied by Europeans to African music. Significantly, the words tell a story that can be understood on both a literal level of individual pain and complaint and on a symbolic plane of social protest. Hamilton, *Voices,* pp. 60, 113.

Ngoni (Afr.)   A group of Bantu settled in Natal, South Africa, around 1800. These early raiders, called *Mazitis* by the Portuguese, were led by three Ngoni chiefs: Gngwana, Nqaba, and Zwangendaha. As early as 1819 they began migrating to the Indian Ocean coast. In 1821 the first Ngoni appeared near Lourenço Marques, Mozambique. They crossed the Limpopo River and in 1824 were in the vicinity of Inhambane. They passed the Sabe River about 1826, and in 1830 they appeared in Manica and Sofala. Up to and including the present, they have retained their separate identity. In 1970 the the Ngoni numbered 35,000. They are scattered in the area south of the Sabe in southern Mozambique, in Swaziland, and along the South Africa borders. Henriksen, *Mozambique*, pp. 154, 247, 250; GEPB.

ngunza (Bant.)   The name for a prophet and religious leader among the Bacongo of São Salvador do Congo, northern Angola, c.1960. Pelissier, *La Colonie*, p. 167(n).

Ngunza (Bant.) A town in west-central Angola, formerly Novo Redondo, located 100 mi. (160 km) northeast of Benguela. In 1769, it was a *presidio* protecting the Benguela-Luanda road against attacks by local chiefs. The fortress was rebuilt and a garrison was stationed there in 1857. A paved road to Lobito, the port on the Atlantic coast, was constructed in 1928. In 1960 it had a population of 12,708. Today Ngunza is an important agricultural and commercial center. GEPB; WNGD.

Ngwila (Bant.) A messianic sect that appeared among the Bacongo in northern Angola in 1916 at a time of social unrest in the region. Around 1960, the sect became involved in the struggle for Angolan independence. Its slogan was, "Africa for the blacks, the whites are intruders." Pelissier, *La Colonie*, p. 164.

Ngwizako (Bant.) A group of traditionalists and monarchists who began working in 1961 to restore the old Congo Kingdom under a Catholic king. After the death of King Antonio II in 1957 the group, presided over by José dos Santos Kasabanga, then in exile in Leopoldville, elected and crowned Kasabanga king with the name Antonio III. This royalist party is also known as Ngwizani-a-Congo. Wheeler, *Angola*, pp. 168-9.

Nhaneca-Humbe (Bant.) An Angolan farming and cattle-herding group that settled in the Huila plateau around 1900. Politically they were pro-Portuguese and helped the government in the agrarian reform of the 1960s. Due to their isolation, they did not take part in the War for Independence of 1960-74. Pelissier, *La Colonie*, p. 12.

Nhungue (Bant.) An ethnic group settled on the south bank of the Zambezi, pacified by the Portuguese c.1580. Newitt, *Portuguese Settlement*, p. 26.

nia (Mand.) Among the Mandingos in Guinea-Bissau, the body and soul of a person, both formed in the womb of the mother. At death, the body disintegrates but the soul is immortal. All living beings whether animal or plant have *nia*. Dalafosse, *The Negroes of Africa*, p. 221.

Niassa Company A Portuguese company established in 1891 by royal charter to explore and trade in the Niassa district, northwest Mozambique. In 1897 the government occupied the territory and declared it a district, ending the trade monopoly of the company. DHP. *See also* Niassa district.

Niassa district A jurisdiction established in 1897 in Mozambique. The Portuguese had explored this region as early as 1590 and subsequently established several settlements and missions. In 1600, João dos Santos a Jesuit, visited the area and came to know local customs and traditions. He wrote an account of his explorations, included in his book, *Etiopia Oriental e Varias Historias*, published in Evora in 1609 and reprinted in Lisbon in 1891. DHP.

Niassa, Lake Now Lake Malawi, the lake and region bordered on the west by Malawi, on the north by Tanzania, and on the southeast by Mozambique. The Portuguese first explored this area in the eighteenth century. At the turn of the twentieth century the Lake Niassa region was a center of production of cotton clothing which Portuguese traders bought then sold for high prices in Tete, Manica, and other settlements in Mozambique. Newitt, *Portuguese Settlement*, pp. 27, 30, 42; GEPB.

nidcua *See* mbuemba.

Niger-Congo languages West African linguistic complex of related languages that at the end of the nineteenth century were called Nigritic languages. The current term is Congo-Kordofanian languages. This latter grouping incorporates the diverse Bantu dialects along with the major West African coastal tongues. HDRGC.

nihimo (Afr.) In Mozambique, the collective land, forests, and hunting grounds occupied by an ethnic lineage. The idea of individual ownership with rights to buy or sell was unknown but each person or household enjoyed access to land assigned and controlled by the headman of the group. In some areas at present, particularly those that are densely populated, private ownership with rights of transmission is recognized. Kaplan, *Area Handbook*, p. 87.

nixibua (Afr.) A variety of watermelon (*Citrulus vulgaris*); this tropical vine is found growing both wild and cultivated around Luanda and in seasonal watercourses in arid and sandy areas of Mossâmedes. Its edible seeds contain a valuable oil and the fruit and vines provide forage for domestic animals. Ficalho, *Plantas Uteis,* pp. 187-8.

njimbu (Kimb.) A copper coin circulated c.1893 in São Salvador do Congo, Angola. EDK.

nkandu (Kik.) (1) The second of the four days of the traditional African week in São Salvador do Congo c.1880. The others, in order, are *nsona, konzo,* and *nkenge.* Henderson, *Angola*, p. 43; BeAD.

nkandu (Kik.) (2) In São Salvador do Congo c.1880, a season when it was forbidden to hunt certain game or to catch any of several species of fish. BeAD.

nkenge (Kik.) The fourth of the four days of the traditional African week in São Salvador do Congo c.1880. The others, in order, are *nsona, nkandu,* and *konzo.* Henderson, *Angola,* p. 43; BeAD.

Nkimba (Bant.) A secret society organized in northern Angola around 1960 by the Bacongo people. It was an aggressive political group preaching messianic goals together with social justice for the oppressed African masses. It was a revival of the *Antonianos* (q.v.) who had appeared in the seventeenth century. Pelissier, *La Colonie,* p. 163.

Nkomati Accord (Afr.) A non-aggression pact signed on March 16, 1984, at Nkomati on the southern Mozambican border by Mozambican president Samora M. Machel and P.W. Botha, the foreign minister of South Africa. The purpose of the agreement, endorsed by the United States and Great Britain, was to work to end hostilities between the two countries. It recognized the differences between the two countries and affirmed that the two nations were indissolubly linked by geography and proximity. The pact was specifically directed against the African National Congress and the Mozambique National Resistance (ANC and MNR, qq.v.). Riley, *Major Political Events,* p. 186.

nkumbi (Kik.) In São Salvador do Congo c.1880, a drum used in ceremonies where libations of animal blood were poured on the grave of a great hunter. BeAD. *See also* nzabu-a-menga.

nkuta (Kik.) In São Salvador do Congo c.1880, provisions for a long voyage; also payment for a small service rendered by a relative or friend. BeAD.

nocha (Afr.) In Angola and elsewhere, a large tropical tree (*Parinarium mobola* Oliv.) having a dense, deep green foliage. During the harvest from November to January its edible strawberry-flavored fruit is consumed in great quantities by Africans. Its seeds contain a commercially valuable oil and its timber is used for construction and to make domestic utensils. Ficalho, *Plantas Uteis,* p. 175.

Nomi societies (Afr.) In Sena, Mozambique, societies of young boys and girls who, after their puberty initiation, form groups that lived together in communal villages. These were highly organized societies whose members hired themselves out to clear new land, harvest crops, and build houses and canoes. At the end of the agricultural season they used their money to hold elaborate banquets in lavish displays of wealth. Vail, *Capitalism,* pp. 71-2.

Nossa Senhora da Luz (Pg.) A small coastal settlement established by Diogo Afonso in 1500 near the Praia de Abaixo, Santiago Island, Cape Verde.

Because the port was inadequate and the area was not suitable for agriculture, the village did not prosper. Fernándes, *Description*, p. 180.

Noticias (Pg.) "News." A daily published in Maputo, Mozambique, by the *Sociedade de Noticias*. In 1926, it was the largest newspaper in the country. Its current daily press run is about 40,000. Darch, *Mozambique*, p. 283.

Novo Estado (Pg.) "New State." The authoritarian regime established in Portugal in 1926 under the leadership of Antonio de Oliveira Salazar. He emphasized a strong Lusocentric racial, religious, and cultural nationalism, proclaiming a spirit of patriotic unity that resulted in the the Colonial Act of 1933. This act ended the autonomy of the African colonies and imposed the policy of forced work enacted, according to Portugal, for the common benefit. The *Novo Estado* stressed cultural revivalism, embodied in the concept of glorifying the Portuguese past, and was run with strict central governmental control of the economic, political, and social aspects of the African colonies. Because many of its goals and methods were deeply rooted in pre-1926 tradition, the *Novo Estado* was perhaps the most powerful of all modern Portuguese governments. Angola and Mozambique were governed from Lisbon by politicians wielding an absolute authoritarism. According to some scholars, the *Novo Estado* profoundly and negatively influenced the African colonies and led to their rebellion that culminated in their independence in 1975. Wheeler, *Angola*, pp. 12, 17-8, 125; GEPB.

Nova Lisboa *See* Gabu.

Nova Oeiras (Pg.) An iron factory established in 1767 by governor F.I. de Sousa Coutinho in the city of the same name in Benguela, Angola. After the forest was cleared, roads were opened and 400 temporary houses for workers were built. Factory masters from Brazil and Viscaya, Spain, were brought in to oversee mining and to process the iron ore and manufacture finished products for export to Portugal. The project failed in 1769 due to economic problems and the sudden deaths of seven of the technicians, including the four known as the Masters of Biscayne (q.v.). Their deaths represented a great loss to the Portuguese government. Silva Rego, *O Ultramar*, pp. 185-7.

npaza *See* nphete.

npepe (Bant.) A tall tropical evergreen tree (*Monodora myristica*) bearing fruit with aromatic and edible seeds in the pulp. Its seeds, sold in the markets, are used as a condiment and stimulant and to treat stomach ailments. They are also used to make rosaries. According to F.M.J. Welwitsch (1807-1872), it is native to West Africa and was taken by slaves to the New World where it is variously called Jamaica nutmeg, calabash nutmeg, and *muscade de calabash*. In São Tomé, it is called *iobó*. Although it is aromatic, it is not true nutmeg (*Myristica fragrans* Houtt.). Almada Negreiros, *Historia*, p. 243; Ficalho, *Plantas Uteis*, pp. 79-80.

nphete (Afr.)   In Mozambique, a symbolic gift that was customary in the *prazo* society around 1750 and indicated a man's willingness to marry his prospective bride. It was also called *npaza*. Isaacman, *Mozambique: The Africanization*, pp. xviii, 45.

NRC (Native Recruiting Corporation)   A Portuguese colonial organization associated with the Transvaal Chamber of Mines. It was founded in 1896 to recruit laborers in southern Mozambique and elsewhere to work in the South African goldfields. By 1906 the NRC and Witwatersrand Native Labour Association (WNLA, q.v.) had established about 200 recruiting centers in Mozambique. Rita-Ferreira, *O Movimento Migratorio*, p. 74; ESA.

nsanga anda (Afr.)   A string of beads used as currency in São Salvador do Congo c.1880. BeAD.

nsona (Kik.)   The first of the four days of the traditional African week in São Salvador do Congo c.1880. The others, in order, are *nkandu*, *konzo*, and *nkenge*. Henderson, *Angola*, p. 43; BeAD.

nsope (Bant.)   A graceful rope-jumping dance accompanied by drums. It is performed by young girls in the Nampula and Cabo Delgado districts, northern Mozambique, usually for recreation during the rainy season when the girls do not work in the fields. Lutero, *Ethnomusicologia*, Africa Literatura, Arte y Cultura, Lisbon, 1980, II:57-83. *See also* timbila, tufo.

nsuka (Bant.)   The Bantu word for dawn, used in São Salvador do Congo c.1880. BeAD.

nsulula (Kik.)   The Kikongo word for abortion or miscarriage, used in São Salvador do Congo c.1880. BeAD.

nsunga (Kik.)   In Angola and elsewhere, any of the several species of baobab (q.v.), a tropical tree (genus *Adansonia*) bearing gourdlike fruit. In the dry season, Africans extract water stored in the fruit and in the pulpy wood. The dried pods are used for drinking cups and tobacco pipes. BeAD.

ntadala (Mak.)   A flat tract of land in Makonde territory, northern Mozambique, c.1963. RLM.

ntaka (Kik.)   A track of low wet soft land; the term for a marsh in São Salvador do Congo c.1880. BeAD.

Nucleo dos Estudantes Africanos Secondarios de Moçambique   *See* NESAM.

Nyaneka (Afr.)   A Bantu ethnic group settled in the Angolan highlands between the Cunene River and the Atlantic coast. In the sixteenth and seventeenth centuries they were established in central Angola where they grew maize and raised cattled. Very little is known about the early history of the Nyanekas, except that they were a branch of the Bantu. In the late 1880s they were mistreated by white settlers and forced to work as slaves on the plantations. Government officials and even missionaries frequently meddled in the Nyanekas' community life. They found these conditions intolerable and fled to the mountains, waging a war of resistance against Portuguese rule until the 1920s. During the War for Independence (q.v.) they again took to the mountains and fought for freedom. When Angola became an independent nation in 1975, they returned to their farming. Clarence-Smith, *Slaves, Peasants*, pp. 9, 84-6, 88. *See also* Nyaneka bandits; Nyaneka, expeditions against the.

Nyaneka bandits (Afr.)   Around 1880 groups of Nyaneka persecuted by the Portuguese authorities took refuge in the rugged territory and thick forests of the southern Angolan highlands among groups of runaway slaves, outlaws, and army deserters. The leaders of these groups, often Nyaneka chiefs, organized a guerrilla war for liberation that lasted until the 1970s. They returned to their traditional farming when Angola became independent in 1975. Clarence-Smith, *Slaves, Peasants*, pp. 85-6. *See also* Nyaneka; Nyaneka, expeditions against the.

Nyaneka, expeditions against the   Around 1880 the Portuguese army organized a formal campaign in Angola to subdue the Nyaneka guerrillas then in open rebellion against white settlers and government officials. The Nyanekas' traditional hierarchy included leaders to oppose outside intrusions into their territory and the *cipakas* (fortresses) they built in the bush became famous. Although the colonial authorities believed they had subdued them in 1900, the Nyaneka people nevertheless remained opposed to outside rule until the late 1920s. During the struggle for the liberation of Angola in the 1960s and 1970s, the Nyaneka again fled to the mountains. Clarence-Smith, *Slaves, Peasants*, pp. 86-8. *See also* Nyaneka, Nyaneka bandits.

Nyassa   English transliteration of a central African placename. *See* Niassa Company, Niassa district.

Nyassa, Lake *See* Niassa, Lake.

nyumbe (Afr.)   A magic charm thought to have the power to neutralize European bullets and other ammunition. These irresistible talismans, believed to carry mysterious religious power, were provided by sorcerers to African chiefs and their forces in the Zambezia region during the bloody rebellions from 1890 to 1900. Isaacman, *Mozambique: The Tradition*, pp. 62, 67, 129; GEPB. *See also* mhondoro, svikiro.

nzabu-a-menga (Kik.)   "Pool of blood." The blood of animals offered in sacrifice. It was used in graveside rituals to honor great hunters. These practices were prevalent among Africans in São Salvador do Congo, Angola, in the 1880s. BeAD. *See also* nkumbi.

Nzambi, Mona N'Engana (Afr.)   "Sons of God." A group of young Africans in Baixa Cassange, Angola, who around 1891 worshipped a prophet who they believed appeared among the Mbundu people living in the grasslands of the Benguela *planalto*. This sect preached a folk religion that was a mixture of Christianity and pagan revivalism. Pelissier, *La Colonie*, p. 184. *See also* kimpasi.

nzanza (Kik.)   In the area of São Salvador do Congo, Angola, c.1880, the term for a flat hilltop, a peneplain tableland formed by erosion. BeAD.

nzimbu (Bant.)   A shell used as currency in the Congo Kingdom from the fifteenth to the seventeenth centuries. *Nzimbus* were collected from special fishing grounds off the island of Luanda under the control of local African chiefs. Around 1575 about 3000 people were engaged in collecting them. In 1650 an African ruler transferred these shellfish grounds to the Portuguese as a guarantee for promised mine concessions. Birmingham, *Trade and Conflict*, pp. 3-4, 47-8, 152. *See also* cowrie.

nzongo (Kik.)   A common measure of weight for gunpowder in São Salvador do Congo c.1880. BeAD.

{ O }

oala (Afr.)   An alcoholic beverage made from millet, sorghum, and scented *muxiri* (q.v.) roots; an African beer found in Pungo Andongo, Malange region, east-central Angola. Ficalho, *Plantas Uteis*, pp. 140-1.

OAU (Organization of African Unity)   The first modern Pan-African organization formed on May 25, 1963, by the independent African nations. The African Liberation Committee of the OAU sought to coordinate political and military support for the several nationalist movements in Portuguese Africa. In 1967 the OAU recognized PAIGC (q.v.) as the sole legitimate representative of the people of Guinea-Bissau and Cape Verde. In November 1973 Guinea-Bissau became the forty-second member of the OAU. The Republic of Cape Verde joined the OAU on July 18, 1975. HDRGC.

oba (Pg.)   One of the tallest trees in the forests of São Tomé, *oba* (*Pentadesma butyraca sabine*) grows over 90 ft. (80 m) high. The seeds are rich in oil and butyric acid. It supplies a valuable timber which tolerates long periods of submersion in water. Also called *pau-oba* (obawood). Ficalho, *Plantas Uteis*, p. 90.

obi (Afr.)   An Angolan name applied in Brazil to a shrub bearing nuts with a edible kernel similar to a walnut. It was brought to Brazil by slaves and today is used in Afro-Brazilian cult rituals in Bahia and elsewhere in Brazil. DHP; WNWD.

OCA (Organizaçao Cultural dos Angolanos) (Pg.)   "Cultural Organization of Angolans." A nationalist group of young Protestant Umbundus founded in Lobito, southern Angola, in 1953 by Julio Afonso and José Belo Chipenda. Greatly influenced by American Protestant missionaries, this group openly opposed the Portuguese government. Both leaders were arrested in 1957 by the police and accused of being in contact with international opposition forces. Pelissier, *La Colonie,* pp. 290, 325; GEPB.

ocambadiona (Afr.)   "Day of the bridegroom." Among the Cuanhamas of southern Angola, the part of the wedding ceremony performed on the fourth day of the long wedding ritual. GEPB.

ochana (Afr.) In Angola and elsewhere, a swampy track or boggy land. GEPB.

ocumbo (Umb.) "Fenced garden." A small piece of ground near a hut where an Umbundu family cultivated cabbage, lettuce, tomatoes, okra, and peppers c.1920. Henderson, *Angola*, p. 49.

OIT (*Organisation Internationale du Travail*) (Fr.) "International Labor Organization." This institution, headquartered in Geneva, made several representations to the Portuguese government regarding African forced labor. The Lisbon government answered by saying that the Convention of September 25, 1926, had forbidden forced labor except for public works and stated that the abuses by private employers would gradually disappear. Cunha, *O Trabalho Indigena,* pp. 273-4.

oitava (Pg.) In Portuguese East Africa, a measure of weight equal to one-eighth of an ounce (3.77 grams). Axelson, *Portuguese in South-East*, p.243.

Oja (Afr.) A stone-built town on the Indian Ocean at the mouth of the Tana River, northern Mozambique, that by the thirteenth century was a trading port. A competitor of Mombasa (q.v.), Oja was taken by the Portuguese in 1507. Axelson, *Portuguese in South-East*, p. 68.

ojotjukoroka (Afr.) "Year of the smallpox." An expression used by the Herero of southern Angola around 1885 to refer to the devastating effects of a smallpox epidemic. Dias, *Famine and Disease,* JAH, Cambridge, 1981, 22(3):363. *See also* ki-ngongo.

Okavango (Afr.) A large marsh on the Cubango River near the Angolan-Namibian border where a group of African agriculturists and fishermen settled in the 1800s. In colonial times these people had little contact with Portuguese settlers. GEPB.

Okavango River *See* Cubango River.

okra (Afr.) Tall annual herbs (*Hibicus esculentus* and *H. abelmoschus*) found in Angola and throughout tropical regions. Okra has been cultivated since ancient times in African kitchen gardens for its young mucilaginous pods used in soups and stews. It is also called *gombo, quiabo,* and *quingombo de cheiro*. Oil from the seeds of *H. abelmoschus* is used in perfumery. In French, okra is called *abrette*. Ficalho, *Plantas Uteis,* pp. 96-7. WNWD.

Olhão (Pg.) A town on the Atlantic coast of southern Portugal that played an important role in navigation and trade with West Africa during the

Discovery (q.v.). Its sailors and merchants crowded the caravels during voyages to Arguim, Guiné, and São Jorge da Mina c.1490. In 1862 a group of fishermen from Olhão settled in Porto Alexandre in southern Angola. They had a long tradition of marine fishing and by 1868 Porto Alexandre had ten fisheries, of which six were operated by Olhenses. In 1892 they introduced steamships to their operations and by 1925 there were fifty boats from Olhão. They also developed a local shipbuilding industry. Iria, *O Algarve no Descobrimento,* Congresso da Historia, Lisbon, 1946, I:206; GEPB.

Olifants A river that rises in southwest South Africa, flows northwest, and empties into the Atlantic Ocean. It was discovered by Bartlomeu Dias in January 1488. Axelson, *Portuguese in South-East,* p. 14; WNGD.

Olivença (Pg.) An African settlement in northwestern Mozambique near the Malawi border. In the 1970s it was transformed into a fortress by the Portuguese who were fighting the guerrillas of FRELIMO (q.v.). Surrounded by rebel forces, Olivença was resupplied by air. Henriksen, *Revolution,* pp. 28, 48.

Olivetta nana (Lat.) A highly desirable and valuable shell currency used in Angola around 1650. These shells from Luanda, noted for their beautiful color, were carried by African servants in straw sacks, in loads of 64 Ibs. (29 kg) each, to the Congo to be exchanged for slaves and bark cloth. Polanyi, *Dahomey,* p. 181. *See also* bark cloth, cowrie as currency, nzimbu.

olo foro (Mand.) Among the Mandingos of Guinea-Bissau, a beverage prepared from the dried leaves of a tropical plant (*Terminalia macroptera*) and used to treat coughs and tuberculosis. Carreira, *Mandingas,* p. 242.

olonguaio (Afr.) Among the Benguelas of southern Angola, a small gourd worn by women as an amulet to expel evil spirits from a sick person. GEPB.

oluina (Umb.) "Maternal lineage." Among the Mbundu c.1920, the term for direct line of descent through the mother binding together members of extended families. Property as well as religious and social rights were inherited through *oluina,* from mother's brother to sister's son. Anderson, *Angola,* p. 50.

OMA (*Organisaçao das Mulheres de Angola*) (Pg.) "Organization of Angolan Women. " A nationalist group established in Luanda in 1963 that closely collaborated with such other radical movements as the MPLA (q.v.). Wheeler, *Angola,* pp. 206, 213. *See also* OMM.

omamilamila (Bant.) "Protective ancestors." In São Salvador c.1920, the term for spirits who were believed to be the protectors of a family, community, or ethnic group. Only the initiated could communicate with these spirits during secret rituals and dances. *Omamilamila* were worshipped by members of the Kimbanguism and Tocoismo sects (qq.v.). Estermann, *O Tocoismo*, Garcia de Horta, Lisbon, 1965, 13(3):340.

Oman   A sultanate on the southeastern Arabian peninsula. Muscat, its capital, was captured in 1508 by the Portuguese who governed the state until 1650 when the sultan, with Dutch and British help, retook it. In 1741 it was seized by Yemen. Beginning in the nineteenth century it was a British protectorate, then in 1954 it became an independent state. GEPB; WNGD. *See also* Omani trade.

Omani trade   Around 1639, traders from Oman on the Indian Ocean coast of the Arabian peninsula became a threat to Mozambique and other areas of East Africa. The Portuguese, unable to compete, established a commercial monopoly by forcing Moslem traders and shippers to purchase licenses from Portuguese officials. This policy failed and free trade again became widespread in the area. Henriksen, *Mozambique,* pp. 29, 46.

ombaca (Afr.)   The term for a large, well organized caravan of Ovimbundu merchants who in the 1880s transported products from the African Lakes Region in the east to the Atlantic coast of Angola in the west. Along their protracted route, these skilled merchants traded beeswax, rubber, ivory, and slaves. Newitt, *Portugal*, p. 17; GEPB. *See also* Ovimbundu traders.

OMM (*Organisaçao das Mulheres Moçambicanas*) (Pg.)   "Organization of Mozambican Women." A group founded in Maputo in 1972 by FRELIMO (q.v.). Opposing the traditions of female inferiority and subordination, it was dedicated to fighting sexual discrimination and aimed to integrate women into both the political and economic systems. Later OMM and FRELIMO vigorously attacked the sexual division of labor in an effort to further emancipate the women of Mozambique. Munslow, *Mozambique.* p. 157. *See also* OMA.

Ombala (Umb.)   In Angola, the seat of an Umbundu settlement c.1900. Henderson, *Angola*, p. 51. *See also* Imho.

omufito (Afr.)   In southwestern Angola, the term for a low sandy forested tract of land. Ervedosa, *Literatura Angolana*, p. 18.

omumbo (Afr.)   A tropical shrub (*Vangueira esculenta*) related to coffee (*Coffea arabica*). It bears seeds, called beans, from which a stimulant similar to coffee is extracted. GEPB.

omuramba (Herero) In southwest Angola, a river bed that carries water for only a few days or weeks each year. GGT.

onaka (Umb.) A seasonally dry riverbed where during the dry season from April or early May to January the Umbundus (q.v.) cultivated maize, sorghum, and millet. Henderson, *Angola*, p. 49.

onça (Pg.) "Ounce." In Portuguese colonial Africa, a unit of weight equal to 1.28 ounces, or 36.3 grams. Duncan, *Atlantic Islands*, p. 259.

"One State, One Race, One Faith and One Civilization" Motto associated with the *Novo Estado* (q.v.) in Portugal, coined in 1930 by President Antonio Salazar. It was meant to tie together the African colonies as an extension of Portugal, proclaimed to be a nation without official racial or geographic distinctions. According to President Salazar, the Portuguese government "Administer[ed] the Minho and Beira provinces in Portugal the same way as Angola and Mozambique in Africa." Duffy, *Portuguese Africa*, p. 272.

Onga Zanga (Afr.) The official center for colonial cotton research in northern Angola. It was organized by the *COTONANG* (q.v.) in the 1950s. Pelissier, *La Colonie*, p. 309.

ongole (Afr.) A communal pastureland among the Ambos of southern Angola, c.1920. Henderson, *Angola*, p. 54.

ongubo (Afr.) Among the Ambos in southern Angola c.1920, a tract of land farmed by a family. The size of most lots varied between fifteen and fifty acres. Henderson, *Angola*, p. 54. *See also* etunda, chilongo.

Onhaqouro (Afr.) An old African town and trading post located on the Cuama River near the junction of the Zambezi and Shire rivers. It held a fair that was well known by coastal chiefdoms, the Monomotapa in Central Africa, and the Kilwa and Malindi on the Indian Ocean. At Onhaqouro c.1514 Portuguese and other Europeans traded cloth, firearms, sugar, and wine with Africans for cattle, goats, coconuts, honey, gold, and ivory. Axelson, *Portuguese in South-East*, pp. 85, 87, 90. *See also* Otonga.

onion Edible bulb of *Allium cepa* with a strong sharp smell, apparently imported to Africa from the Mediterranean and cultivated by the Takrus and Wolofs in Senegal long before the arrival of the Portuguese c.1450. Lewicki, *West African Food*, p. 58. *See also* yoboro.

Ophir Company A corporation founded with British capital in Mozambique in 1884 to conduct coastal shipping and inland trade. In 1888, it was taken over by the *Companhia de Moçambique*. Herrick, *Area Handbook*, p. 38.

Opium Company A large Mozambican corporation organized in 1877 on the Mopeia *prazo* by I.J. de Paiva Raposo to produce and export opium. The *prazo* was near the Kwa-Kwa River north of the Zambezi. This concession, granted by the Lisbon government, was part of a new free trade policy instituted to attempt to replace the slavery-based colonial economy. Paiva Raposo brought fifty experienced opium growers from India, oversaw the poppy cultivation, and expanded production in the Zambezi Valley as far as Tete. In Mopeia, he established a garrison, built a church and houses for the administrators, and created a new town for the workers. The biggest problem with opium production was the labor shortage, often remedied by using military forces to forceably recruit Africans from the villages surrounding the *prazo*. In 1882 A.A. Caldas Xavier became administrator and introduced a policy that allowed *prazo*-holders to pay their taxes by lending laborers to perform government work for two weeks every year. At the time this labor exploitation caused rebellion among the 1,800 African workers on the plantation and in 1884 a mob burned and destroyed the estate. Newitt, *Portuguese Settlement*, pp. 284, 352; Vail, *Capitalism*, pp. 59-60, 76-9.

Oporto slave market Oporto, a seaport in northern Portugal, was an important slave trade center early in the Discovery (q.v.) and by 1500 it had a large slave population. Of the baptisms recorded in the cathedral in 1540, the number of baptisms of slave children was 6 percent of the total while those of freedmen accounted for only 0.2 percent. If these percentages are applied to the 1527 census population of Oporto, the calculations indicate that there were about 700 slaves and 24 freedmen in an urban population of 12,000. Saunders, *A Social History*, p. 53; GEPB.

OPVDC (*Organisação Provincial de Voluntarios e Defesa Civil*) (Pg.) "Organization of Provincial Volunteers and Civil Defense." A colonial paramilitary force established in 1961 in Angola by Portuguese settlers. This force was active in defending plantations and protecting convoys in northern Angola. Wheeler, *Angola*, p. 229.

oral history The strong oral tradition among Africans is understood to be one of the richest and most valid forms of African literature, whether in an African language or in Portuguese. Before and after the arrival of the Portuguese in Angola c.1480, such African groups as the Umbundu, Benguelas, and Ovimbundu had oral historians who received and transmitted tales and stories as well as genealogies. The individual oral historian emphasized diverse images, metaphors, clichés, and plots as he applied his creative skills to make his performance aesthetically as well as historically valuable. Each *lunda* (event) or episode had its own internal logic. Retelling historic events depended on the oral historian's own sense of story development as well as ethnographic evidence, especially with distinct groups of people. Miller, *Kings and Kinsmen,* pp. 23-26. *See also* orature.

orange A subtropical citrus tree (*Citrus sinensis*) producing fruit with a juicy pulp either sour or sweet. Oranges were introduced by the Arabs to Africa from India around 200 AD and were found by the Portuguese on the East African coast in 1498. According to Leo Africanus writing c.1500, feral orange trees were found in the wooded hills of Hausa, Kano province, modern Nigeria. Valentim Fernandes reported having seen oranges on the Guiné coast and on São Tomé in 1506. Fernandes, *Description,* pp. 127, 135, 147; Lewicki, *West African Food,* pp. 72, 182-3.

Orange River River in South Africa about 1,300 mi. (2,100 km) long. It rises in the Orange Free State and continues west across the Cape Province. In its lower course it forms the boundary between South Africa and Namibia, emptying into the Atlantic at Alexander Bay. It was discovered by the Portuguese navigator Bartholomeu Dias in 1488. Axelson, *Portuguese in South-East,* p. 13; WNGD.

orature A term coined by Donald Burness in 1981 to refer to the oral tradition carried down for many generations by Africans, either in indigenous languages or in Portuguese. These oral narratives that incorporate myths, tales, stories, and episodes are considered to be of unique aesthetic value and have inspired many twentieth century African writers. Burness, *Critical Perspectives,* p. 48. *See also* oral history.

orchil A wild dye-yielding lichen (*Roccella tinctoria* L.; syn. *Litmus roccella*) found in mountainous areas of Cape Verde. It yields a reddish-blue pigment used to dye cloth. In colonial times it was collected, processed, and exported to West Africa, Brazil, Genoa, London, Amsterdam, Marseille, and elsewhere in Europe. Also called *urzela* in Portuguese and archil in English. Duncan, *Atlantic Islands,* p. 160; Carreira, *Cabo Verde e Guiné,* BCG, 1967, xxii(87/88):313. *See also* indigo.

ordeal *See* tribal ordeals.

Ordenaçãos Afonsinas "Afonsine Code." A code of laws compiled and published in 1446 under King Afonso V of Spain. Based on Roman and

Canon law, this code dealt with Moslem slaves or Moors at a time when the slave population was small. Then, a slave could receive a full trial with the right of appeal should the verdict go against him. In 1472, due to increased lawlessness among slaves newly arrived from West Africa, Portuguese slaveholders pressed for and obtained more stringent punishments for slaves' crimes. Saunders, *A Social History,* pp. 11, 114, 122; GEPB. *See also* Ordenações Manuelinas.

Ordenaçãos Manuelinas "Manueline Code." A code of laws compiled and promulgated by King Manuel I in 1514. With the amendments of 1521 it remained the definitive Portuguese law for the rest of the century. Unlike the *Ordenacoes Afonsinas* (q.v.), this code provided a set of principles and rules of moral conduct applicable to most cases in a society that felt threatened by the unruly behavior of hundreds of slaves brought from Guiné, the Gulf of Guiné, and Angola at the end of the fifteenth century. Saunders, *A Social History,* pp. 114, 122; DHP.

Ordens da Provincia da Zambezia (Pg.) "Laws of the Zambezia Province." A legal periodical published from 1935 to 1955 in Quelimane, Mozambique, by the provincial government. Dias, *A Imprensa,* p. 89.

Ordens da Provincia de Manica e Sofala (Pg.) "Laws of the Province of Manica and Sofala. " A legal periodical published in Mozambique by the provincial government from 1943 to 1955. Dias, *A Imprensa,* p. 89.

Ordens da Provincia do Niassa (Pg.) "Laws of the Province of Niassa." A legal periodical published by the provincial government from 1935 to July 1955. Its publication was irregular. Dias, *A Imprensa,* p. 89.

Ordens da Provincia do Sul do Sabe (Pg.) "Laws of the Province of South Sabe." A legal periodical published by the provincial government from 1935 to 1955. Dias, *A Imprensa,* p. 89.

Ordens do Distrito de Lourenço Marques (Pg.) "Laws of the District of Lourenço Marques." A legal periodical published in Mozambique by the provincial government. It appeared in Lourenço Marques from 1947 to 1949. Dias, *A Imprensa,* p. 89.

Order of Christ A religious military brotherhood established in Portugal in 1319 by Pope John XXII and always headed by a nobleman whose title was Master of the Order. Its headquarters at Castro-Marim, near the mouth of the Guadiana River, was a fortress built to defend the Algarve, then threatened by Moorish forces. The order received Tomar, Castelo Branco, and other properties confiscated from the abolished Templars. At the time of the Discovery (q.v.), its master was Prince Henry. He devoted the revenues of the order as well as the large subsidies he received from the state to underwrite the voyages of the Discovery (q.v.) that he organized. After his death in 1460 his nephew Prince Fernando, the younger brother of King Afonso V, was appointed master. Before he became king in 1495, Prince Manuel as Duke of Beja had been master. In 1496 the mastership of the order was declared part of the Crown. That same year, the pope granted the members of the Order of Christ the right to marry without forfeiting their ecclesiastic privileges so that the Crown was free to reward a subject with a knighthood from the order. Livermore, *A New History,* pp. 86, 127, 132; GEPB.

ore (Afr.) A tropical legume (*Caesalpinia crista* L.) bearing edible beans. It is found in Guinea-Bissau and elsewhere in Africa. GEPB.

Organic Law for the Overseas Territories Code of laws promulgated in 1972 by the Portuguese government under Prime Minister Marcello Caetano that declared Angola and Mozambique states within the Portuguese nation, a constitutional reform giving limited autonomy to provincial governments. Local elected assemblies had the right to legislate and control finances but a governor-general named by Lisbon still retained control over defense and foreign relations and had the prerogative to veto legislation. Henriksen, *Mozambique,* pp. 210-1.

Organisaçao Cultural dos Angolanos *See* OCA.

Organisaçao das Mulheres de Angola *See* OMA.

Organisaçao das Mulheres Moçambicanas *See* OMM.

Organisação Provincial de Voluntarios e Defesa Civil *See* OPVDC.

Organisation Internationale du Travail *See* OIT.

Organization of African Unity *See* OAU.

Organum Viatorum (Lat.) "Travelers' Guide." A pocket sundial made by the famous guild of Nurenberg metalworkers and set in the meridian by means of a tiny inset magnetic needle. Known early outside Germany, this instrument was called *Os Relogios de Agulha* (Clocks of the Needle) by King Duarte who mentioned it in passing in his book *Leal Counseilhero* (Faithful Adviser) written between 1428 and 1437. Taylor, *History of Technology,* 1976, II:5-11.

orphaes do rey (Pg.) "Orphans of the King." Portuguese orphan girls were educated by the Crown in Lisbon and Oporto orphanages. Once they were of marriageable age, the king provided them with a dowry in the form of some minor government post, and often sent them to the colonies to marry Portuguese settlers. In 1593, a group of these young women arrived in Luanda, Angola. Boxer, *Women,* p. 23.

Oryza glaberrima (Lat.) One of the oldest sub-Saharan grains, a rice native to the upper Niger River in West Africa. Later, its cultivation spread to the region between Lake Chad and the Atlantic coast. Its ancestor is believed to be the wild variety *O. barthii.* It has been cultivated in seasonally flooded areas of West Africa. especially Senegal, for more than one thousand years. Lewicki *West African Food,* pp. 32, 33; GEPB.

ossami (Afr.) In São Tomé and elsewhere, a pungent edible berry borne by the tropical tree *Aframomum melegüeta.* It is used as a pepper substitute and is called *malagüeta* (q.v.) in Portuguese. It was introduced to Cape Verde from the Gulf of Guiné by the Portuguese c.1500. Tenreiro, *A llha,* p. 92.

otarampa (Afr.) In Angola and elsewhere, a tropical tree (*Carpodinus lanceolata*) with roots that are harvested for their high quality latex. Carvalho e Vasconcellos, *As Colonias Portuguesas,* p. 363. *See also* borracha.

Otavi copper mines A mining complex at Otavi, German South-West Africa (now Namibia), developed with German capital beginning in 1898. Between then and 1903, the German government brought pressure to bear on the Portuguese for a concession to build a railroad from Otavi to the Baia dos Tigres or Porto Alexandre in Angola. Portugal refused permission and in 1903 the Germans developed Swakopmund as a port and linked it by rail with Otavi. Wheeler, *Angola,* p. 75.

Otchicango (Afr.) An African town, Baixo Cunene in Portuguese, near Vila Pereira de Eça in southern Angola. By 1959 it was a SWAPO (q.v.) base of operations to help launch and continue the War for Independence (1960-1975). Pelissier, *La Colonie,* p. 293.

Otchinjua (Afr.) An African settlement in southwestern Angola that was part of a large government territory set aside in 1950 for European colonists. Pelissier, *La Colonie,* p. 154(n).

Otondo (Afr.) A small Arab sultanate on the Indian Ocean near Mombasa, Kenya, where Nuno da Cunha's expedition arrived c.1530. Soon after, the

Portuguese established an alliance with the sultan and other Arab potentates along the coast. It is also known as Tondo and Utondwe. Axelson, *Portuguese in South-East*, p. 121.

Otonga (Afr.) A large town on the Cuama River, Quelimane, Mozambique. In 1511 the navigator Antonio de Saldanha explored the region and soon it was settled, becoming a commercial center. In 1521 the town organized an annual fair and important slave trade market frequented by both Moslem and Portuguese traders. Axelson, *Portuguese in South-East,* pp. 77-8, 91.

Ouidah (Whydah) (Afr.) Seaport west of Cotonou, Benin. Originally part of the Ardra Kingdom, in 1470 the region was explored by Pedro Escobar and João Santarem. The French established an important slave trade center there around 1600. In the seventeenth century, Ouidah became an international slave market where British, Dutch, French, and Portuguese merchants bought thousands of slaves for the New World plantations. By 1750 the king of Dahomey controlled the trade in slaves from the interior at the time when the British dominated the international slave trade. In 1970 it had a population of 26,000. Newitt, *Portugal*, pp. 4, 5; DHP; HDB; WNGD.

Ouidah-Bahia Trade This trade was based on the export of slaves from Ouidah and several petty kingdoms along the length of the Gulf of Guiné to Brazilian plantations in exchange for tobacco, sugar, and rum from Brazil. It is estimated that from 1731 until the middle of the nineteenth century, Brazilian traders annually exported between 10,000 and 12,000 slaves, mostly Sudanese, from Ouidah to Bahia. The Sudanese commanded a high price because they were considered better workers than Bantu slaves from Angola. Some of them, ostensibly brought to work in the Bahian sugar and tobacco plantations, were clandestinely re-exported to the more lucrative markets of Minas Gerais in the interior of Brazil and Rio de Janeiro on the coast. This trade was so important that in 1695 the Portuguese in Bahia minted their first gold coins, struck largely from gold obtained in Ouidah in exchange for tobacco. After the discovery of gold in Minas Gerais in 1698, this process was reversed. Henceforth, Brazilian gold was smuggled by the Bahian slave traders into Ouidah, despite the government's efforts to stop this leak. Boxer, *The Portuguese Seaborne*, p. 171. *See also* Brazil ward.

ounce An unofficial unit of currency of unstable value used by British and other Europeans in the Gulf of Guiné to pay Africans for gold in what was known as the "ounce trade." This specious currency was also known as "Guinea value" and "Coast value." At Ouidah (q.v.), where the British and Portuguese used it c.1737, the "ounce" in "ounce trade" was formally recognized at half the rate of ounce gold (q.v.). Polanyi, *Dahomey,* pp. 158, 175.

ounce gold An English monetary unit which c.1793 was worth £4 sterling. It was used to buy goods and slaves in colonial West Africa. Polanyi, *Dahomey*, p. 159. *See also* ounce.

Our Lady of the Conception, Church of In 1513, King Manuel wrote to Pope Leo X expressing concern about the Africans brought to Lisbon from Guiné, many of whom died in transit before they had received baptism. He said it was necessary that the vicar of the Church of Our Lady of the Conception in Lisbon be authorized to baptize those Africans who were willing to receive the sacrament. The king also requested permission for the captains of slave ships bound for Lisbon to baptize, on the vicar's behalf, slaves who were in danger of dying. Pope Leo X granted these requests in his bull *Eximiae Devotionis* and ordered that a font be erected in the church to baptize sick slaves. Saunders, *A Social History,* pp. 40-41; GEPB.

Our Lady of Grace, Church of   Also known as Ave Maria, this parish church, built in 1504 and staffed by the Order of the Hermits of Saint Augustine, was possibly the first in São Tomé. In 1534, when São Tomé became a diocese, this church was raised to the rank of cathedral. Garfield, *History*, p. 258.

Our Lady of Loreto A parish outside the western walls of Lisbon where many freedmen lived. Around 1550 this was in a section of the city not yet developed, so freedmen could raise vegetables in their gardens for family consumption and for sale in the city. The tax roll of 1565 reveals that some of the wealthiest free Africans in Lisbon lived in this parish. Saunders, *A Social History,* pp. 40-41; GEPB.

Our Lady of Mercy, Brotherhood of Generally called Misericordia (q.v.), this fraternity was founded in Lisbon in 1498 by Queen Leonor, wife of King João II. Other branches followed rapidly in Portugal and overseas. No fewer than sixty-one branches had adopted its *compromiso* (rule) by the time of Queen Leonor's death in 1534. The Misericordia brothers concerned themselves with charitable acts such as visiting prisoners, ministering to the sick, and providing food, clothing, and shelter to travelers and the needy. Men joined the brotherhood with their entire families, including servants and slaves. Free Africans, alone or with their families, were allowed to join but were not allowed to hold elective office. Saunders, *A Social History*, p. 151; GEOB.

Our Lady of the Rosary, Church of and Brotherhood of A Lisbon church where in 1513 a brotherhood for African freedmen was organized. King João III gave a royal order on April 15, 1528, that each caravel returning from São Jorge de Mina had to give 500 *reis* as alms to this brotherhood. Brasio, *Os*

Pretos, pp. 76-77, 151; Pinto Rema, *A Primeira Evanligelização,* BCG, 1966, xxi(82):329.

Our Lady of the Rosary of the Negroes, Church of A parish church established in 1627 in Luanda, Angola, to serve the African population. It had a brotherhood for slaves and its chaplain's duties included teaching the catechism, hearing confessions, and celebrating the liturgy in Kimbundu and other dialects. Gabriel, *Angola,* p. 122-3. *See also* Our Lady of the Rosary.

ourique (Afr.) In Guinea-Bissau, an earthen barrier built to hold back flowing water. Such dams are used for irrigating rice, the most important crop in the former colony. Mota, *Guiné Portuguesa,* I:293.

ouro branco (Pg.) "White gold." Name given by Portuguese-speaking Africans to rice in Guinea-Bissau. It is a basic part of the local diet and is the main commercial export crop. Mota, *Guiné Portuguesa,* II:152.

Ovambo (Afr.) An ethnic group settled between the Cunene and Okavango rivers in southern Angola and the northern part of what is now Namibia. In this large area, parts of which are subject to flooding, the Ovambo raise cattle. Starting in 1950 the government began to modernize and improve their public health, education, and mission schools. Forced labor was abolished there in 1962. Communications improved dramatically with the repair and extension of the railway, the building of a new port in Mossâmedes, the construction of an excellent network of tarred roads, and the spread of airfields. At the same time, however, rebellion and separatism increased greatly with the beginning of the War for Independence (1961-75). The Ovambo people, assisted by the MPLA (q.v.) and, after 1975, with the assistance of the new government of Angola, started the reconstruction of an economy shattered by war and destruction. Clarence-Smith, *Slaves, Peasants,* pp. 89, 99, 104; Pelissier, *La Colonie,* p. 12. *See also* Ovambo flood plains.

Ovambo flood plains A large part of the Ovambo region southeast of Lubango lies along the Angola-Namibia border, an area periodically flooded by the Cuvelai River and other smaller streams. The remaining area is densely populated. The sandy soil is infertile and both rainfall and floods are highly irregular, so crop cultivation is limited to hardy and drought-resistant millet. Fishing and hunting were very important until the end of the nineteenth century when cattle raising began to dominate the economy. In 1960 this territory had a population of 450,000. Clarence-Smith, *Slaves, Peasants,* pp. 9-10; GEPB.

Ovambo trade The Ovambo territory, occupying a large region between the Cunene and the Okavango rivers in southern Angola, was almost completely isolated during the colonial period. As mobile trade was the rule for much of

Africa in the nineteenth century, African traders would band together in caravans and make trading expeditions into the Ovambo countryside. Soon some of the Ovambo themselves became involved in the profitable caravan commerce, although most were essentially hunters and fishermen until the ivory boom in 1870 and the boom in the rubber trade in 1900. In 1923, when the railway arrived at Mossâmedes and the interior, Ovambo trade was modernized under Portuguese supervision. Clarence-Smith, *Slaves, Peasants,* pp. 65-7. *See also* Ovambo.

Overseas Provinces This name, referring to Portuguese colonies, appeared for the first time in 1663 although the term "colonies" was the primary designation until 1822 when the first Portuguese constitution covering all overseas provinces was promulgated. This constitution established the principle of individuality of overseas Portuguese territories and granted citizenship to all inhabitants who were legally qualified. The term "Overseas Provinces" was used again in the Republican constitution of 1911 and President Antonio O. Salazar began stamping it on official documents in 1926. In 1962, as the multiple wars for liberation escalated, Salazar appealed to Portuguese pride in her overseas provinces in an attempt to unite Portugal behind the war effort, inundating the country with pamphlets, books, movies, posters, and speeches in praise of the supposedly congenial multiracial society in the Portuguese African Provinces. Bender, *Angola,* pp. xx, xxi; Cunha, *O Trabalho Indigena,* p. xxvi.

Overseas State Council A government agency created by King Joao IV on July 14, 1643. It was in charge of supervising, controlling, and administrating all Portuguese overseas territories. Its specific duties concerned war strategy, taxation, law, and business. DHP.

Ovimbundu (Bant.) The Ovimbundu is a Bantu group who speak Umbundu (q.v.) and trace the origin of their dynasty to King Katekula-Mengo, an elephant hunter. They migrated to Angola from the eastern highlands in the period between 1450 and 1600, settling on the central plateau. During most of the colonial period they lived in geographic isolation. Their economy, which is basically agricultural, prospered when the Portuguese introduced cash crops such as coffee, maize, wheat, and beans in the 1860s. Once inland commerce and trade opened, some became long distance traders, organizing large caravans to transport goods from Tete on the Indian Ocean coast of Mozambique to Benguela, Angola, on the Atlantic. The Ovimbundu were successful as independent farmers and those who became contract laborers on the coffee plantations in northern Angola were known as hard workers. Eventually soil depletion, overpopulation, and various external factors stimulated the Ovimbundu to expand their holdings outside the village structure. With the breakdown of the clans and their village-bound societies, the people became detribalized and self-conscious about being free to work and prosper. In 1973 the *Junta Provincial do Poamento* (Provincial Population Board) began a forced resettlement program that moved them hundreds of miles away to new smaller fields with inferior soil. The Ovimbundu, whose economy was ruined by resettlement, deeply resented this injustice. Today they are the largest ethnolinguistic group and the most homogeneous in terms of social, economic, political, and religious characteristics. In 1970 they constituted one-third of the Angolan population of 5,673,000. Jonas M. Savimbi, a charismatic and popular politician, is their leader. Bender, *Angola,* pp. 170-81, 183, 185; Okuma, *Angola in Ferment,* pp. 8, 878, 107; *The Washington Post,* Washington, D.C., June 1, 1991, p.7A. *See also* Ovibumdu traders.

Ovimbundu kingdoms The Ovimbundus were never united under a single king although before the Portuguese conquered the Benguela plateau around 1600 some thirteen out of twenty-two kingdoms had emerged as powerful entities. Throughout the plateau on which they settled there are massive outcroppings of granite and sandstone that were used as royal habitations, sacred temples, and shelters by them. The Ovimbundu also made military use of these great rock formations, constructing walls made of fragments shaped from them. To the Africans, such stoneworks of the gods and man represented divine and royal acts, while to the Portuguese they were fortified obstacles to their expansion of authority on the plateau. Wheeler, *Angola,* pp. 25-6.

Ovimbundu traders When African slavery officially ended in 1879 and economic expansion developed in central Angola, the Ovimbundu (q.v.) began organizing long-distance caravans, competing with the Portuguese for trade and trade routes across the Benguela *planalto*. They revitalized the trade in ivory, wax, honey, salt, and rubber, going as far away as the Congo (now Zaire), the African Lakes, and the Kalahari Desert. The caravan leaders were well organized and able to round up large numbers of followers, revolutionizing the old social structure with its scattered lineage-based villages. They supplied the Cokwe and other African ethnic groups with firearms, which made them a formidable military power in Central Africa. At this time the Ovimbundu were the most successful African group in redirecting their economic activities. Newitt, *Portugal,* p. 17; Pelissier, *La Colonie,* p. 12. *See also* Ovimbundu kingdom.

oxó (Mand.) In early colonial West Africa, fine well-worked decorative cloth worn by wealthy people. Made by the Mandingos, *oxó* cloth was traded along the Guinea-Bissau coast and in Cape Verde in the period around and after 1580. Duncan, *Atlantic Islands.* p. 12. *See also* barafula.

pacasa (Kimb.) In Angola and elsewhere, any of various wild buffalo such as *Bosbrachycerus* spp. (African buffalo) or *Syncerus caffer* (Cape buffalo). The African buffalo is found in rain forests in the Congo and elsewhere on the Atlantic coast; the Cape buffalo is found in South Africa. Africans hunted *pacasas* for meat and hides long before the Portuguese arrived c.1500. Carvalho e Vasconcellos, *As Colonias Portuguesas*, p. 349; GDLP.

pachiça (Pg.) In Mozambique c.1900, an African miner returning from the South African gold fields. After working there for several years, he had learned some English and often had become a member of the Church of England. A *pachiça* was well respected in his village for his social manners and his superior economic position. PDM.

Padrão Diogo Cão (Pg.) Monument built in the Zaire district, northern Angola, to commemorate the arrival of explorer Diogo Cão in 1482. In July of 1938 at the foot of this *padrão*, King Pedro VII of Congo declared: "We have always been and we shall be forever Portuguese. Angola is Portuguese and it can only cease to be Portuguese by stepping over our dead bodies." Pelissier, *La Colonie*, p. 265; GEPB.

padrão dos descobrimentos (Pg.) "Monument to the discoveries." Around 1425 during the period of the Discovery (q.v.), Prince Henry ordered the building of *padrãos* (stone pillars) surmounted by a block and cross of wood. The cross bore on its face the royal coat of arms and on the other side inscriptions recording the date and the names of the king and the explorer. These *padrãos* stand in the Atlantic Islands, West Africa, and elsewhere where the Portuguese sailed on voyages of exploration. Prestage, *The Portuguese Pioneers*, p. 206; GEPB.

padrão real (Pg.) "Royal patronage." The privilege granted to Portuguese kings by the pope at the time of the Discovery (q.v.). The kings were allowed to present candidates for ecclesiastical benefits in the Atlantic Islands, Africa, and India. On January 8, 1455, Pope Eugene IV issued the papal bull *Inter Coetera* granting Prince Henry the right to building churches, send missionaries to convert the Africans, and administer church institutions in those territories. In 1514 Pope Leo X issued *Dum Fidei Constantian* which allowed the Crown the right to present candidates for bishop, abbot, and administrator of church benefits. The royal patronage extended from Cape Bojador to Goa. DHP; GEPB.

PAIGC (*Partido Africano da Independencia da Guiné e Cabo Verde*) (Pg.) "African Party for the Independence of Guiné and Cape Verde." A militant political group founded clandestinely in Bissau on September 19, 1956, by Amilcar Cabral. It had a program for national liberation and its followers included politicians, craftsmen, and manual workers. In 1959 the PAIGC General Secretariat was moved to Conakry, French Guinée. In April 1961 in Casablanca PAIGC played an important role in linking the movement with Angolan and Mozambican militants. In 1964 PAIGC engaged the Portuguese in an intensive military confrontation on the large southern coastal island of Como. On July 1, 1970, in Rome, Amilcar Cabral and leaders of FRELIMO and the MPLA (qq.v.) were given an audience with Pope Paul VI to explain and defend the ideology of the party. PAIGC's goal was reached with the independence of Guinea-Bissau and Cape Verde on July 5,1975. HDRGC.

Paiva song A song of protest named for José de Paiva-Raposo, holder of the Sena *prazo* in Mozambique. It was sung c.1918 by unhappy laborers on the plantations. The *Paiva* songs voiced anger and criticism for demanding too much and paying too little. It is a musical tradition in Africa, whereby people in authority, whether they were chief, headman, husband, father, plantation owner, or master, could be denounced for their behavior in song in terms that would not be permitted in any other form. These songs, in short, legitimized the criticism and became immensely popular, spreading quickly along the Zambezi River from Mopeia to Caia, where the Sena sugar factory began production in 1908, and thence downstream to Marromeu and eventually to the Sena sugar estates (q.v.), the main plantation at Luabo. These songs include a triple enunciation of the theme followed by an epigrammatic comment exactly repeating the form of traditional canoe-songs, such as Jemwe songs (q.v.). These melodies are more effective in their original Sena language than in English translation because of their accelerating rhythm and final stumping rhyme. Munslow, *Mozambique*, p. 68; Vail, *Capitalism*, pp. 167-8. *See also* work songs.

palaver (from Pg. *palavra*, word) Very early in the Discovery (q.v.), a discussion between a Portuguese slaver and African chiefs regarding the price and conditions of sale of slaves. Later, a jargon based on Portuguese and widely used by European slavers when trading gold, goods, slaves, spices, and other merchandise. By 1500, this oral communication had developed an extensive vocabulary and grammar that are still present in the creolized

Pequeno Portuguese (q.v.) spoken along the Atlantic coast of Angola and in other Afro-Portuguese countries. GEPB; DHP. *See also* fala de Guiné.

palhota taxa (Pg.) "Hut tax." A tax imposed by the Portuguese government around 1760 on each hut occupied by an African family in the Zambezia region of Mozambique. On *prazos* having over fifty hectares the *prazo*-holders had to pay it. In compensation, they were no longer liable for any other dues or service to the government. The *palhota taxa* was still levied on huts and plantations into the second half of the nineteenth century. Newitt, *Portuguese Settlement*, pp. 43, 346. *See also* mussoco.

palm oil A reddish or yellow semi-solid oil obtained from the fruit of several kinds of palm, especially the oil palm (*Elaeis guineensis*), one of the most important commercial plants in Africa. The tree evolved in tropical Africa and is found wild on the west coast in an area 12° north and south of the equator. In the wild it does best in transition zones between tropical forests and savannah, and also appears in tropical forests following the penetration of man. For centuries this tree has been a source of oil for the people of these areas. The fruit pulp, which contains from 50 to 65 percent or more oil, is separated from the seed kernels then pressed to extract the palm oil. This oil is used to manufacture margarine and soap, as well as for cooking oil and lubricants. Another kind of oil is obtained from the kernel, which contains from 44 to 53 percent oil of a different chemical composition. The shell is removed from the kernels then they too are pressed, producing a white semi-solid oil. The cake, the solids left after pressing the kernel, is an excellent animal food. The success and extensive development of oil palm plantations in the nineteenth century contributed to a large degree to the decline of the interior slave trade in Portuguese Africa. In Guinea-Bissau, in areas of less rainfall closer to the eastern savanna region of the Sudan, the oil palm is replaced as a local source of oil by the shea-butter tree (*Buryrosperm parkii*), also known as *karite*. In Portuguese the oil palm is called *palmeira do azeite*. Lewicki, *West African Food*, p. 109. GEPB; HDRGC.

palm wine An alcoholic beverage made from the fermented sap of the oil palm (*Elaeis guineensis*). It is drunk by Africans in Senegal and along the Atlantic coast. Palm wine was made in West Africa long before the arrival of Portuguese explorers in 1450s. Lewicki, *West African Food*, p. 131.

Palma (Pg.) Municipality and city in the Delgado district, Mozambique, with an area of 1,920 sq. mi. (5,000 sq. km). To the north the Rovuma River forms the border between Palma and Tanzania. The city is an important shipping and commercial port and the municipality includes a big-game area and sites of cocoa cultivation near the towns of Nangade and Quionga. All this territory, called the *Triangulo de Quironga*, was returned to Portugal in the 1919 Treaty of Versailles. GEPB.

palmatorio (Pg.) In Mozambique in the colonial period, an instrument to punish petty offenders consisting of a thick perforated wooden paddle attached to a short handle. The decision to punish someone was an administrative one and the person to be punished was held and struck twenty-five times on each upturned palm. The four to five holes in the *palmatorio* "sucked up the flesh" and raised painful welts. The punishment was usually administered in the presence of other Africans to further increase the humiliation. Those minor offenses that required use of the *palmatorio* were usually entered into the official records on crime. Harris, *Palmatorio,* Africa Today, 1958, 24:11-12.

Pan-African Congress *See* Pan-Africanism.

Pan-Africanism A political movement that emerged in the late nineteenth century. Its ideals were to obtain the complete independence of Africa, end its exploitation, and establish a federation of countries with limited national sovereignty. In addition Pan-Africanism promoted the concept of the rebirth of an African society that combined African traditions, mores, and culture with European values. The Berlin Conference of 1884 had dealt with territorial issues and recognized the rights of Portugal, Britain, Belgium, France, and Germany, completely ignoring the rights of Africans and creating a backlash in the overseas African community. The first Pan-African Congress was organized by Henry Sylvester-Williams, a West Indian lawyer, and held in London July 23-25, 1900. Thirty delegates, most from the United States and the West Indies, attended. Leaders who emerged from this new group included W.E.B. DuBois, an American, and Marcus Garvey, a Jamaican, both of whom led groups that advocated African separatism and self-determination. Less radical leaders, such as Blaise Diagne of Senegal and Benito Sylvain, a Haitian who had lived in Paris for many years and who had organized the Black Youth Association in 1896, supported cooperation among the races. This disparate group was united in their dislike of colonialism and their desire to unify, in one way or another, the African world. The movement persisted through two world wars, then in 1945 the first of what might be called a truly African Pan-African Congress was held in Manchester, England. One of the leaders, Kwame Nkrumah of Ghana, proposed a mass African revolution to seize power by force. The meeting, in effect, served notice to the colonial powers that Africans desired independence and were willing to fight for that independence. By 1957 Ghana was granted sovereignty, followed by others, including French Guinée and Mali. Subsequent meetings saw progressively more unification of independent African states, culminating in the 1963 congress at Addis Ababa, Ethiopia, when the Organization of African Unity (OAU, q.v.) was chartered. In the late twentieth century, Pan-Africanism has fragmented, due in part to disparate forms of government ranging from true democracy to military dictatorship and from the inability of many governments to establish sound national economic bases. Martin, *The Pan-African Connection*, pp. 11-12; Thompson, *Africa and Unity*, pp. 3-7, 234-7; DHP; EA.

Pan-Portuguese-African Associations A loose federation of several political groups, based in Lisbon in the 1920s. They attempted to launch a movement led by Africans that would transform the face of Portuguese Africa. They petitioned, pleaded, published, and spoke on behalf of the interests of the African masses. Their newspapers and magazines espoused Pan-Africanism and Pan-Negroism and urged advancement of Africans in all levels of government, both provincial and national, in the face of the exclusivist policies of the nation and the colonies as a whole. They wrote of democracy, constitutionalism, and freedom and urged the economic betterment of Africans and the election of Africans to represent other Africans in legislative bodies. These associations also applied pressure on Portugal to establish relations with the League of Nations and with W.E.B. Du Bois's Pan-African Congress. Wheeler, *Angola*, pp. 118-9; GEPB. *See also* Liga Africana.

pangaio (Hind.) A type of sailboat built in East Africa around 1500. These simple wooden coasters tied with Cairo fiber had one mast, one sail, and oars. They sailed the Mozambique coast during the period of the Discovery (q.v.). Axelson, *Portuguese in South-East*, p. 243.

pangolim (Afr.) In Mozambique, any of a number of related toothless armored mammals (order *Pholidota)* that feed on ants and termites and are able to roll into a ball when threatened. GEPB; WNWD.

panno da costa (Pg.) A crude cotton cloth of inferior quality worn by slaves in the colonial period. It was woven in the interior of West Africa and sold in Guiné, Brazil, and elsewhere. Formerly used to barter for slaves on the West African coast, the sale or trade of *panno da costa* was made illegal in Cape Verde in 1821 to help curb the slave trade. HDRGC. *See also* batan.

panno de palma de Guiné (Pg.) A raw linen-type cloth woven of palm fiber and canvas, traded in Arguim (q.v.) and sold c. 1450 by Portuguese merchants in Lagos, Faro, Silves, and, later, Lisbon. *Pannos de palma*, together with linen from Flanders and damask from India, was sold in Portuguese shops and displayed in churches and monasteries. Iria, *O Algarve no Descombrimento*, Congresso da Guiné, Lisbon, 1946, I:205.

Papagaios, Ilha dos (Pg.) "Island of Parrots." An island in the Gulf of Guiné, off modern Cameroon, discovered c.1470 by Portuguese navigators. In 1668, São Tomean merchants who visited it on their voyages to São Jorge da Mina (q.v) named it *Ilha dos Papagaios.* Mota, *Toponimos,* p. 328.

Papei (Afr.) In Guinea-Bissau, an ethnic group of Senegambian stock, closely related to the Manjaco and Banyun. The Papei are concentrated on Bissau Island and the Geba Estuary. The local petty chiefs have limited authority over these non-Islamic coastal rice-cultivators. They resisted Portuguese expansion and between 1884 and 1915 organized bloody rebellions. In 1960, the Papei population was 50,000. HDRGC.

"Para o ingles ver" (Pg.) "For the Englishman to see." An expression referring to Portuguese reforms and legal changes in colonial administration c.1850 designed to appease the rising indignation of British humanitarians regarding abuses and injustices against Africans in Mozambique and Angola. Henriksen, *Mozambique,* p. 147. *See also* "Para o preto ver."

"Para o preto ver" (Pg.) "For the black man to see." An expression referring to Portuguese reforms and improvement in favor of Africans in Portuguese Africa around 1950. This was the time when nationalist leaders began organizing open rebellions against Portuguese colonialism in Mozambique, Angola, and elsewhere. Henriksen, *Mozambique,* p. 147. *See also* "Para o ingles ver."

pardo (Pg.) "Dark." The light-skinned *mestiço* offspring of a Portuguese father and African mother; an expression coined early in the Discovery (q.v.) in Portugal. GEPB.

Paralelo A monthly magazine that first appeared in August 1952 in Beira, Mozambique. Its name referred to the twentieth latitudinal parallel south (*paralelo* 20°S, q.v.) that passes very close to Beira. This literary periodical signaled the beginning of the soul-searching consideration of the cultural nationalism of Mozambican intellectuals. Its subtitle was *Msaho* ("song" in Chopi) because of the eight Mozambican poets who each contributed one to three poems. The writers were members of a generation that saw poetry as a valid means of participating in a heightened cultural and artistic awakening. Hamilton, *Voices,* pp. 169-70.

paralelo 20°S (Pg.) "Twentieth parallel south." Line drawn on the map of Mozambique marking a position as well as a geographic frontier to regulate the annual flux of workers going to the South African gold fields in the Transvaal. Only laborers living south of this parallel could legally migrate to the Witwatersrand mines. In a series of agreements beginning in 1897 and capped by the Convention of 1928, it was agreed that the Portuguese government would collect custom duties on goods from returning laborers and, most important of all, a percentage of the earnings of each laborer recruited in the region. The worker would receive part of the payment in gold at the mines, and the rest in *escudos* once back in his village. The government also was guaranteed that 47.5 percent of the rail traffic from Johannesburg, Pretoria, and Krugerdorp would go to Lourenço Marques. Mozambique received a substantial income from the 200,000 laborers who migrated every year. This policy ended when Mozambique became independent in 1975. Munslow, *Mozambique*, p. 120; GEPB.

Partido Africano (Pg) "African Party." A political group organized by young Angolans in Lisbon around 1910 at the time of the proclamation of the Republic in Portugal. Most likely inspired by the African-American Back to Africa Movement led by Marcus Garvey, it published the periodical *O Negro* to defend the interests of Africans. Pelissier, *La Colonie*, p. 223.

Partido Africano da Independencia da Guiné e Cabo Verde *See* PAIGC.

Partido Democratico de Angola *See* PDA.

Partido Nacional Africano *See* PNA.

Passa Palavra (Pg.) *"Pass the Word."* Title of a communist political tract published in Lisbon around 1965 and widely distributed to government militia and African urban centers in Portugal. It attacked the authoritarian and abusive regime and invited soldiers and others to abandon what was then thought to be a lost cause. It built awareness and sympathy for the revolutionary cause within the Portuguese military establishment. Henriksen, *Revolution*, p. 193. *See also* Deserter's Voice.

pasta (Pg.) In colonial Mozambique, a sheet of gold weighing 17 oz. (483 g). Axelson, *Portuguese in South-East*, p. 243.

PDA (*Partido Democratico de Angola*) (Pg.) "Angolan Democratic Party," an Angolan independence party founded in 1962 in Leopoldville, Beligan Congo. *See* ALIAZO, ASSOMIZO.

peanut *See* groundnut.

pearl millet *See* bulrush millet.

peça (Pg.) "Slave." A term used in the Zambezi region of Mozambique in the colonial period. Isaacman, *Mozambique: The Africanization*, p. 88. *See also* peça enteira, peça da India.

peça da India (Pg.)   An African slave, male or female, between the ages of 15 and 25, in good health but not physically outstanding. This type of slave was valued at two-thirds of one *peça enteira* (q.v.) in Brazilian markets. Boxer, *The Portuguese Seaborne*, p. 390; Duncan, *Atlantic Islands*, p. 199; DHP.

peça enteira (Pg.)   "Full slave." Term referring to an African slave, male or female, between the ages of 15 and 25 and of normal or superior height and in good health. This was a category of slave commanding the highest price in the Brazilian market. DHP. *See also* meia peça, peça da India.

pellagra   A chronic disease caused by a deficiency of niacin and protein in the diet and characterized by gastrointestinal disturbances, skin eruptions, and central nervous system disorders. It is endemic in many areas of Angola and elsewhere in Portuguese Africa. GEPB; WNWD.

pepino (Pg.)   "Cucumber." A trailing annual vine (*Cucumis sativa*) of the gourd family cultivated for its edible fruit. Introduced by the Portuguese into Africa from Europe c. 1500. A favorite vegetable of the settlers and apparently ignored by Africans. Ficalho, *Plantas Uteis*, p. 185.

pepper   Traded in Europe since antiquity, true pepper is a pungent condiment obtained from the small dried fruits, called corns, of the East Indian woody vine *Piper nigrum*. At the time of the Discovery (q.v.), it was known as *pimenta de Malabar*. In 1482, King João II built a *factoria* (q.v.) at São Jorge de Mina in the Gulf of Guiné to control the trade of spices, mainly pepper. Vasco da Gama reported in 1498 that Arab traders brought pepper from India. Pepper commanded a high price in Portugal and the rest of Europe c. 1500. Bartolomeo Marchionni, a Florentine merchant and representative of Lorenzo de Medici, had control of the pepper trade in Lisbon at this time. In 1520 King Manuel I established a royal monopoly on the importation and sale of pepper. *P. nigrum* has numerous relatives with similar but less pungent oils, including *P. guineense* (also known as *pimenta da Guiné, pimenta de São Tomé*, and *pimenta de Congo*). Such pepper substitutes as *Xylopia aethiopica* (Selim, or Negro, pepper), *X. indulata* (Cameroon pepper), and *Aframomum melehueta* (grains of Paradise) were also traded. GEPB. *See also* malagüeta.

Pequeno Portugues (Pg.)   "Little Portuguese." In Angola and elsewhere in Portuguese Africa, a creolized variation of standard Portuguese spoken by uneducated Africans in urban and semi-rural areas. It is known pejoratively as *Pretogues* (q.v.). Hamilton, *Black from White Language*, in *Ideologies and Literature*, 1976-7, 1(1):29. *See also* Fala de Guiné, pidgin Portuguese.

"Perda da Independencia" (q.v.)   "Loss of Independence." An expression referring to the period of Portuguese history from 1580 to 1640 when the country was ruled by Spain. Following the battle of Alcacer Quibir on April 8, 1578, in which King Sebastião was killed leaving no heir to the throne, Sebastião's uncle Cardinal Henrique became king, ruling until his death in 1580. Because he, too, died without issue, the throne passed to a distant relative, Philip II of Spain, known in Portugal as Filipe I. Two more Spanish Filipes ruled Portugal until the Duke of Bragança retook the throne in 1640, becoming King João IV, known as *O Restaurador* (The Restorer). DHP.

pessegueiro (Pg.) In São Tomé e Príncipe, a small tropical tree (*Chytranthus mannii*) that yields a valuable hardwood and bears fleshy edible fruits. Ficalho, *Plantas Uteis*, p. 121.

PIDE (*Policia Internacional e de Defesa do Estado*) "International Police for the Defense of the State," the secret police organization created by the Portuguese government in 1957 to locate, detain, interrogate, and persecute individuals conspiring against the government in its overseas provinces. PIDE systematically rooted out nationalists and was much feared and hated. So successful was PIDE that the nationalists were forced to maintain only small revolutionary units inside the colonies and could not communicate regularly with those cells that did exist. Around 1970, PIDE was renamed *Direção Geral de Segurança* (DGS, q.v.). Newitt, *Portugal in Africa*, p. 226.

pidgin Portuguese A rudimentary Portuguese jargon originally developed around 1550 for purposes of trade in West Africa during the slave trade. It incorporates the vocabulary of Portuguese and other languages with a simplified form of Portuguese grammar. Some modern scholars have advanced the theory that pidgin Portuguese has given rise to Afrikaans and contributed to the Afro-Dutch dialect called Papiamento that is spoken in Surinam and the former Dutch Caribbean. Carvalho, *As Colonias Portuguesas*, p. 22. *See also* Fala de Guiné, Pequeno Portugues.

Pijiguiti (Afr.) Dockyards at the broad estuary of the Geba River in Bissau. This was where in 1959 PAIGC (q.v.) organized the first longshoremen's strike. The government responded to the strikers with gunfire, killing 50 and wounding 180. The Pijiguiti massacre was the turning point for the founder of PAIGC, Amilcar Cabral, and his followers who then decided that an armed struggle was the only way to achieve independence. HDRGC.

pipa (Pg.) In the colonial period, a Portuguese measure of wine equal to 238.5 liters or 126 English gallons (an Imperial cask, one-quarter of a hogshead). Duncan, *Atlantic Islands*, p. 260. *See also* quartilho.

plague The term applied to bubonic plague, a contagious and often a fatal disease caused by a bacterium (*Pasteurella pestis*) and characterized by swelling (buboes) of the lymph glands, fever, prostration, delirium, and usually swift death. Fleas carry the disease from infected rats to humans. Known since antiquity, it was recorded in China in 224 BC. Beginning in the fourteenth century and continuing throughout the Middle Ages, this disease occurred in Europe in staggering pandemics that destroyed virtually the entire population of cities. These plagues, also known as the Black Death, have occurred in Luanda, Angola, Lourenço Marques, Mozambique, and other Portuguese seaports since colonial times. It was not until 1920, when plague struck Luanda, that its incidence and consequences in a Portuguese-African location were fully described. *Revista Medica de Angola*, Luanda, 1923, pp. 317-24; FWNE.

"Plateau for England, Lowland for Portugal" The slogan of Cecil John Rhodes, coined in 1890 to promote his aim to leave the Manica Plateau of Mozambique in British hands and the coast for Portugal, therefore dividing the colony into two areas of influence. Although the policy was strongly opposed by Lisbon, Rhodes' plan was successful and the Manica Plateau became part of Southern Rhodesia, now Zimbabwe. Duffy, *Portuguese Africa*, p. 220.

Plymouth Brethren A Christian community that founded a mission in Kwanjulu, Bié district, southern Angola, in 1890, linking the hinterland with Benguela on the Atlantic coast. This group was founded in Dublin in 1831 and named for Plymouth, England, from which the first Puritan (Congregational) settlers sailed for Massachusetts in 1620. The Plymouth Brethren was established by Benjamin Wills Newton and others to enjoy Christian fellowship and try to recapture the simplicity of the apostolic church. Axelson, *Portugal*, p. 250.

PNA (*Partido Nacional Africano*) (Pg.) "National African Party." A moderate political group organized by *mestiço* intellectuals in Lisbon in 1921. Its aims were economic reform, better education, and more autonomy for the colonies. The PNA tried to establish relations with the Pan-African Congress led by W.E.B. Du Bois. In a Lisbon meeting in 1923, a group of nationalists endorsed the PNA activities in Angola and São Tomé e Príncipe. The PNA sent representatives to Geneva to the International Labor Organization meetings in 1923 and 1925 where they repeatedly asserted that the African personality was "one of enduring vitality." Marcum, *The Angolan Revolution*, I:21-2; DHP.

poço dos negros (Pg.) "Cemetery for blacks." A pit for the burial of slaves dug in Lisbon in 1515 by order of King Manuel I. Before its establishment slave traders and masters simply left slave corpses to rot on dunghills and refuse heaps, or else buried them in shallow graves where the dogs dug them up and ate them. For fear that the rotting bodies would corrupt the atmosphere, the king ordered that a pit be dug and filled with quicklime to serve as a communal grave for dead slaves. The pit, which gave its name to the present Lisbon street *Poços dos Negros*, was on the western side of the city outside the Santa Catarina gate and near the area where many slave corpses had been found unburied. Saunders, *A Social History*, p. 110; Rodney, *Africa in Europe and the Americas*, CHA, Cambridge, 1975, 4:582; GEPB. *See also* poço seco.

poço seco (Pg.) "Small Cemetery." A common burial ground for slaves dug in 1515 in the city of Elvas by order of King Manuel I. Saunders, *A Social History*, p. 110.

Policia Internacional e de Defesa do Estado *See* PIDE.

political commissar strategy The strategy of the political leadership working for FRELIMO (q.v.) in the Tete area was as follows: after arriving in a village, an agent would explain that he was interested in finding a wife; this enabled him to establish contact with the chief and the people then, having won the confidence of the former, the agent would identify the people who most likely would help the independence effort. When sufficient people were recruited and mobilized, his work ended and he would move on to the next village. Munslow, *Mozambique*, p. 119.

polygamy In Angola and elsewhere, the practice of having two or more spouses (multiple wives are polygyny; multiple husbands polyandry). This traditional custom in pre-Christian Africa was practiced by both animists and Moslems. Even after Christianity had been introduced in the Congo and other regions of Angola, many newly baptized heads of families continued to practice such "pagan" behavior. Manuel Baptista Soares, Bishop of Congo from 1612 to 1619, reported to Rome in his *Visita a Limina* that on a trip to Cambambe, he spoke with seven chiefs, all baptized and all still polygamous; one had 120 wives, another 100, and a third 15. Gabriel, *Angola*, p. 226.

pombeiro (Afr.) A Portuguese white or *mestiço* bush merchant who c.1750 bought slaves in *pombos* (markets) in Angola, then sold them to the Crown or to private contractors in Luanda, Benguela, and other coastal trade centers. The nearly ubiquitous *pombeiros* were found trading slaves from Cunene, southern Angola, on the Atlantic coast to the Zambezi River on the Indian Ocean shores of Mozambique. In the nineteenth century, the *pombeiros* organized caravans across two large routes. The first went from Lunda in northeast Angola, through Cassanje, Melanje, and on to Luanda; the second from the Zambezi to Central Africa. The wealthy and powerful *pombeiros* controlled and monopolized both trade routes and fed the economy of the towns of Luanda and Benguela with profits from slaves, wax, ivory, and, later, rubber. The two most famous *pombeiros* were Pedro João Baptista and António Amaro José who in 1806-14 crossed Central Africa from Cassanje to Tete then back to Luanda on the Atlantic. The *pombeiros* were also called *funantes pretos*. After slavery was abolished, *pombeiro* meant simply a trader. Wheeler, *Angola,* pp. 49-50, 54, 65-7; DHP: GEPB.

pombo (Bant.) "Slave market." In the interior of Angola c.1600, in distant and isolated trade centers, African chiefs exchanged ivory, wax, and other goods for slaves. The first reference to a *pombo* is connected with a market controlled by the Mbundu at Stanley Pool (now Malebo Pool), on the Congo River. A slave trader in a *pombo* was called *pombeiro* (q.v.). Axelson, *Portuguese in South-East,* p. 243; Trimingham, *Trade and Conflict,* p. 17.

Ponta Delgada (Pg.) A seaport and the capital city of the Azores, discovered and settled by Portuguese navigators in 1443. King Manuel I declared it a *vila* (town) in 1499. King João III granted Ponta Delgada the status of "city" on April 3, 1546, and a Jesuit college was opened there in 1591. In 1970 its population was 69,930. Today it is an important commercial and tourist center. It exports pottery, hats, distilled liquors, and citrus fruit. GEPB.

Port Herald Burial Society A society organized by miners at the Shamva Mine Corporation in Southern Rhodesia c.1900. The majority of its members were Mozambican laborers. The high mortality rate in the mines forced these workers to establish the society to provide funerals and burials for its members killed on the job. Munslow, *Mozambique,* p. 57.

Porto Alexandre (Pg.) A fishing village founded in 1853 on the Atlantic coast south of Mossâmedes, southern Angola. The fishermen and their families came from the Algarve, Portugal, and established a prosperous fishing industry. Today it is one of most important economic centers in southern Angola. Duffy, *Portuguese Africa,* p. 98.

Porto Grande, Cape Verde *See* Mindello.

Porto Novo (Pg.) A Portuguese trade center established c.1550 on the Gulf of Guiné to buy gold, spices, and slaves. It was also the seat of the Dahomey Kingdom, ruled by a king, but after 1761 controlled by Portugal. In 1863, it became a French protectorate. Porto Novo is now the capital of Benin (formerly Dahomey) and the second largest city in the country. In 1970 it had a population of 110,000. HDB.

Porto Santo (Pg.) A small island and port in the Maderian archipelago 40 mi. (80 km) northwest of Maderia. It was discovered c.1425 by João Gonçalves Zarco and Bartolomeu Perestrello, the latter the father of Isabel Moniz Perestrello who became the wife of Christopher Columbus. Settled c.1440 by Perestrello, who was granted the title *donatario* (q.v.), this isolated island was often attacked by pirates and privateers. In the period around 1690 about 600 Portuguese colonists settled in Porto Santo. They raised cattle, sheep, goats, and horses and grew barley, rye, and wheat, the last exported to Funchal, Madeira. The island population in 1960 was 3,550. Duncan, *The Atlantic Islands*, pp. 7, 63, 255; GEPB.

portolano (It.) Medieval navigational chart used between 1300 and 1500. The earliest *portolano* still surviving was produced in Genoa by Petrus Visconte in 1311 and is considered to mark the beginning of professional cartography. The *portolani* are characterized by rhomb lines that radiate from the center in the direction of the wind or compass points and were used by pilots to lay courses from one harbor to another. The charts were usually drawn on vellum and embellished with a frame and other decoration. Of the roughly 130 *portolani* surviving, most of them are in Italy or Catalonia; three are in Portugal, including one drawn by Pedro Reinel c.1450. The Italian *portolani* tend to include only Western Europe and the Mediterranean basin, but some from Catalonia can be considered maps of the then-known world. DHP; EB; EI.

Portugal Portugal first became independent from Spain in 1143. Due to internal and international factors, beginning in 1380 under King João I, head of the House of Avis, it began a world maritime expansion. He married the English princess Philippa of Lancaster the same year and among his sons Prince Henry (1394-1460), known in English as The Navigator, is the most famous. Prince Henry conquered Ceuta in 1415, giving his intellectually gifted mind a taste for adventure and discovery. Sailors in his service were sent to explore along the West African coast, passing Cape Bojador in 1434. In 1487, Bartolomeu Dias was the first European to sail around the Cape of Good Hope at the southernmost end of Africa, opening the sea route to India. Under King João III (reigned 1521-1557), Portugal reached the height of its colonial power. In 1578 his son, Sebastião I, invaded North Africa but was defeated and killed, signalling the end of the House of Avis and the decline of Portugal. In 150 years of exploration and conquest, Portugal became an empire and one of the greatest colonial powers in the world. It was the first European nation to colonize sub-Saharan Africa and to begin the settlement of Europeans in these colonies beginning in 1490. The Portuguese partly westernized the continent, introducing maize, wheat, manioc, New World beans, coffee, and European and New World fruits, cattle, and domestic animals. In the process of introducing Christianity and "civilizing the Africans," Portugal, like many other colonial powers, made serious mistakes. Perhaps the most serious was the founding of the slave trade beginning in 1500 and not ending until the middle of the nineteenth century. Because the transport of slaves to Brazil and the rest of the New World was very profitable, Portugal concentrated mainly on the slave trade, neglecting to develop its colonial economies and industries, unlike England, France, and Holland whose plantation economies, while hugely profitable, were dependent on slave labor. Portugal resisted the abolition of slavery, among other reasons, because this trade was compatible with its feudal colonial system. Only by the middle of the nineteenth century did Portugal begin to improve its colonial commerce in beeswax, ivory, and rubber, and start to organize modern colonization. European and American industrialization and capitalism needed workers in Africa to produce the raw materials for their factories, to build roads and railroads to transport those raw materials, and to provide a market for European products. This was more important than supplying slaves to cultivate sugar, cotton, or tobacco in the Americas. The exploitation of African laborers continued well into the twentieth century. It was not until the 1960s that African nationalists, opposed to colonialism, organized the wars for independence that ended in 1974 and resulted in the independence in the next year of five former colonies: Angola, Cape Verde, Guinea-Bissau, Mozambique, and São Tomé e Príncipe. Henderson, *Angola,* pp. 99-102. Marques, *History of Portugal* pp. 133-148; DHP; EB; GEPB.

Portugal and King Gurunhana Gurunhana (1850-1906), king of Gaza in Mozambique, signed a treaty with Portugal in May 1886 that provided military protection to the kingdom, granted him the rank of colonel, and paid a subsidy of 1,000 *contos* a year. In return, Gurunhana (1850-1906) was obliged to secure free transit through the kingdom to Portuguese traders and to promote agricultural development and education. A Portuguese official was stationed in the kingdom to improve relations. By 1895, Gurunhana was unhappy with Portuguese abuses and he and his forces confronted the Portuguese. Gurunhana was defeated, the kingdom was in disarray, and he was exiled to the Azores, where he died. DAHB; ESA; GEPB.

Portugal, Armed Forces Coup of 1974 in *See* Lisbon, Military Coup of 1974 in.

Portugal e o Futuro (Pg.) "Portugal and the Future." An important book by General Antonio de Spinola, a leading army officer, published in 1974 in Lisbon by Arcadia. In it the author argued that Portugal's African wars could not be won by military means, but could only be settled by political negotiation. He went on to expose what he called "Portuguese myths," including Portugal's "civilizing mission" in her overseas territories which he called a false assumption. He called for the decolonization of Portuguese Africa, proclaiming the Africans' right of self-determination. He recommended the creation of a "vast Lusitanian Community" that would comprise the overseas territories, including Brazil. It would be a commonwealth that could build upon the progressive autonomy of each of its parts. More than anything else, *Portugal e o Futuro* brought Portugal's once-great world empire to an end. Bruce, *Portugal*, pp. 21, 102; DHP.

Portugalidade (Pg.) "Portugality." The concept of an idealized style, attitude, or way of life that later writers believed embodied Portuguese civilization at the time of the Discovery (q.v.). It was to them *"Um ideal patrio que um portugues deu ao mundo expressiva liçao de Portugalidade,"* ("A patriotic ideal that the Portuguese gave the world as an eloquent lesson on Portugality,") Simões, *Nós...*, p. 461. *See also* soul of Portugal.

portugaloiser (Fr.) French name for the *cruzado*, a Portuguese gold coin that circulated in northern Europe for centuries. It was also struck in places like Zwolle, Holland, and Hamburg, Germany. The *portugaloiser*, first minted c. 1450 when a great quantity of gold from Guiné entered Lisbon, was stamped with a cross and named the *cruzado*. It had a fixed value and weight and was used in international trade to pay for the maize, wheat, and manufactured goods that Portugal needed. It was this Portuguese gold of West African origin and great purity that made Portuguese coins a major European currency. Boxer, *The Portuguese Seaborne Empire*, p. 31. *See also* cruzado.

Portuguesação (Pg.) Official Portuguese policy aimed at speeding the entry of Africans into the Portuguese economy, culture, and Christian life by educating them and teaching them Portuguese skills, values, and ideals. It was an ambitious goal of the *Novo Estado* (q.v.) of President Antonio O. Salazar c.1927. As late as 1967, the Portuguese president praised the colonists, missionaries, and soldiers for their efforts to make Africa and Africans totally Portuguese, with all its virtues and defects. DHP; GEPB.

Portuguese Africa Until the end of the nineteenth century, Portugal's possessions stretched across southern Africa from the Atlantic to the Indian Ocean, comprising some 780,000 sq. mi. (2,019,327 sq. km), an area equal to Western Europe. In perhaps no other region of Africa has the presence of a colonial power been so clearly impressed as on the cities and towns of Portuguese Africa. "In a sense they are Portugal; the architecture, the streets, the city squares, the gardens and parks are fundamentally Portuguese. But beyond the towns, in the bush, in the African fields and villages, little has changed in four hundred years of domination. In contrast, the urban centers betray the advance of Europe." In 1958 Portuguese Africa's population was about 5,500,000, 99 percent of whom were Africans. Duffy, *Portuguese Africa*, pp. 1-2; GEPB.

Portuguese African citizenship   In the 1960s, when Portugal was facing increasing uprisings among Africans, the Portuguese government promulgated laws eliminating the traditional duality of political and civil status between so-called "civilized" and "uncivilized" Africans. In 1965 Portugal declared that all Africans were to have full Portuguese citizenship, subject to the same obligations and enjoying the same privileges and rights as its other citizens. The government restated that the goals were to create among Africans a sense of being Portuguese and to address the need to raise their educational, social, and economic status within the framework of Portuguese civilization. Herrick, *Area Handbook*, pp. 2-3; GEPB.

Portuguese colonial policy   This policy is reflected in the body of principles, laws, and norms promulgated for several centuries by the Portuguese state to create conditions needed for what the Portuguese perceived to be the welfare and survival of African communities. It was intended to be a pragmatic policy that eventually altered and reoriented customary ethnic laws and values toward a "civilized" Portuguese society. Cunha, *O Sistema Portugués*, p. 5.

Portuguese Congo district   A district of 94,750 sq. mi. (35,141 sq. km) created by the government on May 31, 1857, with Cabinda as its capital. It had five administrative units; Cabinda, Cacongo, Santo Antonio do Zaire, Ambrizete, and São Salvador do Congo. Its first governor was Neves Ferreira who, like all administrative personnel up until 1914, was an army officer. Felgas, *Historia*, pp. 139, 181, 192.

Portuguese Coup   *See* Lisbon, Military Coup of 1974 in.

Portuguese East Africa, explorations in   Portugal's presence in East Africa began with Vasco da Gama's expedition in 1498. After rounding the Cape of Good Hope, he sailed up the East African coast to the area that later became Mozambique. Since the beginning of Portuguese occupation, miscegenation between Portuguese and Africans had given rise to a mixed-race population that around 1650 emerged as the so-called Afro-Portuguese settlers. Members of this new social group controlled government, trade, and politics on the lower Zambezi River and along the Mozambique coast up to Cabo Delgado. During the eighteenth century, they held a strict monopoly on foodstuffs, cotton cloth, ivory, and gold. When gold was discovered in the escarpment north of Tete, some of them began to embark on new conquests north of the Zambezi. In the early nineteenth century, quasi-feudal states were organized by these rich and powerful Afro-Portuguese landholders, called *prazeros* (q.v.). Their wealth, invested in slave trading, mining, and *prazos* (q.v.), brought them still more sources of income. Afro-Portuguese *prazeros* became slave traders, supplying local demand at the time when, in the face of international abolition of the slave trade, Brazilian, Cuban, and American slave traders joined the French and closed down their operation in the former slaving ports in Angola and elsewhere in Africa. Newitt, *Portugal in Africa*, pp. 8-11; DHP.

Portuguese indigenous policy (Pg.)   Since the Discovery (q.v.) the Portuguese goal in Africa was to integrate Africans into Portuguese society, to convert them to Christianity, to teach them the Portuguese language, and to educate them to be citizens of Portugal. On the economic level, Africans, men in particular, were taught European work habits and methods and were expected to support their families. For those cultures where the men traditionally grew cash crops and the women grew the food to feed the family, this was a new concept. This process, described as "civilizing" the Africans, began soon after the first contact in 1480. In the colonial period these ideas were often forgotten because of local wars and Portuguese political instability. From just after the French Revolution in 1789 to the twentieth century, the government tried in vain to organize an egalitarian Portuguese-African society under the banner of liberty, fraternity, and equality. In 1926, the *Novo Estado* (q.v.) struggled to build a selective process of acculturation according to the degree of "civilization" reached by an individual African. In 1954, the Salazar regime attempted to educate them and capacitate them to enjoy all the rights and obligations of Portuguese citizenship. Cunha, *O Sistema Portugués*, pp. 6-7, 131-2; DHP.

Portuguese influence in Benin   Since 1475 when Portuguese navigators discovered the Gulf of Guiné and built São Jorge de Mina as a trade center in the Dahomey Kingdom (modern Benin), this area was controlled by Portugal. The impact of its presence is shown in such place-names as Porto Novo, in the denominations of cowrie currency in which the smallest unit is called a *toque* and the largest a *galhina*, in the Portuguese names for certain fetishes, and in the name for heads of commercial centers, called *cabosseros*. This linguistic influence has also spread to other parts of Portuguese Africa and to Brazil. Polanyi, *Dahomey*, pp. 181-2; HDB.

Portuguese Military Coup of 1974   *See* Lisbon, Military Coup of 1974 in.

Portuguese policy of association   A policy established by the Third Portuguese Republic of 1910. It was based on the principles of subjugation of the "non-civilized" African population in the colonies. While this system of government kept customary laws, it imposed a special penal code, restrictions of freedom, and limited self-determination and economic-industrial control while decentralizing the administration and recognizing the moral, not the political, personality of each colony. Cunha, *O Sistema Portugués*, pp. 21-3.

Portuguese policy, African resistance to The opposition to colonialism in Africa began around 1880 when the *mestiço* intellectual elite in Angola and Mozambique demanded more schools and better education for Africans at a time of great agricultural and industrial expansion. This generation of leaders believed in the cultural integration of the colonial society and rejected discrimination against both African workers on the plantations and *mestiços* in the government bureaucracy. Included in this group of protesters were labor leaders and journalists opposed to government control. The labor shortages at this time were acute, particularly on São Tomé. By 1950, half the African labor on the large plantations on Sao Tomé e Príncipe had to be imported from Cape Verde, Angola, or Mozambique. This caused hardship and resentment in the places from which they came. In 1953 hundreds of African workers on Sao Tomé were massacred by police after they protested labor conditions. Following this savagery the opposition turned violent and in 1961 nationalists took up arms to combat this system of forced labor and social and economic injustice. Chilcote, *Protest,* pp. 238, 294.

Portuguese policy of secrecy during the Discovery For the projects he sponsored, Prince Henry had a policy of keeping from public knowledge the time and length of the voyages of exploration, the territories visited, the new information gathered about ocean currents and prevailing winds, and any other facts or data that might be helpful to competitors. This official policy explained the strange silence maintained by fifteenth century Portuguese chroniclers concerning Portuguese maritime expansion. Around 1480, King João II expanded this policy and was responsible for the disappearance of early ships' chronicles such as those referred to by the fifteenth-century Portuguese chronicler G.E. de Zurara. Prestage, *The Portuguese Pioneers*, pp. 168-9.

Portuguese Town A barrio in Banjul, the capital of Gambia. It lies west of the barracks and MacCarthy Square, fronting the Atlantic. In the nineteenth century, this was the the area in which many Portuguese *mestiço* merchants and traders resided. Today it is still a mulatto neighborhood. HDG.

Portuguese travels and explorations in Africa Portuguese explorers traveled inland from coastal bases in West and East Africa from the beginning of the Discovery (q.v.). Around 1460, navigators sailed to the upper course of the Senegal and and Gambia rivers, distances of about 200 mi. (350 km).

Timbuctu, Tekrur (qq.v.), and the upper Niger River were reached between 1480 and 1487. West Africa was explored under orders of King João II in 1482, reaching what would become São Jorge da Mina in the Gulf of Guiné. That same year Diogo Cão discovered the mouth of the Congo River, sailing up it as far as Congo and arriving at Mbanza, the settlement of the African chief Nzinga-a-Cuum. The chief eventually agreed to be baptized, taking the name King João I of Congo. In East Africa, Vasco da Gama arrived at Mombasa on the Indian Ocean in 1498. In 1514-5, António Fernandes traveled to Monomotapa, now part of Zimbabwe. Pero Covilha reached Abyssinia by way of Cairo in 1492. After that time there were several attempts to explore central Africa, a goal not achieved until the nineteenth century. DHP.

Portuguese West Africa, explorations in   Portugal began its expansion along the West African coast when Gil Eanes passed Cape Bojdor in 1434 and by 1480 Bartolomeu Dias had reached the Cape of Good Hope on the southernmost coast of Africa. The first colonists settled on São Tomé around 1490 and married African women, giving rise to the mixed-race class that became the *mestiço* aristocracy. These Afro-Portuguese were farmers and traders who spoke Portuguese and acquired local habits, values, and beliefs. By the end of the sixteenth century, their new society replaced the original European feudal caste. Newitt, *Portugal in Africa*, pp. 2, 3.

posto (Pg.)   In Portuguese Africa, an administrative unit established in 1907 by the Portuguese government comprised of a group of villages with a population usually totaling several thousand people. In the 1960s, the Portuguese-African population grew so quickly, they numbered upward of 48,000 people in some *postos* in Angola and Mozambique. Henriksen, *Mozambique*, pp. 100-01.

Praia (Pg.)   The capital of Santiago Island, Cape Verde, founded in 1652. In 1769, the Marquês de Pombal upgraded the old village, designating it a city and the capital of the island. In the colonial period, it was a port for the slave trade and a stopping place for fresh water for ships sailing to South America and down the West African coast. Local export of livestock and export of *orchil* (q.v.), a local dye plant, kept the port busy. By 1980 it had a population of 37,480. Today it exports millet, beans, manioc, tobacco, rum, and coffee. Its airport serves the South Atlantic lines. GEPB; HDRGC; WNGD.

Prassum Promontorium (Lat.)   "Commanding Promontory," the southernmost point of Africa, roughly the area of the Cape of Good Hope. Known by Europeans from hearsay, the *Prassum Promontorium* appeared in Fra Mauro's 1459 planisphere over twenty years before its discovery by the Portuguese explorer Bartolomeu Dias in 1480. In 1485, King João II of Portugal, in a formal communication to the newly elected Pope Innocent VIII, referred to the fact that his navigators had reached the *Prassum Promontorium* where he said the barbarian world began. Parry, *The Discovery of the Sea*, pp. 57-58. *See also* Promontorio Sacro.

prazero (Pg.) In colonial Mozambique, the recipient of a royal land grant called a *prazo* (q.v.) which often encompassed an enormous territory. The recipient, usually a Portuguese or Portuguese-Goan, had the obligation to pay an annual tax, provide specific services, and obey the laws promulgated by the government. These *prazeros* had virtual absolute power to rule the estate and the hundreds of slaves who cultivated the land as well as the thousands of free Africans living on it. The *prazero* usually built houses for the administrators and a church and residence for missionaries. Many sent their sons to Lisbon or Goa to be educated. The *prazeros* formed a powerful elite that wielded progressively more economic, political, and military power. During the second half of the nineteenth century the Portuguese authorities made concerted efforts to restrain and control the *prazeros*, a goal not achieved until the close of the century. Isaacman, *Mozambique: From Colonialism*, pp. 29-32, 59-63; DHP.

prazo (Pg.) In Mozambique, a large estate granted by the king of Portugal to Portuguese-African and Goan settlers. This system of placing public land in private hands began c.1650 and continued until c.1850. It was based on the concept that the descendants of the founder be recognized as virtual rulers. An adaptation of the ancient Portuguese feudal system, this land grant system began in Sofala around 1640 when Portuguese captains held jurisdiction over land and people near trade centers and villages on the Indian Ocean coast. By right of conquest, large tracks of land were granted for three lifetimes (a total of 90-100 years) to government officials and African chiefs with the obligation to settle villages and develop the estate. By a treaty signed in 1659 between the Monomotapa king and the Portuguese, the former made a formal surrender of his whole kingdom to Portugal and the Portuguese captain at Tete was confirmed to be in possession of the land, villages, and fair in the area. From the middle of the seventeenth century, the *prazos* south of the Zambezi River had already assumed the form they were to maintain for more than 200 years. Isaacman, *Mozambique: From Colonialism*, pp. 17, 18-19; Newitt, *Portuguese Settlement*, pp. 54-62; GEPB. *See also* prazero; prazo da Coroa; prazo legistation; prazos, abolition of; prazos, policy regarding leasing of.

prazo da Coroa (Pg.) "Crown *prazo*." In Zambezia, Mozambique, *prazos* owned by the king of Portugal and abandoned by their grantees. Consequently, they derived no revenue for the king. From 1750 to 1850, this land was granted with limited rights to settlers. The settlers were obliged to cultivate the land and to pay taxes, but they could not sell, mortgage, or divide the estate except under special circumstances and with express royal permission. Isaacman, *Mozambique: The Africanization*, p. 43; DHP. *See also* prazo.

prazo legislation The granting and renting of *prazos* in Mozambique was a perennial problem for the Lisbon government. In the seventeenth century and up to 1762 when the administration of Mozambique and Goa was separated, anyone who wished to acquire a *prazo* could petition the governor of the town of Dos Rios setting out his particular claim to land. The official, after satisfying himself about the legality of the petition, was free to issue a temporary grant. The papers were sent to Goa and the viceroy of Goa-Mozambique issued a *carta de aforamento* (deed lease) and a confirmation of the grant. If the *prazo* were deeded but unused and there were still one or two years of the lease to run, the heir could apply for renewal after the death of the leaseholder, but in each case the grant had to be confirmed by the government. When Mozambique was separated from Goa, *prazo* leasing was suspended. It was not reinstated until 1778 when the application for a vacant *prazo* was made to the governor of Mozambique. After investigating the circumstances of the vacancy, he fixed the rent and issued a new deed to the leasee. Over the years, *prazo* legislation underwent many reforms. One of the last, in 1888, divided the *prazos* into three categories: isolated *prazos* in danger of invasion by chiefdoms; fiscal *prazos* legally granted by the Crown; and *prazos* held by privileged individuals and corporations. Newitt, *Portuguese Settlement*, pp. 90-2, 353-4; GEPB.

prazo society In colonial Mozambique from 1750 to 1850, an indigenous Afro-Portuguese *prazo* society emerged. It was a social class that evolved from the intermarriage of Portuguese settlers and African women and characterized by African customs and mores clearly defined by pattern of residence, extended family kinship relations, and political loyalties. The basic socioeconomic unit was the leaseholder, married to an African woman, who also kept many mistresses and their children living in large compounds. He took an African name, worshipped local gods, observed local customs, applied traditional laws, and kept hundreds of slaves and freedmen, with their families, in large compounds. Often these *prazeros* (q.v.) organized military forces to protect their vast dominions. Isaacman, *Mozambique: The Africanization*, p. 43; DHP.

prazos, abolition of The *prazo* system, organized around 1640 by the Portuguese in Mozambique, was reformed several times. The last reform took place in 1915. In the 1930s, the Salazar government abolished the *prazos*, which had become monopolies run by Afro-Portuguese settlers. Newitt, *Portuguese Settlement*, pp. 54-60; GEPB.

prazos, policy regarding leasing of In Zambezia, Mozambique, the lease of a *prazo* was for three lifetimes (approximately 90-100 years). By law, a *prazo* could not be mortgaged or divided without royal permission. Actually, many *prazos* were granted but not developed because it would be too expensive. Consequently, the state did not receive any income from them. In 1758 all *prazo* grants were suspended until 1778 when the governor-general of Mozambique, Antonio Manuel de Mello e Castro, surveyed the system and reinstated *prazo* leasing, guaranteeing the rights of the new leaseholders. The Lisbon government agreed with his policy and approved the long-term contracts he had entered into. This policy was economically beneficial to both the leaseholders and the government. Newitt, *Portuguese Settlement*, pp. 93-4.

Preclara tua (Lat.) A bull issued by Pope Leo X on January 10, 1516, authorizing sea captain to baptize sick slaves coming from Guiné. Each captain paid one golden *ducade* to the Church of the Conception in Lisbon by order of King Manuel I for this privilege. Pinto Rema, *A Primeira Evangelização*, BCG, Lisbon, 1966, xxi(82):321.

presidio (Pg.) In Angola and elsewhere, an isolated fort guarded by a garrison established to protect surrounding villages and farms against invaders. Often a *presidio* subsequently became a town. In 1579, Paulo Dias de Novais began construction on a line of *presidios* in the Luanda area from the coast up to the Cuanza River. By 1589, he had set up five more in the territory between the Cuanza and Lukala rivers. Duffy, *Portuguese Africa*, p. 36.

preto (Pg.) "Black." During the colonial period, a term was widely used in Portugal, either affectionately or scornfully. In the nineteenth century the term *indigena* replaced *preto* and in the 1960s *Africano* displaced *indigena*. DHP.

Pretogues (Pg.) A pejorative name for *Pequeno Portugues* (q.v.), a creolized Portuguese. This variation of standard Portuguese is spoken today in some urban and semi-rural areas of modern Angola by semi-assimilated Africans. Hamilton, *Black from White Language*, Ideologies and Literature, 1967-8, 1(1):29.

Primavera plantation Located near São Salvador do Congo, and owned by the Nogueira Company of Leopoldville, Zaire, this was one of the largest coffee plantations in northern Angola, employing about 2,000 African laborers in 1960, the year it was the scene of a bloody nationalist revolt. Portuguese forces responded with the massacre of hundreds of laborers. By

1961 Primavera had become a symbol of Angolan rebellion. Pelissier, *La Colonie*, pp. 475-77.

Príncipe Island An island in the Gulf of Guiné 100 mi. (160 km) northeast of São Tomé. It was discovered by João de Santarem in 1471 and named in honor of Prince Henry the Navigator who had died in 1460. The island's highest peak is 3,000 ft. (4,800 m) and it is of volcanic origin with fertile soil. The coastal lowland is hot and humid, but at higher elevations the temperature is mild and there is abundant rain. In 1550 King Manuel I granted Príncipe to Antonio Carneiro, a wealthy merchant who brought colonists from Portugal and slaves from Angola to establish what became a prosperous sugar industry. Soon after, a fortress was built in Praia Delgada in the northern part of the island. In 1735, the main city of San Antonio was declared the capital of the colony where at the height of the slave trade the *Campanhia de Cacheu e Cabo Verde* established a slaving station. In 1706 the French fleet attacked the island and took the fort. The abolition of the African slave trade in 1811 caused an economic crisis not substantially alleviated until 1850 when the introduction of cocoa and coffee cultivation improved the economic position of the islanders. Soon the colonists began exporting coffee to Portugal and the rest of Europe, creating one of the wealthiest societies in Portuguese Africa. Plantation owners such as the Barão de Agua-Itzé became millionaires. In 1975, the island became part of the independent People's Democratic Republic of São Tomé e Príncipe. GEPB; WNGD.

Promontorio Sacro (Pg.) "Sacred Promontory." The extreme southwestern point in Europe, located in southern Portugal. This headland, which juts deeply out into the Atlantic, has two small capes, São Vicente and Sagres. Around 1437, Prince Henry built his residence, later called *Vila do Infante* (q.v.), on Cape Sagres. The *Promontorio Sacro* was well known and frequently visited by navigators during the Discovery (q.v.). Costa, *Descobrimentos Maritimos*, Congresso da Historia, Lisbon, 1938, II:10-11. *See also* Prassum Promontorium.

Pro parte tuae serenitatis (Lat,) A bull issued by Pope Julius II on January 31, 1508, granting King Manuel I of Portugal the right to convert the indigenous people of the African West coast to Christianity. Once they were properly instructed and baptized, the king had the right to force the new converts to work on his estates. In return, he was obliged to provide food, clothing, and shelter. Pinto Rema, *A Primeira Evangelização*, BCG, Lisbon, 1966, xxi(82):316.

Protestants in Mozambique In the second half of the nineteenth century Protestant missionary activity among Mozambican workers, especially in the

South African mines, greatly increased and the flow of laborers to and from the Rand spread Protestantism to south and central Mozambique. Many people in northern Mozambique also converted to Protestantism while working as migrant laborers in Nyassaland and Tanzania. Beginning in 1926, the Salazar regime restricted Protestant mission activities and in 1928 Portugal withdrew their right to have schools outside their properly registered centers. Protestant missions came to be regarded as advocates and fomenters of African nationalism and by the 1960s, the missions became centers of resistance to colonialism. Several future nationalist leaders were educated in Protestant missions, including Eduardo Mondlane of Mozambique. Munslow, *Mozambique*, pp. 66-7.

provas judiciais *See* tribal ordeals.

Pumbo (Afr.)   An African town in northeastern Angola which had a large slave market in the nineteenth century. Portuguese and African traders from all over the colony came to Pumbo to barter ivory, wax, and gold for slaves. Vansina, *Kingdoms of the Savanna*, p. 53.

Pungo Andongo (Afr.)   An administrative post in the Malanje district, central Angola. This was the seat of the Dongo Kingdom conquered by Luis Lopes de Sequeira in 1669. In 1857, the Portuguese built a fort there that led to an increase in agriculture and commerce. In 1904 the Malanje-Luanda railroad came to Pungo Andongo, bringing prosperity to the region. GEPB.

putu (Afr.)   "Portuguese." In the colonial period, the name given by Africans to Portuguese settled in Angola. Felgas, *Historia*, p. 21.

puul (Afr.)   A rich grassy soil where the Brames (q.v.) of Guinea-Bissau cultivate upland rice, millet, and groundnuts (qq.v.). Mota, *Guiné Portuguesa*, I;303.

{ Q }

Qadiriya Tariqa (Ar.) An Islamic sect that converted many Mandingos in Guinea-Bissau in the 1760s. Around 1770 Moslem missionaries established a Qadiriya Tariqa center on the Futo Toro plateau midway up the Senegal River. From here the sect expanded to western Guinea-Bissau. Gonçalves, *O Mundo Arabo-Islámico*, p. 198. *See also* Tijaniya Tariqa.

Quae Olim (Lat.) A bull signed in Rome by Pope Gregory XVI on January 13, 1845, establishing the São Tomé diocese as a suffragan of the archdiocese of Lisbon and separating it from the São Salvador de Bahia archdiocese in Brazil. GEPB.

quartilho (Pg.) In the colonial period, a measure of wine equal to 0.4 liters or 3.36 English gills (4 gills = 1 pint or 16 oz.). Duncan, *Atlantic Islands*, p. 260.

quarto (Pg.) "Quarter." Tax collected c.1440 at the *Casa dos Escravos* (q.v.) in Lisbon and equal to 25 percent of the cost of a slave. This amount was estimated by dividing a shipload of slaves into four lots and taking one lot as representative of the whole. Saunders, *A Social History*, p. 9. *See also* vintena.

quatro-mil reis (Pg.) "Four thousand *reis*." By order of King José I, a coin minted in 1755 in Mozambique and in 1758 in Rio de Janeiro and Lisbon. GEPB.

Quela (Afr.) The capital city of Bando e Bangala district in east-central Angola. At an altitude of 4,000 ft. (1,210 m), its temperate climate makes it a rich cotton-producing region. GEPB.

Quelimane (Afr.) A seaport on the Indian Ocean north of the mouth of the Zambezi River. Vasco da Gama arrived here in 1498 and found a prosperous community of Swahilis and Afro-Arabs. It was an active trade center dealing in ivory, gold, and slaves. It was also the place where several of his sailors fell ill with yaws, a new disease to Europeans. In 1545 the Portuguese established a fort and a commercial center there to control trading between Goa and the

African coast. It was a busy slave station that in 1814 was opened to foreign ships. Today it is an important commercial center located a few miles inland from the ocean. GEPB; WNGD.

Quelimane do Sal (Afr.) A Mozambican *prazo* on the mouth of the Zambezi River rented by Dona Teodora Temporaria de Matos in 1829. She kept this property under her control until 1875 when it passed into the hands of the Albuquerque family. Newitt, *Portuguese Settlement*, pp. 287, 289.

Quelimane River River of central Mozambique that empties into the Indian Ocean north of the Zambezi. It was partially explored by Vasco da Gama in 1498. In 1545 the Portuguese established a trade center at its mouth that soon became a thriving port of call for ships in the Indian Ocean. Axelson, *Portuguese in South-East*, pp. 24, 134-6; WNGD.

"Quem não esta na Camara esta na Misericordia" (Pg.) "Who is not in the Chamber is in the Misericordia." A proverb from Alentejo, Portugal, which refers to the loyalty of Portuguese colonists who were proud to serve the government in either of these two institutions in Africa and elsewhere in the Empire. Boxer, *Portuguese Society,* p. 206.

"Quem tem raça de preto, sempre se lhe conhece" (Pg.) "A black is always a black." An old Portuguese saying that refers to the fact that African physical features cannot be denied. Chaves, *O Preto da Guiné*, Congresso Commemorativo, Lisboa, 1946, 2:562.

quenafe (Afr.) In Mozambique, a tropical shrub (*Hibiscus cannabimus*) that yields a fiber used to make cordage and mats. PDM.

Querimba Islands (Afr.) A group of over twenty islands in the Indian Ocean off Mozambique between Pemba and Cabo Delgado. Vasco da Gama visited the area in 1498 then Portuguese settlers developed and controlled the region beginning in 1744. In 1808 Muslims from Madagascar attacked and expelled the Portuguese. Boxer, *The Querimba Islands*, Studia, 1963, 11:343-5.

Quessua (Afr.) An American Methodist mission established in 1890 in Malange in eastern Angola. The missionaries founded a school to educate local children, a hospital, and residences for the teachers and medics. Over its many years of service, it was one of the most active mission stations in the area. In 1961 the Quessua missionaries were harassed by followers of the Maria sect, white settlers, and the Portuguese authorities, always distrustful of Protestant missions in Angola and particularly antagonistic during the War for Independence (1965-75) when the missionaries were accused of helping the nationalist forces. Marcum, *The Angola Revolution*, I:23, 124, 149.

Quessundé (Afr.) In Guinea-Bissau, a choir that performs folk songs. The young singers periodically boarded with Balanta (q.v.) families to learn these traditional songs. Monta, *Guiné Portuguesa*, I:330-1.

quiaca (Afr.) A beer made from bark of the *quimbombo* (q.v.) tree mixed with honey, popular among the Bié of central Angola. GEPB.

quianca (Kimb.) "Siren." A popular literary character in modern Angolan poetry. Usually she appears in dreams, taking many different forms including that of a mermaid. This and other literary devices have been studied by Oscar Ribas in his work *Missosso* (Luanda, 1967). Ervedosa, *Itinerario*, pp. 13, 14.

quibaba (Afr.) In Angola, a tall tropical tree (*Celtis henriquesu*) with a thin ash-white trunk and edible fruit. Its extremely valuable wood is used to make furniture and is highly esteemed as firewood. It is found in Golungo Alta east of Luanda and elsewhere in West Africa. Ficalho, *Plantas Uteis*, p. 258; GEPB.

quibaba-da-queta (Afr.) In Angola, a tropical hardwood tree (*Entandophragma angolense* Welw.) reaching the extraordinary height of 140 ft. (43 m). Its bark yields a medicine used to treat fevers and its wood is also considered very valuable. Ficalho, *Plantas Uteis*, p. 116.

quibaba roxa (Afr.) In Angola, a tall tropical tree (*Khaya senegalensis*) with a whitish bark and edible fruit. Its valuable wood, a type of African mahogany, is used to make furniture and is much exported. It is found in Golungo Alta and Serra da Queta east of Luanda and elsewhere in West Africa. Ficalho, *Plantas Uteis*, p. 258.

Quibala (Afr.) The name of both a municipality and its capital city in the Cuanza-Sul district of Benguela, southern Angola. Situated on a tableland 4,265 ft. (1,300 m) high, its temperate climate attracted Portuguese colonists. It is an important commercial and communications center linked by road with Amboim, Libolo, Malanje, and Bié. GEPB.

quibanda (Kimb.) Tax for unmolested passage imposed on outsiders by African chiefs in the Bié territory, southeastern central Angola, c.1870. GEPB.

quibeba (Afr.) A tall tropical tree (*Ficus quibeba* Welw.) of striking appearance with big leaves similar to those of a magnolia. It yields a milky substance used to glue domestic furniture. It grows in the Golungo Alto forests of Angola. Ficalho, *Plantas Uteis*, p. 267.

Quibenjula (Afr.) A small promontory on the Atlantic coast, Benguela district, southern Angola. On English maps it appears as Red Point. GEPB.

quibondo-ça-menha (Afr.) A tall tropical tree (*Sterculia tragacantha* Lindl.) that yields a milky latex that is refined to make a type of rubber. It is found in the Golungo Alto forests of Angola. Also known as *quibondo-de-agua*. Ficalho, *Plantas Uteis*, p. 101.

quibosa (Afr.) In Angola and elsewhere, a generic name applied to several species of tropical shrubs including *Triumfetta semitriloba, T. orthacantha*, and *T. rhomboidea*, the last also found on São Tomé. All these plants yield a strong fiber used by Africans to make cordage, a valuable commercial product. Ficalho, *Plantas Uteis*, pp. 96, 106.

quibosa-ça-iala (Afr.) A tropical tree (*Hibiscus calyphyllus*) found in the Golungo Alto forests of Angola. Africans use its fibers to make textiles. GEPB. *See also* quibosa.

quibosa-ia-muchito (Afr.) In Angola, small tropical trees of the genus *Cordia* that yields a very strong fiber used for cordage. This collective name is applied to several species that grow in dense clumps in the Golungo Alto forests. Ficalho, *Plantas Uteis*, p. 223.

Quiita (Afr.) A Catholic mission founded in 1894 on the fertile banks of the Caculovar River, Huila province, southern Angola. The mission built a church, several schools to educate local children, and an infirmary. Beside religious education, the mission operates a technical station that provides agricultural instruction to increase local production of sugar cane, millet, beans, sweet potatoes, and various fruits. GEPB.

Quilemba (Afr.) A small railroad station on Chela Mountain on the Mossâmedes-Serpa Pinto line that runs into the Lubango Valley, Huila district, southern Angola. GEPB.

Quilengues (Afr.) Town and capital of the Quilengues municipality, Huila district, southern Angola. This old colonial town was founded in 1685 near the Caconda fort. Beginning in 1722 the governor of Benguela used Quilengues as a base for exploration of the territory. A military garrison was established there in 1827 followed by a church, school, and several missions by 1854. Although African unrest prevailed until 1907, the government managed to control the region. It is a rich livestock area where cattle, sheep, goats, and pigs are raised. It is an important market with an annual fair. In 1960, the municipality had a population of 52,525. GEPB.

Quiloa (Afr.)   An island city off the Indian Ocean coast near Sofala, Mozambique. It was founded by Persians in the tenth century and taken by the Portuguese in 1502 when its Islamic ruler Habrahemo requested protection from King Manuel I. Soon it became an important trade center where Portuguese, Arabs, and Africans dealt in gold, ivory, and slaves. It also attracted Indian and Chinese merchants who traded in Oriental merchandise. In the nineteenth century it became an important international market connecting East Africa with the Orient. Before World War I, Germany governed it; the British took it over in 1920. It is now part of Tanzania. DHP.

quilombo (Kik.)   Maroon (q.v.) settlements built in isolated regions by fugitive slaves on São Tomé and elsewhere in Africa. The first *quilombo* on São Tomé was established around 1600. Garfield, *History*, p. 258.

quilombo camps   Temporary Jaga war stations established in central Benguela, Angola, c.1580 during their struggle against the Portuguese. The camps sheltered warriors and their families. The transient and dangerous nature of these settlements is attested to by the custom of forbidding women on pain of death to give birth within its borders. After confinement, the woman could return to the camp with her baby. Childs, *The Peoples of Angola*, JAH, Cambridge, 1960, I(2):275-6.

Quilombo dos Bembos (Afr.)   An agricultural settlement established by the Portuguese government in 1960. This was a multiracial community located in Cuanza-Norte, east of the Lunda. Production was strictly controlled and enforced by government officials. Bender, *Angola*, pp. 104, 116-7. *See also* quilombo.

Quilua (Afr.)   The town seat of the Antonio Enes municipality in Nampula, Mozambique. By 1856 it was an important slave market. Portuguese military forces occupied Quilua in 1918. GEPB.

quimbar (Afr.)   In Angola, a half-urbanized African who returns to his village after working in a city or in the mines. Also spelled *kimbar*. GEPB.

quimbo (Bant.)   In Cape Verde, one's native village. Cape Verdians are deeply attached to their roots, their homes, and their place of birth. The *quimbo* is a symbol of whatever is dear and loved, but of necessity left behind at home. Migrants to São Tomé as well as those settled in New England in the United States feel the call of their distant village and the underdeveloped land, ravaged by drought, that forced them to migrate. For twentieth-century Cape

Verdian writers the *quimbo* is a recurring theme in fiction and poetry. Carreira, *The People*, p. 113.

quimbombo (Afr.) In Angola and elsewhere a tropical wild shrub (*Drepanocarpus* sp.) the bark of which is used to prepare a native beer. GEPB.

Quimbumbe (Afr.) An African village near Ambriz on the Atlantic coast in northern Angola. It is an important manufacturing center that produces sacks, baskets, and other domestic articles. GEPB.

Quimulaza (Afr.) A Congo dynasty in the São Salvador area that c.1636 usurped the throne by ousting the royal Quimpanzu family. The first Quimulaza king was Alvaro VI who reigned from 1636 to 1641. The Quimulaza were defeated in the Battle of Ambuila in 1665 and moved to Quibango Mountain near the origin of the M'brige River in northern Angola. Gabriel, *Angola*, pp. 131-2.

Quinga (Afr.) An administrative post in the Nampula district, northern Mozambique, established in 1901 at the mouth of the Quinga River. GEPB.

Quingenge (Afr.) An administrative town in the Benguela district, southern Angola. It is on the Benguela railroad 104 mi. (170 km) from Lobito on the Atlantic coast and 400 mi. (644 km) from Luanda. In 1960 it had a population of 20,125. It is an important commercial and agricultural center with a Catholic mission, schools, and an airfield. GEPB.

quingombó (Afr.) A tropical cultivated variety of okra (*Hibiscus esculentus* L.). Its unopened flower buds and immature seed pods are eaten by Africans in Angola. A similar plant is cultivated in Brazil where is called *guingombo de cheiro*. Ficalho, *Plantas Uteis*, pp. 96-7.

quinjuanjua (Afr.) In Angola, a tropical plant (*Ampelopsis heracleifolia*) bearing an edible astringent fruit. Africans use it to prepare a fermented beverage, a kind of wine. It is also spelled *xinjuanjua*. Ficalho, *Plantas Uteis*, p. 119.

quintal (Pg.) In colonial Mozambique, a measure of weight equal to 4 *arrobas* (130 lbs or 58.8 kg). Axelson, *Portuguese in South-East*, p. 245.

Quionga Triangle (Afr.) A wedge of territory between Cape Delgado and the mouth of the Rovuma River in northern Mozambique, that the 1919 Treaty of Versailles restored to Portugal after near thirty years of German occupation. Henriksen, *Mozambique*, p. 108.

quipaka (Kimb.) A copper coin equal to 50 *reis* that was used in the colonial period in Ambaca, central Angola. EDK.

Quipeio (Afr.) An administrative town, Huambo district, southern Angola. It is in a rich agricultural area with a temperate climate, located in the Benguela *planalto* near Nova Lisboa. In the twentieth century many Portuguese colonists settled in the region. GEPB.

quipuculo cafeli (Afr.) A tropical nonbranching tree (*Vernonia conferta*) of the Composite (daisy) family with a cluster of leaves at the top, somewhat resembling a palm. Its wood is considered very valuable. It is found in Cazengo, Golungo Alto, and the Bembos forests of Angola. Ficalho, *Plantas Uteis*, p. 204.

quipuculo-poculo (Afr.) A small tree (*Anthocleista macrantha*) with big leaves and a striking and elegant shape. Ash from the burned leaves is used for making soap. It is found in the Golungo Alto forests of Angola. Ficalho, *Plantas Uteis*, p. 221.

quisafú (Afr.) A small tree (*Bixa orellana* L.) of the American tropics introduced into Angola by the Portuguese in the colonial period and now found in Golungo Alto and Cazengo. Its seeds produce a red dye used to stain baskets and other domestic articles; also used in folk medicine. Commercially it is called *rocu, urucu, annatto*, among other names. Ficalho, *Plantas Uteis*, p. 86.

quisanana (Afr.) A tropical weedy plant (*Corchorus tridens*) with edible stalks and leaves. Africans mix them with oil and eat them as greens. It is found in the Luanda district, Pungo Andongo, and elsewhere in Angola and the Zambezia of Mozambique from which it is exported to India. Ficalho, *Plantas Uteis*, p. 106.

Quisiba Island (Afr.) The southernmost island of the Querimba (q.v.) archipelago off Mozambique in the Indian Ocean. In 1744, the Portuguese Moraes family took possession of the island and were granted a *prazo* for three lifetimes (approximately 90 years). Soon after it became a thriving estate. The leaseholder became "Africanized," taking African wives, and adopting an African name, customs, and language. In 1829 Domingo de Moraes, a descendant of the founding family, was still in possession of Quisiba Island. Newitt, *Portuguese Settlement*, pp. 213-5.

Quissama (Afr.) Municipality in the Cuanza-Norte district, Congo province, northern Angola, in an area of sleeping sickness (q.v.). Its capital,

Muxima, is located on the left bank of the Cuanza River in a dense forest that includes the towns of Dembo-Xio, Mumbondo, and Quixinje, all linked by rail with Luanda. Paulo Dias de Novais visited Quissama in 1581 and the Portuguese built a fort there in 1599. They built a new fortress in 1686 to repel attacks by local chiefs and pacify the region. In 1960 it had a population of 11,307. GEPB.

Quissanga (Afr.)   A municipality in the Cabo Delgado district, Niassa province, northern Mozambique, in a region the Portuguese first explored in 1500. An agriculturally rich Swahili-speaking area that produces beans, groundnuts, millet, rice, cotton, and manioc, it includes the towns of Mucojo, Montepuez, and Maconde. In 1960 it had a population of 36,335 including Indo-Portuguese and Indo-British. GEPB.

quitanda (Pg.)   A female African street vendor in nineteenth-century Portuguese African towns. At that time, African women sold goods imported from Portugal and the rest of Europe. Boxer, *Portuguese Society*, p. 129.

quitandeiro (Pg.)   In Angola and elsewhere, a nineteenth-century itinerant African male who peddled cloth, food, medicines, and other goods in hamlets and towns in the interior. Caetano, *Os Nativos*, p. 98. *See also* funante.

Quitengue (Afr.)   An African kingdom in the region of Monomotapa, Mozambique, visited by the explorer Antonio Fernandes around 1513. The area was rich in gold and ivory and Fernandes recommended building a factory on an islet in the Cuama River. The Portuguese established a trade center there to attract gold and ivory merchants from Quiteve and Monomotapa (qq.v.), and at the same time protect Sofala and Angoche, booming cities in the 1600s. Axelson, *Portuguese in South-East*, p. 82.

Quiteva (Afr.)   A colonial fort in southern Angola established on the right bank of the Cunene River. In 1915 it was attacked by rebellious native chiefs who were defeated. GEPB.

Quiteve (Afr.)   An old Moslem kingdom in Mozambique south of the Zambezi River between the Manica Mountains and the Indian Ocean. When the Portuguese arrived in 1513, it was already an established trade center for ivory, gold, and slaves. The African chiefs lost control of the gold mines in 1574 when in a struggle for power Portuguese forces defeated and killed the king of Quiteve and took control of the area. Assisted by the Portuguese, a member of the royal house took over the throne. After that time, Portugal dominated the trade in gold, ivory, and slaves. Axelson, *Portuguese in South-East*, pp. 48, 80.

quitoco (Afr.) In Angola, the name for aromatic herbs (*Blumea* spp. and *Pluchea* spp.) used by Angolan practitioners to treat scurvy and other diseases. The herbs are found in Golungo Alto, Icolo e Bengo, Ambriz, and elsewhere. Ficalho, *Plantas Uteis*, p. 206.

quitundo (Afr.) A tropical tree (*Heeria insignis*) the charcoal of which is used by African blacksmiths to shape copper and iron while they are hot and malleable. It is found in Caconda, Pungo Adondo, Huila, and elsewhere in Angola. Ficalho, *Plantas Uteis*, p. 12.

Quixaxe (Afr.) An administrative town in the Nampula district, northern Mozambique, about 40 mi. (65 km) from the Indian Ocean. This was a military region often disturbed by rebellious African chiefs. Until 1910 it was part of Mossuril military command; afterward it was put under the nearby army post at Mojical. GEPB.

quixibua (Afr.) A tropical tree (*Ampelopsis urenaefolia* Planch.) with astringent fruits, a favorite food for Africans and also used to prepare a local beer. It is found in Golungo Alto, Cacondo, and Bié in southern Angola, and elsewhere in Africa. Ficalho, *Plantas Uteis*, pp. 119-20.

Quizungo (Afr.) Village on the Indian Ocean coast in the Quelimane district of Mozambique. Shipwrecked Portuguese sailors landed there in 1585. By 1837 it was a center of the slave trade and in 1861 became an administrative post. Vail, *Capitalism*, p. 19.

Quizungo River (Afr.) A river in the Quelimane district, central Mozambique. In 1861 it marked the southern border of the Angoche captaincy. Here in 1894 Gungunhana, the last king of Gaza, organized an unsuccessful military rebellion against the Portuguese. GEPB.

Rabil (Afr.)   Village on Boavista Island, Cape Verde. In 1810, Bishop Silvestre de Maria Santissima declared it the capital of the island and built a church there dedicated to São Roche. GEPB.

racial attitudes in Portugal at the Discovery   At the Discovery (q.v.), the Portuguese believed that, while Africans brought from Arguim (q.v.) c.1444 were human beings, by nature they were inferior to whites in physical and mental ability, therefore best suited for bondage. At the time the Latin word *nigrum* (black) was another name for the Devil, and to be black was a misfortune. The playwright Gil Vicente describes slave women as unattractive because of their color, their broad noses, and their kinky hair. These "ugly" features are mentioned by Gomes Eanes de Zurara, the chronicler who saw the first African slaves, captured in Arguim, arrive at Lagos. He described them as "black and deformed individuals coming from the lowest level of the world." Saunders, *A Social History,* pp. 166-7; GEPB.

rama   A large palm (*Raphia pedunculata*) found in Mozambique and elsewhere in Africa. Leaves are used to make hats, baskets, clothes, and light cordage. Sap from the stem is used to make the sweet beverage, *harafa.* Boxer, *Portuguese Society*, p. 125

Ramadan (Ar.)   The ninth month of the Moslem year, a period of daily fasting from sunrise to sunset. In Guinea-Bissau the Islamic Mandingos faithfully observe this fasting and pray daily in the mosques. They call this devotion *Suncaro.* Gonçalves, *O Mundo Arabo-Islámico*, p. 214.

Rand   *See* Rand Mines Ltd., Witwatersrand.

Rand Mines Ltd.   In South Africa, a mining corporation associated with Corner House, a British company formed in 1893 to develop the gold fields at Witwatersrand. Since the 1860s many Mozambicans have been seasonal laborers in this area. In 1894 Best and Williams, a Lourenço Marques company, worked with the Portuguese government to regulate organized legal migration of Africans to work seasonally in the Rand mines. Rita-Ferreira, *O Movimento Migratorio*, p. 15; ESA. *See also* Witwatersrand.

Rand Native Labour Association In Mozambique, an official government agency established in 1897 by the *Câmara das Minas de Transval* (Transvaal Chamber of Mines) to recruit responsible contractors to register Mozambican workers for the South African gold fields. Rita-Ferreira, *O Movimento Migratorio,* pp. 64-65. *See also* Witwatersrand.

rapariga lotada (Pg.) "Highly-priced female slave." The term used to describe a young female slave, 16 to 20 years old, who was healthy, attractive, and well developed. This category of slave was highly sought after by slavers calling at Cape Verde ports c.1756 on their voyage to Brazilian markets. Carreira, *As Companhias Pombalinas,* BCG, 1968, xxxii(91/92):302-4.

real (Pg.) A Portuguese copper coin of low value circulated in Portugal and its overseas possessions early in the colonial period. The *real* was discontinued in the early sixteenth century, but its multiples (e.g., ten *reis*) were retained. Boxer, *The Portuguese Seaborne,* p. 391.

rebita (Kimb.) In Angola, a popular dance among the Kimbundu people. Such modern poets as Viriato da Cruz and Agostinho A. Neto use this dance as a symbol of the spirit of an African world the downfall of which may be the result of having been abandoned by the gods. The subject of the African's lot, embellished by folk tradition and the rhythm of such popular dance music as the *rebita,* has profound meaning for African poets. Hamilton, *Voices,* pp. 95-6.

recrutamento de mão-de-obra (Pg.) "Labor recruitment." Since the 1870s, the Portuguese periodically registered Mozambican migrant laborers to work in the South African gold mines, Rhodesian (Zimbabwean) farms, and other employment out of the country. This migration was strictly controlled, not least because the government was paid a percentage of the laborers' salaries. Caetano, *Os Nativos,* pp. 28, 29. *See also* migracao legalizada.

recrutamento sistematico (Pg.) "Systematic recruitment." In Mozambique, a legal registration system established by the WNLA and the NRC (qq.v.) in 1906 to recruit African laborers for the gold mines. The period of labor (12-18 months), salary, transportation, health care, and other benefits were clearly stated and enforced. Rita-Ferreira, *O Movimento Migratorio,* pp. 114, 115. *See also* migração internacional.

regedor (Pg.) "Administrator." An African administrator of a group of villages called a *posto* (q.v.); he had the duties of assisting in the collection of taxes, persuading people to contract their labor outside their place of residence or on their own fields, enforcing government rules, and gathering information. The *regedor* or *regulo* system was introduced in Portuguese Africa in 1907. A *regedor* came to his position in the colonial administration by succession, election, or appointment by the government for his loyal service in the army or for being an able civil servant. As late as 1965, about 90 percent of the *regedores* were traditional chiefs or government appointees. They were never popular and, during the War for Independence (1960-75), incurred the enmity of the nationalists for their exploitation of workers and their collaboration with the Portuguese. Henriksen, *Mozambique,* pp. 101-2.

regedoria (Pg.) An administrative group of African villages, considered a juridical unit administered by a *regedor* (q.v.) according to Portuguese colonial legislation introduced in 1907 by the Lisbon government. Most Africans lived in *regedorias* and those living outside these jurisdictions were deprived of what few political rights the residents might claim. This system was abolished in 1963 at the start of the War for Independence. Henriksen, *Mozambique,* pp. 101, 142.

regimento (Pg.) "Manual." At the time of the Discovery (q.v.), navigators and explorers before they sailed received detailed instructions and information regarding the route, the places to be explored, and other navigation matters in a document called a *regimento*. The sea captains and later the governors were responsible for seeing that a *regimento* was strictly followed. Prestage, *The Portuguese Pioneers*, p. 202.

Regimento da Altura do Sol (Pg.) "Method to Measure the Height of the Sun." A book delineating the way to calculate the height of the sun. The method was described in 1573 by Pedro Nunes, the chief cosmographer to King João III of Portugal. Prestage, *The Portuguese Pioneers*, p. 202.

Regimento da Inquisicão (Pg.) "Rules for the Inquisition." A code promulgated by King João III on August 16, 1552. In 141 articles it described the necessary qualifications for judges and officials, how a process should be initiated, rules to investigate allegations and take testimony from witnesses, procedures to apply to and conduct the court of appeals, the execution of sentences, and regulations governing prisons. GEPB.

Regimento do Astrolabio (Pg.) "Astrolabe Handbook." A book containing the scientific method to determine latitude while on the high seas, performed by observing the position of the sun and other stars. This revolutionary method to measure solar inclination, previously unknown in Europe, was developed c.1483 by royal cosmographers serving under King João II. Later, it was renamed the astronavigation (q.v.) method and was widely used beginning with Diogo Cao's expedition of 1482-84 to the Cape of Good

Hope. In 1485, the chief mathematician of the office, José Vizinho, was sent by the king to Guiné to test the *Regimento do Astrolabio* method in the Southern Hemisphere. Costa, *A Marinha dos Descobrimentos*, p. 86; DHP.

Regimento do Astrolabio de Munich (Pg.) "Astrolabe Handbook of Munich." An astronomic calendar originally published in 1494 in Munich. A navigational section added to the 1509 edition was based on the work of José Vizinho, a contributor to the *Regimento do Astrolabio* (q.v.). Barbosa, *Novos Subsidios,* Congresso da Historia, Lisbon, 1938, pp. 57-59.

Regimento Nautico (Pg.) "Navigation Manual." A manual prepared by Mester José, a Jewish physician and cosmographer in the service of King João II and widely used between 1480 and 1498 by Portuguese navigators. GEPB.

regioes da fame (Pg.) "Regions of famine. " In Guinea-Bissau and the Cape Verde peninsula of Africa, areas of barren lands destroyed by erosion and improper agricultural practices. These areas, populated by Fulas and Mandingos, are part of the Sahel (q.v.). Mota, *Guiné Portuguesa,* 1:277.

Regulamento de 1878 (Pg.) "Ordinance of 1878." A statute promulgated in Lisbon on November 21, 1878, interpreting and clarifying the Law of 1875 (q.v.). It declared null and void the two-year government protection given to the former *libertos* (q.v.) and reaffirmed the absolute right to work or not to work and the privilege of accepting or rejecting labor contracts. Cunha, *O Trabalho Indigena,* pp. 142-3.

Regulamento para os Contratos de Serviçais de Colonos na Provincias da Africa (Pg.) "Regulations for Labor Contracts of Workers and Colonists of the African Provinces." This was a labor code promulgated by the Portuguese government in 1878 designed to protect the rights and interests of both settlers and workers in Africa. Because it guaranteed basic human rights, this code was an advance and a milestone in Portuguese African policy. Duffy, *Portuguese Africa*, p. 143.

regulo (Pg.) "Chief." In colonial Portuguese Africa, an African chief who attained his dominant position through succession, election by his peers, or as a reward for service to the Portuguese government. Chilcote, *Portuguese Africa*, p. 93.

Rehobother bastards An African ethnic group that emigrated from South Africa to southern Angola and settled in the Huila *planalto* c.1880. They were not connected with the Boers but like them were granted land by the Portuguese government. They prospered as small farmers and by 1900 were fully integrated into Portuguese society. Clarence-Smith, *Slaves, Peasants*, p. 45. *See also* Boers.

reinado (Crio.) "Parade." A religious procession in which a group of three male friends carried a statue of Our Lady the Mother of God around the capital of Fogo Island, Cape Verde, singing, praying, and stopping to eat in neighborhood houses. A traditional festival still popular as late as 1930. Cardoso, *Folclore*, p. 43.

reis (Pg.) Plural of the *real* (q.v.), a Portuguese monetary unit.

Relatorio da Commissao de Trabalho (Pg.) "Report of the Labor Commission." An 1898 Portuguese government ordinance that imposed the right of the state to coerce African laborers and farmers to produce enough food to feed themselves and preferably a surplus by cultivating their own land. The ordinance declared that the people had a moral and legal duty to do this. Cunha, *O Trabalho Indigena,* pp. 150-51.

RENAMO (Resistencia Nacional Moçambicana) (Pg.) "Mozambican National Resistance." An organization established in 1977 to oppose FRELIMO (q.v.) and its Marxist leaders. Portuguese citizens such as Orlando Cristina, a former officer of the secret police, Jorge Jardim, a millionaire businessman from Beira, and other conservative politicians formed RENAMO to overthrow the Portuguese government in Mozambique. Southern Rhodesia, now Zimbabwe, and South Africa provided funds and military forces to help the insurgents. After seven years of civil war, the RENAMO rebels were defeated and forced to sign the Nkomati Accord (q.v.) with South Africa on March 16, 1984. HDM.

renda do verde (Pg.) "Tax on green [vegetables]." A tax imposed in 1880 on the fresh produce sold in city markets and in the streets in Angola and elsewhere in Portuguese Africa. Boxer, *Portuguese Society,* p. 21.

rendza (Afr.) In Mozambique, a tropical vine (*Cissus adenocaulis*) that yields a substance used in folk medicine to treat eye ailments. PDM.

requisitado (Pg.) "Laborer forced to work." In Mozambique and elsewhere after 1898, an African was compelled by law to make himself available for work and the government kept a list of such workers for private employers. In 1927, it was reported that there were 16,308 *requisitados* in Lourenço Marques. Rita-Ferreira, *O Movimento Migratorio,* pp. 158-9. *See also* Mozambique, forced labor in.

resgate de escravo (Pg.) "Slave redemption." In North Africa c.1400, Moslems often enslaved Christian captives. Such Portuguese religious orders as the Trinitarians (q.v.) were dedicated to rescuing these captives by paying money and sometimes volunteering to take a captive's place in slavery. This practice was not applied to the slave trade between Africa and the New World. Duffy, *Portuguese Africa*, pp. 139-40.

retornados (Pg.) "Returnees." In 1961 at the beginning of the War for Independence, Portuguese white and *mestiço* settlers were forced to leave Angola and Mozambique and return to Portugal. By the winter of 1975/76, there were about one million people, *retornados* and their families, registered for government assistance. The majority had nowhere to live and these destitute colonists were herded into refugee camps on the outskirts of Lisbon and other cities. In those encampments many built rough shacks out of cardboard, old crates, dustbins, corrugated iron, and anything else on hand. The overcrowded camps had shortages of food and medical facilities, leading to the threat of serious epidemics. In 1976 the government was forced to establish offices to administer assistance to the *retornados*. Harvey, *Portugal*, pp. 126-8.

revivalism *See* nativism and revivalism.

Revolta Activa (Pg.) "Active Revolt." Within the MPLA (q.v.), a small opposition group formed in Brazzaville, Congo, in May 1974. It was led by left-wing intellectuals including the brothers Mario and Joaquim Coelho Pinto de Andrade. The group played an important role in the early development of the party although it never rallied more than about seventy supporters. Critical of MPLA's military and political policy, the group attacked Agostino A. Neto for what they perceived to be his dictatorial government. In 1976, seven leaders of the group were arrested for a short time by the government. HDA.

Rhonga See Ronga.

ria (Pg.) In Guinea-Bissau, a long narrow wedge-shaped estuary or inlet, widening and deepening as it goes toward the sea. On the West African coast, especially on the Geba, Corubal, and Cacheu rivers, the sea invades the lower reaches of present-day and former riverbeds, transforming them into estuaries and creating a complicated system of channels. The sea comes into these estuaries after passing over extensive underwater banks which can rise to within 70 ft. (21 m) of the surface. The tapering shape of the *rias* increases the height of the tides, the greatest anywhere in West Africa. These *rias* have a beneficial effect on the climate of the coastal interior and stimulate the growth of forests, palm groves, and mangrove thickets. Mota, *Guiné Portuguesa*, I:368.

ribeira (Pg.) In São Tomé, a small stream; also called simply *agua*. Garfield, *History*, p. 258.

Ribeira das Naus (Pg.) The shipyard in the port of Lisbon where *naus* (caravels) and other ships were built and repaired during the Discovery (q.v.). Located near the *Casa da India*, it was destroyed by the earthquake of November 1, 1755, and replaced by the *Arsenal da Marinha* (Naval Shipyard). *Ribeira das Naus* was the major port of departure for navigators and explorers from 1385 to 1500. Godinho, *A Economia dos Descobrimemntos*, p. 33; DMA.

rice An aquatic, occasionally dryland, cereal grass (*Oryza* spp.) that has been grown widely in the warm climate of West Africa for over 2000 years. At their arrival in 1450, the Portuguese found rice growing on the lower Senegal River. This rice was the indigenous species, *Oryza glaberrima*, rather than *O. sativa*, the Oriental species. Today, the Wolof and the Serer still grow rice as well as millet. Lewicki, *West African Food,* pp. 34-5.

rikan (Afr.) In the Western Sudan, the term for the oil palm (*Elaeis guineensis*) which bears clusters of fruit that when pressed yield palm oil (q.v.). For centuries, Africans have used *rikan* as a source of cooking and medicinal oil. Lewicki, *West African Food*, p. 108. *See also* argan.

Rio de Janeiro Convention An international meeting held in 1815 in Rio. After bitter arguments, Portugal and England signed a treaty agreeing to the gradual abolition of the slave trade between the African colonies and the New World. The treaty contained nine articles, three of which were secret. Cunha, *O Trabalho Indigena,* pp. 21-3. *See also* Slave Trade Conference.

Rio do Ouro (Pg.) "Gold River." Discovered by Gil Eanes and Afonso Gonçalves Balaia in 1436, this river flows into the Atlantic from Guiné, West Africa. The legendary Spanish navigator Jaime Ferrer explored Rio do Ouro in 1346. When the Portuguese arrived at the time of the Discovery (q.v.), they found an active market in gold and slaves in the area. Cortesao, *A Espansao dos Portugueses,* pp. 15, 57; Mota, *Toponimos,* pp. 71-72.

Rio do Padrão (Pg.) Name given to the Congo River by Portuguese navigators c.1495 in recognition of the *padrão* (stone memorial) erected in honor of King João II by the explorer Diogo Cão in 1482. Prestage, *The Portuguese Pioneers,* p. 207. *See also* padrão dos descobrimentos.

Rios da Guiné (Pg.) In early Portuguese chronicles from the period around 1490, this name referred to a large territory in Guinea-Bissau that was crossed by several rivers. In this densely populated area the Portuguese traders found one of the main West African sources of slaves for the Lagos and Lisbon markets. Saunders, *A Social History,* pp. 7, 182; GEPB.

roça (Pg.) In Portuguese, the word for a subsistence farm on which crops and animals were raised. The colonists who arrived at São Tomé in 1485 introduced this type of farming into the island, building settlements and clearing the tropical forest to cultivate vegetables, grains, and fruit trees for family consumption. By importing slaves from Angola, these traditional farms, with house and barn, were developed into small commercial enterprises. By 1500 colonists were prosperous enough to export grain and sugar to Portugal. During this early colonial period, the *roças* remained relatively small and underdeveloped. After 1850 the first large *roças*, were established to grow such cash crops as coffee, *cacau* (cocoa), and sugar cane. These were corporate enterprises geared to international markets and spawning a wealthy class of planter. This economic and industrial revolution made São Tomé a world-class competitor in international markets of the time. Tenreiro, *A Ilha,* pp. 141–43; GEPB.

roça-forro (Pg.) "Slave farm." An expression used in São Tomé around 1895 by white landholders to refer to a small farm owned and cultivated by a former slave. Tenreiro, *A Ilha,* p. 145.

rolo do mar (Pg.) "Ocean wave." At the time of the Discovery (q.v.) this term referred to gigantic and dangerous waves caused by seasonal monsoonal storms, called hurricanes on the Atlantic coast of Africa and typhoons in the Indian Ocean. GEPB.

Roman law on slavery *See* slaves, interracial relations in Portugal and.

Romanus Pontifex (Lat.) A bull issued by Pope Nicholas V on January 8, 1454. It granted Prince Henry, on behalf of Portugal, the right to hold the newly discovered African territories as well as ones to be discovered in the future. It specifically included all the lands, ports, islands, and seas from Cape Bojador and Nao to Guiné and granted the right to build monasteries, churches, and chapels under royal patronage. Felgas, *Historia,* p. 17; Pinto Rema, *A Primeira Evangelização,* BCG, Lisbon, 1966, xxi(82):313.

Rombezia (Afr.) A term applied by Mozambican nationalists in the 1960s to the large territory bordered by the Rovuma and Zambezi rivers. Regional political leaders tried unsuccessfully to establish Rombezia as an independent country. Henriksen, *Revolution,* p. 798.

Rome Peace Accord On October 6, 1992, Joaquim A. Chissano, president of the Mozambique Republic, and Afonso Dhalakama, leader of RENAMO (q.v.), signed a peace agreement in Rome. Under its terms there was to be an immediate truce and Zimbabwean troops would be withdrawn within a month. The troops had been guarding two strategic corridors, the Beira Corridor in central Mozambique and the Limpopo railway in the south, against repeated attacks by RENAMO forces. Up to 500,000 Mozambicans had fled into the Beira Corridor seeking protection. The agreement also laid down the provisions that both government and RENAMO troops would move into specific assembly areas within a month and hand over their weapons to United Nations monitors within six months. *Manchester Guardian Weekly,* October 11, 1992, p. 8.

romeira (Pg.) In Angola, the name for the pomegranate (*Punica granatum*), a decorative fruit tree often planted near a house. It was introduced from Portugal early in the colonial period. Ficalho, *Plantas Uteis,* pp. 181-2.

Ronga, also **Rhonga** (Afr.) A small kingdom located on Maputo Bay in southern Mozambique. In 1522, Portuguese merchants established commercial relations with Ronga traders who brought gold, ivory, and other goods from Central Africa to trade at the Maputo market. In 1833, in alliance with the Zulus, the Rongas took part in an attack against Lourenço Marques. The last Ronga rebellion took place in 1895 when they were defeated and the kingdom was taken over by the Portuguese government. They are also known as *Xirongas* (q.v.). Henriksen, *Mozambique,* pp. 48, 76-7, 89; GEPB.

Rossio da Trindade (Pg.) The oldest slave market in Lagos, southern Portugal, it was established in 1453, early in the Discovery (q.v.). It became a center for the sale of thousands of slaves brought from Arguim, Guiné, and São Jorge da Mina in the Gulf of Guiné. Iria, *O Algarve no Decobrimento,* Congresso da Guine, Lisbon, 1946, I:204.

Rota do Cabo (Pg.) "The Cape Route." The maritime passage around the Cape of Good Hope, discovered by Bartolomeu Dias in 1498. From 1498 to 1635 the *Rota do Cabo* was under the exclusive control of Portugal. DHP.

Rotavismo (Pg.) "Rotating government." Name given in Portugal in the 1890s to a system of government in which the two main political parties, the *Progresistas* and the *Regenadores,* alternated in office. The parties were controlled by the political bosses in country towns, the landed gentry, the clergy, and certain municipal leaders. Both parties neglected the interests of the rising professional class as well as the working class of Lisbon, Oporto, and other cities. Its leaders became progressively less able to cope with economic and social pressures emerging in Portugal and Africa. In Mozambique there were serious problems with the forced labor policy and the shortage of workers in the Zambezi region. In Angola the forced labor policy created international tensions. In São Tomé and Cape Verde, migrant workers were forced to sign exploitive labor contracts to work on the plantations. The *Rotavismo* system could not control these problems and was replaced in 1904 by the nationalist movement. Vail, *Capitalism*, p. 183-5; DHP.

roteiro (Pg.) "Ship's log." A book in which is entered the daily record of a ship's progress including the ship's position and any notable events of the day. From 1440 to 1500, the period of greatest Portuguese maritime expansion, the *roteiros* of pilots described in detail the coastal topography, distances traveled, landmarks, ocean currents, vegetation, the color of the water, and the direction of winds. *Roteiros* such as the *Roteiro de Esmeraldo* and the *Roteiro de Valentim Fernandes* (qq.v.) form part of the Portuguese national historical records. GEPB. *See also* conhecenças das terras, conhecenças e sinais, portolano, roteiros Arabes.

Roteiro de Esmeraldo (Pg.) An outstanding ship's log kept c. 1550 by Duarte Pacheco Pereira. It includes detailed observations and descriptions of the West African coast from Tangier to the Cape of Good Hope. Costa, *A Marinha dos Descobrimentos,* pp. 294, 295. *See also* roteiro, Roteiro de Valentim Fernandes.

Roteiro de Valentim Fernandes (Pg.) A log kept in the 1540s by Valentim Fernandes in which the author, a pilot, describes the West African coast from Morocco to the Gulf of Benin, including the coast on which the fortress of São Joao Baptista de Ajuda (q.v.) was built. Costa, *A Marinha dos Descobrimentos*, p. 29. *See also* roteiro, Roteiro de Esmeraldo.

roteiros Arabes (Pg.) "Arab logbooks." These Arab logs, especially those describing the East African Coast, were widely used by the Portuguese during the period of the Discovery (q.v.) because they supplied additional information and covered areas not yet reached by Portuguese navigators. Costa, *A Marinha dos Descobrimentos*, p. 296. *See also* portolano, roteiro, Roteiro de Valentim Fernandes, Roteiro de Esmeraldo.

roupa de Cabo Verde (Pg.) "Cape Verde linen," a distinctive cloth woven in the islands and sold in West Africa and elsewhere. Also called *pano de Cabo Verde* (Cape Verde cloth). Carreira, *Panaria*, p. 21.

Rovuma (Afr.) A river about 450 mi. (720 km) long that rises in southern Tanzania, flows east, and empties into the Indian Ocean north of Mozambique.

Inland sections form part of the boundary between Tanzania and Mozambique. Also spelled *Ruvuma.* WNGD.

Rozvi (Afr.) An African chiefdom related to the Monomotapa Kingdom. It rose to preeminence in the fifteenth century when it controlled the territory south of the Zambezi River, a land rich in gold, ivory, and slaves. Antonio Fernandes, a merchant from Sofala, visited the region in 1512 and established trade with the kingdom. A few years later the Portuguese occupied the territory and ruled the kingdom until late in the nineteenth century. In 1890, the British South African Company took over and the kingdom faded away. Henriksen, *Mozambique,* pp. 6-8; Newitt, *Portuguese Settlement,* pp.22-7.

Ruacana (Afr.) Falls over the lower Cunene River on the southwest frontier of Angola and Namibia. GEPB.

rubber booms in Angola The first rubber cycle in Angola began in 1859 when the Portuguese government ordered the Bacongos in São Salvador province to cultivate rubber-producing plants and sell rubber to the government at preset prices. The enforcement of this compulsory policy by terrorist means alarmed and panicked the population and about half the workers between the ages of 20 and 40 fled to Leopoldville, Belgian Congo (now Zaire). Around 1885 the sudden increase in the rubber trade in southern Angola was caused by the discovery of a tropical shrub (*Carpodinus gracilis*) that produces abundant, if inferior, latex that could be sold on the expanding world rubber market. The shrub grows naturally in the deep well-drained sands in the south. Soon it was also found in even greater quantities in the northern parts of the Kalahari sandveld. Production was largely in the hands of Cokwe and Luvale immigrants. They reduced the roots to a pulp and then used a variety of rudimentary techniques to purify the latex. Export peaked in 1903. Intensive overharvesting resulted in a decrease in supply. The boom came to an end early in 1918 due to dwindling production and international competition, mostly from increased production of *Hevea brasiliensis* (the rubber of commerce) and, to a lesser degree, *Ficus elastica* (India rubber). Clarence-Smith, *Slaves, Peasants,* pp. 65, 95; Pelissier, *La Colonie,* p. 261. *See also* rubber cycle in Angola; rubber tree, India.

rubber, commercial (*Hevea brasiliensis*) *See* rubber tree, India.

rubber tree, India A tall evergreen tropical tree (*Ficus elastica*) that grows wild in eastern Angola and elsewhere. It thrives in moist well-drained soil. At one time, this was the major source of natural rubber. In the rubber boom (q.v.) period between 1874 and 1916, Luanda and Benguela became centers of rubber production. The current source of high grade rubber, *Hevea brasiliensis,* was introduced to São Tomé from its native Brazil in 1860 by the Portuguese but it did not overtake rubber produced from India rubber trees until after World War I. Carvalho e Vasconcellos, *As Colonias Portuguesas,* p. 232; GEPB.

rubrocinta (Afr.) A tropical insect (*Seleno rubrocinctus* Giard.) that attacks and destroys the *cacau* (cocoa) tree. It is believed the *rubrocinta* was introduced into São Tomé and elsewhere in Africa from Brazil, where it is native. It is a well known pest in São Tomé where, before it was brought under control in 1922, it decimated the *cacau* plantations in 1918 and 1921. GEPB.

ruivo (Pg.) A category of teleost fish of the order *Acanthoprerygill* (bass, perch, mackerel, and their relatives) having stiff and spiny anterior rays of the dorsal and anterior fins. A kind of fish well known on the Atlantic coast of Portugal where at least six species are commercially fished. GEPB; WTNID.

rum An alcoholic liquor distilled from fermented sugar cane and molasses. It has been made in Cape Verde since 1470 when sugar cane was introduced to the island by the Genoese. By 1508 rum was already an important industry that greatly increased with the acceleration of the slave trade. Rum was exported to West Africa and Portugal. Duncan, *Atlantic Islands*, p. 21.

runners In Mozambique, a corps of recruiting officials organized around 1901 by the WNLA (q.v.) to register Mozambican laborers for the gold fields of South Africa. In Portuguese, this corp was known as *auxilaries de recrutamento.* Rita-Ferreira, *O Movimento Migratorio*, p. 102.

rupee (Hind.) The monetary unit of India, a silver coin equal to US$21 in 1962. Historically, the Portuguese colony of Goa and the presence of East Indian merchants in Africa assured that the rupee was a currency well known in Mozambique and Portugal. Vail, *Capitalism*, p. 203. *See also* thaler.

Rural Labor Code A body of laws that in 1962 superseded the Native Labor Code of 1928 (q.v.). Passed as a result of international pressure on Portugal to end her colonial forced labor policy, the provisions of this code abolished forced labor and penal sanctions for failure to fulfill a labor contract. It also outlawed labor recruitment by the authorities and the paternalistic guardianship of laborers. To supervise the enforcement of this code, a bureau was created. By this substantial reform, practically every worker in Portuguese Africa was henceforth free to work as and where he wished. Henriksen, *Mozambique*, p. 119; Wheeler, *Angola*, p. 196.

rusambo (Afr.) In the *prazo* society of colonial Mozambique, a symbolic gift that signaled the end of a slave-trading transaction. It served as a type of receipt, formalizing the commercial operation. Isaacman, *Mozambique: From Colonialism,* pp. 203(n.83).

Ruvuma River (Afr.) *See* Rovuma River.

Ruys' Steamer Song Protest song of Pirira popular in the 1950s and sung by villagers on the Luaba *prazo,* lower Zambezi. It referred to José Guillerme, known as Ruys, an overseer on the *prazo.* Ruys spread his terror by descending with his armed agents on villages, taking any food they could lay their hands on. This left the people without adequate supplies and forced them to purchase foodstuff from company-owned stores at high prices. One of the verses of the song went, "Fathers, brothers, The Ruys' steamer / Fear for Pirira, / You must run, you must run!" Vail, *Capitalism,* pp. 321-3. *See also* Jemwe song.

saba (Kik.)   A temporary thatch shelter in São Salvador do Congo c.1880. BeAD.

Sabe River (Afr.)   A river in southeast Mozambique about 400 mi. (644 km) long that rises in Zimbabwe, flows across the border into Mozambique, and continues east emptying into the Mozambique Channel on the Indian Ocean. Originally Sabi, also spelled Save, the Portuguese explored the river early in the Discovery (q.v.) on the same trip on which they found the mouth of the Zambezi River. In this mineral-rich region in the period around 1590, the trading town of Saiha and many nearby villages engaged in commerce between the interior and the coastal towns, including those on the Arab-Swahili Bazaruto Islands on the Indian Ocean. Axelson, *Portuguese in South-East*, pp. 27, 173; WNGD.

Sabi River   *See* Sabe River.

Sacalavas (Afr.)   An ethnic group in Madagascar that raided the Querimba Islands in 1807, burning several prosperous settlements. In a second invasion in 1816, Portuguese forces defeated and killed the intruders. Newitt, *Portuguese Settlement*, p. 215

sachicunda (Afr.)   On the Zambezia *prazos* of Mozambique c.1750, the leader of a group of domestic slaves. *Sachicundas* also served a leaseholder as bodyguards and household retainers. Newitt, *Portuguese Settlement*, pp. 195-7.

Sacrae Religionis (Lat.)   A bull signed in Rome by Pope Martin V on June 10, 1421, granting the Franciscan monastery in Ceuta, North Africa, the same privileges as the Mount Sion monastery in Lisbon. GEPB.

Safim (Afr.)   A seaport and old commercial center on the Atlantic coast of Morocco. Around 1450, its Arab ruler requested Portuguese protection. From 1508 to 1541 Portuguese forces occupied the town and built a fortress. Soon Safim became an important trade center linked with the Western Sahara and the São Jorge da Mina (q.v.) trading post in the Gulf of Guiné. Pressed by constant Arab attacks, King João III ordered his forces to abandon the city in 1541. DHP; GEPB.

Sagres nautical school (Pg.) A nautical center established in 1423 by Prince Henry. The school was founded near Sagres, a town on Cabo São Vicente on the Atlantic coast of southern Portugal, to enable scientists, astronomers, and geographers to study and improve navigation and to train navigators and explorers. Among its scholars were Jaime de Majorca, Mestre Joham, Samuel Goleimo, and Antonio de Noli. Prince Henry, himself a scientist, settled there to study and work. He died there on November 13, 1460. His residence was posthumously named the *Vila do Infante* (q.v.) (House of the Royal Prince) in his honor. Marques, *History of Portugal*, I:50-57; DHP; GEPB.

Sahara, caravans in Since the Middle Ages groups of travelers, especially merchants and Moslem pilgrims on their way to Mecca, crossed this vast desert in North Africa that extends from the Atlantic to the Nile. These long-distance travelers and traders carried supplies and merchandise and grouped together for security. Even today it is a dangerous voyage. Hill, *Markets in Africa*, JMAS, 1963, I:445. *See also* trans-Saharan trade.

Sahara Desert (Afr.) A vast desert region in North Africa encompassing c.3,500,000 sq. mi. (c.9,061,000 sq. km), extending from the Atlantic to the Nile. The Western Sahara attracted Portugal's interest beginning in 1352 when Genoese merchants visited and traded in Timbuctu, a wealthy medieval city built along the middle Niger River. Early in the Discovery (q.v.), navigator João Fernandes explored the Rio do Ouro and the Senegal River on the Atlantic coast c.1445, gathering information about Moslem pilgrims and merchants who often crossed the desert. In 1485 King João II established a trading post at Uadem in the Western Sahara. Later he sent Pedro de Evora and Gonçalvo Anes as ambassadors to the King of Timbuctu. GEPB.

Sahel (Ar.) "Border." The area at the southern edge of the Sahara Desert is commonly referred to as the Sahel. It is characterized by periodic devastating droughts. Historically it was a flourishing region of great markets. Western influence penetrated the Sahel and the western Sahara at the comparatively late date of 1448 when the Portuguese reached Arguim (q.v.) on the Atlantic coast in what is today Mauritania. According to Gomes Eanes de Zurara, the first African slaves brought to Lagos, southern Portugal, in 1444 were from the Sahel. Also spelled Sahil. Lewicki, *West African Food*, p. 33, 65; DHP. *See also* Sahelian drought.

Sahelian drought A prolonged period of dry weather that affects West Africa and the Cape Verde Islands. The Portuguese government have kept statistics for the period 1912-1970, a total of 58 years, that show many periods of sustained drought and consequent famine that has resulted in over 250,000 deaths. The unpredictability of the rains has been accompanied by major migrations of people in this area, especially in Cape Verde. While those on the mainland are able to migrate away from drought areas, those on islands are forced to migrate off-island to obtain work to support their families. For Cape Verdians this has meant migration either to plantations on São Tomé or to New England in the United States. These migrants seldom return to their homeland, so the populations of the islands are disproportionately women, children, and the elderly. Since independence in 1975, the Cape Verde government has established an agency of water management and water conservation, developed a modern drilling and desalinization process, and has begun reforestation and erosion control programs to reduce the disastrous natural and social effects of Sahelian droughts. HDRGC. *See also* Sahel.

sailors, African   *See* African seamen.

sailors, diet of   At the time of the Discovery (q.v.), the crews of Vasco da Gama received a daily ration of food and drink as follows: 1 lb. of biscuit, 1 lb. of beef or ½ lb. of pork, 2½ pints of water, 1½ pints of wine, plus oil and vinegar. On fast days, rice, fish, or cheese took the place of meat. The chief dietary element was doubtless the ships' biscuits. The first reference to royal ovens baking biscuits is from 1460, during the reign of King Afonso V. The ovens in the Valley of Zebro near Lisbon were able to supply 17,847 quintals of biscuits in three years, the equivalent of more than a million daily rations. This shows not only the capacity of the Royal ovens, but the great size of Portuguese marine endeavors. Even these ovens, however, were not sufficient to meet the demand, for six other were built in Lisbon near da Porta da Cruz, and it was sometimes necessary to obtain supplies from Spain. At the end of the fifteenth century, on voyages to São Jorge da Mina (q.v.) and Morocco, the daily ration of biscuits was usually 2 lbs. per man, which is about double that given to the Portuguese navy today. Prestage, *The Portuguese Pioneers*, pp. 334-5. *See also* slaves, diet of.

sailors, wages of   According to Gaspar Correa, writing at the time of the Discovery (q.v.), a seaman received five *cruzados* a month, to which was added two *cruzados* for carpenters, caulkers, blacksmiths, turners, and other skilled artisans. The king gave married men one hundred *cruzados* per trip to cover shore expenses and to leave with their wives. Single men received forty *cruzados*. Prestage, *The Portuguese Pioneers*, p. 335. *See also* sailors, diet of.

sal (Pg.) "Salt." Salt was an important industry in Portugal and Cape Verde at the time of the Discovery (q.v.). In 1476, many African slaves were working in the salt pans of the Sado River in Alentejo, southern Portugal. Parish registers show that in the towns there were large numbers of slaves who specialized in salting fish. In 1515 salt was abundant on the seashores of Cape Verde and passing ships could take any amount. Once the salted fish industry developed in New England in the United States, British ships stopped at Cape Verde to load large amounts of sea salt for the New World. Duncan, *Atlantic Islands*, pp. 4, 21, 51; Lewicki, *West African Food*, pp. 116-8.

Sal Island (Pg.) One of the islands in the northwest part of the Cape Verde archipelago, discovered by Antonio de Noli in July 1455. Although it is an arid wasteland, salt is abundant on its shores and has been gathered throughout history by passing ships. In 1960 Sal Island had a population of 2,626. Duncan, *Atlantic Islands*, pp. 8, 21, 158.

sal moio (Pg.) A Portuguese dry measure equivalent to 52 English bushels (3,325 lbs. or 1,450 kg). In 1846, this measure was made a standard weight in Cape Verde. Duncan, *Atlantic Islands*, p. 261.

samacoa (Afr.) In Mozambique, an African official appointed by the Portuguese to work on the *prazos* c.1880. His tasks were to promote agricultural production and the export of cash crops, especially in the Quelimane area. The *samacoa* helped to take the census, collect taxes, and enforce the policy of forced labor. Isaacman, *Mozambique: The Africanization*, pp. xviii, 160, 162.

Sambizanga (Afr.) A Luanda *musseque* (slum) that in 1964 had a population of about 50,000, composed of Angolans, Portuguese, Cape Verdians, and people from other African colonies. Pelissier, *La Colonie*, pp. 344-45.

Sambo (Afr.) A town in the Huambo district, southern Angola, founded in 1902 in a rich agricultural area well irrigated by the Cunene and Cubango rivers. Its temperate climate attracted Portuguese and other European colonists. GEPB.

samn (Ar.) A butter made from churning whole milk; consumed c.1500 in large quantities by the pastoral Berber nomads on the borders between the Sahara and the Western Sudan. This region today is part of Mauritania. The Portuguese found abundant *samn* butter when they visited various chiefdoms settled along the Senegal River in 1450. Lewicki, *West African Food*, pp. 110-1.

sanababiche (Crio.) "Son of a bitch." A term used c.1930 on Fogo Island, Cape Verde. It is the Crioulo corruption of an American expression, introduced by Cape Verdian migrants returning from New England in the United States. Cardoso, *Folclore Caboverdeano*, p. 31.

San Antonio (Pg.) A castle built by the Portuguese on the African Gold Coast in 1503. It was a trade center with facilities to house hundreds of slaves waiting to be shipped to Brazilian markets. It was taken by the Dutch in 1642, and by the British in 1872. The Ghanan government restored it in the 1950s and now it used by the Accra Town Council for offices and as the local police headquarters. In the colonial period it was called Santo Antonio de Axem. HDG.

Sancho the monkey In Cape Verde, Sancho is a symbol of both defeat and hope that if a cataclysm occurs, he can turn disaster upside down. An idle mischief-maker who laughs at unremitting toil, Sancho symbolizes the frustrations of the islanders, incapable of changing their lot for a better world. Davidson, *The Fortunate Isles*, pp. 35-36.

sandimora (Crio.) In Cape Verde, mourning songs sung by relatives and friends at funerals and burials. Valkhoff, *Miscelanea*, p. 46.

Sane Carissimus (Lat.) A bull signed in Rome by Pope Martin V on April 4, 1418, granting King João I of Portugal spiritual privileges in his war to conquer and convert the Moslems in North Africa. Pinto Rema, *A Primeira Evangelização*, BCG, Lisbon, 1966, xxi(82):312.

Sanga A town in Quibala municipality, southern Angola. It was founded in 1893 by runaway slaves and convicts. Soon after, Portuguese forces occupied the camp. Today is a prosperous town linked by road with Novo Redondo on the Atlantic coast and with Vila Teixeira da Costa in the hinterland. GEPB.

sangira (Afr.) In Zambezian *prazos*, an African judge, often a slave, who heard cases and rendered decisions according to customary law c.1788. He was a respected official in the domestic slave hierarchy. Newitt, *Portuguese Settlement*, p. 199.

San Jago (Pg.) A fortress that served as a trade center, built by the Portuguese in the Gulf of Guiné in 1505. Taken by the Dutch in 1650, they rebuilt it and renamed it *Coenraadsburg*. In 1872 it was taken by the British. The government of Ghana restored the old castle in the 1950s. Today is occupied by the Accra Museum and Monument Board. HDG.

Sansa (Afr.) A *prazo* in the Zambezia region leased in 1712 by João Pereira da Silva. Inherited at his death by his daughter, it was administered by her husband Juliano Rodrigues de Paiva until he passed away in 1749. Ines Pessoa, a granddaughter of the original *prazero*, took possession of Sansa in 1757. Ines and her Afro-Portuguese husband Miguel Pereira Gaio managed the estate. Pereira Gaio died in 1800, and the *prazo* remained in the family until 1884 when it was taken by the government. Newitt, *Portuguese Settlement*, pp. 157, 166-7, 315.

San Sebastian A fortress and trade center built c.1560 by the Portuguese at Shama (q.v.) east of Sekondi near the mouth of the Pra River in the Gulf of Guiné. It was taken by the Dutch in 1640 and occupied by the British in 1872. The Ghanaian government restored this old castle in the 1960s and now it is used for offices. HDG.

Santa Casa da Misericordia *See* Misericordia.

Santa Cruz do Castelo Around 1550 this parish was one of several in Lisbon that served the spiritual needs of the slave population. It was a wealthy church located in a northern district near the Alcaçova royal palace where many masters and their slaves lived. According to the parish records, numerous slaves were baptized and married in this church. Saunders, *A Social History*, pp. 55-57; GEPB.

Santa Luzia (Pg.) One of the Barlovento Islands of the Cape Verde archipelago, discovered by the Portuguese navigator Diogo Afonso in 1461. GEPB.

Santa Manga (Pg.) A *prazo* in the Zambezia region leased in 1860 by Manuel Antonio de Sousa, a member of the wealthy Sousa family of Mozambique. In 1874, Sousa rented the estate back to the Portuguese government. Newitt, *Portuguese Settlement*, pp. 323, 315.

Santantoniozinhos (Pg.) "Little Sons of Saint Anthony." The name of the followers of an Afro-Christian sect founded in Quibango, Angola, in 1704 by a young African woman named Beatriz. Gabriel, *Angola*, p. 35.

Santarem (Pg.) A port and city in central Portugal on the northwest bank of the Tagus River. Around 1520 there were many slaves working on farms and in vineyards and olive groves surrounding the city. Today the area produces oil and wine and is a center of tourism. In 1981 it had a population of 62,243. Saunders, *A Social History*, pp. 54, 207; WNGD.

Santarem Generation Portuguese historians have coined this expression to refer to the children of King João I and his queen, Philippa of Lancaster. These exceptional children, who included the future King Duarte (b. 1391), Prince Henry, known as the Navigator (b. 1394), Isabel (b. 1397), João (b. 1400), and Fernando (b. 1402), played important roles in the Portuguese expansion of the fifteenth century, helping to establish the Portuguese Empire that eventually linked Europe, Africa, Asia, and the Americas and included cultural interactions, the impact of which on land and people shaped civilizations that have survived to modern times. For the people of Africa, this contact with Portuguese explorers in the fifteenth century was their first experience with Europeans since the time of the Roman Empire. *See also* Santarem. Bennett, *Africa and Europe*, pp. 25-6.

Sanctae Memoriae Paulus (Lat.) A brief that Pope Gregory XV sent to King Alvaro I of Congo in 1625. The pope announced to the king and his subjects the departure of a group of missionaries bound for the kingdom. The pope told the king that these missionaries had been selected by his predecessor, Pope Paul V, and that his death had interrupted the preparations for departure. GEPB.

Santiago Island (Pg.) The largest island of the Cape Verde archipelago, discovered in 1456 by the Genoese navigator Antonio de Noli and colonized in 1466. King Afonso V granted its settlers the monopoly of the trade between Arguim (q.v.) and Lisbon. By 1512, many ships were calling at its port and in 1590 Sir Francis Drake attacked the settlement. By 1600 Santiago was an important center of the slave trade. In a two-year period between 1609 and 1610, ten ships carrying a total of 4,439 slaves stopped at Praia Grande, now Praia, the major city and port. In 1702 the total population of the island was 2,026. In 1980, the capital city of Praia had a population of 37,480, the island about 90,000. Its main exports are coffee, sugar, and oranges. Duncan, *Atlantic Islands*, pp. 18-21, 166, 200; GEPB; WNGD.

Santo Antão (Pg.) One of the islands in the extreme northwest of the Cape Verde archipelago. It was discovered by navigator Diogo Afonso in December 1461. In 1532 Ribeira Grande, the island's capital, became the seat of the first bishopric of Cape Verde. In 1614 the bishopric was transferred to Praia on Santiago Island. In 1702 Santo Antão had a population of 2,025 and 43,198 in 1980. The island exports coffee, sugar, and citrus. Duncan, *Atlantic Islands*, pp. 18, 179-80; WNGD.

sanzala-enfermaria (Pg.) In rural Angola around 1950, a small government clinic established to care for Africans in agricultural areas. In 1953 there were thirty *sanzala-enfermarias*. Caetano, *Os Nativos*, p. 141.

sanzoro (Afr.) In the Barué Kingdom of central Mozambique c.1850, a small defensive structure built on the frontier along dangerous roads or streams to protect merchants and travelers. Isaacman, *Mozambique: The Tradition,* pp. xi, 62. *See also* aringa.

São Baptista de Ajuda (Pg.)   A fort and slave trade center built in Ouidah (q.v.) around 1680 by Bernardim Freire de Andrade. By 1720 traders from Bahia, Brazil, exported sugar and tobacco to buy slaves in Ouidah, also spelled *Whydah.* Newitt, *The Portuguese in Africa,* pp. 4, 5; DHP.

São Domingos   The seat of a municipality on the northern bank of the Cacheu River in Guinea-Bissau. Established in 1943, by 1945 it had a population of 20,283, mostly Fulas and Balantas. Abshire, *Portuguese Africa,* pp. 18, 20.

São Januario (Pg.)   An agricultural community established in 1880 in Humpata, north of Sá de Bandeira, central Angola by Boer trekkers. The settlers were granted choice acreage, freedom of religion, freedom from Portuguese taxation for ten years, and the right to use their own language and elect their own municipal representatives, all in return for accepting Portuguese sovereignty. The relationship soured as both sides engaged in hostile activities. The Boers soon became restless and most migrated back to South West Africa or north and east into the Congo; others disdained sedentary farming and took to raiding nearby herds owned by Africans. Wheeler, *Angola,* pp. 71-2; GEPB.

São Jorge de Mina (Pg.)   The oldest and most impressive of all the fortresses built by the Portuguese in the Gulf of Guiné. Planning and preparation of materials began in Edina in 1480. In December 1481 more than 600 men under the command of Diogo de Azambuya sailed from Lisbon bringing much of the building material with them. The group included Bartolomeu Dias, the navigator who would sail around the Cape of Good Hope in 1488, and may have included Columbus. The castle, fashioned after the Tower of London, served as the post headquarters from 1482 to 1637 when the Dutch took it. They occupied it until 1872 when it became a British possession. It was restored by the Ghanaian government in the 1960s and today is used as offices by the Accra City Council. Van Dantzig, *Ghana Castles,* p. 90; DHP; HDG.

São Nicolãu (Pg.)   One of the *Barlovento* (windward) group of islands of the Cape Verde archipelago. It was discovered in January 1461 by Diogo Afonso, sailing in the service of Prince Henry. Due to the prolonged droughts, agriculture was not developed until the nineteenth century. Prior to then, the main business was the slave trade and the collection and export of *urzela* or orchil (q.v.), known in English as archil, a dye-yielding lichen found in mountainous areas. São Nicolãu's bay is well sheltered and in the colonial period was a port of call for ships sailing to Brazil. Duncan, *Atlantic Islands,* pp. 18, 158; HDRGC.

"São pretos e nos brancos" (Pg.) "They are blacks and we are whites." An expression used by Boers in Humpata and Huila c.1880 to express their contempt for Africans who, they believed, were by nature inferior to whites and absolutely incapable of equality. For a Boer, to be associated with or to live with an African woman was the greatest dishonor. This racist reasoning was the basis for the now-abolished policy of apartheid in South Africa. Guerreiro, *Boers de Angola*, Garcia de Horta, 1958, 6(1):25.

São Salvador do Congo (Pg.) The original *mbanza* (settlement) and residence of King Nzinga-a-Cuum of Congo, the first African king met by the Portuguese in 1482. After his conversion and baptism, Nzinga-a-Cuum was known as João I. In 1548 the Jesuits built the Church of Christ the Savior, the name of which also became the name of the city. Soon São Salvador became the center of government, trade, education, missions, and military forces in the region. Around 1510, King Afonso I of Congo, the successor to King João I, built his palace in the western part of the city. Across from the royal residence, the Portuguese established their walled headquarters. In 1596, the city became the seat of the first bishopric of the Congo and Angola Diocese. With Dutch incursions into Portuguese territory in the seventeenth century, the city began a steady decline and by 1690 São Salvador was deserted with its twelve churches, fortress, and royal residence in ruins. The bishopric was transferred to Luanda in 1716 and the following year the last Capuchin missionary left São Salvador. Recovery was slow, but by 1881 the population had increased to 3,500. By 1960, a Holy Ghost Catholic mission had returned. The city's importance continued to grow due to the abundance of natural resources nearby and the development of modern agriculture in the surrounding area, both leading to trade and commerce. After independence in 1975, the city was renamed Mbanza Congo. Gabriel, *Angola*, pp. 142-3; Felgas, *Historia*, pp. 62-64; DHP. *See also* São Salvador do Congo Mission.

São Salvador do Congo Mission A Catholic mission established in 1881 in the old capital of the Kingdom of Congo. It was staffed by diocesan missionaries from the famous *Sernache de Bom Jardim* Missionary College (q.v.). Gabriel, *Angola*, p. 254.

São Tomé e Príncipe, agriculture and economy of The Portuguese introduced agriculture to the islands in 1486. They brought sugar cane, wheat, millet, barley, beans, and such fruits as grape, fig, and olive, plus domestic animals. The colonists settled in the northeast around São Tomé city and Vila Trindade, where most of the population is still settled today. Soon the Portuguese introduced African slaves and plants such as *malagüeta* (q.v.), guinea-pepper, cola, oil palm, yam, and sorghum from Angola. Later, the colonists brought Indian hemp, hashish, and other plants and, from the New

World, maize, potato, manioc, cashew (*Anacardium occidentale*), pineapple (*Ananas* spp.), and others. The Portuguese pioneers' contribution to the world economy has never been surpassed. Early in the settlement, the colonists imported slaves from Angola and built a prosperous sugar industry, exporting sugar to Portugal beginning in 1510. In 1554 São Toméan sugar was sent to Lisbon, and from there re-exported to Flanders, England, and Germany. Usually merchant ships sailed to Cape Verde and Madeira to load wheat and millet to take to Lisbon and other European ports, then returned to São Tomé to start the cycle again. By the end of the century the islands' exports were eclipsed by cheaper Brazilian sugar and the islanders, unable to recover the Portuguese market, turned to the slave trade. After the abolition of that trade, coffee and cacao (*Theobroma cacao*) were introduced c. 1830 and a modern plantation system began to develop. Coconut and oil palm plantations were established on the coastal belt; their production accounted for about 30 percent and 5 percent, respectively, of island exports. On both islands, coffee and cacao are still dominant. Cacao (the source of cocoa and chocolate) is typically cultivated on northeastern slopes at elevations of between 650 and 1,300 ft. (200 to 400 m) while coffee is grown at higher elevations. Until 1905, these islands were the world's leading producers of coffee and cocoa. Since then production has declined to about two-thirds of its peak export value. Fishing is also important, especially for shark. Tenreiro, *A Ilha*, pp. 58-60, 77-8; GEPB.

São Tomé e Príncipe, Diocese of   Created by Pope Paul III on November 3, 1534, at the request of King João III of Portugal, the diocese was split off from the Funchal Diocese (q.v.) and included the islands of São Tomé and Príncipe, the West African coast from Sierra Leone (q.v.) to the Cape of Good Hope, and the Kingdom of Congo in Angola. Gabriel, *Angola*, p. 83.

São Tomé e Príncipe, discovery and settlement of   The islands were discovered by João de Santarem in 1470 and first colonized in 1495. Soon it became a center of sugar production for the Portuguese market. For nearly three hundred years São Tomé was both the center of the slave trade between Angola and Brazil and a center of sugar production and export to Lisbon and England. From 1752 to 1852 the government was transferred to Príncipe Island. In 1951 São Tomé e Príncipe were organized as an overseas province. In 1975 it became the People's Democratic Republic of São Tomé e Príncipe. GEPB; WNGD.

São Tomé e Príncipe, education in   Following the first settlement of the islands in 1495, education was limited to mission schools in São Tomé City, later including another mission school in Santo Antonio, the capital of Príncipe. In 1504 the *Loios Conegos* (Blue Canons) from the Saint Eloy monastery in Lisbon opened a mission school for mulatto children in the parish of Our Lady of Grace in São Tomé city. Around 1830, the economic prosperity brought by the introduction of coffee and cacao allowed the local authorities to greatly improve the level of education. On June 5, 1944, the government modernized the educational system and divided it into primary, secondary, and trade schools. At the time there were ten public and ten mission schools. In 1959 a new secondary school, the Liceo João II, was founded, and a new trade school administered by Catholic missionaries was opened in São Tomé city. In 1965 the student population in the city was 3,436 children in primary schools (of which 2,390 were in public schools, and 1,046 in mission schools), 294 in the lyceum, and 64 in the trade school. The government established courses to prepare students to enter advanced schools in painting, commerce, and technology in Portugal. *Sao Tomé Pequena Monografia*, pp. 28-30; GEPB.

São Tomé e Príncipe, emancipation of slaves in Island slaves were provisionally freed by King Pedro V of Portugal on April 29, 1858. As elsewhere in Portuguese Africa, under the emancipation provisions all Africans then in bondage would become *libertos* (free men) within twenty years. Because the emancipation proclamation included the provision that Africans could no longer be forced to work at a particular job, the immediate effect was a shortage of labor. At that time, too, many planters were in the process of increasing their plantings of coffee and cacao, thereby increasing their need for labor. The planters no longer could enslave people, but they continued to treat their island-bound workers as if they were slaves, despite their new legal status. Hammond, *Portugal and Africa*, pp. 314-16.

Sao Tomé e Príncipe, ethnic diversity of The islands' racial composition is the result of nearly five hundred years of acculturation, intermarriage, and miscegenation. The people are descendants of Portuguese, Spanish, and French colonists and merchants and Angolan slaves brought to work on the plantations. This *Crioulo* (q.v.) society has developed a lifestyle conducive to living and working together peacefully. Ashire, *Portuguese Africa*, p. 23; CE.

Sao Tomé e Príncipe, governors of During the colonial period, there were a total of 124 governors in São Tomé e Príncipe. The first, Francisco de Figuereido, appointed in 1586, governed for only a few months before dying of tropical fever. The last was Antonio Jorge da Silva, appointed October 30, 1963. The names and dates of appointment of all the governors can be found in *São Tomé Pequena Monografia*, pp. 87-102. GEPB.

São Tomé e Príncipe, health in The main public health concerns are malaria, tuberculosis, venereal diseases, and parasites. Between 1911 and

1914 there was an epidemic of sleeping illness that, according to public health authorities, was brought under control after an efficient mosquito eradication campaign. In 1962 there were two central hospitals and two maternity clinics, one each in São Tomé City and San Antonio on Príncipe Island, with a total of 16 physicians in attendance, two central pharmacies, and 38 nurses working in several rural settlements. In addition, some plantations have clinics to take care of their workers. At one time syphilis was epidemic but has since been brought under control. GEPB.

Sao Tomé e Príncipe, literacy in In 1987, the rate of adult illiteracy was 57.5 percent; of this total 34.5 percent were men and 23 percent were women. ASOS.

São Tomé e Príncipe, labor affairs in As has been true in most agricultural economies, the plantation owners historically have perceived that they have had a shortage of labor. After the emancipation of the slaves in 1859, an English-Portuguese Mixed Commission on Slaving reported as early as 1865 that Africans shipped from Benguela, southern Angola, to the island plantations as *libertos* (free men) actually were being treated like slaves. A labor crisis was created in 1899 by the Portuguese forced labor policy being applied on São Tomé and Príncipe on the cacao and coffee plantations. It was a bitter dispute with charges and counter-charges among Portuguese authorities, the English government, and international agencies. The labor problem came to a head as a result of the 1903 report by Judice Biker, the Portuguese governor of Guinea-Bissau. The report documented that between 2,000 and 4,000 Angolan laborers were taken every year to São Tomé and Príncipe as seasonal workers, yet only a few were permitted to return to their homeland. Duffy, *Portuguese Africa*, pp. 157-65; HDRGC.

São Tomé e Príncipe, periodicals in In 1953 there were two periodicals on the islands, *Voz de São Tomé*, a bi-weekly newspaper that began publication in July 1947, and *Boletim de São Tomé e Príncipe*, a government periodical for information, statistics, and propaganda, founded in January 1951. GEPB.

São Tomé e Príncipe, population of In 1890 the total population of both islands was calculated to be about 27,500 of which 6,000 were whites, 6,000 assimilated, 2,000 *forros* (descendants of free slaves), 1,500 Angolares, and 12,000 African contract laborers from the mainland. According to a 1960 census, the population of the islands was 59,102, of which 5,714 were whites living in São Tomé, the capital city. In 1981, the islands had population of approximately 86,000. Tenreiro, *A Ilha*, p. 87; *São Tomé Pequena Monografia*, pp. 16-17; WNGD.

São Tomé e Príncipe Province A Portuguese overseas province created in 1832. It comprised the islands of São Tomé and Príncipe plus São Baptista de Ajuda (q.v.) off Dahomey. In 1975 the province became the People's Republic of São Tomé e Príncipe. GEPB.

São Tomé e Príncipe, shipbuilding in The early settlers began harvesting the island's timber around 1490. From one giant tree, probably a *mafumeira* (q.v.) or *ocá*, they cut enough boards that Captain Fernão de Mello was able to build two small ocean-going ships. In 1493, São Tomean settlers were granted the privilege of trading with São Jorge de Mina (q.v.). The islanders constructed ships of 40 and 50 tons capacity for this purpose. Hodges, *São Tomé e Príncipe,* pp. 13, 19.

São Tomé e Príncipe, slave trade in The first settlers introduced slaves in 1485 and by 1500 the islands were a flourishing center, trading along the Gulf of Guiné and in the Congo. Local traders had a monopoly on the slave trade granted to them by the Crown in 1522. At that time, the colonists controlled the number of slaves sent to Brazil and the West Indies. The abolition of the slave trade in 1811 ushered in a profound economic recession that lasted until coffee and cacao (cocoa), introduced in the 1830s, were produced in sufficient quantities to revitalize the economy. Duffy, *Portuguese Africa,* pp. 12, 17, 51, 135-6; DHP; GEPB.

São Tomé, slaves and sugar cane cultivation in Before 1500, São Tomé islanders had taken a commanding lead in sugar production and slave importation. Sugar cane cultivation had been introduced to the island in 1493, and from then to 1500 a thousand slaves were brought from Angola to work on the sugar plantations. In 1517 there were only two sugar mills, but by 1529 the island was exporting 5,000 *arrobas* (approximately 70 metric tons) and twelve new mills were in construction. By 1520 there were 4,072 slaves working in the fields and the mills. In the 1540s São Tomé was the world's largest producer of sugar, a position it would lose to Brazil and the West Indies. Hodges, *São Tomé e Príncipe,* pp. 18-20.

São Vicente (Pg.) One of the islands in the *Barlovento* (windward) group of the Cape Verde archipelago, discovered and settled by the Portuguese in 1460. It is a rocky wasteland with periodic droughts that limited agricultural development prior to the nineteenth century. The only commercial product was orchil (q.v.), also known as *urzela*, a dye-yielding lichen grown and collected in the mountains, then processed and exported to Portugal. Around 1650 the intense slaving on the Guiné coast stimulated the economy of the island. In 1790, the British established a consulate in Mindelo, the capital, and a coaling station for the British navy. British crews en route to Brazil made regular stops there, and an underwater communications cable reached Mindelo in 1875, which then became the main port for the whole archipelago. Duncan, *Atlantic Islands*, pp. 18, 23, 161-66; HDRGC.

sap-sap (Afr.)   In Angola, and elsewhere, a wild or cultivated tropical tree (*Annona muricata*) called soursop, *guanabana*, or *corossol*, native of the New World and introduced to Africa by the Portuguese early in the colonial period. Its fruit is highly esteemed for drinks and desserts and is used in folk medicine. The tree is found in Icolo e Bengo, Golungo Alto, Novo Redondo, Angola, and on São Tomé where it is called *coração da India*. A concoction called *empebi*, made from its seeds, is used to treat dysentery and stomach ailments. Ficalho, *Plantas Uteis*, p. 76.

Saracens (Ar.)   Dark-complected members of the Moslem Moorish people who c.700 AD conquered and ruled Portugal, Spain, and North Africa. Before and during the time of the Discovery (q.v.), Saracens were pioneers in the arts and sciences, including navigation, and were considered highly civilized by Europeans. GEPB.

Sargasso Sea (Pg.)   A large tract of comparatively still water in the North Atlantic northeast of the West Indies, noted for its abundance of dense floating seaweed. In 1425 it was encountered by Portuguese navigators on their trips to the Azores and Madeira in the service of Prince Henry. By 1500 ships returning from East Africa and India would sail to the latitude of the Sargasso Sea to find favorable west winds to take them to Lagos and Lisbon. Columbus crossed the Sargasso Sea on his first voyage to the New World in 1492. DHP; GEPB. *See also* sargassum, volta do Sargasso.

Sargassum (Lat.)   Various species of floating brown seaweeds (genus *Sargassum*) that bear small but prominent berry-like bladders, found in warmer seas; in the Atlantic they drift with the wind and currents from the southwest and accumulate in the area known as the Sargasso Sea (q.v.) and along the Portuguese coast where the variety *S. megalophyllum* is found. These seaweeds are a rich habitat for fish. GEPB. *See also* Sargasso Sea.

sargento-mor (Pg.)   "Sargeant Major." In Mozambique and elsewhere in Africa, a title of honor granted by the king of Portugal c.1850 to certain settlers and loyal African chiefs for outstanding service. Isaacman, *Mozambique: The Africanization*, p. 144. *See also* capitão-mor do interior.

sassa (Afr.)   "Goiter." In Angola and elsewhere, an enlargement of the thyroid gland caused by a dietary deficiency of iodine, a naturally occuring element in sea salt. With this deficiency there is often a visible swelling, called a goiter, in the lower part of the throat. *Sassa* is widespread in Angola and endemic in the Benguela Plateau. *Revista Medica de Angola*, Luanda, 1923, 5:95-103.

saudade (Pg.) "Sadness, yearning, homesickness." A deep and melancholy feeling for something unattainable; supposedly characteristic of Portuguese culture. *Saudade* is a type of gentle sadness, and feelings of *saudade* are often expressed by such contemporary Afro-Portuguese poets as G. Victor Bessa in *Batuque sem Sanzala* and Ovidio Martins in *Caminha Saudade*. Burness, *Six Writers*, pp. 49-50; Andrade, *Antologia Tematica*, p. 138. *See also* saudosismo.

saudosismo (Pg.) "Lonesomeness." A deep personal sadness and yearning, supposedly characteristic of a Portuguese philosophy often expressed by Afro-Portuguese writers in the 1950s. Based on the concept of *saudade* (q.v.), it is used by Cape Verdian poets to impart the mystic and romantic feeling of longing, once have left, to return to the islands. The Angolan writer Tomaz Viera da Cruz suggests that *saudosismo* implies a quiet melancholic dream rooted in the African past with its legacy of slavery, injustice, and suffering that touches the inner feelings of the Angolan soul. Hamilton, *Voices*, pp. 42, 335.

Saurimo (Afr.) A municipality, Lunda district, east-central Angola. Before 1975 it was called Henrique de Carvalho. In 1918 it became the seat of the Lunda district government and by 1960 comprised the administrative posts of Dala, Mona-Quimbundo, and Xacassau. It is an agricultural center producing cotton, rubber, coffee, and wax, and an important commercial area. GEPB.

savana-pomar (Pg.) In Guinea-Bissau and elsewhere, a cleared field in a forest cultivated in a cycle as part of a type of sustainable agriculture involving ten- to forty-year cycles. Often these fields are sheltered by fruit trees and other useful species left from a previous cycle. Mota, *Guiné Portuguesa*, I:90. *See also* bolanha.

savannah In Africa and elsewhere, a plain or grassland found mainly in tropical or subtropical regions having seasonal rains and characterized by scattered trees. In Angola the savannah gives way to a grassland with greater numbers of trees, many of them of the Ficus family, and leguminous climbers and shrubs. In the more humid savannahs, dense elephant grass (*Panissetum* spp.) grows to 16 ft. (5 m). Historically these regions have supported both agricultural and pastoral peoples. Woodland clearing for agriculture and fuel, continuous grazing by domestic animals, and frequent fires to control and maintain pastures have led to the gradual impoverishment of many savannah regions. Along the various rivers there are extensive tracts of arboreal and grassy savannahs. In Guinea-Bissau many savannah areas are covered by drought-tolerant grasses and the dominant tree in many cases is the oil palm (*Elaeis guinensis*). Mota, *Guiné Portuguesa,* I:88-92; CEA; GEPB.

Save River   *See* Sabe River.

schistosomiasis   *See* bilharziasis.

Scottish missionaries   A group of eight Presbyterian missionaries from Scotland led by David Livingstone (1813-73) arrived at Zambezia, Mozambique, in 1858 and settled in Blantyre, Malawi. All had been students at Oxford University and were members of the Oxford Movement. Among these newcomers Kirk, Livingstone, and Thornton kept diaries, and Thomas Baines painted a series of watercolor sketches of the river. Of this group of energetic Victorians, only Thornton, a young geologist, was sympathetic to the Portuguese. In 1861, the group was joined by a party of Anglican clergymen led by Bishop Mackenzie; the following year a party of women arrived to work in the mission. Soon these missionaries published dozens of letters, diaries, memoranda, tracts, and colored illustrations that horrified abolitionists and raised indignation about the perceived decadence of the Africans and the immorality of the colonists. This publicity created international tensions and angered the Portuguese government. In 1864, Livingstone and the other missionaries left Blantyre, but they returned in 1874 to continue their work and to expose the abuses of the slave traders, still engaged in the internal slave trade. In 1875 Presbyterian missions were established in the Shire Highlands and on the shore of Lake Niassa (qq.v.). More than any other influence, this group of missionaries shaped the future of Zambezia, linked in 1877 with the Congo and the Mashonaland High Veldt, until in early 1890 Britain and Portugal were brought to the verge of war. Newitt, *Portuguese Settlement,* pp. 129-32; GEPB.

"Scramble for Africa"   An expression coined in Europe at the end of the nineteenth century that referred to the struggle among such industrialized countries as England, France, Belgium, and Germany to gain supremacy in the exploitation of raw materials from Africa. They believed it was imperative to establish their own colonies to protect the sources of these raw materials and to establish guaranteed markets for their own manufactured goods. This modern imperialism came into conflict with the historic Portuguese approach based on the consolidation of its colonies. The 1885 Congress of Berlin (q.v.) legalized the partition of Africa and greatly reduced the frontiers of Angola and Mozambique. Munslow, *Mozambique,* pp. 4, 7.

scurvy A tropical disease caused by a deficiency of vitamin C due to a lack of fresh vegetables and fruits and characterized by anemia, a tendency to bruise easily, spongy gums, and loosening of the teeth. It is reported that one-third of Vasco da Gama's crew died or was severely incapacitated by scurvy during his first trip to India (1497-99). This sickness was common in Luanda around 1590. Alexius Abreu, a Portuguese physician who was director of the hospital at Luanda from 1595 to about 1610, treated many patients suffering from scurvy. His treatise, entitled *Mal-de-Luanda*, the name given to scurvy at the time, was published in Lisbon in 1626. GEPB; SMD.

sea money *See* dinheiro do mar.

Sebastianism The belief that King Sebastião, killed in Morocco at the battle of Alcacer-Qibir on August 4, 1578, had not in fact died and would eventually return to Portugal to rebuild the empire. Rumors that he had not died began to circulate in Portugal at the time of the arrival of survivors of the tragedy. With surprising swiftness the belief that he was alive and hidden fused with the Arthurian legend and with various Messianic prophesies current in Portugal at the time. Later, the tragic death of Sebastião became identified with the prophetic verses of G. Troncoso (c.1500-1556), generally known as the *Bandarra*. These verses included themes on the coming of a Messiah-King and the fifth world monarchy prophesied in the Book of Daniel. The popularity of Sebastianism increased during the years of "Spanish Captivity" (1580-1640) that ended when, after sixty years of Spanish rule, King João IV seized the throne of Portugal. Sebastianism persisted in Portugal into the eighteenth century and even longer in the colonies, Brazil and Macao in particular, where people continued to believe that King Sebastião would come back from his enchanted hiding place in the mid-Atlantic to fulfill the apocalyptic prophesies of the scriptures. Boxer, *The Portuguese Seaborne,* pp. 369-74; DHP; GEPB.

secretario (Pg.) In Cape Verde, a self-appointed all-purpose messenger boy found at hotels and at the ports who, for a tip, attached himself to a visitor with unquenchable enthusiasm. Duncan, *Atlantic Islands*, p. 165.

Sede Apostolica A bull issued in Rome by Pope Julius II on July 4, 1505, granting King Manuel I of Portugal the right to trade with the Moslems and heathens in Africa and other lands with the obligation of converting them to Christianity. Pinto Rema, *A Primeira Evangelização,* BCGP, Lisboa, 1966, xxi(2):316.

self-determination, policy of This policy was conceived in 1918 at the end of World War I by the British Prime Minister David Lloyd George as basis for settling territorial disputes and colonial claims. In reference to tropical Africa, the policy stated that colonial powers had a duty to administer their colonies and to protect and educate the indigenous people within them. When Portugal became a member of the United Nations in 1955, she rejected this policy of self-determination as it applied to her African "provinces" and declared that according to the Portuguese constitution the provinces were part of the Portuguese nation. After the 1961 rebellion in Angola, the United States called on Portugal to allow Angolans to exercise their rights to self-determination. Portugal's refusal precipitated the bloody wars for independence that ended in 1975 with the establishment of five new nations: Angola, Cape Verde, Guinea-Bissau, Mozambique, and São Tomé e Príncipe. Abshire, *Portuguese Africa*, pp. 367-69, 379-80.

sekulu (Umb.) "Elder." The head of an Umbundu village, considered to be a descendent of the village founder. In the 1920s the *sekulu* was the authority who could speak of "my village"; for everyone else, it was "our village." Henderson, *Angola*, p. 49. *See also* imbo.

Seló (Pg.) "Sail, Ho!" The name of a literary journal published in 1962 in Mindelo, São Vicente Island, Cape Verde. Although it published only two issues, its editors Oswaldo Osório and Mário Fonseca pledged they would continue the policy of *Certeza* and *Claridade* (qq.v.). Hamilton, *Voices*, pp. 270, 307.

Selvagens (Pg.) A group of small deserted islands off the African coast about 180 mi. (290 km) southeast of Madeira. Discovered by Pedro de Sintra in 1462, they were granted to the Order of Christ and later transferred to the Crown. From the sixteenth century until 1904, they were owned by a Madeiran family who then sold them to Luis da Rocha Machado. They are a volcanic wasteland without fresh water but at the time of the Discovery (q.v.) and afterward they had *urzela* (orchil, q.v.) of high commercial value. Prestage, *The Portuguese Pioneers*, p. 182; GEPB.

"Sem negros não há Pernambuco e sem Angola não há negros" (Pg.) "Without blacks, Pernambuco would not exist, and without Angola, there would be no blacks." A saying written c.1650 and attributed to the Jesuit Antonio Vieira. The Dutch conquered northern Brazil, including Penambuco, in 1632 and in 1640 took Angola because this colony was the major source at the time of the slaves needed on the Brazilian sugar plantations. Cunha, *O Sistema Portugués*, p. 106.

Sena An ancient village on the south bank of the Zambezi River about 125 mi. (200 km) southeast of Tete. The Portuguese first encountered the village in 1520 and soon after established a settlement. The colonists held the first fair in Sena in 1560, trading ornaments and cotton textiles from Cambray (France) with Moslem merchants for gold, ivory, and slaves. In 1704, the Portuguese built a fort to protect this trade center. Sena was declared the capital of the district in 1763. Henriksen, *Mozambique,* pp. 4, 31, 41; GEPB.

Sena people (Afr.)   A group settled in the area between the present-day Mozambican city of Sena and the mouth of the Zambezi River. Its political organization closely paralleled that of the Tonga (q.v.), the principal difference being the absence of a dominant royal clan in the Sena society. In 1500, before the arrival of the Portuguese, several Sena chiefs were already settled in the territory. These small chiefdoms survived into the colonial period under the protection of the *prazeros* (q.v.). Isaacman, *Mozambique: The Africanization*, pp. 4, 10-11, 22.

Sena Sugar Company   A company organized with British capital in 1892. Located on the south bank of the Zambezi River, it was one of the largest sugar plantations in the region. A subcontractor of the Zambezi Company (q.v.), it had cane fields and sugar mills on both sides of the river. The plantation was transferred back to Portuguese control in 1942. In 1960 it was still producing sugar and rum for export. Henriksen, *Mozambique*, pp. 105-6, 118.

Senado da Camara (Pg.)   "Municipal Council." A Portuguese political institution founded in 1495 that, depending on the size and importance of the town, comprised from two to six *vereadores* (counselors), two *juizes ordinarios* (justices of peace), and a *procurador* (prosecuting attorney). They all had voting rights at council meetings and were collectively known as the *oficiais da Camara* (officials of the Council). They were elected through a complicated system of annual balloting from voters' lists drawn up every three years. The annual ballot was usually held on New Year's Day, occasionally on New Year's Eve. The *Senado da Camara* and the *Misericordia* (qq.v.) were the twin pillars of Portuguese colonial society in Africa since early in the Discovery (q.v.). *Senados da Camara* were established in Luanda, Angola, in 1575, and in Mozambique in 1763. This system remained unchanged until 1822. Boxer, *The Portuguese Seaborne*, pp. 273-4, 278, 286.

sene (Pg.)   "Senna." A wild and cultivated tropical medicinal shrub (*Cassia bovata*) traded in commerce and used in pharmaceuticals. It is found in many African regions including Nubia, Kardofan, and Senaar. Frederick Welwitsch (1807-1872) found it on Cape Verde and on the Atlantic coast of Angola from Benguela to Mossâmedes. Ficalho, *Plantas Uteis*, p. 150.

Senegal Kingdom   *See* Wolof state.

Senegal River (Afr.)   A river about 1,015 mi. (1,600 km) long that rises in the Futa-Djallon Highlands in Guinea-Bissau, flows north then west, and empties into the Atlantic. It was discovered by Nuno Tristão, who sailed up it, in 1444. He reported that the area was a beautiful green land with many palms. He added that the river divided the land of the Azenegues and that of the Wolofs. In this area, also in 1444, Portuguese explorers captured the first slaves taken to Lagos and sold in its market. Medieval geographers believed that the Senegal River was one of the branches of the Nile. Prestage, *The Portuguese Pioneers*, p. 74; WNGD.

Senegambia   A loosely defined territory in West Africa in the areas around the Senegal and Gambia rivers. At the time of the Discovery (q.v.) it already was densely populated with the largest cluster of Niger-Congo peoples on the Atlantic coast. These groups included the Balantas, the Manjacos, and the Papeis of modern Guinea-Bissasu. The Portuguese had great difficulty controlling this population, especially the Papeis who engaged in bloody uprisings until the 1930s. Abshire, *Portuguese Africa,* p. 112; HDRGC.

Senussia (Ar.)   In Guinea-Bissau, a branch of an Islamic religious brotherhood that originated in Mauritania in the nineteenth century. Despite the great influence this Moorish fraternity exercised on the animists in the Cacheu-Gabu area of Guinea-Bissau, the latter did not embrace Islam. Gonçalves, *O Islamismo*, p. 152.

sepoys (Hind.)   Indian soldiers brought c.1767 from Goa to Tete and the Zambezia region to protect Portuguese settlers. In 1781, sixty more were brought to Africa. Of these, only fourteen survived the trip and were stationed in Tete, forty-six having died of fever in Zanzibar. In contemporary Mozambique, *sepoy* means an African soldier enlisted for service by local authorities, and often has a negative connotation. GEPB; HDM.

Serer (Afr.)   A Senegambian ethnic group mainly settled in southeastern Senegal. They are related to the Diola of Guinea-Bissau and to the Sine and Salum chiefdoms which between the thirteenth and fourteenth centuries were vassals of the Mali Empire. HDRGC.

Sernache do Bom Jardim (Pg.)   A seminary organized in the 1840s in the Portuguese town of Sernache to train missionaries for the colonies. Prior to its founding, the Portuguese government outlawed religious orders in Africa in 1834 and expelled the missionaries. This college was founded with the encouragement of the Holy See to fill this gap. It successfully functioned until 1911. The *Sernache do Bom Jardim* educated more than three hundred missionaries who later worked in Angola and Mozambique. When the first of the graduates went to Africa they lived among the Europeans in the colony, helping in hospitals and clinics and in elementary and secondary schools. In the 1890s they penetrated the interior of Africa, establishing missions and organizing rural schools. Gabriel, *Angola*, p. 272; DHP.

sertanejo (Braz.) "Backwoodsman." A nineteenth-century Portuguese or Portuguese-African colonial trader in the back country. He was regarded as a typical merchant of the *sertão* (q.v.) in Portuguese Africa and Brazil. GDLP. *See also* sertanejos in Angola, sertanejos in Mozambique.

sertanejos in Angola A Portuguese or *mestiço* owner of a small store in villages in Benguela, Catumbela, and Bié in south-central Angola. Around 1840 when exploration and expansion began in earnest, *sertanejos* (q.v.) specialized in trading ivory, wax, dyestuffs, slaves, and wild rubber. By 1890, they had developed booming businesses in such new towns as Silva Porto, Vila Teixeira da Silva, and Nova Lisboa. Wheeler, *Angola*, pp. 26, 44, 54, 64; GEPB. *See also* sertanejos in Mozambique.

sertanejos in Mozambique A Goan merchant or a mulatto who traded in gold, ivory, firearms, and cloth in the interior of Zambezia. Around 1700, as the *prazo* system and the fairs were established along the Zambezi River and the coastal towns in the colony, these backwoodsmen emerged as a powerful group. Eventually many *sertanejos* (q.v.) became *prazo*-holders, controlling large estates and many villages. Newitt, *Portuguese Settlement*, pp. 34-38, 54-8, 129-30; GEPB. *See also* sertanejos in Angola.

sertão (Braz.) "Interior, backwoods." A Brazilian term used in Angola, Mozambique, and elsewhere to refer to distant and isolated regions. HDA. *See also* sertanejo.

serviçais (Pg.) "Servants." In Portuguese Africa, former slaves who after the abolition of slavery in 1869 were bound under a five-year labor contract to work for their former masters, the government, or corporations on plantations, in factories, or in domestic service, in many cases in inhumane conditions. In contemporary São Tomé, *serviçai* is an African or *mestiço* plantation worker who speaks the local dialect. In 1921, there were still over 3,000 *serviçais* on the islands. Duffy, *Portuguese Africa*, p. 153; GEPB.

Service in Rural Communities A community civic action program organized by Portuguese authorities in the 1960s in Mural, Mozambique, and elsewhere to improve the health and social conditions of Africans in rural and isolated settlements at a time when political unrest was greatly increasing. The aim was to integrate rural and urban African people into Portuguese society. The service sent out mobile teams of seven people including agriculturists, medics, social workers, teachers, and craftsmen. They taught basic farming and domestic crafts, inoculated children, practiced emergency medicine, distributed government propaganda, and monitored signs of discontent. By late 1963 twenty units were reported to be operating in Mozambique, concentrating on the remote northern areas and in central urban districts. Henriksen, *Revolution*, pp. 23, 99, 104.

sesame An East Indian tropical herb (*Sesamum indicum*) believed to have been introduced into Africa by the Portuguese around 1500. Its flat seeds yield an edible oil used in cooking and medicine. In Angola and Mozambique, another species of sesame (*S. angolense* Welw.) is cultivated by Africans in rocky, sandy soils where *S. indicum* does not do well. GEPB.

sesmarias, lei das (Pg.) "Land grant law." A medieval law established in Portugal by which all owners or leaseholder of uncultivated land had to find men to cultivate it. The royal justices were empowered to see that anyone who was ready to farm vacant land could obtain draft oxen at a reasonable price. If a landowner did not cooperate, the local authorities could intervene, find cultivators, and collect the rent for the royal treasury. All *sesmarias* had to be approved by the Crown. This law was incorporated into the first compilation of Portuguese laws, the *Ordinações Afonsinas* (q.v.) completed in 1446. By royal decree, on April 3, 1760, the *lei das sesmarias* was transferred to Mozambique where in Zambezia and elsewhere the *prazos* were considered *sesmarias*. Newitt, *Portuguese Settlement*, pp. 1-2, 104-5; GEPB.

Setubal (Pg.) Capital of Setubal district and seaport on the Bay of Setubal, southwestern Portugal. The city played a decisive role during the Discovery (q.v.) when in 1458 the fleet of King Afonso V sailed from this port to begin the conquest of North Africa. King João II married Eleanor of Lancaster here in 1471 and established his residence in the city. In 1505 Tristão da Cunha sailed for India from Setubal. King João III built several palace and government buildings there and fortified the port in 1531. GEPB; WNGD.

shahm (Ar.) "Rendered animal fat." An important element in the diet of Africans and Berbers in Mauritania. They eat dried meat moistened with melted *shahm*. Lewiki, *West African Food*, pp. 111-2.

Shama (Afr.) A town on the West African Gold Coast with a population of 800 c.1472. The Portuguese used it as a center for trade in gold and spices until 1483 when the São Jorge de Mina (q.v.) fortress was completed. The town was occupied by the Dutch in 1648 and became British territory in 1872. It is now part of the Republic of Ghana. In 1970 its population was 7,739. HDG.

shamba (Swah.) In Mozambique, a family vegetable plot cultivated by the head of a household. The *shamba* allows an African family to be more self-sufficient. FRELIMO (q.v.) institutionalized this deeply rooted family institution in the 1975 Mozambican constitution. Henriksen, *Mozambique*, p. 203.

"Shamwale ngawona" (Afr.) "My friend, look at this." An 1890s song of protest expressing the bitter feelings the African workers felt for the administrators of the Mopeia (q.v.) plantation. It was a response to the hard labor levies imposed by the government and to the quasi-military routine of field cultivation. *Shamwale ngawona* was also the name given to the four-pronged hoe introduced by the sugar company in 1890. Vail, *Capitalism*, pp. 123, 167.

Sharia (Ar.) "The law." The Islamic legal system that includes both the teachings of the Koran and the traditional sayings of Mohammed. Among the Mandingos in Guinea-Bissau, the *Sharia* is a guide to normal rules of conduct although deviations from it are very common. Silva, *Usos e Costumes*, BCG, 1968, xxiii(91/92); 249-50; DI.

shibalo *See* chibalo.

Shiite (Ar.) "Follower." A member of the one of the two great sects of Islam, the other being Sunni (q.v.). Shiites consider Ali, Mohammed's son-in-law and the fourth of the caliphs, as the first Imam and rightful successor to Mohammed. They also do not accept the Sunna (q.v.) as an authoritative supplement to the Koran. Shiites are considered heretics by the Sunni. The Shiites have had great influence in Mozambique, especially after 1918 when Mustafa Kemal Paxa abolished the Turkish Sunni caliphate. Gonçalves, *O Mundo Arabo-Islámico*, p. 31; DI.

Shire Highlands An area in the hill country east of the Shire River (q.v.) in southern Malawi. Its elevation of 3,000 ft. (4,800 m) is great enough to render the area free of the heat and many of the diseases of the lowlands. The region has been inhabited at various times by the Makua, Yao, Marave, and Makololo. In 1875, this territory was visited by Portuguese and Swahili traders searching for slaves. Scottish Presbyterians established a mission in this area in 1875. Newitt, *Portuguese Settlement*, pp. 30, 231; WNGD.

Shire River (Afr.) A river about 250 mi. (400 km) long that flows from Lake Niassa (q.v.) south into the Zambezi River in central Mozambique. It has several cataracts including the impressive Murchison Falls. The vast Shire River region north of the Zambezi was practically unknown to the Portuguese until the eighteenth century when the discovery of gold lured prospectors and traders into the area. It is also spelled *Chire* and *Xire*. Newitt, *Portuguese Settlement*, pp. 27-8, 30, 88.

Shona (Afr.) An ethnic group settled in Mozambique south of the Zambezi River and in Zimbabwe. Their ancestors organized several chiefdoms, built settlements protected by stone walls, and practiced a complex religion. Among the most important Shona sub-groups are the Karanga, Manyka, Teve, Barué, and Ndau. Around 1500 the early Portuguese explorers applied the name Karanga to all Shona, whether or not they inhabited the Mashonaland Plateau where the Karanga kingdom (q.v.) was situated. The Tawara and the Tonga (qq.v.) have cultural and linguistic links with the Shona and are considered to have a common origin. In 1970, the Shona numbered over 3,000,000. Henriksen, *Mozambique*, p. 250; HDM.

Sierra Leone (Sp.) "Lion Mountain." A nation in West Africa on the Atlantic between Guinea-Bissau and Liberia. Located on the low coastal belt of the Atlantic, it is characterized by mangrove swamps and an upland plateau. The Portuguese explorer Pedro de Sintra reached this region in 1460. Between 1550 and 1650 it became an active center of commerce. Slaves, ivory, wax, and amber were exchanged for cotton, black Indian cloth, basins, and beads. In 1787, a local chieftain granted land for a settlement for runaway and freed English and American slaves, and under the sponsorship of English philanthropists, the capital, Freetown, was established. In 1795, the British Sierra Leone Company built a port that was declared a British Crown Colony in 1808. In 1896 it became a Protectorate and in 1961 it achieved independence. In 1974 the country had a population of 2,735,000. Freetown had 314,340 people in 1974. Duncan, *Atlantic Islands,* pp. 199, 201, 214-5; WNGD; WNWD.

Silves (Pg.) A town on the Algarve, an area on the Atlantic coast of southern Portugal. It was an important commercial and trading port during the Discovery (q.v.) when Silves' fishermen, sailors, and merchants filled the caravels going to Arguim, Guiné, and São Jorge de Mina (qq.v.). Nearly destroyed by the 1755 earthquake, it is an historic city with a Gothic cathedral and a Moorish castle. In 1981 it had a population of 31,352. Iria, *O Algarve no Descobrimento*, Congresso da Guiné, 1946, I:196; WNDG.

sinais da terra pelas aves (Pg.) "Signs of land from observing birds." Early in the Discovery (q.v.) navigators sailing in the South Atlantic could identify the presence of and certain features of the coast by looking for birds and determining their distance and the direction and altitude of their flight. Among the larger birds mentioned are hawks, harpy eagles, white and purple herons, albatross, and lannerets. The smaller birds included falcons, egrets, sea gulls, sparrows, quail, and skylarks. Costa, *A Marinha*, pp. 346-7. *See also* conhecenças e senais, conhecenças das terras.

sinais da terra pelas plantas maritimas (Pg.) "Signs of the coast from observing sea plants." Early in the Discovery (q.v.) navigators sailing in the South Atlantic could recognize certain features of the coast by observing the marine vegetation growing on the continental shelf. They differentiated among many species of multicelled algae (seaweeds) that grow in shallower waters near the coast. Costa, *A Marinha*, p. 349. *See also* conhecenças e sinais, conhecenças das terras.

sinais das tormentas (Pg.) "Signs indicating storms." Early in the Discovery (q.v.) navigators sailing in unknown seas carefully observed atmospheric phenomena they believed presaged disturbances. These phenomena included a red sunrise or sunset, clear static air, lightning on one side of the ship, or the presence or absence of calm waters, clouds, thunder, and, most of all, prevailing winds. These signs are recorded in the 1604 *Roteiro* (ship's log, or itinerary) of Gaspar Manuel. At sea between the Cape of Good Hope and Natal, lightning in the night means a sudden storm, but beyond that point in the Indian Ocean, neither lightning nor calm waters precludes a storm. Costa, *A Marinha*, p. 350. *See also* conhecenças e sinais.

"Sina Mama" (Afr.) "Without a Mother." A lullaby sung in villages and towns in Central Africa during the 1870s and 1880s, heard and noted by British travelers. The British disembarked at Quelimane, Mozambique, on the Indian Ocean coast then would travel by canoe up the Kwa-Kwa River as far as the village of Mogurumba, then be carried in *machilas* (slings) past the poppy plantations of the new opium company to Mzaro on the north bank of the Zambezi, and there hire boatmen who sang this song that went, "I have no mother, I have no father. I have no mother to nurse me. Senhora Mariya [The Lady Mary] is my mother." Missionaries and traders concluded that David Livingstone understood the song to refer to the Virgin Mary, a last trace in local culture of ancient Jesuit endeavors. The song became something of a tourist attraction, rivaling only the grave at Chupanga (q.v.) of his wife, Mary Moffat Livingstone, also called Senhora Mariya. Vail, *Capitalism*, p. 7. *See also* Shamwale ngowona.

sisal in Mozambique Sisal is a strong fiber used for cordage, mats, and related articles and obtained from the leaves of the agave (*Agave sisalana*), a succulent plant native to southern Mexico. The agave was introduced to

Mozambique by the Portuguese late in the nineteenth century. The commercial cultivation of sisal began just after the beginning of the twentieth century. In 1918 German planters formally established sisal plantations in Tanganyika and along the northern coastal strip of Mozambique. In 1961 there were twenty-seven plantations covering 132,000 acres, mainly inland from the ports of Mozambique. A substantial share of Mozambique's sisal harvest is destined for the United States. Abshire, *Portuguese Africa*, p. 272-3.

Sisters of Saint Dorothy   An Italian religious order founded by Paula Frasinetti in 1820 and dedicated to the education of poor children. Its first members arrived in Lisbon on June 16, 1866. They opened schools in such Portuguese cities as Lisbon, Covilha, Evora, Tomar, and Vila Real. These sisters also came to Angola and opened schools for African children in Mossãmedes in 1934, in Sá de Bandeira in 1937, and in Benguela in 1939. GEPB.

Sisters of Saint Joseph of Cluny   A French religious order founded by Ana Maria Javouhey in 1807 and dedicated to working in overseas missions. The order arrived in Lisbon in 1879 and soon sent sisters to Portuguese Africa. They founded schools, hospitals, and other charitable institutions in Luanda in 1883, Huila in 1885, Coconda in 1892, and in Cabinda and Malanje in 1893. During the same time they also opened schools and hospitals in Inhambane and in several towns on the upper Zambezia in Mozambique. Around 1900 there were about 85 Portuguese and 54 African sisters working and teaching in the order's Portuguese African missions and schools. The order also is known as the Mission Sisters. GEPB.

Sisters of Saint Nicholas   An order founded on São Tomé made up of devout widows. This congregation was dedicated to working in schools and hospitals. Around 1900 the order was still very active in the island. Almada Negreiros, *Historia*, p. 160.

slattee   A unit of slaves of varying numbers classified according age, health, and origin, then offered for sale in the markets of Dahomey (q.v.). The individuals in a *slattee* were chained together and sold as a group. This system of wholesaling slaves was established around 1672 as sugar production on Brazilian and West Indian plantations became enormously profitable. Established and new planters needed more and more laborers and the exportation of slaves escalated. Polanyi, *Dahomey*, pp. 22, 140. *See also* coffle.

slave   A human being who is owned as property by another and is absolutely subject to his will. Slaves had been held in Portugal since Roman times.

Before the fifteenth century in Portugal the term "slave" was usually applied to a *Mouro* (Moor). At the Discovery (q.v.) the term was applied mainly to African slaves brought from the west coast of Africa. According to Gomes Eanes de Zurara in his *Cronica da Guiné*, in 1444 the Portuguese captured 300 slaves in Guiné, took them to Lagos, and sold them in the market. After 1450, African slaves were numerous in Portugal. In 1466 there were 3,000 in Evora and by 1550 there were 10,000 in Lisbon. The *Ordenações Manuelinas* (q.v.) of 1514 and the *Leis Extravaganters* (q.v.) of 1559 legally defined slaves as chattel. Capella, *Escravatura*, pp. 44, 171; GEPB.

slave broker By 1500 Lisbon had the largest slave market in the country and there about 12,000 slaves in Portugal. In 1550 there were eight brokers in Lisbon who dealt exclusively in slave transactions. A few other brokers mainly sold cattle, dealing occasionally in slaves. A dealer received a two-percent commission for each slave, paid equally by seller and buyer. Saunders, *A Social History*, pp. 18-19; GEPB.

slave children, baptism of The practice of baptizing the children of the slaves arriving in Lisbon probably began c.1500. In 1514 King Manuel I ordered all slave children under the age of ten to be baptized within a month of their arrival. Slave children born in Portugal were to be baptized soon after birth. Although parish registers indicate that the baptism of slave children was customary, it is doubtful whether the ordinance was ever rigidly enforced. Indeed, in 1568 the archbishop of Lisbon found it necessary to order all masters who owned slaves over the age of seven to have them baptized. Saunders, *A Social History,* p. 41; GEPB. *See also* slaves, baptism of.

slave children, manumission of From the time of the Discovery (q.v.) the Portuguese Crown ruled that children of slaves could be legally freed from slavery under special circumstances. In 1536 Nicolas Clenardus noted that in most houses, the birth of a slave child was greeted warmly. Whether or not he was the father, the master of the household often became fond of his slaves' children. A deep affection for a slave born or brought up in the house was frequently cited as a reason for manumission. Frequently a Portuguese man who had fathered the child of a slave woman paid the master for their child's freedom. Saunders, *A Social History*, pp. 91-2, 139; GEPB.

Slave Coast The region along the Gulf of Guiné roughly from the Volta River to the Niger Delta. The Portuguese discovered and explored this territory in 1471. From 1500 to 1800, many of the slaves taken to the New World plantations by the Portuguese and other Europeans were obtained from this region. GEPB.

slave festivities in Portugal From soon after the arrival of the first African slaves in Lisbon in 1444, slaves participated in church festivities. There are reports from 1466 of dancing in the churches as one of their "strange customs." In 1633, a Capuchin friar in Lisbon described how they celebrated the day of *Nossa Senohra das Neves* (Our Lady of the Snows) on August 5 by donning their African dress consisting of loincloths or skirts and tying ornamental bands around their heads, arms, and chests. So attired, they marched and danced, some in African fashion, through the streets. Saunders, *A Social History,* p. 150; GEPB.

slave-interpreters In the early period of the Discovery (q.v.), many Portuguese vessels carried African interpreters, often slaves themselves, to facilitate negotiations between the slave-traders and the African chiefs. Captives were taken to Portugal with the hope that some of them might understand the language of slaves already in the country and teach them Portuguese. At the time of the first voyage of Alvise Cadamosto to Guiné in 1454, there were many interpreters among the African slaves in Lisbon and other cities. These slave-interpreter were well treated aboard ship, receiving special food and wages. In 1497 there were many slave-interpreters in all the Portuguese trading posts along the West African coast. Saunders, *A Social History,* pp. 12, 62; DHP.

slave market in Lisbon Early in the Discovery (q.v.), Lisbon had become the center of the African slave trade starting in 1481 when by royal order the *Casa da Guiné* and the *Casa da Mina* (qq.v.), the agencies entrusted with collecting duties from the slave trade, were transferred from Lagos to the capital city. From the time of King Afonso V, Lisbon increased in wealth derived mainly from this trade. From 1450 to 1500, over 150,000 slaves were brought from West Africa to Portugal and most of them passed through one of the two trade agencies. A 1554 census fixed the number of slaves in Lisbon at about 10 percent of a population of 100,000. By 1750, the Lisbon slave market had disappeared. Capela, *Escravatura,* p. 101; Duffy, *Portuguese Africa,* p. 134; GEPB.

slave names In Portugal c.1490, slaves were baptized and their godparents gave them Christian names such as Afonso, Antonio, João, or Pedro. Names were often taken from the church calendar. The most popular name was Antonio, in honor St. Anthony who was born in Lisbon. In 1559, four female slaves bought for Queen Catarina were each given the name Catarina in her honor. Often the master's or mistress's name became the name of his or her slave. Thus, the daughter of Catarina, a slave owned by Guiomar Silveira, was named Guiomar, and another slave child was christened Afonso after his mother's owner, Maria Afonso. It was mandatory in the parishes to register the names of white and slave children in the same book. Non-Christian slaves usually kept their African names. Saunders, *A Social History*, p. 90; GEPB.

Slave River   *See* Rio dos Escravos.

slave sailors   *See* African seamen.

slave ships, crew of   Aboard a caravel there were 10-30 officers, a captain, a pilot, a scrivener (trade overseer), a crew of *marinheiros* (able seamen), *grumetes* (ordinary sailors), and *pagens* (cabinboys). Early in the sixteenth century, Europeans worked alongside Africans, with no distinction in terms of pay. Saunders, *A Social History*, p. 11; GEPB. *See also* sailors, diet of.

slave ships, legal capacity of   Early in the Discovery (q.v.) Portuguese kings set standards for the trip from Arguim, and later from São Jorge de Mina (q.v.), to Lisbon. Portuguese legislation regarding the physical welfare of slaves was evidenced by laws like those passed on March 28, 1684, regarding overcrowding aboard ships. The law required all slave ships be measured by competent officials, their tonnage (cubic volume) ascertained exactly, and official records of these measurements be kept. The tonnage would set the limit on the number of slaves a vessel could legally carry; specifically, a ship could carry seven slaves for every two tons, provided the slaves were below deck or under shelter, but only five slaves for every two tons if the slaves were carried on an open deck without shelter. Thus a 100-ton ship would be allowed to carry a maximum of 350 slaves under shelter, or a maximum of 250 without shelter; if she carried equal numbers of sheltered and unsheltered slaves, not more than 300 in all. Usually a lateen-rigged vessel of 50-100 tons could carry about 130 slaves; smaller ships such as caravels of 20-25 tons could take 30. Saunders, *A Social History*, pp. 11, 231-32; GEPB.

slave trade   The buying and selling of enslaved Africans, mainly to New World plantations, flourished between c.1550 and 1807. The abolition of the extremely profitable slave trade began in 1803 when Denmark outlawed the importation of slaves to its colonies followed by Great Britain in 1807 when the trade was essentially stopped because Britain controlled half of all slave trading. Later legislation, including that in the United States in 1808, France in 1817, Holland in 1818, Spain in 1820, and Sweden in 1824, reinforced the ban. From that time, the international slave trade was illegal and greatly reduced. In 1836 Portugal formally abolished slavery, but a clandestine market continued in her African colonies, particularly Mozambique. Cunha, *O Trabalho Indigena*, pp. 16-17. *See also* Slave Trade Conference.

slave trade, Africanization of   Early in the history of this commerce, Portuguese slavers experienced the impact of the African kings' and chiefs' long history of dealing with slavers, an activity that predated the arrival of Europeans. Around 1600, the Portuguese were forced to hire Africans and *mestiços* (q.v.) to travel inland to find slaves and bring them to such coastal ports as Ouidah and São Jorge da Mina (qq.v.). Selection of slaves by sex, age, and health required a tough *palaver* (q.v.). Also, dealing with African middle men became a necessity because Europeans could not endure the climate, the diseases, the hostile environment of the forest, or the isolation imposed by long and dangerous trips inland. Wheeler, *Angola*, p. 49; DHP.

Slave Trade Conference   An international meeting called by Belgium in Brussels on November, 1880, to organize a European crusade against the continuing slave trade in Central Africa. Hammond, *Portugal and Africa*, pp. 121-2. *See also* slave trade.

slave trade in Angola   Since the beginning of Portuguese contact with Angola, slaves were considered a commodity. Gifts of slaves by King Afonso I of Congo to the Portuguese Crown were common. On September 19, 1571, Paulo Dias de Novais, the Lord Proprietor, was given the right to annually export forty-eight slaves duty-free. In 1575 alone, 52,000 slaves were sent to Brazilian plantations. In the seventeenth century, a network of trade routes into the interior was opened and long-distance caravans contributed the main share of slaves. Government officials and local chiefs sold slaves in markets where *pombeiros* (bush merchants) went to buy slaves to ship to Brazil. By the eighteenth century, the slave trade was the foundation of the Angolan economy. The Portuguese Crown officially abolished the trade in 1836, but it continued clandestinely as long as the demand from Brazil and São Tomé existed. Even in the twentieth century, the legacy of centuries of slave trading remained and forced labor, a form of modern-day slavery, was seen by white planters as a remedy to chronic labor shortages. Duffy, *Portuguese Africa,* pp. 15, 17, 137-8; HDA.

slave trade in Cape Verde Islands   The Cape Verde Islands' location between Africa and the New World made them an important center for the slave trade beginning inn December, 1466, when the King of Portugal authorized settlers to engage in slaving. Ribeira Grande, the capital of Santiago Island, became an important slave center in the sixteenth century. In a three-year period from 1513 to 1515, 29 ships brought 2,966 slaves to Ribeira Grande in transit to Brazil and the Caribbean. In the seventeenth century, the *Companhia Geral do Grão-Para e Maranhã* (q.v.) and other slavers opened stations in Praia to process thousands of slaves to work the sugar plantations and gold mines in Brazil and elsewhere in America. Duncan, *The Atlantic Islands,* pp. 195, 211; GEPB.

slave trade in Guinea-Bissau   Guinea-Bissau was a highly populated territory that from 1446 onward provided Portugal with a great number of slaves, mainly taken to Brazil and the Caribbean. From 1500 to the end of the eighteenth century, about 5,000 slaves a year were exported. On September 1, 1664, the *Companhia da Costa da Guiné* had an exclusive monopoly on exporting slaves for a period of eight years. At this time slavers were permitted to participate in the plantation profits on condition that they undertake to procure laborers. The economic pressure of slavers' fleets off the coast of Guinea undermined the inland states of West Africa by wars and raids to capture slaves to supply the foreign trade. The trade diminished greatly when King Pedro V abolished slavery in Africa on April 29, 1858. Cunha, *O Trabalho Indigena,* pp. 135-6; Polony, *Dahomey*, pp. 18, 22, 140.

slave trade in Mozambique   Before 1500, the Arab slave trade was carried on in the interior of Africa, along the Mozambique coast, and on the Manica Plateau. Since early in the Discovery (q.v.), the Portuguese controlled the African slave trade and, until 1550, most of the slaves were sold in East Africa. After that time the balance began to swing toward the New World. After the Dutch made in-roads into Africa, Portuguese West Africa in particular, in the 1640s, the Portuguese shipped all their slaves to the Brazilian plantations. From 1780 to 1800, it is reported that about 10,000 were exported each year, this figure rose to 15,000 a year, and soared for a decade to perhaps 25,000. By 1800, slaves formed the bulk of Mozambique exports to the New World. In October 1858, Portugal abolished slavery in Portuguese Africa and the international trade ended. Herrick, *Area Handbook*, p. 32; Hammond, *Portugal and Africa*, p. 41.

slave trade in Portugal   Portugal had been engaged in the West Africa slave trade since the 1440s, first at Arguim and by 1480 in the Gulf of Guiné. On the coast from Arguim to the Congo, Portugal sought slaves for the New World plantations. From 1500 to 1575 São Tomé was the center of the trade. By 1600 Portugal's monopoly began to fragment under growing competition, first from Dutch slavers, then from other European powers. In the last 150 years of legal trade (1657-1807), it is estimated that several million slaves were shipped from Luanda and Benguela to the New World. Duffy, *Portuguese Africa,* pp. 132, 136, 142.

slave warehouses   Huge barracks, called *factorias* (q.v.), were built c.1574 in São Tomé to keep slaves brought from Angola, São Jorge de Mina (q.v.), Guiné, and others parts of Portuguese Africa to be shipped to Brazilian markets and elsewhere in the New World. Tenreiro, *A Ilha*, p. 72.

slavery, abolition of   *See* abolition of slavery in Portugal, abolition of slavery in Portuguese Africa.

slavery in Mozambique Slavery was practiced by the Arabs of East Africa long before the Portuguese came in 1500. After their arrival, the Portuguese organized their own system of slavery, following the African traditions of voluntary domestic slavery, forced servitude as a result of war, and crimes committed by individuals. The *prazos* (q.v.) had gangs of slaves employed to clear land around towns and fortresses. Slaves also served as soldiers and laborers on the manioc plantations and scattered Portuguese farms. Traditional African slavery was less demanding than that in Brazil and elsewhere in the New World, but under the Portuguese in Africa it was not without its brutalities and excesses. On the estates and *prazos*, cruel masters were not unknown, and those who kept a seraglio of African women were even more common. Generally, however, the abuses of slavery in Mozambique and elsewhere in African colonies were a nineteenth-century phenomenon. The Portuguese government officially abolished all types of slavery in Mozambique and elsewhere in April 1858. Duffy, *Portuguese Africa*, pp. 64, 141-2; DHP.

slavery in Portugal A regular slave trade began once the Portuguese reached the Senegal River in 1444. The first African slaves in Portugal were taken in 1444-45 and sold at auction in a field outside Lagos (q.v.). In 1445 Gomes Pires, a navigator and merchant, concluded transactions with the Idzagen people of the Rio de Oro who exchanged some of their slaves for trade goods. After 1448 direct contacts were made with African princes who had prisoners of war and criminals for sale. In 1466 the island of Santiago in the Cape Verde group was settled as a base for trade with Upper Guiné. Five years later the factory at São Jorge da Mina (q.v.) in the Gulf of Guiné extended their commerce. Saunders, *A Social History*, pp. 5, 62; Capela, *Escravatura*, pp. 44, 171.

slavery, voluntary *See* mitete.

slaves aboard ships to West Africa, food for In 1519, King Manuel I established a standard ration for slaves aboard ships going to West Africa. During the voyage, the captain had to provide sufficient amounts of yams, peaches, bananas, and *malagüeta* pepper (q.v.), as well as sticks to gnaw to assuage pangs of hunger. In addition, the ship carried maize, biscuits, and dried antelope's meat. It is not known whether the royal edicts were obeyed. Saunders, *A Social History,* pp. 13-14; GEPB. *See also* slaves, diet on shipboard.

slaves as agricultural workers In Portugal c.1514 slaves cleared land and gathered nuts, berries, hay, and honeycombs. These products were part of their diet, and the surplus was sold to profit their masters. In wild rocky places in the Algarve, slaves cut and bound *esparto* (broom) grass into sheaves to be sold for the manufacture of rope and matting. In the summer in central

Portugal, some slaves guarded fields, vineyards, and olive groves while others tended flocks and herds. In autumn they picked grapes and drove animals laden with wine to the cellars. South of the Algarve, slaves were renowned for their skill in operating olive presses and in the manufacture of oil. Saunders, *A Social History*, p. 69; GEPB.

slaves, baptism of Since the Discovery (q.v.), the Portuguese had been concerned with baptizing African slaves after teaching them the Christian faith. Pope Eugene IV in his 1455 bull *Romanus Pontifex* referred specifically to the need to baptize the slaves brought to Portugal. King Manuel I became concerned about slaves who died without baptism after being brought from Guiné. In 1513 he empowered the vicar of the Church of Nossa Senhora da Conceição in Lisbon to baptize those Africans who were willing. He also ordered captains of slave ships bound for Lisbon to baptize those who were in danger of dying. In 1516 Pope Leo X granted the king permission to erect a fountain in the Church of Nossa Senhora da Conceição in Lisbon exclusively for the baptism of slaves. Capela, *Escravatura*, p. 93-4; Duncan, *Atlantic Islands,* p. 230; GEPB. *See also* slave children, baptism of.

slaves, baptismal tax on In Angola c.1600, a Portuguese tax of 300 *reis* was paid by slavers for the baptism of every captive who was sent to Brazil. Davidson, *Black Mother,* p. 158.

slaves, branding of King Manuel I decreed in 1519 that all slaves landed at São Tomé from Benin, the Slave River (Guiné), and the Congo were to be branded with a cross on their right arm. This was later changed to the letter "**G**," (q.v.) for "Guiné." Saunders, *A Social History*, p. 13; GEPB.

slaves' burial at sea Since the Discovery (q.v.) it was the practice to bury at sea slaves who died during the voyage. In such a case c.1500, the scrivener checked whether the victim had been marked as belonging to the king or to a private party and entered the relevant information in a special section of the log. The corpse was then thrown overboard. Occasionally, living slaves suffered the same fate. During two voyages from the coast of Africa in 1506 and 1507, one captain threw nursing infants alive into the sea "so that their mothers would not die," and ordered an African male to be thrown overboard as well. Saunders, *A Social History,* p.14; GEPB.

slaves' burial in Portugal Since the Discovery (q.v.) it was a practice to give slaves a full Christian burial. In 1513, the *almoxarife* (treasurer) of a government manufacturing plant at the Vale de Zebro in Lisbon, made sure that an African slave who had worked in the mill had a shroud, a funeral complete with candles, and a mass with wine and bread. When the Misericordia (q.v.) was called upon to undertake a slave's funeral, the slaveholder offered alms to cover the ceremony and the gravediggers' fees. Municipal authorization was sometimes necessary for a slave to be buried inside the city, although there were usually no objections to burying slaves in churchyards and even in the churches themselves. Indeed, by 1530, the Portuguese expected slaves to have Christian burials. Saunders, *A Social History,* p.110; GEPB.

slaves, civil law regarding   At the Discovery (q.v.) slavery was legal in Portugal. Since their arrival in Portugal in 1444, African slaves were considered members of society with the right to life and to due process of law; they also were considered *cousa* (chattel). As objects slaves could be used as security for a debt and they could also be pawned. On the other hand, the civil law spoke of a slave as a human being, having fundamental rights of life although temporarily deprived of personal freedom and totally owned by another man. This double status was recognized in Portugal and the colonies. In 1516 Portuguese law prescribed the death penalty for anyone who murdered a slave, although no evidence exists of any executions. A slaveholder found guilty of a capital crime was either exiled to Morocco or fined substantial amounts of money. Saunders, *A Social History,* pp. 113-5; GEPB; HDP. *See also* slaves, commercial law regarding.

slaves, commercial law regarding   In Portugal since the Middle Ages, the commercial code and royal ordinances regarded slaves as *cousas* (chattel). A barrel of wine or oil, an animal or a slave, all were considered commodities. The buyer of a damaged animal could claim his money back; the purchaser of a slave found to be sick or crippled could recover his money within a month of the transaction. Saunders, *A Social History,* pp. 114-5; GEPB; HDP. *See also* slaves, civil law regarding.

slaves, diet on shipboard   Although Portuguese kings since the Discovery (q.v.) were concerned with the feeding of slaves on shipboard, there is scanty information about it. In 1684 the amount of food for slaves in transit to Brazil was legally regulated. Aboard ship slaves were to be fed three times a day and given 3½ pints of water per person. Based on the probable duration of the trip, ships' captains had to store sufficient quantities of food and drink. The law specified that for a trip from Lisbon to Pernambuco, the ship had to carry supplies for thirty-five days; from Angola to Bahia, food sufficient for forty days; from Angola to Rio de Janeiro, enough for fifty days. Sick slaves were to be isolated to prevent the spread of infection and be given special care. Violators were punished with heavy fines, confiscations, even exile, based on the status of the offender. Attendants and ships' guards were to be punished with severity. In some cases penalties could be exile varying from six years to a lifetime in India. There is little evidence that these rules were in fact carried out. Saunders, *A Social History*, pp. 231-2; GEPB. *See also* sailors' diet on shipboard, slaves welfare on shipboard.

slaves, disease among Early in the Discovery (q.v.) c.1440, some slaves arriving in Lisbon were suffering from so-called tropical fevers. These included yellow fever, dengue fever, malaria, yaws (qq.v), measles, and others not easily identified. Sick slaves were held at the *Casa dos Escravos* (q.v.) in Lisbon and often were entrusted to a private healer for treatment. As a rule hospitals did not treat them because it was assumed that a master wealthy enough to buy slaves was also wealthy enough to pay a physician to look after them. Once recovered, the factor (q.v.) evaluated and sold these slaves, generally at reduced prices. Saunders, *A Social History*, pp. 16, 109-10; DHP; GEPB. *See also* slaves, medical services in Portugal for.

slaves, education of Early in the Discovery (q.v.) Portugal began educating African slaves in Lisbon. After 1444 the Crown held that although they "were in a state of perdition by living so like beasts, with no law of reasonable creatures," they were men with souls who could be educated. Indeed, one youth seized in 1445 became so well educated in reading, writing, and Christian doctrine that he came to know the Bible and other basics of civilized Portuguese life. João Pinto, a Wolof slave converted to Christianity, had an elaborate signature and asserted that he was able to read a *Book of Hours* in his possession. In 1535, the humanist Nicolaus Clenardus taught Latin to his three slaves so that they could assist him in his school in Evora. Saunders, *A Social History*, pp. 29, 91, 101-2; GEPB.

slaves, employment in hospitals of Around 1500 at the *Hospital dos Todos-os-Santos* (q.v.) in Lisbon and in small hospitals in other cities, there was often a shortage of workers. Because the Portuguese were reluctant to work in hospitals since it was a menial as well as a dangerous task, the Crown authorized the employment of male and female slaves to take care of the sick and the dying. In 1504 the *Hospital dos Todos-os-Santos* had a staff of twenty-six people, of whom six were slaves. The four male slaves were assigned only the most menial physical tasks such as sweeping the floors, changing the bed linen, and emptying the patients' chamber pots; the two women helped wash the bed linen and the patients' clothes. The hospital gave the same meal to all its staff, slave or free. All ate together in the hospital refectory, where stories from lives of the saints were read out to them during the meal. In 1515 King Manuel I greatly increased the annual supply of slaves for all the hospitals and infirmaries in the country. Saunders, *A Social History*, pp. 67, 97; DHP; GEPB. *See also* slaves, food in Portugal for.

slaves, food for, in Portugal Around 1500, the Portuguese government became concerned with the welfare of the slaves and stored enough food to feed all the slaves in Lisbon and other cities. Around 1510 African slave workers as well as Portuguese staff in *Hospital de Todos-os-Santos* in Lisbon were fed two meals a day in the refectory. A serving was ¹/₃ kg meat or fish, ¹/₂ kg bread, and one liter of wine. Stories of saints were read during meals. At the Royal Ovens at the Vale de Zebro on the southern bank of the Tagus, slaves ate about the same ration. In 1515 lamb was added to the diet. In these institutions, the yearly allowances of food per slave was between 925 and 1,075 lbs. (420 and 488 kg). This amount was more than double the 440 lbs. (200 kg) that Fernand Braudel estimates was the yearly average consumption of a person in the Mediterranean area at the time. Saunders, *A Social History,* pp. 97-98; GEPB. *See also* slaves, employment in hospitals of.

slaves, intermarriage of, with Portuguese and free Africans In Portugal since the sixteenth century slaves freely intermarried, both in church or, informally, by common law. Free African men usually married African women, free or slave. Poor Portuguese laboring men married African or mulatto women more frequently than African or mulatto men married Portuguese women. In Evora in 1551, an African woman held by the Inquisition mentioned that another African woman was married to a Portuguese migrant from Beira, apparently by common law. Afonso Alvares, a mulatto grammar teacher in Lisbon, married a Portuguese woman, the daughter of a pack-saddle maker, in 1530. Saunders, *A Social History,* pp. 146-7, 215; GEPB. *See also* slaves, marriage of.

slaves, interracial relations in Portugal and Roman and Portuguese law considered a slave both a "thing" and a " man" deprived of his natural freedom, and racial relations were relatively friendly. Around 1565 the day-to-day social intercourse among slaves, freedmen, and Europeans seems to have been fairly good, especially among the lower classes of Portuguese society. Poor Africans and poor Portuguese mingled easily; they played games and enjoyed social evenings together, and some Portuguese appear to have received Africans in their homes and to have accepted Africans' hospitality. The Lisbon tax roll of 1565 shows that there were no African ghettos in the city and that Africans took lodgings in the same houses as Europeans. Its was a common practice among Portuguese couples to serve as godparents to the children of their domestic slaves. Saunders, *A Social History,* p. 146; GEPB. *See also* baptism of slaves.

slaves, legal status of *See* slaves, civil law regarding; slaves, commercial law regarding.

slaves, marriage of In Portugal at the Discovery (q.v.), marriages between slaves or between slaves and freedmen were recognized by canon law (q.v.) as they had been since the Middle Ages. Records of such unions as early as 1530 are found in parish registers in the larger centers of slave population such as Lisbon, Lagos, and Evora. In any Portuguese household the number of slaves was usually small so slaves often found partners from among slaves belonging to neighboring masters. In such cases, they visited each other on occasional nights. A slave married to a freedman also probably had the same arrangement. Common law liaisons between slaves were often casual, though some slaves considered these marriage to be binding. Inspired by the Council of Trent (1545-63) and its definition of the doctrines of the church, the bishops found that slave couples were unaware that they could marry in the church, and that many masters had forbidden their slaves to do so. The bishops decreed that slaves who knew the fundamentals of the Christian religion could lawfully marry even if their masters opposed the union, and that a master committed mortal sin if he either denied this right or tried to separate them once married. Saunders, *A Social History*, pp. 103-15; GEPB. *See also* slaves, intermarriage of, with Portuguese and free Africans.

slaves, medical services in Portugal for As early as 1466 Portugal had established public medical services to take care of sick slaves arriving from Guiné. They were housed in the *Casa dos Escravos* where a private medic undertook to treat them. Often an unsold slave was taken either to the house of a pious benefactor for treatment at their own expense or to the Misericordia (q.v.). If the slave lived, his benefactor could buy him from the *Casa dos Escravos* for about half the market price. No slaves were treated in the charity hospitals which usually admitted only Portuguese, although these institutions did not exclude free Africans. They prohibited slaves because it was assumed that a master had means to pay a physician to care the sick in his home. After King Joao II established the *Hospital de Todos-os-Santos* in Lisbon in 1492, the policy of admitting sick slaves was introduced. Some masters made efforts to maintain their slaves in reasonable physical condition and provided them with medical treatment if needed. Home remedies were the usual treatment, but professional assistance might be sought to treat severe maladies. In 1520, King Manuel I ordered a permanent hostel to be built in the Lisbon suburb of Alcantara so that sick or diseased slaves could be isolated from the rest of the population. In 1523, the infirmary was reserved for male slaves and workers. On several occasions in 1526, the *almoxarife* (tax collector) of Vale de Zebro took a slave to a barber-surgeon to have a tooth pulled. He also secured medicine and a doctor to look after slaves suffering from a range of ailments including pleurisy, a blow to the head, an injured foot, and fever. Slaves belonging to the Crown or the nobility always received better medical care than those belonging to less affluent masters. Saunders, *A Social History,* pp. 16, 89, 109-10; DHP. *See also* slaves, disease among.

slaves, mutilation of   In Portugal, the Manueline Code of 1521 allowed a royal court, after due process of law, to punish an African slave by cutting off his ears if he were convicted of stealing goods worth between 100 and 400 *reis.* The convicted slave had the right of appeal should the verdict go against him. Saunders, *A Social History,* pp. 102-3; GEPB.

slaves, number exported from Angola   Portugal dominated the Angolan slave trade from 1500 to 1850. Although the records are neither complete nor accurate, enough studies have been made of various parts of Africa, and also of each country to which slaves were shipped, to make presently accepted estimates fairly reliable. The total number of slaves arriving in the Americas from all parts of Africa is estimated at about 13 million. Angola is estimated to have shipped about 4 million, or 30 percent of all slaves in the trade, over a period of 350 years and would seem to have been the largest supplier of slaves in the world. Because Portugal imposed a tax on all slaves exported, it had a vested interest in keeping records of those slaves who actually embarked. There are no records, only calculations, of the number of persons originally captured and those lost between delivery at the coast and embarkation. One observer of conditions during the 1780s used a working estimate of 50 percent of slaves dying during the forced march to the coast and 40 percent of the remainder dying in Luanda, or a total of 70 percent of the original number captured dying before they even set foot on a Portuguese ship. If this estimate can be taken seriously, it means that 13 million persons were captured in the hinterlands of Angola alone, the same as the total number that arrived in the Americas, to supply 4 million slaves for actual shipment from Angola. If the loss during the middle passage (q.v.) from Africa to the Americas is added to the loss from capture to embarkation, Basil Davidson's estimate of a total of 50 million Africans lost in the slave trade may not be excessive. Henderson, *Angola,* pp. 94-5.

slaves, runaway, in Portugal   That African slaves often fled from captivity to other Portuguese cities or to isolated places was a problem from early in the Discovery (q.v.). In 1498 King Manuel I ruled that runaway slaves, once found, should be brought before a judge in the main town of the district in which the slave had been captured and be made to reveal the name of his master. The magistrate was authorized to administer up to thirty lashes in his attempt to elicit this information. The slave was then kept in jail until his master took him back. Unlike other places in the empire where runaways established maroon settlements (q.v.), there was no secure place in Portugal to hide and slaves did not have the right to sanctuary in churches. Should a slave seek sanctuary, a judge could evict him or her by force from the church and bring the slave to justice. Saunders, *A Social History,* pp. 134b; GEPB.

Slaves' Square A market in the Alfama borough, north of Lisbon where as early as 1502 slaves were bought and sold alongside wine, horses, and cattle. In 1550 it was called *Pelourinho Velho.* Saunders, *A Social History*, p. 17; GEPB.

slaves, taxes on *See* dizima.

slaves, transportation in chains of In the Zambezi region of Mozambique during the colonial period, captured slaves were transported bound together with chains, leather, or bamboo for the long march to distant markets where they would be sold. Isaacman, *Mozambique: The Tradition*, p. 88.

slaves, wages paid to Since early in the Discovery (q.v.) in Portugal, slaves were paid for work done for outside employers and these earnings were shared with their masters. They performed work of different kinds and the record of compensation varies a great deal. Around 1530 in Lisbon a male carrier of baskets of meat, fish, or produce to the market received 40 *reis* per day; a longshoreman working on the waterfront loading and unloading ships was paid 100 *reis* per day, the highest wage for slaves at the time. Around 1550, a male carrier of baskets of meat and fish in the market still earned 40 *reis* per day; a female water carrier was also paid 40 *reis* per day, but of this, 20 to 35 *reis* went to her master, and the rest the slave kept for herself to buy food while at work; a washerwoman's salary was 30 to 35 *reis* per day. As policy, an employed slave, male or female, was required to share part of his or her earning with the master and part was saved to purchase the individual's manumission (q.v.), a legacy of the practice since medieval times of allowing Moorish slaves to work and earn money to free themselves. Saunders, *A Social History*, pp. 77-9, 138-9; GEPB.

sleeping sickness (Pg.) An infectious disease especially common in forested areas of tropical Africa and caused by either of two trypanosomes (*Trypanosoma gambiense* or *T. rhodesiense*) that are transmitted by the bite of a tsetse fly (*Glossina* spp.). The disease is characterized by fever, weakness, tremors, and lethargy, often ending in prolonged coma and death. In Angola, Guinea-Bissau, and elsewhere there are four recognized species of tsetse fly: *G. palpalis*, *G. sub-morsitans*, *G. longipalpis*, and *G. fusca*, the last one being very rare. In 1871, sleeping sickness was reported in the areas of Cazengo, Golungo Alto, and the Cuanza River, Angola. It appeared in Luanda in 1873. *Revista Medica de Angola*, Luanda, 1923, 2:91-95, 4:159-64; GEPB; WNWD.

smallpox An infectious disease, often fatal, ushered in with severe febrile symptoms, which, in the course of two or three days, are followed by papular eruptions appearing over all parts of the body. The eruptions pass successively through the states of maculation, vesiculation, pustulation, and later crust formation; after this pits of the skin (pockmarks) are produced. In Angola this disease apparently has recurred, especially in Luanda, since the beginning of the colonization because this seaport, like others in Portuguese Africa, was a port of call for ships traveling to and from India and other areas of contagion, although the first official acknowledgment of a smallpox epidemic in Luanda was not reported until 1864. Smallpox later was classified as endemic in the country. *Revista Medica de Angola*, Luanda, 1923, 2:453-54; SMD. *See also* vaccination.

soap In São Tomé, Africans made a type of soap for domestic washing and cleaning even before the arrival of the Portuguese in 1480. They mixed potassium or sodium salts from ashes with fatty acids from tropical shrubs that contained high amounts of emulsifiers. In the sixteenth century one plant often used for soapmaking was *Solanaum saponaceum* Welw., introduced from Peru to the island specifically for this purpose. This plant, called *jindondolo* by Africans and *afurra* by Portuguese, was used later by colonists to make a well-esteemed soap exported in the seventeenth and eighteenth centuries to Portugal and the rest of Europe. Ficalho, *Plantas Uteis*, pp. 229-30; Hodges, *São Tomé e Príncipe*, p. 24.

soba (Bant.) Among ethnic groups in Angola, an absolute chief; an hereditary title of authority for life. GEPB.

sobado (Afr.) In colonial Angola, a loosely defined territory and its residents under the absolute authority of a chief or *soba* (q.v.). There were hundreds of *sabados*, each ruled by a *soba* who often controlled a number of settlements and forced travelers to pay heavy taxes on their goods. GEPB.

Sociedade Agricola Algodoeira Voluntaria dos Africanos de Moçambique (Pg.) "Private Agricultural Cotton Society of Mozambican Africans." A cooperative group established by Lazaro Kavandame in Mueda, Cabo Delgado, Mozambique, in 1957. Its aim was to encourage Africans to increase cotton production without government intervention or coercion. By 1958 the cooperative had 1,000 members and was flourishing. The cotton company that controlled cotton production in North Mozambique offered Kavandame a salary to work for it, a proof of the cooperative's success. By July 1959 there were more than 1,500 members in the cooperative, and the company then started putting pressure on the government to stop unfair competition by rivals. The companies sent agents to destroy the society's fields under the pretense that their cotton was of inferior quality. Some of the members of the cooperative were threatened and forced to hire contract laborers on cotton plantations. In September 1959 Kavandame and others of the group were imprisoned. They were later released, but were forced to cooperate with the government. Munslow, *Mozambique*, pp. 70-1.

Sociedade de Comercio das Ilhas de Cabo Verde (Pg.) "Commercial Society of the Cape Verde Islands." A Portuguese chartered trade company established on September 18, 1780, to exploit the sale of merchandise and the slave trade along the upper Guiné coast and the Cape Verde Islands. This corporation, the successor of the *Companhia Geral do Grão-Pará e Maranhao* (q.v.), failed a few years later through a combination of lack of capital and poor management. Carreira, *As Companhias Pombalinas*, BCGP, 1968, Lisbon, xxiii(89/90):45. *See also* Companhia da Costa de Guiné.

Sociedade de Geografia de Lisboa (Pg.) "Geographic Society of Lisbon." A private organization of academics, geographers, statesmen, and explorers established in Lisbon in 1875. It represented a new generation of colonialists eager to study and foster new economic development and to advance Portuguese occupation in Africa. DHP.

Sociedade Propagadora de Conhecimentos Geographico-Africanos (Pg.) "Society for the Promotion of Knowledge of African Geography." A Luanda-based organization founded in 1881 by Urbano de Castro, the editor of the society's *Boletim*. It was also known as *Sociedade de Geografia de Luanda* (Geography Society of Luanda). Lopo, *Jornalismo*, p. 30.

Society of Jesus *See* Jesuits.

sócópé (Criol.) "With only one foot." A slow measured rhythmic dance performed in unison, very popular on São Tomé. It is reminiscent of a staid military quadrille performed at a formal ball. Dancers move very slowly, as if they had only one foot. Originally the dance had no lyrics, but today a dancer tells jokes during the dance. The first part, of European origin, is slow; the second is African, and quicker and livelier. This combination of European and African dance is peculiar to São Tomé. Although the dance originally was held in low esteem, modern São Tomeans think of the *sócópé* as a national symbol and its performance an indication of high social standing. Garfield, *History*, pp. 31, 248; Tenreiro, *A Ilha*, p. 188.

Sofala (Afr.) A seaport on the northern coast of the Mozambique Channel, it was the main port of call of the Portuguese fleet at the end of the fifteenth century. As early as the seventh century it was a trade station under Arab domination dealing in gold, ivory, slaves, and Chinese goods. It was conquered by the Portuguese in 1505 and soon after became an important commercial center for trade with South and Central Africa, Portugal, Aden, Ormuz, Goa, Macão, and Japan. It was the precursor of modern Maputo, capital of Mozambique. Axelson, *Portuguese in South-East*, p.45.

Solemnibus Conventionibus (Lat.) A bull signed by Pope Pius XII in Rome on September 4, 1940, that abolished the Mozambique Prelacy and instituted the Dioceses of Beira and Nampula. HDM.

"Soldiers United Will Win!" The slogan of a powerful military interest group organized in Portugal in 1968. The goals of this new generation of army officers were to improve the working conditions in the armed forces and to minimize military discipline. Bruce, *Portugal, The Last Empire*, p. 63.

Songhai A West African empire of the middle Niger. At the end of the ninth century the Songhai were active in the trans-Saharan trade. By the end of the fourteenth century the empire was controlled first by Ghana, then by Mali. The new empire of the fifteenth and sixteenth centuries was created by Ali Sunni who wrested it from Mali and reigned from 1465 to 1492. Its capital was Gao, situated near the Niger River. Under Ali Sunni the Songhai Empire reached its greatest extent, stretching from the Senegal River in the west to Kano in the east and as far north as Taghaza. He also restored Timbuctu as a cultural center in 1495. DHP; GEPB.

Soninke (Afr.) A powerful ethnic community that evolved from nuclear Mande stock of the Niger-Congo language family in West Africa. They are related to the Susu and Dyula of Guinea-Bissau and eastern Senegal. Their most notable achievement was the founding of the Ghana-Sudanic Empire. HDRG. *See also* Songhai.

sope (Afr.) In Mozambique, an alcoholic drink distilled from fermented sugar cane and molasses, very popular among Africans. It was first manufactured in Inhambane in the 1890s when sugar replaced the cashew and coconut economy. Hammond, *Portugal and Africa*, p. 154.

sorghum Also known as Guinea corn; tropical Old World grain-producing grasses that have solid stems bearing large, compact panicles of flowers followed by numerous seeds. *Sorghum vulgare* is grown for grain, *S. saccharatum* for its sweet syrup, and these and other sorghum species, including *Sorghum arundinaceum* var. *sudanense*, called Sudan grass, are grown for fodder and pasturage. Apparently it had two centers of cultivation, Ethiopia and Western Sudan where Leo Africanus noted it growing in 1526.

According to Valentim Fernandes writing in 1506, sorghum was harvested twice a year in March and September. In African cultivation the seed is scattered in an irregular pattern on prepared fields, not grown in furrows as is customary in Europe. Before it flowers, sorghum can be confused with maize (*Zea mays*), the New World corn to which the more drought-tolerant sorghum and millet (q.v.) are related. It is a basic food for a considerable portion of West Africa. The Portuguese found this grain early in the Discovery (q.v.) in Western Sudanese and Senegalese markets. Fernandes, *Description*, pp. 15, 137, 191; Lewicki, *West African Food*, pp. 28, 116, 215; GEPB.

soul of Portugal, The An expression used in the 1950s by the English writer F.C.C. Egerton to suggest that the Portuguese character fluctuates between sound judgment and hero madness. When the former prevails, the country is stable; when the latter, instability sets in. According to Egerton, the Salazar regime restored a balance of sorts by stressing Portugal's traditional civilizing mission in Africa. Wheeler, *In Search*, p. 15.

South Africa Act A formal treaty signed in 1909 between South Africa and Portugal ensuring that the port of Lourenço Marques would receive fifty percent of the total traffic in goods between Transvaal and southern Mozambique. Hammond, *Portugal and Africa*, p. 331.

South West African People's Organization *See* SWAPO.

Southern Cross A constellation of the southern hemisphere whose four brightest stars form a Latin cross. It was used as a point of reference by early Portuguese navigators to determine their position in southern latitudes. In 1454 the navigator Alvise Cadamosto observed six large bright stars which he identified as the Southern Cross. Pilot João de Lisboa in his letter to King Manuel I sent a drawing of the constellations he had seen, among which was the Southern Cross. Prestage, *The Portuguese Pioneers*, pp. 321-22; WNWD.

Soyo (Afr.) Soyo was the first area of Angola reached in 1482 by Diogo Cão. It is a town that occupies a key position on the southern bank of the Congo River and along the Atlantic coast. It was known in the colonial period as Santo António de Zaire. Due to the offshore oil reserves, it is a growing commercial center. HDA.

spice (Pg.) Any of numerous vegetable substances, usually from plant parts other than leaves, such as clove, cinnamon, nutmeg, pepper, and others. Early in the Discovery (q.v.) this term was the generic name for a group that included condiments, household medicines, chewing gums, stimulants, narcotics, perfumes, and several kinds of oils. DHP. *See also* malagüeta

spice trade This trade across the Indian Ocean to India, China, and the East Indies was monopolized by the Portuguese around 1510. Afonso de Albuquerque brought cinnamon, black and white pepper, chewing gums, clove, and nutmeg from Asia to the Lisbon court. Soon the trade in spices attracted the interest of such German financiers as Anton Welser, George Imhoff, and other bankers from Augsburg. Abshire, *Portuguese Africa*, p. 40; DHP.

Stella Maris (Lat.) "Sea Star." Another name for the North Star, a fixed (unmoving) celestial body positioned in the heavens at true north. It was a standard point of reference for navigators, including the Portuguese at the time of the Discovery (q.v.). Cortesão, *History*, I:206-7.

Strange Adventures of Andrew Bettell of Leigh, The A classic narrative written 1589-90 by Andrew Bettell, an English adventurer. He describes the Cuango Valley, the Congo Kingdom, the life and settlements of the Africans he encountered, and Portuguese activities in Angola. It is an interesting account of the author's twenty-one months in captivity among the savage Jagas. This journal was published by the Hakulyt Society in London in 1901. Duffy, *Portuguese Africa*, pp. 63-3, 351; DHP.

Sub-Guinea People People settled on the Atlantic coast within the tidal and mangrove belt, mainly in Guinea-Bissau. Their agriculture, whether irrigated or not, was and is the most developed in the region. On higher ground, their clearing of the forest for farming gives the landscape its settled look in sharp contrast to the interior. In the depressions and along strips of land, mostly reclaimed from the sea, they have laid out an intricate system of high-yielding rice paddies. This type of farming has made possible a more intensive utilization of land which, in turn, supports a greater population and a higher standard of living. Mota, *Guiné Portuguesa*, I:379-80.

sucha (Afr.) A pressed and molded mixture of sugar and tea leaves that resembles a chocolate bar, first manufactured and sold in 1935 by the Sena Sugar Company on the lower Zambezi River. Vail, *Capitalism*, p. 262.

sucupira (Braz.) In Angola, a magnificent tree (*Pentaclethra macrophylla*) that reaches 100-120 ft. (30-36 m). Its wood is used for shipbuilding and other industrial uses. The seeds, which are edible and can be made into a bread, are also a source of fat for soap and candles. Ficalho, *Plantas Uteis*, p. 168.

Sudan *See* Bilad-es-Sudan.

Sudan grass A tall annual grass (*Sorghum arundinaceum* var. *sudanense*) that has been cultivated in the Sudan since antiquity for forage and fodder and, occasionally, food. Lewicki, *West African Food*, p. 28. *See also* sorghum.

Sudanese black Historically in Guinea-Bissau and elsewhere, the name for a type of tall Sudanese African, a racial mixture of Ethiopian, Nubian, and Berber. Mota, *Guiné Portuguesa,* I:165.

Sudanese Moslems A large group of followers of Islam concentrated in Mauritania, the Sahel, Futa-Djallon, and Guinea-Bissau. They are tightly linked through their clerics with either the *Qadiriyya* or *Tijaniyya tariqas* (qq.v.). In the nineteenth century, Islam greatly expanded in Western Sudan. The *Fadiriyya* order, which was founded in 1860, became a powerful group among the Senegalese. Trimingham, *A History of Islam*, pp. 159-60.

Suez Canal The ship canal across the Isthmus of Suez joining the Mediterranean and the Gulf of Suez, a distance of 107 mi. (172 km). It was opened on November 17, 1869, and put Mozambique and East Africa on a direct sea route to Portugal and Europe. The canal ended Portugal's 370-year isolation in the Indian Ocean. Hammond, *Portugal and Africa*, p. 75.

sugar *See* sugar cane.

sugar cane (Ar.) A tall perennial South Asian grass (*Saccharum officinarum* L.) cultivated since antiquity as the main source of sugar in tropical and subtropical regions. According to the Arab geographer al-Bakri, there were large plantations of sugar cane south of the Sahara in the eleventh century. The Moors introduced sugar cane to Sicily and it was brought from Sicily to Portugal around 1350. In 1452, early in the Discovery (q.v.), on Prince Henry's initiative it was introduced to Madeira and Diogo de Teive was given a contract to build a water mill in Sao Miguel to grind the cane. By 1455 Teive already was manufacturing 6,000 *arrobas* (8.4 metric tons) of sugar a year, a figure that soon increased greatly. The first cargo of Madeiran sugar arrived at Bristol, England, in 1456. Later it was also exported to Flanders, Castile, France, and Portugal. Sugar cane cultivation was brought to Cape Verde by the Genoese c.1455, and it overtook Madeira as a major supplier. In the late sixteenth century it was introduced to Brazil, then in 1640 to Barbados from which it spread to the rest of the Caribbean, precipitating the need for African slaves. In Arabic, sugar is *qasab as-sukr*. Lewicki, *West African Food,* pp. 144-5; Duncan, *Atlantic Islands,* pp. 9, 21, 85, 191; DHP. *See also* cultura de canna, sugar cane in Cape Verde, sugar cane in São Tomé e Príncipe.

sugar cane in Cape Verde The Genoese introduced sugar cane to Santiago Island, Cape Verde, c.1455 where it developed into an important export item. By 1508, sugar also was used to produce rum, a trade article sold in Guinea-Bissau and nearby African settlements. In 1533, sugar cane was taken to São Vicente Island, Cape Verde, by the Genoese brothers Francesco, Giuseppe, and Paulo, traders from Genoa. Cape Verdian sugar cane plantations were small and vulnerable to drought and the hot, dry winds from Africa. By 1600 cheaper Brazilian sugar forced Cape Verde out of the market and the industry never recovered, although sugar is still cultivated in the archipelago for local consumption. Duncan, *Atlantic Islands*, pp. 21, 160, 167; DHP.

sugar cane in São Tomé e Príncipe Donatario Alvaro Caminha and the settlers who came with him introduced sugar cane into the islands around 1490. The local system of sugar cane cultivation was established by colonists from Madeira c.1493. The industry soon prospered due to the climate, the fertile soil, and the abundance of slaves imported by the *roçeiros* (planters). After 1600, the industry survived the competition from Brazilian sugar that ruined the Cape Verde sugar cane industry. Duncan, *Atlantic Islands*, pp. 21, 191; *São Tomé Pequena Monografia*, pp. 22-3.

sugar mill A mill used to extract the juice of sugar cane or sorghum to manufacture sugar. In the colonial period the millstone had a pair of large, flat, round stones or a set of two or three vertical rollers between which the sugar cane was ground and the juice expressed. A mill was operated by wind, water, animals, or slaves. Apparently the first Portuguese colonial sugar mill was built by Diogo de Teive in São Miguel, Madeira, in 1452 at the request of Prince Henry. From there, the technology was taken to Cape Verde and São Tomé e Príncipe. In 1495 Alvaro Caminha settled in São Tomé and built several sugar mills. By 1529 there were upward of twenty sugar mills on the islands. Tenreiro, *A Ilha*, pp. 68-9; DHP.

sungilando (Kimb.) "Story-telling." Among the Kimbundu (q.v.) of Angola, tales and stories orally transmitted by parents to children. *Sungilando* as a concept is a symbol of the past that inspires many Portuguese and African writers and poets. Hamilton, *Voices*, p. 46. *See also* griot.

Sunna, Sunnah (Ar.) "Shining path." Moslem law followed by the Sunni (q.v.) sect and based, according to tradition, on the teachings and example of Mohammed. It is observed by orthodox Sunni Moslems in Guinea-Bissau and elsewhere. Brito, *As Fontes do Direito Islámico*, BCGP, 1966, xxi(82):167; WNWD.

Sunni (Ar.) Any member of one of the two great sects of Islam, the other being Shiites (q.v.). Sunnis approve the historical order of the first four caliphates as the rightful line of succession to Mohammed and accept the Sunna (q.v.) as an authoritative supplement to the Koran. The Moslem sect settled in Guinea-Bissau belong to the Sunni tradition. Brito, *As Fontes do Direito Islámico*, BCG, 1966, xxi(82):176.

sunturu (Afr.) A community assembly in a mosque. This is a practice common among the Fulas in the Gabu area of northern Guinea-Bissau. Mota, *Guiné Portugues*, I:279.

suoma (Afr.) "Sleeping sickness." An often-fatal illness of sheep and goats carried by African tsetse flies (*Glossina malpali* and *G. trypanosoma uniformae*). The illness is indigenous in river areas, dense forest, and open woodland in Angola and São Tomé. GEPB. *See also* nagana.

Super Specula Militantis Ecclesiae (Lat.) A letter signed by Pope Clement VIII on May 20, 1596, creating the Diocese of Congo with the seat at the cathedral of São Salvador do Congo. There was a chapter with dean, secretary, notary, and nine canons. Gabriel, *Angola*, p. 84.

sura (Afr.) In Guinea-Bissau, an alcoholic beverage produced by fermenting coconut water (also called coconut milk) from the fruit of the coconut palm (*Cocos nucifera*). In Mozambique and elsewhere, it is also called palm wine. Newitt, *Portuguese Settlement*, p. 385; GEPB.

Sura (Ar.) "Chapter." There are 114 *suras* in the Koran. The first "The Introduction" and the last "The Men," contain seven and five verses, respectively. Each *sura* has a name, a different topic, and a distinctive vigorous style. All but sixteen were dictated by the prophet Mohammed in Mecca, the remainder were dictated in Medina. The *suras* are seriously studied and followed by orthodox Moslems in Guinea-Bissau and elsewhere. Among the first slaves taken by the Portuguese in 1446, nearly all were orthodox Sunnis (q.v.) familiar with the *suras*. Brito, *As Fontes do Direito Islámico*, BCG, 1966, xxi(82):169-74.

svikiro (Afr.) "Spiritual medium." The term for a messenger of the supreme divinity who puts the king of the Shonas in touch with his ancestors. The *svikiro* played an important part in governing the people, especially in times of social crisis or internal revolt. The *svikiro* prescribed a medicine that was believed to make the warriors invincible and no important decision was taken without previously consulting him. Henriksen, *Mozambique*, p.10.

Swahili coast In East Africa, the Indian Ocean coast from southern Mombasa down to Sofala and modern Beira, Mozambique. Before the arrival of the Portuguese in 1500, it was occupied by a Swahili-speaking Arabic people engaged in trade and commerce. At that time they ruled such wealthy cities in the region as Malindi, Pemba, Angoche, and Kilwa. In 1498 Vasco da Gama and his expedition were surprised to see the level of their comfort and luxury. This region enjoyed great prosperity until the middle of the eighteenth century. Axelson, *Portuguese in South-East*, pp. 54, 84, 180; GEPB.

Swahili-Islamic culture At their arrival in 1498, the Portuguese found an old prosperous civilization that extended throughout East Africa from Mombasa south to Beira in Mozambique and inland to the Congo area in Central Africa. It was a predominantly Islamic society shaped by long contact with animistic Bantu people and used Swahili (q.v.) as a *lingua franca*, speaking it from the Indian Ocean to Congo in Central Africa. Trimingham, *Islam in East-Africa*, p. 66-7.

Swahili language (Ar.) A Bantu language with an uncomplicated sound system and a vocabulary with many Arabic, Portuguese, English, and Indian loanwords. It is spoken by 1.5 million people in East Africa in an area roughly from southern Somalia to Mozambique, and including Zanzibar and the Comoro Islands. In the mid-twentieth century, Swahili, also spelled *Kiswahili*, became a symbol of national unity in what became Tanzania. For African-Americans, it is the language of "Black Power." Kaplan, *Area Handbook*, p. 20.

Swahili merchants Swahili-speaking traders who engaged in trade and commerce along the Swahili coast (q.v.) and Central Africa for centuries before the arrival of the Portuguese in 1498. One of their trade routes was inland along the Zambezi River to the Congo River basin. These Arab-African, later Afro-Portuguese, entrepreneurs originally dealt in gold, ivory, and slaves, later adding European and Indian goods. They were active up to the end of the nineteenth century. The Portuguese named the first administrator of these people in Sofala in 1506. Axelson, *Portuguese in South-East*, p. 84; DHP.

Swahili people In East Africa, a large Islamic-Bantu population settled between the mouth of the Ligonha River, northern Mozambique, and the Tanzanian border. They occupy the extreme northern part of the coast and are related to Bantu coastal peoples in Kenya, Tanzania, and Zanzibar. They are Moslems who have been influenced for centuries by Arab and Persian traders. In 1970, they constituted about 500,000 people. Kaplan, *Area Handbook*, pp. 83, 101-2.

Swahili society In East Africa, a large community of Arab-Bantu people constituting a somewhat homogeneous sociocultural entity in which patrilineal, patriarchal, patrilocal, and endogamous traditions coexist with the traditions of independent Bantu household family unity, dominant headman, kinship ties, animistic beliefs, and village and territorial organization. In 1498 Vasco da Gama's party were surprised to see the wealth of their cities and their booming commerce along the Indian Ocean coast. Trimingham, *Islam in East-Africa*, pp. 143-9.

Swahili Zone In Mozambique, the area known as the Swahili Zone extends along the Indian Ocean coast from Moma at the mouth of the Ligonha River into northern Tanzania, where Swahili is spoken by the Makuas. West of the coast and north of the Zambezi, Swahili is the *lingua franca* of various ethnic groups. Non-African merchants easily learned it and used it in their transactions. After 1916, however, Swahili was not allowed to be used in Portuguese legal documents. This policy has been changed since Mozambique became a republic in 1975. Herrick, *Area Handbook*, p. 58.

SWAPO (South West African People's Organization) A nationalist party formed in 1960 by the Ovambo ethnic group of Angola and Namibia. Its leader, Hermann ja Toivo, demanded reunion of the Angolan Ovambos with their brothers to the south in the Baxo Cuenene region of Angola, the capital of which was Vila Pereira d'Eça. SWAPO continued its fight against the Luanda government long after the War for Independence was over in 1975. Newitt, *Portugal in Africa*, pp. 54, 56.

sweet potato A tropical farinaceous plant (*Ipomoea batatas* L.) with tuber-like roots. It was introduced from the New World into Angola by the Portuguese c.1520. Soon it brought great economic and social change in Portuguese Africa because Africans adopted it as a basic food, using it to make a type of flour. Today it is a primary foodstuff for millions of Africans. Ficalho, *Plantas Uteis*, p. 230. *See also* yam.

Swiss missionaries In 1887 Swiss Protestant missionaries arrived at Lourenço Marques (today Maputo) and Paul Berthoud, their first leader, opened educational and health facilities in the town. From the beginning, Swiss as well as other Protestant schools taught Africans in their own languages. In 1910 the Republican government in Lisbon welcomed non-Catholic education in Mozambique and elsewhere, but by 1933 the Salazar government accused them of undermining Portuguese sovereignty. As a result they were forbidden to use African languages in their schools. Despite this, the Swiss missionaries continued their educational work and by 1973 there were forty missions in Mozambique. Henriksen, *Mozambique*, pp. 144, 212, 215.

Swiss Romande missionaries A group of Protestant missionaries from the Romande province of Switzerland led by Henri A. Junod, an ethnologist. They came to Lourenço Marques, Mozambique, in the late nineteenth century, opened a mission, and studied and used local languages. In 1898, they published an essay entitled *Les Ba-Ronga* (The Ronga People). This account, based on interviews with three African informants, was published in 1912 in two volumes in Switzerland by Neuchatel-Imprimerie Attinger Frères. A second edition published in New York by AMS Press appeared in 1977. This work has been translated from the French into Portuguese under the title, *Usos e Costumes dos Bantos: A Vida duma Tribo Sul-Africana* (Manners and Customs of the Bantu: The Life of a Southern African Tribe), Lourenço Marques; Imprensa Nacional, 1944-47, 2 vols. This study is still considered an important historical document. Darch, *Mozambique,* pp. 92-3.

syphilis An infectious venereal disease caused by a spirochete (*Trepanoma pallidum*). The origins of syphilis are not completely known, but there is archeological evidence that native Americans as well as people of the Old World suffered from it. Many historians believe the syphilis did not exist in the Old World until it appeared in Naples shortly after the return of Christopher Columbus from his first voyage to the New World in 1492. Following the fall of Naples in 1495, the army of King Charles VIII of France spread a perhaps more virulent strain of the disease throughout Europe. In 1530, Girolimo Frascataro, an Italian physician and poet, wrote a long poem entitled "Syphilus, sive Morbus Gallicus" ("Syphilis, or the French Disease"). The central character in this poem is an infected shepherd named Syphilus. From this book, the name syphilis was applied to this illness. Apparently Portuguese explorers and sailors spread syphilis to Angola and São Tomé where it appeared among the islanders around 1550. In the twentieth century the Portuguese government provided efficient medical service in the islands. In São Tomé in 1982, there were only five cases of syphilis in a population of 82,000. Hodges, *São Tomé e Príncipe,* pp. 52, 69, 72; EA; GEPB; SMD.

tabanca (Afr.)   On Santiago Island, Cape Verde, a processional dance performed at certain festivals, especially during the Feast of Saint John on June 24. In the course of this dance, the participants walk in loose formation through the town singing, clapping, and dancing to the accompaniment of drums, conches, and whistles. The dance is a vestige of African religious tradition brought by slaves to the island during the colonial period. Hamilton, *Voices,* p. 243; HDRGC.

Table Bay   A slip of land 6 mi. (9.6 km) wide forming the harbor of Cape Town in Cape province, Republic of South Africa. Table Bay was discovered by the Portuguese navigator Antonio de Saldanha c.1503 and originally named *Aguada de Saldanha* (Saldanha's Watering Place.) Valkhoff, *Miscelanea,* pp. 267-8.

tabua (Afr.)   "Board." In Guinea-Bissau, a small wooden board painted or engraved with Arabic proverbs and used by children in Islamic schools. It is common in Mandingo (q.v.) and other African Moslem communities. Gonçalves, *O Mundo Arabo-Islámico,* p. 206.

tacamaca (Afr.)   A gum resin extracted from either of two tropical rubber trees, *Clintranda henriquesina* or *Carpodinus lanceolata.* It is found on the Zanzibar coast, on the Querimba Islands, in Mozambique, and elsewhere in tropical Africa. Ficalho, *Plantas Uteis,* p. 155.

tacula (Afr.)   In Angola in Libongo, Zenza do Golungo, and Golungo Alto and elsewhere, a tall tropical hardwood tree (*Pterocarpus tinctorius* Welw.) bearing a fine red wood. Its bark and leaves are used in folk medicine and in sorcery; its sap is employed in dyeing. In wedding rituals and other festivities, Africans use it to paint their feet. In the colonial period, Africans developed an active trade in it. It has several names, including *lucula* and *hula.* Ficalho, *Plantas Uteis,* pp. 143-44.

tahibadjo (Ful.)   Among the Fula (q.v.) and other Islamic communities in Guinea-Bissau, a student of the Koran; also, the assistant to a teacher of Islam. Gonçalves, *O Mundo Arabo-Islámico,* p. 214.

taka (Kik.) A wooden hook or hitch; a short straight piece of wood fastened at the center to a fishing line. When the *taka* is swallowed by a fish, it lodges crosswise and allows the fish to be pulled out. The *taka* was popular around São Salvador in the 1880s. BeAD.

talo (Afr.) Name given by Mandingos in Guinea-Bissau to a tall tropical tree (*Erythrophleum guinense*) that provides a hard wood for construction, firewood, and other domestic uses. In colonial times its poisonous resin gave it the reputation of being sacred. This resin, also called *mancone*, was used in tribal ordeals (q.v.). Carreira, *Mandingas*, p. 133, 172. *See also* cassa, muave.

tamarind (Ar.) Tropical tree (*Tamarindus indica* L.) found wild and cultivated in Portuguese Africa, Mali, northern Sudan, and Senegambia. It is a beautiful tree with pinnate leaves and edible yellow flowers striped with red. Its fruit is eaten raw for refreshment, made into jam or sherbet, or pressed into cakes. Its acid pulp is used for preserves and to make a cooling laxative drink. It was known by the Greeks and Romans as well as East Indians, who brought it to Africa. Ficalho, *Plantas Uteis*, pp. 153-4; Lewicki, *West African Food*, pp. 66-7.

tambacumba (Afr.) In Guinea-Bissau a tropical shrub (*Parinarium macrophyllum*) that grows in sandy and brackish lowlands often flooded by rivers or the Atlantic. Mota, *Guiné Portuguesa*, p. 50.

Tambara (Afr.) A *prazo* (q.v.) located along the Pungue River and extending up to the Lupata Mountains south of the Zambezi River, Mozambique. This *prazo*, once held by Dona Ines Garcia Cardoso and afterward by Dona Ursula de Sá, was taken in 1827 by José Francisco Alves Barbosa, an Afro-Portuguese. He asked that the *prazo* be conferred in perpetuity upon his family, an unusual petition at the time. Newitt, *Portuguese Settlement*, p. 99.

Tanda (Kik.) Around 1880, a Portuguese born in São Salvador do Congo, Angola. BeAD.

tanga (1) (Afr.) A garment that covers the groin, worn by Angolan slaves on their arrival at Brazilian markets. GEPB.

Tanga (2) (Afr.) A town on Zanzibar Bay visited by the Portuguese in 1498. At the time, it was a busy port, trading with other East African cities and with India. GEPB.

Tangier Seaport at the extreme north of Morocco on the western end of the Strait of Gibraltar. It was taken by the forces of Prince Henry in 1437 to secure control of the northernmost part of the West African coast. King Afonso V personally occupied the port in 1471, and it continued to be a Portuguese possession until it was lost to Spain in 1580. It became an English possession in 1662 and in 1684 they gave it to the king of Morocco. In 1924 it was declared an International Zone, a status that was not abolished until October 29, 1956. In 1962 it became the royal residence of the King of Morocco. Prestage, *The Portuguese Pioneers*, pp. 46, 58, 177; WNGD.

tangomãu (Afr.) A Portuguese trader who gave up his European way of life, adopting African customs and marrying an African woman. In 1490 King Manuel I referred to *tangomaus* as being Africanized or Kaffiralized (made infidel) Portuguese. By 1550 the *tangomãus* handled much of the coastal and interior bartering in Ghana. Duncan, *Atlantic Islands*, p. 212; Pinto Rema, *As Primeiras Missões*, BCG, 1967, xxii(87/88):232-3. *See also* lançado.

tanguin (Afr.) A poisonous beverage extracted from the bark of a tree (*Tanghinia venenifera* Dup.), found in Angola and elsewhere in Portuguese Africa. The beverage, a decoction made with ground bark and water, is used in tribal ordeals (q.v.). A sorcerer forced an accused person to drink *tanguin* to prove his innocence or guilt. This potion taken in small amounts is extremely purgative and the individual dies immediately of cardiac arrest. If taken in large quantities, it is emetic and the individual vomits and survives. Portuguese law punished this practice as a serious crime. Ficalho, *Plantas Uteis*, pp. 164-5, 167. *See also* agua-vermelha, eseré.

tantam (Afr.) A percussion instrument consisting of a hollow cylinder with an animal-hide membrane stretched tightly over the ends. A traditional instrument used in Cape Verde and elsewhere in Portuguese Africa to play a lover's melody; consequently, the *tantam* is a symbol of love and beauty. Fernando de Castro, a Cape Verdian poet living in Guinea-Bissau, wrote a book-length poem entitled *Africa Raiz* (Africa Root, 1966) where, at the start of the *tantam* rhythm, the poet yields to erotic fantasies. Hamilton, *Voices*, p. 360; GDLP.

Tanzania (Afr.) The former Tanganyika, a German colony which, together with the island of Zanzibar, became an independent republic in 1961. Many Tanzanians were sympathetic with the Mozambican nationalists and Tanzania's capital, Dar es-Salaam (q.v.), became a center of anti-Portuguese political activity in the 1960s. MANU and FRELIMO (qq.v.) were organized in this city in 1961 and 1962, respectively. Since that time, Tanzania has been a close ally of Mozambique. In 1975, when Mozambique became an independent country, the governments established official relations and a permanent joint commission for economic development. Henriksen, *Mozambique*, pp. 153, 169, 229; GEPB.

Targa (Ar.) A Moroccan settlement taken by the Portuguese in 1490 in their effort to secure the whole North African coast west of the Strait of Gibraltar preparatory to further conquests south along the Atlantic coast. Newitt, *Portuguese Settlement*, p. 5.

tarikh (Ar.) "Family history." Among the Moorish Sunni Moslem Arabs in Western Sudan, the genealogical and legal history of a family. In the Sahel (q.v.) and the southwestern Sahara, the *tarikh* included inheritances, inventories, commercial documents, deeds of manumission, protocols for performing rituals, and lists of officeholders. One of the most important *tarikhs* is that of Abd ar-Rahman's *Tarikh as-Sudan* (Genealogical History of the Negroes), completed in 1655. Trimingham, *A History of Islam*, pp. 4-5.

Tariqa (Ar.) In Western Sudan and the Maghreb c.1800, a Sufi Moslem brotherhood often devoted to the cult of an Islamic saint or to a particular form of worship or ritual. Spreading across the Maghreb, the brotherhood was active from the end of the eighteenth century through the nineteenth. It spread to Guinea-Bissau around 1820, and soon each *Tariqa* had its own ritual, prayers, and initiation rite. Gonçalves, *O Islamismo*, p.162; Johnson, *The Maghrib*, CHA, Cambridge, 5:102. *See also* Qadiriyya Tariqa.

Tarrafal (Pg.) In the Cape Verde Islands, a notorious political prison located at the northern end of Santiago Island. It was established in 1936, during the time of Portuguese fascism under President António Salazar, to hold people who opposed the government, including Communist Party members and their sympathizers. During the War for Independence (1963-1975), the prison was filled with African as well as Portuguese nationalists. *Tarrafal* had a particularly odious reputation for torture, brutality, and death. Its extremely isolated location made escape impossible. By 1971 more than one hundred agents of PIDE (q.v.), the Portuguese secret police, had arrived in Cape Verde to infiltrate and arrest partisans of PAIGC (q.v.). PIDE arrested many nationalist and foreign activists, usually incarcerating them in Tarrafal's dungeons. HDRGC.

tarrafe (Pg.) In Portugal, a small tree or shrub (*Tamarix gallica*) used for firewood. The Portuguese introduced it to Cape Verde and elsewhere in the empire during the colonial period. Also called *tamaigueira*. Ficalho, *Plantas Uteis*, p. 88.

Tavira (Pg.)   A seaport in the Algarve, southern Portugal, on the Atlantic coast 18 mi. (28.8 km) northeast of Faro (q.v.). At the time of the Discovery (q.v.), it was an active commercial port trading with Arguim, Guiné, São Jorge da Mina, and other West African factories. Navigators, explorers, sailors, and merchants crowded the town. In 1980 it had a population of 24,182. Today Tavira is still a prosperous city, trading in white wines, mineral waters, tuna, and sardines. Iria, *O Algarve*, Congresso da Guiné, Lisbon, 1946, I:196; WNGD.

tavoleta (Pg.)   Name given by João de Lisboa in 1415 to two kinds of navigational instruments called *kamal* (q.v.), one the *tavoleta pequena* and the other the *tavoleta grande*. Both had graded knots, one for each degree. The *tavoleta pequena* was used to measure the height of stars, mainly the Pole Star, at latitudes 5° to 14° and its cord had 10 knots. It is believed the *tavoleta grande* was used to measure latitudes 15° to 24°, also with 10 knots. Costa, *A Marinha dos Descobrimentos*, p. 35, 36; DMA.

Tawara   An isolated, fiercely independent, ethnic community settled between the upper Zambezi and Ruia rivers in Monomotapa, Mozambique. As early as 1561, the Tawaras opposed the activities of early Portuguese missionaries. During the colonial period many of their chiefs remained distrustful of foreigners. In the many rebellions of the late nineteenth century, the Tawara were anti-Portuguese and joined such anti-colonial leaders as Hanga, Samacande, and Mapondera. The Tawara fought in various rebellions between 1902 and 1917. In defeat, they often fled across the border into Southern Rhodesia, obtaining protection from the British. Isaacman, *Mozambique: The Tradition*, pp. 36, 142-3, 195; GEPB.

taxation in Angola   A tax was levied on African people in Angola in 1908. This tax had two purposes: to raise revenue for government expenses and to force Africans into a monetary rather than barter economy, thus bringing traditional societies into European economic orbits. At that time, tribute paid to indigenous authorities was a regular part of African culture. A visitor might take salt or a chicken as tribute to a king or the chief of a subkingdom. The new tax, however, had to be paid in Portuguese currency, not in shells, salt, cloth, or personal service, the traditional means of exchange. Angolans who did not pay and could not flee were forced to work as contract laborers. As late as 1920, a British engineer working on the Benguela railway noted that currency was still unknown and cotton and salt continued to be used for barter. Henderson, *Angola,* pp. 119-20.

tcherno (Afr.)   "Theologian." A learned man who is a teacher and counselor among the Fulani and Mandingo Moslems in Guinea-Bissau. He was in charge of maintaining Islam orthodoxy and periodically called on families to give advice on the correct way to perform rituals and to pray. A *tcherno* was paid for his services by the faithful. Gonçalves, *O Mundo Arabo-Islámico*, p. 196. *See also* almani.

tchikove (Afr.)   Among the Ambos in southern Angola c.1920, a loosely defined family farming area inside Ambo land. Henderson, *Angola*, p. 54.

Tchipumbule (Afr.)   An African nativist cult that originated around 1950 in the Quioco-Lunda area of northeast Angola on the border with the Belgian Congo. In 1956 its members became involved in the anti-Portuguese struggle for independence. As it grew, the movement further expanded toward the Malange territory. Pelissier, *La Colonie*, pp. 181-82.

tea   A white-flowered evergreen shrub (*Thea sinensis*), grown in China, India, Japan, India, and other countries. In 1920 the Portuguese introduced tea cultivation from India to Mozambique where it is now widely grown. The first factory to process tea leaves was built in Milange, Quelimane district, in 1924. Two years later 27 tons of tea were exported. By 1959 Mozambique ranked third, after Kenya and Malawi, in the production of tea in East Africa. It is grown in the western half of the Zambezia district, extending from the forest-clad slopes of Mount Milange, which stands astride the common border with Malawi, to Gurue, Milange, Tacuane, and Cosocone, the highest mountain massifs of the province. In 1969 approximately 37,800 acres were under cultivation, annually producing between 9,000 and 10,500 tons. Abshire, *Portuguese Africa*, p. 272; Ficalho, *Plantas Uteis*, p. 90.

teke (Kik.)   Around 1880 in São Salvador do Congo, Angola, an idol that Africans believed had the magic power to help or hurt. This statue did not represent a god or gods, but it was thought to be endowed with supernatural powers. Sometimes it was directly addressed, and spoken of, as the dwelling of a spirit. BeAD.

Tekrur (Afr.)   One of the earliest Islamized states of the Western Sudan, known by the Arabs as *Bilad-es-Sudan* (Land of the Blacks); the area where the Fulas of Guinea-Bissau originated. The Tekrur state arose in the third century, at the same time as ancient Ghana (q.v.). From the eighth to the tenth centuries, Tekrur was a fully autonomous state on the middle Senegal River, actively competing with Ghana for control of the trans-Saharan trade. During its height, Tekrur was linked to Morocco by an overland trade route two hundred miles inland from the Atlantic coast. Berber invaders from North Africa took the Tekrur state in the eleventh century. From this admixture, the

Fula people emerged and spread throughout much of the sub-Saharan Sahel (q.v.), the savanna lands, and the region of modern-day Guinea-Bissau. Tekrur was under the control of the Mali Empire (q.v.) from 1230 until the Portuguese arrived in 1546. The Tekrur people, known as the Tukulor (now the Tokolor), and the Fulas are members of the Niger-Congo language group. Trimingham, *A History of Islam*, pp. 26, 28, 32; HDRB.

tembanza (Afr.) An official title reserved for women in the Matamba kingdom of Angola c.1628. It conferred both military and political powers which were exercised at that time by Queen Nzinga in her war against the Portuguese. Miller, *Nzinga of Matamba*, JAH, 1975, 16(2):209. *See also* Kasanje.

Tembo (Afr.) A small island in the Indian Ocean off the southern coast of Mozambique. Its ownership as well as that of the islands of Inhaca, Maputo, and Dos Elefantes was disputed by Britain in 1872. The contention was settled in favor of Portugal by Adolphe Thiers, president of France, on September 25, 1872. GEPB.

temo (Kik.) Among the Bacongo of São Salvador do Congo, Angola, c.1888, a gang of three or four men banded together for mutual aid in building a house, or of women for clearing a farm. For compensation, each individual contributed a small amount of money every market day. Once the job was done, the money collected was used to pay each contributor for his or her work. BeAD.

Tempo (Pg.) "Time." The title of FRELIMO's (q.v.) official magazine, first published in Maputo in 1975. It reflected the views of the new government, although articles are often written by individuals not directly associated with editing the magazine. HDM.

tempo das aguas (Pg.) "Rainy season." In Cape Verde, this season lasts from August to October. During this period, the temperature rises to 92°F (33°C), humidity is high, and a hot wind from the southwest prevails. Carvalho e Vasconcellos, *As Colonias Portuguesas*, p. 44. *See also* tempo das brisas.

tempo das brisas (Pg.) "Windy season." In Cape Verde, this season lasts from November to July. During this time, the temperature dips to 60°F (15°C) and a dry northeast wind from the Sahara prevails. These winds bring cooler air than the prevailing winds of the African continent at the same latitude. Carvalho e Vasconcellos, *As Colonias Portuguesas*, p. 43. *See also* harmattan, tempo das aguas.

Tenerife   The largest of the Canary Islands, discovered in 1341 by Nicolo da Recco, a Florentine in the service of Portugal. According to sailors, its volcanic mountain Pico de Tenerife (12,172 ft., 3,710m) was visible from a distance of 250 Italian miles. In 1479 the control of the island was transferred to Spain as part of the Alcaçovas Peace Treaty (q.v.), signed between Portugal and Castile. Tenerife's 8,000 inhabitants lived in caverns in the mountains. Their food was meat, barley, goat's milk, and some fruits, especially figs. Prestage, The *Portuguese Pioneers*, pp. 6, 48, 98.

tenga-tenga (Pg.)   An African porter, male or female, used to transport goods on the *prazos* (q.v.) and in urban centers of Zambezia and elsewhere in Mozambique. The African carriers were very popular and in 1920 their number in Quelimane alone was estimated to be 90,000. For their work, the men were paid 1,600 *escudos* a month, while women received a few yards of cloth or 500 *escudos*. The Boror Company (q.v.) forced young people to work as *tenga-tenga*; youths 12 to 14 years of age and small children worked 120 days a year for between 200 and 600 *escudos* a month. Vail, *Capitalism*, p. 223.

Terçeira (Pg.)   An island in the central Azores, discovered by Portuguese navigators in 1427. It appears in the 1375 Catalan map of Gabriel Valseca under the name of *Insule de Brazil* (Brazilwood Island) after the red dyewood trees found there; these trees were also the source of the name of the South American country, first called Land of the Holy Cross. In 1450 Prince Henry gave the captaincy of Terçeira to his Flemish servant Jacques de Bruges, who wanted to colonize it. Prestage, *The Portuguese Pioneers*, pp. 48-9, 50, 52.

terço (Pg.)   A measure of wine equal to 42 English gallons or 158.98 liters, used on the Atlantic Islands in the colonial period. Duncan, *Atlantic Islands*, p. 260.

terra assentada (Pg.)   The name for a flat, well-irrigated tract of fertile arable land. These areas have been cultivated on São Tomé since its settlement in 1495. The relative abundance of this fertile soil has transformed the island into a rich, highly developed agricultural area. *Roças* (farms) are scattered throughout the territory today. Also called *terra assente*. Tenreiro, *A Ilha*, p. 18, 46.

terra de Lemnos (Pg.)   "Lemnos earth." Name given in early colonial times to the pulp of the baobab tree (q.v.). It was exported to Europe for use as a medicine to treat dysentery, hemoptysis, and fevers. Ficalho, *Plantas Uteis*, p. 93.

Terra do Natal (Pg.) "Nativity Land." Name given by Vasco da Gama to the Natal Province in South Africa, discovered on December 25, 1497, and named in honor of the birth of Christ. GEPB.

terras da coroa (Pg.) "Crown lands." Lands owned by the Portuguese Crown in colonial Africa, acquired by right of conquest c.1500 and later. In the colonial period, the king granted them to *donatarios* and captains for a maximum of three lifetimes (90 to 100 years). Their possession had to be acknowledged by the resident grantee by paying taxes and cultivating the land. Isaacman, *Mozambique: The Africanization*, p. 97.

Terras dos Negros (Pg.) "Lands of the Blacks." Name given to Guiné by such early Portuguese navigators as Dinis Dias and Alvise L. Cadamosto. It was the area along the Atlantic coast roughly encompassing Senegal and Mauritania, and inland to include the Sahara Desert. Mota, *Mar, alem Mar*, p. 90, 172. *See also* Bilad-as-Sudan.

terras em fatiota (Pg.) "Land grants." *Prazos* granted in the eighteenth century in perpetuity to religious orders in the Zambezia region of Mozambique. The concept justifying these generous grants was that the Church never ceases to exist, and therefore has no generations or lifetimes, the usual span of three being the basis for land granted to private citizens. Around 1780 exceptions to this rule occurred when *terras em fatiota* were granted in perpetual lease to a few settlers in Tete and Zambezia, requiring only loyalty to the Crown and a small rent. Henriksen, *Mozambique*, p. 57; GEPB.

terras firmes (Pg.) "Firm continental lands." In Mozambique, an expression used until the nineteenth century to refer to an area encompassing the Mossuril Peninsula, Cabeçeira Grande, and Cabeçeira Pequena. It covers about 500 sq. km and it had a population of 15,000 in the mid-nineteenth century. HDM.

Tete (Afr.) A town and capital of the Tete district in western Mozambique. It is on the Zambezi River 270 mi. (435 km) northwest of Beira (q.v.) and was founded by the Portuguese in 1540 as a gold trading center. Later, according to David Livingstone (1813-1873) who visited it in 1864-5, it became a slave market. In 1960 it had a population of 38,962 and in 1980 the district, now a province, had a population of 831,000. Duffy, *Portuguese Africa*, pp. 35, 88-9, 184; WNGD. *See also* Sena.

Tete Agreement An international agreement signed in 1913 between the Portuguese government and Southern Rhodesia (now Zimbabwe) regulating the migrant workers in the latter's mines. Under strict controls, the Mozambique government registered the laborers, thereby receiving a bonus in gold for each man plus a percentage of his wages on his return home from the mines. At the time, this strictly monetary system gave the colony a sound economy. Vail, *Capitalism*, p. 202. *See also* Mozambique-Transvaal Convention.

Tete railroad line A state-owned Mozambican line 160 mi. (258 km) long, built between 1947 and 1950. It begins at Dona Ana on the north side of the Zambezi, proceeding northwest to Tete then Moatize and its coal fields which supply the entire Beira network. Abshire, *Portuguese Africa*, pp. 330, 332.

Tete silver mines Francisco de Sousa, a Jesuit writing in 1610, referred to the rumor of silver mines found by a slave in the Tete district. After obtaining the rights to some of the mining area for his order, de Sousa reported their discovery to King Pedro of Monomotapa. In 1696, Manuel Pires Saroa, a Portuguese *prazero*, actually located the mines at Nhacasse, a five-day journey from Tete, and secured them for Portugal by persuading the local African king to give them to the colonial government. Newitt, *Portuguese Settlement*, pp.80-1.

Texas fever An infectious disease of cattle caused by a sporozoan organism (*Bebesia bigeminaan*) that invades the red blood cells. It is carried by the cattle tick *Boophilus annunlatus.* By the 1890s it was reported to be widespread in the Zambezia region. By 1903 Texas, or tick, fever had devastated cattle in the Tawar homeland in the Tete district and in western Southern Rhodesia. Local sorcerers used the occasion to connect this natural disaster with the European presence. Isaacman, *Mozambique: The Tradition*, pp. 131, 140; WNWD.

thaler (Ger.) An obsolete monetary unit of some German states, also known as the Maria Teresa thaler. By the end of the eighteenth century this coin was produced by the Royal Mint in London for circulation in East Africa and many Arab countries. In Portuguese, it is called a *therezinha*. Freeman-Grenville, *East African Coins*, JAH, 1960, 1(1):39; PDM. *See also* ceitil, larin.

Thonga *See* Tonga.

thornbelt In Mozambique and elsewhere, a tropical xerophytic woodland of the savanna type, commonly dominated by short, thorny, seasonally leafless acacia trees. This type of vegetation is also known as thorny forest. Rita-Ferreira, *O Movimento Migratorio*, p. 36. WNWD.

tick fever   See Texas fever.

Tigres Peninsula (Pg.)   A peninsula in southern Angola that runs northwest to southeast parallel to the Atlantic Ocean. Currently this land formation is 23 miles long and 2.5 miles deep (37 by 4 km), much larger due to landfill than it was in 1775. GEPB.

Tijaniyya Tariqa (Ar.)   A West African Muslim brotherhood founded in the Sudan c.1798 by Ahma at Tijani who was inspired by the great Islamic revival at the end of the eighteenth century. This vigorous new order spread rapidly across the western Islamic world. Its expansion was peaceful, preaching a *jihad al-qawl* (holy war of words) among Moslems as well as among infidels. By 1853 it had brought vast regions between Senegal and Niger under its influence, declaring *jihad* against the pagan Bambara people of the mid-Niger River and extending their movement into western Senegal, where they clashed with the French. They then advanced from the Atlantic coast into the interior of Africa. *Tijaniyya Tariqa* was introduced into Guinea-Bissau at the end of the nineteenth century. Today this popular brotherhood is centered in southeastern Guinea-Bissau and many Fula and Beafada (qq.v.) are members. Gonçalves, *O Mundo Arabo-Islámico*, pp. 199-200; Trimingham, *A History of Islam*, pp. 155, 159, 163. *See also* Qadiriyya Tariqa.

timbila (Afr.)   A percussion instrument, a kind of xylophone, popular among the Chopi in southern Mozambique. It consists of a series of wooden bars graduated in length so as to sound the notes of a scale when struck with a small wooden hammer. Performers frequently form a band or orchestra in which the *timbila* is the main instrument and is accompanied by between 18 and 23 stringed instruments. This musical tradition appears to be descended from chamber orchestras introduced by missionaries in the colonial period. *Timbila* music was first reported by the Jesuit Andres Fernandes in 1582. Lutero, *Ethnomusicologia in Africa*, Lisbon, 1980, II:583-89.

Timbuctu (Afr.)   A remote city built midway up the Niger River at the south edge of the Sahara in the agreeable Sudanese zone between the desert and the rain forest. It has houses and mosques of sun-dried mud brick. Most of its inhabitants are people converted to Islam around 1200 by Berber adventurers. From 1250 to 1350 it was incorporated into the Mandingo Empire of Mali. Around 1330 it was a prosperous city with substantial trade with North African Berber merchants in gold dust, spices, and slaves. In 1352-53, Timbuctu was visited and described by the Arab geographer Ibn Battuta. In 1486, King João II of Portugal sent an ambassador to the ruler of Timbuctu, believing the city-state was vassal to Prester John. In the nineteenth century

Timbuctu was successively ruled by several African chiefs. By 1893, when the French occupied the city, it was in ruins with a population of only about 7,000. Today it is part of Mali. It had a population of 20,483 in 1976. Cortesão, *A Expansão*, pp. 261-2; GEPB; WNGD.

Tirre (Afr.) A Zambezian *prazo* that in 1830 was in the process of being granted to the Misericordia brotherhood (q.v.). Although it was forbidden by law to hold such an estate in land, the chief justice of the Mozambique colony, Joaquim Xavier Dinis Costa, recommended that the *prazo* be leased to the Misericordia on condition that the brotherhood sublease it to the Velasco family, who had a claim on it. Newitt, *Portuguese Settlement*, pp. 100-1.

tobacco Any of a number of solanaceous plants (*Nicotiana tabacum* and other *N.* spp.) with white or pink flowers and large, lance-shaped leaves: it is cultivated throughout the temperate and tropical zones for its leaves which are prepared for smoking, chewing, or snuff. It is a New World plant introduced by the Portuguese to Angola and Mozambique around 1590. Locals soon became addicted to it. There are two species cultivated in Africa: *N. tabacum*, grown throughout the continent, and *N. rustica*, cultivated in the Sudan. In Portugal in the 1600s, it was known as *erva santa* (holy herb) because theologians had stated that "Smoking is a pleasure, not a sin." Since its introduction to Guinea-Bissau in the 1600s, the Bijagos people have developed an elaborate technique of cultivation. In the nineteenth century, it was cultivated in Lubango and in the Huila area of southern Angola, in Mozambique in the Zambezia region north of Sofala, and on the Chironde *prazo*. Ficalho, *Plantas Uteis* pp. 231-4; Newitt, *Portuguese Settlement,* p. 208.

Tocoism (Afr.) A nativist messianic sect organized by Simão Gonçalves Toco c.1949 in Kinshasa, Zaire. It is an amalgam of traditional African folks rituals and Christian liturgical ceremonies. Ancestor and spirit worship with initiation rituals are combined with the cult of the Holy Trinity, Jesus Christ, baptism, and marriage. The sect is pervaded by vague nationalism, anti-conventional Christianity, and anti-European feelings. Its members reject the use of alcohol and abstain from eating pork. Estermann, *O Tocoismo*, Garcia de Horta, 1965, 13(3):327-8, 331-3.

Tokolor Revolution (Afr.) This revolution, launched in 1848, was perhaps the most militant attempt to use Islam as a large-scale instrument to form a state in the Western Sudan. Led by al-Hajj' Umar, the *khalif* (chief, or prince) of the *Tijaniyya Tariqa* (q.v.) in West Africa, the Tokolor aristocracy sought to establish a new theocratic regime in Segu, Kartam, and some parts of Senegambia. Hajj' Umar's attempt to extend his domination into the Bambara chiefdom in Senegal threatened to shut off the French from the waterway vital to the gum arabic trade with the Moors of southern Mautritania. Hajj' Umar's ambition resulted in a bloody confrontation with French troops coming from the Atlantic coast. His forces were defeated and he was killed. After his death, this confrontation between Tokolor social and political institutions, as expressed by the ethos of *Tijaniyya Tariqa*, suddenly ended the same year. Ajayi, *West Africa in the Anti-Slavery Trade Era*, CHA, Cambridge, 1976, 5:200-1; 203-4. For the origin of the Tokolor people, *see* Tekrur.

toleta de marteloio (Pg.)   A navigational table used by Portuguese navigators c.1440 to estimate the position of the sun and one's deviation from a true course. It had eight entries, one for each quarter (11°15'), and consisted of the resolution of right-angle triangles, as summarily described by Ramon Lull. Also called *raxon*. Cortesão, *History*, I:217.

tombo (Afr.)   A 1780 survey that described the land and set the borders of a *prazo* in the Zambezia. In 1786 Antonio Manuel de Mello e Castro, a government official, ordered a compilation of the *tombos* in the area and decided that the Tete town council should be the custodian of them. Newitt, *Portuguese Settlement*, pp. 89-90.

tonga (1) (Afr.)   In São Tomé, a name given to children born on the island to parents from Cape Verde and elsewhere in Portuguese Africa. Henriksen, *Mozambique*, pp. 247, 250, 251.

Tonga (2) (Afr.)   In the colonial period, an ethnic group settled on the Indian Ocean in the Inhambane and Gaza districts of southern Mozambique. Today they occupy most of the lands just north of the Save and Maputo rivers on the South African-Mozambican frontier. Related to the Shona to the north, this Bantu people, together with their neighbors the Chopi, are a patrilineal group whose hereditary chiefs have had wide political, military, and religious power. The Tonga are the second-largest ethnic group in Mozambique and are divided into the following sub-groups: Ronga, Shangana, Hlengwe, and Tswa. Until FRELIMO (q.v.) took control of the country in 1975, about 40 percent of Tonga males journeyed to work legally and illegally in South African gold fields and even in the mines of Southern Rhodesia, now Zimbabwe. The Portuguese government encouraged legal migration for the financial revenues it received. This labor migration drew sharp criticism because it resulted in agricultural underdevelopment of the southern region of Mozambique as well as imposing hardships on the workers and their families. For some of the laborers, one consequence of their working in foreign countries was they learned to speak and read English. Some also brought back independent African religions such as the Ethiopian Movement founded in South Africa. In 1970 the Tonga and Chopi numbered 1,850,000. Both groups have been greatly influenced by Methodist and Catholic missionaries. Tonga is also spelled Thonga. Henriksen, *Mozambique*, pp. 247, 250-1.

toque (Pg.)   A currency unit that circulated in Mozambique and East Africa c.1700; it was equal to forty cowries (q.v.), marine shells found especially in the Luanda coastal region. GDLP. *See also* Cypraea annulus.

Tordesillas, Treaty of A treaty between Spain and Portugal signed on June 7, 1494, to settle conflicts arising from Christopher Columbus's first voyage to the New World in 1492. In 1494, Pope Alexander VI issued *Inter Caetera*, a document setting a line of demarcation from pole to pole 100 leagues west of the Cape Verde Islands. Spain was given exclusive rights to the region west of this line in return for converting the heathen people they encountered. Portuguese expeditions were to keep to the east of this line. King João II of Portugal was dissatisfied because Portugal's rights were not specifically affirmed and the Portuguese would not have sufficient sea room for their African voyages. To solve the conflict, Spanish and Portuguese ambassadors met in Torsedillas, northern Spain, where they reaffirmed the papal division but the line itself was moved to 370 leagues west of the Cape Verde Islands. Papal sanction for this change was finally given on January 24, 1506. DHP; GEPB. *See also* volta do mar, volta do Sargasso.

tornado (Pg.)   In Guinea-Bissau and elsewhere in West Africa and the adjacent Atlantic, a brief and violent thunder squall with a whirling column of air extending downward from a cumulonimbus cloud at the time that the rain begins. Beginning c.1440, Portuguese navigators reported having seen *tornados* on the Atlantic coast of West Africa. They are also known as *tornados secos* (dry tornadoes) and *travoadas*. Mota, *Guiné Portuguesa*, I:31-2. *See also* tropical storms, force of.

tornador-mor (Pg.)   A Portuguese agriculture inspector, a post created in 1759 in the Zambezia region. He was in charge of collecting the *prazos*' taxes and seeing that *prazos* were not left unoccupied. This administrative position was introduced from India, apparently without Lisbon's approval. Newitt, *Portuguese Settlement*, p. 106.

torreira do sol (Pg.)   "Intense heat of the sun." The heat of the day, from noon until two or three p.m., when the heat of the sun seems to scorch. Portuguese explorers experienced *torreiras do sol* for the first time at their arrival in Guiné in 1440. GDLP.

Torwa (Afr.) An African dynasty of the Butua kingdom south of Monomotapa in the Manica region, Mozambique. Under pressure from Arab Moslem traders it disappeared in 1648 and was replaced by a new dynasty. Newitt, *Portuguese Settlement*, p. 53, 69.

tostão (Pg.) An old Portuguese silver unit of currency equivalent c.1700 to US$100. The expression *dez tostães* (ten tostães, US$1000) is still heard in Portugal, and was common in Brazil until the 1940s. Duncan, *Atlantic Islands*, p. 264.

Toto (Pg.) In Angola, a *colonato* (government farming settlement) of Africans under the guidance and management of Portuguese. They were organized in 1957 to improve and increase agricultural products. Caetano, *Os Nativos*, p. 85.

trabalho compelido, sistema de (Pg.) "System of forced labor." A law promulgated in the African colonies in 1889 by the Portuguese government to regulate African forced labor. It was replaced in 1928 by the *Codigo de Trabalho* (Labor Code), which outlawed compulsory labor for Africans. Rita-Ferreira, *O Movimento Migratorio*, p. 167.

trabalho correcional do indigena (Pg.) "Indigenous correctional labor." Penal labor without compensation, imposed by a court of justice on a convicted African. Cunha, *O Trabalho Indigena*, p. 253.

trabalho e bom para o preto (Pg.) "Work is good for a black." An old Portuguese saying, originating c.1550 and reflecting the notion of African laziness, supposedly characteristic of those who had to be pressured to work. An African was often disciplined with the lash, so that he not fall into indolence, unwilling to work or exert himself. Chaves, *O Preto da Guiné*, Congresso Commemorativo, Lisbon, 1946, 2:562.

trabalho escravo do nativo (Pg.) "Native slave labor." In the colonial period, compulsory work imposed on Africans in Portuguese colonies. Cunha, *O Trabalho Indigena*, p. 5.

trabalho independente do indigena (Pg.) "Independent native labor." Wage-earning work done freely by an African for an employer of his own choice. This practice was established by the labor statute of 1928. Cunha, *O Trabalho Indigena*, p. 5. *See also* trabalho compelido do indigena.

trabalho indigena (Pg.) "Native labor." Wage labor performed by an African. According to statutes of 1899 and 1911, an African had a moral and legal obligation to voluntarily perform physical work under penalty of being forced to work by the authorities. Cunha, *O Trabalho Indigena*, pp. 147-48.

trabalho militar do indigena (Pg.) "Native military labor." Work performed by an African soldier or draftee in military forts and barracks. It involved land-clearing for road construction and other services required by the armed forces. Military labor was sanctioned by law in 1898. Cunha, *O Trabalho Indigena*, p. 175.

trabalho obrigatorio do indigena (Pg.) "Compulsory native labor." Work imposed by the government according to the 1928 *Codigo de trabalho dos indigenas das Colonias Portuguesas de Africa* (Labor Code of natives of the Portuguese colonies). The code was restricted to public works for common benefit and included compensation. Duffy, *Portuguese Africa*, pp. 319-20. *See also* trabalho livre do indigena.

trabalho penal (Pg.) "Penal labor." Work imposed by a court of law on African prison inmates c.1936. It was conceived as a way to rehabilitate and educate criminals. Cunha, *O Trabalho Indigena*, p. 178. *See also* trabalho militar do indigena.

Tractatus Instrumenti Astronomi *See* De Instrumento Secretorum.

trade caravans in Angola Groups of traders traditionally traveled together for safety in southern Angola and elsewhere. Prior to 1800, due to the chronic shortage of head porters, Portuguese traders formed their own caravans using employees or slaves. For most of the nineteenth century caravan trade was the rule because markets were generally found in villages and settlements scattered in rural areas. Only at the height of the ivory boom c.1870 and the rubber boom c.1900 was trade carried out on ranches and farms by merchants such as those from Ovamboland, central Angola. Ox-drawn wagons, introduced during the rubber boom, were well suited to the role of mobile shops; wagons were able to take over most of the roving trade in the interior of Angola. The advent of trucks and railroads beginning c.1910 spelled the end of an era of peripatetic traders, increasingly replaced by a network of fixed stores. Clarence-Smith, *Slaves, Peasants*, pp. 65-6. *See also* trade caravans in Mozambique.

trade caravans in Mozambique Organized groups of traders were led by African guides on long journeys through hostile territory. They dealt in gold, cloth, ivory, and slaves. These traders and their packs of animals were very active in the greater Zambezia region; their trips usually lasted between eight and eighteen months. Among the various trade centers were Zumbo, Abutua, Manica, Tete, and Bisa. Isaacman, *Mozambique: The Africanization*, pp. 82, 84, 87. *See also* trade caravans in Angola.

transfrontiersmen A term for European settlers in Portuguese Africa in the colonial period. Many of these were *prazo*-holders who cultivated the land, paid taxes annually, provided specific services to the government, and obeyed the law. These pioneers resided permanently on their estates, married African women, and maintained many concubines. They created a large Afro-Portuguese kinship system that completely isolated them from their European roots and progressively absorbed them into indigenous racial and cultural groups. Isaacman, *The Prazeros as Transfortiersmen*, JAH, 1975, 8(1):6, 8, 36. *See also* prazero.

trans-Saharan trade (1400-1800) Throughout medieval times and later, the trans-Saharan trade was mainly carried out by caravans led by Moslems and Sudanese. From North Africa the main goods imported into Central Africa were silks, fine cloth, glassware, perfumes, and aromatics of all kinds; exports to Europe and the East included gold, salt, leather, cola nuts, and slaves, the last the most important. White slaves were also taken and sold in Sudanese kingdoms. Around 1445, the Portuguese began trading with pilgrims to Mecca and established relations with Arab traders and African chiefs in Arguim (q.v.). By 1800, the Kanuri language of Central Africa had become a *lingua franca* along the Saharan trade routes. Kanuri speakers might be found as far apart as Cairo, Egypt, and Freetown, Sierra Leone, a total distance of 3,415 mi. (5,500 km). Fisher, *The Central Sahara and Sudan*, CHA, 1975, 4:26, 79, 87, 121, 125; DHP. *See also* Azenegues.

trans-Zambezia railroad This private rail line was inaugurated in 1922. It began at the town of Dondo in the Beira-Umtali area of Mozambique, crossed the Zambezi River at Sena, and pushed northward to the Malawi border. Owned by Portuguese and British interests, it was built by the British-capitalized Trans-Zambezia Railways Company. It formed one of three integral parts of the 600-mile (960 km) connection serving Malawi, Central African railways, and the Mozambique-Malawi railways. Abshire, *Portuguese Africa*, p. 332.

Transvaal A province in South Africa that prior to 1800 was inhabited by Bushmen, Hottentots, and Zulus. In 1836 it was settled by Boers and in 1852 England recognized its independence. The discovery of gold in the Transvaal in 1886 and the construction of a railroad between the Boer Republic and Lourenço Marques in Mozambique the same year, emphasized the importance of southern Mozambique as a source of labor for the mines. The 1897 Transvaal-Portuguese Agreement, augmented by the Portuguese-South Africa Convention of 1928, regulated trade privileges and the flux of workers. In 1936 about 250,000 African laborers from Mozambique went to work in the Witwatersrand gold fields. In return for rights to recruit labor from south of the 22nd parallel, the Portuguese received a guarantee of 47.5 percent of the sea-bound rail traffic from Johannesburg and Pretoria. It also collected payment for each worker recruited, customs duties on the goods of returning laborers, and deferred wages from the miners, given to the Portuguese in gold, that the laborers accepted in *escudos* once in Mozambique. When Mozambique became a Republic in 1975, all the previous agreements were replaced by new bilateral accords. Henriksen, *Mozambique*, pp. 87, 120-1.

tratos de escravos (Pg.) "Slave trade." Portugal first engaged in this commerce in the 1440s, originally at Arguim (q.v.), then by 1480 in the Gulf of Guiné. The government licensed traders and established Lisbon as the port of entry for African slaves and European trade goods. All this commerce was supposed to be done through such government agencies as the *Casa da Guiné* and *Casa da Mina* (qq.v.). Carreira, *As Companhias Pombalinas*, BCG, 1968, xxiii(89/90):12; GEPB. *See also* resgate de escravos.

travessia de Africa (Pg.) "Crossing Africa." To cross Africa from Angola to Mozambique had been a goal of Portuguese policy since the time of King Manuel I. Around 1510 the king made known his wishes to establish overland contact between the Congo Kingdom (q.v.) in Angola and the land of Prester John in Abyssinia, now Ethiopia (q.v.). In his 1563 essay, *Coloquios des Simples e Drogas da India*, Castelo Garcia de Horta refers to a secular priest who went from West Africa to India, passing through Mozambique and the town of Sofala without using the sea. In 1627 the Jesuit Antonio Machado revived the Manueline idea of a voyage from the Congo to Ethiopia. The first documented round-trip crossing of Africa was accomplished by Pedro João Baptista and Antonio Amaro José, who undertook this trip beginning in 1803 and returning in 1815. In 1884-5, Hermenegildo Carlos de Brito Capelo and Roberto Ivens crossed the continent from Benguela on the Atlantic coast to the Zambezi River and the Indian Ocean coast of Mozambique, then returned to Luanda, Angola. The details of these explorations are recorded in two books by Capelo, *De Benguela a Terras de Iaca* and *Angola a Contracosta*. Duffy, *Portuguese Africa*, pp. 188-9; DHP.

trekboere (Afrk.) "Migrant Boer farmers." After a five-year trip from Transvaal, South Africa, through the Kalahari desert, Boer farmers settled in Humpata and Huila, southern Angola, in 1880-1. Guerreiro, *"Boers" de Angola*, Garcia de Horta, 1958, 6(1):11. *See also* Boers in Angola, voortrekkers.

tribal ordeals Ancient African method to determine guilt or innocence in which the accused was exposed to physical danger from which he was supposed to be divinely protected if he were innocent. Such a method of judgment was common in Angola, Mozambique, and elsewhere in Portuguese Africa. A sorcerer forced the accused to drink a concoction prepared from certain trees or plants known to contain poisons. These plants included *aguavermelha*, *cassa*, *muave*, and *tanguin* (qq.v.). In most cases drinking these beverages produced one of two effects. If the poison were taken in small amounts, it was purgative, causing violent peristalsis followed by sudden death from cardiac arrest. In large amounts, the drink was emetic, inducing vomiting and the person survived. In Angola, tribal ordeals were known as *provas judiciais*, in the Gulf of Guiné as *fava de prova* (bean of proof). Purgative beans often were the base of the drink. Ficalho, *Plantas Uteis*, pp.162-5.

Tribuna, A (Pg.) "The Tribune." A newspaper founded in Lourenço Marques, Mozambique, in 1960 by Antonio de Gouveia Lemos, Ilidro Rocha, and João Reis. *A Tribuna* started off as a morning paper and later briefly became a weekly, disappeared, and re-emerged as an evening paper. Soon after it commenced publication it was taken over by the *Banco Nacional Ultramarino* (q.v.). In the 1960s, in its Arts and Letters section, the paper published polemics regarding the nature and scope of Mozambican literature. In 1963 its publication was suspended for ten days by the government for offenses against censorship regulations. In May 1975 it again became a weekly, but did not survive the departure of its then-current editor, Fernando Malgalhes, for Portugal. Darch, *Mozambique*, pp. 170-2; Hamilton, *Voices*, pp. 170-2; HDM.

Trinitarians A Catholic religious order officially named the Order of the Most Holy Trinity for the Redemption of Captives. It was established in France by St. John de Matha (d. 1213) and approved by Pope Innocent III in 1198. It had the unique mission of freeing Christians held captive by Moslems. For more that six centuries, Trinitarians performed heroically, ransoming prisoners in Moslem Spain and North Africa. The Trinitarians are believed to have obtained the freedom of about 140,000 Christians between 1199 and 1855. DHP; EA. *See also* resgate de escravo.

tropicais (Pg.) "Tropical ones." A term applied to illegal Mozambican workers who c. 1937 entered South Africa to work in the Transvaal (q.v.) gold mines without proper documentation. The Witwatersrand National Labour Association named them *tropicais* to avoid paying them the legal salaries or giving them housing or health care. The South African government imposed severe penalties on those employers who were found to have admitted undocumented laborers coming from north of the 22nd parallel in Mozambique. Rita-Ferreira, *O Movimento Migratorio*, p. 107.

tropical medicine *See* Instituto de Medicinca Tropical.

tropical storms, force of Tropical cyclones, storms with winds that move counterclockwise, are designated by international agreement as having winds of gale force (39 miles per hour) but less than hurricane force (73 miles per hour). Tropical cyclones and hurricanes (called typhoons in the Indian and Pacific Oceans) occur in all tropical oceans with the exception of the South Atlantic. In the northern hemisphere they are more numerous from June through November; in the southern hemisphere they are concentrated in the period of December through March. Tropical storms, however, have been known to occur in both hemispheres during any month of the year. Around 1440 Portuguese navigators reported that when they reached the southern hemisphere they encountered tropical storms, including gales, squalls, hurricanes, and violent whirlwinds, in the waters off the Atlantic coast of West Africa. Mota, *Guiné Portuguesa*, I:40. *See also* tornado.

trovoada (Pg.) See tornado.

trucimão (Pg.) An African slave serving as an interpreter for early Portuguese navigators along the West African coast c.1440. According to Alvise Cadamosto, a *trucimão* was taken to Portugal where he learned Portuguese, returning c.1450 to Guiné and Senegal where he served as an interpreter to African chiefs and Portuguese merchants and slave traders. Pinto Rema, *As Primeiras Missões*, BCG, 1967, xxii(87/88):232-3.

true ebony In Angola and elsewhere in tropical Africa, trees in the genera *Diospyros*, *Maba*, and *Euclea* that yield a hard, heavy, durable wood that takes a fine gloss, used for furniture and decorative woodwork. The usual color is black, but red and green varieties are also found. Ficalho, *Plantas Uteis*, p. 211; WNTID.

trypanosomiasis An infectious tropical disease caused by one of several trypanosomes (genus *Trypanosoma*), flagellate protozoans that live as parasites in the blood of man and other vertebrates. The disease is usually transmitted through the bite of a mosquito. At least two species of trypanosomes (*T. gambiense* and *T. rhodesinse*) affect man, causing a different form of African sleeping sickness from that transmitted by the tsetse fly. *Trypanosomiasis* is a fatal disease widespread in some parts of Africa. It has greatly discouraged the economic development of various regions that are heavily infested. The disease is widespread in Equatorial Africa, including the Manica, Sofala, Tete Niassa, and Porto Amelia districts of Mozambique, but the extent of infection is restricted by the relative sparseness of the human population. Simmons, *Global Epidemiology*, II:219; GEPB. *See also* tsetse.

tsachikunda (Afr.) The African subchief of a military unit composed of ten to twelve slaves on a Zambezian *prazo* (q.v.) c.1800. The *tsachikunda* was a trusted servant appointed by a *prazero* (q.v.) to secure the internal security of the estate. Isaacman, *Mozambique: The Africanization*, p. 34.

tsetse (Bant.) A muscid fly (*Glossina morsitans*) of central and southern Africa that transmits the parasite *Trypanosoma brucei*, the cause of *nagana* (q.v.), the sleeping sickness of cattle, horses, and other animals; also, the related fly (*G. palpalis*), the carrier of *Trypanosome gambiense* and *T. rhodesinse* that cause sleeping sickness in man. GEPB; SMD. *See also* trypanosomiasis.

tubabo-moné (Afr.) A Portuguese or other European farmer with a swarthy complexion settled among the Balantas in southern Guinea-Bissau. In Portuguese, a *tubabo-moné* is called a *branco-preto* (white-black). Mota, *Guiné Portuguesa*, II:159.

tucorim (Hind.) A coarse fabric brought by Goan merchants from India to Mozambique and traded in Sofala, Manica, Quelimane, and the Zambezia *prazos* c.1600. PDM.

tufo (Afr.) A popular type of song accompanied by a dance. It is performed on Mozambique Island by young girls on a small freestanding stage encircled by the audience. Accompanied by drums, the dancers' rhythmic movements elicit enthusiastic clapping by the audience at the grace and dignity of the performers. Apparently it was originally a religious performance and shows Bantu and Arabic influences. Lutero, *Ethnomusicologia in Africa*, Africa, Lisbon, 1980, ii:576-79.

tuna industry (Pg.) A large food industry in Portugal. Tuna is a generic term for several species of fish found in the Atlantic, including *Orcynus, Thunnus*, and *Scomber*. Since ancient times the Atlantic coast along the Algarve has been one of the most important fishing areas of Portugal. Genoese and Sicilian fishermen introduced commercial tuna fishing to southern Portugal c.1305. In 1433 King Duarte granted Prince Henry a monopoly on commercial tuna fishing in that region. Even today the Algarve is the site of a substantial tuna industry. Early in the Discovery Portuguese fishermen brought their tuna-fishing skills to West Africa where commercial fishing for tuna and other fish is still an important industry. GEPB.

Tunduru (Afr.) A FRELIMO (q.v.) camp in Tanzania established in 1965 as a rehabilitation center for wounded soldiers. It became a children's camp in 1966 when one FRELIMO soldier, on his own initiative, collected about twenty-five abandoned children in the Niassa area and took them to Tunduru. Toward the end of 1966 the camp was formally placed under FRELIMO's Department of Education and later it became a primary school. Children who wished to enter one of the few secondary schools were required to complete this level before moving on. Munslow, *Mozambique*, p. 99.

tunga penetrans (Afr./Lat.)   In Angola and elsewhere, a flea-like insect (*Sarcopsylla penetrans*) commonly known as a chigger, jigger, chigoe, or sand flea. The tiny red female penetrates the skin under the toenails and, as she becomes distended to about pea size with eggs, causes a painful ulcer and inflammation to form. Infested slaves took these insects to the New World where they became a source of constant concern among slave owners because these insects could incapacitate or cripple a slave. GEPB; SMD.

Tungue Bay (Afr.)   A bay on the north Mozambican border between Cabo Delgado and Funzi Point on the Indian Ocean coast near Vila de Palma. In 1510 Portugal gave this bay to the Arab ruler in Quiloa. In 1886 it was established as the northern frontier of the Portuguese colony, dividing it from Tanganyika, a German territory. GEPB.

{ U }

ualió (Afr.)   In Guinea-Bissau, a prophet who occupies the top hierarchical rank among Islamized Fulas. Gonçalves, *O Islamismo*, p. 214.

UAM (*União Africana de Moçambique*) (Pg.)   "African Union of Mozambique," a nationalist party organized in Malawi in 1961 by exiles and workers from the Tete district, Mozambique. Its first president was José Baltazar de Costa Chagonga, a former medical orderly. It had few followers and a limited influence in the War for Independence (1960-75). Henriksen, *Mozambique*, p. 169.

uanga (Kimb.)   "Spell." A term constantly used in modern Afro-Portuguese literature to express deep nationalistic feeling inspired by the African past. *Uanga*, a novel by the Angolan writer Oscar Ribas (Luanda, 1951), describes Luanda urbanization and progress in the 1880s. He laments a by-gone era of magic, enchanted beauty, and scenic landscapes, now lost forever. Hamilton, *Voices*, pp. 46-7.

uapaca (Afr.)   In Angola, a tall tropical tree (*Uapaca guineensis* Muell.) that grows in the Maiombe and Zau regions. It yields a timber used in construction and for making furniture. GEPB.

uaque-uaque (Ar.)   "Vagabond." In Mozambique, an Arabic term referring to a vagrant drifter who wanders among towns and villages along the Indian Ocean coast. PDM.

uba (Afr.)   In rural towns in São Tomé, a chicken coop. Tenreiro, *A Ilha*, p. 125.

Ucua (Afr.)   A small African town located 52 mi. (83.5 km) east of Luanda on the paved highway between Luanda and Carmona. It is an active Methodist center that was attacked and burned by African nationalists on March 18, 1960. Thirteen European civilians and many *mestiços* and Africans were massacred. Deep nationalistic hate for the Europeans was one of the reasons for the killing. In 1960 it had a population of 5,576. Pelissier, *La Colonie*, p. 558.

ucuba (Afr.) A wild and cultivated tropical tree (*Brachystegia tamarindoides* Welw.) very common in the Huambo forests of Angola. It yields a valuable hardwood used for construction and the manufacture of furniture. It is also called *ossasa*. Ficalho, *Plantas Uteis*, p. 153.

UDCV (*União Democrática de Cabo Verde*) (Pg.) "Democratic Union of Cape Verde," a political group established in the 1950s to work for independence. In 1962 it merged with FLING (q.v.). HDRGC.

UDG (*União Democrática da Guiné*) (Pg.) "Democratic Union of Guiné," a small political group formed in the 1950's that soon merged with other nationalist parties to fight for independence. In 1962 it associated itself with the *Frente de Luta Pela Independencia Nacional da Guiné-Bissau*. HDRGC.

UDMGCV (*União Democrática das Mulheres da Guiné e Cabo Verde*) (Pg.) "Democratic Union of the Women of Guiné and Cape Verde," a political group organized in 1960 to assist in the liberation and mobilization of women and to work for the independence of the colonies. HDRGC.

UDNM (*União Democrática Nacional de Moçambique*) (Pg.) "National Democratic Union of Mozambique," a party organized in Bulawayo, Zimbabwe, on October 2, 1960, by a group of migrant workers and discontented secondary school students from southern and central Mozambique. One of the founders was Uria Simango, a Protestant pastor from the Beira area. When the embryonic nationalist UDNM later merged with FRELIMO (q.v.), Simango became its vice president. Henriksen, *Revolution*, p. 20; Munslow, *Mozambique*, p. 79.

UGEAN (*União-Geral dos Estudantes da Africa Negra*) (Pg.) "General Union of Students of Black Africa," a group formed in Paris in 1960 by young Portuguese-African nationalists then attending universities in Europe. Later the movement merged with PAIGC and MPLA (qq.v.). HDRGC.

Ughoton A seaport in modern Benin, Gulf of Guiné. Beginning in 1514 Portuguese merchants bought many slaves at this port for the Lisbon market. Saunders, *A Social History*, p. 13.

Uige (Afr.) Town and province in northeastern Angola, it is part of the old district of São Salvador do Congo inhabited by the Bacongo people (q.v.). This important coffee-growing area has its administrative and commercial capital at Uige, previously named Vila Marechal Carmona. Following an African uprising against European settlers in March 1961 and a violent reaction by Portuguese militia and civilians, thousands of Congo refugees left the area and fled to Zaire. From 1961 to 1974, Uige, together with the neighboring province of Zaire, was the main area of operations for UPA (q.v.) guerrillas. HDA.

Ujamaa (Afr.)   Name given by Tanzania in 1976 to a group of villages located south of the Rovuma River in northern Mozambique. In this area, Africans cultivate cassava and maize introduced by the Portuguese early in Discovery (q.v.). These settlements were camps used by FRELIMO (q.v.) as centers of indoctrination. Henriksen, *Revolution*, p. 151.

Ukwashi wa Chokwe (Afr.)   "Self-Help Association." A mutual-aid society founded in 1956 in Southern Rhodesia by Ambroise Muhunga to help refugees from Angola. In 1959 Smart Cha, an ebonist (carpenter) became its president and continued assisting victims of the war. Pelissier, *La Colonie*, p. 293-5.

ulama (Ar.)   Among the Moslems of Guinea-Bissau, an individual or group dedicated to the study and interpretation of the Koran. *Ulamas* are found in various urban centers and serve as teachers, consultants, and interpreters of the Moslem legal system. A *ulama* is the highest religious authority and, since 1500, they have played important roles in the expansion of Islam in the Sudan (q.v.). The members form an aristocratic class, revered as political leaders in several countries in West Africa. Trimingham, *A History of Islam*, pp. 5, 95-7, 132.

Ulenje (Afr.)   A market town in present-day Zambia. In the 1750s caravans of merchants from the East African coast, Central Africa, and the Angolan Atlantic coast traded cloth, firearms, and beverages for ivory, copper, and slaves. Axelson, *Portugal*, p. 82.

uli-elo (Afr.)   Name given by the Mandingos of Guinea-Bissau to a purgative prepared from the ground bark of a tropical tree (*Spathodea campanulata*) that grows in the area. Carreira, *Mandingas*, p. 242. *See also* cidja-ó.

ulima (Umb.)   "Cycle of land cultivation." A traditional and sound method of rotational cultivation used by speakers of Umbundu (q.v.) in Angola and nearby areas. It begins in September with tilling the land before the first rain. Corn is planted in stages from early October into December, depending on the weather. The crop is hoed from January to March and the harvest takes place in April. The *ulima* is a yearly cycle that moves inside a larger twenty-to-forty-year cycle made up of six to fifteen years of cultivation, two to four years of grass fallow, and sixteen to twenty years for the regeneration of shrubs and small trees. This cycle was applied to the upland fields, but not to the more fertile, periodically flooded, river bottoms. Henderson, *Angola*, p. 48.

ulo (Afr.) In Angola and elsewhere, a tall tropical shrub (*Cassia didymobotrya*) that yields a substance used by Africans to stupefy fish. This herb is also called *igongo, calembe, cafoto, tchingando*, and other names, a testimonial to its usefulness. Ficalho, *Plantas Uteis*, p. 129.

Ultimatum, The A final demand with a threat to break relations and use military force, presented on January 11, 1890, to the Portuguese government by Britain's prime minister, Lord Salisbury. The British called for the withdrawal of Portuguese military forces from Makolo, Shire, and Mashonaland in east-central Africa. The British also were intending to temporarily occupy Mozambique Island, and requested the promise that the Portuguese not interfere with British settlers and friendly African chiefs. The British were ready to send their fleet to Lourenço Marques in Mozambique, Cape Verde, and Lisbon if their claims were not accepted. Owing to the time limit imposed by the ultimatum, the Portuguese king and his council of state recognized that the country was not prepared for war and that any resistance would be futile. Consequently, they yielded to Britain's demands. Axelson, *Portugal*, pp. 228-231.

Umbanda (Afr.) In Mozambique, a wide-spread Afro-Brazilian sect apparently evolved from the *macumba* cult. It includes Indian, African, and Catholic elements and has a priesthood, a set of dogma, and a liturgy that emphasizes the strong belief in ancestor worship. This sect was imported from Brazil in modern times. Its members are called *Ubandistas*. DALAC.

umbaúa (Afr.) In Portuguese Africa and elsewhere, large tropical trees of the Melianthaceae family that yield a soft wood used to make boxes and other domestic utensils. It grows on riverbanks and in low moist ground. PDM.

Umbundu (Bant.) A Bantu language spoken by the Ovimbundu people settled on the highland plateau of central Angola from the Benguela Atlantic coast to the Zambezi watershed and beyond. This language is widely understood in south-central Angola and it has played an important role in Angolan regionalism and nationalism. During the War for Independence (1960-1975), UNITA (q.v.) used the Umbundu language as a means of communication. In 1970 there were about 1.5 million people who spoke Umbundu. Hamilton, *Black from White,* 1966-7, I(1):29; GEPB.

Umfuli (Afr.) A river near the modern town of Hartley, Zimbabwe. Along this river c.1600 the Portuguese found gold fields and established several camps for miners and traders. In 1965, archaeologists found that this seventeenth-century community had exploited the gold fields for many years. Newitt, *Portuguese Settlement*, pp. 44, 46.

umpumpa (Kik.) The unmarried state of an adult male or female and of a widow or widower, a state not in accord with African tradition. In São Salvador do Congo around 1880, adults who were not married carried a social stigma. BeAD.

UNATA (*União dos Naturais de Angola*) (Pg.) "Union of Natives of Angola," a political party organized in 1955 by the *mestiço* pharmacist Eduardo Victorio Pereira in Sá de Bandeira and Mossâmedes, Angola, to pressure the Portuguese government for political reforms and eventual independence. In 1958 the party sent a memorandum to the government that resulted in the arrest by the secret police of Pereira and other leaders of the movement. Pelissier, *La Colonie*, p. 292.

undai (Afr.) A small tropical tree (*Gardenia jovis-tonantis*) found in rocky soil in Cazengo, Colungo Alta, and Ambaca, Angola. Africans considered the *undai* to be a sacred tree. They carved magical objects such as fetishes from its hard fine-grained wood and placed sticks from the trees in the rafters of their huts for divine protection. Ficalho, *Plantas Uteis*, pp. 196-7.

undoki (Kik.) "Witch." A term used in São Salvador do Congo c.1880. BeAD. *See also* unganga.

undul (Afr.) *See* Portugal, African dances in.

undumba (Kik.) In Kikongo, Angola, a term applied to a young unmarried woman. The term "virgin" was not in the Kikongo language as it was spoken around 1880 in São Salvador do Congo. BeAD.

UNEM (*União Nacional dos Estundantes de Moçambique*)(Pg.) "National Union of Mozambican Students," a political party organized in Paris in 1963 by Portuguese-African students then in Europe and the United States. Their mission while abroad entailed publicizing the nationalist struggle. In 1965 UNEM's headquarters was moved to Dar es-Salaam, Tanzania. Attempts were made to integrate its members with FRELIMO (q.v.), but in December 1967, FRELIMO condemned these students as traitors. Munslow, *Mozambique*, pp. 65, 98-9.

UNDM (*União Nacional Democratica de Moçambique*) (Pg.) "National Democratic Union of Mozambique," a nationalist party organized in Bulawayo, Zimbabwe, on October 2, 1960, by Paulo José Gumane, David Mabunda, Uria Simango (the Protestant pastor from the Beira region), workers, and exiles, mostly from south and central Mozambique. Henriksen, *Mozambique*, p. 169.

unganga (Kik.) "Medicine man." A term used in São Salvador do Congo c.1880. BeAD.

UNGP (*União dos Naturais da Guiné Portuguesa*) (Pg.) "Union of Natives of Portuguese Guiné," a political group seeking independence without revolution or violence that was organized around 1960 by Benjamin Pinto Bull. Its leader went to Lisbon in July 1963 to negotiate with Portugal. These negotiations failed, prompting UNGP to unite with FLING (q.v.). In 1966, Benjamin Pinto Bull's brother, Jaime, was elected president of FLING. HDRGC.

ungudi (Kik.) Term of endearment used for and among siblings of the same mother but different fathers, current in São Salvador do Congo c.1880. BeAD.

UNHCR (United Nations High Commission for Refugees) This international agency played an important role in helping the 1.4 million Mozambicans forced to flee to neighboring countries during the civil war that the government fought against RENAMO (q.v.) from 1975 to 1992. The ravages of the struggle dislocated a large rural population and the UNHCR helped them to find protection in Zimbabwe, Malawi, Zambia, Swaziland, and South Africa. Andersson, *Mozambique*, pp. 111-3.

União Africana de Moçambique *See* UAM.

União das Populações de Angola *See* UPA.

União das Populações das Ilhas do Cabo Verde *See* UPICV.

União das Populações do Norte de Angola *See* UPNA.

União Democrática da Guiné *See* UDG.

União Democrática das Mulheres da Guiné e Cabo Verde *See* UDMGCV.

União Democrática de Cabo Verde *See* UDCV.

União Democrática Nacional de Moçambique *See* UDNM.

União dos Naturais de Angola (Pg.) *See* UNATA.

União dos Naturais da Guiné Portuguesa *See* UNGP.

União-Geral dos Estudantes da Africa Negra *See* UGEAN.

União Nacional (Pg.) "National Union." A loose organization established in Lisbon in 1957 by President Antonio O. Salazar. Its purpose was to publicize Portuguese government policies, organize elections in the colonies, and publish economic and administrative reforms in Europe. Pelissier, *La Colonie*, pp. 103-4.

União Nacional Democratica de Moçambique *See* UNDM.

União Nacional dos Estundantes de Moçambique *See* UNEM.

União Nacional de Moçambique Independiente *See* UNMI.

União Nacional dos Trabalhadores de Guiné *See* UNTG.

União Nacional para a Independencia Total de Angola *See* UNITA.

União Progressiva *See* UP.

Unidade Tribal *See* UT.

UNITA (*União Nacional para a Independencia Total de Angola*) (Pg.) "National Union for the Total Independence of Angola." A political party founded in March 1966 in Muanga, Moxico district, by Jonas M. Savimbi, an Angolan nationalist, and his followers. It was an ethnic self-reliance group that concentrated on underground resistance inside Angola. In December 1966, UNITA guerrillas opened up an eastern front and attacked the Benguela railway near Teixeira de Sousa. The railway, which carried Zambian copper to the Atlantic port of Lobito, was temporarily cut. In retaliation, Zambia exiled Savimbi and his UNITA followers. Until 1974, the movement retained a low profile, but following the cease-fire with Portugal in June 1974, UNITA moved into the central highlands, its natural political stronghold. When the war ended, UNITA joined with Portugal, FNLA, and MPLA (qq.v.) in the transitional government. Soon the party disagreed with the new Angolan government. In November 1975, UNITA turned to South Africa for arms and a civil war began in south-central Angola. In March 1976 the party went underground in eastern and southeastern Angola, mainly in Moxico, Bié, and Cuando-Cubango provinces, until May 1991 when Savimbi and President José Eduardo dos Santos of Angola signed the Lisbon Accord (q.v.) that ended sixteen years of civil war. They set elections for the fall of 1992. HDA; *New York Times*, June 1, 1991: HDA.

United Nations Charter In October 1945, the United Nations prepared a charter that included protection of the rights and interests of indigenous populations in Portuguese-African colonies. It stated the need for education and for the establishment of autonomy and self-government. Cunha, *O Sistema Portugués*, pp. 49-50.

United Nations High Commission for Refugees *See* UNHCR.

universities *See* Angola University, Mondlane University.

UNMI (*União Nacional de Moçambique Independiente*) (Pg.) "National Union of Independent Mozambique," a party established in Malawi in the 1960s by exile migrant workers from central Mozambique. It was a proto-nationalist group whose members were mainly from the Tete district. It spent a good deal of energy petitioning the United Nations for assistance for its economic and social problems. Munslow, *Mozambique*, p. 80.

UNTG (*União Nacional dos Trabalhadores de Guiné*) (Pg.) "National Union of Guinean Workers," a small labor group founded in Guinea-Bissau in 1959 and affiliated with PAIGC (q.v.). Its first constitution was drafted in 1961 by Luis Cabral, its secretary general and, after independence, the president of Guinea-Bissau. UNTG functioned clandestinely until the end of the War for Independence in 1975. HDRGC.

UP (*União Progressiva*) (Pg.) "Progressive Union," a nationalist party founded in 1953 in the Manica-Sofala district. They demanded independence for Mozambique and its founders claimed to have the backing of the MPLA (q.v.). Henriksen, *Mozambique*, pp. 163-4.

UPA (*União das Populações de Angola*) (Pg.) "Union of the Peoples of Angola," an ethno-nationalist political party organized by Alvaro Holden Roberto in Leopoldville, Zaire, in 1960. It was a Marxist movement that spread to Angola where it had 53,183 members in 1970. Pelissier, *La Colonie*, pp. 91, 252-57.

UPICV (*União das Populações das Ilhas do Cabo Verde*) (Pg.) "Union of the People of the Cape Verde Islands," a political organization formed in the United States in 1959 by José Leitão da Graça and his wife, Maria Querido Leitão. Its aim was to preserve the Cape Verdian "personality" within limited social change. In the mid-1970s it was renamed the Peoples' Liberation Front of Cape Verde. Following the independence of Cape Verde on May 23, 1975, the leaders of this group who were then living in Cape Verde were exiled to Portugal. HDRGC.

UPNA (*União das Populações do Norte de Angola*) (Pg.) "Union of the Peoples of North Angola," a political party organized in Leopoldville, Zaire, in July 1957 with Barros Necaca as president and Borralho Lulendo as secretary. Antonio III, king of Congo and head of the party, wanted to establish an independent Catholic kingdom within the Portuguese community. Pelissier, *La Colonie*, p. 269-71.

Upper Guinea Term applied c.1500 to the coastal region of West Africa between Gambia and Cameroon. Upper Guinea is mentioned in the chronicle of Jaime Ferrer, a Spanish explorer who c.1346 sailed along the Atlantic coast and apparently visited the Mandingo Kingdom, at the time a gold trading center in the Sudan. The first reference to Guiné made by Portuguese navigators is dated 1450. Early traders gave various sections of coastal Upper Guinea different names, including Grain Coast, Pepper Coast, Ivory Coast, Gold Coast, and Slave Coast. All but the Pepper Coast persist to this day. Cortesão, J., *Expansão Portuguesa*, pp. 57-58.

Upper Zambezia A northeastern Angolan province bordering on Zaire and Zambia. This region is part of Central Africa and contains the watershed for the upper Zambezi and Kasai rivers. Much of it is a deserted plateau that descends in the east into marshy malarial basins. Wheeler, *Angola*, p. 4.

urca (Pg.) A type of medieval ship of German origin introduced into Portugal at the beginning of the fifteenth century. By 1452, there were many *urcas* in the service of Portugal, as is attested to by a document by King Afonso V dated 1456. DHP.

Urupandi fair (Afr.) A Mozambican trade center very active c.1615 due to several gold fields discovered on the Mazoe River and its tributaries, south of Tete. This fair faded away c.1700, mostly due to wars among Africans for control of the mining. This upheaval put an end to the gold panning on which the fair depended for its prosperity. Newitt, *Portuguese Settlement*, p. 45.

Urze arborea (Pg.) In São Tomé and elsewhere, an arboreal sweet broom (*Philippia thomensis*) that grows in waste places in tropical and subtropical regions. Tenreiro, *A Ilha*, p. 52.

urzela (Pg.) "Orchil weed." See orchil.

ussua (Afr.) In São Tomé, an African dance, a kind of waltz, popular in the 1920s. *Ussua* dancers formed cooperative groups that included musicians and a treasurer. They performed and shared tips from the public. Tenreiro, *A Ilha*, p. 188.

UT *(Unidade Tribal)* (Pg.) "Tribal Unity." A political party organized in Lorenço Marques, Mozambique, in the 1960s. This union of ethnic groups aimed at establishing an independent Mozambique based on the principle of ethnic unity of all Mozambicans, Portuguese, and mine workers in the South African gold fields. This movement was rejected by the nationalist politicians in the colony. Rita-Ferreira, *O Movimento Migratorio*, p. 141.

Utrecht, Peace Treaty of A peace accord signed in 1713-15 by England, France, and Spain that ended the Spanish War of Succession. Among other provisions, it gave England exclusive world maritime and commercial hegemony and the exclusive privilege of providing African slaves to the Spanish American colonies. Portugal rejected the treaty because it ignored her right to participate in the slave trade, a right held by Portugal since the Discovery (q.v.). Silve Rego, *O Ultramar*, p. 4; GEPB. *See also* "Inglaterra, la nação mais negreira de Europa."

vaccination The practice of inoculating with cowpox vaccine to prevent or mitigate an attack of the more virulent smallpox originated in the Middle East where the concept of vaccination was noted by Europeans in Turkey. It was refined and tested in 1796 in England by the physician Edward Jenner (1749-1823). Vaccination was introduced in Luanda, Angola, in 1802 by governor Saldanha da Gama, greatly reducing the deadly effects of the smallpox epidemic so prevalent in that city and in other regions in West Africa. Dias, *Famine and Disease*, JAH, Cambridge, 1981, 22(3):363(n); *Revista Medica de Angola*, Luanda, 1923, I:107; GEPB. *See also* vaccine.

vaccine Originally a quantity of lymph, or a preparation of a serum from cowpox vesicles containing the causative virus, used in vaccination to prevent smallpox. *Revista Medica de Angola*, Luanda, 1923, I:107; GEPB. *See also* vaccination.

Va-Dema (Afr.) A small chiefdom on the banks of the Zambezi River beyond the Cabora Bassa Falls (q.v.) in Tete, Mozambique. This highly populated region was occupied by the Portuguese early in the Discovery (q.v.). Newitt, *Portuguese Settlement*, pp. 25-6.

vadio (Pg.) "Vagrant." According to Portuguese law promulgated in Portuguese Africa in 1875, an apparently non-productive former slave who could be forced to work under a five-year contract for his former master. *Vadios* provided cheap labor for planters. Bender, *Angola*, p. 139. *See* vagrancy clause.

vagrancy clause This clause, introduced into Portuguese law in 1875, considered any apparently non-productive African a *vadio* (vagrant) and thereby subject to forced labor. The determination of productivity was usually left to local administrators who had no difficulty finding enough "vagrants" to meet the settlers' demands for free labor. Bender, *Angola*, p. 139.

vaka (Kik.) A chicken coop in São Salvador do Congo c.1880. BeAD.

Vale de Loge (Pg.) A planned government agricultural settlement established in the Uige province, Angola, in 1968. It was a a system of land development that usually had a mixed group of ten to thirty Portuguese and African workers laboring together. This social experiment ended in failure. Bender, *Angola*, p. 117. *See also* colonato.

"Vamos descobrir Angola!" (Pg.) "Let's discover Angola!" The slogan of a group of young intellectuals c.1948 who, after graduation from Angolan secondary schools, came to Portuguese universities. Their objectives while working for degrees were to read and learn about their homeland's physical and cultural landscape, its traditions and values. This awareness gave rise to the *Movimento dos Novos Intellectuais de Angola* (Movement of the Young Intellectuals of Angola) and in 1950 to the founding of the *Associação dos Naturais de Angola* (Association of the Native Sons of Angola). This outstanding new generation of well educated men and women, black, white, and *mestiço*, came mainly from urban areas. Many kept to the original precepts although some of them evolved into a Europeanized elite, far removed from their original goal of knowledge of the history and culture of their native land. Ervedosa, *Itinerario*, pp. 99, 100.

vanilla (Pg.) Commercially important orchid (*Vanilla planifolia*) of tropical America with fragrant greenish-yellow flowers and long thin pods (vanilla beans) filled with nearly microscopic seeds. Treated unripe pods yield the vanilla flavoring of commerce. Vanilla cultivation was introduced into São Tomé by the Portuguese naval officer Custodio Borja in 1879. Carvalho e Vasconcellos, *As Colonias Portuguesas*, p. 213.

vara (Pg.) Cloth measure equivalent to 43.11 English inches (109.5 cm) in use in the 1600s. Duncan, *Atlantic Islands*, p. 261.

varajim (Afr.) "Song of protest." A song of dissent, named by African laborers after Fernando Vaz Valezim, a Portuguese administrator of the huge Mopeia (q.v.) plantation in the 1950s. He was a notorious overseer who abused men and women employed in the fields. Workers accused him of seizing babies from their mothers' backs and hiding them in a box to force the women to work. Although Valezim's behavior was approved by his employers, this policy did not pay because the plantation continued to lose money. It was not until 1959, when Mozambique exported 35,051 tons of cotton to Portugal worth 540 million *escudos*, that the company for the first time in nine years made a small profit on cotton. Later he was assigned to the Luabo sugar estate in the lower Zambezi. Vail, *Capitalism*, pp. 321-2. *See also* Jemwe.

vargen (Afr.) A small plot of land rented by a settler to grow vegetables for his family in the Zambezian region in the 1750. It was also called a *horta* (garden). Newitt, *Portuguese Settlement*, p. 95.

varzea (Pg.) In São Tomé c.1490, an alluvial flood plain irrigated by small streams and heavily cultivated with sugar cane. A *varzea* was excellent for agriculture that required low, level, well-irrigated land. Tenreiro, *A Ilha*, p. 70.

vassal of the king of Portugal A personal allegiance of servitude to the king of Portugal. In 1572, the King Alvaro I of Congo became a vassal of the king of Portugal in gratitude for the restoration of his throne which had been siezed by the Jagas. He promised to pay the king a fifth of the annual harvest of *jimbos* (shells for currency) gathered off the island of Luanda. Gabriel, *Angola*, p. 63.

vatakana (Kik.) A field prepared for planting corn or other grains in São Salvador do Congo, Angola, c.1880. BeAD.

vedor de fazenda (Pg.) "Royal comptroller." In the 1600s, a Crown inspector in charge of collecting taxes and revenues owed to the royal treasury. In 1630, *vedores de fazenda* were sent to Zambezian settlements to review the titles of the *prazos* (q.v.) and investigate frauds in the payment of taxes. Axelson, *Portuguese in South-East*, p. 244.

vegeculture In central and south-central Africa, an early method of cultivating vegetables, grains, and rootcrops. This incipient stage of agriculture, characteristic of the later stages of the Stone Age, was practiced in Angola and elsewhere in the region. Both vegeculture and ironworking were introduced to central Africa by Bantu migrants around the fourteenth century. Vegeculture was an important cultural advance that made possible a steady production of food, including sorghum and millet, that in turn sustained local population growth. Kaplan, *Angola*, p. 101; OED.

vegetarianism In Guinea-Bissau, especially during times of privation and famine, the term is used to refer to the custom of eating all kinds of wild fruits and roots indiscriminately. Mota, *Guiné Portuguesa*, II:95.

vela (Kik.) A sacred hut in a compound where people were initiated into the mystery of *ndembu* (q.v.), a cult fetish in São Salvador do Congo, Angola, c.1880. BeAD.

vendus (Fr.) In Guinea-Bissau, a transient marshy area, the consequence of flooding from seasonal rains. Mota, *Guiné Portuguesa*, I:73.

Venice, Portugal's relations with Portugal and Venice developed close relations during the late Middle Ages. Between 1420 and 1460 Venitian navigators explored the African coast in Prince Henry's service. There is no doubt that the Venitians had discussed the travels of Marco Polo (1254-1324?) to China c.1271 with Prince Henry. Polo's journal was published in English with the title of *The Book of Ser Morco Polo* in which the author wondered at the splendors he saw and of which he heard. Prince Pedro, brother of Prince Henry, brought a copy of this account back to Portugal in 1428. During the Renaissance, this book was the chief, almost the sole, source in the West for information on the East. For many parts of central Asia there was no other European material available until the late nineteenth century. Prince Henry found encouragement in this work for his quest for a maritime route around Africa to India. This goal was accomplished by Vasco da Gama in 1498, nearly forty years after Prince Henry's death in 1460. Cortesão, *History*, I:297; CE.

vento leste (Pg.) "Easterly wind." Name given by the Portuguese in Guinea-Bissau to the *harmattan* (q.v.), a hot and dry Sarahan wind that erodes the soil, seres the vegetation, and weakens the population. It blows continuously east to west and leaves a reddish-brown iron-rich cover over the soil that renders it barren, especially in the interior. Mota, *Guiné Portuguesa*, I;30.

ventos gerais (Pg.) "Trade winds." Winds that blow steadily toward the equator from the northeast in the tropics north of the equator, and from the southeast in the tropics south of the equator. Portuguese navigators encountered these winds early in Discovery (q.v.). They found that these *ventos gerais* speeded their ships' course from Lisbon to the Atlantic islands and to the Cape of Good Hope. On their return voyages, however, they had to sail west toward the Sargasso Sea (q.v.) to find favorable winds to take them east to Lisbon. In the India Ocean, the trade winds or seasonal *monsoons* (q.v.) allowed the navigators to follow the *carrera da India* (Indian course) in their trips to and from Goa. Costa, *A Marinha dos Descobrimentos*, p. 351. *See also* volta do mar, volta do Sargasso.

vezo-vezo (Kik.) A trade knife with a single sharp edge and a haft, set with bone, on each side; used in São Salvador do Congo, Angola, c.1880. BeAD.

viagem a contra costa (Pg.) "Trip from coast to coast." A transcontinental journey of exploration that had both commercial and political value. Attempts to travel from Angola to Mozambique or the reverse were organized by the Portuguese government on several occasions at the end of the eighteenth and the beginning of the nineteenth centuries. The most successful of these took place in 1804 under the leadership of two *pombeiros* (q.v.), Antonio Amaro José and Pedro João Baptista. They started on November 11, 1804, at Cassanje, Angola, headed for Sena, Mozambique. After crossing the

Cuando and Cassai rivers they reached Cazembe, where they stayed for four years. The expedition arrived in Tete, Mozambique, on February 11, 1811, returning to Luanda, Angola, in 1815. The account of the expedition was published under the title *Travesia da Africa* (Crossing Africa, Lisbon, Agencia Geral das Colonias, 1936). In English it appeared under the title *Lands of Kazembe* (London, 1873), translated by Richard F. Burton, the English orientalist. Cunnison, *Kazembe and the Portuguese, 1798-1832*, JAH, Cambridge, 1961, II(1):62.

viagens triangulares (Pg.) "Triangular voyages." Triangular trips from Europe to Africa to the Americas carrying European merchandise to sell in West Africa to buy slaves for the New World markets and then, after delivering the slaves, returning to European ports with sugar, rum, lumber, dyewoods, and other goods. Apparently the first of these triangular trips were organized by Portuguese merchants from São Tomé around 1500, followed by the Englishman John Hawkins in 1570. After 1580, when Portugal became a dependency of Spain, English merchants controlled these markets. According to some historians, these commercial voyages have been some of the most profitable ever undertaken. Mota, *Guiné Portuguesa*, II:17; GEPB.

victory clothes   Colorful garments selected by King João II c.1490 for African slaves serving in the royal palace to wear as a symbol of his victory over African chiefdoms. He also authorized pagan slaves to keep their African names which included Cumba, Tanba, Tonba, and Babry. Those converted to Christianity enjoyed the king's affection, receiving popular names such as Antonio, Maria, Pedro, Caterina, and Afonso. Saunders, *A Social History*, p. 40; GEPB.

vielo (Afr.) In Angola and elsewhere, an edible leguminous plant (*Voandzeira subterranea*) much cultivated in warm climates; when the flower falls, the stalk supporting the seedpod lengthens and bends downward until the oil-rich pod reaches the ground where it begins to enlarge and ripen. In Angola the *vielo* is also called *mendubi-de-Angola*. Ficalho, *Plantas Uteis*, pp. 133, 137.

Vila do Infante "Village of the Prince." A village founded by Prince Henry c.1437 in Sagres in southern Portugal on the Algarve. It included the Church of Our Lady of Grace, a palace, a fortress, and buildings for the institution he established for scholars and navigators engaged in research. Its original name was *Tercanabal*, later changed to *Vila do Infante*. Prince Henry resided, worked, and studied here. He died in this village on November 13, 1460, and was buried in the church he founded. In 1587 the English pirate Sir Francis Drake attacked and sacked the village. Iria, *O Algarve no Descobrimento*, Congresso da Guine, Lisbon, 1946, I:195. *See also* Sagres nautical school.

Vila Formosa (Pg.)   The seat of a small settlement outside Boror (q.v.), a *prazo* located north of the Zambezi River. On February 20, 1892, João de Azevedo Coutinho occupied and burned the *prazo* and the village. Newitt, *Portuguese Settlement*, p. 291.

Vila Luso (Pg.)   The capital city of Moxico district, central Angola. Founded in 1901, the municipality includes the villages of Caxipoque, Camanongue, Lucusse, Muangai, and Sandando within an area of 25,760 sq. mi. (67,000 sq. km). After independence it was renamed Luena. Kaplan, *Angola*, p. 8.

Vila Marechal Carmona   *See* Uige.

Vila Salazar   A town and county seat of Cazengo in Cuanza del Norte district, central Angola. On May 28, 1956, it was elevated to the rank of city and named Vila Salazar. After independence the new government renamed it Ndalatado in 1977. GEPB.

Vili   Nineteenth-century long distance merchants, members of a Kikongo-speaking community in the Loango kingdom. They flourished in northern Angola throughout the seventeenth century and controlled much of the trade between and among chiefdoms in gold and, later, rubber from the seventeenth through the nineteenth centuries. They faded away with the end of the rubber boom and the closing of the colonial frontiers at the end of the ninetenth century. HDA (2).

vintem (Pg.)   "Twenty." An old Portuguese silver coin equivalent to US 20 cents. This currency circulated in East Africa c.1650. Axelson, *Portuguese in South-East*, p. 244.

vintena (Pg.)   "Twenty percent." This was the royal tax levied on goods and slaves brought directly from trading posts in West Africa and Asia to Portugal early in the Discovery (q.v.). Under royal order, the *vintena* on slaves was to be collected in Portugal at the *Casa dos Escravos* (q.v.) although this tax was often paid in Cape Verde or São Jorge de Mina, clearinghouses for the slave trade in the Gulf of Guiné. Saunders, *A Social History*, pp. 69, 269; GEPB.

violence, justification for   In 1968, as the Angolan War for Independence intensified, Portugal decided to use military force to fight what it considered nationalist sedition. The government established strict control over dissidents and other Africans, restricting and regulating people's movements, creating a network of paid informers, and sowing distrust among villagers and nationalists. Eventually the secret government police agency PIDE, later DGS (qq.v.), managed to drive the nationalists into neighboring countries from which they continued their struggle. The Portuguese government called this policy a vindication that justified the extreme control and persecution of its opponents. Bender, *Angola,* p. 162.

"Virar Mandingo" (Pg.)   "Mandingo Conversion." In Guinea-Bissau c.1890, Islamic clerics began a largely unsuccesful campaign to convert Mandingos from animism to Islam. Mota, *Guiné Portuguesa,* I:264.

Virgin Mary, apparition of In 1960 it was reported that the Virgin Mary, the protector of Africans, appeared to two Congolese adults in Cassulo Cuenda, Malange, Angola. The Virgin foretold the liberation of the Angolan people and the coming of a Messiah who would usher in a new era of peace and happiness for the oppressed. Pelissier, *La Colonie,* p. 412.

Viuva Bastos e Filhos An Angolan corporation established in Mossãmedes in 1895 by the family of M.J.A. Bastos. By 1903 it was the largest corporation as well as the largest landowner in the Atlantic coastal strip of Mossamedes, controlling 34 percent of a total of 11,000 acres cultivated in the area. The company produced 31 percent of the rum in the province and by 1920 dominated the salt market and had invested heavily in the fishing industry. Clarence-Smith, *Slaves, Peasants,* p. 51; GEPB.

Voice of Liberty A radio program first broadcast in 1964 in Algiers by Afri-can nationalists to coordinate political propaganda, war information, and anti-Portuguese indoctrination among the forces fighting in Africa. In 1966, the Voice of Liberty was appealing to Portuguese army deserters and civilians in Africa and soldiers in Portugal for moral support of the war effort. They also asked for international assistance for FRELIMO, MPLA, UPA (qq.v.), and other nationalist groups. It had a positive effect on the ideological inte-gration of the revolution as well as undermining the morale and loyalty of the enemy forces. Munslow, *Mozambique,* pp. 8-9. *See also* Voz do Desertor.

Volta River   Discovered by the Portuguese c.1460, it was called *volta* (turning) because of its meandering course; Africans called it *Firao, Frao,* or *Atirri.* It begins as three branches, the Black, Red, and White, in Upper Volta. A fourth branch originates as the *Pendjari* in Benin and becomes the *Oti* as it enters Togo. The distance from the source of the Black Volta to the Gulf of Guiné at Ada is about 1,000 mi. (1,600 km). At Ada it is a mile (1.6 km) across. The river is at its lowest in March and at its highest at the end of September. HDG.

volta do mar (Pg.) "Turn around from the sea." An expression referring to safely navigating out into the open sea west of Grand Canary Island and

Madeira Island early in the Discovery (q.v.). At this point, navigators had to take a route by way of the Azores to find favorable northwest and then northeast winds to take them to Lisbon. In the period around 1480 the *volta do mar* involved a long passage in open waters to find predictable winds. Once found, they had to take a rough estimate of polar latitude. Mastering the *volta do mar* gave sea captains the necessary confidence to further explore along the unknown Atlantic coast. Parry, *The Discovery of the Sea*, pp. 102, 253. *See also* volta do Sargasso.

volta do Sargasso (Pg.) "Turn around from the Sargasso." An expression used by Portuguese navigators c.1490 to describe their trips west past Madeira and the Azores to an area of westerlies that helped the caravels returning from Guiné to reach Lagos and Lisbon. Cortesão, *History*, p. 114. *See also* Sargasso sea, volta do mar.

voluntarios (Pg.) "Volunteers." In South Africa, the name given by the Witwatersrand Native Labour Association (WNLA, q.v.) to Mozambican contract workers illegally employed beyond the period of their residence permits c.1906. They were also called *locais* (locals). Rita-Ferreira, *O Movimento Migratorio*, p. 123.

voluntary slavery In Mozambique before the arrival of the Portuguese, voluntary slavery was a traditional institution. This domestic slavery or, more precisely, adopted dependency, persisted in its customary form in Zambezian society into the period when the *prazos* were organized around 1600. During periods of famine and drought Africans voluntarily enslaved themselves to a wealthy chief in exchange for food, clothing, and protection. They worked in the fields, collected firewood, and guarded the herds. This slave status was never for more than one generation and could not be transmitted to their children. Isaacman, *Mozambique*, pp. 47-50; GEPB.

voortrekkers (Afrk.) Boer colonists under the leadership of J.F. Botha who arrived at Humpata, southern Angola, on December 22, 1880, after a long journey from the upper velt region in South Africa. A group of about 55 families established the São Januario colony (q.v.) north of Sa de Bandeira. They opened two schools to teach their language and religion, but soon became unhappy with the economic and political conditions and by 1885 all but twelve families had left. Guerreiro, *Boers in Angola*, Garcia de Horta, 1958, 6(1):12. See also Boers in Angola, Transvaal, trekboere.

Voz Africana (Pg.) "African Voice." A weekly catering to African readers and first published in 1969 in Lisbon by Miguel Murupa, a defector of FRELIMO (q.v.). Although pro-Portuguese, the weekly criticized the government for failing to provide health and education services for the African population. Henriksen, *Mozambique*, pp. 181-2.

Voz Africana (Pg.) "African Voice." A newspaper founded in Beira, Mozambique, by the *Centro Africano de Manica e Sofala*. It was published between 1932 and 1975. Henriksen, *Mozambique*, p. 282.

Voz da Revolução (Pg.) "Voice of the Revolution." A newspaper first published by FRELIMO (q.v.) in Lourenço Marques, Mozambique, in 1965. Its publication was irregular because of the war then in progress. This journal is a source of considerable importance for historical and political information. Around 1970, it replaced *Boletim Nacional* and *Boletim de Informação* both also published by FRELIMO (q.v.). *Voz da Revolução* was published in three series. The first was mimeographed and ran for about five years. The second, comprising twenty-two issues, was printed. Publication was suspended from 1971 until after independence. In May of 1978, *Voz da Revolução* was revived and modernized. Darch, *Mozambique,* p. 162.

Voz de Africa, A (Pg.) "The Voice from Africa." A newspaper founded in Lisbon in 1911 by the *Junta de Defesa dos Direitos de Africa* (Committee for the Defense of African Rights) to promote justice for Africans and self-government for the Portuguese colonies. It was published ephemerally from various presses in Lisbon, Oporto, and Geneva from 1911 until 1930. Pelissier, *La Colonie*, pp. 224-25.

Voz de Africa (Pg.) "Voice of Africa." A journal published in Mindelo, Cape Verde, around 1915. It promoted *nativismo*, an emerging Pan-African ideology, and stressed freedom and justice for the colonies. Government censorship caused the paper to fold in 1919. Davidson, *The Fortunate Isles*, pp. 44, 48, 50.

Voz de Moçambique (Pg.) "Voice of Mozambique." A daily published in Lourenço Marques as an organ of the Association of Mozambican Natives. It played an important role in the cultural and literary development of Mozambique. In 1960 it published a vivid polemic on the value of regional poetry and literature in the colony and in 1971 it reported the publication of *Os Noivos, ou Conferencia Dramatica sobre o Lobolo* (The Newlyweds, or a Dramatic Consultation on the Lobolo), a play by Lindo Hlong. Hamilton, *Voices*, pp. 167, 170-9, 223. *See also* lobola.

Voz do Desertor (Pg.) "Deserter's Voice." A periodical published in Lourenço Marques, Mozambique, in the 1970s. At the time the Portuguese military power in Mozambique began to crumble from internal dissention in their armed forces and increasing opposition in Lisbon. Nationalist infiltration into the colonial army further weakened the troops' loyalty to Portugal. *Voz do Desertor* played an important role in this deterioration and in the struggle for independence (1960-1975). Munslow, *Mozambique,* p. 126.

Vuhoca (Afr.)   One of the Bazaruto Islands off the Indian Ocean coast of Mozambique, occupied in 1722 by the Portuguese. It was declared a Crown *prazo* and named Manbone. In 1762 it was leased to Sebastião Rodrigues who that same year paid a tax of 75 *cruzados*. The last holder of the *prazo* was his grandson. In 1806 it passed out of the Rodrigues family and was divided into four parts and granted by the government to four *donas* (ladies) in an attempt to tighten up its administration. Newitt, *Portuguese Settlement*, pp. 208-09.

vuku (Kik.) The term for bubonic plague in São Salvador do Congo, Angola, c.1880. BeAD.

Vumba fair   An important fair held in Manica, Mozambique, near a gold-mining area. It was established around 1630 by Afro-Portuguese traders under the protection of local chiefs. This fair, active until the 1850s, was one of the commercial centers in the hinterland where gold, ivory, wax, pearls, rock crystal, and animal skins were traded for European cloth, liquor, firearms, and gun powder. Newitt, *Portuguese Settlement*, pp. 46, 74.

{ W }

walakaji (Kik.) "Orphan." In São Salvador do Congo, Angola, around 1880 there were numerous *walakajis*, many of whom were wards of the Misericordia (q.v.). BeAD.

wali (Afr.) The highest dignitary in the Islamic hierarchy. Considered a living saint, the *wali* was a teacher deeply revered by Moslems in Senegal during the colonial period. Today among the Mandingos and Fulas in Guinea-Bissau, the *wali* presides over services in the mosque and teaches the Koran. Gonçalves, *O Mundo Arabo-Islámico*, p. 196.

walumuka (Kik.) A ritual to secure the germination of grains, believed to bring a good harvest, performed by sorcerers in São Salvador do Congo, Angola, around 1880. BeAD.

Walvis Bay An inlet on the Atlantic coast of Namibia explored by the Portuguese navigator Bartolomeu Dias in 1488 and named *Angra da Concepção*. In 1886, Portugal relinquished this bay to Germany, which at the time was in the process of establishing a colony in the area and gave the bay its present name. Valkhoff, *Miscelanea*, p. 270.

wanda (Kik.) The term for a net or hammock in São Salvador do Congo, Angola, c.1880. BeAD.

wandu (Kik.) Edible kidney-shaped beans of the New World genus *Phaseolus*, introduced by the Portuguese and widely cultivated in São Salvador do Congo, Angola, and elsewhere in Africa. *Phaseolus* spp. are much better soil-nitrogen fixers than Old World *Vigna* spp., so they also increase soil fertility. BeAD.

wantu (Kik.) The term for mankind, used in São Salvador do Congo, Angola, c.1880. BeAD.

war for the acquisition of slaves Since the Middle Ages Portugal had enslaved prisoners of war, a policy greatly escalated in West Africa at the time of the Discovery (q.v.). In 1441 two caravels landed at Rio do Ouro and sailors attacked several Berber settlements near the coast, capturing a few men and women. These captives became the first African slaves brought to Lagos and sold in the market. In 1444, the merchants of the Algarve sent an expedition to the same region and brought back 235 prisoners, also sold at auction at the Lagos market. These expeditions marked the beginning of the highly profitable slave trade. This trade lasted until the middle of the nineteenth century. Saunders, *A Social History*, p. 4-5; GEPB.

"War of Exhaustion" An expression first used in Mozambique and elsewhere in Portuguese Africa in mid-1973 by middle-level members of the Portuguese army. The ideology of an aggressive Portuguese nationalism, promoted by the Lisbon government, had worn thin among combat officers in the colonies. Dispirited by French and American setbacks in Vietnam, Portuguese officers compared their country's poverty to the wealth of France and the United States and drew pessimistic conclusions. In the 1970s Portugal's position was seriously weakened by nationalist guerrillas in Angola; in Mozambique protracted fighting had drained Portugal's energy and self-confidence. Henriksen, *Revolution*, p. 101. *See also* flagellation.

watermelon A trailing vine (*Citrulus vulgaris*) that grows wild in tropical Africa, especially in transiently flooded gullies. Among the Berbers and other groups, it serves to quench thirst when other sources of water are unavailable. At certain times of the year in the driest regions of the continent it can be the only source of water for men and beasts. Watermelon has been cultivated in Egypt and other parts of the continent for millennia. It is widespread both wild and cultivated in the sub-Sahara. In 1335, it was reported to be cultivated on the banks of the Niger River between Timbuctu and Gao, and was grown by the Wolofs and Mandingos of Guinea-Bissau. In 1506, Valentim Fernandes reported that this vine was known by Africans in Senegal. In Luanda it is called *nxibua*, in Mossamedes *ditangue*, and in Zambezia *mavembe* and *pateca*. Ficalho, *Plantas Uteis*, p. 187; Lewicki, *West African Food*, pp. 21, 58, 64-5.

water yam The fleshy edible root of a tropical climbing plant (*Dioscorea alata*) widely cultivated in Senegal and Guinea-Bissau among the Tokolor (q.v.). Together with cassava (q.v.), water yam provides some of the most important sources of carbohydrates for Africans. Its various names, *al-quafi* in Arabic, *kappe* in Tokolor, *khabi* in Susu, a Mandingo group, and *kape* in Fulani, suggest both its antiquity and its popularity in West Africa. Lewicki, *West African Food*, p. 49; GEPB.

weaverbird In Portuguese Africa and elsewhere, any of a number of Old World finch-like birds (family *Ploceidae*). They are mostly characterized by their construction of elaborate nests of interlaced grass and other vegetation hanging from a branch with an entrance at the bottom or on the side. These large structures, shaped like inverted domes, are inhabited by many pairs of birds. Weaverbirds are also called *cherico*. PDM.

Welser bankers A wealthy German family of merchants and financiers based in Ausburg c.1470. It reached the height of its prosperity under Bartholomew Welser who died in 1484. His brothers Luca and Ulrich continued the commercial relationships with Venice, Milan, Cologne, Florence, Frankfurt, and Lisbon. A Welser agent participated in the 1505 expedition to India led by Francisco de Almeida. The factories (q.v.) of the Welser group were established in Lisbon, Cape Verde, Madeira, and Palma in the Canary Islands between 1503 and 1531. The Welser family was active in Lisbon until 1599. DHP.

Welwitschia mirabilis (Lat.) A low-growing woody plant of extraordinary appearance and structure. Although there is no known relative to it living or in the fossil record, it shares characteristics of both gymnosperms and angiosperms. *Welwitschia mirabilis* was customarily classified as a gymnosperm (Gnetaceae family). Now it is rightfully placed by itself in the class *Welwitschiaceae*. Named after its discoverer, the Austrian botanist Frederick Welwitsch (1806-1872), the single species *Welwitschia mirabilis* is known locally as *n'tmboa* or *tumboa*. It is limited in distribution to a narrow inland belt of grassland and desert extending from the Mossâmedes Desert of Angola southward to an area 100 miles (160 km) north of Swakopmund in South Africa. It produces only two leaves and the stout, roughly bow-shaped, trunk remains close to the ground, tapering down into a deep taproot that may reach from 10 to 15 ft. (3 to 4.5 m) in circumference. It has been estimated to live 1,000 years or more. Young plants produce two succulent cotyledons, and, at right angles to them, two low-lying twisted leathery leaves eventually 10 ft. (3 m) or more long that continue to grow from their base in the crown of the trunk while dying down at the tips. Male and female cones, 1 in. and 3-4 in. (2.54 cm and 7.6-10 cm), respectively, appear in clusters on separate plants at about the same time from January to April. After pollination by insects, the fertilized cones become woody as in conifers and the bracts turn bright red. Seeds mature in May and their broad wings allow them to be easily dispersed by the wind. In the considerable fog common at that time of year they germinate readily. Africans use the dried wood as firewood and the older trunks as seats. No other uses are known. In South Africa it is known as *nyanca-hycancop* and among the Hottentots as *gories*. Ficalho, *Plantas Uteis*, p. 276; EA; GEPB.

West African exploration Portugal was the first European nation to explore the West African coast. Early in the Discovery (q.v.), Gil Eanes reached Cape

Bojador (q.v.) in 1434 and in 1444 Portuguese navigators discovered Arguim (q.v.), an important commercial center at the time. This contact initiated the slave trade, first with Portugal then after 1550 with Brazil and the rest of the New World. In the seventeenth and eighteenth centuries England, France, Holland, and Denmark were attracted to the area to trade with African chiefs in slaves, gold, and ivory. In 1796, Mungo Park, sent by the English African Association, explored the course of the Niger River at Segu and proceeded 300 mi. (480 km) upstream to Bamako. This successful mission opened West Africa for nineteenth century commercial development, necessary after the abolition of the slave traffic in 1811 and the abolition of slavery itself in 1836. DHP; GEPB.

West African food crops The rise of the Sudanic states in West and Central Africa may be attributed in part to the variety of plants that provided abundant food for the growing population of the region. Among these were wild and cultivated grains including *fonio* (q.v.), sorghum, and millet, Guinea yams, water yams, okra, watermelon, calabash gourds, and kola. Sudanic crops with important commercial value include cotton, palm oil, palm kernel oil, and sesame. Lewicki, *West African Food*, pp. 108, 126; HDRGC. *See also* cassava, fonio, malagüeta, sorghum.

West African states, pre-Portuguese At their arrival at the Senegal River in 1444, the Portuguese found four historic chiefdoms: the Serer, Wolof, Fula, and Tokolor (qq.v.), all Islamized to various degrees. These Senegalese states were at the westernmost region of the continent. Toward the east there were the Soninke and Mandingo (qq.v.) states between the Niger and Senegal rivers, and the Songhai (q.v.) on the upper Niger. Trimingham, *A History of Islam*, p. 34. *See also* West African exploration.

Western Sudan The Portuguese came in contact with the Western Sudan in 1450 when they discovered the Senegal River. At the time this area was a loosely defined sub-Saharan territory extending to the Atlantic coast. In the eleventh century this area had been dominated by the empires of Ghana and Mali plus a number of amorphous agglomerations of indigenous groups having little in common except the vague recognition of a far-distant suzerain to whom they were vassals. Today the area comprises Guinea-Bissau and parts of the republics of Senegal, Gambia, and Upper Volta. Trimingham, *A History of Islam*, pp. 34, 36; GEPB; WNGD. *See also* Sudan; West African states, pre-Portuguese.

whaling industry in Angola Whale hunting began in Mossãmedes on the Atlantic coast c.1900. From about 1909, Norwegian and British whalers established shore factories in southwestern Africa to process their catches.

This led to a phenomenal boom in exports from Mossâmedes in the period between 1911 and 1915 which brought atypical profits to the colony and nearly succeeding in eliminating the southern Angolan trade deficit. This boom was short-lived because World War I and the development of factory ships combined to reduce the activities of shore factories to a very modest level after 1915. Clarence-Smith, *Slaves, Peasants*, p. 23.

whaling industry in Cape Verde   Whale hunting began off Cape Verde in 1675. By 1686, Portugal began to lease out whaling rights to capitalize on the foreign competition. A royal provision of March 14, 1732, regulated the trade in whale oil and collecting tithes on ambergris (q.v.). According to these regulations, whales were Crown property. From 1844 to 1891, American whalers based at the islands of Brava and São Nicolau were very active. Whaling disappeared from the area around 1915. Carreira, *The People*, pp. 42, 44, 45.

whaling industry in Portugal   Commercial whale hunting, centered in Lagos on the Algarve, had been an important activity since 1258. In 1367, King Fernando I imposed a tax to be paid to the Bishop of Silves by whalers in Tavira and Lagos. King João I granted Estevão Vasco Filipe permission to whale off the Algarve coast in 1424. After 1450, the whaling industry disappeared from the southern coast of Portugal. Godinho, *A Economia*, p. 33.

White Fathers in Mozambique   The White Fathers (Society of Missionaries of Africa) was founded by the French cardinal Charles Marie A. Lavigerie in 1868 to promote the conversion of Africans, especially Moslems, to the Catholic faith. The White Fathers, a French-speaking group, arrived in Mozambique around 1876. King Leopold II of Belgium requested the Holy See to trust to this order the newly founded Apostolic Vicariate of the Belgian Congo. Henriksen, *Mozambique*, pp. 13, 212, 215.

white women in Angola   The first European women known to have come to Luanda, Angola, arrived in 1595. All twelve were married to European men then in Angola, but only one left descendants. In 1772, the then-current governor of Angola was the first governor to bring his wife with him to Luanda. As late as 1902 there were only just over one hundred European women settled in the capital of the colony. Of all the women who came to Luanda in the colonial period only eight were wives of *degredados* (criminals deported to Angola). Hammond, *Portugal and Africa*, pp. 38-39.

Whydah   See Ouidah.

wimi (Kik.)   Fish poison used by fishermen in São Salvador do Congo, Angola, c.1880. BeAD

Windsor Treaty An Anglo-Portuguese accord signed on October 14, 1899, by which Portugal received loans from Britain and Germany for the development of her African colonies. As collateral, Portugal put up the custom duties from Angola and Mozambique. The treaty also allowed free navigation on the rivers and authorized Britain to transport war materiel through Portuguese possessions into the Transvaal, then in the midst of the Boer War. At the same time, Britain and Germany promised to protect Portuguese rights in Africa. DHP.

Windward Coast In the colonial period, this area comprised the Upper Guinea coast from Cape Palmas, Liberia, to the Saloum River north of Gambia. In the seventeenth century and later, this large area was variously known as the Grain Coast, the Malagüeta (pepper) Coast, and the Kwa-Kwa Coast. The Mali Empire that flourished between 1650 and 1750 was located in this loosely defined territory. At that time, Portugal established commercial relations with Mali to trade gold, ivory, and, most of all, slaves. Rodney, *The Guinea Coast*, CHA, Cambridge, 1975, 4:294; WNGD.

Wiriyamu (Afr.) An African village 16 mi. (26 km) south of Tete, Mozambique, where a large-scale massacre of African rebels by Portuguese security forces took place on December 6, 1972. This incident, reported by missionaries and subsequently published in European newspapers in July 1973, resulted in about 400 deaths. Henriksen, *Mozambique*, pp. 168, 214-5.

witch doctors in Mozambique Folk medicine practitioners involved in black magic were widespread in rural Mozambique in the 1970s. During the civil war (1975-1992) the leaders of RENAMO (q.v.) enlisted many witch doctors, often women, to help in the fight against the Marxist FRELIMO government. The witch doctors used rituals, spells, and charms to give courage and fearlessness to young fighters before they went into action. Andersson, *Mozambique*, pp. 61, 144.

witchcraft in Portugal, Africans and The practice of witchcraft and black magic was common in Portugal at the time of the Discovery (q.v.). After its founding in 1495 the Portuguese Inquisition often investigated cases of sorcery. One incident reported in 1560 involved Filipe Cruz, a freedmen from Setubal, who was accused before the Inquisition of having said that he had a lump on his little finger which he gave to Satan so that he now kept company with the Devil. Apparently the judges did not prosecute Cruz. In an other case, a female slave from Evora was called as a witness in a trial for invocation of devils. She condemned herself by admitting she knew one spell. The incantation was meant to bind in love a man and a woman and consisted of keeping one's eye fixed on the star nearest the moon and murmuring the words "Through her you must enter, and through her you must leave." The inquisitors held her for interrogation from 24 October 1551 until she died in prison the following May. There were numerous other cases involving African magic and unorthodox Christian practices. African witchcraft was a widespread tradition in what was once Portuguese Africa, and was brought to Portugal by African slaves. Saunders, *A Social History*, pp. 162-4; GEPB.

Witwatersrand gold fields An uplifted rocky region of Transvaal province, Republic of South Africa, and the most productive gold mining district in the world. The uplift runs in an east-west direction for about 62 mi. (95 km), has a maximum width of about 25 mi. (40 km), and reaches an elevation of more than 2,000 ft. (600 m) above the surrounding plateau. Surface gold was discovered in 1884 and active mining operations began in 1886. Since then, Mozambican laborers have migrated to work the mines. In 1894, Best and Williams (q.v.), a company from Lourenço Marques, organized the legal migration of Africans to work seasonally in these gold mines, known also as the Rand. Rita-Ferreira, *O Movimento Migratorio*, p. 74.

Witwatersrand Native Labour Association *See* WNLA.

WNLA (Witwatersrand Native Labour Association) A large organization, associated with the Transvaal Government and the Chamber of Mines, that recruited African workers from outside the Transvaal. Its operations extended to Mozambique, Malawi, and other regions. In 1906, the WNLA together with the Native Recruiting Corporation (q.v.) had about 200 recruiting posts in Mozambique alone. Rita-Ferreira, *O Movimento Migratorio*, p. 74.

Wolof slaves Venetian navigator Alvise Cadamosto, in the service of Prince Henry, came in contact with the Wolof people when he reached the Senegal River in 1454. Long before his arrival the Wolof had been Islamized, intermingling Moslem and animistic practices. Around 1490 slaves sold to the Portuguese by the Wolof were taken to Lisbon, Evora, and other cities. Some of these newcomers converted to Christianity yet still kept some attachment to their Moslem faith. In the 1550s a few became well known because they were accused of heresy before the Inquisition, as was the case of a slave called Amaçambat. Trimingham, *A History of Islam*, pp. 16, 29, 99.

Wolof state (Afr.) An Islamic chiefdom established around 1360 on the south bank of the mouth of the Senegal River 400 mi. (640 km) south of Cape Branco. It is in a flat countryside bounded on the east by the Tekrur (q.v.) state, on the south by the Gambia Kingdom, and on the west by the Atlantic. The Wolof people dominated the region from 1400 to 1450. Explorer Alvise

Cadamosto observed in 1454 that the Wolof, ruled by King Zuccolin, then 20 years old, mixed Moslem and animistic rituals. In 1500 the chiefdom was made a part of the Soninke Empire (q.v.), a group from the east. For many years the Portuguese bought slaves from the Wolof. Prestage, *The Portuguese Pioneers*, p. 107; Trimingham, *A History of Islam*, pp. 46, 47. *See also* Senegal River, Wolof slaves.

work songs   A revealing collection of extracts from songs and interviews with migrant workers in the Witwatersrand gold fields (q.v.) and their wives was made by Alpheus Manghezi in 1970. The miners described in their own words the sufferings and humiliations involved in the process of recruitment, the journey to South Africa, the working conditions, and the return home; their wives reported their stories of life without their husbands. There are two songs in particular, *Maghalangu* (Leaving for the Mines) and *Xikewembu xa Muhliwa* (Working in the Mines), both considered poignant and representative of the life of an African mine laborer. Work songs are well known in Mozambique. Darch, *Mozambique,* pp. 119, 209. *See also* Paiva song.

{ X }

Xa-Muteba (Afr.)   Town in northeastern Angola that in the colonial period (c.1500) was ruled by Lunda kings. It is in a prosperous cotton-producing area that in 1961 was greatly affected by the War for Independence (1960-1975). Miller, *Kings and Kinsmen,* p. 33.

Xandel (Afr.)   A modern African town in central Angola. President Francisco Higinio Craveiro Lopes of Portugal inaugurated a railroad terminal at Xandel in 1954. It is in a rich cotton-producing region where in 1955 COTONANG (q.v.) imposed the system of forced cotton cultivation. African farmers were obliged to produce cotton and to sell the harvest at fixed prices imposed by the government. From 1961 until it was abolished in 1969 this policy resulted in bloody rebellions and the jailing of many opponents. Pelissier, *La Colonie,* pp. 480, 414(n), 561.

Xarife (Pg.)   In Guinea-Bissau, the title given to a pious Moslem after his third visit to Mecca, an honor that entitles him to wear a green turban. GEPB.

Xa-Xa (Afr.)   In Ouidah (q.v.) c.1820, the chief representative of the king of Dahomey. In 1821 Felix de Sousa, a Brazilian slaver and city merchant was appointed governor of the trade center. King Gezo (1818-58) considered Sousa his white brother, in charge of the administration of the port. Polanyi, *Dahomey,* p. 136.

Xai-Xai   *See* João Belo.

xémã (Afr.)   In Cape Verde, a medicinal bath taken by women after giving birth. It is prepared by boiling *bafureira* (q.v.) leaves. Ficalho, *Plantas Uteis,* p. 257.

xerafine (Pg.)   A Portuguese silver coin that circulated in Mozambique c.1600. Its official worth was 300 *reis,* but it varied greatly in weight and intrinsic value. It was also called a *pardau.* Boxer, *Portuguese Society,* p. 116.

Xhosa (Bant.)   A Bantu group settled in southern Mozambique and South Africa long before the arrival of the Portuguese. In June 1522 sailors of the caravel *São João,* wrecked on the Indian Ocean coast, met a group of Xhosa for the first time. Later in the colonial period the Xhosa migrated to the Zambezian region in the north. Today there are several subgroups, each with different names. Their social organization is matrilineal; men raise cattle and women work in agriculture. In 1970 the number of Xhosa in Portuguese Africa was unknown, but there were 2.5 million in Trankeis, their homeland in South Africa. Isaacman, *Mozambique: The Tradition*, p. 189; SESA.

xibalo *See* chibalo.

xica (Kik.) In São Salvador do Congo, Angola, c.1880, the action of beating a drum, blowing a wind instrument, or firing a gun. BeAD.

Xicapa (Afr.) A river that rises in Alto Xicapa on the northern border of Angola and empties into the Cassai River. It forms the northern frontier between Angola and Zaire. GEPB.

Xicongo (Bant.) An African ethnic group settled in the Congo, northern Angola, when the Portuguese arrived in 1482. At the time, the Xicongo was comprised of Congos, Iacas, Pombos, Sucos, Sussos, Sorongos, and Zombos. They identified themselves with the centralized monarchy established in São Salvador do Congo around 1490. During the colonial period they unified the kingdom and inspired a strong nationalism centered on the monarchy. In modern Angola, the Xicongo rallied with the Portuguese to combat the nationalists during the War for Independence between 1960 and 1975. Henderson, *Angola*, pp. 41-2.

Xicongussa (Afr.) A plain in Morrumbene municipality, Inhambane district, southern Mozambique, where in 1888 chief Gungunhana fought and defeated the Portuguese army. GEPB.

Xiconhoca (Afr.) "The Snake." A character in a play entitled *La Sagrada Familia, ou Critica do Javali, do Camaleo, e Don Xiconhoca* (The Holy Family, or, The Judgment of the Boar, the Chameleon, and Mr. Xiconhoca). In this highly political piece, the boar with his nose always in the trough represents greed, the chameleon with ever-changing colors represents opportunism, and Xiconhoca is a universally understood character representing treacherous collaboration with the enemy. This play was presented by the Theatre Group of FRELIMO (q.v.) formed at Nachingwea in southern Tanzania in the 1970s. Darch, *Mozambique,* p. 271.

Xiconhoca o Inimigo (Pg.) "Chico Nhoca, the Enemy." A highly esteemed volume of popular political cartoons built around the character Xiconhoca (q.v.), who represents everything that Mozambicans consider politically and socially undesirable. Xiconhoca is a parasite, a bureaucrat who complicates the life of the people, and an agent of the enemy. Darch, *Mozambique,* p. 264.

xidi (Kik.) A frog having a very dark back and light yellow belly found in São Salvador do Congo, Angola. BeAD.

ximbi (Kik.) The word for a nymph, used in São Salvador do Congo, Angola, c.1880. BeAD.

xina (Kik.) Wealth acquired in trade, a term used in São Salvador do Congo, Angola, c.1880. BeAD.

Xinge (Afr.) An ethnic group settled in the northeast Cuango-Cassai province of Angola who were greatly influenced by the Katanga rebellions and the French Zaire independence movement. These isolated Africans were sympathetic to the UPA (q.v.) and took part in the 1961 uprising centered in the cotton territory of Malange. Pelissier, *La Colonie,* pp. 593, 608.

Xipaminine (Afr.) A suburb of Lourenço Marques, Mozambique, built in 1921 for a small number of *assimilados* (q.v.) who were legally entitled to register their property and to rent out apartments. In Xipaminine, as opposed to Munhuanna, the nearby complex built ten years later, property had higher value and rents exceeded the monthly salary of middle-range civil servants. This meant that only the most affluent *assimilados* could afford to live there. Although the residents had been promised free water, a garden, a market, and regular bus service, they had to pay for water, the garden never materialized, and the bus rates were so exorbitant that most had to walk to work. Isaacman, *Mozambique: From Colonialism,* pp. 57, 58.

Xire River *See* Shire River.

xirja (Xir.) Among the Xirongas of Mozambique, the grave plus the area around an abandoned hut, left empty after its owner's death. To define this area was a traditional practice among the Xirongas until the 1950s. DX.

xirjamba (Xir.) Among the Xirongas in southern Mozambique, a family vegetable garden worked either by the husband or his sons. This tradition persisted until c.1950. DX.

Xironga (Bant.) A Tonga dialect spoken in the Maputo district by about 100,000 people in 1906. Also called *landim.* DX.

xisense (Xir.) The residue or lees left in a bottle of an alcoholic beverage. The Xirongas considered this the best drink, suitable only for a chief or a person of honor in the community. DX.

xivu (Kik.) The cool season that begins about May 15 in the area of São Salvador do Congo, Angola. BeAD.

xiwaywayo (Xir.) A beverage prepared from fermented sugar cane juice and molasses, popular among Xirongas in southern Mozambique around 1950. DX.

xixi (Kik.) Partially burned firewood or charcoal in São Salvador do Congo, Angola, c.1880. BeAD.

xoem (Ar.) "Regiment." A Moorish army unit operating in North Africa at the time of the Discovery (q.v.). After the Portuguese conquered Ceuta in 1415, this type of Moorish guerrilla force attacked the city several times. GEPB.

xoqua (Afr.) In Mozambique, a tribal ordeal (q.v.) in which the accused was exposed to physical dangers from which he was supposed to be divinely protected if he were innocent. Ficalho, *Plantas Uteis*, p. 166. *See also* muave, tanguin.

X-Ray Code name for a South African column that on December 11, 1975, took the town of Luso in southwest Angola. For a while it seemed possible that the X-Ray Column might be able to push eastward from Luso, a railway station, to the border of Zaire. This action was planned by Jonas M. Savimbi, leader of UNITA (q.v.), with the idea of using the railway to bring troops and supplies from Zaire and Zambia. Bridgland, *Jonas Savimbi, A Key to Africa,* p. 144.

xuanga (Afr.) An involuntary slave on a *prazo* in Zambezia, Mozambique, c.1600. GEPB. *See also* voluntary slavery.

Xupanga (Afr.) An African village in the Beira district, central Mozambique, where Mary Moffat Livingstone, the wife of David Livingstone, died and was buried on April 27, 1862. GEPB.

xylophone (Gr.) The generic name for a type of African musical instrument quite widespread in Angola, Congo, Central Africa, and elsewhere and having many local names. It consists of a series of wooden bars graduated in length so as to sound the notes of a scale when struck with small wooden hammers. GEPB.

{ Y }

Yaka (Bant.)   A subgroup of Congo people settled in Zaire, Uige, and Cabinda in northern Angola under the rule of the Manicongo (q.v.) when the Portuguese arrived in 1483. The Yaka remained isolated until the nineteenth century. Around 1920 they rejected Portugal's domination and forced labor policy. They took part in the War for Independence against the Portuguese. Today the Yaka, the third largest group in Angola, still remember the once-great state of the Manicongo, a unifying factor and source of inspiration. HDA.

yam (Afr.)   The edible starchy tuberous root of any of several tropical climbing plants (genus *Dioscorea*), including *D. cayennensis* and *D. rotundata*, that grows wild and is widely cultivated in Angola and elsewhere in West Africa. In the Western Sudan yam cultivation is presumed to be very ancient because there are over 200 known varieties. Lewicki, *West African Food*, pp. 21, 50, 54, 161; GEPB. *See also* sweet potato.

"Yana!" (Afr.)   "Let them come!" An expression used by President Samora Machel of Mozambique, in a speech given on February 14, 1981, in the Matola district of Maputo after a bloody attack by South African forces in which twelve political exiles, members of the African National Congress, were killed. Mozambican writer Samuel Munguanmbe, Jr., took the slogan "Yana!" as the refrain to a song he composed. The song is slow and sad, yet powerful, accompanied by a simple acoustic guitar that allows the listener to concentrate on the often highly political words. The song became popular and was sung in political meetings, schools, and the streets of cities and villages. Darch, *Mozambique*, p. 267.

Yangowe (Afr.)   An African settlement on the Indian Ocean near Sofala where Pero de Anaia and his soldiers took refuge in 1505 after being attacked by Kaffir warriors. Welch, *South Africa under King Manuel*, p. 235.

yanvalou (Afr.)   A sacred dance from Angola brought by early Yoruba slaves to the New World, including Cuba, Brazil, and Haiti. In Haiti *yanvalou* is a ritual dance that honors Legba, guardian of crossroads, highways, and the entrances of houses, yards, and gardens. Legba is one of the most important deities in the Voodoo pantheon. Jahn, *Muntu,* pp. 39, 42-3; DALAC.

Yao (Afr.) A Bantu group settled in the Niassa district between the Lugenda and the Rovuma Rivers, west of the Cabo Delgado in Mozambique. In the eighteenth and nineteenth centuries the Yao controlled the local slave trade and acted as middlemen for Arab traders, exchanging ivory and iron for cloth, ornaments, and eventually firearms. Their long contact with Moslem traders influenced their decision to adopt Islam, wear Arab dress, and accept customs and social manners compatible with Islamized Bantu culture. In 1859, because of internal struggles, attacks by the Ngoni, and locust plagues, some of them moved to Tanzania and Malawi. In Yao villages the huts are not round, but rectangular, additional evidence of their long association with Arabs. The Yao have intermixed with the Nyanja and Ngoni as well as Arabs, and this heterogenous composition contributes to friendly relations with their neighbors. In 1970, the Yao numbered 175,000; Henriksen, *Mozambique*, p. 247-8.

Yao Grammar (Afr.) A scholarly work on African linguistics written by W.H. Whiteley (Oxford, Clarendon Press, 1966). It is important for its conceptual approach and the material it provides on the Yao language, widely spoken in northern Mozambique, Malawi, and southern Tanzania. Whiteley describes the elements that are used to build sentences, their grammatical relationships, and a range of sentence types. Darch, *Mozambique,* p. 109.

yaws An infectious tropical disease caused by a spirochete (*Treponema pertenue*) closely related to that of syphillis (q.v.). Yaws is characterized by a primary ulcerated lesion on the skin followed by a secondary stage in which ulcers develop all over the body. In the tertiary stage the bones are affected. This disease was well known in Portugal by 1490. In 1498 King Manuel I issued detailed regulations for the treatment of this illness by the *Casa das Boubas* (Clinic for Ulcerative Disease) that was attached to the *Hospital de Todos-os-Santos* (q.v.) in Lisbon. Yaws was widespread among Africans in Mozambique and Angola after 1500. At the time it was known as *Polypapilloma tropicum*. For a long time this disease was considered to have originated in Africa; now it is known to be pantropical. In Portuguese, yaws is called *framboesa*. GEPB; WTNID.

yellow fever A tropical and subtropical viral disease transmitted by a mosquito (*Aedes aegypti*) and characterized by sudden onset, prostration, fever, relatively slow pulse, albuminuria, jaundice, and a tendency to hemorrhage, especially from the stomach. The first yellow fever epidemic in Luanda and Massangano was in 1595 and the next in 1860. Today it has been established that the area in which the infection occurs includes a broad belt in Central Africa, bounded in the north by the Sahara and extending across Angola, the Congo, northern parts of Zambia, Tanzania, Uganda, Kenya, the southern Sudan, and Ethiopia. It is known that the infection was endemic among forest animals, particularly primates and monkeys, and that it was spread among them by forest mosquitoes. It is also called yellow jack. *Revista Medica de Angola*, Luanda, 1923, 2:433; SESA. *See also* malaria, sleeping sickness.

Yemaya (Yor.)   In Angola and elsewhere, a Yoruban female deity often identified with the sea. In Nigeria, Yemaya was considered the mother of all things and a symbol of fertility. Yoruba slaves brought her cult to Brazil and Cuba. Today in Afro-Cuban rituals, Yemaya, or Yemanya, is honored as the goddess of rivers and springs. A ritual dance performed in her honor imitates the waves of the sea to which Yemaya surrenders herself then rumbles and rolls until she becomes a hurricane. Jahn, *Muntu,* pp. 65, 95; DALAC.

yevogan (Afr.)   In the colonial period in Ouidah (q.v.), Dahomey, a high official of the local king, a position created in 1733 during a period of great commercial activity in Dahomey. The *yevogan* supervised trade and foreign traders, collected taxes from all ships in the port and the sale of the local king's slaves, and inspected coastal areas to prevent smuggling. He was a powerful and trusted official. Sometimes he is referred to as the viceroy of Ouidah. The *yevogan*'s power and influence greatly decreased by the end of the eighteenth century although the most famous *yevogan* was the Afro-Brazilian Francisco de Sousa, appointed in 1818, a man considered eminently trustworthy. HDB.

ye-ye (Afr.)   *See* African dances in Portugal.

yoboro (Man.)   The onion (*Allium cepa*), a member of the lily family having an edible bulb with a strong sharp smell. It is widely cultivated in the Western Sudan by the Mandingos, Fulani, and other groups. *Yoboro* cultivation was noted by the Portuguese in the Mali state in the fourteenth century and in the middle of the nineteenth century in Timbuctu and in the nearby town of Kabara, not far from Mandingo country. The remarkable number of local names given to this plant in Senegal and the middle Niger testifies to the long-standing and very widespread cultivation and consumption of onions in these areas. Lewicki, *West African Food*, pp. 58-9.

Yombe (Bant.)   A Bantu subgroup settled in northern Angola. At the arrival of the Portuguese in 1483, the Yombe were subjects of the Manicongo (q.v.). Like many other African groups, they fought Portuguese rule and fiercely opposed the slave trade in the colonial period. In the twentieth century the Yombe took part in the War for Independence. The memory of the Congo kings, still alive among the Yombes, is a unifying link among them. HDA.

Yoruba (Afr.)   The Yoruba were united by a common language and cultural base but were divided politically into independent kingdoms at the time the Portuguese came in contact with them c. 1450. Even before their contact with Europeans, the Yoruba grew cotton, wove cloth, smelted iron, practiced smithery, cast bronze, and made glass. The Yoruba produced the greatest wealth of art of any African people, and the ancient bronze castings at the Yoruba city of Ife rank among the great artistic masterpieces of the world. In the region occupied by the Yoruba in Nigeria, Portuguese explorers introduced such New World plants as maize, manioc, and beans, today staple crops. Historically the Portuguese, long before the English and Dutch, dominated the slave traffic to the New World plantations. In the nineteenth century Yoruba slaves were taken in large numbers to Brazil and Cuba where the Yoruba language is still spoken and their deities still worshipped. Today they are the third largest ethnic group in West Africa, mostly settled in the western region of Nigeria and numbering over ten million. EA; GEPB; HDB.

Yufi (Afr.) An ancient area of gold mining, today identified with Mashonaland in Zimbabwe, from which Bantu people led by Arab traders brought gold and ivory to Kilwa (q.v.) on the Indian Ocean. The Portuguese arrived at Sofala and Kilwa in 1520 and took control of the trade originating at Yufi. Welch, *Europe's Discovery*, pp. 53, 281.

yuka (Afr.) In Angola and elsewhere, a sacred dance apparently brought by slaves from Nigeria to Brazil and Cuba. In Africa, it was a dance of the Ekue secret society of the Efik, identified with tilling the fields, building roads, and casting iron. It was also associated with a deity who protected the growth of grains and food plants. In the New World, Yuka is a goddess identified with the sea, somewhat similar to the Yoruba goddess Yemaya (q.v.). This dance was particularly enjoyed by slaves in the Caribbean. Around 1698 Père Labat, a French missionary in the West Indies, described the dance as "highly obscene that decent masters should forbid their slaves to dance." Jahn, *Muntu*, pp. 79, 81-82, 95; DALAC.

Yuphuro (Afr.) A Mozambican musical group considered one of the best of their type. Their music is firmly rooted both melodically and linguistically in the local traditions of their home area, Nampula, in the north. It should be noted that Mozambican popular music has been dominated for many years by musicians from the south, especially speakers of Chopi and Shanganan. Yuphuro has toured in western and eastern Europe with great success. The band has recently taken to spelling its name Eyuphuro. Darch, *Mozambique*, p. 26.

Yusuf (Ar.) A Portuguese fortress built on the site of a Moslem sheikdom of the same name at Sofala on the Indian Ocean, it is one of the oldest and most famous European fortifications in southeast Africa. The surrounding African people spoke Shona and kept cattle, used iron implements, and ate meat, fish, and shellfish. Vasco da Gama arrived at Yusuf in 1498 and was surprised by the skeikdom's wealth and comfort. Darch, *Mozambique*, p. 35; GEPB.

{ Z }

Zaara (Ar.) An Arab village on the far side of the Benegorfate Mountains five leagues from Arzila (q.v.), taken by the Portuguese in 1471. They fortified the town and it served as base for their expansion in North Africa early in the Discovery (q.v.). GEPB.

zaburro Any of various tropical annual grasses called sorghum (q.v.) (*Sorghum vulagare* and other *Sorghum* spp.) found in Angola and elsewhere in Africa. Sorghum is closely related to millet (q.v.) and New World maize (q.v.) or corn (*Zea mays*). Lewicki, *African Food*, p. 26; GEPB.

zaia (Afr.) Any of several varieties of the New World manioc (genus *Manihot*) of the spurge family, having edible starchy roots. The Spanish found it cultivated by the Arawaks in the Caribbean. It was brought to Europe and Africa and soon became a dietary staple among Africans and colonists. GEPB.

Zaire (Afr.) Formerly the old kingdom of Congo in northern Angola. The Portuguese arrived in this area in 1483 and founded São Salvador do Congo which has remained the capital of the district up to the present. In the colonial period this area was developed by Portuguese colonists and African farmers. In the eighteenth century the city of São Salvador do Congo fell into decay and remained so until around 1860 when coffee plantations were established in the area. Soon commerce and trade greatly expanded, bringing prosperity to the region. In 1940 many acres of land formerly owned and cultivated by African farmers were bought by Portuguese and other European colonists despite Portuguese laws that protected African lands. Subsequently, numerous bush stores burgeoned. During the War for Independence, the Zaire district was one of the most active anti-Portuguese centers in Angola. In 1970 the district had a population of 41,766. GEPB; HDA.

Zala (Afr.) An Angolan administrative post in Luanda district populated mainly by Dembos people who have been highly influenced by the Portuguese since the sixteenth century. Coffee was introduced around 1850 and today Zala is a densely populated and prosperous area with numerous coffee plantations. Pelissier, *La Colonie*, pp. 505, 626-7.

Zalala (Afr.)   A large coffee plantation located near Carmona in the northwest Luanda district. In 1960, under the political leadership of the UPA (q.v.), Zalalan Africans formed well-organized opposition groups made up of workers and farmers to fight for the independence of Angola, obtained in 1975. Pelissier, *La Colonie*, pp. 503, 636.

zalale (Afr.)   Dense tropical forest and source of sleeping sickness, located in the hinterland of the Quelimane district in Mozambique. In 1933 the French commercial Madal Society (q.v.) cleared the region for cultivation. Draft animals and machinery were introduced to this vast territory and it was transformed into a large-scale plantation for copra and foodstuffs. Vail, *Capitalism*, p. 256.

Zambezi Company (Afr.)   This was one of the largest Mozambican commercial corporations. It was organized in 1892 without a charter and occupied today's Tete and Zambezi districts, regions of good agricultural land and the heart of the traditional *prazo* system. In 1917 the company was attacked by Barué irregular forces, but soon the Portuguese government restored order and the company continued its operations. In 1928 the Zambezi Company along with other companies, was asked by the Salazar government to surrender its contract to the government in return for compensation. From the beginning, the company subcontracted a number of its *prazos* to specific agricultural firms. One of the most successful was a British concern, the Sena Sugar Estates. They had mills on both sides of the lower Zambezi producing sugar and distilling alcohol until 1960. Henriksen, *Mozambique*, pp. 105, 109.

Zambezi Consortium   *See* ZAMCO.

Zambezi district (Afr.)   An administrative post created in 1933 with its seat in Mopeia (q.v.) on the lower Zambezi River, Mozambique. In the nineteenth century the Zambezi district comprised the whole basin of the Zambezi and Limpopo rivers. By the early twentieth century, the term was restricted to mean only the Zambezi basin. In 1935 the government put African chiefs in charge of groups of villages with the obligation of providing cheap labor for the plantations and to collect taxes so heavy that they forced many Africans to flee to nearby countries to escape the tax laws. The district had a population in 1980 of 2,500,200. GEPB; WNGD. *See also* ZAMCO.

Zambezi, voluntary slavery in   From 1750 to 1850, voluntary, or domestic, slavery and the manumission of slaves were fully institutionalized in Tete, Sena, and other towns in the region. Slave status was never more than one generation deep. This customary form of domestic servitude was accepted by the *prazo* (q.v.) system and in the Moslem sheikdoms in northern Mozambique. Isaacman, *Mozambique*, pp. 47-48, 50-1; HDM. *See also* voluntary slavery.

Zambezi Navigation Company   A corporation founded in 1912 by J.P. Hornung to control the transportation of sugar, rum, and other products along the Zambezi from the interior to the port of Chinde on the Indian Ocean coast. The share capital was equally divided between the Sena Sugar Company (q.v.) and J.P. Hornung himself. The new company guaranteed to carry all Sena Sugar Company products at an agreed charge of 10 shillings per ton from Caia to Chinde and 6 shillings per ton from Marromeu to Chinde. Vail, *Capitalism*, pp. 152-3. *See also* Zambezi Company.

Zambezi partition   In 1891 the vast territory along the Zambezi River was divided between England and Portugal. Land west of the Zumbo village and the region covered by the Luanga River north of the Zambezi became British. Soon after, this region was granted to the South African Company for development. In 1902 an administrative post was established by the company in the Luanga Valley. For many years this territory was dominated by the British settler John Harrison. Newitt, *Portuguese Settlement*, pp. 308-9.

Zambezi province   This province was established at the end of the nineteenth century with Quelimane as its capital. In 1900 it comprised all the Zambezi region in Mozambique from Tete to the Indian Ocean about 250 mi. (400 km) away. Along the course of the Zambezi there were many *prazos* on both banks. In 1942 it included the municipalities of Quelimane, Chinde, Maganja da Costa, Mopeia, and Vila Junqueiro. In 1945 Quelimane had a population of 1,000,000 of which only 4,500 were whites. GEPB.

Zambezi River (Afr.)   A river in southern Central Africa about 1,700 mi. (2,700 km) long, flowing from northwestern Zambia south across Angola to the border of Botswana. It then turns east to form the boundary between Zambia and Zimbabwe, crosses central Mozambique, and empties into Mozambique Channel at Chinde. It is navigable in three long stretches, separated by rapids and Victoria Falls. It has many headstreams in the marshlands of southeastern Angola and western Zambia. The first European to reach the mouth of the river was Vasco da Gama on January 22, 1498. He named it *Sinais de Deu* (God's Miracle). The Portuguese soon began trading with the interior and in 1531 established a fair at a town on the river about 150 mi. (240 km) from the sea. A few years later as trade increased, the Portuguese founded Sena and Tete, located about 250 mi. (400 km) from the coast. The first European explorer to reach the upper Zambezi was the Scot, David Livingstone, in 1851. He came near Linyanti Falls and later traveled downstream where on

January 22, 1855, he discovered Victoria Falls, which he named for Queen Victoria. In 1858, Livingstone sailed up the river from the coast on the steamboat *Ma Robert*, reaching the lower end of the gorge which he referred to as Kebrabasa, today Cabora Bassa (q.v.). GEPB; SESA; WNGD.

Zambezi wars   These wars between *prazeros* (q.v.) and African, mostly Afro-Portuguese, chiefs took place in the period between 1840 and 1902 in the territory stretching on both sides of the Zambezi River from the Indian Ocean coast inland to Zumbo and beyond (q.v.). The major Afro-Portuguese warlords involved in these conflicts were referred to collectively as the Pereiras, Cruzes, Sousas, and Vas do Anjos. The most prominent of these was Manuel Antonio da Sousa. By 1870 the Portuguese government ended these protracted struggles by introducing a system of direct administration. All the *prazos* were nationalized and rented to private companies, putting an end to these conflicts. Henriksen, *Mozambique*, p. 78-89, 109; GEPB.

Zambia (Afr.)   Portuguese commercial penetration in the colonial period involved three regions of modern Zambia: the basins of the Kafue, the Luangwa River and the upper Zambezi River including the Shire Valley, and the Mashonaland (q.v.) high velt. These were all areas explored and controlled by the Portuguese in the 1600s, long before England and other European countries began competing for Africa. In the Shire region, Scottish missionaries (q.v.) established an unofficial frontier in 1889 that Portugal tried unsuccessfully to overcome. The Shire area was later known as Northern Rhodesia and was administered by the British South Africa Company from 1889 to 1923, when it became a British colony. The rush to seize Mashonaland was the work of Joaquim Paiva de Andrada who, with the assistance of local warlords, tried to occupy Mashonaland in 1890. In 1892 Cecil John Rhodes, a British financier operating in South Africa, moved in and occupied the territory. Zambia, a member of the Federation of Rhodesia and Nyassaland from 1953 to 1963, became an independent republic in 1970. Newitt, *Portugal in Africa*, pp. 28-9; GEPB; WNGD.

ZAMCO (Zambezi Consortium)   A corporation headed by South Africa with Portuguese and Southern Rhodesian capital, established in the 1950s to dam the Zambezi River at Caboro Bassa (q.v.). The plans entailed the creation of a man-made lake 115 mi. (185 km) long with a width of 10 to 20 mi. (16 to 32 km), creating a formidable barrier to southward infiltration and cutting Tete province in half. The hydroelectric energy the dam produced would feed into the South African grid. ZAMCO thought that this huge undertaking would ensure increased support for Portugal's military effort against FRELIMO. While the dam was under construction, guerrillas attacked it unsuccessfully in 1964 and 1968. Munslow, *Mozambique*, p. 46; GEPB.

Zangado (Afr.) A *musseque* (slum) southeast of Luanda that in 1960 was populated by poor Africans living in shacks without running water or electricity. Pelissier, *La Colonie*, p. 339(n).

Zangala (Afr.) A crowded *musseque* (slum) in southeast Luanda with poorly built huts lacking water, electricity, or roads. In 1960 most of its residents were Angolans and refugees from nearby countries. Pelissier, *La Colonie*, p. 339.

Zanzibar (Ar.) An old Arab trade center on an island off modern Tanzania, taken by the Portuguese in 1506. By 1580 it had a large European population engaged in trading gold, ivory, and slaves. In 1698 Ottoman Arabs drove off the Portuguese and occupied the town, Under their control it attained its greatest historical importance. By 1842 it had become an important slave trade center. In 1873 the British pressured the Sultan to close the slave market. It became a British Protectorate in 1890 and on January 12, 1964, part of the Republic of Tanzania. Axelson, *Portuguese in East-Africa*, p. 35; GEPB.

zaonia (Afr.) In Guinea-Bissau and elsewhere, a center with a mosque, school, and facilities for social services. Usually it is a place where members of Moslem brotherhoods meet to observe such occasions as Ramadan and others. Gonçalves, *O Islamismo*, p. 162.

zecchin (It.) A Venetian copper coin that circulated in Mombasa, East Africa, c.1776. Freeman-Grenville, *East African Coins*, JAH, Cambridge, 1960, I(1):40. *See also* larin, thaler.

Zenza (Afr.) A river that rises in west-central Angola south of Carmona and flows south, emptying into the Bengo River west of Luanda, Angola. It irrigates a rich coffee plantation region in Cuanza Norte. This territory was a center of nationalist guerrillas during the War for Independence from 1960 to 1975. Pelissier, *La Colonie*, pp. 603, 629-637.

Zenze do Lucula (Afr.) An African village in Cabinda, northern Angola, where in 1961 nationalist forces under the leadership of Alexander Tary organized a strong resistance to the Portuguese government. Pelissier, *La Colonie*, p. 563.

Ziguinchor (Afr.) A Portuguese settlement on the Casamance River north of Guinea-Bissau in modern Senegal. Around 1800 this was an important slave trading center under Portuguese control. Mandingo and Fula slaves were brought from the hinterland and sold in local markets to Portuguese slavers for the New World plantations. Newitt, *Portugal in Africa*, pp. 4-5.

zimba (Afr.) (1)   In Mozambique and elsewhere, a divided tray consisting of two squares. It is used by miners to wash soil and gravel in search of gold and other precious metals. Isaacman, *Mozambique: TheAfricanization*, p. 71.

Zimba (Afr.) (2)   A Bantu ethnic group that had settled in the Malawi Kingdom south of Lake Malawi long before the arrival of the Portuguese in 1500. In the 1850s internal struggle forced them to migrate to the area called the middle Zambezi. In 1900 Portuguese chroniclers spoke of a Zimba community in the Tete region. In 1917 during the Barué War, the Zimbas joined other groups rebelling against the Portuguese. Henriksen, *Mozambique*, pp. 12, 51, 108.

Zimbabwe (Afr.)   Originally part of the old Monomotapa Kingdom (q.v.), the area was explored by the Portuguese in 1505 and described by Diogo de Alcaçova in 1506. Dominican missionaries established missions in the area in the colonial period. Between 1850 and 1890 it was known as Mashonaland (q.v.), the area where Cecil John Rhodes obtained mining concessions in 1888. This region was under the administration of the British South Africa Company beginning in 1889 and became the British colony of Southern Rhodesia in 1923, then an independent republic in 1970. In 1969 it had adopted the name of Zimbabwe. DHP; WNGD. *See also* Zimbabwe ruins Zimbabwe settlement.

Zimbabwe ruins   A broad term applied to numerous groups of ruins scattered in Southern Rhodesia (now Zimbabwe), northern Transvaal, and Botswana. Generally, however, the term refers to Great Zimbabwe, a place 16 mi. (26 km) southeast of Fort Victoria in west-central Mashonaland (q.v.). In 1505 this area was explored by the Portuguese, who called it Monomotapa (q.v.). These ruins still hold unsolved mysteries regarding their builders and their history. The remains indicate that this was an important bartering center where gold and ivory was exchanged for European goods most likely brought from the Indian Ocean coast. Archaeologists have recovered Dutch gin bottles, Arab glass, Venetian beads, and numerous gold and iron ornaments of African origin. All these items appear to be from the sixteenth and seventeenth centuries. GEPB; SESA.

Zimbabwe settlement   Early in the sixteenth century, the Portuguese built a fort in Central Africa with a garrison and a mission to protect the Monomotapa Kingdom (q.v.) and convert pagans. Around 1758 the government reorganized the administration of the town, built barracks, a church, and facilities for the missionaries. In 1760 Portugal withdrew the garrison but kept the missionaries to take care of the spiritual needs of the people and educate the young. At the time the missionaries were charged with crowning Monomotapa kings, a ritual a new king felt necessary to be recognized as ruler. In 1823 the military post was re-established and Caetano Camillo Vas dos Anjos, a militia colonel, was appointed commandant of the garrison. Newitt, *Portuguese Settlement*, pp. 72, 118, 152, 174.

zimbo (Afr.)   In Angola, a small trumpet-shaped marine shell used in the Luanda region as currency in the fifteenth and sixteenth centuries. In 1574 King Sebastião granted Captain Paulo Dias de Novais a monopoly to harvest *zimbo* shells south of the Dande River. These shells were also called *buzio*. Caetano, *Os Nativos*, p. 102. *See also* cowrie.

zo (Kik.)   A small lot set aside to cultivate fodder for horses and cattle in São Salvador do Congo c.1880. BeAD.

zumbi (Kik.)   A fetish which was supposed to bring good luck to its worshipper. It used in São Salvador do Congo c.1880. BeAD.

Zumbo fair (Afr.)   A trade center established around 1716 in the village of Zumbo at the confluence of the Luangwa and the Zambezi rivers beyond Cabora Bassa Falls. It was frequented by Portuguese, Goan, Moslem, and itinerant African traders who exchanged gold, ivory, rock crystal, and wax for cloth, guns, gunpowder, and liquor. Located in a region of seasonal and permanent mining camps, it attracted traders from central Africa eager to trade goods with coastal merchants. At the end of the eighteenth century, increasing unrest and anarchy began to disturb the traders, and in 1836 it was closed due to the chaos created by wars among local chiefs. Newitt, *Portuguese Settlement*, pp. 75-9.

Zumbo, Vila do (Afr.)   A settlement founded in 1716 at the confluence of the Luangwa and Zambezi rivers by Francisco Rodrigues, a Portuguese merchant from Goa. Portugal declared it a vila (town) on April 27, 1763. Because it was established on the north-south trade route along the Zambezi, it became the chief point of contact between Portuguese and African traders c.1840. Portuguese traders were not allowed to penetrate beyond this town. When David Livingstone visited the region in 1853, Zumbo had disappeared altogether. Because it had been the closest town to the Angolan border, it was rebuilt in 1861 by Albino Manuel Pacheco, the military commander of Tete district. Although Zumbo was attacked by African chiefs in 1917, it soon after became an important center for cattle and agriculture of all kinds, growing rice, wheat, beans, sweet potatoes, and other produce. Today it is an administrative post where commerce and trade are carried on with neighboring countries such as Zambia and Zimbabwe. Newitt, *Portuguese Settlement*, pp. 79, 215, 296; GEPB.

Zunga e Nkimba (Kik.) The ritual of initiation into the mysteries of Nkimba (q.v.), a secret society in São Salvador do Congo c. 1880. BeAD.

zuza (Kik.) Meat preserved by drying it over a fire, in São Salvador do Congo around 1880. BeAD.

BIBLIOGRAPHY

BIBLIOGRAPHY

I.   Encyclopedias, Dictionaries, Glossaries, Journals

ACR   Africa Contemporary Record, Annual Survey. New York, London: Africana Publishing Company, 1981.

Africa   Africa, the Journal of the International African Institute. London: Oxford University Press, 1928-

ASOS   Africa South of the Sahara. London: Europa Publications, 1983.

BCG   Boletim Cultural da Guinea Portuguesa. Porto, Portugal: 1966.

BeAD   Bentley, W. Holman. Appendix to the Dictionary and Grammar of the Kongo Language as Spoken at San Salvador, the Ancient Capital of the Old Kongo Empire, West Africa. London: Kegan Paul, 1895.

BICAP   Boletim de Informação de Cabo Verde. Praia, Cape Verde: 1960.

BPICV   Boletim de Propaganda e Informação. Praia, Cape Verde: 1949.

CE   Columbia Encyclopedia. New York: Columbia University Press, 1963.

CEA   Cambridge Encyclopedia of Africa. London: Cambridge University Press, 1981.

CHA   Cambridge History of Africa. London: Cambridge University Press, 1975.

Claridade: Revista de Arte e Letras. Mindelo, Cape Verde: March 1937, January 1947, September 1947, July, 1948, December 1949, May 1958, December 1960.

DAHB   Dictionary of African Historical Biography. Mark R. Lipschutz and R. Kent Ramussen, eds. Berkeley: University of California Press, 1986.

DALAC   Dictionary of Afro-Latin American Civilization. Benjamin Núñez, ed. Westport, Conn.: Greenwood Press, 1980.

DEI   Dizionario Enciclopedico Italiano. Rome: Institutto della Enciclopedia Italiano, 1961.

DHP   Dicionario de Historia de Portugal. Joel Serrão, A.A. Doria, et al., eds. Lisbon: Iniciativas Editoriais, 1971.

DI   Dictionary of Islam: Being a Cyclopaedia, Ceremonies, and Customs, together with the Technical and Theological Terms of the Muhammadan Religion. Thomas P. Hughes, ed. Clifton, N.J.: Reference Books, 1965.

DMA   Dicionario de Marinha Antigua e Actual. Lisbon: Centro de Estudos Ultramarinos, 1963.

DN   Dicionario de Numinástica. Porto Alegre, Brazil: Livraria Sulina, 1969.

DPC   Dicionario de Portugués-Chopé e Chopé-Portugués. Luis Feliciano dos Santos, ed. Lourenço Marques, Mozambique: Imprensa Nacional, 1949.

DRP   Dicionario Ronga-Portugués. Jose Luis Quintão, ed. Lisbon: Junta de Investigações do Ultramar, Centro de Estudos Politicos e Sociais, 1960.

DX   Dicionario de Xironga-Portugués, Portugués-Xironga. Jose Luis Quintão, ed. Lisbon: Agencia-Geral das Colon Divisão de Publicações e Biblioteca, 1951.

EA   Encyclopedia Americana, International Edition. Chicago: Americana Corporation, 1974.

EB   Encyclopaedia Britannica. Chicago: Encyclopaedia Britannica, 1979.

EDK   Ensaio de Dicionario Kimbundu-Portuguez. J.D. Cordeiro de Matta, ed. Lisbon: A.M. Pereira, 1893.

EI   Enciclopedia Italiana de Scienze, Letteri e d'Arti. Milan-Rome: Instituto Giovanni Trecani, 1928.

EJ   Encyclopedia Judaica. Jerusalem: Keter, 1972.

FWNE   Funk and Wagnalls New Encyclopedia. New York: Funk & Wagnalls, 1973.

FWNSD   Funk and Wagnalls New Standard Dictionary of the English Language. New York: Funk & Wagnalls, 1963.

FWSDF   Funk and Wagnalls Standard Dictionary of Folklore, Mythology, and Legend. New York: Funk & Wagnalls, 1972.

GH   Garcia de Horta. Lisbon: Junta das Missões Geograficas, 1959.

GDLP   Grande Dicionario de Lengua. Antonio Moraes de Silva, ed. Lisbon: Editorial Confluencia, 1949.

GEDL   Grande Enciclopedia Delta Larousse. Lisbon: Studia, 1963.

GEPB   Grande Enciclopedia Portuguesa e Brasileira. Lisbon and Rio de Janeiro: Editorial Enciclopedia Limitada, 1960.

GGT   Glossary of Geographical Terms. Dudley Stamp. London: Longman, Green, 1962.

GSE   Great Soviet Encyclopedia. New York: Macmillan, 1973.

HD   Harvard Dictionary of Music. Cambridge, Mass.: The Belknap Press, 1969.

HDA   Historical Dictionary of Angola. Phillis Martin, ed. Metuchen, N.J.: The Scarecrow Press, 1980.

HDA(2)   Historical Dictionary of Angola (2). Susan H. Broadhead, ed. Metuchen, N.J.: The Scarecrow Press, 1992.

HDB   Historical Dictionary of Benin. Samuel Decalo, ed. Metuchen, N.J.: The Scarecrow Press, 1987.

HDD   Historical Dictionary of Dahomey (People's Republic of Benin). Samuel Decalo, ed. Metuchen, N.J.: The Scarecrow Press, 1976.

HDG   Historical Dictionary of Ghana. D.M. McFarland, ed. Metuchen, N.J.: The Scarecrow Press, 1985.

HDM   Historical Dictionary of Mozambique. Mario Azevedo, ed. Metuchen, N.J.: The Scarecrow Press, 1991.

HDRC   Historical Dictionary of the Republic of Cape Verde. Richard Lobban and Marilyn Haller, eds. Metuchen, N.J.: The Scarecrow Press, 1988.

HDRG   Historical Dictionary of the Republic of Guinea-Bissau. Richard Lobban, ed. Metuchen, N.J.: The Scarecrow Press, 1988.

HDRGC   Historical Dictionary of the Republics of Guinea-Bissau and Cape Verde. Richard Lobban, ed. Metuchen, N.J.: The Scarecrow Press, 1979.

HDT   Historical Dictionary of Togo. Samuel Decalo. Metuchen, N.J.: The Scarecrow Press, 1987.

HDWS   Historical Dictionary of Western Sahara. Tony Hodges. Metuchen, N.J.: The Scarecrow Press, 1982.

IESS   International Encyclopedia of Social Studies. New York: Macmillan and the Free Press, 1968.

JAH   Journal of African History. London: Cambridge University Press, 1981-

JMAS   Journal of Modern African Studies. London: Cambridge University Press, 1963-

JNH   Journal of Negro History. Washington, D.C.: Association for the Study of the Negro Life and History, 1916-

JSS   Journal of Semitic Studies. Jerusalem: 1950-

NCE   New Catholic Encyclopedia. New York: McGraw-Hill, 1967-79.

NDLP   Novo Dicionario da Lengua Portuguesa e Ingleza. Leipzig: F.A. Brockhaus, 1932-

NEB   New Encyclopaedia Britannica. Chicago: Encyclopaedia Britannica, 1985.

OED   Oxford English Dictionary. Oxford: The Clarendon Press, 1989.

PDM   Pequeno Dicionario de Moçambique: Moçambicanismos e Terms Mais Corrientes. Lourenço Marques, Mozambique: Edição do autor, 1972.

Revista Medica de Angola. Luanda, Angola: 1921-1928.

RLM   Rudimentos de Lingua Mocande. Guerriero M. Viegas. Lourenço Marques, Mozambique: Instituto de Investigações Cientificas de Moçambique, 1963.

SED   Swahili-English Dictionary. Charles William Rechenbach. Washington, D.C.: Catholic University of America Press, 1967.

SEI   Short Encyclopedia of Islam. H.A.R. Gibb. Ithaca, N.Y.: Cornell University Press, Photomechanic Reprint, 1961.

SESA   Standard Encyclopedia of Southern Africa. Eric Rosenthal. London: Frederic Warne, 1970.

SMD   Stedman's Medical Dictionary, Illustrated. Baltimore: Williams & Wilkins, 1982.

WBE   World Book Encyclopedia. Chicago: Field Enterprises, 1935.

WNGD   Webster's New Geographical Dictionary. Springfield, Mass.: Merriam-Webster, 1988.

WNTCD   Webster's New Twentieth Century Dictionary, Unabridged. Second Edition. New York: Collins World, 1975.

WNWD   Webster's New World Dictionary of the American Language. New York: Simon and Schuster, 1980.

WTNID   Webster's Third New International Dictionary of the English Language, Unabridged. Springfield, Mass.: Merriam-Webster, 1971.

II. Books, Journal Articles, and Monographs

Abshire, David M., and Michel A. Samuels. Portuguese Africa: A Handbook. London: Pall Mall Press, 1969.

Ajayi, J.F. Ade. West Africa in the Anti-Slavery Trade Era. *In* Cambridge History of Africa, 5:202-207. London: Cambridge University Press, 1976.

Almada Negreiros, Antonio de. Colonies Portugaises: Île de Sao Tomé avec Cartes. Paris: A Challamel, 1901.

_____. Historia Ethnografica da Ilha de São Tomé. Lisbon: Companhia Nacional Editora, 1895.

Almeida, Raymond A., and Patricia Nyham. Cape Verde and Its People: A Short History, Adapted from an Unpublished Manuscript by Dreide Meintel Machado. Boston: American Committee for Cape Verde, 1976.

Andersson, Hilary. A War Against the People. New York: St. Martin's Press, 1992.

Andrade, Elisa. The Cape Verde Islands: From Slavery to Modern Times. Dakar, Senegal: United Nations African Institute for Economic Development and Planning, 1973.

Andrade, Mario de. Antologia Tematica de Poesia Africana. Lisbon: Lavraria da Costa Editora, 1975, 2 vols.

-------. La Poesie Portugais: Anthologie Precédée de "Evolution et Tendances Actuelles." Jean Todrani et Andre Joucla-Ruaua, trans. Paris: P.J. Oswald, 1969.

Anonymous. *See* Libro del Conscimiento.

Antonio, Mario (Fernandes de Oliveira). African Writers in Portuguese. *African Arts*. Los Angeles, Winter, 1970.

Araujo, Norman. A Study of Cape Verdean Literature. Boston: Boston College Press, 1966.

Axelson, Victor E. Portugal and the Scramble for Africa, 1875-1891. Johannesburg: Witwatersrand University Press, 1967.

-------. Congo to Cape: Early Portuguese Explorers. New York: Harper and Row, 1973.

-------. Portuguese in South-East Africa. Johannesburg: Witwatersrand University Press, 1973.

-------. Portuguese Settlement in the Interior of South-East Africa in the Seventeenth Century. Lisbon: Congresso Internacional da Historia dos Descobrimentos, 1961.

Barbosa, Antonio. Novos Subsidios para Historia de Ciencia Nautica Portuguesa da Epoca dos Descobrimentos. Lisbon: Congresso da Historia, 1938.

Barreto, João. Historia da Guiné, 1418-1918. Lisbon: 1938.

Battell, Andrew. The Strange Adventures of Andrew Battell of Leigh in Angola and the Adjoining Regions. Nendeln, Liechtenstein: Kraus Reprint, 1937.

Beier, Ulli. Contemporary Art in Africa. New York: Praeger, 1968.

Bender, Gerald J. Angola under the Portuguese: The Myth and the Reality. Berkeley: University of California Press, 1978.

Bennett, Norman Robert. Africa and Europe from Roman Times to the Present. New York: Africana Publishing Company, 1984.

-------. New England Merchants in Africa: A History through Documents, 1802 to 1865. Boston: Boston University Press, 1965.

Birmingham, David. Carnival in Luanda. *Journal of African History*. London: Cambridge University Press, 1988, vol. 29, pp. 93-103.

--------. Trade and Conflict in Angola: The Mbundu and Their Neighbors under the Influence of the Portuguese. 1483-1790. Oxford: The Clarendon Press, 1960.

Boleão, Jose de Oliveira. Moçambique. Lisbon: Divisão de Publicações e Biblioteca, Agencia-Geral do Ultramar, 1966.

Boxer, Charles R. Four Centuries of Portuguese Expansion, 1414-1825: A Succinct Survey. Johannesburg: Witwatersrand University Press, 1965.

--------. Portuguese Seaborne Empire, 1415-1825. London: Hutchinson, 1969.

--------. Portuguese Society in the Tropics: The Municipal Councils of Goa, Macao, Bahia and Luanda. Madison: University of Wisconsin Press, 1965.

--------. The Querimba Islands in 1744. Lisbon: *Studia*, 1963, 77:43.

--------. Race Relations in the Portuguese Colonial Empire, 1415-1825. Oxford: The Clarendon Press, 1963.

--------. Salvador de Sá and the Struggle for Brazil and Angola, 1602-1686. London: University of London, 1952.

--------. Women in Iberian Expansion Overseas, 1415-1815. New York: Oxford University Press, 1975.

Brasio, Antonio. Historia e Missiologia. Luanda, Angola: Instituto de Investigação Cientificas, 1973.

--------. Monumenta Missionalia—Africa Ocidental. Vol. I (1471-1531); vol. II (1600-1622). Lisbon: Agencia-Geral do Ultramar, 1952.

--------. Os Pretos em Portugal. Lisbon: Agencia-Geral do Ultramar, 1944.

-------. Seminario de Cabo Verde. In BPICV, 12(133):3-7. 1960.

Bridgland, Fred. Jonas Savimbi: A Key to Africa. New York: Paragon House, 1986.

Brito, Eduino. As Fontes do Direito Islámico. In BCG, 1966, vol. 22(82), pp. 167-176.

Bruce, Neil F. Portugal: The Last Empire. New York: John Wiley and Sons, 1975.

Burness, Donald. Critical Perspectives on Lusophone Literature from Africa. Washington. D.C.: Three Continents Press, 1981.

--------. Fire: Six Writers from Angola, Mozambique and Cape Verde, Washington, D.C.: Three Continents Press, 1977.

Caetano, M. Os Nativos na Economia Africana. Coimbra, Portugal: Editora, 1954.

Capela, Jose. Escravatura: Empresa de Saque, O Abolicionismo (1810-1875). Porto, Portugal: Afrontamento, 1974.

Cardini, Franco. Europe in 1492: Portrait of a Continent Five Hundred Years Ago. New York, Facts on File, 1989.

Cardoso, Pedro. Folclore Caboverdiano. Porto, Portugal: Edição Maronus, 1933.

Carreira, Antonio. As Companhias Pombalinas. In BCG, 1968, vol. 23(89/90), p. 325.

--------. Cabo Verde e a Companhia do Grão-Pará e Maranhão (Um Documento Inédito para Su Historia). In BCG, 1967, vol. 22(87/88), pp. 309-324.

--------. Evolução do Islamismo. In BCG, 1966, vol. 21(84), pp. 417-9.

--------. Mandingas da Guiné Portuguesa. Lisbon: Centro dos Estudos da Guiné Porutuguesa. Publicação Commemorativa do V Centenario do descobrimento da Guiné, 1947, p. 324.

--------. Panaria Cabo-Verdiano-Guineense: Aspectos Históricos e Socio-Económicos. Lisbon: Junta de Investigaçó do Ultramar, 1968.

--------. The People of Cape Verde Islands: Explotation and Emigration. Christopher Fyfe, trans. and ed. London: C. Hurst, 1982.

Carvalho e Vasconcellos, Ernesto Julio de. As Colonias Portuesas: Geografía Física, e Económico e Politica. Lisbon: Varia Classica Editora de A.M. Texeirra, 1921.

Castro, Armando. O Sistema Colonial Portugues em Africa (Medeados do Seculo XX). Lisbon: Editora Camacho, 1978.

Chatelain, Héle. Folk-tales of Angola: Fifty Tales, with Kimbundu Text. Lancaster, Penn.: American Folklore Society, 1894.

Chaves, Luis. O "Preto da Guiné" no Folclore. Congresso Commemorativo, Sociedade de Geografía de Lisboa, 1946, 2:557.

Chilcote, Ronald R. Portuguese Africa. Englewood Cliffs, N.J.: Prentice-Hall, 1967.

--------. Protest and Resistance in Angola and Brazil: Comparative Studies. Berkeley: University of California Press, 1972.

Childs, Gladwyn Murray. The Peoples of Angola in the Seventeenth Century according to Cadornega. Journal of African History. London: Cambridge University Press, 1960, vol. 1, pp. 1-2.

Clarence-Smith, William G. Slaves, Peasants and Capitalists in Southern Angola, 1840-1926. London: Cambridge University Press, 1976.

Comhaire, Jean. Sociétés Secrètes et Mouvements Prophetiques au Congo Belgique, Afrique. London: International African Institute, 1955.

Conflict Studies. London: Institute for the Study of Conflict, 1969-

Congresso Commemorativo do Quinto Centenario do Descobrimento da Guiné. Lisbon: Sociedade de Geografia de Lisboa, 1946.

Congresso da Historia da Expansão Portuguesa no Mondo. Lisbon: Sociedade de Geografia de Lisboa, 1937-1938.

Congresso da Historia de Guiné. Lisbon: Sociedade de Geografia de Lisboa, 1938, 1946.

Congresso da Historia dos Descobrimentos Marítimos. Lisbon: Sociedade de Geografia de Lisboa, 1938.

Cortesão, Armando. History of Portuguese Cartography. Lisbon: Junta de Investigação do Ultramar, 1966-1967, 2 vols.

Cortesão, Jaime. A Expansão dos Portuguese no Periodo Henriquino. Lisbon: Portugalia Editora, 1965.

--------. Los Portugueses en Ballesteros, Historia de America. Barcelona: Salvat Editores, 1961.

--------. Os Portugueses em Africa. Lisbon: Portugalia Editora, 1960.

Costa, A. Fontoura da. Descobrimentos Marítimos Africanos dos Portugueses com D. Henrique, D. Afonso V e D. João II. Lisbon: Congresso da Historia, 1938, vol. 2, pp. 10-26.

-------. A Marínhara dos Descobrimentos. Lisbon: Agencia Junta-Geral do Ultramar, 1960.

Coutinho, J. Siqueira. Os Portugueses na Ethiopia. Lisbon: Congresso da Historia, 1938.

Cunha, Joaquim Moreira da Silva. O Sistem Portugues Depolitica Indigena, (subsidios para o seu estudo). Coimbra, Portugal: Coimbra Editora, 1953.

--------. A Trabalho Indigena: Estudo de Direito Colonial. Lisbon: Agencia-Geral das Colonias, Divisão de Publicaões e Biblioteca, 1949.

Cunnison, Ian. Kazembe and the Portuguese, 1798-1832. *Journal of African History*. London: Cambridge University Press, 1961, vol. 2, pp. 61-76.

Danzig, A. van. A Short History of the Forts and Castles of Ghana. Accra: Ghana Museums and Monuments, 1971.

Darch, Colin. Mozambique. Oxford: Clio Press, 1987.

Dathorne, O.R. African Literature in the Twentieth Century. Minneapolis: University of Minnesota Press, 1975.

Davidson, Basil. Black Mother Africa: The Years of Trial. Boston: Little Brown, 1961.

--------. The Fortunate Islands. London: Century Hutchinson, 1989.

Delafosse, Maurice. The Negroes of Africa: History and Culture. F. Fligelman, trans. Port Washington, N.Y.: Kemikat Press, 1968.

Delgado, Ralph. Historia de Angola. Benguela, Angola: Edição de Tipografia do Journal de Benguela, 1948.

Dias, A. Jorge. Portuguese Contribution to Cultural Anthropology. Johannesburg: Witwatersrand University Press, 1961.

Dias, Jill R. Famine and Disease in the History of Angola c.1830-1930. *Journal of African History*. London: Cambridge University Press, 1981, vol. 22, pp. 340-378.

Dias, Raul Neves. A Imprensa Periodica em Moçambique, 1854-195411. Lourenço Marques: Imprenta Nacional de Moçambique, 1956.

Dias Farinha, A. Lingua Arabe e Ilamismo. Junta de Investigaçó do Ultramar. Lisbon: 1973.

Duffy, James. Portuguese Africa. Cambridge, Mass.: Harvard University Press, 1959.

Duncan, T. Bentley. Atlantic Islands, Madeira, the Azores, and the Cape Verdes in Seventeenth Century Commerce. Chicago: University of Chicago Press, 1972.

Ervedosa, Carlos. A Literatura Angolana: Resenha Histórica. Lisbon: Casa dos Estudantes do Imperio, 1963.

--------. Itinerario de Literatura Angolana. Luanda: Editorial Culturano, 1972.

Espirito Santo, J. Nomes Vernáculos de Algumas Plantas Venenosas e Medicinais da Guiné Portuguesa. *In* BCG, 1948, pp. 398-404.

Estermann, Carlos. O Tocoismo como Fenomeno Religioso. Garcia de Horta. Lisbon: Junta de Investigações do Ultramar, 1965.

Estudos Ultramarinos. Lisbon: Instituto Superior dos Estudos Ultramarinos. 1939-

Felgas, Helio A. Esteves. Historia do Congo Portugues. Carmona, Angola: 1958.

Fernandes, Valentim. Description de la Côte Occidental d'Afrique (Sénégal au Cap de Monti Archipelago, 1506-1510). Bissau, Guinea-Bissau: Centro de Estudos das Guiné Portugues, 1951.

Ferreira, Manuel. Literatura Africana de Expressão Portuguesa. Lisbon: Instituto de Cultura Portuguesa, 1977.

--------. No Reino do Caliban: Antologia Panoramica da Poesia Africana de Expressão Portuguesa: Cabo Verde, Guinea-Bissau, Angola, São Tomé e Príncipe, e Mozambique. Lisbon: Empresa de Publicidade Seara Nova, 1975.

Ficalho, Francisco Manuel Carlos de Mello, Conde de. Plantas Uteis da Africa-Portuguesa. Lisbon: Agencia-Geral das Colonias, 1947.

Filesi, Teobaldo. Le Relazioni tra Il Regno Negro del Congo e la Sede Apostolica nel 1600, Nueve Testimonianze. Como, Italy: P. Carioli, 1968.

--------. Roma e Congo all'Inizio del 1600, Nuovo Testimonianze. Como, Italy: P. Cairoli, 1970.

Fisher, H.J. The Central Sahara and Sudan. *In* Cambridge History of Africa. London: Cambridge University Press, 1975, vol. 4, pp. 26, 79, 84, 121, 125.

Flint, John E., and I. Geiss. Africans in South America. *In* Cambridge History of Africa. London: Cambridge University Press, 1975, vol. 5, pp. 428-30.

Freeman-Grenville, G.S.P. East African Coin Finds and Their Historical Significance. *Journal of African History*. London: Cambridge University Press, 1960, vol. 1, pp. 31-43.

Gabriel, Manuel Nunes. Angola, Cinco Siglos de Cristianismo. Queluz, Portugal: Literal-Sociedade Editora, 1978/79.

Garfield, Robert. History of São Tomé Island, 1470-1800. Chicago: Northwestern University, unpublished Ph.D. dissertation, 1971, Microfilm 72-07784.

Gérard, Albert S. European-Language Writing in Sub-Saharan Africa. Budapest: Akademiai Kiadó, 1986, 2 vols.

Godinho, Victorino de Malgalhes. A Economia dos Descobirmentos Henriquinos (1385-1580). Lisbon: Livraria Sá da Costas, 1962.

Goemaere, Pierre. Le Portugal Rentera-t-il en Afrique? Brussels: A. Goemaere, 1968.

Gonçalves, Jose Julio. O Islámismo na Guiné Portuguesa: Ensaio Socio-Missionologico. Lisbon: n.p., 1961.

--------. O Mundo Arabo-Islámico e o Ultramar Portugues. Lisbon: Junta de Investigações do Ultramar, Centro de Estudos Politicos e Sociais, 1972.

Guerra, Manuel dos Santos. Terras da Guiné e Cabo Verde. Lisbon: Tipografía Silva, 1956.

Guerreiro, Manuel Veigas. "Boers" de Angola. Lisbon: Garcia de Horta, Missões Geograficas e de Investigação do Ultramar, 1958.

Hamilton, Russell G. Black from White and White on Black: Contradictions of Language in the Angolan Novel. *Ideologies and Literature*. Minneapolis: University of Minnosota Press, 1976, vol. 1, pp. 25-58.

--------. Voices from an Empire: A History of Afro-Portuguese Literature. Minneapolis: University of Minnesota Press, 1975.

Hammond, Richard James. Portugal and Africa (1815-1910). A Study in Uneconomic Imperialism. Stanford, Cal.: Stanford University Press, 1966.

Hanlon, Joseph. Mozambique: The Revolution under Fire. London: Zed Books, 1990.

Harris, Marvin. Palmatorio. *Africa Today*. Denver: 1958, vol. 24, pp. 11-12.

Harvey, Robert. Portugal: The Birth of Democracy. London: Macmillan, 1978.

Henderson, Lawrence W. Angola: Five Centuries of Conflict. Ithaca, N.Y.: Cornell University Press, 1979.

Henriksen, Thomas H. Mozambique: A History. London: Collins, 1978.

--------. Revolution and Counter-revolution: Mozambique War of Independence, 1964-1974. Westport, Conn.: Greenwood Press, 1983.

Herbert, Eugenia W. Smallpox Inoculation in Africa. *Journal of African History*. London: Cambridge University Press, 1975, vol. 21, pp. 539-59.

Herdeck, Donald E. African Writers. Washington, D.C.: Black Orpheus Press, 1973.

Herrick, Allison Butler, et al. Area Handbook for Mozambique. Washington D.C.: American University Foreign Studies Series, 1969.

--------, et al. Area Handbook for Angola. Washington, D.C.: U.S. Government Printing Office, 1967.

Hill, Paul. Markets in Africa. *Journal of Modern African Studies*. London: Cambridge University Press, 1963, vol. 1, p. 445.

Hisket, M. The Nineteenth-Century Jihads in West Africa. *In* Cambridge History of Africa. London: Cambridge University Press, 1976, vol. 5, p. 163.

Hodges, Tony, and Malyn Newitt. São Tomé and Príncipe: From Plantation to Macro State. Boulder, Colo.: Westview Press, 1988.

Iria, Joaquim Alberto. Breve Noticia Acerca da Expansão e Esforço Colonisador dos Pescadores Olhanenses no Sul de Angola. Lisbon: Congresso da Historia, 1938, vol. I, pp. 9-31.

--------. O Algarve no Descobrimento e Cristianização da Guiné no Seculo XV. Congresso Commemorativo da Guiné, 1946, vol. I, pp. 193-206.

Isaacman, Allen F. Mozambique: The Africanization of a European Institution, 1750-1902. Madison: University of Wisconsin Press, 1972.

--------. Mozambique: From Colonialism to Revolution, 1900-1982. Boulder, Colo.: Westview Press, 1983.

---------. The Prazeros as Transfortiersmen: A Study in Social and Cultural Change. *International Journal of African Historical Studies,*. New York: Africana Publishing Company, 1975, vol. 8, pp. 1-39.

--------. Mozambique: The Tradition of Resistance; Anti-Colonial Activity in the Zambezi Valley, 1850-1921. London: Heinemann, 1976.

Jahn, Jahnheinz. Muntu. An Outline of the New African Culture. New York: Grove Press, 1961.

--------. Neo-African Literature: A History of Black Writing. Oliver Coburn and Ursula Lehrburge, trans. New York: Grove Press, 1968.

Johnson, Douglas. The Maghrib. Cambridge History of Africa. London: Cambridge University Press, 1976, vol. 5, p. 102.

Kaplan, Irvin. Angola: A Country Study. Washington, D.C.: American University Foreign Studies Series, 1978.

--------, et al. Area Handbook for Mozambique. Washington, D.C.: American University Foreign Studies Series, 1977.

Kilson, Martin L., and Robert I. Rotberg. The African Diaspora. Cambridge, Mass.: Harvard University Press, 1976.

Leathart, Scott. Trees of the World. New York: A & W Publishers, 1977.

Leite de Vasconcelos, Jose. Antroponia Portuguesa. Lisbon: Imprensa Nacional, 1928.

Levitzon, Nehemia. North West Africa from the Maghrib to the Fringes of the Forest. *In* Cambridge History of Africa. London: Cambridge University Press, 1975, vol. 4, pp. 142-222.

Lewicki, Tadeusz, and Mariano Abramowicz. West African Food in the Middle Ages According to Arabic Sources. London: Cambridge University Press, 1974.

Libro del Conscimiento de todos los Reynos y Tierra Señorios que son por el Mundo y de las Señales y Armas que han cada Tierra y Señorio. Written c.1350 by a Spanish Franciscan. First published in Madrid by Imprenta de T. Fortanet, 1877, edited by Marcos Jiménez de la Espada. English translation by Clements Markham. London: 1912.

Livermore, H.V. A New History of Portugal. London: Cambridge University Press, 1966.

Lopes da Silva, Baltasar. O Dialecto Crioulo de Cabo Verde. Lisbon: Junta das Missões Geograficas e de Investigações do Ultramar, Centro de Estudos Politicos e Sociais, Dialectos Portugueses do Ultramar, 1957.

Lopo, Julio de Castro. Jornalismo de Angola. Luanda, Angola: Edição do Centro de Informação e Turismo de Angola, 1964.

Lutero, Martinho, and C. Martins Pereira. a Musica Tradicional em Mozambique. *Africa*, 1960, vol. 2, pp. 575-88.

Mantero, Francisco. Manual Labour in São Thomé e Príncipe. New York: Negro Universities Press, 1969.

Marcum, John A. The Angolan Revolution. Vol. I: The Anatomy of an Explosion; vol. II: Exile Politics and Guerilla Warfare (1962-1976). Cambridge, Mass.: MIT Press, 1978.

Margarido, Alfredo. Estudos sobre Literatura das Nações Africanas da Lingua Portuguesa. Lisbon: A Regra do Jogo, 1980.

Marques, Antonio Henrique R. de Oliveira. History of Portugal. New York: Columbia University Press, 1976.

Martin, Toni. The Pan-African Connection from Slavery to Garvey and Beyond. Dover, Mass.: Majority Press, 1983.

Meintel, Deirdre. Race, Culture and Portuguese Colonialism in Cabo Verde. Syracuse, N.Y.: Syracuse University Press, 1984.

Miller, Joseph C. Kings and Kinsmen: Early Mbundu State in Angola. Oxford: The Clarendon Press, 1976.

--------. Nzinga of Matamba in a New Perspective. *Journal of African History*. London: Cambridge University Press, 1975, vol. 16, pp. 201-16.

Moser, Gerald. African Literature in Portuguese: The First Written, the Last Discovered. African Forum Series. New York: The American Society of African Studies, 1967, vol. 2, pp. 78-96.

--------. Essays in Portuguese-African Literature. University Park, Penn.: The Pennsylvania State University Press, 1969.

Mota, Avelino Teixeira da. Guiné Portuguesa. Lisbon: Agencia-Geral do Ultramar, 1954.

--------. Mar, alem Mar: Estudos e Ensaios de Historia e Geografia. Lisbon: Junta de Investigações do Ultramar, 1972.

--------. Topónimos de Origem Portugues na Costa Ocidental de Africa desde o Cabo Bojador ao Cabo Santa Catarina. Bissau, Guinea-Bissau: Centro de Estudos da Guiné Portuguesa, 1950.

Munslow, Barry. Mozambique: The Revolution and Its Origins. London: Longman, 1983.

Newitt, M.D.D. Portugal in Africa, The Last Hundred Years. London: Longman, 1981.

--------. Portuguese Settlement in the Zambezi: Exploration, Land Tenure and Colonial Rule in East Africa. New York: Africana Publication Company, 1973.

Nunes Nabarro, Margaret D. The Background and Development of the Fado in Moçambique up to 1973. In Marius F. Valkhoff, Miscelanea Luso-Africana. Lisbon: Junta de Investigações Cientificas do Ultramar, 1975.

Okuma, Thomas. Angola in Ferment: The Background and Prospects of Angolan Nationalism. Westport, Conn.: Greenwood Press, 1974.

Oliveira, Fernão. A Arte de Guerra do Mar [por] Fernando Oliveira. Lisbon: Ministerio de Marinha, 1969.

Oliver, Paul. Shelter in Africa. New York: Praeger, 1971.

Parry, John H. The Discovery of the Sea. Berkeley: University of California Press, 1981.

Pelissier, René. La Colonie du Minotaure: Nationalism et Revoltes en Angola (1926-1961). Montanet, France: privately published, 1978.

Pereira de Lima, Alfredo. Edificios Históricos de Lourenço Marques. Lisbon: Livraria Academica, 1966.

Pereira de Lima. Joaquim Alberto: Epítome de Historia da Medicina Portuguesa. Porto, Portugal: Portocalence Editora, 1943.

Pinto Rema, Henrique. A Primeira Evangelizão do Guiné (1533-1640). In BCG, 1966, vol. 21(82), p. 307.

--------. A Primeiras Missões da Costa de Guiné (1533-1640). In BCG, 1967, vol. 22(87/88), pp. 225-268.

Polanyi, Karl. Dahomey and the Slave Trade. Seattle: University of Washington Press, 1966.

Portugal: Agencia Geral do Ultramar. Cabo Verde: Pequena Monografia. Lisbon: 1970.

Prestage, Edgar. Portuguese Pioneers. New York: Barnes & Noble, 1967.

Preto-Rodas, Richard R. Negritude as a Theme in the Poetry of the Portugues-Speaking World. Gainesville, Fla.: University of Florida Press, Humanities Monograph no. 31, 1970.

Proceedings of the American Philosophical Society. Philadelphia: 1973.

Randles, W.G.L. L'Ancien Royaume du Congo: Des Origines à la Fin du XIXe Siècle. Paris: Mouton, 1968, pp. 234-5.

Riley, Eileen. Major Political Events in South Africa, 1948-1990. Oxford and New York: Facts on File, 1991.

Rita-Ferreira, Antonio. O Movimento Migratorio de Trabalhadores entre Moçambique e a Africa do Sul. Lisbon: Junta de Investigações do Ultramar, 1963.

Rocha, A. O Filho do Emperor do Monomotapa. Lisbon: *Ultramar*, 1973, vol. 2(5/6), pp. 206-8.

Rodney, Walter. The Guinea Coast. *In* Cambridge History of Africa. London: Cambridge University Press, 1975, vol. 4, pp. 223-4.

--------. Upper Guinea and the Significance of the Origins of Africans Enslaved in the New World. *Journal of Negro History*, 1969, vol. 54, pp. 276-96.

Ronciere, Charles G.M.B. de la. La Decouverté de l'Afrique au Moyen Age, Cartographes et Explorateurs. 2 vols. Cairo: Société Royale de Geographie, 1925.

Rosario, Morais de. Genoveses na Historia de Portugal. Lisbon: 1977.

Russell-Wood, A.J.R. A World on the Move: The Portuguese in Africa, Asia and America, 1415-1808. Manchester: Carcanet Press, 1992.

Saunders, A.C. de C.M. A Social History of Black Slaves and Freedmen in Portugal, 1441-1555. London: Cambridge University Press, 1982.

Silva, Artur Augusto. Usos e Costumes Jurídicas dos Mandingas. *In* BCG, 1968, vol. 23(89), pp. 233-300.

Silva Rego, Antonio da. O Ultramar Portugues no Seculo XIX (1830-1910). Lisbon: Agencia-Geral do Ultramar, 1966.

--------. Portuguese Colonization in the Sixteenth Century: A Study of Royal Ordinances (Regimentos). Johannesburg: Witwatersrand University Press, 1959.

Simmons, James S. Global Epidemology: A Geography of Disease and Sanitation. Philadelphia: Lippincott, 1944.

Simões, Antero. Nós . . . Somos Todos Nós. Luanda, Angola: Tipografia Angolana, 1972.

Sloan, Irvin J. The Blacks in America, 1492-1977: A Chronology and Fact Book. Dobbs Ferry, N.Y.: Oceana Publications, 1971.

Soremekum, Fola. Angola: The Road to Independence. Ile-Ife, Nigeria: University of Ife Press, 1983.

Spinola, Antonio de. Portugal and the Future. Johannesburg: Perskor Publishers, 1974.

Taylor, Eva G.R. English Debt to Portuguese Nautical Science. Lisbon: Congresso da Historia da 16th Seculo, 1938.

--------. History of Technology, vol. 2, pp. 5-11. London: Mansell, 1976.

Tendeiro, João. Esboço Epizootologico da Guiné. Congresso Commemorativo do Quinto Centenario de Descobrimento da Guiné. Lisbon: Sociedade de Geograpfía, 1946.

Tenreiro, Francisco. A Ilha de São Tomé. Lisbon: Junta de Investigações do Ultramar, 1961.

Thompson, V.B. Africa and Unity: the Evolution of Pan-Africanism. New York: Humanities Press, 1969.

Trimingham, John Spencer. A History of Islam in West Africa. London: Oxford University Press, 1956.

--------. Islam in East Africa. Oxford: The Clarendon Press, 1964.

--------. Islam in West Africa. Oxford: The Clarendon Press, 1970.

U.S. Board on Geographic Names Gazetteer. Angola: Official Names Approved by the United States Board on Geography. Washington, D.C.: U.S. Office of Geography, 1956.

--------. Mozambique: Official Names Approved by the United States Board on Geography. Washington, D.C.: U.S. Office of Geography, 1969.

--------. Portugal and the Cape Verde Islands: Official Names Approved by the United States Board on Geography. Washington, D.C.: U.S. Office of Geography, 1961.

--------. Portuguese Guinea: Official Names Approved by the United States Board on Geography. Washington, D.C.: U.S. Office of Geography, 1963.

--------. São Tomé e Príncipe: Official Names Approved by the United States Board on Geography. Washington, D.C.: U.S. Office of Geography, 1962.

Urdang, Stephanie. Fighting Two Colonialisms: Women in Guinea-Bissau. New York: Monthly Review Press, 1979.

Vail, Leroy, and L. White. Capitalism and Colonialism in Mozambique: A Study of Quelimane District. Minneapolis: University of Minnesota Press, 1980.

Valkhoff, Marius F., ed. Miscelanea Luso-Africana: Colectanea dos Estudos Coligidos. Lisbon: Junta de Investigações Cientificas do Ultramar, 1975.

--------. New Light on Africans and "Malayo-Portuguese." Louvain, France: Editions Puters, Imprimiere Orientalist, 1972.

Vansina, Jan. Kingdoms of the Savanna. Madison: University of Wisconsin Press, 1966.

Welch, Sidney R. Europe's Discovery of South Africa. Cape Town: Juta, 1937.

--------. Portuguese and the Dutch in South Africa, 1641-1806. Cape Town: Juta, 1951.

--------. South Africa under King Manuel, 1495-1521. Cape Town: Juta, 1948.

Wheeler, Douglas L. A Note on Smallpox in Angola. *Studia*, 1964, vol. 13-14, pp. 355-62.

--------. In Search of Modern Portugal: The Revolution and Its Consequences. Madison: University of Wisconsin Press, 1983.

-------, and René Pelissier. Angola. New York: Praeger, 1971.

Wilson, W.A.A. The Crioulo of Guiné. Johannesburg: University of Witwatersrand, 1962.

Wiseman, John A. Political Leaders in Black Africa. Aldershot, U.K., Edward Elgar Publishing, 1991.

Youssuf, Kamal. Monumenta Cartographica Africae et Aegyptie. Cairo: privately published, 1926-51.